STRATEGIES OF INQUIRY

HANDBOOK OF POLITICAL SCIENCE

Volume 7

STRATEGIES OF INQUIRY

Edited by
FRED I. GREENSTEIN Princeton University
NELSON W. POLSBY University of California, Berkeley

 ADDISON-WESLEY PUBLISHING COMPANY

Reading, Massachusetts
Menlo Park, California • London • Amsterdam • Don Mills, Ontario • Sydney

This book is in the
ADDISON-WESLEY SERIES IN POLITICAL SCIENCE

PREFACE

Early in his career, the fledgling political scientist learns that his discipline is ill-defined, amorphous, and heterogeneous. This perception will in no way be rebutted by the appearance of a presumably encyclopedic eight-volume work entitled *The Handbook of Political Science*. Indeed, the persistent amorphousness of our discipline has constituted a central challenge to the editors of the *Handbook* and has brought to its creation both hazards and opportunities. The opportunities were apparent enough to us when we took on the editorial duties of the *Handbook;* the hazards became clearer later on.

At the outset, it seemed to us a rare occasion when a publisher opens quite so large a canvas and invites a pair of editors to paint on it as they will—or can. We immediately saw that in order to do the job at all we would have to cajole a goodly number of our colleagues into the belief that our canvas was in reality Tom Sawyer's fence. We did not set out at the beginning, however, with a precise vision of the final product—i.e., a work that would be composed of these particular eight volumes, dealing with the present array and number of contributions and enlisting all the present contributors. Rather, the *Handbook* is the product of a long and in some ways accidental process. An account of this process is in order if only because, by describing the necessarily adventitious character of the "decisions" that produced this work, we can help the reader to see that the *Handbook* is not an attempt to make a collective pronouncement of Truth chiseled in stone, but rather an assembly of contributions, each an individual scholarly effort, whose overall purpose is to give a warts-and-all portrait of a discipline that is still in a process of becoming.

We first became involved in discussions about the project in 1965. Addison-Wesley had already discussed the possibility of a handbook with a number of other political scientists, encouraged by their happy experience with a two-volume compendium of highly respected review essays in social psychology (Lindzey, 1954), which has since been revised and expanded into a five-volume work (Lindzey and Aronson, 1968–69).

Of the various people to whom Addison-Wesley aired the handbook idea, we evidently were among the most persistent in encouraging such a project. No doubt the reason was that we were still close to our own graduate work in a department where a careful reading of many of the chapters in *The Handbook of Social Psychology* was in some ways more fundamental to learning our trade than a comparable exposure to many of the more conspicuous intellectual edifices of the political science of the time. Gardner Lindzey, in writing his introductory statement to the first edition of *The Handbook of Social Psychology* (reprinted in the second edition), described *our* needs as well as those of budding social psychologists in saying that

> the accelerating expansion of social psychology in the past two decades has led to an acute need for a source book more advanced than the ordinary textbook in the field but yet more focused than scattered periodical literature. . . . It was this state of affairs that led us to assemble a book that would represent the major areas of social psychology at a level of difficulty appropriate for graduate students. In addition to serving the needs of graduate instruction, we anticipate that the volumes will be useful in advanced undergraduate courses and as a reference book for professional psychologists.

With the substitution of "political science" in the appropriate places, Lindzey's description of his own purposes and audiences reflects precisely what we thought Addison-Wesley might most usefully seek to accomplish with a political science handbook.

In choosing a pair of editors, the publisher might well have followed a balancing strategy, looking for two political scientists who were poles apart in their background, training, and views of the discipline. The publisher might then have sought divine intervention, praying for the miracle that would bring the editors into sufficient agreement to make the planning of the *Handbook*—or *any* handbook—possible at all. Instead they found a pair of editors with complementary but basically similar and congenial perspectives. We were then both teaching at Wesleyan University and had been to graduate school together at Yale, at a time when the political science department there was making its widely recognized contribution to the modernization of the discipline. Each had recently spent a year in the interdisciplinary ambience of the Center for Advanced Study in the Behavioral Sciences. Moreover, we were both specialists in American politics, the "field" which in 1973 still accounted for three-quarters of the contributions to *The American Political Science Review*. There were also complementary divergencies. Within political science, Polsby's work and interests had been in national politics and policy-making, whereas Greenstein's were more in mass, extragovernmental aspects of political behavior. Outside political science, Polsby's interests were directed more toward sociology and law, and Greenstein's tended toward psychiatry and clinical and social psychology.

To begin with, neither we nor the publisher could be sure without first gathering evidence that the discipline of political science was "ready" for a handbook comparable to the Lindzey work. We were sure that, if it was at all possible for us to bring such a handbook into being, we would have to employ the Aristotelian tack of working within and building upon existing categories of endeavor, rather than the Platonic (or Procrustean) mode of inventing a coherent set of master categories and persuading contributors to use them. First, at our request the publisher inquired of a number of distinguished political scientists whether they felt a need would be served by a handbook of political science similar to *The Handbook of Social Psychology*. This inquiry went to political scientists who had themselves been involved in extensive editorial activities or who were especially known for their attention to political science as a discipline. The responses were quite uniform in favoring such a handbook. The particular suggestions about how such a handbook might be *organized,* however, were exceptionally varied. But fortunately we had asked one further question: What half-dozen or so individuals were so authoritative or original in their contributions on some topic as to make them prime candidates for inclusion in any political science handbook, no matter what its final overall shape? Here agreement reemerged; the consultants were remarkably unanimous in the individuals named.

Seizing the advantage provided by that consensus, we reached the following agreement with the publisher. We would write the individuals who constituted what we now saw as a prime list of candidates for inclusion as authors and ask whether they would be willing to contribute to a handbook of political science, given a long lead time and freedom to choose the topic of their essay. (We did suggest possible topics to each.) It was agreed that unless we were able to enlist most of those with whom we were corresponding as a core group of contributors, we would not proceed with a handbook. Since all but one of that group indicated willingness to contribute, we signed a publishing agreement (in September 1967) and proceeded to expand our core group to a full set of contributors to what we then envisaged as a three-volume handbook, drawing on our core contributors for advice. Our queries to the core contributors were a search not so much for structural and organizational suggestions as for concrete topics and specific contributors to add to the initial list.

The well-worn term "incremental" suggests itself as a summary of how the table of contents of *The Handbook of Political Science* then took shape. As the number of contributors increased, and as contributors themselves continued to make suggestions about possible rearrangements in the division of labor and to remark on gaps, the planned three volumes expanded to eight, most of which, however, were shorter than the originally intended three. Throughout, Addison-Wesley left it to us and the contributors, within the very broadest of boundaries, to define the overall length of the project and of the individual contributions. And throughout, we urged the contributors not to seek intellectual anonymity in the guise of being "merely" summarizers—or embalmers—of their fields but rather to endeavor to place a distinctive intellectual stamp on their contributions.

A necessary condition of enlisting the initial group of contributors was a production deadline so far in the future as to dissolve the concern of rational individuals about adding to their intellectual encumbrances. As it turned out, our "safely remote" initial deadline (1970) was in fact a drastic underestimation of the number of postponements and delays.* Along with delays there have been occasional withdrawals, as individual contributors recognized that even with a long fuse the task of preparing a handbook article would be a major one and would inevitably preempt time from other projects and interests. Departing contributors were often helpful in suggesting alternatives. Both through the late enlistment of such substitutes and through the addition of collaborators taken on by invited contributors, we feel we have been spared a table of contents that anachronistically represents only the cohort of those individuals who were responsible for the shape of political science circa 1967.

Whether one builds a handbook table of contents a priori or ex post facto, *some* basis of organization emerges. We might have organized a handbook around:

1. *"political things"* (e.g., the French bureaucracy, the U.S. Constitution, political parties);

2. *nodes or clusters in the literature* (community power, group theory, issue voting);

3. *subdisciplines* (public administration, public law, comparative government, political theory, international relations);

4. *functions* (planning, law-making, adjudication);

5. *geography* (the American Congress, the British Cabinet, the politicoeconomic institutions of the U.S.S.R.);

6. or any combination of the above and further possibilities.

Any of our colleagues who have tried to construct a curriculum in political science will sympathize with our dilemma. There is, quite simply, no

---

* For the comparable experience of *Handbook of Social Psychology* editors with delays, see Lindzey, 1954, p. vii, Lindzey and Aronson, 1968–69, p. ix.

sovereign way to organize our discipline. Although much of our knowledge is cumulative, there is no set beginning or end to political science. Apart from certain quite restricted subdisciplinary areas (notably the mathematical and statistical), political scientists do not have to learn a particular bit of information or master a particular technique at a particular stage as a prerequisite to further study. And the discipline lacks a single widely accepted frame of reference or principle of organization. Consequently, we evolved a table of contents that to some extent adopted nearly *all* the approaches above. (None of our chapter titles contains a geographical reference, but many of the chapters employ one or more explicitly specified political systems as data sources.)

The protean classifications of subspecialization within political science and the ups and downs in subspecialty interests over the years are extensively reviewed by Dwight Waldo in his essay in Volume 1 on political science as discipline and profession. A further way to recognize the diversity and change in our discipline—as well as the persisting elements—is to note the divisions of disciplinary interests used by the directories of the American Political Science Association, the membership of which constitutes the great bulk of all political scientists. A glance at the three successive directories which have been current during our editorial activities is instructive.

The 1961 *Biographical Directory of the American Political Science Association* (APSA, 1961) represents a last glimpse at a parsimonious, staid set of subdisciplinary categories that would have been readily recognizable at the 1930 Annual Meeting of the Association.

1. American National Government

2. Comparative Government

3. International Law and Relations

4. Political Parties

5. Political Theory

6. Public Administration

7. Public Law

8. State and Local Government

In the next *Biographical Directory* (APSA, 1968), there appeared a categorization that was at once pared down and much expanded from the 1961 classification. A mere three "general fields" were listed. The first was "Contemporary Political Systems." Members electing this general field were asked to specify the country or countries in which they were interested, and those countries were listed parenthetically after the members' names in the subdisciplinary listing, presumably out of a desire to play down the importance of "area studies" as an intellectual focus and to accentuate the importance of functional or analytic bases of intellectual endeavor. "International Law, Organization, and Politics" was the second general field, and "Political Theory and Philosophy" was the third. But the 26 categories in Table 1 were provided for the listing of "specialized fields." They included some venerable subdivisions, perhaps in slightly more fashionable phrasing, and other distinctly nonvenerable subdivisions, at least one of which (political socialization) did not even exist in the general vocabulary of political scientists ten years earlier. In this *Handbook*, the 1968 categories have many parallels, including the general principle of organization that excludes geography as a specialized field criterion while at the same time recognizing that political scientists can and should study and compare diverse political settings. Diplomatically avoiding the presentation of a structured classification, the editors of the 1968 *Directory* relied on the alphabet for their sequence of specialized fields.

TABLE 1 Subdisciplinary categories used in *Biographical Directory* of the American Political Science Association, 1968

1. Administrative law
2. Administration: organization, processes, behavior
3. Budget and fiscal management
4. Constitutional law
5. Executive: organization, processes, behavior
6. Foreign policy
7. Government regulation of business
8. International law
9. International organization and administration
10. International politics
11. Judiciary: organization, processes, behavior
12. Legislature: organization, processes, behavior
13. Methodology
14. Metropolitan and urban government and politics
15. National security policy
16. Personnel administration
17. Political and constitutional history
18. Political parties and elections: organizations and processes
19. Political psychology
20. Political socialization
21. Political theory and philosophy (empirical)
22. Political theory and philosophy (historical)
23. Political theory and philosophy (normative)
24. Public opinion
25. Revolutions and political violence
26. State and local government and politics
27. Voting behavior

Even with this burgeoning of options, many members of the discipline evidently felt that their interests were not adequately covered. Goodly numbers took advantage of an opportunity provided in the questionnaire to the APSA membership to list "other" specialties, referring, for example, to "political sociology," "political behavior," "political development," "policy studies," "communication," "federalism," and "interest groups."

The 1973 *Biographical Directory* (APSA, 1973) attempted still another basis of classification, a revised version of the classification used in the 1970 *National Science Foundation Register of Scientific and Technical Personnel.* Braving a structured rather than alphabetic classification, the authors of this taxonomy divided the discipline into nine major classes and a total of 60 specialized classifications, with a return to the antique dichotomy of foreign versus U.S. politics. The specifics of the 1973 listing are given in Table 2.

TABLE 2 Subdisciplinary categories used in *Biographical Directory* of the American Political Science Association, 1973

I	Foreign and Cross-National Political Institutions and Behavior
1.	Analyses of particular systems or subsystems
2.	Decision-making processes
3.	Elites and their oppositions
4.	Mass participation and communications
5.	Parties, mass movements, secondary associations
6.	Political development and modernization
7.	Politics of planning
8.	Values, ideologies, belief systems, political culture
II	International Law, Organization, and Politics
9.	International law
10.	International organization and administration
11.	International politics
III	Methodology
12.	Computer techniques
13.	Content analysis
14.	Epistemology and philosophy of science
15.	Experimental design
16.	Field data collection
17.	Measurement and index construction
18.	Model building
19.	Statistical analysis
20.	Survey design and analysis
IV	Political Stability, Instability, and Change
21.	Cultural modification and diffusion
22.	Personality and motivation
23.	Political leadership and recruitment
24.	Political socialization
25.	Revolution and violence
26.	Schools and political education
27.	Social and economic stratification

(continued)

As will be evident, the present *Handbook* contains articles on topics that appear on neither of the two recent differentiated lists and omits topics on each. Some "omissions" were inadvertent. Others were deliberate, resulting from our conclusion either that the work on a particular topic did not appear ripe for review at this time or that the topic overlapped sufficiently with others already commissioned so that we might leave it out in the interests of preventing our rapidly expanding project from becoming hopelessly large. There also were instances in which we failed to find (or keep) authors on topics that we might otherwise have included. Hence readers should be forewarned about a feature of the *Handbook* that they should know without forewarning is bound to exist: incompleteness. Each reviewer will note "strange omissions." For us it is more extraordinary that so many able people were willing to invest so much effort in this enterprise.

It should be evident from our history of the project that we consider the rubrics under which scholarly work is classified to be less important than the caliber of the scholarship and that we recognize the incorrigible tendency of inquiry to overflow the pigeonholes to which it has been assigned, as well as the desirability that scholars rather than editors (or other administrators) define the boundaries of their endeavors. Therefore we have used rather simple principles for aggregating essays into their respective volumes and given them straightforward titles.

The essays in Volume 1 on the nature of political theory which follow Waldo's extensive discussion of the scope of political science are far from innocent of reference to empirical matters. This comports with the common observation that matters of theoretical interest are by no means removed from the concerns of the real world. And although we have used the titles *Micropolitical Theory* and *Macropolitical Theory* for Volumes 2 and 3, we have meant no more thereby than to identify the scale and mode of conceptualization typical of the topics in these volumes. Here again the reader will find selections that extensively review empirical findings.

Similarly, although the titles of Volumes 4, 5, and 6 on extragovernmental, governmental, and policy-output aspects of government and politics may appear to imply mere data compilations, the contents of these volumes are far from atheoretical. This is also emphatically true of Volume 8, which carries the title *International Politics*, a field that in recent decades has continuously raised difficult theoretical issues, including issues about the proper nature of theory. Volume 7 carries the title *Strategies of Inquiry* rather than *Methodology* to call attention to the fact that contributors to that volume have emphasized linking techniques of inquiry to substantive issues. In short, contributions to the eight volumes connect in many ways that can be only imperfectly suggested by the editors' table of contents or even by the comprehensive index at the end of Volume 8.

It can scarcely surprise readers of a multiple-authored work to learn that what is before them is a collective effort. It gives us pleasure to acknowledge obligations to five groups of people who helped to lighten our part of the load. First of all, to our contributors we owe a debt of gratitude for their patience, cooperation, and willingness to find the time in their exceedingly busy schedules to produce the essays that make up this *Handbook.* Second, we thank the many helpful Addison-Wesley staff members with whom we have worked for their good cheer toward us and for their optimism about this project. Third, the senior scholars who initially advised Addison-Wesley to undertake the project, and who may even have pointed the publishers in our direction, know who they are. We believe it would add still another burden to the things they must answer for in our profession if we named them publicly, but we want to record our rueful, belated appreciation to them. Fourth, Kathleen Peters and Barbara Kelly in Berkeley and Lee L. Messina, Catherine Smith, and Frances C. Root in Middletown kept the paper flowing back and forth across the country and helped us immeasurably in getting the job done. Finally, our love and gratitude to Barbara Greenstein and Linda Polsby. And we are happy to report to Michael, Amy, and Jessica Greenstein, and to Lisa, Emily, and Daniel Polsby that at long last their fathers are off the long-distance telephone.

Princeton, New Jersey	F.I.G.
Berkeley, California	N.W.P.

REFERENCES

American Political Science Association (1961). *Biographical Directory of The American Political Science Association,* fourth edition. (Franklin L. Burdette, ed.) Washington, D.C.

American Political Science Association (1968). *Biographical Directory,* fifth edition. Washington, D.C.

American Political Science Association (1973). *Biographical Directory,* sixth edition. Washington, D.C.

Lindzey, Gardner, ed. (1954). *Handbook of Social Psychology,* 2 volumes. Cambridge, Mass.: Addison-Wesley.

Lindzey, Gardner, and Elliot Aronson, eds. (1968–69). *The Handbook of Social Psychology,* second edition, 5 volumes. Reading, Mass.: Addison-Wesley.

CONTENTS

CONTENTS OF OTHER VOLUMES IN THIS SERIES

SOURCES FOR POLITICAL INQUIRY: I LIBRARY REFERENCE MATERIALS AND MANUSCRIPTS AS DATA FOR POLITICAL SCIENCE

CLEMENT E. VOSE

Political science is a willing prisoner in the library cycle, which I think of as the progression of the reporting of events in daily newspapers to weekly, monthly, and quarterly journals, to books, and then to the indexing and cataloging that refers readers back to the beginning of the cycle, even though an increasing amount of professional research occurs outside of it and sparse attention has been given to library instruction. The discipline's origins in history and law 50 to 100 years ago account, in part, for this. There has always been a dependence on government documents and historical reference sources. The escape to the real world as exhibited by personal observation, field work, interviews, and surveys results in publications that enter the library cycle, too. While political science will never again be exclusively a library subject, its importance and potential for clarification is not safely slighted.

The most ardent library enthusiast can, therefore, agree with V. O. Key's dour assessment:

> Professional students of public affairs, both by the limiting circumstances of their employment and the habits of work induced by their tradition and training, have been far too dependent upon the library, the document, and excogitation. Projects that rely on firsthand observation and utilize the appropriate techniques for the accumulation of data relevant to the analytic problems deserve priority. All this is not to deny the utilities of the printed or archival source. The point is simply that heavy reliance on such materials severely restricts the range of questions open to investigation. Over the past quarter of a century social scientists have in varying degree extricated themselves from the toils of the library, but the political scientists have made the least progress in this direction. (Key, 1956, p. 30)

The fact that the library provides only a part of the data for political science is no reason to neglect it. The work of the discipline will be improved by understanding that the modern library world is inordinately complex and considerable sophistication is required to tap its resources intelligently.

Political science would be broadened by training students in the organizing principles of libraries, government documents, law collections, and archives. Each of these areas may be regarded as information systems made up of subsystems with almost endless variations of detail. They are, at the same time, also significant organized structures with deeply important historical and political significance. The political scientist should approach them with an awe appropriate to other professional edifices but with sufficient confidence to act as an intelligent, aware critic. Such a multitude of considerations go into the publication, acquisition, cataloging, and use of written information, and into the planning, financing, and building of depositories of knowledge that political science should revel in and seek to understand these phenomena.

The objective of this chapter is to discuss some of the areas concerning the use of sources that political scientists are likely to find valuable. There are a number of systems or sets of materials that are important for their own sake; and if several of these are viewed in depth, they may then be used to develop principal points to be applied to other sets.

The need for particular kinds of information varies so widely among political scientists that any essay on the subject is certain to be highly idiosyncratic. Political scientists do not read the same newspapers and magazines, nor the same books, nor the same articles in the same professional journals. Specialization and the possibility of different approaches and emphases have engendered remarkable disparities even in what accomplished scholars do in the same subfield. This chapter, then, discusses some of the considerations one political scientist, influenced by legal training and with an amateur interest in librarianship, finds intriguing about libraries and their contents.

ERRORS AND ODDITIES IN REFERENCE MATERIALS

Standard library reference sources reflect such matters as the publisher's financial and ideological aims and the constraints imposed on the editors, whether they be an early deadline, ignorance, guile, or high-handedness. However noble the quest for objectivity in formulating, editing, and publishing reference materials, it is difficult to pass beyond such barriers as culture, historical time, nationalism, religion, race, and partisanship.

These caveats about archives and reference sources will be supported by examples in this chapter, but this is only one emphasis. One of equal, if seemingly contradictory, weight for working political scientists is the profusion of materials at hand. They are plentiful, they are remarkably usable, and they are relatively inexpensive. The application of intelligence and industry will yield an astonishingly complete picture of any number of political moments. The scholar needs an acute balance between an appreciation of the weaknesses of his sources and an appreciation of their validity and usefulness. Indeed, in their writings about politics, more scholars need to display precisely what limits their information has and what sources are most germane.

Toward others' ignorance of sources one can be surly, constructive, or excusing. It is naturally attractive to think, as Isaac Stern remarked of Jack Benny's violin playing, "He has all the skill required for his needs." Thus some scholars feel confident they need learn about the sources only when they are about to use them. Few of the reference books or manuscript collections to be recommended in this chapter, on the other hand, present technical barriers. It is probable that the abilities of political scientists can be improved if they treat the extent, reliability, and utility of sources as a subject to be studied in itself.

There are several attitudes that are useful in approaching libraries and archives, reference sources and manuscript collections. Already imbued with a grab bag of fact and fiction, of outlook and assertions, of supporting sources of one kind or another, the individual student looks to books and periodicals for many things: corroboration, the original source of a fact or idea, renewal for specifics that slip the mind, and for new or more detailed information on a subject. All too often the quest for information is regarded as a bore when it can be seen as intellectual joy itself. When contradictory information is found, and it is far more common in standard sources than one would suppose, the student has a chance to win the game of wits against the world's accumulated knowledge. A brief indication of the type and range of errors and oddities to be found in library sources will illustrate this point.

Anonymous authors. Two famous instances of anonymity of authorship are measures of differences in political style during two eras, the Federalist period and modern America. "Publius" was a pseudonym of the former period, "X" of the latter. In the eighteenth century most newspaper contributors wrote anonymously but in the twentieth century the opposite is true.

The 85 essays in defense of the new Constitution appeared in New York newspapers between October 1787 and May 1788. Their purpose was to convince the state of New York to ratify the proposed Constitution and they succeeded. While many contemporaries knew that Hamilton, Madison, and Jay had written *The Federalist,* it was not until 1807 that a list of authors of specific essays was published. Positive identification of the authors of some essays remained elusive for 150 years. In our time the authorship of only 15 of the essays remains in doubt and Jacob E. Cooke now seems to have settled this definitively (1961, pp. xi–xxx). As is well known, content analysis is finding increasing uses and obtaining strong sophistication as one means of examining communication (Mosteller and Wallace, 1964; Riley and Stoll, 1968).

The X-Article presents more a curiosity of form than a patent mystery. Entitled "The Sources of Soviet Conduct," it was published in the July 1946 issue of *Foreign Affairs*. The author is identified only as "X." It had been prepared by George F. Kennan, a career diplomat thought to have important influence in the Truman Administration. Within a week or so, following an article in the *New York Times* by Arthur Krock, "the authorship of the article became common knowledge" (Kennan, 1967, p. 356). Cleared by the Committee on Unofficial Publications of the State Department, Kennan asked the editor of *Foreign Affairs* to publish the article anonymously. Although he says it was entirely inadvertent, Kennan did assure attention when he named "X" as the author. The essay was given wide publicity, became in the popular mind the intellectual basis for the Truman doctrine of containment, and was subsequently disowned as inapplicable to new situations faced by American diplomacy after 1953 (Kennan, 1967, p. 356; Halberstam, 1972, p. 107).

Political writing, like anthropological diggings, old masters, and credit cards, may sometimes present puzzles of authorship and authenticity. This is evident in the practices of large organizations, as in Congress and the Presidency, where ghost-writing is institutionalized and the practice well understood. As such it is a definite byway of the discipline and therefore one with which library users should have a nodding acquaintance. An example is the publication of a Lincoln document of importance in 1879 in the *North American Review:* a diary purported to have been kept during the winter of 1860–1861 but identified only as "The Diary of a Public Man" with the name of the author withheld. Historians did not agree until the 1940s that the diarist was Samuel Ward, brother of Julia Ward Howe. (See Anderson, 1948, pp. 146–156.)

Hoaxes. Publication of the "Pentagon Papers" in the *New York Times* (June and July 1971) led the staff of the *National Review* to prepare several bogus memoranda and reports and publish them as further, authentic government documents concerning the development of American policy toward Vietnam in the 1960s. These reports were accepted as genuine by the chief wire services and by hundreds of newspapers that treated the documents as straight news. A day later the editor of the *National Review* announced the episode as a hoax (*National Review*, 27 July 1971; *New York Times*, 22 July 1971; *Time*, 2 August 1971). Such hoaxes are sometimes believed to be accurate for longer than one day; there may yet be some that remain undiscovered, although one doubts that these pertain to significant events. One dictionary reports the "moon hoax" as "a fabricated account of wonderful discoveries in the moon, said to have been made by Sir John Hershel, written by Richard Adams Locke and published in the New York *Sun* in 1835" (*Funk & Wagnalls New Standard Dictionary*, 1955).

Later convictions for perjury or conspiracy to commit perjury, occurring months or years after an event, often make nonsense out of earlier pious interviews, tight-lipped denials, widely quoted news releases and other forms of published news. In late 1971, McGraw-Hill Book Company and *Life* magazine boasted of plans to publish an authorized biography of Howard Hughes, the reclusive billionaire. Claims of authenticity were questioned and for weeks the country was treated to a seemingly endless dispute that culminated in the admission by Clifford Irving that his book on Hughes was a hoax. His earlier claims were officially discredited when he pleaded guilty to charges of conspiracy (*New York Times Index,* generally under "Hughes, Howard," 1971, 1972; *New York Times,* 14 March 1972, p. 1). Vice-president Spiro Agnew also protested rumors of scandal for weeks in 1973 before he entered a plea of no contest to one count of income tax evasion and simultaneously resigned his office (*New York Times,* 10 October 1973). The Watergate story is replete with a succession of denials and admissions from many persons. An awareness of subsequent events is required for readers of dated newspapers and periodicals. This awareness ought, really, to make more newspaper readers and TV viewers agnostics, if not cynics, even though the printing of lies as events is unintended by reporters and is only occasional.

Aliases and fictitious persons. False armistices, mistaken information, and hoaxes may be perpetrated through the media of fast-breaking news more readily than in publications enjoying less severe deadlines. The rarity of deceit against editors of reference books is shown in the following entry in *Who Was Who in America, 1897–1942* (pp. 263–264):

> COSTER, Frank Donald. The sketch of the then president of McKesson & Robbins, Inc., published in Volume 20 under this name is the only instance—during nearly five decades of continuous publication involving over 77,000 biographees—of a fictitious biographee foisting himself on the editors of *Who's Who.* Those holding certain outstanding civilian and official positions, including the presidencies of concerns whose securities are quoted on the New York Stock Exchange, are arbitrarily listed in *Who's Who.* This imposter became so qualified on being elected president of the important drug house of McKesson & Robbins, Inc. He had for years successfully hoodwinked banks, boards of directors, famous clubs' admission committees, trade organizations, stock exchanges and scores of leading business men and officials. It later developed he had had falsified birth certificates filed which apparently substantiated his biographical data, to which he added fraudulent educational information. Although buried as Coster, he was actually Phillip Musica, an ex-convict.

Musica had entered *Who's Who in America* as part of a larger swindle (Shaplen, 1955). A similar result occurred in the 1880s when an author in quest of money succeeded in submitting and having published in *Appleton's Cyclopedia of American Biography* accounts of some 50 completely nonexistent South American scientists (Schindler, 1936, pp. 680–690).

Even census figures have been tampered with through the addition of thousands of fictitious names to population returns. This occurred in 1910 in twelve cities in the West. Investigations by the Census Bureau "found that a total of 102,967 fictitious names had been added to the census schedules for these cities, ranging from 909 for Walla Walla to 32,527 for Tacoma" (*Annual Report of the Attorney General of the United States for the Year 1912*, p. 37). While 47 defendants were convicted of fraud, only nine jail sentences were imposed and modest fines collected. The Department of Justice prosecuted the cases with vigor but made this report after they were settled:

> The investigations in these cases showed that the padding of the census returns was due principally to the "boosting" spirit, and a feeling of rivalry prevailing in some cities, and that the general sentiment of some of the communities was largely responsible. It was on this account that the sentences, as a rule, were light. In one case the judge, in sentencing a defendant who plead guilty, said: "I am going to be lenient with you because I feel that a majority of the community is just about as guilty as you are."

It was nevertheless believed that the prosecutions would have a deterrent effect against "similar frauds in connection with future census taking" (*Annual Report of the Attorney General of the United States for the Year 1912*, p. 37).

Omissions and quirks in publications. It may take considerable acumen to discover that factual information may have been omitted from a publication purporting to carry it. It is well known, for instance, that official telephone directories in the United States omit names and numbers for persons who ask, and pay, to be "unlisted." In Manhattan alone there are 100,000 unlisted numbers. This tribute to privacy makes the telephone directory something less than ideal as a reference tool for present and future historians. Moreover, telephone directories do not carry any indication of this practice. Directories of other kinds possess a similar kind of reliability when they follow the dictates of members, subscribers, graduates, and the like.

It is an obvious political maxim that persons controlling a publication have printed only what they wish about themselves. This is also true of government control. The *Great Russian Encyclopedia* deleted the entry on Beria, downgraded Stalin, and praised Khrushchev as an expression of new Soviet leadership in the 1950s (Benton, 1958, pp. 552–568). In 1971 Vishinsky was demoted in the *Great Russian Encyclopedia* (*New York Times*, 16 August 1971). In the United States, the *Congressional Directory* is utterly reliable on certain facts such as committee assignments, seniority lists, district lines, and spelling. But the editors of the *Directory* are completely at the mercy of members of Congress in compiling the biographical section. For example, former Maine Senator

Margaret Chase Smith for years permitted only her name to be entered, and nothing further. An adequate outline of her career, including her birth date of 14 December 1897, however, is included in the decennial *Biographical Directory of the American Congress, 1774–1971,* as well as in the biennial *Who's Who in America.* Other members of Congress make up for this meager entry. In several inches of copy in the *Congressional Directory,* Ken Hechler, a representative from West Virginia who eschews no full first or middle name, notes that his grandfather was wounded at Antietam, that his own personal motto is "Better to jump the gun than not to move when the gun goes off," and confides for the benefit of concerned constituents that at about 60 years of age he is "not yet married." Actually, offbeat twists are more than welcome to alleviate some of the boredom of reading deadpan career biographies.

Continuous revision of encyclopedias. In a withering critique of the old *Encyclopaedia Britannica,* Harvey Einbinder has shown how the editorial practice of "continuous revision" maintains errors, keeps dated information, and introduces contradictions. The *Britannica* took its present shape with the famous 11th edition of 1878. Two additional editions appeared and then, in 1929, the editors held all type, stuck to the same volume organization and length, and set in motion the practice of revising and rewriting some of the articles each year. This has meant that several hundred articles were reprinted intact from their first appearance 30, 40, and 50 years ago. These include many articles on literature, history and politics, although far fewer concerning scientific areas (Einbinder, 1964). The publication of the *New Encyclopaedia Britannica* in 1974 is built on an architectural design formulated by Mortimer Adler, a modern Thomist. This is to say that *all* the world's knowledge claimed to have been set down through a grand scheme of concepts that places details within a hierarchical framework. While it is clear that everything in it is freshly written, it is unclear how future developments will be accommodated.

CATALOGS AND INDEXES TO BOOKS AND PERIODICALS

It is a wise researcher who appreciates the differences that exist among the many kinds of keys to library resources. Only a *concordance*—an index of the principal words of a particular author or book with their immediate contexts—begins to be a complete key to the whole subject. There are many full indexes to a particular circumscribed source. A card catalog will include an index to the titles, authors, and subjects embraced in a given library's book collection. The national union catalogs are examples of published works of many volumes, available in college libraries of any size, that provide information about all published books. The books themselves may be difficult to obtain although most can be obtained with ease and swiftness, by means of interlibrary loan and photocopying.

Periodical sources are tapped through a complex set of indexes. The most valuable type of index is one for a single journal, provided one's interest in the particular periodical is high. Political scientists are likely to have a use for the *Cumulative Index to the American Political Science Review, Volumes 1–62: 1906–1968*. It would be very useful if the several major political science journals in the United States joined forces to prepare a joint index. Most academic journals provide annual indexes and these are handy when checking through a long run of volumes in search of particular authors, titles, and topics. The type of index provided and the general index in which a journal is included can be found in *Ulrich's International Periodicals Directory.* Among other journals with full indexes are the *Harvard Law Review* and the *Yale Law Journal.* More detailed information about articles in the discipline can be found in the *International Political Science Abstracts,* begun in 1950. Published in both French and English, the abstracts are confined to articles published in nearly 80 social science journals in some 25 countries. In a handful of periodicals, all the articles, without exception, are abstracted. In most, only the articles concerning political science are selected. This is a solid index, making it an invaluable source of information for a scholar seeking a comprehensive view of writings on a given subject treated by professional students of politics.

There are numerous indexes to single publications of interest to political scientists besides those already named. The *New York Times Index*, the *Subject Index of the Christian Science Monitor,* and the *Wall Street Journal Index* are really the only ones published for daily newspapers although the special libraries maintained by large circulation metropolitan papers such as the *Baltimore Sun* have their own unpublished aids. This is true of some libraries also. For example, the University of Minnesota Library has for many years kept a card index to the chief news stories in the major Minneapolis newspapers. The indexes to the *Congressional Quarterly Weekly Report,* the *National Journal Reports,* and *United States Law Week* contribute to the value of those publications.

In the periodical index field, the H. W. Wilson Company is preeminent. Its 12 publications mostly limit the number of periodicals indexed, presenting a total altogether of about 1200. The *Readers' Guide to Periodical Literature* is its best seller, indexing articles from 150 publications of general circulation: *Atlantic, Harper's, Saturday Review, New Republic, Nation, Time, Newsweek,* the *New Yorker* and the best-known and established magazines representing a group outlook: *America* and *Commonweal* for Catholics, the *Christian Century* for liberal Protestants, and *Commentary* for the American Jewish Committee. The list indexed has been changed many times since the *Reader's Guide* took up where *Poole's Index* left off at the turn of the century.

The Wilson Company has been eminently practical in satisfying the needs of libraries. Its prices are scaled to accord with the number of indexed periodicals purchased by specific libraries. In turn, the selection of the magazines indexed is made by these libraries. Some of the details of this practice are an interesting reflection of the particular population of voters. Every seven years lists are prepared by the Committee on Wilson Indexes, which is appointed by the Reference Services Division of the American Library Association. Most of the votes cast are from small public libraries and from many high school and junior college libraries. Large university libraries and large public libraries each have one vote. While it is difficult to believe that this arrangement can ever be altered through litigation to accord with a library's circulation or user figures, it is tempting to recommend changes to accommodate professional readers. This is not to say that the Wilson Company policy is anything but proper within the bounds of its assumptions and its tried-and-true commercial experience. When the voting lists are sent out:

> The subscribers are asked by the Committee to cast their votes carefully and objectively, with primary emphasis on the reference value of the periodicals upon which they are voting. They are also urged to give serious consideration to the maintenance of a good subject balance so that no important field will be overlooked in proportion to the overall coverage. Suggestions for additions or deletions of titles should be brought to the attention of the Committee in care of The H. W. Wilson Company.

Most political scientists will find the list of periodicals indexed in the *Social Sciences Index,* as of June 1974, with too many gaps to be a dependable guide to all current work in the discipline. Happily, those included in the index are the *Annals of the American Academy of Political and Social Science, American Political Science Review, Canadian Journal of Political Science, Journal of Politics, Orbis, Political Quarterly, Political Science Quarterly, Political Studies, Public Administration Review, Public Opinion Quarterly, Social Research, Soviet Studies, Western Political Quarterly,* and *World Politics.* Among the omissions are journals that are included in other Wilson indexes. Their *Readers' Guide to Periodical Indexes* already carries *Foreign Affairs* and the *Yale Review,* for example, so these are not repeated. Important among the missing in any of these standard indexes are relatively new journals. These include the *British Journal of Political Science,* the *American Journal of Political Science* (formerly the *Midwest Journal of Political Science*), *Polity,* and the *Social Science Quarterly* (formerly the *Southwest Journal of Social Sciences*). But its subscribers are not likely to advocate that *every* discipline have anything like full representation for its publications. Precisely 263 periodicals are now covered in the *Social Sciences Index.*

An important rite of passage for a new magazine from an uncertain business venture to an established position is anointment by inclusion in the Wilson indexes. Owing to reliance on infrequent elections, it is a certainty that the first volume of a new periodical would not be included in, say, the *Readers' Guide.* A check of back issues of this index reveals that *Time* magazine, started in 1923, was first included in the *Readers' Guide to Periodical Literature* 12 years later, in 1935. The *New Yorker,* perhaps the foremost political weekly in the broad sense over its first 50 years, was counted in 1930, five years after its first issue. Even *Life,* begun in 1936, and *The Reporter,* begun in 1949, each took four years to be included.

William F. Buckley's conservative *National Review* made a fight for it. He considered exclusion to be a result of liberal bias against his weekly, begun in 1955. The campaign included a series by columnist George Sokolsky attacking what he asserted to be a liberal bias in the *Readers' Guide to Periodical Literature.* Periodical librarians also received a round robin appeal from 14 well-known librarians, publishers, and scholars, led by Clinton Rossiter. Its appeal opened with these words:

> I should like respectfully to suggest that you recommend the magazine *National Review* for indexing in the *Readers' Guide to Periodical Literature.* If you have read any of my books, you are aware that I am out of sympathy with many of the views expressed by the editors and contributors to *National Review.* However, as a professor of government, I recognize that these views express a significant point of view, and I consider it a part of my responsibility as an educator to help as best I can to give to students of current affairs the opportunity to know what these views are and what journal of opinion expresses them regularly, together with the arguments that are being used in their support. (Letter, Rossiter *et al.* to Periodical Department, Wesleyan University Library, 16 November 1960. Copy in possession of author.)

The campaign succeeded in 1963, after a wait of eight years.

Other standard Wilson indexes deal with agriculture, business, education, and technology and will be of interest to political scientists with a curiosity in those fields. The *Index to Legal Periodicals* shows further the advantages and limitations inherent in indexing a list of journals. Yes, even beginning law reviews are included from their very first volume, for the advisory committee speaks for the Association of American Law Schools. But the chief weakness in coverage lies in the omission of all the articles on legislation, litigation, lawyers, and law topics in periodicals of general circulation like the *New York Times Magazine,* and in the history and social science journals. The index is correctly named, in any event, but is a departure from the *Index to Legal Periodical Literature* by Jones and Chipman for the years 1803 to 1937, for this included a selection of publications in addition to law reviews. It is clear, however, that no one key will do and so the bright researcher must develop peripheral vision in order to notice how helpful at the margins other particular indexes may be.

There are a handful of keys to periodical sources likely to be of utmost interest to political scientists. For writings by political scientists the *Interna-*

tional Political Science Abstracts is superb. For books and pamphlets, as well as articles, on public issues and developments of the day the *Public Affairs Information Service Bulletin* (*PAIS*) is excellent. Begun at the New York Public Library in 1914 by a progressive reformer in order to enable his associates and compatriots to back up their proposals with references, the orientation of *PAIS* concerns topics and issues. Indexers compiling the *PAIS* search widely among hundreds of periodicals and other sources to provide the best sources on current topics.

The subject of "subject headings" is unavoidable for anyone concerned at all with problems of terminology in political science, politics, and public affairs. Library users benefit from an acquaintance with the one-volume guide called *Subject Headings Used in the Dictionary Catalog of the Library of Congress,* 7th edition, 1966, which has quarterly supplements. The H. W. Wilson Company periodical indexes follow the dictates of that volume. Library catalogs throughout the United States are also organized around this book of subject headings. The Card Division of the Library of Congress studies each book processed and indicates the most suitable subject entries for the catalog card prepared for a book. These are listed on the printed card issued by the Library of Congress and several identical cards are purchased by most libraries that acquire a given book. A library's card catalog will include references to a single book many times over. Consider the book *Jumbos and Jackasses: A Popular History of the Political Wars* by Edwin P. Hoyt (New York: Doubleday, 1960). Six cards are needed: one is an author entry and another a title entry. Then there are four subject entries: (1) U.S. Politics and Government; (2) U.S. Presidents. Election; (3) Democratic Party; and (4) Republican Party. The common sense of the Card Division is attested by the fact that the book was *not* cataloged under genus *elephantidae* or genus *equus*.

Political scientists must, nevertheless, take a sharply critical view toward the Card Division and its *Subject Headings Used in the Dictionary Catalog of the Library of Congress*. While a book is likely to touch on hundreds of topics, as will be seen in checking an index, the card catalog is necessarily limited to major subject headings. But too few are ordinarily applied. Only one subject heading is granted *The American Party System and the American People* by Fred I. Greenstein (Englewood Cliffs, N.J.: Prentice Hall, 1963), and that is U.S. Politics and Government. 1945–   . Although an inspection of this book shows its subjects to include local and state politics, political parties, and electoral behavior, it will not be found under these headings in the card catalog. Nor does the book, strictly speaking, limit its examination to the years since 1945. Another book, *Politics and Social Life: An Introduction to Political Behavior* by Nelson W. Polsby *et al.* (Boston: Houghton Mifflin, 1963), wins two subject entries: (1) Political Science—Addresses, essays, and lectures; and (2) U.S. Politics and Government—Addresses, essays, and lectures. The student looking in the card catalog under Political Science is lucky; one look-

ing under Sociology is not. This absence of imagination has serious conse-
quences for bibliographies because those who prepare them are so dependent
on the card catalog. Among the omissions in *Sociology of the Law: A Research
Bibliography* compiled by William J. Chambliss and Robert B. Seidman
(Berkeley, Calif.: Glendessary Press, 1970), for example, is a book called
*Caucasians Only: The Supreme Court, the NAACP and the Restrictive
Covenant Cases* by Clement E. Vose (Berkeley, Calif.: University of California
Press, 1959). The compilers report trying "to be complete and to include all
relevant literature" and "surveyed the literature of sociology, law, economics,
psychology, anthropology and political science" (Chambliss and Seidman, p. v).
Alas, *Caucasians Only* is not to be found in the card catalog under Political
Science or Sociology or Law. It is also not cataloged under Race, although it
will be found under (1) Discrimination in housing; (2) Negroes—Housing; and
(3) National Association for the Advancement of Colored People. Nor is it
cataloged under Law although it appears under Real Covenants—U.S.
Caucasians Only, like most books in political science, fails to be picked up by
bibliographers for many of the compilations in which it should appropriately
appear. It is not even cataloged under the heading U.S. Supreme Court. If it
had been titled as an exploration of interest group behavior, which is its chief
point, *Caucasians Only* might then, at least, have been cataloged under Pressure Groups or Lobbying. *Subject Headings Used in the Dictionary Catalog of
the Library of Congress,* when checked in 1974, does not include the heading
"interest groups," although the term has been widely used in political science
for many years.

While the number of subject headings in the Library of Congress system
for books is infinitely expandable, the subject list used in legal digests is
ordinarily limited. The West Publishing Company's digests, constituting the
most comprehensive subject approach to case law, divides American law into
some 420 broad topics. These are then broken down into subdivisions and
subtopics running into the thousands. Since the subject terminology was
determined in the 1880s there are considerable differences in the ways in which
the subject headings (with their West key numbers) have been filled out. All
the writers on legal research have praised the usefulness of digests in terms such
as these:

> The case digest is the lawyer's indispensable tool. It is a vastly detailed
> subject index to the law as set forth in the reported cases. (Price and Bitner,
> 1962, p. 183)

> ...judicial decisions are published in chronological order, both in their
> official and unofficial reports. This body of law consisting of almost three
> million decisions every year, could hardly be searched for relevant pre-
> cedents, unless there were some means of subject access. (Cohen, 1968, pp.
> 41–42)

Such access is, in fact, provided by various finding-tools—the most important of which are case digests. A digest to judicial decisions superimposes a subject classification upon chronologically published cases. The classification consists of an alphabetically arranged scheme of legal topics and subtopics which can be approached through a detailed index. Brief abstracts of the points of law in decided cases are classified by subject and set out in the digests under appropriate topical headings. They are then located and retrieved by the researcher through the index to the digest. (Cohen, 1968, pp. 41–42)

Through subject headings, then, the comprehensive American Digest System and other systems for particular courts or jurisdictions give all researchers a relatively easy path to the location of precedent. There are a number of cautions to mention concerning legal digests, however, for they oversimplify, give unevaluated "squibs" about cases, do not conveniently show changes in the law, and ignore the social context and intellectual movement outside of court decisions.

An awareness of subject headings is useful to anyone who reads, clips, or refers to newspapers and to anyone who maintains files on contemporary affairs and writes and indexes books. Here a new reference will be helpful because it has been prepared in association with the *New York Times Index* to coordinate all the information facilities at the *Times*. This new key to subjects comes in two large loose-leaf binders and is called *The New York Times Thesaurus of Descriptors*. Its editors observe that descriptors are primarily subject headings and do not ordinarily include geographic names, personal names, and other proper names. The descriptors do handle many matters in the daily news that are of particular interest. The introduction includes these points of practice that will indicate something of the nature of *The New York Times Thesaurus of Descriptors*:

Descriptors include terms current in the news (such as BLACK Power or BRAIN Drain) even though they are not found in standard library catalogues or dictionaries.

Abbreviations and acronyms are used as descriptors, usually with "see" references to the name spelled out (NATO. See North Atlantic Treaty Organization). The practice may be reversed when the abbreviation is much better known than the term it represents (DICHLORO-Diphenyl-Trichloroethane. See DDT). No attempt has been made to compile an exhaustive list of abbreviations and acronyms.

There are similar notes on alphabetization, geographic versus subject terms, foreign names, and religious denominations.

ENCYCLOPEDIAS, YEARBOOKS, DIRECTORIES, AND HANDBOOKS

To get one's bearings, to refresh one's mind about details, and to learn fresh information, an article in an encyclopedia, handbook, or yearbook can be ideal. By following cross-references to related entries on a subject it is possible to capture very quickly an amazing range of information and thought. By moving among several encyclopedias and other books in the encyclopedia family, it is possible to learn a great deal in an afternoon. There will be gaps and snags along the way but the variety of encyclopedias and yearbooks is so great and their general quality so high that attention to the opportunities will pay off.

In addition to an acquaintance with leading reference books, political scientists need a standard in order to measure quality, pertinence, and utility. The library market is ripe for well-named, aggressively promoted but shoddy reference books. But not all encyclopedias are encyclopedic, nor are all dictionaries based on sound principles of word definition. There are so many types of reference books devoted to such a variety of subjects that each beckons special, intrinsic criticism. When all is said and done, however, we look for high standards of scholarship in all reference sources: clarity of purpose, appropriate design, accuracy and consistency, intellectual taste, completeness and rationality, attribution of information sources, and similar qualities. The examples of reference books given below indicate how some succeed and others fail, but for discussions of still other references of interest to political science, those interested will wish to look elsewhere. (See Schattschneider, Jones, and Bailey, 1973; Vose, 1968, 1974.)

The *United States Government Manual* describes the executive departments, provides citations to the statutes, reorganization plans, and executive orders that created them, and outlines their functions. The divisions of each department are described and numerous leading officials identified. In the span of a few pages it is easy to gain a basic picture of the organization, a useful thing to have even though one knows that the political, legal, fiscal, and social character of the organization is quite thoroughly left aside. It could hardly be otherwise. This is made evident when one discovers that the American National Red Cross, "chartered under the act of Congress approved January 5, 1905 (33 Stat. 599, as amended; 36 U.S.C. 1), pursuant to the treaties of Geneva or the treaties of the Red Cross to which the United States is a party," is described in 3½ pages, while the Council of Economic Advisers, the Central Intelligence Agency, the Office of the Solicitor General, and the Federal Bureau of Investigation are described in less than a page each. Yet the *United States Government Manual* contains more than mere listings, for it describes and delineates, even though all is done within the confines of bureaucratic blandness.

The directory feature is sometimes the entire content of a volume but most directories go beyond simple listings to depict, in a more or less complete manner, the organizational and procedural makeup of the institution or association. The *Biographical Directory of the American Political Science Association* is a case in point, for while most of the six editions of that work have the barest biographical listing, the 1952 edition carried an analysis of the profession prepared by James L. McCamy. The *Foundation Directory,* now in its 4th edition (1971), has always included essays about foundations, their size, governance, and tax problems. In this instance the *Foundation Directory,* published about every five years, is handsomely supplemented by the *Foundation News.* Behind this is a headquarters of The Foundation Center in New York which not only accepts researchers but through national advertising invites them to visit.

The best directories have complex indexes that yield much information if used carefully. The *Congressional Staff Directory,* the *Congressional Directory,* the *United States Government Manual,* and the *Foundation Directory* are among the best examples of this. But even the best directories need a little help from their friends and if, say, one wished to nail down details about partners in a prominent Washington law firm, it would be possible to make good headway by using the *Martindale-Hubbell Law Directory* for brief biographies of the firm members. Published annually since 1868, *Martindale–Hubbell* back through the years would show changes over time in recruitment and advancement in the firm. The more detailed biographies of individual lawyers could be found in *Who Was Who in America* (volume 4 contains a cumulative index) that would tend to list those with high government service. *Who's Who in America* would carry this up to date. A difficulty with using this reference is that lawyers, even prominent ones, gain entrance into *Who's Who* more slowly than educators, prominent businessmen, and government officials.

Professional users of directories, handbooks, almanacs, and encyclopedias ought to notice the source of the information placed so effortlessly at their disposal. In the United States many of the highly touted commercially published books of this sort derive their information very substantially from government publications that are entirely in the public domain and have no copyright. The best-loved source is the *Statistical Abstract of the United States* (and various pirates in cheaper editions), published annually since 1878. Like the daily newspaper, the almanac is commonly the retailer of information (which is its right and proper thing to do), but a professional reader can be grateful for the convenience and take care in his serious work to locate the original source. Professor Manley O. Hudson at the Harvard Law School, the great teacher of international law, is recalled as insisting that the *New York Times* was not a proper source for a legal citation because it was (1) not official, (2) not a publisher of complete decisions, and (3) not free of error. Professor Hudson, like Professor Kingsmith in the movie *The Paper Chase,* did not suffer students gladly who adduced casual information from uncertain sources.

> . . . Nor would it do even for them to cite in general terms or even by name, some supporting decision or treaty. "Where's the document?" Hudson would growl. "Bring in the document!" And that was the end of that promising line of discussion for a while, unless, as they gradually learned to do after the year began, some of them had anticipated the difficulty and "brought in the document" with them. But, as often as not, even when the document was brought in, it received short shrift, and there had to be a further postponement. "What are you reading from? What *is* that?" Hudson would ask sharply. "Who wrote that?" The student, stopped short in his tracks as he glimpsed the summit of his argument, would again falter and stumble. But he would recover, perhaps with a touch of triumph, to say, "This is the Anglo-French Treaty of so and so, concluded only six months ago." "How do you know that?" The implacable challenge would still come. To answer that this was what the title page said the document was, or that the text had been found in the *New York Times,* or in the Compilers' *Commercial Treaties,* or even in the *Supplement to the American Journal of International Law,* or similar convenient sources, would (on the surface, but in part also actually) stir Hudson almost to anger and contempt. "That document is worthless! We can't discuss a text found in a place like that—can we gentlemen?" (appealing to the class)—"Where is the official text? Why don't you bring in a document that we can trust?" (Stone, 1960, pp. 215, 219–220)

The ultrarespectable, and certainly very good, *New York Times Encyclopedia Almanac* (later to become *The Official Associated Press Almanac)* has also been careless with sources. Its 1970 edition (p. 305) offers a table of Negro Population of Large U.S. Cities and gives its source as the Congressional Quarterly, Inc. The perfectionist researcher knows that the Congressional Quarterly makes no census tallies and so this is an instance of one unofficial source citing a second unofficial source—undoubtedly relying on estimates of the United States Bureau of the Census. This same 1970 *New York Times Encyclopedia Almanac* lists population estimates for 1969 that were "supplied by the editorial staff of the Rand McNally Commercial Atlas & Marketing Guide" (p. 198). The identical fault: good for bedtime reading and quick checking but unreliable, unofficial, and incomplete!

Although the *New Columbia Encyclopedia* (4th ed., 1975) is handy (is only one volume) and appeals to mature readers, the multivolumed general encyclopedias such as the *Britannica* are not apt to be as useful to political scientists as are specialized encyclopedias. Those published before 1950 represent an older strand of knowledge and outlook and are superb for many purposes so long as their dates of origin are understood. Specialized works for that time include Hastings' *Encyclopedia of Religion and Ethics* (13 vols., 1912), the *Encyclopaedia of the Social Sciences* (16 vols., 1934), and the *Universal Jewish Encyclopedia* (10 vols., 1939). Hastings' encyclopedia displays impressive scholarship on ancient religious and political beliefs and practices. The *Encyclopaedia of the Social Sciences* continues to be exceedingly strong on legal history, with brilliant articles by Frankfurter, Pound, Powell, Llewellyn, and other legal realists of that day. The 50-page essay on political parties in numerous countries is classic; its contributors include Arthur Holcombe on theory, Harold F. Gosnell on organization, Arthur W. MacMahon on the United States, Frank H. Underhill on Canada, Sigmund Neumann on Germany, Lindsay Rogers on France, and so on. The *Universal Jewish Encyclopedia* has maps, photographs, and illustrations, is truly international in scope, and is much more like a general encyclopedia than the *Encyclopaedia of the Social Sciences,* in that numerous concise entries identify minor people and places.

The usual hallmark of a specialized encyclopedia is the long essays, fashioned by an individual scholar working under a generous editor. This has been evident in several works published in recent years. The *International Encyclopedia of the Social Sciences* (17 vols., 1968) admirably represents the best thought in the following disciplines: anthropology, economics, political science, psychology, sociology, social thought, and statistics. This work goes far beyond the general encyclopedias in providing information and ideas oriented toward the informed reader that often fill in cracks between the social science disciplines. The six articles on geography, for example, deal in 35 pages with political, economic, cultural, social, and statistical geography. These also refer the reader to other articles within the encyclopedia on Area, Cartography, City, Conservation, Ecology, Environment, Land, Location Theory, Planning, Population, and Region and Water Resources, among others. There is an open invitation to read and learn. There is also a challenge to improve on and add to this monument of social science learning. One may also check facts against it. An instance of this is shown in puzzling over the following statement: "As far as I know, the French historian Marc Bloch (shot by the Nazis in 1944) was the first to insist on the importance of the generation—as opposed, say, to the century or the reign—as a unit of historical time" (Bliven, 1969, p. 203). The two articles on generations, however, show this belief to be indisputably wrong, one asserting that "since the early nineteenth century there has been developed a social and historical concept of generations as comprising the structure not only of societies but of history itself" (Marias, 1968, p. 88). This is supported by a discussion of the importance of the generation in the writings of Auguste Compte, John Stuart Mill, Antoine Cournot, and others in the nineteenth century and of Karl Mannheim and Ortega y Gasset and others before Marc

Bloch in the twentieth. The *International Encyclopedia of the Social Sciences* is thus an argument settler and its depth of treatment may just now be beginning to be appreciated.

The *Encyclopedia of Philosophy* (8 vols., 1967) is organized in a similar manner and also includes hundreds of brief intellectual biographies. There are fine sections on the philosophy of law, political philosophy, ethics, racism, and democracy in the *Encyclopedia of Philosophy*. The recent *Encyclopedia of Education* (10 vols., 1971) will also hold an interest for political scientists, in both their specialized research and in their teaching and other career activities. There are many articles on libraries, specialized education such as for law, government programs such as the G.I. Bill of Rights, and particular organizations such as the Brookings Institution, the Social Science Research Council, and the American Association of University Professors. The article on academic regalia may be a bit too much but those on academic due process, academic freedom, and the academic marketplace are closer to home. There is even an article on faculty fringe benefits. There are several other specialized encyclopedias in fields generally thought to be further distant from political science such as art and science and technology, some of which will be superb starting points to gain knowledge in another field. Also, the *New Catholic Encyclopedia* (15 vols., 1967) merits praise for its excellent editing at The Catholic University of America because its articles on church-state law, freemasonry, and the history of public education in several countries, among others, are so fully informed and fairly presented. It also carries many biographies of prominent Catholic figures, both lay and clerical. Finally, the *Encyclopedia Judaica* (17 vols., 1972) is also specialized and thorough on many political subjects.

DOCUMENTS BY AND ABOUT THE UNITED STATES GOVERNMENT

Congress

An understanding of the documents published by and about Congress is reinforced by a knowledge of the history of the institution and its place in American politics. The opposite is also true, for the history contained in the documents and the history of their publication is also a rich vein of politics in itself.

The two greatest functions of Congress, the deliberative and the lawmaking, are registered in a series of publications that dates from the very first Congress in 1789. Congress contracted for their publication with commercial publishers and, while there was some switching of publishers from time to time, there has never been a real break in the issuance of these two series of documents. The laws passed by Congress have been published chronologically in the *United States Statutes at Large*. The debates of Congress have also been published continuously but under different titles: the *Annals of Congress* from 1789 to 1824, the *Register of Debates* from 1824 to 1837, and the *Congressional Globe* from 1833 to 1873. When the Government Printing Office was established in 1861, commercial printers soon lost these two publications to the new establishment. The *United States Statutes at Large* was continued under the same title but a new title was adopted in 1873 for the publication of debates, the *Congressional Record,* which has continued in use since that time.

The development of a committee system and the frequent use of investigation and research as Congress developed produced many documents apart from the debates and laws. Since 1817 these have been published in a unique series called the Congressional Serial Set. It is made up mostly of House and Senate documents in American history. The number of volumes in the Serial set reached approximately 15,000 in 1971.

Congress was gradually developing a principle of public information in the publication of its laws, debates, and reports, and this was particularly well expressed by the establishment of the Government Printing Office. This office is part of the legislative branch of government and is supervised by a joint committee of Congress. It is, of course, headed by the Public Printer who is appointed by the President with the advice and consent of the Senate. Although the Government Printing Office lies officially within the boundaries of the legislative branch of government, it serves the entire government and indeed even conducts a printing operation in the basement of the Supreme Court Building in order to set up in advance of delivery the opinions of the justices.

A depository library system for government publications is based on a theory that information printed by the government should be distributed and kept permanently in every part of the country for citizens to consult. This notion is certainly fundamental to the American theory of democracy. Indeed it is more easily justified in terms of enlightening the citizenry than third class mailing rates for pulp magazines.

A steep growth in the number of depository libraries has accompanied the proliferation of United States government publications. The number of depository libraries is listed annually in September in the *Monthly Catalog of United States Government Publications*; there are now approximately 1100. As many as 300 of these have been added in the last decade and most represent the movement of junior colleges and community colleges to enlarge their library programs by acquiring government documents inexpensively. This could be shortsighted for while the documents themselves are free, the cost of their storage is high and the easy acquisitions of these publications may not, in the long run, be beneficial to such small institutions. In any event, the addition of depository libraries is in harmony with their steady growth since 1859 when a few depository libraries were begun under an act charging the Department of the Interior with the publication and distribution of government documents. National growth is evidenced by the dates at which libraries in the country were designated as depositories. The Boston Public Library, the Harvard University Library, and the Yale University Library all became depositories at the inception of the program. By 1900 depository libraries existed at the land grant colleges, at most of the large city libraries in the country, and at prominent private colleges. State libraries were also included in the program. The upshot is that these older libraries continue to have some edge on newer institutions because the older libraries have holdings that run back through the nineteenth century.

Returning to Congressional publications per se, the next significant step for students of politics was the more common printing of committee hearings and their inclusion in the depository program. Beginning in 1924 all hearings published by committees and listed in the *Monthly Catalog* have been mailed to depository libraries for safekeeping. It is possible to detect in the literature of political science the impact of the availability of these hearings to scholars in various parts of the country. For example, the study of politics and the Smoot-Hawley Tariff by E. E. Schattschneider was based largely on a scrutiny of the nearly 20,000 pages of testimony in the public hearings on the tariff bill in 1929–1930 (Schattschneider, 1935, p. 3). Excerpts from hearings before the House Committee on Un-American Activities from 1938 to 1968 were made into a commercial best-seller and a play by a leading critic, playwright, and editor (Bentley, 1971).

The *Congressional Record*, like Congress itself, is frequently held up to ridicule for its wordiness and its inclusion of extraneous material published at the behest of congressmen. There is also the genteel practice permitting members of Congress to change their remarks on the floor after they have been spoken but before entry into the *Record*. Yet the *Record* is one of the publishing marvels of American government and politics. By the 1940s it had achieved the usable form it has today. The *Congressional Record* is often thought of as the world's largest daily newspaper because it contains a daily verbatim account of everything said on the floor of both Houses of Congress, includes extensive additional reprinting of national editorial and other comment, and provides a résumé of events scheduled for the day of publication. This latter feature, called the *Daily Digest,* was introduced in 1946. The value of this schedule lies not only in its immediate use as a guide to hearings, bills reported, and so on. The *Daily Digest* is also combined in sequence for the entire year and published in a separate part of the permanently bound *Congressional Record,* thereby constituting a veritable institutional diary. An additional aid is provided every two weeks in the form of the *Congressional Record Index,* which includes a history of bills and resolutions for both the House and the Senate. This is also collated and bound as a separate book as a key to an entire term. Because a single daily issue of the *Congressional Record* may run to more than 200 pages, the total for the year often takes up as much as five linear feet of shelf space. In approaching a single year of the *Congressional Record* it will be evident very quickly that the entire year constitutes a single volume. Thus the deliberations of the Second Session of the Ninety-first Congress between 19 January 1970 and 2 January 1971 are embraced in Volume 116, paginated consecutively to 44621. Happily, this massive material occupying over six linear feet of shelf space is divided into 35 numbered parts, easily searched by using the last two books in the volume, the *Congressional Record Index* and the final book, Part 35, the *Daily Digest*. The *Daily Digest* also contains a résumé of congressional activity, a disposition of executive nominations, a table of bills enacted into public law during the session, and an elaborate and exceedingly valuable history of bills enacted into public law during the session with details of citations at various stages of enactment.

The clarification of binding law and its publication for the information of all residents of the country has presented the most complex intellectual public policy and publishing task of Congress. The chronological appearance of the series called the *Statutes at Large,* now past its 180th year of consecutive publication, contains too many additions, deletions, and contradictions to make it a feasible key to the law in force for an accomplished lawyer, let alone an ordinary citizen. This is not to say that the *Statutes at Large* can be disregarded, only that its uses are limited. Congress recognized this difficulty and sought in 1873 to begin a codification of the laws in a series of publications called the *Revised Statutes.* But there was insufficient appreciation of the difficulty of the task and also an unawareness of the stretch of time that Congress should provide for in order to achieve a satisfactory codification. In a word, the *Revised Statutes* muddied rather than solved the problem; weak editing produced numerous contradictions and difficulties for users. In the 1890s Congress appointed a commission that ultimately prepared the Criminal Code of 1909 and the Judicial Code of 1911 but, as Charles J. Zinn has pointed out, "Almost immediately after that Congress enacted laws which affected those codes but did not specifically amend them, again two bodies of law grew up side-by-side" (Zinn, 1952, p. 5). Finally, in 1925 the first edition of the *United States Code* was adopted by Congress and this, since brought up to date, stands as a monumental, yet relatively easy, collection of books to use.

The codifiers had to work through the entire set of statutes in force at that time and classify them under one of the fifty subject titles of the *Code.* Although classification is a matter of opinion and judgment, the expert lawyers who have worked on the *Code* have done an impressive job. The *United States Code* has continued under a program of constant updating and revision with the result that today when a public law is enacted by Congress, its place in a title of the *United States Code* is already settled. This is true even though the *Code* is officially published every six years.

Congress is such a vast institution and the results of its deliberations are so important that its work is necessarily characterized by an enormous variety of publications that are sped through the printing presses. These include in each Congress more than 15,000 different bills with additional prints on many, all published quickly at the behest of the persons in Congress introducing them. There are also numerous committee prints as well as hearings, reports, calendars, and guides to major legislative actions. When these are added to the list of publications, streaming off the presses, concerning the executive branch and the courts, as well as the political literature in newspapers, magazines, and books, one can see that Congress is almost literally overwhelmed by the printed page.

The growth of government publications has been so great and the practice of printing and disseminating information so lacking in flair that commercial publishers that had been squeezed out of the business in the late nineteenth century have now returned with enormous vigor and imagination. Thus the classic guide *Government Publications and Their Use* (Schmeckebier and Eastin, 1969) is published privately by the Brookings Institution, while another important key, the indispensable *Monthly Catalog of United States Government Publications,* is issued by the Government Printing Office. For the historical record there are also the statutes and debates printed privately and discussed earlier. There are examples of the newer commercial interest in the *Congressional Quarterly Almanac* and the West Publishers' *U.S. Code Congressional and Administrative News,* both of which date from the early 1940s. Among documents of a current session these publishers provide up-to-date information in the form of the *Congressional Quarterly Weekly Report* and the fortnightly additions to the *Congressional and Administrative News.* Another privately published document is the *Congressional Staff Directory.* It has always been true that newspapers reveal information about the government to the public but today's information is so extensive and complex that the newspapers themselves have become the most consistent subscribers to the *Congressional Quarterly Weekly Report,* the *National Journal Reports, United States Law Week,* and other keys to current developments. Because these publications are carefully documented, imaginatively edited, regularly published, thoroughly indexed, bound in loose-leaf, widely available in libraries, and easily obtained by individuals at faculty and student rates, they are also heavily used by political scientists. They merit extended comment.

A phenomenal range of political and legislative developments are covered in depth by the *Congressional Quarterly Weekly Report* published by Congressional Quarterly, Inc. since 1944. This includes the full text of presidential press conferences and messages, details on lobbying expenditures, redistricting developments in every state, and election campaigns, costs, and results. The most important innovation of Congressional Quarterly is the careful preparation of roll call votes of all members of both Houses. These are not only published in the *Weekly Report* but have also been compiled annually since 1945 in a special single volume, *Congressional Quarterly Almanac.* In turn, the total studies produced by Congressional Quarterly have been published in volumes of longer range summaries called *Congress and the Nation,* the first covering the years from 1945 to 1964, and the second covering the Johnson administration from 1965 to 1969. Congressional Quarterly really operates as a type of newspaper research service, selling its words to regular newspapers throughout the country and placing its information in libraries as well. It is strong on objectivity, emphasizes up-to-dateness, and regularly provides considerable depth in its reporting. Its very ample indexes have made it a service very highly regarded among political scientists.

A second notable service concerning Congress, designed particularly for lawyers, is the *United States Code Congressional and Administrative News,* a legal service pamphlet of the West Publishing Company of St. Paul, Minnesota. This is published every two weeks and includes the text of all public laws. In addition, selected official committee reports constitute the legislative history of these laws, and the *Congressional and Administrative News* also includes the text of presidential executive orders and proclamations and certain other key administrative rules and regulations. There is almost no editorial or descriptive comment in this publication but it is a quick and useful text paralleling the *Statutes at Large* and the most important documents of Congress that pertain to the enactment of legislation. It too is collected and bound in annual volumes and consequently makes up an historical record since its initiation in 1940.

One other source that deserves to be pointed out is the *National Journal Reports,* a weekly publication patterned after the *Congressional Quarterly Weekly Report* but emphasizing research and evaluative journalism, and resulting in substantial and detailed analyses of particular phenomenon associated with Congress. Its in-depth stories may deal in several pages with lobbies, with a particular committee's work, or with a particular public policy. The *National Journal Reports,* established in 1968, is now heavily depended on by political scientists in the field of American government who wish to have the kind of political science report on current events that ordinarily is available only after a scholar has worked on the subject. In common with the other commercial services dealing with Congress and with national government problems, the *National Journal Reports,* the *U.S. Code Congressional and Administrative News,* and the Congressional Quarterly Service are each exceedingly expensive. While student subscriptions are available, the regular library fees for each run into the hundreds of dollars.

The Federal Executive

Over 90 percent of United States government publications emanate from the executive branch. This is out of an annual total of about 30,000 entries in the *Monthly Catalog.* A convenient way to grasp the extent and character of this enterprise is to examine the *Monthly Catalog.* This provides information concerning publications available in the depository libraries and also introduces the concept of "government authors." The President is rarely considered a government author in the official sense because the Office of the Federal Register publishes the *Weekly Compilation of Presidential Documents,* the *Public Papers of the President,* and is consequently the government author for *Monthly Catalog* purposes. The Office of the Federal Register also prepares the daily newspaper of the executive branch, begun in 1936 and called the *Federal Register.* This is the legal place of publication of presidential executive orders and departmental and agency scheduling of hearings and the issuance of rules and regulations. At a lower level of law the *Federal Register'*s contents match those of the *Statutes at Large* and, comparably, the *Code of Federal Regulations* presents administrative law in codified form just as the *United States Code* does for statutory law.

Prepared annually by the Office of the Federal Register, the *United States Government Manual* contains several sections about the printing and publishing programs of the government. The description of the Government Printing Office mentions that a special brochure, *How to Keep in Touch with U.S. Government Publications,* is available by writing to the Superintendent of Documents, Washington, D.C. 20402. Government bookstores are also opening in a number of cities. The *Government Manual* also includes a description of the Office of Federal Register. Thus the *Monthly Catalog* and the *Government Manual,* together with *Government Publications and Their Use,* will afford a sound beginning to working with the numerous sources that display the work of the executive branch.

The Constitution of the United States: Analysis and Interpretation contains a huge body of knowledge stressing Supreme Court rulings with more than 100 pages on the national executive. These annotations treat tenure, succession, the Commander-in-Chief, pardons, executive agreements, removal power, the legislative role of the President, and impeachment. A new edition of this annotated Constitution was published in 1973. A streamlined version created years ago by Edward S. Corwin is now back in print in paperback and, complements the large government publication very well indeed. This new version of *The Constitution and What It Means Today* is now being revised annually after each Supreme Court term ends (Corwin, 1973). Titles that apply to the president and executive branch in the *United States Code* and the *Code of Federal Regulations* are pointed out. Other publications of interest concerning the presidency include the listings of all Administrations in the *Biographical Directory of the American Congress, 1774–1961,* budget and other economic documents, reports of Presidential commissions, and annual reports and periodic bulletins issued by departments and agencies about their programs.

Many nongovernmental publications must be consulted to learn about the president and the executive branch of government. The *New York Times* in 1971 again showed itself to be noteworthy by publishing "The Pentagon Papers" and later, the memoirs of Lyndon B. Johnson. It is the only newspaper in the United States with a published index to all issues from its inception, in this instance from 1856 to the present. While the *New York Times Index* is remarkably informative in itself and may be used with great profit quite apart from the newspaper, *Facts on File* is more complete since it is a condensed news service published weekly and indexed cumulatively through each year. *Keesings Contemporary Archives,* published since the 1930s, is also a formidable but easily used source of the same character. Other publications discussed at length as shedding light on Congress are equally useful guides to activities in the executive branch. These include the *U.S. Code Congressional and Administrative News,* the Congressional Quarterly Services, including the superb reference *Congress and the Nation* (Vol. 1 for 1945–1964, Vol. 2 for 1965–1968, and Vol. 3 for 1969–1972), and the *National Journal Reports.*

An official, contemporary, and permanent publication of presidential writing and utterances was not begun until 1957. Bound volumes of the *Public Papers of the Presidents* are now prepared for publication by the Office of the Federal Register. The calendar year is the basic unit, with adjustments for inaugural years, or years in which unexpected, abrupt transitions of office occur. (One book per year was published for Presidents Truman, Eisenhower, Kennedy and Nixon but two each for Johnson.) The volumes come out about ten months after the period covered ends. Upon the recommendation of the National Historical Publications and Records Commission the *Public Papers of the Presidents* will cover previous Presidents back to Herbert Hoover, the volumes for Eisenhower and Truman already having been published. The chief documents for earlier administrations will be found in a compilation by James D. Richardson called the *Messages and Papers of the Presidents, 1789–1897,* in ten volumes. The public papers of Franklin D. Roosevelt were edited by Samuel Rosenman and published commercially in the 1930s and early 1940s. The press conferences, messages to Congress, and political campaign speeches found in the *Public Papers of the Presidents* are updated every Monday by the *Weekly Compilation of Presidential Documents.*

The manuscripts of the presidents in the Library of Congress and the presidential libraries will be discussed in a later section of this chapter dealing with manuscripts and archives.

The Courts

The private or commercial tracking of the work of the federal judiciary is even more extensive and significant than that accomplished for the legislative branch of the United States government. The same holds true for courts throughout the country. Everything begins with the publication of official reports. The decisions of the Supreme Court from its beginning in 1790 are gathered together in the *United States Reports.* This series contains all the opinions of the justices issued in connection with any litigation that came to the Court. But the editing and printing of these decisions have been overseen by a reporter, a succession of men designated by the justices. As in English practice, the first 90 reports of the Supreme Court decisions were named for the reporter who handled their publication, but they have also been known and cited as *United States Reports.* This is really an arcane matter because when the printing of the *Reports* was taken over in 1875 by the United States Government Printing Office, the *Reports* came generally to be known *not* by the name of the reporter, although men still serve in such a position, but by the title *United States Reports,* cited simply as "U.S." By 1973, these totaled over 412 volumes. The *United States Reports* are indispensable for students of constitutional law and of judicial behavior. Thus a compiler of a constitutional law textbook would ordinarily use little else besides the opinions found in the *United States Reports*; this is true also of the authors of standard histories of constitutional law. The *United States Reports* are not only essential in describing the development of constitutional doctrine, the judicial philosophies of individual justices or of whole courts as they appear in the opinions, but they also have been crucial in some of the pathbreaking intellectual work in political science on judicial behavior. For example, the work of Pritchett, represented particularly in his *Roosevelt Court* (1947), was accomplished by an almost exclusive use of the *United States Reports,* as he emphasized the division among the justices that could easily be learned from this service. Thus the official decisions of the Court are not only useful in historical and conventional descriptions of the Court, but also in ascertaining the social and political dynamics among the justices.

One further point should be made about the great significance of the *United States Reports* as a source in understanding the work of the Supreme Court. This series includes the orders of the Court and all the petitions that are received by it. Consequently it is a starting point for numerous types of intellectual enterprise. Studies of what the Court did not do start here. Many observations predicting the future course of decision begin with attention to details in the opinions. Detective work in the *United States Reports* often tells a great deal about the Supreme Court as an institution.

The power, prestige, and magic of the Supreme Court of the United States is reflected in the fact that *four* commercial publishers copy the *United States Reports* verbatim as the basis of law reporters offered for sale, and successfully so, to lawyers and others who follow legal developments. *United States Law Week* photographs and prints new decisions within hours of their release by the Court. This is the most comprehensive, and costly, service concerning the Supreme Court because all cases docketed are summarized, all orders on such cases are indicated, oral arguments are summarized, and the status of the Court's work is frequently summarized. The *Supreme Court Bulletin* by the Commerce Clearing House is also based on the *United States Reports* but is the least valuable of the four commercial reporters. The two other services, each of which is a system of information about the rulings of the Supreme Court, are the *Lawyer's Edition of the United States Supreme Court Reports* and the *Supreme Court Reporter.*

Among reference books on this subject one of the best and probably the most neglected by political scientists is *Supreme Court Practice* by Robert L. Stern and Eugene Gressman (1969). The operations of the Supreme Court are constantly changing and this reference book is needed by anyone who wishes to be well versed in Court procedures as they evolve.

Stern and Gressman show the Supreme Court to be a creative governing body with initiative in all kinds of matters. For one, they amplify the well-understood significance of the Judiciary Act of 1925 restricting the Court's obligatory jurisdiction and increasing the scope of its discretionary power of review. Some 150 pages of the book treat the writ of certiorari in instructive detail which underscores the Court's "active and effective role in the realm of public administration" (Stern and Gressman, 1969, p. 148). For another, they clarify the less-known discretion of the modern Court in refusing to review 75 percent of the cases coming by way of appeal and, therefore, presumably within its obligatory jurisdiction. This power of choice was gained by shaping a Rule of the Supreme Court, in four steps in 1928, 1936, 1942, and 1954, requiring counsel on appeal to show, in a preliminary statement, that the questions involved in his case are "substantial." Stern and Gressman conclude that the requirement that substantiality be shown "means that the Jurisdictional Statement now performs a function similar to that of the petition for certiorari" (Stern and Gressman, 1969, p. 393). As with other subjects treated, the book includes statistics, reviews history, cites commentaries, quotes the views of the justices, and comes forward with its own interpretation. Another available procedure contributing to the image of an active court, administering its business with initiative, is the utilization of its certiorari jurisdiction *before* rendition of judgment by a court of appeals, a choice the Court utilized in the case over the Nixon tapes in 1974. These and other features show that a handbook on a court can do more than recite wooden rules and formal practices.

Political scientists with a further interest in the law, and in judicial decisions and behavior, might note details about many other sources by consulting the superior books on the study of law such as *Effective Legal Research* by Price and Bitner. *Legal Research in a Nutshell* by Morris Cohen deals with the fundamentals most concisely. Both describe the sources of statutes and administrative decisions, as well as judicial rulings. They are the books, above all others, that students should refer to to learn many specific points about the law library that are beyond the scope of this chapter.

Archives and Manuscript Collections

Today vast offices of files from government agencies, voluntary associations, and individuals are culled, processed, and preserved by professional archivists in hundreds of repositories around the country. These manuscripts are sources of data concerning political behavior, professional careers, human relationships, social movements, organized strategies, and tactics in seeking or stopping new public policies. The "developmental analysis" for Woodrow Wilson by George and George synthesized well-known facts of Wilson's career but also depended on the Wilson, Baker, Hitchcock, and Lansing Papers at the Library of Congress and the House Papers at the Yale University Library (George and George, 1956, p. 323). New light on tactics in decision making by the Supreme Court was shed by Alexander Bickel's discovery and publication of unpublished opinions of Mr. Justice Brandeis that were in the Brandeis Papers at Harvard University Law School (Bickel, 1957). Political scientists with an historical bent, especially in public law (David Danelski, Woodford Howard, Peter McGrath, Alpheus Mason, Walter Murphy, Marvin Schick, Sidney Ulmer, Clement E. Vose, and Alan Westin among them) have made heavy use of manuscripts for judicial biographies and studies of litigation. As the volume of papers grows and their availability increases, it is probable that political scientists with widely disparate interests will utilize manuscript collections.

National Archives

The National Archives and Records Service, under the direction of the Archivist of the United States and begun in 1934, "selects, preserves, and makes available to the Government and the public the permanently valuable noncurrent records of the Federal Government" *(United States Government Organization Manual,* 1971/72, p. 456). These include official files and detailed records of every executive department including the Defense, State, and Justice Departments and independent agencies as well. The Bureau of the Census files, for example, include forms prepared by enumerators in house-to-house canvassing for decennial censuses. Applications for National Science Foundation grants, blueprints of every Navy ship, and papers from the Court of Claims are among the millions of records in the National Archives. The National Archives Building in Washington, D.C. has been supplemented since 1954 with the development of thirteen Federal Records Centers in ten regions of the country, and the Washington National Records Center at Suitland, Maryland, and the National Personnel Records Center in St. Louis. With its millions of cubic feet of government records the National Archives holds materials of interest to political scientists in all fields. Scholars should feel welcome to make known their interests and appreciate that the Archives is as open and available for information as their friendly neighborhood druggist. The Archivist of the United States has formed the National Archives Advisory Council with a representative of the American Political Science Association as a member, to advise on policies that will make the entire archival system of greater service to scholars. There are also many publications concerning the National Archives, the best being

H. G. Jones's *The Records of a Nation: Their Management, Preservation, and Use* (New York: Atheneum, 1969).

A unique institution came into existence in 1941 with the establishment of the Franklin D. Roosevelt Library at Hyde Park, New York. From the time of George Washington, presidential papers had been regarded as the personal property of the president. Some of them were destroyed, others acquired by private individuals or institutions, and much of 23 other presidents' deposited in the Library of Congress. The idea of a personal presidential library was President Roosevelt's and he donated part of his Hyde Park estate for the location. The library was dedicated on 30 June 1941. The Hayes Library in Fremont, Ohio, run privately since 1917, is the only similar memorial to a nineteenth century President.

The idea of the Hyde Park library was incorporated into law by Congressional enactment of the Presidential Libraries Act of 1955. The Act provides that the National Archives and Records Service of the General Services Administration may accept and operate new Presidential libraries. The Harry S. Truman Library at Independence, Missouri, was built and furnished without cost to the government from funds donated by thousands of individuals and organizations. It was dedicated 6 July 1957, and President Truman had his office there until his death in 1973.

The Dwight D. Eisenhower Library in Abilene, Kansas was planned and completed within the framework of the Presidential Libraries Act of 1955. In 1960 President Eisenhower gave to the government the bulk of his personal papers on the condition that they be deposited and maintained by the United States in perpetuity at the library. The library building and the papers of many of Eisenhower's associates, during his time as general and as president, were also donated. The Eisenhower Library was dedicated on 1 May 1962.

The Herbert Hoover Library in West Branch, Iowa, was accepted by the federal government and dedicated on 10 August 1962. The nucleus of the library's holdings is the large collection of papers accumulated by Mr. Hoover during his long years of public service, especially while he was Secretary of Commerce and President of the United States. The papers do not include those on "war and peace" which he long ago gave to Stanford University.

The cataclysmic events surrounding the American presidency, highlighted by the Kennedy assassination in 1963, the Vietnam War, and the Watergate scandals, have opened serious issues over the continued expansion of the Presidential library idea. Appearances have sometimes concealed the doubts. Thus did Lyndon B. Johnson, on 9 August 1965 at the height of his prestige, accept a proposal by the regents of the University of Texas to pay fully for a personal presidential library to be built on the Austin campus, along with a Lyndon B. Johnson Institute of Public Service. The building was erected while he was still in office, and he took up office space there prior to his death in 1973. During his final months in the White House Johnson obtained from Congress a substantial appropriation for all the libraries in the system, enabling each one to have larger staffs and to undertake new projects to collect papers and do oral histories.

The events associated with Watergate have seriously jeopardized plans for a library for President Nixon. A number of the trustees in charge of planning for a library in southern California were implicated in the scandals. In addition, the controversy over the value of the Nixon vice-presidential papers raised questions about ownership, appraisal, and tax practices of presidential materials generally. The central White House files that make the centerpiece for most Presidential libraries are not really sufficient to make a first-class library, and this is why the archivists in charge of developing the Kennedy Library in Massachusetts have reached out to obtain the life papers of such leading economists as John Kenneth Galbraith, Seymour Harris, Walter Heller, and Paul Samuelson. They have also undertaken one of the most substantial oral history programs in the country. But Nixon's associates present more problems than can be seen by reading the headlines. Former Vice-President Spiro Agnew simply donated his papers to the University of Maryland, while Gerald Ford has been placing his noncurrent files with the Michigan Historical Society. If a Nixon Library could somehow be established, there would be inevitable gaps in the eventual holdings.

Since the mid-1960s the papers and attic-like museum objects of John F. Kennedy, his brothers, and his associates have been maintained at the Federal Archives and Records Center in Waltham, Massachusetts always with the expectation of moving one day to a new and permanent home near Harvard Square in Cambridge, ten miles away. A fund-raising committee took up residence in a Beacon Hill apartment once lived in by the late President. The Kennedy family chose the prominent architect I. M. Pei to design the library. Harvard University proferred cooperation by starting a John F. Kennedy Institute (later to be named the John F. Kennedy School of Government) directed by Professor Richard Neustadt, and arranged to have Pei design a building to be nearby the government-run Kennedy Library. The Commonwealth of Massachusetts donated more than 12 acres of choice land adjoining the University and fronting the Charles River. There would be a museum aspect to the enterprise, associated with the Library. In 1973 a grandiose and costly plan for all of this was unveiled by Pei, Senator Edward Kennedy and others. The expectation that one million tourists would visit the site during its opening year sent chills down the spines of the sons of Harvard, the denizens of Radcliffe, and many of the citizens of Cambridge, while innkeepers and fast-food managers and their lawyers, contractors, and bankers spent many a day examining records of deeds and zoning regulations. The 1973 plans were adjusted the following year to provide for smaller buildings and lower costs. A pedestrian park would take up much of the space, thus alleviating pressure from crowds of visitors (*New York Times,* 8 June 1974, p. 46).

The sad part of the story of the reduced Kennedy Library is that only about one-third of the 22 million papers in the Kennedy collection, as it presently stands, would be housed in the new edifice. The others would remain in Waltham. In a trenchant essay, Ada Louise Huxtable attacked the museum provision of the Presidential Libraries Act of 1955 by asserting that a meaningless museum catering to well-intentioned tourists is senseless national policy. Scholars will suffer while the masses are deceived (Huxtable, 1974).

In preserving documents across the whole national government, the National Archives and Records Service acts in accordance with its established "records management" function. As part of the General Services Administration, the staff of the National Archives has developed guidelines of what is disposable as well as what is appropriate to preserve. The archivists work closely with all agencies of the federal government to weed out and destroy multiple copies of items, duplicates with modest variations, and other types of material of minimal probable archival interest. It is said that this practice of records disposal frees filing cabinets and space sufficiently to pay in large part for the preservation work of the National Archives.

Records come into the central archives from the departments and agencies in Washington, into the Federal Records Centers from the lower federal courts around the country and from the many regional and district offices of federal administrative office, and into the presidential libraries from individual administrations. In addition, the National Archives acquires manuscript and other valuable materials of interest to scholars from an astonishing variety of sources. When the National Archives was established in 1934, many national records were in private hands and some were purchased by the federal government. The family of Franklin D. Roosevelt donated memorabilia of his family life to the library at Hyde Park. Mrs. Ernest Hemingway has donated a vast archive of her husband's manuscripts to the Kennedy Presidential Library. At the end of World War II a vast captured German archive from the German Foreign Office and other parts of the government came into the possession of the National Archives. The Ford Motor Company motion picture film collection was donated to the National Archives.

True, the National Archives, under the Federal Records Act, may accept "documents, including motion-picture films, still pictures, and sound recordings, from private sources that are appropriate for preservation by the Government as evidence of its organization, functions, policies, decisions, procedures, and transactions" (Act of 5 September 1950, 64 Stat. 578, Sec. 507 (e) (2)). One authority asserts that "the act in no way was intended to open the door to the institution's competition with established repositories for nonfederal materials" (Jones, 1969, p. 111). The presidential libraries have a freer hand under their statutory authority and can be more aggressive in seeking materials from the private sector. But while the National Archives accepts some manuscript materials from outside the government it holds a virtual monopoly in law over federal records and may even force records that have escaped back into federal custody. This it sought to do in the 1950s when field notes of the Lewis and Clark Expedition of 1804–1806 turned up in the attic of a home in St. Paul, Minnesota and were transferred to the Minnesota Historical Society. "The case's central issue was the United States government's claim to sixty-seven pieces of paper—most of them in the handwriting of William Clark—on the ground that they had been created by a federal employee in the course of his official duties, and that all such documents, including rough notes, belonged rightfully to the federal government" (Tomkins, 1966, p. 105). The National Archives lost the case in two lower federal courts because of the evidence that these rough notes made during the expedition were private papers rather than public documents executed in discharge of official duties [*United States* v. *First Trust Company of St. Paul,* 251 F.2d 686 (1958), affirming 146 F.Supp. 652 (1956)]. While the case seemed hopelessly lost, the choice of the Archivist not to appeal the decision of the Court of Appeals in the case of the Lewis and Clark papers is said to indicate "that the concern of the National Archives will be the preservation of such records rather than a narrow interpretation of the law as to their custody" (Jones, 1969, p. 110).

Policies governing access to the records of the United States government are tied up between conflicting values of information for the public, disclosure to the press, and unfettered inquiry by scholars on the one hand, as against secrecy in the national interest, the orderly control of communications for governmental efficiency, and the maintenance of privacy for individual citizens whose lives may be documented in census, tax, and social security records. Public policy in these matters is in conflict in statutes, in administrative rulings and practice, and in court rulings. Thus the Freedom of Information Act of 1967 (P.L. 90–23, amending 5 U.S.C. sec. 552) seeks to make it easier for private citizens to secure government information. This broadened the provisions of the Administrative Procedure Act of 1942 designed to achieve the same purpose.

During its first three years, about 100 lawsuits had been filed under the Freedom of Information Act, with most filed against the government (*U.S. Law Week* 1970, 39:2115). Yet there were nine categories of information exempted from disclosure, and a federal court ruled against an historian's claim that the army should declassify documents on forced postwar repatriation of Soviet citizens. Since the original top secret classification was held not to be arbitrary and capricious and was periodically reviewed, the army was upheld (*Epstein* v. *Resor,* 9 CA in *U.S. Law Week* 38:2473, 10 March 1970; case decided 6 February 1970). Despite these court rulings, applications for access to once sensitive records appear increasingly to be handled by administration agreeableness. Cases in point include the opening of the FBI records of Ezra Pound and of

Julius and Ethel Rosenberg. When Daniel Ellsberg provided newspapers with the contents of a classified study entitled "History of U.S. Decision-Making Process on Viet Nam Policy" and published or wished to publish them, the Supreme Court would not forbid them. The government was unable to convince the Court that irreparable harm would result from publication of "The Pentagon Papers" [*New York Times Company* v. *United States,* and *United States* v. *The Washington Post Company,* 403 U.S. 713 (1971)]. But Mr. Justice White's concurring opinion cautioned that the Court's decision did not mean that the law invited newspapers or others to publish sensitive documents or that they would be immune from criminal action if they did so. There is wide agreement that documents of the national government have been overclassified, a point testified to by President Nixon's adoption of a program of swifter review (*Weekly Compilation of Presidential Documents,* 9 August 1971, p. 1117).

Among numerous Archives' records closed to researchers (for reasons of confidentiality to protect the privacy of citizens) are census enumerators' schedules. The census-takers fear that disclosure would make the public reluctant to supply information. As early as 1851 the Superintendent of the Census ruled there should be no "unnecessary exposure of facts relating to individuals." The principle of confidentiality was gradually embodied in legislation, and reinforced by sterner instructions to enumerators and stronger assurances of privacy to respondents. The 1909 Census Act authorized furnishing individuals' data from the population schedules "as may be desired for genealogical or other proper purposes," yet retained rules favoring confidentiality—a conflict that existed for some years. Uncertainty was resolved against easy access by adoption of the so-called "72-year ruling" made by the Director of the Census in a letter of 26 August 1952 to the Archivist of the United States. Under this *no* schedules would be open until after a lapse of 72 years from the enumeration date of a decennial census. After 72 years information would be opened to qualified researchers but information is not to be used to the detriment of any person whose records were involved (Davidson and Ashby, 1964, pp. 97–99). Under this policy the records for 1880 became fully available in 1952. This was inapplicable in 1962 because most of the 1890 population schedules were so badly damaged in the Commerce Department building fire of January 1921 that they were authorized for disposal; thus only a few schedules from some of the states survived. The prospect of seeing the 1900 records cheered genealogists as 1972 approached. Alas, the Director of the Census made a preliminary decision to raise the number of years required before disclosing these records from 72 to 100. This policy was questioned by the Archivist of the United States and the National Archives Advisory Council, which helped gain a grudging concession from the Census Bureau allowing access to the 1900 records by qualified scholars and genealogists.

Political scientists will gain from a heightened awareness of the size, variety, and generally easy access to the collections of the National Archives, Federal

Records Centers, and presidential libraries. Knowledge of these riches is provided in articles such as "The use of archives for historical statistical inquiry" (Hays, 1969, pp. 7–15) and "Government archives afield: the federal records centers and the historian" (White, 1969, pp. 833–842). There are numerous items of information about sources in the Truman Library in the 1967 book (now being revised) *The Harry S. Truman Period as a Research Field* (Kirkendall, 1967). The best sources for current archival thinking and news of new available materials are two journals, *The American Archivist* since 1938 and *Prologue: The Journal of the National Archives* since 1969. The following points of information are suggestive:

Item: The government operates over 4000 computers and is producing about 1,200,000 magnetic tapes a year in three categories: fiscal, statistical, and scientific. The National Archives is constantly reviewing its retention programs for these tapes (*Prologue,* 1969, 1:38–39).

Item: Over 600 stenographic tape recordings of all oral arguments before the Supreme Court for the 1955 through 1966 terms have been received from the Marshal of the Court (*Prologue,* 1969, 1:47). Copies are available at cost from the Archives upon approval by the Marshal. An hour's oral argument on tape costs about $15.

Item: The House of Representatives has transferred the greater part of its records relating to the 88th Congress (1963–1964) to the National Archives. This accession consists of general correspondence, committee papers, and petitions (*Prologue,* 1971, 3:43).

Manuscript Collections

Philip Hamer's *A Guide to Archives and Manuscripts in the United States* (1961) makes plain the number one position of the Library of Congress among repositories for private papers. Simple listings run to 74 columns for the Library of Congress, compared to about 20 each for the notable holdings in the New York Public Library, the Huntington Library in San Marino, California, the Southern Regional Collection of the University of North Carolina, the University of Pennsylvania, Yale University, Harvard University and the Massachusetts Historical Society. Comparisons based on this count would merit little weight if not supported by impressions of comparative depth, importance, and use and also by the national leadership in manuscript policy exhibited over many years by the Library of Congress.

The quality of the historic collections of the colonial period, of the eighteenth and nineteenth centuries, and current acquisition policy makes the materials in the Library of Congress unrivaled in comprehensiveness. Most of the papers of 23 presidents are there, along with those of hundreds of congressmen, diplomats, and judges. The Hamer *Guide to Manuscripts* will give the best quick grasp of the range. Otherwise news of accessions will be found in the *Annual Report of the Librarian of Congress,* the *Quarterly Journal of the Library of Congress,* and the acquisition notes in the weekly *Library of Congress Information Bulletin.*

Although systematic conceptions of the world of manuscript collections are undeveloped, there are images that may interest political scientists. So far as manuscripts go, the Library of Congress is *not* the legislative equivalent of the National Archives. Rather it is a great national collection representative of cultural, intellectual, and political life. The Library of Congress even declines gifts of papers from congressmen, while eagerly seeking the office files of The National Woman's Party and the National Association for the Advancement of Colored People or the musical scores of Irving Berlin and Aaron Copland. In 1939 when Felix Frankfurter recommended that President Roosevelt appoint Archibald MacLeish, not a professional librarian, to be Librarian of Congress he took this large view of institutions:

> The need for qualities other than those which are trained in a professional librarian are accentuated in the case of the head of the Congressional Library. That Library is not merely a library, and in the immediate future even more so than in the past it will be concerned with problems quite outside the traditional tasks associated with collecting, housing and circulating books. For one thing the Library of Congress is a museum as well as a library. It has a distinguished collection of etchings and engravings—an aspect of the library which was of the greatest importance and edification to a person like Mr. Justice Holmes. It has a great collection of music—especially manuscript music—and its general manuscript materials, especially recent acquisitions like the Taft papers and the [Theodore] Roosevelt papers, present delicate questions which can be adequately dealt with only by a person of sympathetic and imaginative insight. (Freedman, 1967, p. 493)

In this letter Frankfurter also mentioned the advent of radio, film, and television, stressed that MacLeish was the father of the so-called radio play and had pioneered with film documentaries, and ventured that libraries would have to learn to cope with such records. Mr. MacLeish was appointed Librarian of Congress, serving from 1939 to 1944. There is an attractive mix of professional librarians, archivists, and scholars in the disciplines at the Library of Congress. Thus the specialist in twentieth-century politics in the Manuscript Division is a political scientist who is ready to guide researchers to materials easily overlooked in a formal search.

The Manuscript Division of the Library of Congress has excelled in developing "registers" as finding aids, guides, or organizational surveys of manuscript collections. In two articles in the early 1950s Katherine E. Brand showed convincingly the many valuable ways the register served research (Brand, 1953, 1955). The Division now has a register of most papers in its custody and has published a number of them, thereby influencing practices in other repositories. They are mimeographed but polished, well-edited guides available from the Division, with those for Felix Frankfurter, Andrew Carnegie, Frederick Law Olmstead, Tom Connally, and Booker T. Washington excellent examples of the genre. The standard preface in these registers tells their nature and purpose as concisely as can be:

> The register is a necessary implement in the Division's handling of massive unindexed collections. It serves a variety of purposes, providing a means for exercising custodial control over a collection; assistance to the reading room staff in issuing the collection to readers and to the reference staff in drafting replies to written inquiries; and a source of the information necessary to enable a cataloger to prepare a catalog entry for a collection in accordance with established rules for cataloging groups of manuscripts.

> By their publication, registers may be useful to other repositories by illustrating the Library's methods of organizing collections. The information on the size and organization of a collection furnished by a register may also enable a distant research student, with reasonable knowledge of his subject, to decide whether or not to come to the Library to consult the collection and, if he comes, to make more profitable use of limited time.

> Frequently a register describes a collection largely left in the arrangement it had as a "live" file and which has been accorded only external processing. A register does not describe the piece-by-piece arrangement or contents of a collection. It is not a definitive finding aid, catalog, calendar, or index. Ordinarily it will not enable the Library to furnish from a collection photocopies of itemized pieces, all the correspondence of an individual, or all the material on a given subject. Even the most detailed register will not preclude the necessity of research in locating specific documents. It is merely an aid to research, not a substitute for it.

The most complete registers are the Presidents' Papers Index Series for the 23 presidents whose papers are in the Library of Congress. This series may be used with the publication, in the medium of microfilm, of the papers themselves. Libraries in nearly every state are purchasing the film reels and the individual index books thereby opening to researchers some two million presidential manuscripts. The purchase price for the full set of positive films is about $35,000.

It remains only to say that this chapter has barely suggested surface opportunities for political science research in original manuscript sources, for outside the Library of Congress lie hundreds of fine smaller collections. These may be tapped usefully by consulting the *National Union Catalog of Manuscript Collections* begun in 1958 with annual supplements prepared in the Descriptive Cataloguing Division of the Library of Congress. The volume for 1969 brought the total number of collections described to 25,145, representing holdings in 758 repositories. Because the editors of the *Catalog* depend on reports, there are many collections not listed, among them the papers of the Roman Catholic archbishops of New York located at St. Joseph's Seminary, Yonkers, New York, and of James Weldon Johnson, first executive secretary of the NAACP, located at Yale University.

Oral history collections are deliberately excluded from the *National Union Catalog of Manuscript Collections,* which simply means that the zealous researcher must locate items in these riches by other means. This may be done through reports and catalogs published by the Oral History Association. An example of oral history successfully transcribed is seen by the memoir *Felix Frankfurter Reminisces* (Phillips, 1962). There are endlessly fascinating interviews of political figures now preserved in oral history programs that provide invaluable data about politics. Most have been transcribed and are easy to read and use. William E. Leuchtenburg *et al.* has illustrated how oral history is helpful to an historian needing a source of vivid expression:

> ... in writing about the Supreme Court, I have to explain at one point that the National Grange was opposed to the Court-packing plan presented by President Roosevelt. This is in itself a rather dull statement. Louis Taber's memoir, the memoir by the head of the Grange, at Columbia, however, has a vivid account of the morning on which he got a phone call from Henry Wallace, asking him for lunch, when he had never had a call from Wallace asking him for lunch in a private dining room before; how he knew he didn't trust himself to have lunch with Wallace before the position of the Grange had been announced; how he went to the mimeograph machine and hand-cranked it himself, and turned out the statement of the Grange in opposition to the Court plan; and how, when he finished cranking them, the copies of the statement were still wet, so he peeled off two or three of the copies and handed them out to each of the press association reporters in Washington, so he would be sure before he spoke to Wallace that the position of the Grange would be on record.
>
> Then at some length, and again quite vividly, he explains what happened when Wallace began to ask him to give support to the Court-packing bill, and put the Grange behind it, and how he sprang the surprise of what had happened that morning. (Leuchtenburg *et al.,* 1968, p. 3)

The spread of manuscript sources across the country can be looked at as so intimidatingly vast that one should forget the whole subject, but it also means that modest objectives can be achieved. A single set of papers can yield a fine study, as the papers of Edward G. Ryan in the State Historical Society of Wisconsin did in Alfons Beitzinger's (1960) biography, originally a doctoral dissertation. But one cannot be blind to interlocking possibilities and will profit from appreciating the variety of sources. Most repositories tend to have a regional flavor; this cuts across all subjects, which means that movements like abolition and populism will be depicted in many collections. Yet attention is called to the notable collections on women and women's rights at Radcliffe College (Cambridge, Massachusetts) and Smith College (Northampton, Massachusetts). Collections on blacks and black politics will be found at Yale University, in the Schomberg Center for Research in Black Culture of the New York Public Library at 125th Street in New York City, in the Martin Luther King Center in Atlanta, in the Amistad Research Center, Dillard University, New Orleans, and at Howard University in Washington, D.C. The papers of Booker T. Washington, of the NAACP and many of its leaders, and of the Urban League are at the Library of Congress. The Peace Collection at Swarthmore College, Swarthmore, Pennsylvania includes many of the papers of Jane Addams and of Hull House. There is a collection on settlement houses and other facets of the twentieth-century movement for social welfare at the University of Minnesota Library, Minneapolis. Two emphases of the Michigan Historical Collections are prohibition and conservation. There are substantial collections of papers of labor leaders and files of trade unions at the University of California in Berkeley, the University of Wisconsin in Madison, the Walter Reuther Library at Wayne State University in Detroit, the New York Public Library, and the Library of Congress. The papers of the American Civil Liberties Union since its organization in 1920 are in the manuscript collection of Princeton University. Papers of legislators and jurists and legal action groups are in the new Collection on Legal Change, Wesleyan University, Middletown, Connecticut. The Jewish Archives in Cincinnati include papers of many figures prominent in public life such as the lawyer Louis Marshall. A monumental collection on American scientists is held by the Library of the American Philosophical Society, Philadelphia.

Political scientists will recognize that political data come in many forms, are found in many places, and give shape to propositions in the discipline. This is not so much a subject in itself as it is an ancillary to the research that enlarges the scope, refines the verities, and enhances the spirit of political science. New wrinkles in methodology and in sources and types of data provided by recordings, the computer, video, field studies, and interviews are most welcome. Certainly the discipline can never again be *confined* to libraries and archives, but the early closeness of political science to history deserves renewal. This renewal should focus on improved knowledge of reference sources, possibly by inventing economical and lucid courses of instruction on libraries and archives. It is full of policy problems, of fascination, of abiding joy in learning.

REFERENCES

The reference materials and books described in this article are, for the most part, not included in the bibliography. The works listed below are primarily guides to and criticisms of those materials.

Anderson, Frank Maloy (1948). *The Mystery of "A Public Man": a Historical Detective Story*. Minneapolis: University of Minnesota Press.

Barzun, Jacques, and Henry F. Graff (1957). *The Modern Researcher*. New York: Harcourt.

Beitzinger, Alfons J. (1960). *Edward G. Ryan: Lion of the Law*. Madison: State Historical Society of Wisconsin.

Bentley, Eric (1971). *Thirty Years of Treason*. New York: Viking Press.

Benton, William (1958). *"The Great Soviet Encyclopedia." Yale Review* 47:552–568.

Bickel, Alexander M. (1957). *The Unpublished Opinions of Mr. Justice Brandeis*. Cambridge: Belknap Press.

Bliven, Naomi (1969). Review of *The Battle of Silence* by Jean Bruller. *New Yorker*, 8 November, p. 203.

Borden, Ruth B., and Robert M. Warner (1966). *The Modern Manuscript Library*. New York and London: Scarecrow Press.

Brand, Katharine E. (1953). "Developments in the handling of recent manuscripts in the Library of Congress." *American Archivist* 10, no. 2:99–104.

——————— (1955). "The place of the register in the manuscript division of the Library of Congress." *American Archivist* 13, no. 1:59–67.

Butler, Pierce (1961). *An Introduction to Library Science*. Chicago: University of Chicago Press.

Clapp, Verner W. (1964). *The Future of the Research Library*. Urbana: University of Illinois Press.

Clarke, Jack A. (1959). *Research Materials in the Social Sciences*. Madison: University of Wisconsin Press.

Cohen, Morris L. (1968). *Legal Research in a Nutshell*. St. Paul, Minn.: West.

Cooke, Jacob E., ed. (1961). *The Federalist*. Middletown, Conn.: Wesleyan University Press.

Corwin, Edward S. (1973). *The Constitution and What it Means Today*. Revised by Harold W. Chase and Craig R. Ducat. 13th ed. Princeton: Princeton University Press.

Davidson, K. H., and C. M. Ashby, eds. (1964). *Preliminary Inventory of the Records of the Bureau of the Census*, Record Group 29, pp. 97–99. Washington, D.C.: National Archives.

Einbinder, Harvey (1964). *The Myth of the Britannica*. New York: Grove Press.

Freedman, Max, ed. (1967). *Roosevelt and Frankfurter: Their Correspondence, 1928–1945*. Boston: Little, Brown.

George, Alexander L., and Juliette L. George (1956). *Woodrow Wilson and Colonel House: a Personality Study*. New York: John Day.

Halberstam, David (1972). *The Best and the Brightest.* New York: Random House.

Hays, Samuel P. (1969). "The use of archives for historical statistical inquiry." *Prologue* 1, no. 2:7–15.

Hoselitz, Bert F., ed. (1960). *A Reader's Guide to the Social Sciences.* Glencoe, Ill.: Free Press.

Huxtable, Ada Louise (1974). "What's a tourist attraction like the Kennedy Library doing in a nice neighborhood like this?" *New York Times,* 16 June, sec. 2, pp. 1, 28.

Jones, H. G. (1969). *The Records of a Nation: Their Management, Preservation, and Use.* New York: Atheneum.

Kennan, George F. (1967). *Memoirs, 1925–1950.* Boston: Little, Brown.

Key, V. O. (1956). "Strategies in research on public affairs." *Social Science Research Council Items* 10:29–32.

Kirkendall, Richard S., ed. (1967). *The Harry S. Truman Period as a Research Field.* Columbia: University of Missouri Press.

Leuchtenburg, William E., Frank Freidel, Cornelius Ryan, and James MacGregor Burns (1968). "A panel of historians discuss oral history." In Louis M. Starr, ed., *The Second National Colloquium on Oral History.* New York: Oral History Association.

Liebling, A. J. (1961). *The Press.* (Much of this material appeared originally in the *New Yorker,* 1946–1961.) New York: Ballantine.

Manley, Marian C. (1954). "Personalities behind the development of PAIS." *College and Research Libraries,* July, pp. 263–276.

Marias, Julian (1968). "The concept of generations." In D. E. Sills, ed., *International Encyclopedia of the Social Sciences.* Vol. 6, p. 88. New York: Macmillan and Free Press.

McCormick, Mona (1971). *Who-What-When-Where-How-Why Made Easy.* Chicago: Quadrangle Books.

Mosteller, Frederick, and David F. Wallace (1964). *Inference and Disputed Authorship: The Federalist.* Reading, Mass.: Addison-Wesley.

Murphey, Robert W. (1958). *How and Where to Look It Up: A Guide to Standard Sources of Information.* New York: McGraw-Hill.

Phillips, Harlan B., ed. (1962). *Felix Frankfurter Reminisces.* Garden City, N.Y.: Doubleday.

Price, Miles O., and Harry Bitner (1962). Student revised ed. *Effective Legal Research.* Boston: Little, Brown.

Riley, Matilda White, and Clarice S. Stoll (1968). "Content analysis." In D. E. Sills, ed., *International Encyclopedia of the Social Sciences.* Vol. 3, pp. 371–377. New York: Macmillan and Free Press.

Schattschneider, E. E. (1935). *Politics, Pressures and the Tariff.* New York: Prentice-Hall.

Schattschneider, E. E., Victor Jones, and Stephen K. Bailey (1973). Reprint ed. *A Guide to the Study of Public Affairs.* Westport, Conn.: Greenwood Press.

Schindler, Margaret C. (1936). "Fictitious biography." *American Historical Review* 42:680–690.

Schmeckebier, Laurence F., and Roy B. Eastin (1969). Second revised ed. *Government Publications and Their Use*. Washington, D.C.: Brookings Institution.

Shaplen, Robert (1955). "The metamorphosis of Philip Musica." *New Yorker,* 22 October, p. 29.

Stern, Robert L., and Eugene Gressman (1969). *Supreme Court Practice*. Fourth edition. Washington, D.C.: Bureau of National Affairs.

Stone, Julius (1960). "Manley Hudson: campaigner and teacher of international law." *Harvard Law Review* 74:215, 219–220.

Tauber, Maurice F. (1954). *Technical Services in Libraries*. New York: Columbia University Press.

Tomkins, Calvin (1966). "Annals of law: the Lewis and Clark case." *New Yorker,* 29 October, p. 105.

United States Office of the Federal Register (1971). *United States Government Organization Manual 1971/72*. Washington, D.C.: Government Printing Office.

Vose, Clement E. (1964–1966). *Understanding Congress. Understanding the Presidency. Understanding the Supreme Court*. Three wall charts. Washington, D.C.: Congressional Quarterly.

——————— (1968). "Reference materials and books." In D. E. Sills, ed., *International Encyclopedia of the Social Sciences*. Vol. 7, pp. 318–326. New York: Macmillan and Free Press.

——————— (1973). "In a gift-horse's mouth." *New York Times,* 28 December, p. 28.

——————— (1974). "Political dictionaries: a bibliographical essay." *American Political Science Review* 68:1696–1705.

——————— (1975). *A Guide to Library Sources in Political Science: American Government*. Instructional Resource Monograph, No. 1. Washington, D.C.: Division of Educational Affairs of the American Political Science Association.

——————— (1975). "Presidential papers as a political science concern." *PS* 8:8–18.

Wheeler, Stanton, ed. (1969). *On Record: Files and Dossiers in American Life*. New York: Russell Sage Foundation.

White, Carl M., ed. (1964). *Sources of Information in the Social Sciences: A Guide to the Literature*. Totowa, N.J.: Bedminster Press.

White, Gerald T. (1969). "Government archives afield: the federal records centers and the historian." *Journal of American History* 55:833–842.

Winchell, Constance M. (1967). 8th ed. *Guide to Reference Books*. Chicago: American Library Association.

Zinn, Charles J. (1952). "Codification of the laws." *Law Library Journal* 45:2–7.

2

SOURCES FOR POLITICAL INQUIRY: II QUANTITATIVE DATA

JEROME M. CLUBB

The value of computer technology for empirical social research requires no elaboration. Even a cursory glance at any one of a number of professional journals provides ample demonstration of the widespread use of computers and other forms of electronic data processing equipment by students of political and social phenomena. Indeed, it would be difficult to imagine the state of research without these devices. Computers allow utilization of larger and more varied bodies of empirical data and permit application of more powerful and more diverse methodologies than would be conceivable if methods of hand tabulation were to be solely relied upon. Thus, the availability of modern computers has contributed significantly to broadening the scope of social research and to developing a methodological diversity and sophistication that was practically inconceivable even a few short years ago. Nor has the value of computers been limited to original research. Computers have proven to be powerful instructional aids that facilitate training in statistics and related skills and allow even beginning students to gain experience in the manipulation and analysis of empirical data.

The mere availability of computers, however, is not sufficient to allow realization of these and related benefits. Computers obviously cannot collect research data, nor can these devices themselves convert data to a form suitable for machine digestion and analysis. Where large bodies of data are concerned the accomplishment of these tasks requires major investments of human energy and financial resources. An abundance of data of potential value to political researchers is, of course, now available in computer-readable form. Numerous academic, governmental, and commercial organizations, as well as individual scholars and research groups, collect or produce machine-readable data files in the course of research projects or as a by-product of their daily activities. Indeed, one of the consequences of the so-called computer revolution has been a staggering increase in the volume of information that is routinely collected and stored. Utilization of such materials is another matter. The storage and preservation of collections of machine-readable data require techniques and procedures significantly different from those that are applicable to more traditional forms of information. Reference and catalogue systems for machine-readable data resources are not well developed, and the researcher who attempts to use these materials confronts major difficulties in identifying, locating, and evaluating data of potential value. Even when useful machine-readable data are obtained from other scholars or commercial or governmental sources, extensive and costly further manipulation is usually required to convert them to a form suitable to the specific requirements of locally available computational facilities.

Moreover, although most students of political phenomena have access to computational equipment of some form, effective use of these facilities requires technical skill and supporting resources. Specialized computer programs appropriate to the data and research problems of concern to investigators are required, and for the development of such programs advanced technical training and expertise are necessary. Indeed, even routine data processing using available computer programs and program systems requires technical skill and experience that are not possessed by many scholars. It is now generally recognized, at least at the present stage in the development of computer technology, that for each individual to carry out these varied and demanding tasks would require an inordinate and impractical investment of time and energy in acquisition of requisite technical expertise. In any event, it is obvious that for every scholar to attempt to serve as his own data collector, programmer, and data processor would constitute an irrational utilization of labor that could only be productive of wasteful duplication of effort and be detrimental to the general research enterprise.

Computer technology, in short, has opened major new intellectual opportunities for students of politics and for social scientists in general. That technology has also posed new challenges and has given rise to the need for a variety of supporting resources that are not a part of the traditional research and instructional environment. This chapter is concerned with these new challenges and oportunities. The initial section discusses new facilities that have developed to support computer-based research and instruction. A second section is devoted to sources of machine-readable and nonmachine-readable data for the study of politics. In these discussions attention is directed both to the advantages of these new resources and to the problems confronted in their utilization. It should be recognized at the beginning that no brief essay can provide a fully adequate introduction to the new information resources that are available for the empirical study of political phenomena. The rapidly changing nature of computer technology and the equally rapid development of supporting resources for empirical social research are such that any essay concerned with these topics is inevitably obsolete virtually before publication. Thus the discussion that follows should be seen as, at best, a minimal starting point for the interested student.

SOCIAL SCIENCE DATA ARCHIVES

In recent years substantial human and financial resources have been allocated to the development of a variety of organizations that capitalize on computer technology and are intended to facilitate the application of that technology to empirical social research. These facilities include limited "data laboratories" designed to serve a purely local community of students and scholars. Ordinarily these local organizations maintain limited bodies of data, aid in the acquisition and processing of additional data, and provide consultation and assistance in the research and instructional use of data and local computational resources. At the opposite extreme are relatively large-scale data archives and data banks that perform more varied functions for national and even international constituencies. Although these organizations vary widely in function, orientation, and organization, as well as in size, they perform essentially common services, providing data and other resources to support computer-aided social research. (For discussions of the development and characteristics of social science data archives see, for example, Rokkan, 1966; Rokkan and Valen, 1966; Converse, 1964, 1966; Deutsch, 1966; Miller, 1969; Bisco, 1966, 1970; and Clubb, 1970a.)

In their early development, data archives were primarily concerned with the data of sample survey research, and it is probably fair to say that data of this form remain the predominant concern of most of these organizations and of the students of politics who use them. During the past few decades, survey research has come to be a principal means for the investigation of mass political phenomena. But despite the great value of this approach, the cost of conducting a meaningful and well-designed survey is well beyond the means of all but the most fortunate researchers. The research value of a major collection of survey data, however, is rarely exhausted by a single researcher or research project. Thus the concept of sharing data resources for "secondary analysis" (Hyman, 1972) has been generally accepted, although often honored more in principle than in reality. Individual survey investigations, moreover, are usually cross-sectional in nature and concerned with political phenomena at a single point in time. The accumulation of survey investigations over the years, on the other hand, opens the possibility of combining data from even very diverse studies to allow longitudinal investigations of political processes and phenomena over an extended period of time, thereby adding new and increased value to the data of individual surveys. The pages of the *American Political Science Review,* as well as a variety of other journals and books, provide numerous examples of successful, and not-so-successful, secondary analyses.

Hyman (1972) provides an excellent discussion of the procedures, opportunities, and problems of secondary analysis of survey data and calls attention to important studies that rest upon this mode of investigation. The development of data archives can be seen as an effort to realize more fully these potential values. Data archives are developed to provide institutional mechanisms for data sharing and to facilitate more economical research, more widespread use of data, and more varied use of costly data resources. By making data generally available in machine-readable form, they also encourage replication of original investigations and in this way contribute to improvement of the quality of research.

The functions of many data archives have now expanded beyond initial concern with the preservation and dissemination of sample survey data received from original researchers. In many cases data are received in a form that, though adequate for the needs of the original researcher, is far from adequate for the needs of others. Various archives now devote substantial effort to converting such data to more generally and readily usable form. Detailed documentation is prepared to supplement and augment information provided by the original investigator; extensive error-checking procedures are carried out to detect and correct or document errors and anomalies characteristic of original data files. The data are then converted to consistent coding conventions and standard formats that are more readily compatible with a variety of computational and program systems. In this way archives overcome some of the obstacles to data use that would otherwise be confronted by the secondary analyst.

The data archive concept has also been extended to other types of research data, in addition to survey research materials. The holdings of a number of data archives now include such materials as systematically organized biographical records, data from national censuses and other enumerations, as well as data created as by-products of ongoing social, political, and economic processes. In the latter category are such materials as election returns, the voting records of national and international legislative and deliberative bodies, national budgetary data, public policy data, and the records of events on the international scene and of the interactions between nations. In a few cases, these holdings include data in very substantial historical depth that allow investigation of long-term processes of political change and development and permit comparative investigation of political phenomena in differing historical contexts. These developments, of course, look toward the creation of complex data bases that combine, for example, survey and elite data with aggregate data for differing units of analysis in order to allow mass and elite behavior to be linked directly to contextual phenomena.

Extension of the activities of data archives and broadening of the holdings of various archives to include these other categories of data was an obvious and logical step. Collections of such data, although originally organized for specific research projects, often have the same potentiality for secondary analysis as do sample survey collections. At least one data archive, the Inter-university Consortium for Political Research, has also broadened its holdings by carrying out projects that involve original collection, organization, and processing of such data. Major bodies of public record data often present complex problems of data collection, processing, and documentation, and the accomplishment of these tasks requires large-scale financial resources (Miller, 1967, 1969; Clubb and Allen, 1967; Benson, 1968; Clubb, 1971). It has seemed apparent that the collection and conversion of such data to a standard machine-readable form can be carried out more efficiently and economically through a centralized project than by relying on the efforts of individual scholars. In several cases, the Consortium has undertaken collection and processing of bodies of data that have been identified by informed scholars as being of great and general research value.

It is justifiable, of course, to look with some suspicion on data collection and processing activities that are carried out more or less independently of research projects. These suspicions are particularly justifiable in view of the absence of well-developed theory to guide the process of selecting particular bodies of data for collection and automation from among the many competing categories of source materials. Obviously the monetary resources available to support social science research are far too limited to be wasted on the expensive work of collecting and processing data for which no research need exists. The danger of wasting scarce resources seems relatively limited, however, in the case of major national data sources such as the reports of censuses and other systematic enumerations, election returns, legislative voting records, and the like. The importance of such materials to a wide range of research interests, and their obvious value for comparative investigations, may seem to justify centralized collection and processing even in advance of the formulation of specific research projects, and it is likely that efforts of this sort will continue at least on a limited scale.

The activities of data archives, of course, are not limited to the collection, processing, and dissemination of research data. In fact, these organizations perform a rather wide variety of additional services. In addition to supplying raw data, most archives are able to perform at least limited analysis work at the request of researchers and other users. These services range from identifying and retrieving variables of interest, through computation of marginal frequencies and the preparation of cross tabulations, to the execution of relatively extensive and complex analyses. Archives also perform various training functions. In some cases, this function is limited to essentially *ad hoc* technical consultation provided to individuals who spend varying periods in residence at the archive; in other cases, the training function takes the form of sponsorship of special conferences or even continuing formal training programs. Similarly, data archives, and particularly those that have developed in the context of research organizations, have contributed to the development of generalized computer programs and systems for data management and analysis. Archival work requires the development of supporting computer programs, and in several cases archives have been able to make such programs available for use at other installations. Finally, and in more general terms, data archives and other supporting facilities have attempted to encourage general adoption of standard formats, coding conventions, documentation, and processing procedures for data preparation and storage. Although these efforts have been far less than universally successful, they look toward maximizing the availability and general utility of research data.

Although the number of existing data archives is not great, it is large enough to preclude detailed description of every such organization that attempts to provide services for a more than purely local constituency. As noted above, archival organizations and related supporting facilities vary significantly in terms of functions, services provided, and orientation. Moreover, local facilities whose principal function is to serve the needs of students and investigators at a single university, or even a single department, sometimes maintain unique bodies of data that can be provided to individuals at other institutions. Thus it is only possible to mention a few of the better known archival organizations. The appendix that follows this chapter provides a more extended, but still incomplete, list of such organizations with current addresses.

The Roper Public Opinion Research Center located at Williams College (Williamstown, Massachusetts) is the oldest of the nationally oriented data archives. The Center was founded in 1946 with the data of some 177 surveys conducted by the Roper Research Associates as its initial holdings. At this writing, these holdings have grown to more than 9000 surveys conducted by well over 100 academic and commercial survey research organizations—including Gallup, the National Opinion Research Corporation, and numerous others —in 68 nations. Data from approximately 100 additional surveys are acquired by the Roper Center each year. Thus the Center's holdings are growing rapidly and include survey data pertinent not only to the United States but to numerous other nations as well. These holdings, moreover, span virtually the entire period of survey research (the oldest survey dates from 1936) and constitute an incomparable resource for the investigation of popular attitudes over the past four decades. Although the Roper Center provides a variety of services including selective retrieval of data bearing upon particular subjects, technical consultation, and analysis, its principal and most invaluable service has been that of collecting and conserving valuable research materials that surely would otherwise have been lost. Because of the magnitude of its holdings, the Center has not attempted to clean and convert every survey to standard form. As a consequence, a significant portion of the Center's holdings require substantial processing to achieve usable form. Many of its studies are, however, readily usable, and the Center is equipped to clean and convert data to usable formats on request.

A second nationally oriented data archive, the Inter-university Consortium for Political Research located in the Center for Political Studies (one of the component research centers of the Institute for Social Research, The University of Michigan), has followed a somewhat different strategy from that of the Roper Center. The Consortium was founded as an institutional mechanism to provide political scientists and other interested scholars with access to the political survey data collected by the Survey Research Center, and more recently by the Center for Political Studies of the University of Michigan, at national elections since 1948. Subsequently, numerous additional collections of survey data have been added to the Consortium's holdings, including data relevant to other nations as well as the United States. In adding data to the archive, however, considerable selectivity has been exercised. An effort has been made to add only data that informed scholars have judged to be of high quality and extensive research utility. Considerable energy, moreover, is invested in documenting, cleaning, and converting data to a standard form compatible with the requirements of a variety of computational systems. Thus, Consortium holdings of survey data are more restricted than those of the Roper Center, but they also tend to be more readily usable.

Expansion of Consortium holdings has also involved the addition of other categories of data, including major bodies of "public record" data in historical depth and materials concerning international relations and politics. In the category of historical data, Consortium holdings now include, for example, aggregate returns at the county level for all elections to the offices of president, governor, and United States senator and representative since 1824, comprehensive congressional roll call records for the years since 1789, selected socioeconomic data at the county and state levels from the United States census reports, 1790 to the present, as well as more limited bodies of similar data for various other nations. Data concerning international politics include comprehensive voting records for the United Nations, aggregate indicators of the attributes of nations, data bearing upon international conflict, and a variety of other materials.

Consortium activities are not limited, however, to the processing and dissemination of research data. From its foundation in 1962 through the time of writing, the Consortium has maintained an annual summer training program in quantitative research methods and has sponsored a large number of specialized research conferences. More recently, the Consortium has become active in the development of undergraduate instructional materials and it also disseminates a major computer program system (OSIRIS III), which was jointly developed by the component centers of the Institute for Social Research, the University of Michigan. This system includes a wide range of capabilities of value for social research and is now in use at a large number of installations in the United States and other nations.

The Roper Center and the Inter-university Consortium for Political Research are the largest and the best-known of the data archives of concern to students of politics. A variety of other organizations also provide similar services. Many of these organizations are more specialized in their activities, and some are primarily oriented toward local clienteles, although they also make data and other services available to researchers and students at other institutions. The International Data Library and Reference Service located at the Survey Research Center of the University of California, Berkeley, has extensive data holdings that tend to concentrate on, but are by no means limited to, survey materials concerning Latin America and the developing nations more generally. As in the case of other similar organizations, the International Data Library and the Survey Research Center have devoted substantial attention to the development of specialized data management and analysis software. As its name suggests, the Latin American Data Bank at the University of Florida has specialized in Latin America and includes substantial holdings of election returns and census materials pertaining to these nations. The National Opinion Research Center at the University of Chicago and the Louis Harris Political Data Center at the University of North Carolina provide access to political survey data collected by NORC and by Louis Harris and Associates. Located at the University of Iowa, the Laboratory for Political Research has holdings of survey data, including several unique continuing surveys relevant to the immediate region, as well as data concerning the United States Congress and other legislative agencies, studies of the Supreme Court, and materials pertaining to local government; the Laboratory has also devoted attention to the development of instructional materials. The Minnesota Data Archive at the University of Minnesota includes a major collection of aggregate national indicators bearing upon a large number of nations which is of particular value for comparative studies of national development. The holdings of the Social Science Data and Program Library Service of the Social Systems Research Institute, the University of Wisconsin, include survey materials and large numbers of extended economic and demographic time series. The Data Program and Library Service has also undertaken a major project (National Program Library and Central Program Inventory Service) that involves the development of a comprehensive and continuing inventory of computer programs relevant to social science research. The goal of this effort is to reduce the localistic and divergent practices and the wasteful duplication of effort that have plagued the development of computational capabilities for the social sciences.

To this list of organizations can be added a number of similar organizations that also provide data and related services. Among these organizations are the Archive on Political Elites in Eastern Europe (located at the University of Pittsburgh), the Bureau of Applied Social Research at Columbia University, the Data Repository Section of the Survey Research Center at the University of Illinois, Northwestern University Information Center, and the Social Science Research Archive, a fledgling organization located at the Institute for Social Research, the University of Michigan. Nor has the development of data archives been limited to the United States. Data archives have also appeared in various European and other nations and include, among others, the Institute for Behavioural Research Data Bank at York University, Canada; DATUM at Bad Godesberg, West Germany; the Social Science Research Council Survey Archive at the University of Essex; the Steinmetz Archives, Amsterdam; and the Zentral-archiv für Emperishe Sozialforschung at the University of Cologne. It is quite predictable, moreover, that the number of data archives and similar organizations, both in the United States and other nations, and the magnitude and variety of their holdings will continue to grow in the future.

Operation and Utilization of Data Archives

Data archives constitute a resource of major importance for the study of political and social processes and behavior. Through these facilities the individual scholar—whether undergraduate, graduate student, or senior scholar—can gain access to data from thousands of empirical studies collected at a total cost ranging in the millions of dollars. This data draws upon the advanced technical and substantive expertise of numerous scholars. Thus these organizations provide a mechanism by which even impecunious students can avail themselves of the product of the most advanced, and the most costly, data collection techniques. At present, however, a number of difficulties confront the scholar who attempts to utilize these facilities. To a considerable degree these difficulties are related to questions of the precise role and responsibilities of data archives and of individual scholars in the research process.

One of the most serious, and the most obvious, problems in the utilization of data archives is that of obtaining information as to their holdings. The preceding discussion has suggested something of the number of data archives and other organizations that are equipped to provide data and related resources of interest to students of politics. Unfortunately, there is at present no comprehensive and continuing guide to the data holdings and services provided by these organizations, although at various times major but unsuccessful effort has been directed to this end. As a consequence, scholars confront considerable difficulty in attempting to access the holdings of data archives in order to locate materials, services, and other resources relevant to their research and instructional interests. With a few possible exceptions, however, most of the organizations referred to above can provide lists of data holdings on request, and a number of them periodically publish information on data holdings and related activities. The Roper Center publishes a biannual newsletter that describes data acquisitions and other activities, while the Inter-university Consortium for Political Research publishes a yearly *Guide to Resources and Services* which provides comprehensive information on data holdings and other services and resources. Various other organizations, including the Behavioural Research Institute at York University and the Survey Research Center at the University of Illinois, also publish periodic newsletters that provide information concerning their holdings and other services.

In this area, *SS Data* (published quarterly since 1971), a newsletter published by the Laboratory for Political Research of the University of Iowa, constitutes a contribution of signal importance. This newsletter provides social scientists with information on data acquisitions by cooperating data archives as well as a more extended description of participating archives. A somewhat similar newsletter, *European Political Data* (published irregularly since 1971), is published by the European Consortium for Political Research under the editorship of Stein Rokkan of the University of Bergen, Norway, and provides information on the data acquisitions and activities of European data archives and research centers. A number of scholarly publications of a more general nature also provide information more or less consistently on the activities of data archives and related organizations. *Social Science Information* (published quarterly since 1962), published under the auspices of the International Social Science Council, and the *Historical Methods Newsletter* (published quarterly since 1967) are probably the most noteworthy in this respect. *Computers and the Humanities* (published quarterly since 1966) periodically publishes descriptions of computer-based work in progress in the social sciences, as well as the humanities, which indicate machine-readable data files that may become available for secondary analysis. The recently published *Directory of Data Bases in the Social and Behavioral Sciences* (Sessions, 1974) provides references to the machine-readable data files held by more than 650 organizations in the United States and other nations. But despite the value of these and other publications, it remains a fact that no detailed, comprehensive, and continuing guide to the data and other resources of data archives is now available.

Communication of information concerning data holdings and services constitutes a major problem for both the operation and utilization of data archives. There can be little doubt that inadequacy of communication has hindered scholarly utilization of these facilities and that given a more adequate mechanism for disseminating information, use would be significantly increased. Numerous scholars probably fail to capitalize upon rich archival holdings of survey data simply because they do not know of their existence or because they are unaware of the ease with which such materials can be acquired and analyzed. By the same token, there are numerous examples of scholars who have devoted extensive time and energy to collecting, coding, and processing legislative roll call records, election returns, census materials, and other similar data in ignorance of the fact that the required materials were available in readily usable machine-readable form from a data archive.

It is also clear that without major effort, this problem will steadily grow as the magnitude of archival holdings increases and as scholarly interests shift toward combining the data from several surveys and other bodies of data to facilitate cross-national comparisons and longitudinal investigations. The various journals and newsletters referred to above are of great importance as mechanisms for providing information as to the holdings of data archives. Even so, the information that they provide falls significantly short of the optimum. Indeed, even a comprehensive, up-to-date, and centralized listing and description of the studies and other bodies of data included in data archives would fall short of the needs of potential users of these materials, although such a listing, which is now nowhere available, would be a considerable advantage. In an ideal world, what is needed is a comprehensive information retrieval system that would list, index, and cross-reference all questions and variables included in archival collections. (In this regard see, for example, Scheuch and Stone, 1966; Janda, 1968.) Such a system would allow the researcher to rapidly search for, identify, and locate all questions and variables pertaining to the problem of interest and, if properly developed, would also provide technical information concerning such matters as data collection procedures, sample design and size, reliability, and the like for each of the questions and variables so identified.

From some points of view, the absence of a comprehensive, automated retrieval and indexing system is all the more frustrating in view of the current state of computer technology. Development of a facility of this sort is fully feasible in terms of contemporary technology, although major substantive difficulties would be encountered in its implementation, and it is possible to conceive of a centralized facility that could be readily and inexpensively employed by individual scholars at remote locations. It is obvious, of course, that the cost of developing and implementing such a facility would be large, indeed, and unjustifiable in terms of the limited financial resources now available for social science research. Even so, it is also obvious that major if less ambitious effort is needed to make specific information bearing upon the contents and characteristics of archival holdings readily and generally available if these materials are to be widely used and their research and instructional potentiality more fully realized.

Further problems in the operation and utilization of data archives concern their obligation and capacity to provide error-free and readily usable data. In this area a matter of central importance concerns the kinds of supporting information (documentation) that are required to facilitate effective secondary analysis of data collections. Where data from sample surveys are concerned, extensive and detailed information is needed as to sample size and design, the precise wording of questions, the interviewing techniques used, the time period during which the survey was conducted, errors and discrepancies characteristic of the data, as well as a variety of other matters.

In recent years, moreover, social scientists have devoted increased attention to comparative studies across nations, cultures, and temporal periods and to the investigation of processes of development and change. Studies of this sort frequently rely on various forms of public record data including voting records, data collected through national censuses and other enumerations, budgetary accounts, and a variety of other categories of information collected through "social bookkeeping" systems. As a consequence, data of this sort are increasingly finding their way into the holdings of social science data archives. Unfortunately, social scientists frequently approach such materials with little regard for their many frailties, shortcomings, and idiosyncracies. In fact, effective use of materials of this sort often requires even greater care and sensitivity to error and even more imposing arrays of supporting information than is required in the case of survey materials. At a minimum, supporting documentation should include precise citations to the sources employed, explanations of the original purposes and techniques of data collection, exact definitions of variables, and explanations of changes in these definitions. Similarly, information as to changes in the boundaries of geographical and political units, explanations of missing data, and assessments of accuracy are necessary for effective use of such materials. (For discussion of these and related problems see, for example, Scheuch, 1966; Deane, 1968; Ohlin, 1968; Tilly, 1969, 1972; Clubb, 1970b).

Various scholars have pointed out that given adequate supporting information of this sort the analyst can often make productive use of even quite imperfect data (Narroll, 1970; Deutsch, Lasswell, Merritt, and Russett, 1966). If the direction and magnitude of bias is known or can be estimated, corrective estimates can be made; if error is known to be random, the consequences can be anticipated and allowed for; if detailed information concerning sample design is available, appropriate weighting and other adjusting procedures can sometimes be employed; if the original modes of data collection are known, error margins and the direction of bias can sometimes be estimated and the effects of error and bias on analytical findings can be assessed. Although not concerned with political phenomena, Goldhamer and Marshall (1953), in their investigation of the frequency of mental illness from the mid-19th century to the 1950s, provide a near classic illustration of these possibilities. By carefully defining the objectives of their study, by estimating the likely effects of the error and bias characteristic of the available data, and by taking into account variations in definitions of mental disease and in recording procedures, these investigators were able to make effective use of limited and imperfect data to develop credible findings. Their study and the excellent discussion of their procedures provided by Wallis and Roberts (1956, pp. 28–45) would well repay the attention of any student.

Converse (1966) reminds us, however, that information pertaining to error, bias and other limitations of data is not characteristically available in the required detail and that the data supplied to archives by original investigators frequently do not meet optimum standards. Academic researchers often, although by no means always, develop and compile relatively elaborate documentation to support the data that they collect and ultimately supply to archives, and monographs reporting substantive findings usually also provide information concerning study design, data characteristics, and other technical matters. Although practices vary, and the variation is probably greatest among nonacademic suppliers, even at best the documentation provided by researchers when supplying data to archives is rarely sufficient to provide fully adequate support for secondary analysis.

Moreover, the data supplied to archives by original investigators often departs from the optimum in still other respects (Bisco, 1966; Converse, 1966). The data supplied are often marked by errors and inconsistencies that, although insignificant for the purposes of the original research, can pose major obstacles to effective secondary analysis. Similarly, data are usually supplied in technical form which, though suitable to the requirements of the original investigator, are far from adequate for purposes of archival storage, dissemination, and use by other scholars.

As a consequence, archival personnel face the difficult decisions of whether, and in what magnitude, to invest organizational resources in preparing improved documentation, in carrying out error and consistency checks and correction procedures, and in technically reorganizing data to increase compatibility with other computers and computer systems. These procedures require extensive time, demand considerable technical and substantive expertise, and involve significant expenditures of monetary resources; obviously decisions in these areas have major consequences for the costs of maintaining and operating data archives. As suggested elsewhere, the practices of data archives vary widely in this respect. Some archives, perhaps primarily as a consequence of limited financial support, pursue a policy that can best be described as *caveat emptor*. Data are accepted, stored, and made available in essentially the form in which they were supplied by the original investigator, and usually little selectivity is exercised where decisions to acquire particular bodies of data are concerned. In such cases the secondary analyst must assume all the tasks and the risks of interpreting data, of developing additional supporting information, and of coping with errors and discrepancies, as well as assume the costs and labor of reorganizing data to conform to the requirements of local computer installations.

At the opposite extreme various other data archives devote substantial time and resources to documenting and cleaning the studies that they receive; elaborate codebooks are prepared, extensive error checks are carried out and corrections made or irreconcilable discrepancies documented, and attention is devoted to attaining maximal compatibility with a wide variety of computer and program systems. To perform these tasks relatively elaborate computational capabilities are required both to perform requisite data management and to facilitate reformatting and other reorganization of data. Obviously, a large staff with varied skills and relatively large-scale capitalization are required to support these activities. These archives thus carry out many of the tasks that would otherwise be performed by secondary analysts; they attempt to provide maximally accurate and usable data in a form that can be used even by analysts without extensive technical expertise, who do not have access to advanced machines or to sophisticated program capabilities. The cost of achieving these goals, however, is such that the number of studies and data collections that these archives can accept and process is limited, and their holdings tend to be relatively selective.

It is worth remembering in this connection that secondary analysis involves large elements of vulnerability. Unrecognized errors and discrepancies in data can be productive of misleading analytic results, and failure to recognize the characteristics of data collections can result in mistaken applications and erroneous findings. Moreover, whatever the practices of individual archives, these organizations cannot relieve the secondary analyst of all scholarly responsibility. Even the most extensive data cleaning efforts often do not serve to eradicate all errors and discrepancies; the most elaborate documentation usually does not provide all supporting information required to facilitate effective use of data files; and at the present stage of the development of computer technology it is impossible to attain complete compatibility with all computer systems. Thus secondary analysis inevitably requires substantial effort and scholarly sensitivity on the part of the analyst.

Difficulties of this sort tend to be most serious in those cases where data collections gleaned from public record sources are concerned. In many instances, such collections are based on a large number of diverse and sometimes unpublished original sources; others draw on a single original source that is available in only one or a few remote repositories. Moreover, compilation and organization of such collections frequently involve elaborate coding procedures and numerous complex substantive decisions by the original investigator. Thus it is often impractical for the archival staff or the secondary analyst to return to original sources to check the accuracy of recorded data, and in the absence of extensive documentation the nature and consequences of coding and substantive decisions cannot be effectively assessed. The standards of accuracy and the documentation and supporting information provided by many original investigators approaches the optimum to say the least. (See, for example, Shapiro, 1965, 1974; Tilly, 1969, 1972; Singer, 1972; Singer and Small, 1972.) In other instances, the documentation and supporting information for collections of public record data tend to be quite rudimentary. In either case, however, both the data archive and the secondary analyst are heavily dependent on the accuracy and reliability of the original investigator and on the supporting information that he provides.

Archival Development

The growth of social science data archives came about as a response to parallel developments in the area of information technology and in the focus, conduct, and methodology of social research. These same factors may suggest the likelihood that, in the future, these organizations will continue to grow in number, in the magnitude and diversity of their holdings, in the range of services that they provide, and in the sophistication with which these services are performed. The number of major empirical investigations conducted by social scientists increases each year, and with it, the number of bodies of data that are candidates for incorporation into the holdings of data archives. The work of social scientists has steadily broadened to include ever more diverse categories of data, and it can be anticipated that the holdings of data archives will increasingly reflect that diversity. Continuing development in computer technology has opened, and will continue to open, new possibilities in the methodology, organization, and conduct of research and it is predictable that data archives will be called on to contribute to the realization of these possibilities within the sphere of their activities. Thus it is possible to conceive of these organizations as holding the potential for major breakthroughs in the social sciences. Indeed, various observers, perhaps in flights of hyperbole, have seen data archives as potentially analogous to the electron microscope for the cellular biologist or the cyclotron for the physicist.

Without denying their present and potential importance, it is possible to entertain with Angus Campbell (1970) "some questions about the New Jerusalem" which data archives are sometimes said to promise. Not the least of these concerns their cost and their sources of support. As the preceding discussion has suggested, data archives are costly indeed to maintain and operate. The cost of documenting and cleaning the data from a major survey investigation usually runs to the thousands of dollars, and the cost of recovering and processing an extensive body of public record data has, in at least one instance, exceeded the million dollar mark. Moreover, data archives face continuing maintenance costs apart from initial cleaning and documentation of data files. Errors discovered through continual use of data collections must be tracked down and corrected; ongoing data collections, such as election returns and legislative roll call records, must be periodically updated to incorporate new materials; data tapes should be periodically renewed to guard against deterioration of magnetic signals; and, to the degree that data archives attempt to capitalize on change and improvement in computer technology, resources must be invested in the development of requisite computer programs.

It is also true, of course, that various developments look toward reducing at least some of the costs involved in operating and maintaining data archives. The quality of data collection and processing carried out by original investigators has steadily improved and will continue to improve in the future. Thus data will reach archives in better condition than in the past, and the costs of documentation, cleaning, and converting data to archival form will diminish. On the other hand, increases in the number of studies conducted, and thus in the volume of data available for incorporation into archival holdings, are likely to offset such savings. Similarly, improvement and innovation in computer technology will undoubtedly reduce the costs of some aspects of the operation of data archives.

It is worth remembering, however, that the development and continued advance of computer technology has worked to increase rather than decrease the costs of social research. Growth in the capacity of computational equipment to manipulate larger and more complicated bodies of data, more rapidly and in more complicated ways, has only stimulated the appetites and ambitions of researchers and has prompted them to attempt to capitalize on these new potentialities. As a consequence, the costs of conducting research have not declined but have increased. The operation of data archives obviously confronts much the same prospect. The ambitions of archival managers, and the demands researchers place on them, will reflect improvement and innovation in computer technology. Indeed, the state of that technology is already such as to allow archives to provide services much in advance of those now performed. As indicated elsewhere, comprehensive information retrieval systems are technically feasible, much larger data bases can be effectively manipulated and controlled, complex data bases can be created linking diverse types of data at multiple levels of aggregation, and computer networks can be developed using telephonic transmission to provide researchers at distant locations with direct access to archival holdings. And these are but a few of the technical opportunities that are available at present. Realization of such opportunities, however, would require expenditures that would offset and exceed any operational savings in other areas that might result from technological advance.

It is clear, in short, that the resources available to data archives must be greatly increased if they are to fulfill the rather exalted visions of some commentators. Indeed, it is probable that even maintenance of current patterns of archival services will involve steadily growing operating costs, if only as a consequence of the increasing supply of valuable research data. Yet realistic consideration of existing data archives indicates that, although they differ significantly in this respect, their financial base tends to be relatively precarious, and that they compete for financial support with the research process itself. Sources of support for existing archives include fees for services, the budgets of individual universities or even university departments, and institutional membership subscriptions; in many instances support relies on some combination of these sources. The fees that archives are sometimes compelled to charge for services may provide an indication of the inadequacy of their financial base. Although these fees are by no means exorbitant in terms of the intrinsic value of the services rendered, they are nonetheless sometimes large enough to foreclose access to archival holdings for some scholars. As a consequence a central goal of data archives, to provide access to research data for all scholars, however impecunious, is contradicted. Moreover, the fact that most data archives have been compelled to turn to research foundations for support for particular activities or special projects is perhaps a further indication of the inadequacy of their present financial base.

The financial characteristics and requirements of data archives raise obvious questions about their continued expansion and growth and their future role. As suggested above, data archives compete for support with research itself. As Campbell (1970) and many others have pointed out, however, social research is seriously underfunded. The marks of inadequate support are numerous. Samples are smaller than would be desirable, reliance on case studies is excessive, and rich bodies of data are only partially exploited. In the latter connection it is predictable, for example, that the research potentialities of the massive and detailed data collected by the 1970 census will be at best imperfectly realized as a consequence of the high cost of access to these data and of effectively manipulating and linking them to other categories of information. In general, the social sciences do not cope adequately with processes of change, and findings and theories may be limited in their applicability to a narrow temporal period. Yet panel studies and other forms of longitudinal inquiry are rare, and researchers are seldom able to support collection and analysis of data to extend their investigations into the past, again as a consequence of the inadequacy of available support.

The holdings of data archives, furthermore, reflect in some sense the social research of the past. The possibilities for secondary analysis of even a single major data collection are numerous. When one envisions linking data from diverse studies and sources, the possibilities for innovative research become almost limitless. Indeed, the data accumulated by archives look toward facilitating longitudinal analysis and toward comparative explanation of behavioral phenomena in a variety of contexts. Even so, if the resources available to support social research are finite, excessive investment in the growth and expansion of data archives could restrict opportunities to explore new research directions and to adopt innovative approaches. Moreover, undue emphasis on data archives and secondary analysis could lead to neglect of other, less costly modes of data collection and research. Campbell (1968) calls attention to the value of small, independently designed, and in some ways unsystematic studies and suggests implicitly that progress of scientific knowledge of political and social phenomena does not rest exclusively on large-scale surveys and other highly expensive forms of data collection. In short, excessive investment in data archives could have a stultifying effect on social research.

Data archives are now and will probably remain for the foreseeable future a vital and increasingly important element of the research enterprise. To unduly restrict their growth and development would be detrimental to that enterprise. It is clear, however, that limitless growth and expansion in the holdings and services of these organizations, and in their consumption of research resources, would be both impossible and undesirable. Thus it is unlikely that archives will realize all the potentialities that have been foreseen. Clearly, considerable selectivity will be necessary both in terms of additions to archival holdings and in terms of development of new and more advanced services. It is to be hoped that the broad community of social scientists will play a larger role in determining the direction of their growth than has been true in the past.

The future growth and development of data archives also depends on the practices and attitudes of social scientists in other ways. In recent years, much attention has been given to the growing acceptance by scholars of the ethic of data sharing and cooperation in the development of research resources. Such an ethic obviously looks toward maximizing the utility of research resources and serves the scientific principle of replication. In practice, however, social scientists have been relatively slow to honor fully the obligations that this ethic entails. As noted elsewhere, investigators who collect original bodies of data often do not prepare adequate documentation, and detailed error-checking procedures are frequently not carried out. Similarly, social scientists have been slow to adopt standardized procedures for data processing and organization. While these failings are often explicable in terms of the inadequacy of available financial support and the necessity of relying on locally available facilities, they limit the utility of data for others and increase the costs of secondary analysis and archival processing. Similarly, subordinate data categories are often combined to superordinate categories. Thus the detail of original data is lost and their utility for secondary analysis diminished. Along these lines, Campbell (1970) and others have suggested that in some cases the utility of major surveys and their value for secondary analysis might be significantly increased if a limited set of additional questions were added to capture otherwise unavailable information, even though these questions might not be directly relevant to the problem under investigation. In short, there is much that individual scholars can do to facilitate secondary analysis and to reduce the costs of data archives.

For both legitimate and questionable reasons, social scientists are also sometimes slow, or unwilling, to release data for use by others. Researchers who invest time, intellectual energy, and scarce financial resources in data collection are often, and legitimately, unwilling to release data until their own research is completed. However, the time lag between data collection and completion of research can stretch out into years, with the result that the value of data for secondary analysis is sometimes seriously diminished. It is clear that in such cases expedients need to be found that will allow more immediate secondary use of data without jeopardizing the interests of the original investigator. In general, it is probably accurate to say in this connection that, despite the legitimacy of these concerns, the fear that the original investigator who conceives of, designs, and executes a study will be "scooped" by a secondary analyst is often unjustifiably exaggerated. (For an example of studies that are based on the same data collection but do not involve significant substantive overlap, see Hess and Torney, 1967; and Easton and Dennis, 1969.)

On occasion, researchers are also unwilling to release data apparently out of concern that in the hands of others, data will be misused and produce erroneous findings or lead to conclusions which the original investigator considers politically or ideologically undesirable. The scientific merit of such a position is obviously questionable and requires no discussion. On the other hand, there are also more legitimate concerns that are sometimes taken as precluding general dissemination of particular bodies of data for secondary analysis. Social scientists are rightly concerned for the privacy, confidentiality and well-being of individual respondents and subjects. (For discussion of these problems, see, for example, Miller, 1971; Hofferbert, 1972; and British Association for the Advancement of Science, 1974.) Where data concerning mass populations are concerned, careful effort is usually, and should be consistently, made to remove all information that would allow identification of individuals before releasing data for general use. In the case of limited and special populations, such as elite groups, that are marked by unique characteristics, the data themselves often allow identification of individuals. Hence the need for safeguarding the privacy and well-being of respondents and research subjects is at odds with the need to disseminate data for general scholarly use. In such cases, most researchers prefer to honor their obligation to protect individual confidentiality. It is probably fair to say, however, that even in many of these instances expedients can be found to allow dissemination of data without threatening the right of individuals and special groups to privacy.

The future of social science data archives involves, then, a variety of serious problems and as yet unanswered questions. The appearance and growth of data archives reflects, of course, the transitions that the social sciences have undergone in the past few decades and are still undergoing. Only a few short years ago the single scholar laboring alone who asked and received little in the way of supporting facilities or monetary resources was the hallmark of social research. It is trite to say that the image, the aspirations, and the technology of social research have radically changed. Social scientists now attempt to capitalize on the most powerful and the most expensive technology, they require major resources, coordinated and programmatic research is increasingly common, and an ethic of cooperation in research endeavors is apparently replacing an older ethic of individualism. Data archives are one element of this change. Their growth and the role that they assume will obviously depend on their value to the research enterprise and on the magnitude of the resources available to support social research more generally.

Data Sources

The advent of computer technology has resulted not only in a vast and continuing increase in the magnitude and diversity of information that is routinely collected and stored, but also in a major change in the form in which information is recorded. As a consequence, the volume of information of potential value to social scientists has greatly increased, and the form of that information is potentially more susceptible to manipulation and analysis. At the same time problems of conservation, storage, and access have also increased. It is obvious that information recorded on punched cards, as electrical signals on magnetic tapes or disks, or in other complicated forms requires different modes of storage and conservation than more conventional textual materials. Moreover, information stored in this fashion is potentially more transitory, and access to such information is a more complicated process than in the case of printed or written words and numbers. Complex electronic equipment programmed in particular ways is required to translate punched cards or magnetic tape, and information stored in one technical form and usable on one machine is not always directly usable on other machines. Such information is also susceptible to a kind of technological obsolescence. As a consequence of technological change, information stored at one time may not be usable without extensive transformation on machines introduced at a later date.

Social science data archives can be regarded as a response to one aspect of this set of problems and needs. Such organizations developed as mechanisms to store and conserve machine-readable data created by social scientists in the course of their research and to disseminate that data to a wider community. It is clear, however, that only a small, indeed an infinitesimal, portion of the growing body of machine-readable information of relevance to social research has, or is likely, to find its way into social science data archives. A host of public and private organizations generate vast quantities of potentially relevant information on a daily basis. Indeed, the quantity of that information verges on the unimaginable. The data produced by the 1970 census of the United States require, for example, some 2000 magnetic tapes for storage in their original form and include literally billions of cell entrys organized at a dozen or more levels of aggregation. This rich and detailed trove of information concerning the characteristics and activities of the American people is further enhanced by a wide variety of special censuses, studies, and surveys that are regularly conducted by the Bureau of the Census.

Nor, of course, is the generation of data by the federal government limited to the census. Numerous other governmental agencies, such as the Bureau of Labor Statistics, routinely collect statistical information pertaining to a variety of issues or generate machine-readable data files as a consequence of special investigations (the many studies conducted by the Department of Health, Education and Welfare) or as records of daily operations. Much of this information is, in principle, available to social scientists, and still other categories of confidential information can also be mentioned, including the files of the Internal Revenue Service and the Social Security Administration, among other agencies. It would be impossible to list the numerous sources of potentially relevant data within the federal government or to assess the character and magnitude of these resources. In the latter connection it may be worth noting, however, that it has been estimated that the federal government produces each month approximately 1000 magnetic tapes that record information of sufficient potential value to be considered for acquisition and storage by the National Archives and Records Service, which has responsibility for the disposition of federal records.

The information produced by the federal government is, of course, only an illustration of the increasing supply of relevant data that is available in machine-readable form from sources outside the academic community. To the federal government can be added state and local governments, numerous public interest groups such as the International City Management Association, the governments of other nations, and a host of private agencies and enterprises in the United States and elsewhere, not to mention the numerous international organizations that collect or produce data of potential value for political and social research. As in the case of the holdings of social science data archives, there is no single reference or consolidated catalogue that provides an effective guide to these sources of machine-readable information. Indeed, the scholar who attempts to assess these resources and identify and acquire materials pertinent to his research faces a major and sometimes virtually insurmountable task.

A number of useful guides and catalogues are available, although only a few of these can be mentioned here and in the bibliography that follows this chapter. The National Technical Information Service of the United States Department of Commerce is a central source for the acquisition of machine-readable data files produced by the federal government and of government-sponsored research and analysis reports. The publications and the wide range of information services provided by this organization make it a resource of major importance for social scientists. Despite its high price, the *Directory of Computerized Data Files and Related Software Available from Federal Agencies, 1974* (National Technical Information Service, 1974) is, for example, an important reference tool. The periodic catalogues issued by the Bureau of the Census provide continuing information concerning the data resources available from that agency, and *Small Area Data Notes,* a continuing newsletter also published by the Bureau, provides information on the machine-readable holdings of the United States census and other data of a variety of organizations. The *Federal Statistics Users' Conference Newsletter* provides continuing information regarding statistical information developed by the various agencies of the federal government, and the *Guide to Recurrent and Special Govern-*

mental Statistics, published by the Bureau of the Census, provides information on some 80,000 governmental agencies, including state and local as well as federal agencies. The Statistical Office of the United Nations and various other international organizations, including the Organization for Economic Cooperation and Development and UNESCO, are sources of data relevant to the nations of the world and their interactions. *The Yearbook of International Organizations* (published yearly since 1948) is a useful and, indeed, indispensable guide to international agencies and their activities and an important bibliographical source. Aiken (1972a, 1972b) has prepared two highly useful guides to machine-readable data resources concerning Western Europe, and publications sponsored by the Council of European Studies also often provide references to machine-readable data resources. (See *European Studies Newsletter,* published bimonthly since 1972.) The footnotes and source citations included in a number of statistical handbooks and compendia provide a useful indication of the range and sources of quantitative information that is available both in machine-readable and nonmachine-readable form for the study of political and social phenomena in cross-national and international perspective. These include, among others, the two volumes of the *World Handbook of Political and Social Indicators* (Russett, Alker, Deutsch, and Lasswell, 1964; Taylor and Hudson, 1970), *Cross-Polity Time-Series Data* (Banks, 1971), and *The Wages of War, 1816–1965: A Statistical Handbook* (Singer and Small, 1972). Moreover, the contents of these volumes are available in machine-readable form and constitute major data resources in their own right.

The information resources produced in growing volume by public and private agencies and recorded and stored in machine-readable form present major problems of preservation and access. As suggested above, information stored in machine-readable form is potentially highly transitory. Punched cards are bulky to store; they also degenerate and become unusable even with the best of care, and it is easy to inadvertently erase information stored on magnetic tapes, disks, or the like. Moreover, tapes, disks, and other similar storage media are costly and reusable. Thus the economy-minded are inevitably tempted to erase valuable information to permit reuse of storage devices, although, indeed, not all machine-readable information has sufficient value to merit the cost of preservation. It has also been suggested that without adequate documentation, files of machine-readable data often become useless. A magnetic tape cannot be visually scanned to ascertain its content. In short, in the absence of documentation, machine-readable data are effectively lost. Difficulties encountered in gaining access to machine-readable data files have already been alluded to in terms of the inadequacy of available indexes, catalogues, and guides. But even when relevant information is located and copies obtained further difficulties are usually encountered. Even within the federal government, for example, a very large number of different computer systems are employed, and data are recorded in a variety of different formats and technical forms. Thus the researcher who obtains data from these sources often faces the further task of conversion to forms compatible with the computer system available to him.

Considerable progress is being made toward alleviation of some of these difficulties. It is likely, for example, that continuing technological change will work to reduce problems involved in the storage and preservation of machine-readable information. Devices are now being developed that allow more compact storage of machine-readable data in more durable and more accessible forms. The practice of recording supporting information in machine-readable form linked directly to the data that it documents has become increasingly widespread and may provide at least a partial solution for documentation problems.

Numerous conventional archives have also made significant progress in developing programs for the acquisition and preservation of machine-readable records. Such archives have the responsibility for the disposition of the records of particular organizations and have custody of organizational records that are considered to hold sufficient utility and intrinsic value to merit preservation. Archivists have developed highly effective procedures for the evaluation, preservation, and management of textual records. In recent years, however, many archives have been confronted with the new problems presented by a growing flood of machine-readable records for which existing procedures were inadequate. The National Archives and Records Service has taken major steps to cope with the problems presented by the machine-readable records produced by the United States government. As a consequence, the Machine-Readable Archives Branch of the National Archives is rapidly becoming a major source of data of interest to social scientists. Numerous other archives have also made noteworthy progress in this area and are also becoming important sources of machine-readable social science data. (The best source of information on the activities of archives in this area are articles published in recent years in *The American Archivist,* the official journal of the American Society of Archivists.)

In general, however, and with noteworthy exceptions, archival programs for evaluating, preserving, and providing access to the machine-readable data files produced by government and private organizations are not yet well advanced. The funds available to support such efforts are far less than adequate in terms of the magnitude of the problem. It is probably also fair to say that many archivists are not attuned to the research interests and needs of political and social scientists but tend instead to be oriented toward more traditional historical problems and interests. Thus the danger of loss of valuable information produced by governmental and private organizations is very real.

But preservation and accessibility of the massive information resources produced by government and private organizations has another side. Numerous observers have cautioned that these resources present real and serious dangers (see, for example, Miller, 1971; and Hofferbert, 1972; and British Association for the Advancement of Science, 1974). Many of the data files produced by such organizations record extensive, detailed, and often highly sensitive or damaging information concerning the activities, characteristics, and behavior of countless individuals and groups. Through the use of computers, diverse data files can be linked and rapidly searched, and detailed and specific information can then be retrieved. Thus these resources could allow a kind of surveillance and investigatory activity that would constitute a grievous threat to individual privacy, well-being, and liberty. These justifiable concerns have assumed particular salience as a consequence of periodic discussions of a "national data center" which would be assigned responsibility for centralized management and control of such information resources. Such an agency has been seen as holding the potentiality for major invasion of individual privacy and as a threat to individual liberties. Exploration of the relative merits of a national data center is beyond the purposes of the present discussion. However, it is perhaps worth suggesting that centralized control might be a more effective and more dependable means of regulating access to these resources and preventing their misuse than the current state of divided, and hence sometimes ineffective, responsibility and control. But whatever the merits of this case, it is clear that the vast bodies of information produced by government and private agencies constitute both major resources for social research and, potentially, a serious danger.

In discussing data resources primary emphasis has been placed on materials available in machine-readable form. It is obvious, of course, that the supply of valuable quantitative and quantifiable research data available in nonmachine-readable form is many times greater. Such materials include the voting returns from popular elections, the voting records of legislative and administrative bodies, judicial records, biographical information for political figures, national accounts, and budgetary information, as well as a wide variety of other source materials. Much of this material is readily available in published form, and more can be found in unpublished form in archives, libraries, and other repositories. Information of this sort is available for most nations and for a variety of subnational units, frequently in substantial historical depth. Data resources such as these have been extensively used in the past by political scientists and other scholars. The availability of modern computers means, however, that these research resources can now be exploited on a larger scale and with greater effectiveness.

Unfortunately, here again it is impossible to suggest more than a small sample of the many indexes and guides to such materials. However, a number of the publications indicated above provide references to published and unpublished source materials, as well as to machine-readable data sources. Several additional references can also be suggested here and in the bibliography that follows. Rokkan and Meyriat (1969) is a basic guide to sources of election data for western European nations, and projected volumes in the same series will indicate sources of similar data for other nations. Mackie and Rose (1973) is a compilation in historical depth of election results in Western nations which also provides useful source citations. Burnham (1963) is a guide to comparable data for the United States which will shortly be republished in revised and expanded form. A bibliography of state manuals, "blue books," and other publications of the various states of the United States that frequently include election returns, biographical and budgetary information is provided by Press and Williams (1962). Dubester (1948, 1950) has prepared two comprehensive bibliographies of the publications of state and national censuses conducted in the United States. The essays and bibliographies, included in Lorwin and Price (*The Dimensions of the Past,* 1972) describe the historical data sources available for non-North American nations. For those interested in historical political phenomena, any one of the number of guides and handbooks for historians provide a beginning point in the search for research materials. (See, for example, Gray *et al.,* 1964; and Poulton, 1972.) *Historical Statistics for the United States, Colonial Times to 1957* (Bureau of the Census, 1961), which will shortly be republished in revised form, is a treasure trove of information and a valuable guide of interest to social scientists. Fishbein (1973) suggests some of the many opportunities for quantitative research afforded by the holdings of the National Archives, and the *Guide to the National Archives of the United States* (1974) describes numerous collections that include quantitative information of value for the study of politics and government. The chapter by Vose that is included in this volume also provides many important references. Although not concerned with quantitative data, many of the resources indicated in that chapter are also relevant to quantitative research interests. It should be recalled, moreover, that through procedures such as content analysis, textual materials can be converted to quantitative form and subjected to systematic analysis.

CONCLUDING COMMENTS

The preceding pages have been devoted to discussion of the information resources and facilities that are available to social scientists as a consequence of the development of computer technology. Particular emphasis has been placed on the problems and difficulties which these resources present in terms of data storage and preservation, accessibility and use of data, costs, and individual privacy. Such problems have at best been partially met. It is clear, however, that the research opportunities presented by these resources merit equal, if not greater, emphasis. It is now realistic to conceive of investigating human behavior and social processes in all their diversity, on a scale, and with a detailed intensity and methodological sophistication that far outstrips anything that was possible even a decade ago. And opportunities are increasing. It is not an exaggeration to say that these opportunities can look toward a revolution in knowledge of human behavior and social phenomena and toward major practical social benefits. Discovery of means to realize these potentialities should be a matter of vital concern for social scientists.

PARTIAL LIST OF SOCIAL SCIENCE DATA ARCHIVES AND RELATED FACILITIES

Archive on Political Elites in Eastern Europe
Department of Political Science
2312 Cathedral of Learning
University of Pittsburgh
Pittsburgh, Pennsylvania 15219

Behavioral Sciences Laboratory
University of Cincinnati
Cincinnati, Ohio 45221

Belgian Archives for the Social Sciences
Van Evenstraat 2A, Room 04–45
2000 Louvain, Belgium

Bureau of Applied Social Research
Columbia University
New York, New York 10025

Center for Comparative Political Research
State University of New York
Binghamton, New York 13901

Data and Program Library Service
4451 Social Science Building
University of Wisconsin
Madison, Wisconsin 53706

Data Bank
Institute for Behavioural Research
York University
4700 Keele Street
Downsview, Ontario, Canada

Data Library
Computing Centre
University of British Columbia
Vancouver 8, British Columbia
Canada

European Consortium for Political Research
Data Information Service
Gamel Kalvedalsveien 12
N-5000 Bergen, Norway

International Data Library and Reference Service
Survey Research Center
University of California
Berkeley, California 94720

Survey Research Archive
Historical Archive
International Relations Archive
Inter-university Consortium for Political Research
P.O. Box 1248
Ann Arbor, Michigan 48106

Latin American Data Bank
Room 471, International Studies Building
University of Florida
Gainesville, Florida 32601

Machine-Readable Archives Branch
National Archives (NNPD)
Washington, D.C. 20408

National Dualabs, Inc.
1601 North Kent Street, Suite 900
Rosslyn, Virginia 22209

National Opinion Research Center
University of Chicago
6030 South Ellis Avenue
Chicago, Illinois 60637

National Technical Information Service
U.S. Department of Commerce
5285 Port Royal Road
Springfield, Virginia 22151

Northwestern University Information Center
Vogelback Computing Center
Northwestern University
Evanston, Illinois 60201

Project TALENT Data Bank
American Institutes for Research
P.O. Box 1113
Palo Alto, California 94302

Polimetrics Laboratory
Department of Political Science
Ohio State University
Columbus, Ohio 43210

Political Data Archive
Department of Political Science
Michigan State University
East Lansing, Michigan 48823

Political Science Laboratory and Data Archive
Department of Political Science
248 Woodburn Hall
Indiana University
Bloomington, Indiana 47401

Public Opinion Survey Unit
University of Missouri
Columbia, Missouri 65201

Roper Public Opinion Research Center
P.O. Box 624
Williams College
Williamstown, Massachusetts 02167

Social Data Exchange Association
333 Grotto Avenue
Providence, Rhode Island

Social Science Archive
Institute for Social Research
Box 1248
Ann Arbor, Michigan 48106

Social Science Data Archive
Laboratory for Political Research
321A Schaeffer Hall
University of Iowa
Iowa City, Iowa 52240

Social Science Data Archive
Survey Research Laboratory
414 David Kinley Hall
Urbana, Illinois 61810

Social Science Data Archive
UCLA Survey Research Center
Los Angeles, California 90024

Social Science Data Archives
Department of Sociology
Carleton University
Ottawa 1, Ontario, Canada

Social Science Data Center
University of Connecticut
Storrs, Connecticut 06268

Social Science Data Center
3508 Market Street, Suite 350
University of Pennsylvania
Philadelphia, Pennsylvania 19104

Social Science Data Library
Room 10 Manning Hall
University of North Carolina
Chapel Hill, North Carolina 27514

Social Science Information Center
621 Social Science Building
University of Pittsburgh
Pittsburgh, Pennsylvania 15213

Social Science User Service
Princeton University Computer Center
87 Prospect Avenue
Princeton, New Jersey 08540

Sociomedical Research Archives
Columbia University School of Public Health
Black Research Building
630 West 168th Street
New York, New York 10032

SSRC Survey Archive
University of Essex
Colchester, England

Steinmetz Archives
Information and Documentation Centre for the Social Sciences
Royal Netherlands Academy of Arts and Sciences
Keizersgracht 569–571
Amsterdam, The Netherlands

Urban Data Service
International City Management Association
Suite 201
1140 Connecticut Avenue, N.W.
Washington, D.C. 20036

Zentralarchiv für Empirische Sozialforschung
Universität zu Köln
5 Köln
Bachemer Str. 40
Germany

REFERENCES

Aiken, Michael (1972a). "A guide to sources of ecological and survey data for western European nations." Pittsburgh: Council for European Studies.

_____ (1972b). "An inventory of machine-readable data on sub-national units in western Europe and the United States." Pittsburgh: Council for European Studies.

Alger, Chadwick (1970). "Research on research: a decade of quantitative and field research on international organization." *International Organization* 24:414–450.

Banks, Arthur S. (1971). *Cross-Polity Time-Series Data*. Cambridge, Mass.: MIT Press.

Benson, Lee (1968). "The empirical and statistical basis for comparative analysis of historical change." In Stein Rokkan, ed., *Comparative Studies Across Cultures and Nations*. Paris and The Hague: Mouton.

Bisco, Ralph L. (1966). "Social science data archives: technical considerations." In Stein Rokkan, ed., *Data Archives for the Social Sciences*. Paris and The Hague: Mouton.

_____, ed. (1970). *Data Bases, Computers and the Social Sciences*. New York: Wiley-Interscience.

Bowman, Raymond T. (1970). "The idea of a federal data center—its purposes and structure." In Ralph L. Bisco, ed., *Data Bases, Computers and the Social Sciences*. New York: Wiley-Interscience.

British Association for the Advancement of Science (1974). "Does research threaten privacy or does privacy threaten research? Report of a study group." London: British Association Publication 74/1.

Burgess, Philip, and Donald Munton (1971). "An inventory of archival and fugitive international relations data." Mimeographed. Columbus: Ohio State University.

Burnham, Walter Dean (1963). "Sources of historical election data: a preliminary bibliography." Bibliographic Series No. 10. East Lansing, Mich.: Institute for Community Development and Services, Michigan State University.

Campbell, Angus (1970). "Some questions about the New Jerusalem." In Ralph L. Bisco, ed., *Data Bases, Computers and the Social Sciences*. New York: Wiley-Interscience.

Campbell, Donald T. (1968). "A cooperative multinational opinion sample exchange." *Journal of Social Issues* 24, no. 2:245–256.

Clubb, Jerome M. (1970a). "Data archives for comparative studies of national development." Paper presented at the Eighth World Conference of the International Political Science Association, Munich, Germany, August–September. Mimeographed. Ann Arbor, Mich.: Center for Political Studies.

——————— (1970b). "Ecological data in comparative research: report on a First International Data Confrontation Seminar." *Reports and Papers in the Social Sciences,* 25. Paris: UNESCO.

——————— (1971). "Historical politics: American elections, 1824–1970." *Items,* 25, no. 4:46–50.

Clubb, Jerome M., and Howard W. Allen (1967). "Computers and historical studies." *The Journal of American History,* 54.

Computers and the Humanities, published quarterly since 1966. Flushing, N.Y.: Queens College.

Converse, Philip E. (1964). "A network of data archives for the behavioral sciences." *Public Opinion Quarterly,* 28 (Summer): 273–286.

——————— (1966). "The availability and quality of sample survey data in archives within the United States." In Richard L. Merritt and Stein Rokkan, eds., *Comparing Nations: The Use of Quantitative Data in Cross-National Research.* New Haven and London: Yale University Press.

Deane, Phyllis (1968). "Aggregate comparisons: the validity and reliability of economic data." In Stein Rokkan, ed., *Comparative Research Across Cultures and Nations.* Paris and The Hague: Mouton.

Deutsch, Karl W. (1966). "The theoretical basis of data programs." In Richard L. Merritt and Stein Rokkan, eds., *Comparing Nations: The Use of Quantitative Data in Cross-National Research.* New Haven and London: Yale University Press.

——————— (1970). "The impact of complex data bases on the social sciences." In Ralph L. Bisco, ed., *Data Bases, Computers and the Social Sciences.* New York: Wiley-Interscience.

Deutsch, Karl W., Harold D. Lasswell, Richard L. Merritt, and Bruce M. Russett (1966). "The Yale political data program." In Richard L. Merritt and Stein Rokkan, eds., *Comparing Nations: The Use of Quantitative Data in Cross-National Research.* New Haven and London: Yale University Press.

Dubester, Henry J. (1948). *State Censuses: An Annotated Bibliography of Censuses of Population Taken After the Year 1790 by States and Territories of the United States.* Washington, D.C.: Government Printing Office.

——————— (1950). *Catalog of United States Census Publications, 1790–1945.* Washington, D.C.: Government Printing Office.

Easton, David, and Jack Dennis (1969). *Children in the Political System: Origins of Political Legitimacy.* New York: McGraw-Hill.

European Studies Newsletter, published bi-monthly since October, 1971. Pittsburgh: University of Pittsburgh.

European Political Data Newsletter, published irregularly since April, 1971. Bergen, Norway: European Consortium for Political Research, Data Information Center, University of Bergen.

Federal Statistics Users' Conference Newsletter, published monthly since 1958. Washington, D.C.: Federal Statistics Users' Conference.

Finster, Jerome, ed. (1974). *The National Archives and Urban Research.* Athens, Ohio: Ohio University Press.

Fishbein, Meyer H., ed. (1973). *The National Archives and Statistical Research.* Athens, Ohio: Ohio University Press.

Garcia-Bouza, Jorge (1969). "The future development of social science data archives in Latin America." In Mattei Dogan and Stein Rokkan, eds., *Quantitative Ecological Analysis in the Social Sciences.* Cambridge, Mass., and London: MIT Press.

Goldhamer, Herbert, and Andrew W. Marshall (1953). *Psychosis and Civilization: Two Studies in the Frequency of Mental Disease.* Glencoe, Ill.: The Free Press.

Gray, Wood, *et al.* (1964). *Historian's Handbook: A Key to the Study and Writing of History.* Boston: Houghton Mifflin

Gustafson, Milton O., ed. (1974). *The National Archives and Foreign Relations Research.* Athens, Ohio: Ohio University Press.

Hartenstein, Wolfgang, and Klaus Liepelt (1969). "Archives for ecological research in West Germany." In Mattei Dogan and Stein Rokkan, eds., *Quantitative Ecological Analysis in the Social Sciences.* London and Cambridge, Mass.: MIT Press.

Hess, Robert D., and Judith V. Torney (1967). *The Development of Political Attitudes in Children.* Chicago: Aldine.

Historical Methods Newsletter, published quarterly since December, 1967. Pittsburgh: The University of Pittsburgh.

Hofferbert, Richard I. (1972). "Data archiving and confidentiality in the international comparative study on the organization of research units." A working paper prepared for the Science Policy Division, UNESCO. Mimeographed. Ann Arbor, Mich.: Center for Political Studies.

Hyman, Herbert H. (1972). *Secondary Analysis of Sample Surveys: Principles, Procedures and Potentialities.* New York: John Wiley and Sons.

International City Management Association, published yearly since 1934. *The Municipal Year Book.* Washington, D.C.: International City Management Association.

Janda, Kenneth (1968). *Information Retrieval: Applications to Political Science.* Indianapolis: Bobbs-Merrill.

Key, V. O. (1966). *The Responsible Electorate: Rationality in Presidential Voting, 1936–1960.* Cambridge, Mass.: Belknap Press.

Lorwin, Val R., and Jacob M. Price, eds. (1972). *The Dimensions of the Past: Materials, Problems and Opportunities for Quantitative Work in History.* New Haven: Yale University Press.

Lowry, Roye L. (1970). "Federal information systems—some current developments." In Ralph L. Bisco, ed., *Data Bases, Computers and the Social Sciences.* New York: Wiley-Interscience.

Mackie, Thomas T. and Richard Rose (1974). *The International Almanac of Electoral History.* New York: The Free Press.

Marvick, Dwaine, and Jane H. Bayes (1969). "Domains and universes: problems in concerted use of multiple data files for social science inquiries." In Mattei Dogan and Stein

Rokkan, eds., *Quantitative Ecological Analysis in the Social Sciences.* London and Cambridge, Mass.: MIT Press.

Mason, John Brown (1968). *Research Resources: Annotated Guide to the Social Sciences.* Vol. 1: *International Relations, and Recent History Indexes, Abstracts and Periodicals.* Santa Barbara, Calif. American Bibliographical Center, Clio Press.

Mickiewicz, Ellen (1973). *Handbook of Soviet Social Science Data.* New York: The Free Press.

Miller, Arthur R. (1971). *The Assault on Privacy: Computers, Data Banks and Dossiers.* Ann Arbor: The University of Michigan Press.

Miller, Warren E. (1967). "Promises and problems in the use of computers: the case of research in political history." In Edmund Bowles, *Computers in Humanistic Research.* Englewood Cliffs, N.J.: Prentice-Hall.

——————— (1969). "The development of archives for social science data." In Mattei Dogan and Stein Rokkan, eds., *Quantitative Ecological Analysis in the Social Sciences.* London and Cambridge, Mass.: MIT Press.

Morrison, Donald George, *et al.* (1972). *Black Africa: A Comparative Handbook.* New York: The Free Press.

Narroll, Raoul (1970). *Data Quality Control: A New Research Technique.* New York: The Free Press.

National Archives and Records Service (1974). *Guide to the National Archives of the United States.* Washington, D.C.: Government Printing Office.

National Technical Information Service (1974). *Directory of Computerized Data Files and Related Software Available from Federal Agencies, 1974.* Washington, D.C.: United States Department of Commerce.

Ohlin, Goran (1968). "Aggregate comparisons: problems and prospects of quantitative analysis based on national accounts." In Stein Rokkan, ed., *Comparative Research Across Cultures and Nations.* Paris and The Hague: Mouton.

Park, Tong-whan (1968). "A guide to data sources in international relations: annotated bibliography with lists of variables." Mimeographed. Evanston, Ill.: Northwestern University.

Poulton, Helen J. (1972). *The Historian's Handbook: A Descriptive Guide to' Reference Works.* Norman: The University of Oklahoma Press.

Press, Charles, and Oliver Williams (1962). *State Manuals, Blue Books and Election Results.* Berkeley, Calif.: Institute of Governmental Services, University of California.

Rokkan, Stein, ed. (1966). *Data Archives for the Social Sciences.* Paris and The Hague: Mouton.

——————— (1968). *Comparative Research Across Nations and Cultures.* Paris and The Hague: Mouton.

Rokkan, Stein, and Jean Meyriat, eds. (1969). *International Guide to Electoral Statistics.* Vol. 1: *National Elections in Western Europe.* The Hague: Mouton.

Rokkan, Stein, and Henry Valen (1966). "Archives for statistical studies of within-nation difference." In Richard L. Merritt and Stein Rokkan eds., *Comparing Nations:*

The Use of Quantitative Data in Cross-National Research. New Haven, Conn., and London: Yale University Press.

Rose, Richard, ed. (1973). *Electoral Behavior: A Comparative Handbook.* New York: The Free Press.

Russett, Bruce M., Hayward R. Alker, Karl W. Deutsch, and Harold D. Lasswell (1964). *World Handbook of Political and Social Indicators.* New Haven, Conn., and London: Yale University Press.

Scheuch, Erwin K. (1966). "Cross-national comparisons using aggregate data." In Richard L. Merritt and Stein Rokkan, eds., *Comparing Nations: The Use of Quantitative Data in Cross-National Research.* New Haven, Conn., and London: Yale University Press.

————— (1968). "The cross-cultural use of sample surveys: problems of comparability." In Stein Rokkan, ed., *Comparative Research Across Cultures and Nations.* Paris and The Hague: Mouton.

Scheuch, Erwin K., and Philip Stone (1966). "Retrieval systems for data archives: the general inquirer." In Richard L. Merritt and Stein Rokkan, eds., *Comparing Nations: The Use of Quantitative Data in Cross-National Research.* New Haven, Conn., and London: Yale University Press.

Schmeckebier, Lawrence F., and Roy B. Eastin (1961). *Government Publications and Their Use.* Washington, D.C.: The Brookings Institution.

Sessions, Vivian S., ed. (1972). *Directory of Data Bases in the Social and Behavioral Sciences.* New York: Science Associates/International.

Shapiro, Gilbert (1965). "Public opinion in the revolutionary process: a quantitative analysis of the *Cahiers de Doleances* of 1789." *Public Opinion Quarterly* 29, no. 3:459–460.

Shapiro, Gilbert, John Markoff, and Sasha R. Weitman (1974). "Quantitative studies of the French Revolution: a progress report on a research program." *History and Theory,* forthcoming.

Singer, J. David (1972). "The 'Correlates of War' Project: interim report and rationale." *World Politics* 24 (January).

Singer, J. David, and Melvin Small (1972). *The Wages of War, 1816–1965: A Statistical Handbook.* New York: John Wiley and Sons.

Stiefbold, Rodney (1969). "Ecological data on Austria." In Mattei Dogan and Stein Rokkan, eds., *Quantitative Ecological Analysis in the Social Sciences.* London and Cambridge, Mass.: MIT Press.

SS Data: Newsletter of Social Science Archival Acquisitions, published quarterly since September, 1971. Iowa City: Laboratory for Political Research, The University of Iowa.

Social Science Information, published quarterly since February, 1962. Paris: International Social Science Council.

Taylor, Charles L., ed. (1968). *Aggregate Data Analysis: Political and Social Indicators in Cross-National Research.* Paris: Mouton.

Taylor, Charles L., and Michael C. Hudson (1970). *World Handbook of Political and Social Indicators II*. New Haven, Conn., and London: Yale University Press.

Tilly, Charles (1969). "Methods for the study of collective violence." In Ralph W. Conant and Molly Apple Levin, eds., *Problems in the Study of Community Violence*. New York: Praeger.

——————— (1972). "How protest modernized in France." In William O. Aydelotte, Allan G. Bogue, and Robert William Fogel, eds., *The Dimensions of Quantitative Research in History*. Princeton, N.J.: Princeton University Press.

United States Bureau of the Census. *Bureau of the Census Catalog*. Washington, D.C.: Government Printing Office.

——————— (1972). *Guide to Recurrent and Special Governmental Statistics,* Vol. 1. Washington, D.C.: Government Printing Office.

——————— *Small-Area Data Notes,* published monthly since January, 1966. Washington, D.C.: United States Department of Commerce.

——————— (1961). *Historical Statistics of the United States, Colonial Times to 1957*. Washington, D.C.: Government Printing Office.

Wallis, W. Allen, and Harry V. Roberts (1956). *Statistics: A New Approach*. New York: The Free Press.

Wasserman, Paul, Eleanor Allen, and Charlotte Georgi, eds. (1971). Third revised edition. *Statistics Sources: A Subject Guide to Data on Industrial, Business, Social, Educational, Financial and Other Topics for the United States and Selected Foreign Countries*. Detroit: Gale Research.

Yearbook of International Organizations, published yearly since 1948. Brussels: The Union of International Organizations.

3

CASE STUDY AND THEORY
IN POLITICAL SCIENCE

HARRY ECKSTEIN

INTRODUCTION

The extent to which certain kinds of study are carried out in the field of political science seems to be a poor indicator of their perceived utility for building theories.

The type of study most frequently made in the field is the intensive study of individual cases. Case studies run the gamut from the most microscosmic to the most macrocosmic levels of political phenomena. On the microlevel, we have many studies of conspicuous political personalities (political leaders such as Lincoln, Stalin, Gandhi), and of particular leadership positions and small leadership groups (the American presidency, the British Cabinet, the prime minister in British government, the operational code of the Soviet leadership, and so on). At the level of political groupings, the literature of the field teems with studies of particular pressure groups, political parties, party systems, revolutionary and protest movements, and political "elites," both on the national and local levels. More abundant still are studies of individual polities in all corners of the world and at many stages of history and development. Many of these treat polities as overall macrocosms; many deal with their subsidiary organizations (administrative apparatuses, legislatures, judiciaries, systems of local government), or with their programs and policies, or their particular electoral, legislative, executive, or judicial decision processes. Beyond that level, one finds a similar profusion of case studies of transnational phenomena: specific processes of and organizations for transnational integration, particular "systems" of international politics, particular crises in international relations, and the like.

The abundance of examples is such that it seems pointless to provide bibliography. Precisely because the genre is so common, political scientists can easily construct a representative list of examples for themselves. If not, a brief visit to the political science section of the library will serve. It is not much of an exaggeration to say that the case study literature in the field comes close to being coterminous with its literature as such.

This plenitude of case studies is not associated with any perception that they are a particularly useful means for arriving at a theoretical understanding of the subject matter of political study. Most political scientists who do case studies appear to have no views at all, or only ambiguous views, on the role that case studies can play in theory building. For them, the case study is literally a genre, not a method. If they do express views on the subject, they usually disparage the genre as a method—for instance, by holding that case studies can at most stir up becalmed theoretical imaginations. One might explain this apparent paradox by holding that political scientists do not place a high value on theory building. No doubt this is true for many of them. But it is much less true nowadays than it used to be, and the volume, or proportion, of case studies in the field has not notably decreased.

It is in order, therefore, to raise three questions: What general role can case study play in the development of theories concerning political phenomena? How useful is the case method at various stages of the theory-building process? And how is case study best conducted for purposes of devising theories?

I intend here to propose answers to these questions that run sharply counter to the now conventional wisdom in political science, especially in the division of the field we call "comparative politics." The quotation marks no doubt give the dénouement away. Readers are supposed to conclude that "comparative" studies are by no means necessary (and often not even wise strategy to follow) in pursuing the objective for which they are usually conducted: the discovery of valid generalizations about political phenomena. Indeed, I hold that the conventional wisdom has things virtually upside down. Case studies, I will argue, are valuable at all stages of the theory-building process, but most valuable at that stage of theory building where least value is generally attached to them: the stage at which candidate theories are "tested." Moreover, the argument for case studies as a means for building theories seems strongest in regard to precisely those phenomena with which the subfield of "comparative" politics is most associated: macropolitical phenomena, i.e., units of political study of considerable magnitude or complexity, such as nation-states and subjects virtually coterminous with them (party systems or political cultures). More precisely, the abstract brief in favor of the case study as a means of building theories seems to me to hold regardless of level of inquiry, but at the macrocosmic level practical research considerations greatly reinforce that brief.

Extensive argument is necessary to make these points. But while the fun is in arguing against conventional views (especially if, as in this case, they seem truistic), arguments do not make sense, and counterarguments are unlikely to be apropos, unless major terms are first defined. In political science the safe bet usually is that even widely used concepts are not widely understood in a uni-form, unambiguous manner. Readers must therefore bear with me for a while as I clarify some basic terminology.

DEFINITIONS

Case Study and Comparative Study

1. The conception of case study commonly held in the social sciences is de-rived from, and closely similar to, that of clinical studies in medicine and psychology. Such studies are usually contrasted dichotomously (as if they were antitheses) to experimental ones, which furnish the prevalent conception of comparative study. Contrasts generally drawn between the two types of study cover virtually all aspects of inquiry: range of research, methods and techniques, manner of reporting findings, and research objectives. (See, for example, Riley, 1963, pp. 32–75.)

As to *range of research:* Experimental studies are held to be conducted with large numbers of cases, constituting samples of populations, while clinical studies deal with single individuals, or at most small numbers of them not statistically representative of a populous set. Experimental studies thus are sometimes said to be "extensive" and clinical ones "intensive." These adjectives do not refer to numbers of individuals alone, but also involve the number of variables taken into account. In experimental studies that number is deliber-ately and severely limited, and preselected, for the purpose of discovering rela-tionships between traits abstracted from individual wholes. Clinical study, to the contrary, tries to capture the whole individual—"tries to" because it is, of course, conceded that doing so is only an approachable, not an attainable, end.

As for *methods and techniques:* The typical experimental study, first of all, starts with, and adheres to, a tightly constructed research design, whereas the typical clinical study is much more open-ended and flexible at all stages. The clinical researcher may have (probably must have) in mind some notions of where to begin inquiry, a sort of checklist of points to look into during its course, or perhaps even a preliminary model of the individual being studied; but actual study proceeds more by feel and improvisation than by plan. Sec-ond, the techniques most commonly associated with such inquiry in the case of "collective individuals" (i.e., social units) are the loose ones of participant observation (simply observing the unit from within, as if a member of it) and *Verstehen* (i.e., empathy: understanding the meaning of actions and interactions from the members' own points of view). The typical techniques of experimental inquiry, per contra, are those rigorous and routinized procedures of data proc-essing and data analysis concocted to ensure high degrees of "nonsubjective" reliability and validity—the techniques of the statistics texts and research methods primers.

Reports of the findings of clinical study are generally characterized as narrative and descriptive: they provide case histories and detailed portraiture. Such reporting might therefore also be termed synthetic, while that of experimental studies is analytic, since it does not present depictions of "whole" individuals but rather of relations among components, or elements, of them. Beyond description, clinical studies present "interpretation"; beyond raw data, experimental ones present rigorously evaluated "findings."

It follows that the *objectives* of the two types of study also differ. That of experimental study is generalized knowledge: theoretical propositions. These may certainly apply to individuals but never exhaust the knowledge it is possible to have of them. Being general they necessarily miss what is particular and unique, which may or may not be a lot. The objective of clinical study, on the other hand, is precisely to capture the particular and unique, for if anything about an individual whole is such, so must be the whole per se. It is conceded that in describing an individual configuration we may get hunches about the generalizability of relations not yet experimentally studied, but only hunches, and even these only by serendipity (Merton, 1957, p. 103). Clinical study is therefore associated more with action objectives than those of pure knowledge. In the case of single individuals, it aims at diagnosis, treatment, and adjustment; in that of collective individuals, at policy. This association of clinical study with adjustive action is based on the assumption that therapy and policy can hardly proceed without something approximating full knowledge of its subjects, however much general propositions may help in proceeding from clinical knowledge of a case to the appropriate manipulation of a subject. Clinical and experimental objectives draw near, asymptotically, as "pure" knowledge becomes "applied" (i.e., in engineering models), but application is merely a possible extension of experimental knowledge while generally being an intrinsic objective of clinical research.

2. Anyone familiar with the modern history of comparative politics (for a brief review, see Eckstein and Apter, 1963, pp. 3–32) will realize that its development since the early 1950s involves a transition, or shift, from the clinical to the experimental mode of study. Macridis and Brown (1955) criticized the old "comparative" politics for being, among other things, noncomparative (concerned mainly with single cases) and essentially descriptive and monographic (not substantially concerned with theory and, at least in aim, wholistic); and he implies that it had a dominant therapeutic objective: to find ways of diagnosing the ills of unstable democracies and making them more stable. Such studies, conforming to the model of clinical research, still abound, but the proportion of those conducted in accordance with that of experimental study has steadily grown, as has the proportion of monographic studies seeking, somehow, to tie into the other variety.

However, while the distinction between clinical and experimental studies is useful for contrasting the old and new comparative politics, it does not serve nearly so well in distinguishing the case study from other modes of research. At best, it can provide an initial inkling (but only an inkling) of the differences among them. Certainly this chapter, which argues in favor of case studies, is not by any stretch of the imagination to be taken as a defense of the kind of work Macridis assails and the field has downgraded. The distinction offers a useful denotative definition of case studies in the social sciences (that is, what people usually mean by the term) but a far from useful connotative and generic one (how the term ought to be used if it is not to raise serious difficulties of meaning and classification and not to define merely one of numerous types of case study).

3. The essential objections to equating case study with clinical and comparative study with experimental inquiry all revolve on one basic point: nothing compels the clustering (hence, dichotomization) of the various characteristics used to distinguish clinical and experimental studies. Although that clustering in fact occurs very frequently in the social sciences, it does so chiefly because of dubious beliefs and assumptions. At most, the characteristics have a certain practical affinity, e.g., the fewer the cases studied the more intensive study may be, other things being equal. But no logical compulsion is at work and the practical considerations often are not weighty.

We may certainly begin with the notion that case studies, like clinical studies, concern "individuals," personal or collective (and, for tidiness of conceptualization, assume that only one individual is involved). From this, however, it does not follow that case studies must be intensive in the clinician's sense: nothing like "wholistic" study may be attempted and the researcher may certainly aim at finding relationships between preselected variables—unless he assumes, a priori, that this is foolish. The research may be tightly designed and may put to use all sorts of sophisticated research techniques. (An excellent example is Osgood and Luria's [1954] "blind analysis," using the semantic differential, of a case of multiple personality.) Its results need not be cast in narrative form, and its objective can certainly be the development of general propositions rather than portraiture of the particular and unique; nor need case studies be concerned with problems of therapeutic action when they go beyond narration, depiction, and subjective interpretation.

The same applies, *mutatis mutandis,* to studies of numerous cases, even leaving aside the fact that the cases need not be, and often are not, very numerous, and certainly not a "sample." This leaves a large residual no-man's-land, even from the standpoint of numbers, between the clinical and experimental. Studies of numerous cases can also take into account numerous variables. Modern data processing capabilities have, in fact, encouraged a kind of omnibus approach even to cross-national research, à la Banks and Textor (1963), in which anything one can think of is cross-tabulated and correlated with just about everything else. Even before these capabilities existed some comparative works treated the various aspects of complex whole, like polities, as comprehensively as any clinical investigation (e.g., Finer, 1949; and Friedrich, 1968). Studies of numerous cases also leave room for improvisation in research. They are not always tightly designed, do not always use rigorous research techniques, are sometimes reported in the descriptive vein, often have few or no theoretical pretensions, and also often seek direct answers to policy and other action questions, not answers that amount to the deduction of applied from pure theory.

These points of overlap and ambivalence in the distinction between the clinical and experimental have led to a concerted attack on the dichotomy in psychology itself. One typical attack argues that the dichotomy originates in an archaic and absurd *Methodenstreit* between "mechanistic" and "romantic" views of human nature (Holt, 1962). Another argues that experimental modes of study can also be used profitably in research into single cases; this is the theme of a notable book of essays, *N = 1* (Davidson and Costello, 1969). This work implies the most important definitional point of all: if case study is defined as clinical study in the traditional sense, then we not only construct a messy generic (not necessarily classificatory) concept, but also foreclose the possibility of useful argument about case study as a tool in theory building. The definition answers the question: case study and theory are at polar opposites, linked only by the fortuitous operation of serendipity.

4. This attack on the conventional idea of case study serves a constructive as well as destructive purpose. It provides ammunition for later arguments against highly restrictive views concerning the role of case study in theory building, and also points the way toward a better, and simpler, definition of what case studies are.

An unambiguous definition of case study should proceed from the one sure point that has been established: case study is the study of individuals. That is about as simple as one can get—but, because of one major problem, it is too simple. The problem is that one man's single individual way may be another's numerous cases. Take an example: In order to help break down the dichotomy between the clinical and experimental, Davidson and Costello (1969, pp. 214–232) reprint a study by Chassan on the evaluation of drug effects during psychotherapy. Chassan argues for the greater power of single-case study over the usual "treatment group" versus "control group" design—in this case, for determining the relative effects of tranquilizers and placebos. Readers can catch the flavor of his argument through two of his many italicized passages:

> . . . the intensive statistical study of a single case can provide more meaningful and statistically significant information than, say, only end-point observations extended over a relatively large number of patients.

... the argument cited against generalization to other patients, from the result of a single case intensively studied, can actually be applied in a more realistic and devastating manner against the value of inferences ... drawn from studies in which extensive rather than intensive degrees of freedom are used. (Davidson and Costello, 1969)

And so on, in the same vein. The whole paper is an object lesson to those who seek theoretical safety only in numbers. But there is a catch. Chassan studied only one patient, but used a large number of treatments by drug and placebo: "frequent observations over periods of sufficiently long duration." The "individual" here surely is not the patient, although he may be for other purposes; it is each treatment, the effects of which are being compared. It is easy enough to see the advantages of administering different treatments to the same person over a long period (hence, safety in small numbers of a sort), as against using one patient per observation (although it is to Chassan's credit that he pointed them out in contrast to the more usual procedure). But n, despite the title of the book, in this case is not one.

If this problem arises with persons, it arises still more emphatically with "collective individuals." A study of six general elections in Britain may be, but need not be, an $n = 1$ study. It might also be an $n = 6$ study. It can also be an $n = 120,000,000$ study. It depends on whether the subject of study is electoral systems, elections, or voters.

What follows from this is that ambiguity about what constitutes an "individual" (hence "case") can only be dispelled by not looking at concrete entities but at the measures made of them. On this basis, a *"case" can be defined technically as a phenomenon for which we report and interpret only a single measure on any pertinent variable.* This gets us out of answering insoluble metaphysical questions that arise because any concrete entity can be decomposed, at least potentially, into numerous entities (not excluding "persons": they differ almost from moment to moment, from treatment to treatment, and consist of highly numerous cells, which consist of highly numerous particles, and so on). It also raises starkly the critical problem of this essay: what useful role can single descriptive measures (not measures of central tendency, association, correlation, variance or covariance, all of which presuppose numerous measures of each variable) play in the construction of theory?

If case study can be thus defined, *comparative study is simply the study of numerous cases along the same lines, with a view to reporting and interpreting numerous measures on the same variables of different "individuals."* The individuals, needless now to say, can be persons or collectivities, or the same person or collectivity at different points in time, in different contexts, or under different treatments. And the term "measure" should of course here be treated with latitude: it might be a highly precise quantity (34.67% of all Britons always vote Labour) or a rather imprecise observation (the American Republican party is a chronic minority party).

Theory and Theory Building

We will be concerned with the utility of case studies in the development of theories in macropolitics—their utility both in themselves and, to an extent, relative to comparative ($n =$ many) studies. While nearly everyone in the field at the present time agrees that the development of good theories is the quintessential end of political inquiry, conceptions of theory, and of the processes by which it may be developed, vary extremely in our field. This makes unavoidable a definitional exercise on theory and a review of the normal steps in theory building.

1. Two polar positions on what constitutes theory in our field can be identified. While positions range between them, they have recently been rather polarized, more often on, or very near, the extremes than between them.

On one extreme (the "hard" line on theory) is the view that theory consists solely of statements like those characteristic of contemporary theoretical physics (or, better, considered to be so by influential philosophers of science). A good summary of this view, tailored to the field of political science, is presented in Holt and Richardson's discussion of the nature of "paradigms" (1968, pp. 4–8), but even better sources are the writings of scientist-philosophers such as Kemeny (1959), Popper (1959), and Hempel (1965).

Theories in this sense have four crucial traits: (1) The concepts used in them are defined very precisely, usually by stating definitions in terms of empirical referents, and are less intended to describe phenomena fully than to abstract from them characteristics useful for formulating general propositions about them. (2) The concepts are used in deductively connected sets of propositions that are either axioms (assumptions) or theorems deduced from them. (3) The object of the propositions is both logical consistency and "empirical import," i.e., correspondence to observations of phenomena. And (4) empirical import is determined by tests themselves deduced from the propositions, and these are designed to make it highly probable that the propositions will flunk the tests, confidence in propositions being proportionate to the stiffness of the tests they manage to survive. In our own field, theories of this type are sometimes called "formal theories," mainly because of the large role of formal deduction in their elaboration; and economics is generally taken as the nearest social science model for them, not only in general form but also in regard to substantive "rationality" axioms (Downs, 1957; Riker, 1962; Buchanan and Tullock, 1967; Curry and Wade, 1968).

On the other pole (the "soft" line), theory is simply regarded as any mental construct that orders phenomena or inquiry into them. This qualifies as theory many quite diverse constructs, including classificatory schemes that assign individual cases to more or less general classes, "analytic" schemes that decompose complex phenomena into their component elements, frameworks and checklists for conducting inquiry (e.g., the "systems" approach to macropolitics, or "decision-making" checklists for the study of foreign policy formation), any empirical patterns found in properly processed data, or anything considered to underlie such patterns (e.g., learning processes or class position).

2. If the term theory were always prefaced by an appropriate adjective, wrangling about these, and less extreme, positions could be avoided. But this would not take us off the hook of having to specify how "good theory" as an objective of inquiry in our field should be conceived. The best position on this issue, it seems to me, is neither hard nor soft but does come closer to the hard than the soft extreme. It rests on two major premises.

The first is that it makes no sense whatever to call any mental construct a theory. Such constructs differ vastly in nature and purpose, so that they can hardly be considered to be of the same species. With some of them, not much more can be done than to assign names to phenomena or to order one's filing cabinets. And it can be demonstrated that, strictly speaking, the soft position compels one to regard as theory any statement whatever in conventional or technical discourse.

Second, it makes little more sense to restrict the term to constructs like those of theoretical physics, or those abstracted from that field by philosophers of science. While such constructs have proved extremely powerful in certain senses, one may doubt that they alone possess power (even in these senses). If constructs like them are not attainable in a field such as our own at its present stage of development (which is at least an open question, since constructs like them have in fact not been attained), commitment to theory in such a narrow sense may induce one to forego theoretical inquiry altogether. Most important, theories in the "hard" sense are a particular form developed, over considerable time, to realize the purposes—the motivating goals, animus, telos—of an activity; and while they do this very well, it does not follow that they are absolutely required for realizing these purposes.

Consequently, even if the constructs of theoretical physics are taken as a model, it seems unwise to restrict the notion of theory entirely to such constructs. It seems better to label as theory any constructs designed to realize the same ends and formulated with the same animus as those which characterize the fields in which hard theory has been developed—leaving open, anyway provisionally, the forms such constructs may take consistent with reasonable achievement of the ends. On this basis, theory is characterized by a telos, or animus, of inquiry rather than by the particular form of statements. The only requirement (which, however, is far from soft) is that the forms of theoretical statements must be conducive to the goals of theoretical activity.

Such a teleological conception of theory requires that the goals be made explicit. They can be characterized under the following headings: *regularity, reliability, validity, foreknowledge,* and *parsimony*.

a). The quintessential end of theorizing is to arrive at *statements of regularity* about the structure, behavior, and interaction of phenomena. "Regularity" here means, literally, "rulefulness": the discovery of rules that phenomena observe in the concrete world, as players do in games or logicians in logic. Such regularity can exist in many senses. The rules may describe simple relations among variables without specification of their exact nature; or they may describe sequences like causal paths or historical and genetic patterns; or they may be statements of the conditions of persistence or efficacy of structures. The rules may also be more or less "ruleful." They may be "probability statements" that permit no inferences about individual cases but only more or less confident ones about sets of them, or they may be "laws" in which probability is at unity. Both of these can further vary in "rulefulness" according, for example, to the number and significance of variables held constant or ignored, or whether they state necessary, sufficient, or both necessary and sufficient conditions if causal sequences or conditions of viability or performance are specified.

b). The animus of theoretical inquiry requires not merely empirical rules, but also that the rules be as *reliable and valid* as possible. Reliability exists to the extent that inquirers, proceeding in the same manner, arrive at the same results; validity to the extent that a presumed regularity has been subjected, unsuccessfully, to tough appropriate attempts at falsification. Not all presumed or discovered regularities are subject to tests of reliability and validity, and certainly not to equally tough ones: e.g., a statistical inference about a set of cases observed by a researcher that cannot be restudied at all or in much the same way can never be reliable and is unlikely to be valid (i.e., successfully tested). Hence, just as concepts become theoretical by being used in regularity statements, so such statements become theoretical if they are subject to tough reliability and validity tests.

c). *Foreknowledge* is the correct anticipation, by sound reasoning, of unknowns (whether the unknown has or has not yet occurred). Theory not only does, but needs to, aim at that objective, because the toughest, hence most conclusive, test of any rule is the correct deduction from it of unobserved experience. In most cases, theories are shaped to fit observations already made, and this is fine, so long as observations are not deliberately selected to fit theories. The manner in which theories are shaped to fit observations does tell us something about their probable validity. But generally there are numerous rules that fit well any body of observations and numerous techniques that yield different results when the question of degree of rulefulness arises. Even if this were not so, all we can really learn from rules shaped to fit knowns is that they hold (in some degree) for the cases observed under the whole complex of conditions prevailing when they were observed, not that they hold for all such cases, under all conditions or under other precisely specifiable conditions. Only foreknowledge, in the sense above, can provide confidence that the regularities are less tenuous.

The objective of foreknowledge has been neglected in recent political science studies because of a fixation on the power of sophisticated data processing to yield valid rules (rather than just rules likely to be validated). Even more, it has been neglected because of a belief that foreknowledge always involves literal prescience of events in the future of the natural world, which, in view of the complexity of macropolitics, seems as near to impossible as anything can be. In fact, theoretical foreknowledge rarely takes the form of prescience. More often it involves experimental prediction (anticipating, by correct reasoning from presumed regularities, the results of activities in which variables are fully controlled), or concrete prediction (anticipating, by such reasoning, what will occur in the natural world if and only if specified initial conditions obtain), or forecasting (anticipating, by such reasoning, the probabilities of specified events occurring, given the initial conditions that do obtain). These types of foreknowledge all fall short of prescience and are not all equally conclusive for theory. The failure of a single forecast, for example, is generally (not always) less conclusive than that of an experimental prediction, although repeated forecasting failures are pretty definitive. All, however, give an essential insight into validity that the mere fitting of regularity statements to known data can never provide.

It should be evident that constructs exactly like those of theoretical physics are not needed for foreknowledge: certainly not for every type of it. All that is required of theory in the generic sense is that some unknown be strictly deducible from the posited regularities, whether the unknown is the outcome of an experiment, or the probabilities of natural events under obtaining conditions, or the occurrence of natural events under conditions specified by the theorist.

d). The notion of *parsimony* is hard to define precisely. The philosophers of science seem themselves to have had inordinate trouble with the concept. I take it to mean that regularity statements are parsimonious in proportion to (i) the variety and number of observations they order; (ii) the number of discrete theoretical constructs (i.e., constructs not strictly deducible from one another) used to order a constant volume and variety of observations; (iii) the number of other theoretical constructs subsumed to or derivable from them; and (iv) the number and complexity of variables used in the statements. On this basis, regularity statements are never parsimonious or unparsimonious (although the concept is often used dichotomously) but always more or less so, especially since trade-offs among the criteria of parsimony are possible.

The ideal of parsimony is to an extent aesthetic, but a high degree of it is required by the objective of foreknowledge and thus hangs together with the general animus of theoretical inquiry. The reason is simply that regularity statements can be made so cumbersome and complex that nothing (or, much the same, too many different things) can be strictly deduced from them, even when the cardinal sin of hypothesis saving is not committed. A case in point is Easton's "systems analysis" of macropolitics (1965). By my reading, Easton identifies at least twelve crucial stresses that can arise in the political system's input-conversion-output-feedback cycle, each potentially fatal and each capable of being more or less reduced ("managed") by different adaptations to stress. Since the stresses can occur in various combinations and sequences, deducing what may ensue from any given initial condition in a polity becomes a matter of permutation, and $12! = 479$ million (approximately); hence, any state of political affairs can lead to something like half a billion subsequent states of affairs without violating Easton's theory. Given that fact, the probability of correct forecasting of any sort seems a bit low. So does that of finding a unique solution for why any given state of affairs exists, or that of failing to account for anything within the terms of Easton's theory. This is precisely why parsimony is essential: only a high degree of it can ensure that regularity statements may fail, and therefore also succeed.[1]

Theories can, of course, be more or less powerful, or "good," depending on the rulefulness of regularity statements, the amount of reliability and validity they possess, the amount and kinds of foreknowledge they provide, and how parsimonious they are.[2] The animus of theoretical inquiry is constantly to increase their power to some unattainable absolute in all these senses. And while that absolute might have a unique ideal form to which the forms of theoretical physics might provide a discerning clue, it should be evident that it can be approached through many kinds of formulations, and always only approached. This is why "theory" is better conceived of as a set of goals than as statements having a specified form.

At the same time, no mental construct qualifies as theory unless it satisfies the goals in some minimal sense. This minimal sense is that it must state a presumed regularity in observations that is susceptible to reliability and validity tests, permits the deduction of some unknowns, and is parsimonious enough to prevent the deduction of so many that virtually any occurrence can be held to bear it out. If these conditions are not satisfied, statements can still be interesting and useful; but they are not "theory."

These are the sort of constructs we want about macropolitics. It should be evident that the pivotal point in the whole conception is that regarding foreknowledge: validity is held to depend on it, parsimony is mainly required for the sake of establishing validity, and regularity statements are not an end unless valid. Any general appraisal of the utility of a method of inquiry must therefore also pivot on that point, as will my brief for the case study method.[3]

3. It should also be evident that foreknowledge is most closely bound up with the testing of theories and that the process of theory building involves much that precedes testing, and some activities subsequent to it as well. It follows that modes of inquiry might be highly serviceable at one state of the process but not at others, and this also must be considered in arguments about them.

a). The process of theory building, needless to say, always begins with *questions* about experience for which answers are wanted—and raising questions, especially penetrating ones, is anything but a simple matter; indeed it is perhaps what most distinguishes the genius from the dullard (for whom common sense, the sense of ordinary people, leaves few mysteries). It is also an ability that, conceivably, could be sharpened or dulled by various modes of inquiry.

b). Questions, to be answered by theories, must usually be restated as *problems* or *puzzles*. This is a complex process that I have discussed elsewhere (Eckstein, 1964, Introduction) and that consists essentially of stating questions so that testable rules can answer them (which is not the case for any and all questions) and determining what core-puzzles must be solved if questions are to be answered. (A familiar example is the subtle process by which Weber arrived at the conclusion that the question of the Protestant Ethic ("Why did modern capitalism as an economic system develop spontaneously only in the modern West?") boils down to the puzzle "what engenders the (unlikely) attitude of continuous, rational acquisition as against other economic orientations?"

c). The next step is *hypothesis:* formulating, by some means, a candidate-solution of the puzzle that is testable in principle and sufficiently plausible, prima facie, to warrant the bother and costs of testing. Like the formulation of theoretical problems, this initial step toward solving them generally first involves a "vision," then the attempt to state that vision in a rigorous and unambiguous form, so that conclusive testing becomes at least potentially possible. The candidate-solution need not be a single hypothesis or integrated set of hypotheses. In fact, a particularly powerful alternative is what Platt (1966, pp. 19–36) calls "strong inference" (and considers characteristic of the more rapidly developing "hard" sciences, such as molecular biology and high-energy physics): developing a set of competing hypotheses, some or most of which may be refuted by a single test.

d). After that, of course, one searches for and carries out an appropriate, and if possible definitive, *test*. Such tests are rarely evident in hypotheses themselves, especially if questions of practicability are added to those of logic.

Testing is, in a sense, the end of the theory building process. In another sense, it is not: if a test is survived the process of theorizing does not end. Apart from attempting to make pure knowledge applied, one continues to keep an eye out for contradictory or confirmatory observations, continues to look for more definitive tests, and continues to look for more powerful rules that order larger ranges of observations, or the same range more simply, or subsume the tested rule under one of a higher order, capable of subsuming also other tested rules.

We now have the basic conceptual equipment needed to discuss sensibly the usefulness of case studies in the building of theories in our field, both in general and at different stages of the theory building process. The "scenery-setting" has been long, and perhaps tedious, but nothing in political case studies (which are many) or writings about them (which are very few) suggests that the stage is overstocked with props. Others may, of course, argue for different constructions of the props—in which case, they will also reject much that follows.

OPTIONS ON THE UTILITY OF CASE STUDIES: AN OVERVIEW OF THE ARGUMENT

The Options

In taking positions on the value of case studies for theory building, both in themselves and relative to comparative studies, one can choose between six, not all mutually exclusive, options. These have been derived from a review of actual political case studies, the scant methodological literature about them (and counterparts in other social and behavioral sciences), and my own reflections on unconsidered possibilities. They are listed in order of the value seen in case studies, especially as one progresses along the path of theory building—a progression in which, arguably, intuitive vision plays a constantly decreasing role relative to systematic procedure.

Option 1 holds case studies and comparative studies to be wholly separate and unequal. They are separate in that the two modes of inquiry are considered to have so little in common that case studies are unlikely to provide more than a severely limited and crude basis for systematic comparisons (e.g., variables of major importance in "$n = $ many" studies might be wholly ignored in studies of pertinent cases or might not be treated in readily comparable ways, and so on). The two modes of study are unequal in that only comparative studies are associated with the discovery of valid theories, case studies being confined to descriptions and intuitive interpretations.

Option 2 desegregates case studies and comparative studies, but hardly lessens their inequality. It holds that the two modes of inquiry draw near (asymptotically) in the interpretation of cases, because such interpretations can be made only by applying explicit or implicit theoretical generalizations to various cases. Case study, however, remains highly unequal, because it is certainly not required, nor even especially useful, for the development of theories. There is an exception to this principle, but it is very limited. One never, or, at least very rarely, has all the theories needed to interpret and treat a case; hence, something in the process of case interpretation must nearly always be left incomplete or to intuitive insight (which is why the two modes may approach closely but not intersect). Any aspects of case interpretation in regard to which theory is silent may be regarded as questions on the future agenda of theory building, as any intuitive aspects of interpretation may be regarded as implicit answers to the questions.

Option 3 grows out of the exception to Option 2. It holds that case studies may be conducted precisely for the purpose of discovering questions and puzzles for theory, and discovering candidate-rules that might solve theoretical puzzles. The idea is simply that, if subjects and insights for comparative study are wanted, case study can provide them, and that case study might be conducted precisely for that purpose, and perhaps satisfy it by something less chancy than serendipity, or at least by affording larger scope to serendipitous discovery than studies that sacrifice intensive for extensive research. This still confines the utility of case study to the earlier stages of theorizing and makes it a handmaiden to comparative study. But it does tie case study into the theory building process by something less contingent than possible feedback flowing from the "clinician" to the "experimentalist."

Option 4 focuses on the stage in theory building at which one confronts the question whether candidate-rules are worth the costs (time, effort, ingenuity, manpower, funds, etc.) of testing. It holds that, although in the final analysis only comparative studies can really test theories, well-chosen case studies can shed much light on their plausibility, hence whether proceeding to the final, generally most costly, stage of theory building is worthwhile. This clearly involves something more than initial theoretical ideas. It begins to associate case study with questions of validity, if only in the grudging sense of prima facie credibility.

Option 5 goes still another step further, to the testing (validation) stage itself. It might be held (no revelation forbids it) that in attempting to validate theories, case studies and comparative studies generally are equal, even if separate, alternative means to the same end. The choice between them may then be arbitrary, or may be tailored to such nonarbitrary considerations as the particular nature of theories, accessibility of evidence, skills of the researcher, or availability of research resources. A corollary of this position is, of course, that case studies may be no less systematic in procedure and rigorous in findings than comparative studies.

Option 6 is the most radical from the comparativist's point of view. It holds that case studies are not merely equal alternatives at the testing stage, but, properly carried out, a better bet than comparative studies. It might even be extended to hold that comparative studies are most useful as preliminary, inconclusive aids to conclusive case studies, i.e., that the former may suggest probabilities and the latter clinch them. (Beyond this, of course, lies the still more radical possibility that comparative studies are good for nothing, case studies good for everything. But all inquiry suggests that this is wrong, and while the history of ideas also suggests that the unthinkable should be thought, there is no point in doing so unless a good case can be made for Option 6.)

Arguments on the Options: An Overview

The options discussed above tell us how we might answer the first two questions posed in the introduction to this chapter, while the answer to the third depends on the others. Since the answers to be proposed are complex and the manner of the presentation is far from simple (being intended to present others' views as well as my own), I will outline them before arguing them, as a sort of map to the discussion.

1. First of all, a taxonomic point should be emphasized. This is that "case study" is in fact a very broad generic concept, whether defined technically as "single-measure" study or by the simpler "single-individual" criterion. The genus can and, for our purposes, must be divided into numerous species, some of which closely resemble, some of which differ vastly from, the model of clinical study. The species that need distinction are: *configurative-idiographic studies, disciplined-configurative studies, heuristic-case studies, case studies as plausibility probes,* and *crucial-case studies.* There may be still other types, but these five occur most frequently or are of most consequence to us.

Two things are notable about these species. They are intimately associated with the options on the utility of case studies in theory building: each option is linked to a special type of case study (except that options 5 and 6 make no difference to the type of case study used). And as the utility attributed to case study increases, especially in progression through the phases of theory building, the associated type of case study increasingly departs from the traditional mode of clinical research and, except for numbers of individuals studied, increasingly resembles that of experimental inquiry.

2. As for choice among the options, and associated types of case study, it seems that the modal preference of contemporary political scientists is the third and/or second (not so different, except in nuance, that they preclude being chosen in conjunction); that few choose the fourth (more for reasons of unfamiliarity than methodological conviction); that options 5 and 6 are not chosen by anyone, or at least by very few. The evidence for this is mostly what political scientists actually write, reinforced by reactions to a preliminary version of this paper by a pretty fair cross-section of fellow professionals and a desultory poll among colleagues and students (only one of whom chose any option beyond the third, and that only because he reckoned that no one would list other possibilities unless up to tricks).

The prevailing preferences seem worth challenging on behalf of the options more favorable to case study. The latter appear to be rejected (better, not considered) for reasons other than full methodological deliberation, more as a result of overreaction against one weak type of case study than because of full consideration of the whole range of alternatives. In consequence, potentially powerful types of case study are neglected and case studies are carried out less rigorously than they might be. Arguably, as well, this incurs liabilities in the conclusiveness of theories and the definitiveness of findings.

I propose to conduct the argument to this effect by evaluating each option, and associated type of case study, seriatim. In gist, the argument runs as follows:

a). Option 1 is hardly worth arguing against. Its basic premise—that comparative and case studies are, for all intents and purposes, antithetical—has been exploded for good and all by Verba (1967) in our field, and has been widely attacked in other social sciences as well (e.g., Holt, 1962; Davidson and Costello, 1969). Nevertheless, it is worth discussing because the type of case study associated with it was once dominant (and is still fairly common), and still provides the most widely prevalent notion of what case study is all about and of its potential for theory building.

b). All the other options are tenable, but only because there are different types of case study that have different power in regard to theory building, and because the utility of case studies is not fully determined by logic (abstract methodology) but depends also on practical considerations (e.g., characteristics of one's subject matter).

c). Options 2 and 3 identify perfectly legitimate uses of case study and methods of carrying them out. They are implicit in a host of meritorious political studies, but these studies do not come near exhausting the utility of case study for theory building. Case studies may be used not merely for the interpretative application of general ideas to particular cases (i.e., after theory has been established) or, heuristically, for helping the inquirer to arrive at notions of problems to solve or solutions worth pursuing, but may also be used as powerful means of determining whether solutions are valid.

d). Option 4 deserves special consideration for two reasons. It identifies an objective for which case study of a particular type is eminently serviceable and which can be of vast importance in theory building, but which is rarely pursued, by case study or other means. In addition, the utility of case study for that objective prepares the ground for arguing the case for the more radical options remaining.

e). Option 5 will be held to state the logically most defensible position: to attain theory in political inquiry, comparative studies and case studies should be considered, by and large, as alternative strategies at all stages, with little or nothing to choose (logically) between them. Since that argument will be most difficult to sustain—at least against the conventional wisdom—for the testing stage, the argument will concentrate on the type of case study suitable to it.

f). When practical considerations are added to logic, option 6 seems still more sensible, at least for studies of politics on the macrolevel. Case study is generally a better choice than comparative study for testing theories in macropolitics, but the type of case study useful for this purpose requires a kind of prior knowledge for which preliminary comparative study (of a limited kind) may often be useful or even necessary. This amounts to saying that comparative study can, in some circumstances, be treated as a handmaiden to case study, not vice versa, and thus, in a sense, stands the popular option 3 on its head.

Before working through all this in detail, I want particularly to emphasize two points. First, nothing that follows should be regarded as an attack on the utility of comparative study in theory building, simply because case studies are defended. (Some readers of an early draft of this chapter concluded from this that comparative and case studies were not distinguishable after all. This is wrong: they have been distinguished. The point is that, logically at any rate, the distinction is not necessarily consequential for theory building.) Comparative studies have proved their utility. To the extent that they are invidiously evaluated vis-à-vis case studies, this is done on two grounds only: on practical grounds of limited applicability and because "$n =$ many" studies invite avoidable errors of method (psychological, not logical hazards) in theory building that case studies are more likely to preclude.

Second, it is not to be inferred that any old case study will do for the purposes of theory building. Some readers of a draft of this chapter concluded that it constituted a defense of "traditional" political studies against the "behavioralists." This is ludicrous, but it occurred. *The discussion presents an argument for both case studies and carrying them out in a particular way.* Since the type of case study for which it argues is very demanding, implying great rigor of thought and exactitude of observation, it is hardly "anti-behavioralist"; and since that type of case study, to my knowledge, is as yet virtually nonexistent in our field, the argument can hardly be "traditionalist."

TYPES AND USES OF CASE STUDY

Configurative-Idiographic Study

1. In philosophy and psychology a distinction has long been drawn between nomothetic (generalizing, rule-seeking) and idiographic (individualizing, interpretative) types of, or emphases in, science. The philosophic progenitor of this terminology (and, in part, the ideas that underlie it) is Windelband (1894), the most notable contemporary defender of the distinction Gordon Allport (for bibliography, see Holt, 1962, p. 402). Idiographic study is, in es-

sence, what was earlier described as clinical study and configurative-idiographic study is its counterpart in fields, like macropolitics, that deal with complex collective individuals. (Verba [1967] calls them configurative-idiosyncratic studies, but the difference in terminology is of no consequence.)

The configurative element in such studies is their aim to present depictions of the overall *Gestalt* (i.e., configuration) of individuals: polities, parties, party systems, etc. The idiographic element in them is that they either allow facts to speak for themselves or bring out their significance by largely intuitive interpretation, claiming validity on the ground that intensive study and empathetic feel for cases provide authoritative insights into them.

If configurative-idiographic studies are made from philosophic conviction, the following assumptions usually are at work (Holt, 1962, pp. 388–397): (a) In the study of personalities and the collectivities they form, one cannot attain prediction and control in the natural-science sense, but only "understanding," in the Germanic sense—and thus, from understanding, limited, nondeductive conceptions of probable futures and prudent policy. (b) In attaining understanding subjective values and modes of cognition are crucial, and these resist quantification. (c) Each subject, personal or collective, is unique, so generalizations can at most be only about their actions (persons) or interactions (collectivities). And (d) the whole is lost or at least distorted in abstraction and analysis—the decomposition of the individual into constituent traits and statements of relations among limited numbers of these; it is "something more" than an aggregate of general relations, rather than "nothing but" such an aggregate.

As already stated, configurative-idiographic studies were long the dominant mode of case study in political science. They still are common, although harder nowadays to distinguish from other types of case study in the field because, as Verba points out (1967, p. 112), homage is now often paid to the behavioral "revolution" in the field by using "some systematic framework to preface or organize the chapters of such studies and by including new variables and aspects of political systems" in them—frameworks and variables, that is to say, developed for nomothetic purposes.

2. Configurative-idiographic studies are certainly useful, and, at their best, have undeniably considerable virtues. They may be beautifully written and make their subject vivid. They may pull together and elegantly organize wide and deep researches. The intuitive interpretations they provide may be subtle and persuasive, and suggest an impressive feel for the cases they treat.

Their most conspicuous weakness is that, as Verba puts it, "they do not easily add up"—presumably to reliable and valid statements of regularity about sets of cases, or even about a case in point. (See also Kaufmann, 1958, and Lowi, 1964.) This is plain in regard to sets of cases, the summation regarding them being at most factual (information about similar subjects, e.g., legislatures, parties, etc., in different contexts) and, because of idiosyncrasies in fact-collecting and presentation, rarely involving even the systemic accumulation of facts. Anyone who has used secondary sources for compiling comparable data on numerous cases knows this to his pain, and, even more painfully, that inventories of interpretative propositions culled from case studies usually contain about as many distinguishable items as studies. The point is less plain, but just as true, for regularity statements concerning individual cases. The interpretations, being idiosyncratic, rarely come to an agreed position, or even to a point of much overlap. For example, in the configurative-idiographic literature on France there seems to be overlap on the position that there are "two Frances," but nearly everyone has his own conception of what they are and where they are found. This situation is hardly surprising: in configurative-idiographic study the interpreter simply considers a body of observations that are not self-explanatory, and, without hard rules of interpretation, may discern in them any number of patterns that are more or less equally plausible.

The criticism that configurative-idiographic study does not add up to theory, in our sense, is mitigated by the fact that its capability to do so was never claimed by its exponents: in fact it is often explicitly repudiated. What is really troublesome about configurative-idiographic study is the repudiation itself (i.e., the claim that case study in the behavioral and social sciences can only be idiographic) and its consequences for the way in which the nomothetic utility of case studies in these fields is regarded.

For a thorough refutation of the idiographer's position, and a broad attack on the distinction between the nomothetic and idiographic itself, readers should consult Holt (1962). His argument, in gist, is (a) that both the position and distinction have "peculiar origins"—misunderstandings of Kant by lesser German philosophers and "romantic" assumptions prevalent during the early nineteenth century ("Teutonic ghosts" raised against classical ideas and styles) that led to unreasonably sharp lines between nature and mechanisms on one hand and behavior and organisms on the other; and, more important, (b) that none of the postulates of idiographic study, as outlined above, withstands examination. As for the consequences of the claims of idiographers, the most stultifying has been the association of nomothetic study in macropolitics with study different from that favored by idiographers in all respects: not only study based on more systematic methods of collecting and processing data and on explicit frameworks of inquiry intended to make for culmination, but "comparative" (i.e., multicase, cross-national, cross-cultural) studies.

If case study could only be configurative-idiographic in character, the conclusions that case studies and comparative studies are wholly antithetical and that theories about politics require comparative study, or are unattainable, could not be avoided. But case study need not have that character, and the comparativists themselves have pointed the way to other varieties—without, however, overcoming a fundamental bias against case study of any kind in theory construction, largely anchored to the archetype of such studies in our field.

Disciplined-Configurative Study

1. The comparativist's typical reaction to the theoretical poverty of configurative-idiographic studies is to hold that, while theories cannot be derived from case interpretations, such interpretations can, and should, be derived from theories. "The unique explanation of a particular case," says Verba (1967, p. 114), "can rest on general hypotheses." Indeed, it *must* rest on them, since theoretical arguments about a single case, in the last analysis, always proceed from at least implicit general laws about a class or set to which it belongs, or about universal attributes of all classes to which the case can be subsumed. The logic involved has been succinctly stated in Hempel's discussion of "nomological" explanation, the essence of which is the explanation of particular phenomena (in my terms "case interpretation") "by showing that (their) existence could have been inferred—either deductively or with a high probability —by applying certain laws of universal or of statistical form to specified antecedent circumstances" (Hempel, 1965, pp. 299–303). Those who consider this the only way of interpreting cases "scientifically" hold that the theoretical bases of case interpretations should always be made explicit, and that *ad hoc* additions to a framework of case interpretation should always be made as if they were general laws, not unique factors operating only in the case in point. The bases of case interpretation, in other words, should be established theories or, lacking them, provisional ones, and such interpretations can be sound only to the extent that their bases are in fact valid as general laws.

Case studies so constructed are "disciplined-configurative studies." The terminology is Verba's, who recommends such studies to us. Studies of this type are in fact very common in contemporary political studies—although, because of our disciplinary *embarras de pauvreté* in regard to validated, or even provisional, "general laws," they more frequently involve the application to cases of frameworks of inquiry, hopefully intended to help knowledge become nomothetic, not deductions from theory in any strict sense of the term. (I take the following to be leading examples: Apter, 1956, 1961; Almond and Coleman, 1960; Dahl, 1966; Lipset and Rokkan, 1967; and the works on political development produced by members of the SSRC Comparative Politics Committee, such as Pye and Verba, 1965.)

Disciplined-configurative studies need not just passively apply general laws or statements of probability to particular cases. A case can impugn established theories if the theories ought to fit it but do not. It may also point up a need for new theory in neglected areas. Thus, the application of theories to cases can have feedback effects on theorizing, as Hempel (1965) recognizes. In addition, it is unlikely that all aspects of a case can be nomologically explained.

As in the field of engineering, where general theories are applied to achieve conscious ends in particular circumstances, there are nearly always elements of prudence, common sense, or "feel" in case interpretations. Theory building, however, aims at the constant reduction of those elements, by stating notions that fit particular cases as general theoretical rules and subjecting them to proper theoretical tests.

In essence, the chain of inquiry in disciplined-configurative studies runs from comparatively tested theory to case interpretation, and thence, perhaps, via *ad hoc* additions, newly discovered puzzles, and systematized prudence, to new candidate-theories. Case study thus is tied into theoretical inquiry—but only partially, where theories apply or can be envisioned; passively, in the main, as a receptacle for putting theories to work; and fortuitously, as a catalytic element in the unfolding of theoretical knowledge. This is, of course, still close to the clinician's conception of his role, and configurative studies that are disciplined in intent are not always easy to distinguish from unadulterated idiography. The two types are often intermixed, and easily blend together.

2. The essential basis of Verba's argument about the relations between general theory and particular case interpretation is surely correct. If the interpretations of a case are general laws correctly applied to the case, the interpretations may be valid or invalid, depending on whether the laws are valid; otherwise, their validity simply cannot be known at all. Moreover, if cases are complex, the number of possible alternative interpretations, equally plausible because not at variance with the facts of the case, is usually vast, so that undisciplined case-interpretation in much-studied cases usually yields large inventories of quite different propositions, none of which is clearly superior to any other. Preferences among them depend on personal tastes or general intellectual fads.

This point can be illustrated by a long quote from an essay of mine on the causes of revolutions. Studying the etiology of internal wars, I argued,

> poses a difficulty ... how to choose among a rare abundance of hypotheses which cannot all be equally valid nor all be readily combined. This problem exists because most propositions about the causes of internal wars have been developed in historical studies of particular cases (or very limited numbers of cases) rather than in broadly comparative, let alone genuinely social-scientific, studies. In historical case-studies one is likely to attach significance to any aspect of pre-revolutionary society that one intuits to be significant, and so long as one does not conjure up data out of nothing one's hypotheses cannot be invalidated on the basis of the case in question.

That most studied of all internal wars, the French Revolution, provides a case in point—as well as examples in abundance of the many social, personal, and environmental forces to which the occurrence of internal wars might be attributed. Scarcely anything in the French *ancien régime* has not been blamed, by one writer or another, for the revolution, and all of their interpretations, however contradictory, are based on solid facts.

Some interpreters have blamed the outbreak of the French Revolution on intellectual causes, that is to say, on the ideas, techniques, and great public influence of the *philosophes* (who were indeed very influential). This is the standard theory of post-revolutionary conservative theorists, from Chateaubriand to Taine, men who felt, in essence, that in pre-revolutionary France a sound society was corrupted by a seductive and corrosive philosophy.

Other writers have blamed the revolution mainly on economic conditions, although it is difficult to find very many who single out as crucial the same conditions. The revolution has been attributed to sheer grinding poverty among the lower classes (who were certainly poor); to 'financial profligacy and mismanagement on the part of the government (of which it was in fact guilty); to the extortionate taxation inflicted on the peasants (and peasant taxation verged upon brutality); to short-term setbacks (which actually occurred and caused great hardship) like the bad harvest of 1788, the hard winter of 1788–89, and the still winds of 1789 which prevented flour from being milled and made worse an already acute shortage of bread; to the over-abundant wine harvests of the 1780s (one of the first historic instances of the harmful effects of overproduction); to the increased wealth and power of the bourgeoisie in a society still dominated to a significant extent by aristocrats, the growth of the Parisian proletariat and its supposedly increasing political consciousness, and the threatened abrogation of the financial privileges of the aristocracy, particularly their exemption from taxation—all unquestionable facts producing manifest problems.

Still another set of writers locates the crucial cause of the revolution in aspects of social structure. Much has been made, and with sufficient reason, of the fact that in the last years of the *ancien régime* there occurred a hardening in the lines of upward mobility in French society—for example, a decline in grants of patents of nobility to commoners and the imposition of stringent social requirements for certain judicial and administrative positions and the purchase of officerships in the army. This, many have argued (following Mosca's and Pareto's famous theory of the circulation of elites), engendered that fatal yearning for an aristocracy of wealth and talent to which the *philosophes* gave expression. Much has also been made, with equal reason, of popular dissatisfaction with the parasitic life of the higher nobility, with its large pensions and puny duties, its life of hunting, love-making, watch-making, and interminable conversation.

And much has been attributed to the vulnerability of the privileged classes to the very propagandists who wanted to alter the system that supported them ("How," asked Taine, "could people who talked so much resist people who talked so well?"), reflected in the Anglomania which swept through the higher aristocracy toward the end of the *ancien régime* and in the rush of many aristocrats to the cause of the Americans in their war of independence.

There are also certain well-founded "political" explanations of the French Revolution: that the revolution was really caused by the violation of the tacit "contract" on which the powers of the monarchy rested (a contract by which the aristocracy surrendered its powers to the monarchy in return for receiving certain inviolable privileges), or that the revolution was simply a successful political conspiracy by the Jacobins, based on efficient political organization. Personalities, needless to say, get their due as well: the revolution has been blamed, for example, on the character, or lack of character, of Louis XVI (who was in fact weak, vacillating and inconsistent), the supposed immorality of the Queen (who indeed was the subject, justly or not, of many scandals), the effect on the public of the dismissal of Necker, and, of course, on the "genius," good or evil, of unquestionable geniuses like Mirabeau, Danton, Marat, and Robespierre.

We could take other internal wars and arrive at the same result—similarly large lists of explanations, most of them factual, yet inconclusive. The more remote in time and the more intensively analyzed the internal war, the longer the list of hypotheses. . . .

. . . How can this embarrassment of interpretative riches (one hesitates to say theoretical riches) be reduced? If the examination of any single case allows one to determine only whether an interpretation of it is based on facts, then broad comparative studies in space and/or time are needed to establish the significance of the facts on which the interpretations are based. Was a blockage in the channels of social mobility a significant precondition of the French Revolution? We can be reasonably confident that it was only if it can be shown that elite circulation and political stability are generally related. Was the Chinese population explosion really an important cause of the Chinese revolution?

Surely this is unlikely if demographic pressures do not generally affect the viability of regimes. (Eckstein, 1965, pp. 137–139)

The argument of this passage still strikes me as correct. However, the operative sentence in the last paragraph should have read that "valid theory is needed to establish the significance of the facts on which the interpretations are based," leaving open the extent to which the formulation of valid theories requires "broad comparative studies." For the problem here is one of case interpretation, not theory building, and the possibility that sound bases for case interpretation might be furnished by case studies themselves cannot be dismissed, unless one assumes (as Verba does, and I did) that no types of case study other than the configurative-idiographic or disciplined-configurative varieties exist. But this, as will soon be evident, is far from the case—and concedes far too much to idiographers or those who, opposing idiography, nevertheless accept the dichotomy between the clinical and experimental that ultimately gives rise to idiographic studies.

It remains to add a point insufficiently stressed in writings on disciplined-configurative studies. The application of theories in case interpretation, although rarely discussed, is not at all a simple process, even leaving aside the question of how valid theory is to be developed. Such applications only yield valid interpretations if the theories permit strict deductions to be made and the interpretations of the case are shown to be logically compelled by the theories. In the case of revolutions, for instance, it is not enough to know that a regularity exists and that a case somehow "fits" it (i.e., does not manifestly contradict it). One should also be able to demonstrate, by correct reasoning, that, given the regularity and the characteristics of the case, revolution must have occurred, or at least had a high probability of occurring. Not all theories permit this to be done, or at least equally well. For example, a theory attributing revolution to aggressions engendered by social frustrations will hardly fail to fit any case of revolution, nor tell us exactly why any case of it occurred. Unless it specifies precisely how much and what sort of frustration engenders revolution, on whose part, and under what complex of other conditions (Gurr, 1970, comes very close to achieving this, but others of the same school do not), the frustration-aggression theory of revolution, applied, say, to the French Revolution, can yield about as many plausible case interpretations as can configurative-idiographic study (there having existed many sources of frustration in the *ancien régime,* as in all regimes).

This point brings out a major utility of attempting disciplined case interpretation. Aiming at the disciplined application of theories to cases forces one to state theories more rigorously than might otherwise be done—provided that the application is truly "disciplined," i.e., designed to show that valid theory compels a particular case interpretation and rules out others. As already stated, this, unfortunately, is rare (if it occurs at all) in political study. One reason is the lack of compelling theories. But there is another, which is of the utmost importance: political scientists reject, or do not even consider, the possibility that valid theories might indeed *compel* particular case interpretations. The import of that possibility, assuming it to exist, lies in the corollary that a case might invalidate a theory, if an interpretation of the case compelled by the theory does not fit it.

But this goes too far ahead, toward a crucial argument that will require much discussion below. The point for the present is merely that exponents of disciplined-configured study have insufficiently considered both the difficulties and promises of the relations between general theories and particular case interpretations.[4]

Heuristic Case Studies

1. Disciplined-configurative study simply assumes that "general laws" are available. It is not thought of as a part of the process of theory building as such, except in that the interpretation of cases may lead to *ad hoc,* serendipitous additions to existing theories in order to cover puzzling aspects of a case. However, the feedback effect in Verba's (1967) recommended sequence of inquiry can be isolated from the rest of the sequence and case study deliberately used to stimulate the imagination toward discerning important general problems and possible theoretical solutions. That is the essence of heuristic case-studies (heuristic meaning "serving to find out"). Such studies, unlike configurative-idiographic ones, tie directly into theory building, and therefore are less concerned with overall concrete configurations than with potentially generalizable relations between aspects of them; they also tie into theory building less passively and fortuitously than does disciplined-configurative study, because the potentially generalizable relations do not just turn up but are deliberately sought out.

Heuristic case studies do not necessarily stop with one case, but can be conducted seriatim, by the so-called building-block technique (Becker, 1968), in order to construct increasingly plausible and less fortuitous regularity statements. This technique is quite simple in principle. One studies a case in order to arrive at a preliminary theoretical construct. That construct, being based on a single case, is unlikely to constitute more than a clue to a valid general model. One therefore confronts it with another case that may suggest ways of amending and improving the construct to achieve better case interpretation; and this process is continued until the construct seems sufficiently refined to require no further major amendment or at least to warrant testing by large-scale comparative study. Each step beyond the first can be considered a kind of disciplined-configurative study, but is better regarded as heuristic case study proceeding with increasingly refined questions and toward increasingly more specific ends. It is important not to confuse the whole process with comparative study. The latter seeks regularities through the simultaneous inspection of numerous cases, not the gradual unfolding of increasingly better theoretical constructs through the study of individuals. Of course, comparative studies can also employ the building-block technique by successively refined theories through a series of multicase studies.

Heuristic case studies should also not be confused with pedagogic ones, which abound in politics and closely related fields. Pedagogic cases in politics generally have the aim of teaching policy and administrative skills by putting students into the positions of policymakers and administrators through detailed narrative accounts of real action problems. They are derived from case-method teaching in the law and business schools, and are most akin to configurative-idiographic studies, except that the idiography is supplied by students, under the guidance of pedagogues assumed to possess special practical wisdom or experience. Theory is not supposed to emerge, and to my knowledge never has emerged, from them.

2. The claim that theoretical puzzles and insights can be usefully (perhaps most usefully) sought in case study is the standard defense of case study by theory-oriented social scientists. Equally commonplace is the belief that this is all that case study can usefully accomplish in the process of theory building (see, for example, Becker, 1968, p. 233; Holt, 1962, p. 399; and Riley, 1963, p. 69). Consequently, studies of this type abound in political science, and have recently crowded or displaced configurative-idiographic studies as the predominant species (no actual frequency count has been made); and there has been little exploration of case studies that might take one beyond the stage of hypothesizing. (Examples of the type are legion, but the following may suffice as illustrations: Weiner, 1957; Pye, 1962; Rudolph and Rudolph, 1967; and Eckstein, 1960.) In many cases, such studies are carried out in light of preconstructed checklists of variables or frameworks of analysis, such as the "functional" framework associated with Almond and his associates (1960, 1966). As one might expect in case study oriented toward theory, these frameworks focus attention on special variables, but not so narrowly as is common in extensive experimental work.

The justification for heuristic case studies runs as follows: (a) Theories do not come from a vacuum, or fully and directly from data. In the final analysis they come from the theorist's imagination, logical ability, and ability to discern general problems and patterns in particular observation. (b) There are ineffable differences in such imaginative and other abilities, but various aids can be used to stimulate them: among them, the printouts from data banks or other comparative studies (which, however, never obviate the use of theoretical imagination, e.g., for interpreting the printouts into proper regularity statements and for determining what data banks should contain or how comparative studies should be designed in the first place). (c) The track record of case studies as stimulants of the theoretical imagination is good. (d) One reason it is good is precisely that, unlike wide-ranging comparative studies, case studies permit intensive analysis that does not commit the researcher to a highly limited set of variables, and thus increases the probability that critical variables and relations will be found. The possibility of less superficiality in research, of course, also plays a role here.

   3. Arguments in favor of heuristic case studies surely have merit. Whatever logic might dictate, the indubitable fact is that some case study writers in macropolitics have come up with interpretations notably incisive for their cases and notably plausible when taken as generalizations for sets of them, with or without the benefit of special frameworks or approaches. See, for example, the works of such men as de Tocqueville, Bagehot, Halévy, Bryce, and Bodley, or, in another field, anthropologists too numerous to mention.

   Nevertheless, one may argue that too much is made of heuristic case studies, for two related reasons. One is that those who defend them sometimes seem to do so simply because they can see no more ambitious function to be served by case study. The other is that, not wishing to make other claims but to defend case studies, they claim too much for such studies as heuristic tools, especially in comparison to "$n =$ many" studies. Scenting a valid claim, they exaggerate it—and miss the possibility that a more persuasive brief might be based on a greater sense of limitation at the heuristic stage of theory building and a lesser one at others.

   The point that case studies are good for more than getting clues will concern us later. But the anticipation of that point in the previous section can be supplemented here by a further suggestive argument. Case studies intended to serve a heuristic function can proceed much in the manner of "clinical" study, i.e., with a minimum of design or rigor, and tackle any case that comes to hand. In that event, however, nothing distinguishes the study from configurative-idiographic study, except the researcher's hopes and intentions, and results can only turn up by good fortune—which the bright will seize and the dull miss, but which the researcher can do nothing to induce. The alternatives are to use at least a modicum of design and rigor in research and not to choose just any case on any grounds but a special sort of case: one considered likely to be revealing, on some basis or other. The suggestive point in this for later argument is not that case study may often depart markedly from the archetype of clinical study (although that is noteworthy), but that *certain kinds of cases may be regarded as more instructive for theory building than others.* Actual heuristic case studies seem in fact generally, even if often just implicitly, to make that claim for the cases selected. The grounds are often obscure, and the claim often seems *post hoc* and intended to disarm charges of idiography. The point nevertheless remains that the brief for heuristic case study is strong only to the extent that cases especially instructive for theory, and subject to rigorous inquiry, can be identified. And if that possibility exists, then the further possibility arises that some cases might be especially instructive also at other stages of the theory-building process.

If the prevalent emphasis on heuristic functions is too modest, in what senses does it also exaggerate? First of all, the fact that case study writers have often spawned ideas notable as generalizations proves nothing. The de Tocquevilles or Bagehots might have been successful in spawning plausible theories without writing case studies, since their imagination and incisiveness clearly matter more than the vehicles chosen for putting them to work. If they had used comparative studies they might have been even more successful, and more successful still if they had had available modern technology for accumulating, coding, storing, and processing data—not to mention the fact that they do always make implicit, sometimes explicit, use of comparisons in their case studies (e.g., Bagehot's contrasts between Britain and America, de Tocqueville's between America and France), even if only to demonstrate that factors used to interpret their cases do in fact differ in different cases. Moreover, for every case study that has notably succeeded in spawning theory, there are scores that have notably failed—and this does not refer to idiography alone. Case study certainly furnishes no guarantee that theoretical abilities will be awakened or sharpened. And comparativists have been at least as successful in spawning theories as configurativists; for every de Tocqueville or Bagehot we can produce an offsetting Aristotle, Machiavelli, Mosca, Pareto, or Weber.

Second, the benefit of being able to take into consideration more variables in case study incurs the cost of highly circumscribed breadth of inference. And it is probable that the number of hypotheses suggested, hence also the number of invalid ones to be pursued, will be proportional to the number of variables considered. Heuristic case studies have a demonstrable tendency, as in the case of studies of the French Revolution, to spawn a crushing and chaotic number and variety of candidate-generalizations, or hypercomplex multivariate theories, especially when these studies are made by imaginative men. And, unlike comparative studies, they cannot even yield initial clues about the generalizability of relations selected from all those that constitute the case—unless, to repeat, the case is considered, on some good basis, especially revealing for sets of phenomena, i.e., one for which breadth-of-inference problems may be claimed to be slight.

These problems have led some to identify "grounded theory" (theory that is initially derived from observations, not spawned wholly out of logic and imagination) with comparative inquiry rather than case study (Glaser and Strauss, 1967, especially Part I). The reasons for doing so are rather convincing. But the more sensible position surely is that, if we are really only concerned with the initial formulation of candidate-theories as a phase of theoretical inquiry (and not theory leaping full-blown out of data), case study is useful but by no means indispensable, as also is comparative study or any other exercise of theoretical imagination. It is manifestly more useful for some people than others. It also would be generally more useful than it has been if more case studies were deliberately undertaken as exploratory means for arriving at candidate-theories, rather than simply allowing these to occur fortuitously, and if special characteristics of heuristically instructive cases could be specified and something like a heuristic "method" could be developed.

If nothing more were to be said for case studies than that they may be helpful in initially formulating candidate regularity statements, we could only conclude that there is no special reason for either making or not making such studies. It follows that if there is a strong justification for case studies as tools in developing theories, it must be found in the special utility of such studies at some later stage of the sequence of inquiry by which theories are established, or, at a minimum, their availability as reasonable alternatives to comparative studies during the later, no less than earlier, stages of the theory-building process.

Plausibility Probes

1. After hypotheses are formulated, one does not necessarily proceed immediately to test them. A stage of inquiry preliminary to testing sometimes intervenes, and ought to do so far more often than it actually does in political study (or the study of other social sciences). It involves probing the "plausibility" of candidate-theories. Plausibility here means something more than a belief in potential validity plain and simple, for hypotheses are unlikely ever to be formulated unless considered potentially valid; it also means something less than actual validity, for which rigorous testing is required. In essence, plausibility probes involve attempts to determine whether potential validity may reasonably be considered great enough to warrant the pains and costs of testing, which are almost always considerable, but especially so if broad, painstaking comparative studies are undertaken.

Such probes are common in cases where costly risks have to be run. These probes are roughly analogous to the trials to which one subjects a racehorse before incurring the costs of entering and preparing it for a major race: success cannot be guaranteed but some kind of odds (ratios between certain costs and probable benefits) can be established. The simple principle at work is that large investments in less likely outcomes are worse propositions than large investments in more likely outcomes. Here the analogy between theorizing and horse racing becomes a little specious, for in probing the plausibility of a theory we can hardly expect to know much, or anything, about previous performance or to have exact estimates of probability like those given by a stopwatch. But we do not lack means for at least getting a reasoned, not merely intuitive, "feel" for the odds against a theory.

At a minimum, a plausibility probe into theory may simply attempt to establish that a theoretical construct is worth considering at all, i.e., that an apparent empirical instance of it can be found. I take that (together with heuristic objectives) to be the purpose of Dahl's influential study of power in New Haven (1961). Dahl, as I read him (contrary to some other interpreters of his work), wants to establish that power in democracy may be "pluralistic," or may not be "monolithic," not that it must be the former and cannot be the latter. The study certainly succeeds in that regard, although it would succeed even more if New Haven had been selected for study because it is typical of a specified class of cases.

Some ways of surmising the plausibility of a theory beyond that minimal point are nonempirical, and since they entail only the cost of thought, these should generally be used before, or instead of, empirical probes. We may have confidence in a theory because it is derived logically from premises that have previously yielded valid theory in a field, or because it is derived from premises contrary to those that have led to major failures. We may also have confidence in a theory if it is able to account for both strengths and weaknesses in existing relevant hypotheses, or otherwise seems to organize considerable volumes and varieties of unexplained data. An example of both these methods of estimating plausibility is furnished by those passages of my monograph on stable democracy (Eckstein, 1961) that show the grounding of its main proposed regularity statement in (as I then thought) validated psychological theories and those that try to show how the strengths and weaknesses of three alternative hypotheses, all rather powerful yet flawed in certain ways, can be explained by the main proposed regularity statement. Demonstrating logically that proposed regularity statements can potentially explain data not yet explained, and/or provide a common foundation for previously validated but quite discrete and unconnected hypotheses, and/or extend assumptions found powerful in some areas to other areas, all create presumptions in favor of testing the statements independently, even by costly means.

Plausibility probes can also be directly empirical, i.e., in the nature of preliminary, rather loose and inconclusive, but suggestive tests before more rigorous tests are conducted. Such probes confront theory with lesser challenges that they must certainly withstand if they are not to be toppled by greater ones. If, for example, it were posited that democratic power structures are normally monolithic (which is in fact often done in political theories) and one had strong reason to believe that New Haven was unlikely to be a deviant case (which is also arguable), then Dahl's study of its power structure would establish much more than that the counteridea of pluralism in democratic power is not completely vacuous. It would cast serious doubt on the posited regularity. Such empirical probes are especially important where nonempirical probes yield very uncertain results, and there is also reason to use them, as additions to others, as cheap means of hedging against expensive wild-goose chases, when the costs of testing are likely to be very great.

2. There is no reason why empirical plausibility probes should not take the form of modest or rather diffusely designed comparative studies, as preludes to more ambitious and tighter ones. Indeed, most systematic comparative studies in macropolitics make more sense as plausibility probes (or as "heuristic comparative studies") than as what they are generally claimed or regarded to be: that is, works presenting definitive results. Almond and Verba's *The Civic Culture* (1963) is surely a case in point. The sample of cases covered by the study is hardly large and dubiously representative; the regularity statements about "democratic stability" emerging in its final chapter could certainly be made more exact, are mainly afterthoughts imputed to the evidence, and are hardly conclusively compelled by that evidence. But they seem sufficiently rooted in data and reasoning to warrant their statement in more precise form and their thorough testing, preferably by logically deduced predictions about findings in a project specifically designed not to get interesting data but to get those crucial to establishing the validity of the work's central propositions. (One may consider it reprehensible that so many comparativists are willing to stop where only that much, or little more, has been accomplished, and then go on to new, still merely plausible, ideas on new subject matter. We certainly have no right to bewail the fact that others do not take up our ideas if we ourselves drop them far short of the point to which they could be taken.)

The essential point for us is that, as empirical plausibility probes, case studies are often as serviceable as, or more so than, comparative ones—and nearly always a great deal cheaper (a prime consideration in probing plausibility). The economic case for them is strongest where required information is not readily available in aggregate data or good secondary sources and is intrinsically hard to get. Case studies can certainly serve the purpose well if well selected, that is, if they are such that a result, for or against a theory, cannot readily be shrugged off. It is true that case studies have been little used in political studies as plausibility probes, but this is largely due to the fact that the idea of any sort of plausibility probe is foreign to the field, plus the fact that comparative studies to amass data from which finished theories supposedly emerge have been its dominant contemporary genre. (Comparative studies as plausibility probes are equally uncommon, except only in the sense that some of them appear better tailored for that purpose than the purposes they pretend to serve.)

Because of the rareness of plausibility probes in the field, an example may be more instructive than abstract discussion. The example I shall use involves my work on governmental performance, following up the monograph (1961) on stable democracy. Self-advertisement is not intended, and no claims about the quality of the work are made. But cases in point are, as stated, rare; one always has special familiarity with one's own work; and the work in question does illustrate the circumstances under which probing plausibility becomes important and case study is used to achieve the intended aim.

As to circumstances that indicate the advisability of plausibility probes: After first formulating the hypotheses on stable democracy, it seemed imprudent to plunge immediately into concerted testing, even assuming that an argument for more than minimal potential validity had already been made. Although the propositions were simple and parsimonious, there is unfortunately no close relationship between the simplicity of propositions and the ease or economy of testing them; in this case, in fact, the effort required was bound to be immense. Concepts used in the propositions had to be more precisely and rigorously formulated. Virtually all the data required to test them had to be produced by extensive fieldwork: one could certainly not base cross-national research into "congruence" among authority patterns (the main independent variable used in the hypotheses) on conveniently available statistical annuals and the like. This called for resources—time, language skills, historical and cultural knowledge—that a single scholar never himself commands. Consequently, it would be necessary to involve others in the work, an effort likely to fail, or to be wasteful, while ideas are still little more than mildly plausible. Furthermore, testing the propositions would not be possible without developing an elaborate scheme of concepts for getting at the multifarious facets of authority relations: concepts unambiguously defined, standardized to apply to interactions in virtually all kinds of social units, and operationalized to make field observations reliable and some sort of measurement of resemblances among authority patterns possible. To relate the independent variable to levels of governmental performance (the main dependent variable), it was necessary also to develop a set of categories and techniques for reliably determining different levels of such performance. And all this done, a large number of taxing field studies had (as it then seemed to me) to be carefully designed, thoroughly carried out, rigorously processed, and their results collated. Under such circumstances it surely is reasonable, even imperative, to seek some decent, however inconclusive, estimate of probable success before any concerted attempt at testing, better than that provided in the initial work.

As to the utility of case study as plausibility probes: Several things were done to arrive at that estimate (Eckstein, 1969, pp. 280–281), but the most important was a study of Norway. That country was selected in part for extraneous reasons (language, personal connections, the high development of social research in the country). The main reason for selecting it, however, was that Norway seemed somehow critical for the theory to be tested, in the sense that the theory could hardly be expected to hold widely if it did not fit closely there. The theory purported to account for high, but not necessarily low, levels of governmental performance—and such performance had been outstandingly high in Norway for a long time on all the criteria initially used to gauge it. Moreover, the theory related social (i.e., nongovernmental) structure to governmental performance, but selected from all facets of such structure one special aspect that intrinsically could remain unchanged while all or most others changed, or, conversely, could change while others remained constant. As it happens, there had been virtually no significant change in governmental structure, but much in social structure, in Norway since late in the nineteenth century. Two things consequently had to be found if the theory were to be considered plausible. The proposed correlates of high governmental performance had to be unmistakably present in high degree and the aspect of social structure selected for emphasis had to be constant over time despite considerable other changes in Norwegian society. Neither was known in advance and both were in fact the case, or so it seemed; hence confidence that the theory might withstand concerted comparative study was greatly increased, to a level more in line with expected costs. The essential point is that Norway seemed to have special characteristics particularly illuminating for the theory: in short, it appeared to be a specially instructive case, of the sort that might be particularly useful for heuristic inquiry but that is more readily identified if candidate-theory already has been formulated.

3. The study was not conclusive for the theory; it merely strengthened its prospects. One reason for its inconclusiveness was that the methods used in it were less rigorous, and the research less thorough, than they might have been, precisely because economies are a major consideration in probing plausibility. Another reason was the prevalent belief that the study of a case could, at most, yield a subjective estimate of the theory's plausibility, simply because it was case study, hence that no massive research assault on it, which would long postpone comparative inquiry, was needed or even justifiable.

And here again we come to a critical possibility. If studies of well-selected cases, no less than comparative studies, can serve the purposes of plausibility probes (the idea of which is, after all, to form estimates of probable validity), could they not also serve, painstakingly selected and rigorously carried out, as tests of validity itself, with similar economies in the work required? The possibility should at least be entertained and the case for it argued, since the potential practical gains could be enormous. It arises, at bottom, from the obvious fact that cases are not all equal in their import, even for the modest purposes of heuristic exploration. The question is whether their inequality extends to the point where certain types of cases, and modes of case study, can serve to test theories for validity—the step most demanding on rigor and in which breadth-of-inference problems seem most damaging to case studies.

To explore this question further, we shall have to look more closely at a suggestion made in the discussion on disciplined-configurative study: that if theory can compel particular case interpretations, then particular cases could invalidate or confirm theories.

Crucial-Case Studies

1. The position that case studies are weak or useless for testing theories rests, at bottom, on the mistaken application of a correct principle—a principle that applies more, but still imperfectly, to the discovery of theories in data than to their testing.

We can think of theory-formulation as a process that leads one to postulate a curve or line to which observations of reality are expected to correspond; and we can think of theories as valid if the curves or lines that best fit relevant observations in fact match the theoretical expectation, or, put in a different manner, if the points yielded by measurements of relevant observations fall on or very near the postulated curve at logically specified locations. The principle that seems to rule out case study for the purpose of finding valid theory is the elementary one holding that any single instance of a relationship yields only one observed point, and that through any single point an infinite number of curves or lines can be drawn. (A less abstract variant of this principle is the argument above that any number of different explanations, not contrary to fact and thus at least minimally plausible, can be offered for any political event.)

The principle is, as stated, incontestable. But we are not constrained to conclude from it that comparative studies are indispensable to the development of valid theories and case studies useless for the purpose, unless we inject between the premise and conclusion a major fallacy that apparently dies hard: the inductive fallacy. The essence of that fallacy is the belief that theories, being contained in phenomena, can be fully derived from observations by simple inspection or, at any rate, sophisticated data processing. This is fallacious in several senses that should be disentangled, although they are all of a piece and usually all committed at once.

a). One aspect of the fallacy involves confusion between the discovery of candidate-theories and their testing: in deriving theory from observations ("grounded theory") one may be tempted to think that curves suggested by comparative data are themselves valid theories. This hazard is not logically inherent in comparative study but contemporary political science, among other fields, suggests that it is extreme in practice, most of all where the behavioral sciences' model of experimental study is closely followed. Such study, regardless of how punctiliously carried out, cannot, in and of itself, reveal general laws guaranteed to be valid. It *only provides more or less powerful clues as to what they are:* i.e., helps to discover them. In some cases these clues may be so powerful that testing may seem superfluous or not worth the cost; but this is highly exceptional.[5]

Strictly speaking, generalizations directly inferred from data only hold (probabilistically) for the phenomena observed under the conditions prevailing during observation. If the observations are voluminous and accurate, and if the conditions of observation are highly various or controlled, one may have very high confidence that the curve that best fits the observations in fact manifests, in graphic form, a valid theory. Nevertheless, the element of surmise in going from data to theory always is considerable, and the "epistemic gap" between them, as Northrop calls it, ineluctable. And such great limitations usually exist, in practice, on the volume, accuracy, and variety or control of observations (including, of course, the obvious limitation that we cannot observe the future) that the risk in identifying an empirical generalization with a theoretical rule usually cannot be defended unless special testing of the presumed rule is carried out.

b). A second aspect of the fallacy concerns the discovery of candidate-theories in the first place. It is the principles that give rise to empirically discovered curves that constitute theories, not the curves as such: these only represent the principles, i.e., show them at work. When an empirically grounded curve has been drawn, therefore, the principles it expresses must still be elucidated. Often this is not much of a problem, and statistical techniques (like causal path analysis) can help solve it. Nevertheless, curves can deceive as well as instruct, regardless of such techniques; and they most resist the discerning of *simple* regularities governing phenomena because the data from which they are constructed usually express all the complex interactions of factors in the concrete world, or sometimes even the laboratory. Nature, as Bacon realized, is a tough adversary capable of innumerable disguises. More than routine method is often required to strip these disguises off.

It seems, in fact, unlikely that the more powerful laws of physical science could have been discovered (their testing aside) by the mechanical processing of observations, however "sophisticated." Certainly one is struck by the small role played by systematic comparative observation in both their formulation and critical testing—in effect, by the thorough lack of correspondence between the psychologist's and physicist's conception of "experimentation." As illustration, take that touchstone of ancient, modern, and contemporary physics: conceptions of gravity and the closely associated law of the acceleration of freely falling objects.

The Galilean challenge to the Aristotelian conception of free fall (the heavier the object, the faster it falls), accepted as gospel for nearly two millennia, did not grow out of observation at all but out of a simple "thought-experiment" (simple in retrospect, but apparently not at all obvious until performed). In gist (and with apologies for a layman's bowdlerization): if Aristotle is correct, then two bricks of the same weight, dropped at the same instant from the same height, must strike the ground at the same instant. If the two bricks are dropped side by side, as if cemented, the rate of fall of each must be the same as if dropped separately; but if cemented, they would be twice as heavy as a single brick and must therefore drop much faster; hence, since both conclusions cannot be right, the theory must be wrong. And the only way to square the two conditions logically is to make the weight of the falling objects irrelevant to acceleration in free fall, with the relevant variables being only the gravitational forces that account for falling and, possibly, the duration of the fall.

There is no observation here at all (and much doubt even about whether Galileo ever climbed the Tower of Pisa to check out, by a single "probe," the plausibility of his conclusion). Had systematic comparative measurements been used, anomalies in the Aristotelian conception would certainly have turned up, at least in the fall of objects "heavy" above a certain threshold. But if a well-chosen sample of objects had been dropped from a well-selected sample of heights under a well-selected sample of wind and other conditions, the likely conclusions would surely have been something like this: that the whole process of falling, like macropolitical phenomena, is "immensely complicated and cannot be accounted for by one or two simple causes" (Verba, 1967, p. 114); that weight is a factor (as it is at certain heights and other conditions); and that weight, size, shape, and density of object, and wind conditions account for such and such a (no doubt high) percentage of the variance in rates of fall, singly or in various combinations. A radical, deductively fertile simplification of the whole complex process might, but almost certainly would not, have emerged.

The Galilean notion was widely disputed until a crucial experiment could be conducted to check it out. Objects of different weights did demonstrably fall at different, sometimes vastly different, rates. So the Galileans' extraneous factors, having no place in the law, remained other people's favored explanatory variables. Only with the invention of the air pump, about 1650, was a definitive experiment possible: dropping a heavy object (coin) and a light one (feather) in an evacuated tube. Again, no systematic comparative measurement was used, only a single experimental observation that foreclosed weaseling out by ad hocery to Galileans and Aristotelians alike.

Newton's theory $(F \propto mm'/r^2)$ was certainly suggested by observations of the movement of astronomical bodies (although Singer [1959] argues that all Newton's laws are quite abstract and not concerned directly with phenomenal observations), but the value of the universal gravitational constant G, needed to convert the expression of Newton's theory into an equation, was worked out initially by Lord Cavendish (in 1798) through a single experiment and the measurement derived from it. And Einstein's revision of Newton's theory could certainly not have been derived from quantitative analysis of observations, while its conclusive test involved a single critical phenomenon: the deflection of light as it passed close to the rim of the sun (Newman, 1963, vol. 2, p. 528).[6]

Comparative observations may be significant in fleshing out basic conceptions of regularities (e.g., determining that the acceleration of freely falling objects is described by $s = 1/2 \ gt^2$, or measuring any specific value g). But they are far from necessary, and quite likely to deceive, when these basic conceptions—critical variables and their basic relationship—are to be formulated.

c). The inductive fallacy has a third facet, pertaining exclusively to testing. It might be conceded that discovering and testing theories are different processes, but not that testing requires data different from those that help in discovery. The analysis of data may be so convincing that one might not consider it worthwhile to test rules derived from them but, despite this, the experiences in light of which theories are constructed cannot be used again as tests of them. Testing involves efforts to falsify, and anything giving rise to a theory will certainly not falsify it; nor will any body of "replicated" observations do so, if replication indeed is faithful. (Replication pertains to reliability, not validity.) The object of testing is to find observations that must fit a theory but have a good chance of not doing so. Nothing that suggests a theory, therefore, can also test it.

2. Having established a need for the independent testing of theoretical curves (on the grounds that the discovery and testing of theories are intrinsically different activities, that no method of discovery can guarantee validity, that even painstakingly gathered and analyzed data can deceive, and that data which suggest regularities cannot also validate them), we come to the crux: the argument of the fifth option that, *in principle, comparative and case studies are alternative means to the end of testing theories, choices between which must be largely governed by arbitrary or practical, rather than logical, considerations.*

Comparative studies can certainly be used to test theories. If we use them for this purpose, our object, as stated, is to demonstrate that a curve that fits their results well in fact closely coincides with a curve postulated by theory, however that may have been worked out. In the case of a law like that of the acceleration of falling objects, for example, one might try to demonstrate that the curve yielded by a set of observations sustains the expectation that the postulated law is an increasingly better predictor as one increasingly approximates the conditions under which the law is considered to hold absolutely.

However, there is available (not necessarily in all cases, but in many) an alternative to that rather cumbersome procedure, and it involves a kind of case study. One can use a well-constructed experiment, conducted to simulate as closely as possible the specified conditions under which a law must hold, and compare its result with that predicted by the law. In the history of science the decisive experiments have been mostly of that kind, a fact that makes one wonder how the comparative observation of unmanipulated cases could ever have come to be regarded as any sort of equivalent of experimental method in the physical sciences. (The main reasons are, by my reading, the influence of J. S. Mill's *Logic,* the intuitive decision reached by some influential contemporary social scientists that their regularity statements must unavoidably be "probabilistic" in form, origin, and testing, and the fact that much experimentation in the physical sciences is simply hopeful fishing for regularities in masses of data.) And if a well-constructed experiment can serve the purpose, then so may a well-chosen case—one that is somehow as crucial for a theory as are certain experiments (or indeed natural observations) in the physical sciences.

This argument is not at all impugned by the incontestable principle regarding the relations between points and curves with which we started. For there is another principle about those relations that is equally incontestable. This is that any given point can fall only on an infinitesimal fraction of all conceivable curves: it will not fall on any of the curves, the number of which is also infinity, that do not in fact pass through the point. (A less abstract variant of this principle is that for every plausible explanation of a political event, there is an infinite number that are not even minimally plausible.) The fact that a point falls, or does not fall, on a curve, therefore, is not at all insignificant. If the curve is not constructed to pass through the point but *preconstructed* to represent a theory, and if, given the nature of a case subsequently examined, we can predict, according to the theory, that it must fall on, or very near, the curve at a specified location, the fact that it does so is of the utmost significance, and its location far from the predicted point will impeach the theory no less than the tendency of several points to describe a divergent curve. At any rate, this is the case if the bases for predicting the location of an unknown point are really compelling—which is the object of crucial case study. In such case study, the compelling instance "represents" a regularity as, in comparative study, a sample of individuals "represents" a population.

3. Crucial-case study presupposes that crucial cases exist. Whether they do or not in macropolitics can hardly be settled abstractly. All one can say on the subject is the following: (*i*) If they do not, no reasonable alternative to testing theory by comparative study exists. (*ii*) The inability to identify cases crucial for theories may not be the result of their nonexistence but of the loose way theories are stated, their relative lack of what we earlier termed "rulefulness." (*iii*) Any *a priori* assumption as to their nonexistence manifestly is a self-fulfilling prophecy, and it is difficult to see with what compelling reasoning such an assumption might be justified. (*iv*) If that reasoning rests on the inability to use controlled laboratory experiments in macropolitics, it suffices to point out that crucial measures in the physical sciences can be of natural observations

(as, for example, the confirmation of Einsteinian relativity). And, obviously most important, (*v*) both hypothetical and actual examples of (apparently) crucial observations in the social sciences, including observations of complex collective individuals can be found—and would almost certainly be found more often if deliberately sought more often.

A more important question, therefore, is how a crucial case can be recognized. What guidelines can be used?

The essential abstract characteristic of a crucial case can be deduced from its function as a test of theory. It is a case that *must closely fit* a theory if one is to have confidence in the theory's validity, or, conversely, *must not fit* equally well any rule contrary to that proposed. The same point can be put thus: in a crucial case it must be extremely difficult, or clearly petulant, to dismiss any finding contrary to theory as simply "deviant" (due to chance, or the operation of unconsidered factors, or whatever "deviance" might refer to other than the fact of deviation from theory per se), and equally difficult to hold that any finding confirming theory might just as well express quite different regularities. One says difficult and petulant because claims of deviance and the operation of other regularities can always be made. The question is therefore not whether they are made but how farfetched or perverse the reasons for them (if any) are.

Generally speaking, "must-fit" cases are those that naturally have the characteristics of a well-designed experiment, so that mere forecasts must be as accurate as concrete, or even experimental, predictions. The case of Norway, as discussed above, is a case in point, if what is claimed about it is indeed true: i.e., that governmental performance has been continuously high while social structure has thoroughly changed. It would also be in point if social structure had remained nearly constant while a substantial change in level of governmental performance had occurred. But it may be admitted that such cases, naturally paralleling the artificial controls of the laboratory, will not commonly occur, and that one will need unusual luck to find them out economically even if they exist.

An alternative is to focus inquiry on "most-likely" or "least-likely" cases— cases that ought, or ought not, to invalidate or confirm theories if any cases can be expected to do so. The best-known example in political study probably is Michels' inquiry into the ubiquitousness of oligarchy in organizations (Michels, 1962), based on the argument that certain organizations (those consciously dedicated to grass roots democracy and associated ideologies, representing classes whose interest lies in such democracy, having highly elaborate and pure formal democratic procedures, and leaders from the same social strata as the membership) are least likely, or very unlikely, to be oligarchic if oligarchy were not universal. (One may argue with Michels' choice of social units, his methods, or his findings [see Willey, 1971], but the principle of the idea is surely sound.) Another example is Malinowski's study (1926) of a highly primitive, communistic (in the anthropological sense) society, to determine whether automatic, spontaneous obedience to norms in fact prevailed in it, as was postulated by other anthropologists. The society selected was a "most-likely" case—the very model of primitive, communistic society—and the finding was contrary to the postulate: obedience was found to result from "psychological and social inducements." A similar example is Whyte's study (1943) of a Boston slum society, a collective individual that should, according to prevailing theory, have exhibited a high level of "social disorganization," but in fact exhibited the very opposite.

The "least-likely" case (as in Michels) seems especially tailored to confirmation, the "most-likely" case (as in Whyte and Malinowski) to invalidation. Methodological purists will find this a curious sentence. They will find it odd because philosophers of science deny that there is a distinction between confirmation and invalidation (Popper, 1959, being the prime example). The philosophers are right to the extent that they argue that nothing can categorically prove theories in the manner of logical proofs, but that some findings may categorically invalidate them. But to the working scientist the distinction between confirmation and disconfirmation does have meaning, even if logic compels one ultimately to equate "validates" with "fails to falsify." There is a difference in nuance between saying "this can't be so if a theory is weak" and saying "this must be so if a theory is powerful." [7] Per contra, of course, any most-likely case for one theory becomes a least-likely case for its antithesis, and vice versa (e.g., the Boston slum was a least-likely case for the ubiquity of social "organization"), so that the distinction is one of research design and objectives rather than the inherent characteristics of a case. For the same reason, crucial case study obviously proceeds best when a case is treated in both senses and confronted with both theory and countertheory.

Cases that are extreme on pertinent measures can usually be regarded as crucial in the sense of being least-likely and most-likely cases. If, for example, one holds that democratic stability is directly proportional to level of economic development and inversely proportional to rate of economic growth ($S_d \propto E_d/E_r$), a very high value of S_d (as in Norway) should predict a high value of E_d and a low value of E_r; if either is not the case grave doubt is *de rigueur*, and if both are not the theory simply cannot be right. Ditto, of course, if the starting point is the economic variables, or if one starts with extremely low stability (as in Republican Spain). And ditto, in spades, if the extreme measure is of change on the stability measure: a marked change, for example, from instability to stability. This appears to have occurred in Germany, which was highly unstable during the Weimar Republic but, by one calculus (Hurewitz, 1971) ranks third out of twenty only to New Zealand and Sweden (with a score of 112.56 on a range from 118.42 to 67.19) in the post-World War II period. (This measure is not greatly at odds with a different and more complex one of change in German "political performance" made by Gurr and McClelland [1971].) If, in that case, a relatively low level of E_d and high level of E_r turned up, and the regularity statement were not rejected, any theory at all could be saved, presumably by casually adding explanatory factors or casually dismissing cases as "deviant."

Measures need not always be extreme to be considered crucial for theory, nor will any extreme measure do as well as any other. It depends on the theory and the circumstances of the case that provides the measure. For example: I have proposed elsewhere that (1) high governmental performance requires congruence between the government's authority pattern and the authority patterns of other social units in the society; that (2) other specified factors also affect performance levels; and that (3) the effects of congruence on performance are considerably greater than those of the principal other factors, which, by and large, work only to depress fractionally the level of performance predictable from congruence (Eckstein, 1969). If all these propositions are valid, any case of very high performance becomes crucial: it must permit accurate predictions about the independent variable, congruence. But a less extreme case may still be crucial, if a marked change in performance has occurred and noncongruence factors remain constant or change little (no doubt hard to know in advance of intensive study), or (not so hard to know) if a *positive* change in performance is considerable enough to make it very unlikely that it has nothing to do with increased congruence but only expresses the amelioration of other factors that previously depressed performance. For this purpose, a change from near the bottom to somewhere near the middle of a scale may suffice, although the more considerable the change the better.

These arguments about most-likely and least-likely cases, cases in which some pertinent variables change and others remain constant, extreme cases of most kinds and some that are not extreme, have a bearing on the question whether crucial cases may be found in macropolitics. It seems rather unlikely that all cases should be equally unlikely or likely, equally changeable or constant in all respects, equally short of extreme values on pertinent variables, and equally modest in change on the variables. More and less crucial cases should therefore be available *en masse,* and some of the more crucial ones identifiable without taxing preliminary studies—on their face value or because the special work required has already been done, even if for other purposes. The possibility, of course, remains that a particular theory, even if suitably stated, cannot be confronted by a clearly crucial case, or that such a case can only be found by wide-ranging preliminary observations and measures of many cases. But these prospects should now appear less daunting than might have been the case, and not at all inevitable.

4. To this point, the discussion has presented the case only for option 5: that case and comparative studies are best conceived as equally useful, alternative means for testing theories. The utility of case study and the weaknesses of comparative studies have been stressed only because the reverse is far more common in our field.

If logic does not intrinsically favor one method or another, the method to be used must be selected for other reasons, i.e., out of practical, prudential considerations. One such reason may be the unavailability of clearly crucial cases. But assuming that not to be the case, probable costs and benefits become the pertinent calculus. On that calculus rests the case for the sixth option on case study, which pertains only to macropolitics. Inquiry into macropolitical units involves problems of scale and of sound comparison that point strongly toward crucial case study as the preferable method; the same considerations might also apply to stages of inquiry other than testing but are less telling there since rigor is at a lesser premium.[8]

The most manifest practical advantage of case study is, of course, that it is economical for all resources: money, manpower, time, effort. The economies are not strictly equal to $1/n$, where n is the number of cases studied comparatively, since some resources usually have to be devoted to the identification of crucial cases, and some work needed to prepare rigorous case study is similar to that required by rigorous comparative studies. But even so they are likely to be considerable. This economic advantage is especially important, of course, if studies are inherently costly, as they are if units are complex collective individuals. Sociologists of knowledge might note, in this connection, that the growth of comparative studies coincided with the influx of unprecedented research monies and other facilities (research institutions, crowds of postgraduate students) into political study, and that my revisionism coincides with a sudden shrinkage in these factors. If that shrinkage compels us to develop less costly means to the same ends, it will be a blessing in disguise.

A second practical advantage involves access to the subjects of study. Samples of macropolitical units are always likely to be poor and highly uncertain in result: small in number (the population being small) despite the likelihood of a sizeable range of variation. If, as is usually the case, they consist of contemporary cases, they are also bound to be a badly biased sample for all cases relevant to general laws. These problems in principle are compounded by practical problems of access resulting from the political exclusion of researchers (as in Burma), the inaccessibility of subjects in other cases, the lack of local research facilities (e.g., survey research organizations), and language problems for foreign researchers, among many other factors. As a result, contemporary comparative studies in macropolitics predominantly have one or more of three characteristics: (1) small numbers of cases chosen by intuition or for convenience; (2) the use, in wide-ranging studies, of readily available, aggregate data that are often quite untrustworthy and dubious indicators of traits they supposedly represent or (3) think-pieces based on discussions of cases by "country-experts" in light of a common framework that are usually not at all well coordinated (e.g., Almond and Coleman, 1960; Lipset and Rokkan, 1967; Dahl, 1966; and the various books in the SSRC Comparative Politics Committee's series "Studies in Political Development"). Crucial case study may, of course, also suffer from problems of access. However, since crucial cases rarely appear singly, the likelihood of being unable to study properly even one of them seems considerably smaller than the likelihood of working with poor samples in comparative studies or that of having to tailor theoretical research to practical possibilities rather than the far more desirable vice versa.

A huge practical problem in comparative research involves special knowledge of the cultures being studied. The arguments made by the German exponents of the view that the *Naturwissenschaften* and *Kulturwissenschaften* are ineluctably different (see especially Dilthey, 1883; and Rickert, 1899), and the arguments of the clinicians inspired by them are surely right insofar as they hold that "social facts," personal or collective, are embedded in widely varying, even in each case unique, cultural systems of meaning and value, and that one can neglect these only at great peril. Their position may not imply that "social laws" are therefore unattainable, but they do imply that the cultural sciences impose a requirement of special cultural "understanding" that does not exist in natural science. Crucial cases can often be selected to satisfy this requirement for individual researchers, and it is always possible to acquire a great deal of cultural *Verstehen* in the course of in-depth study of a case if one does not already possess it. Even if we reject the notion of a special inherent requirement for cultural science, this point can still be made to rest convincingly on the question of special language skills and special historical and sociological knowledge of cases, for lack of which comparativists are often justly criticized.

At the very least, one can obviously, other things being equal, go more deeply into a single case than a number of them, and thus compensate for loss of range by gains in depth: to that extent, at least, the clinicians have a foolproof case. In crucial case study, the advantages of traditional scholarship, as displayed in configurative-idiographic studies, can thus be combined with those of modern technique and rigor. And it is also more possible to apply in crucial case study certain techniques developed in social science for overcoming the imperfections of single measures, especially the "triangulation of imperfect measures" technique developed in social psychology and applied, impressively, by Greenstein and Tarrow in political socialization research (1971). As an aside: the problems of *Verstehen*, depth, and imperfect measures are especially great in research into "political culture"; hence, it is rather astonishing to find that exponents of the political culture approach should also be devoted comparativists.

Specialists in macropolitics have tried to overcome these problems by spawning general frameworks to be applied by different individuals in different cases or by deliberately organizing group research, hoping that the results will add up to coherent comparative study. The results have been uniformly disappointing. The frameworks have not been widely taken up, except as terminology, or have been widely butchered, and a whole volume could be written on the difficulties and meager results of different organizational frameworks for group research. At least until macropolitics develops a consensual paradigm, there seems to be no adequate collective substitute for the work of isolated researchers or, much the same, small and intimate teams of close collaborators.

At this point it should be clear that the practical advantage of crucial case study does not lie merely in resources. Case studies yield methodological payoffs as well. This is in large part due to the fact that they help avoid difficulties that are hard to reduce or abolish in cross-cultural research. Not the least of these are two related difficulties not yet mentioned: the problem of the proper cross-cultural translation of research instruments, a subject rapidly becoming a methodological field in itself and one that absorbs ingenuity and thought better devoted to theory construction and testing themselves. In addition, if we conduct crucial case studies, we are far more likely to develop theories logically and imaginatively, rather than relying on mechanical processing to reveal them. More important still, we are more constrained to state them tightly and in proper form, suitable to testing: that is, in a manner that permits their deductive and predictive application to cases. Sloppiness in the forms of theory compatible with the criteria developed in the section on "Definitions" above is not inherent in comparative studies (certainly not in the "disciplined" variety), but crucial case study involves far more compelling practical demands for the proper statement of theories, or else exposes far more manifestly when theories are not properly stated: i.e., when nothing—or 470 million different things—can be deduced for any case from regularity statements about it.

More thought, more imagination, more logic, less busy-work, less reliance on mechanical printouts, no questions about sampling, possibly firmer conclusions (including that extreme rarity in political study, the conclusively falsified hypothesis), fewer questions about empathy: these surely establish a heavy credit. It remains to see whether any debits may cancel it out.

OBJECTIONS TO THE ARGUMENT (AND REPLIES TO THE OBJECTIONS)

A number of arguments that might be, or have been, raised against my brief for crucial case studies should now be considered.[9] None seem unanswerable, except in ways not very damaging to the argument. But others may see more merit in the objections than in the ways they are answered—and it is also possible that the really telling objections have been missed, or subconsciously avoided to restrict discussion to those that can be answered. The most telling objection of all, of course, would be that crucial cases simply are not available in macropolitics, but that has already been ruled out as unlikely for most, or many, theories. It is true that the literature of political science is not rich in crucial cases, but neither does it abound in efforts to find them, the most likely reason being that the very idea of crucial case study is alien to the field.

Objection 1.

Comparative studies have the advantage over case studies of allowing one to test for the null hypothesis that one's findings are due to chance. Case studies may turn up validating or invalidating results fortuitously, not because theories are actually valid or invalid, but because one cannot determine by single measures whether or not this is so.

Answers. (a) The possibility that a result is due to chance can never be ruled out in any sort of study; even in wide comparative study it is only more or less likely. Now, it is surely very unlikely that, out of all possible states of affairs (which normally are vastly more than the two faces of a coin and sometimes approach infinity), just that predicted by theory should fortuitously turn up in a case carefully chosen as crucial for the theory, and also unlikely that in such a case the predicted result should, just by chance, be greatly out of line with actual observation. The real difference between crucial case study and comparative study, therefore, is that in the latter case, but not the former, we can assign by various conventions a specific number to the likelihood of chance results (e.g., "significant at the .05 level"). Thus, if a theorist posits that democratic stability varies directly with level of economic development and inversely with rate of economic growth, and finds a case of extreme instability with high E_d and low E_r, he cannot rule out plain bad luck, but the presumption that he has an invalid theory surely is vastly greater.

(b) Any appreciable likelihood of unlucky chance findings in a crucial case study arises from the fact that very short-run fluctuations generally occur in any measure of a variable. (Think of air temperature, or rainfall, or the climate of a marriage.) For example, a polity generally high in performance will probably experience some peaks and troughs in its level, and peaks and troughs will also occur in variables used to explain levels of performance. If we then measure a dependent variable at a peak and an independent variable at a trough, a deceptive result will certainly be obtained. But the remedy is obvious: observe over a reasonable period of time.[10]

(c) There is, of course, also a possibility of observer bias in the observation of a case (seeing only what one wishes to see), hence of misleading, if not literally fortuitous, measures. That problem exists also in comparative studies, but not so acutely because of the prophylaxis provided by statistical measures of significance. But again, simple remedies are available. The most obvious is to recognize that falsifying a theory is to be reckoned as success rather than failure, and thus to redefine what one generally wants: knowing what is valid tells one more than knowing what is not, but knowing something to be invalid does signify progress, and often provides very powerful clues as to what is valid. It is true that the reward structure of the social sciences overvalues positive findings, especially in publication—which may be why methods that maximize the probability of some sort of positive result (e.g., multiple regression) are so widely used. But such prizing of positive results, however tenuous, indicates scientific immaturity or insecurity, and ought not to be perpetuated. It works like Gresham's law: bad theory crowds out good. (In fact, the question most frequently, and fearfully, asked about the preliminary version of this paper was: "What do you do if a prediction about a crucial case fails?" Answer: You publish the result—if editors permit and the failure is informative, as it is almost bound to be—and you go on, trying to do better.) Apart from that fundamental point, the problem of observer bias arises more in configurative-idiographic studies than in the more rigorous varieties of case study—hence the stress on it in existing critiques of case study (e.g., Becker, 1968)—and can certainly be reduced in the study of collective individuals by the same methods used to reduce it in comparative studies, such as the correct sampling of the microunits that constitute the case.

(d) In crucial case studies a powerful substitute for the null hypothesis can be put to work: testing for a theory's "countertheories," i.e., likely alternative solutions if a theory is invalid, or a theory's "antithesis," if one is available. (This can also be done in comparative research, but economic considerations make it more feasible in case study, especially if theory and countertheories cannot be tested by exactly the same data.) The process of testing simultaneously for alternative hypotheses ("strong inference") has been held persuasively by Platt (1966) as the correct way to put Baconian empiricism to work and, also persuasively, as the hallmark of the most rapidly developing hard sciences (high-energy physics and molecular biology). An example (not yet acted upon) from my own work on the relations between governmental performance and resemblances among governmental and other authority patterns may again provide a useful illustration of the procedure. "Congruence" theory rests, at bottom, on psychological learning theory in general and some of its specific variants. Since learning theory emphasizes the operation in behavior of gradually internalized orientations (something like habit, although not in the crude sense of the term), its obvious countertheory is one that postulates rational calculations in the light of one's current life-situation, untrammeled by the accretive influences of past learning: in short, an "economic" model of behavior. A theory of political performance could be rigorously developed on that basis (and in fact has been, by Rogowski, 1969). A crucial case study can readily be designed not only to determine whether a case lies off a predicted point on one curve but also whether it lies on, or nearer, a predicted point on a crucial countercurve. Since only one case is involved, the cost of doing both will not be much greater than that of performing one operation alone. Several advantages accrue. We may not merely establish that a theory is false but also why, at bottom, it is false, and what sort of theory would serve better. Furthermore, a finding near a predicted point on one curve but far off such a point on the countercurve, adds to one's case enormously. One may thus not only shed special light on one's theory, but also more general light on the more fundamental bases for further theory construction. And if both theories are confirmed, a false contradiction is exposed; if neither is, the same result is obtained, or sloppy deduction is unmasked. All this takes one far beyond the mere void of statistical nullness.

Objection 2.

If preliminary comparative studies are required to identify crucial cases (e.g., cases extreme on pertinent measures, or highly changeable on a measure, or having the characteristics of natural experiments), the practical advantages of case study are severely reduced. And if they are severely reduced, certain practical advantages of comparative studies, such as their ability to provide data for reanalysis or simply data from numerous contexts, tend to tip the scales in their favor.

Answers. (a) Independent comparative study is not always required to identify crucial cases, simply because in an ongoing discipline the evidence needed to identify a crucial case often is already available. One may want to recheck that evidence or try to improve on it, but that is not tantamount to starting from scratch.

(b) Even if one starts from scratch, comparative studies specifically designed to uncover crucial cases can be very limited in scope, even confined to a single variable, and so much reduced in costs of all kinds. (For example, in the case of congruence theory, one might not initially do research on both performance and congruence, but on performance alone—a fact which, if realized earlier by the author, would have saved funding agencies much money and himself much effort and time in designing research projects and carrying them out.) Common knowledge, no less than disciplinary knowledge, can also reduce problems of sampling in the search for such cases. For example, if the object were to discover a long stable polity, it would take more than ordinary ignorance to include, say, Germany in the search. Comparative studies to uncover crucial cases thus have little in common, in regard to required breadth of study or data requirements, with comparative studies as presently conducted.

(c) The fact that comparative studies provide "extensive" data from many contexts can be offset by the usual claim for "intensive" study: that it can provide more varieties of data (and is likely to do so not only if study is clinical but also if strong inference procedures are used). Such data, moreover, are as much subject to reanalysis as any others. They may not suit well the purposes of others, but then neither might those produced by comparative study; and virtually any body of data has import for a variety of purposes.

Objection 3.

Several crucial case studies are always better than one. Some degree of additional safety is always provided by additional numbers. If therefore the intent is to be conclusive, crucial-case study ends as comparative study anyway.

Answers. (a) The basic problem here again is the equation of success with confirmation. A single crucial case may certainly score a clean knockout over a theory (as Galileo's thought-experiment would have, had it been a real experiment, and as the falling feather and coin in the evacuated tube later did). The problem arises only if confirmation occurs. Because distrust is a required element of the scientific culture, confirmation only eggs us on to allay our own always remaining doubts and disarm those of carping adversaries: and thus we may want to know whether a theory that fits crucial case X also fits cases Y and Z, assuming these are also crucial, and whether, despite precautions and great unlikelihood, chance has tricked us after all. But the further examination of other cases can be restricted much more than in comparative studies that rest their case on sampling, and in such studies "added confirmation" may also be deemed advisable—in fact, is necessary if the studies merely establish curves rather than matching them.

(b) Conceivably, the most powerful study of all for theory building is neither the presently common form of comparative study (of cases studied randomly, or intuitively selected, or simply studied because they seem readily available or accessible) nor the study of single crucial cases, but, so to speak, "comparative crucial case studies." The case for such studies, however, is strong only to the extent that the most crucial cases available are not very crucial, so that high confidence in the results they yield needs the increment of other crucial case findings. Thus, the feather and coin falling in a vacuum leave virtually no doubt to the skeptic or the inquirer devoted to the tested theory, while a case of change in governmental performance highly unlikely to be due merely to the disappearance of performance-depressing factors, as against the factor posited to be required for high performance, probably leaves enough doubt to both to make desirable a further study or two of equal import. The study of such a more tenuous case might also, in some instances, be considered an especially powerful "plausibility probe," warranting the (costly) comparative testing of a probabilistic hypothesis like that logically implied in the congruence theory of governmental performance (Eckstein, 1969, p. 282): that "in all cases, the correlation between performance and congruence will be high." The comparativist may treat any and all crucial case studies as plausibility probes, warranting the costs of using his favored method. The notion of the crucial case study was, after all, devised largely from that of the plausibility probe. The point is that he need not do so, unless the crucial case falls far short of the ideal.

Objection 4.

Crucial-case studies turn out to be comparative studies in disguise. For instance, when dropping a coin and feather through an evacuated tube we take two simultaneous measures and compare them; or, when studying the correlates of a change from low to high governmental performance we again take two measures at different points in time and compare them. The distinction between comparative studies and case studies thus vanishes, along with that between the clinical and experimental modes of inquiry.

Answers. (a) Not all crucial measures are like that. Observing the deflection of light near the rim of the sun compares nothing with anything (unless it is claimed that it compares deflection with nondeflection). The same holds true if only high governmental performance, not change toward it, is the critical observation.

(b) It is by no means sophistic to maintain that the supposedly dual measures above are single measures, i.e., measures of the amount of change in performance between an earlier and a later period or the amount of difference in the rate of fall of two objects. Such changes and differences can be used as points on a curve no less than measurements of static conditions at a particular point in time, and thus satisfy the exacting technical definition of case study.

(c) Measures of "more than," "less than," and "equal to" do presuppose two anchoring measures (see also Objection 5, Answer (d) below), but are not to be confused with comparative measures of samples, and $n = 2$ always suffices to establish them. Thus the distinction between case studies and comparative studies is watered down little, even if points (a) and (b) are disregarded.

Objection 5.

Social science, especially on the macrolevel, does not have available measures precise and discriminating enough to make the sort of predictions needed for crucial-case study.

Answers. (a) If this is true, the fact must bedevil comparative studies as much as any others, unless there is some magic by which many poor measures are equal to one that is good. Numerous poor measures can, of course, cancel one another out, or increase confidence in any one of them. But they can also make for increased distortion, i.e., reinforce one another, and will certainly do so if a measuring instrument contains a consistent bias.

(b) What gospel ordains that social measures must be highly inexact and undiscriminating? That of experience? Perhaps; but perhaps only because of the prevalent assumption that nothing precise can be done in social study—surely a self-fulfilling prophecy if ever there was one. And while there is research there is hope: most of the natural sciences had to live long, and managed quite well, with rather imprecise measures too, and ours have been improving.

(c) Highly discriminating measures are *not* required to put crucial case study to work. If the measure to be predicted is, let us say, the level of democratic stability in postwar Germany, it is not necessary to be able to say that the level is at 112.56 (à la Hurewitz), with reasonable assurance that it is not then at 112.57. It may quite suffice to say that the measure must come out somewhere between 8 and 10 on a ten-point scale, either because theory permits or because of recognized possible error in a measuring technique. The possibility of disconfirmation then still exists, and is, after all, about four times as likely as confirmation. There must, of course, be a limit on imprecision. The minimum requirement is that measures must not be so inexact that any measure considered to validate (or invalidate) a theory could also, because of inherently possible measurement error, be taken to imply the opposite. If we cannot do much better than that in the social sciences, we might as well not measure at all, in any kind of study. Therefore, arguments about imprecision impugn quantitative social science, not crucial case study only.

(d) If no more than a single point is measured, however, crucial case study does presuppose interval measures (even if measurement techniques do not allow discrimination between minute intervals). If only ordinal measures are available, then (and only then) one must have two measurements to confirm, or invalidate, the prediction that a variable will have a higher, or lower, value at one time than another, or under one condition than another. Ordinal measures only state "more than," "less than," or "equal to," and that always requires two points of reference, as stated above. And, as also already stated, this still concedes next to nothing to comparative study, and perhaps nothing at all if the predicted measure is interpreted as the measure of a difference of some discernible magnitude.

Objection 6.

Crucial-case studies cannot confirm multivariate theories, in which one deals with one dependent and several independent variables. The social sciences (especially on the macrolevel, where crucial case study is most advantageous) deal with multivariate phenomena: phenomena in which a variety of determinants converge upon observed experience.

Answers. (a) Again one wants to know: What gospel ordains that social phenomena must be multivariate, or decisively more so than any others? One might answer, the phenomena themselves: look, for instance, at all the factors associated with revolution, or authoritarian political behavior, or political instability, or nonvoting. True—but not decisive, and quite probably pernicious. In the natural sciences, too, "causes" converge in phenomenal experience, but notable successes have been achieved in cutting through the phenomenal complexities to simple theoretical constructs that are powerful tools in explaining particular occurrences or, by engineering, for bringing them about. (For example, the law of acceleration of freely falling objects consists of one dependent variable, acceleration, and one independent variable, time, gravitational force being a constant; but actual "falling" depends on many more factors, although some operate only with infinitesimal effects.) The problem of multivariate complexity largely dissolves if theory is thought of as a *tool of explanation* of the behavior of concrete individuals rather than as total explanation. And the probable perniciousness of the assumption that theories must be multivariate if phenomena are resides precisely in the fact that then they will be, and thus miss beautiful and powerful simplicities, even if they might be found.

(b) Multivariate theories do *not* necessarily rule out crucial case study in testing, provided that one does not simply list independent variables that affect a dependent variable (x has some relationship to a, b, c, ... n) but specifies precisely the relationship of each to the dependent variable and their effects on one another. Newton's theory of gravity, for example, is multivariate: the dependent variable, gravitational force, is determined by two independent variables, mass and distance. But it specifies a direct relationship to one and an inverse relationship to the square of the other. Given the constant necessary to turn these ideas into an equation, predictions can be made for any case that may conclusively confirm or invalidate. The problem then lies more in the way multivariate theories are stated than in multivariation as such. The job of avoiding that problem is immensely difficult (most of us probably need not apply) but it ought to be tackled, even though here again the prevalent reward structure of the social sciences discourages the attempt to do the better work that is more likely to fail, or to be perceived as failure.

(c) A real problem is that a case-finding may be the result of complex "interaction effects." The careful choice of a case may allow one to discount that as a probability, but never altogether, and the fact that the problem might also queer comparative findings (more factors are nearly always interacting than a research design takes into account or allows one to separate) does not abolish the difficulty. The only sensible response is to treat the possibility as reason for continued doubt of some magnitude or other, and thus for further research. If the findings confirm a theory, that simply implies that one might want additional assurance in another pertinent instance. The point here is exactly the same as that regarding the possibility of "chance" results. If the findings disconfirm, and one has strong prior reasons to consider a hypothesis valid (e.g., because of various sorts of estimates of plausibility), the sensible course is simply not to give in all at once but to try another crucial test. In neither case is comparative study the required solution. The responses simply involve added confirmation, or added disconfirmation, by further crucial case study. And studies of additional cases for added assurance are not, strictly speaking, "comparative" studies.

Objection 7.

Crucial-case studies cannot test probabilistically stated theories.

Answers. (a) Agreed.

(b) Theories need not be probabilistic, and the more powerful are not, even if the occurrence of phenomena is. Here, once again, the difficulty lies in confusion between theory as a tool of explanation and theory as the full explanation of concrete events. (That confusion is especially reprehensible in this case because probability statements, inherently, are not total explanations either.) The position rests also on two further fallacies: that if something is true probabilistically of a numerous set of cases, then the probability of its being true is equal for each individual in the set (which is true only in rare cases, like tossing fair coins); and that no mere probability can be deduced from a "law" (it can, to the extent that the conditions under which a law is supposed to hold absolutely do not in fact exist, or to the extent that a law treats variables as constants).

(c) Probability statements are used more often than they need be in political study because of the uncompelled belief that they must be, which works, like other methodological assumptions, as self-fulfilling prophecy.

Objection 8.

Even if all these objections are answerable, it is highly suspicious that so many should arise. Case study seems more susceptible to challenge than comparative study, in regard to which most of these problems are not even raised.

Answer. The essential difference here is not the volume of issues, but that the issues differ because the methods differ. Moreover, comparativists have only recently begun to raise important difficulties inherent in their method, especially on the macrolevel. But, in a relatively short time, an impressive number of difficulties in the method have turned up. After all that has recently been written about difficulties in comparative cross-national study, or even in microlevel studies—problems concerning the selection and proper number of cases, the feasibility and trustworthiness of research instruments (like survey research schedules), the comparability of data, or the utility of various data processing techniques and modes of inferring regularities from numerous data (e.g., various types of significance tests, attributions of causal paths to correlations, attributing longitudinal characteristics to synchronous data)—it is impossible to take seriously the position that case study is suspect because problem-prone and comparative study deserving of benefit of doubt because problem-free.

CONCLUSION

Case study in macropolitics begins in idiography and is rooted in the traditional conception of clinical study. In recent years the position that case study cannot be "nomothetic" has been increasingly attacked in psychology, the very field that made the distinction between idiographic and nomothetic study sharpest and most insuperable. But the notion of nomothetic case study has not been taken far. If not conceived as the application of established theory to case interpretation, it has merely been represented as case study in which rigorous methods, similar to those of "experimental" study, are used and/or in which individual experience is used to help find clues to general theories. If more has been claimed, as by Chassan, it has turned out that the term case study ("$n = 1$" study) is indefensibly applied, by confusing a case with a concrete person rather than a measure.

My object has been to take the argument for nomothetic case study far beyond this point, following up clues provided by examination of more modest arguments in favor of it. The point has been to relate "$n = 1$" studies to all phases of theory building and particularly to stress the utility of case study where rigor is most required and case studies have been considered least useful. Comparative studies have not been attacked, except on practical grounds in limited fields of inquiry; nor is it claimed that appropriate case studies are always available for all theoretical purposes, and certainly not that any kind of case study will serve all purposes. The types of case study are numerous, and that recommended for going beyond formulating candidate-theories is extremely rare in our field or related disciplines.

The argument thus is mainly abstract. There is no track record worth mentioning. But if the horse is run, the results just might be astounding—or, possibly, abysmal. The point is that trials seem in order, not in place of but alongside comparative researches.

It should be evident that case study can be nomothetic only if cases are not selected for the theoretically trivial reasons that nowadays predominate in their selection: because one knows the language, finds a culture congenial to live and work in, can get money for study in it through an affluent area program, considers the case important for foreign policy or otherwise publicly marketable, finds it exotic, and the like. Considerations of congeniality or publicity are well and good if other things are rather equal, not otherwise. And not the least advantage of crucial case studies is that they may permit one to study attractive or convenient cases without sacrifice of disciplinary conscience.

NOTES

1. This statement may be somewhat unjust to Easton: the point is not to criticize him but to make a general argument often violated in political studies. The possible

injustice to Easton arises from the fact that it would be possible, logically and/or empirically, to rule out many combinations and sequences—although, by my reading, Easton has not done so—and there are quite a few to rule out before his framework could permit confident forecasting or unique accounts of existing states of affairs.

2.   The power of theories can also be assessed by another criterion, not included in the text because it strikes me as something for which theorists generally hope, rather than something at which they consciously aim. This is "deductive fertility": not just unexpected knowledge but knowledge in unexpected areas, i.e., reliable and valid accounts of observations outside tne original fields of interest. That criterion can, of course, be consciously pursued when one asks whether a single regularity statement can account for observations that several separate ones cover, or whether the separate regularities can be deduced from a higher-order rule.

3.   The foreknowledge criterion also seems pivotal for economic theorists. Thus, Friedman (1953, p. 41) writes: "The belief that a theory can be tested by the realism of its assumptions independently of the accuracy of its predictions is widespread and the source of much of the perennial criticism of economic theory...." It seems pivotal as well in contemporary philosophy of science, for the emphases on the deductive elaboration of propositions and parsimony are mainly attributable to the stress on nonintuitive foreknowledge (i.e., foreknowledge that is not prophecy or clairvoyance, but rigorously deduced from "rules") as the crucial test of theories. I agree with these positions, except for holding that the ends sought do not manifestly require a unique form of theory. (For a somewhat different "hard," but not overdemanding, view of theory—also based on natural science models but making central "generality" (i.e., range of applicability) and parsimony (i.e., the number of factors needed for complete explanation of a class of events)—see Przeworski and Teune, 1970, pp. 17–23.)

4.   If the essence of disciplined-configurative study is its application to cases of preestablished theories or tools for building theories, we can in fact distinguish four subspecies of this type of case study. It does not seem important to discuss all of them in detail, but it may be useful at least to mention and differentiate them: (1) *Nomological case studies,* so to speak, are studies of the sort Verba has in mind: studies that interpret cases on the basis of theories considered generally valid. (2) A second subspecies may be called *paradigmatic case study*: it involves the application to a case of a preestablished framework, or checklist, for analysis, such as Almond's functional framework or the decision-making framework used in some studies of foreign policies. (3) A third subspecies might be called *methodical case study*: in studies of this sort rigorous methods associated with experimental study are applied to the study of individual cases, as in the studies reprinted in Davidson and Costello's $N = 1$ (1969). (4). The fourth variety may be called *therapeutic case study,* its essence being to apply validated theories and rigorous methods to diagnose problems and difficulties and to arrive at likely ways of eliminating or reducing them, without losing sight of the individual as a "whole."

The first subspecies is uncommon in all the social sciences, except economics, for reasons mentioned in the text. The third is more common in psychology, the fourth more common in psychiatry, than in other human sciences. In political science, the second subspecies predominates, exceeded in frequency only by configurative-idiographic studies.

5.   These statements do not imply that *acting* on clues provided by empirically drawn curves is foolish. Usually it is wise (e.g., not smoking if one wants to keep one's good health) and often nothing better is available for making prudent decisions. The preemi-

nent function of statistical analyses, as Wallis and Roberts (1962, p. 11) emphasize, is precisely to help one to make "wise decisions in the face of uncertainty." Hence they are best used to help cope with action problems (e.g., traffic control problems, public health problems, problems of increasing agricultural yields, etc.) where valid theory provides no better guide and common sense is inadequate. As statistics has become more and more powerful for this purpose, statistical findings have become increasingly confused with theories; but the distinction remains, and is eluctable.

6.   This discussion provides a particularly splendid example of the process of theory building. The process begins with the perception of a puzzle—in this case in the logical implications of a theory (which might also have been discovered in the actual behavior of objects). A "vision" of an alternative way of looking at experience then occurs. The vision is transformed into a tight rule; then a critical test of it, and its alternative, is sought. The test may not be available immediately, but its general nature is apparent in the theory. If it confirms the theory, inquiry is not ended, but resumes with the discovery of new puzzles and/or alternative, better regularity statements.

7.   Take as examples the following: "If the theory of the universality of oligarchy is weak, oligarchy simply *can't* turn up in Social-Democratic organizations (least-likely case, hence confirmation)." "If the theory of spontaneous obedience in primitive societies is strong, such obedience *must* turn up among the Trobriand natives (most-likely case, hence disconfirmation)."

8.   Macropolitics was defined in the introduction to this chapter as the study of overall polities (e.g., nation-states) as units of analysis and of phenomena virtually coterminous with them. That use of the term "macropolitics" needs some elucidation.

    There is a continuum that runs from simple, personal political behavior to the behavior of complex "collective individuals," like nation-states. It seems reasonable to distinguish four major levels of analysis on that continuum. One is *micropolitics:* the political attitudes and activities of individual persons. A second is *group politics:* the political attitudes and activities of collectivities within polities, like classes, pressure groups, or parties. The third is *macropolitics:* politics at the level of polities themselves. Beyond that level are systems and interactions of polities—*megapolitics,* if a neologism is wanted.

    These distinctions, however, are not quite so clean as they might be. For one thing, it might be better to distinguish microstudy and macrostudy more abstractly, treating microstudy as the study of components of systems and macroanalysis as the study of the systems in which they interact. In that case, studies of collective individuals of any size or complexity can be microstudies or macrostudies, depending on how they are treated. The fact would remain, however, that macrostudies are concerned with more inclusive and complex phenomena than are microstudies, which is the point of the distinctions made here. In addition, a continuum being involved, there can be overlap between the levels of politics from the standpoint of inclusiveness and complexity: some political groups are certainly more sizeable and complex than some polities. Still, it is generally the macrounits, as here defined, that are more inclusive and complex. Finally, it is probable that some theories will apply to both less and more inclusive political units and it is possible that behavior at a more complex level of analysis can be "reduced" to behavior at a simpler one; that, however, is something that remains to be established rather than being a matter for postulation.

    For the present purpose, then, macropolitics is used to denote political study at a level where the most inclusive and complex systems of political interaction generally are found. At that level special problems of research and theory building may arise partly just because complexity is great, partly because of the very fact that particular kinds of decision structures are involved. However, the possibility that arguments in favor of case study at the level of polities may also apply, for similar reasons, at lesser, still highly complex, levels is not ruled out. The point argued is, in the most general terms, that the more inclusive and complex are units of political analysis, the stronger is the "practical" case for using case studies to test theories.

9.   Most of the objections were anticipated in the paper's preliminary version. For others, and some possibilities of answers, I am indebted to Philip Converse, Ronald Rogowski, and Sidney Verba.

10.   What constitutes a reasonable period of time for observations cannot be specified even in general terms. It depends on what one is studying and can generally be determined only by a combination of reasoning and reflection on findings as they turn up. The idea, needless to say, is to find time spans over which findings are unlikely to be significantly distorted by fortuitous short-term events. For example, in my discussion of the evaluation of political performance (Eckstein 1969), I argued, upon reasoning, that valid measures of performance require observations of polities over about a ten-year period, at the least. Gurr and McClelland (1971), in an empirical follow-up study, suggest, upon evidence, that a shorter time span might be serviceable for certain measures of performance.

REFERENCES

Almond, G. A., and J. S. Coleman, eds. (1960). *The Politics of the Developing Areas.* Princeton, N.J.: Princeton University Press.

Almond, G. A., and G. B. Powell, Jr. (1966). *Comparative Politics, A Developmental Approach.* Boston: Little, Brown.

Almond, G. A., and S. Verba (1963). *The Civic Culture.* Princeton, N.J.: Princeton University Press.

Apter, D. E. (1956). *The Gold Coast.* Princeton, N.J.: Princeton University Press.

———— (1961). *The Political Kingdom in Uganda.* Princeton, N.J.: Princeton University Press.

Banks, A. S., and R. B. Textor (1963). *A Cross-Polity Survey.* Cambridge, Mass.: The MIT Press.

Becker, H. S. (1968). "Social observation and case studies." *International Encyclopedia of the Social Sciences* 11:232–238.

Buchanan, J. M., and G. Tullock (1967). *The Calculus of Consent: Logical Foundations of Constitutional Democracy.* Ann Arbor: University of Michigan Press.

Curry, R. L., Jr., and L. L. Wade (1968). *A Theory of Political Exchange: Economic Reasoning in Political Analysis.* Englewood Cliffs, N.J.: Prentice-Hall.

Dahl, R. A. (1961). *Who Governs?* New Haven, Conn.: Yale University Press.

Dahl, R. A., ed. (1966). *Political Oppositions in Western Democracies.* New Haven, Conn.: Yale University Press.

Davidson, P. O., and C. G. Costello (1969). *N = 1: Experimental Studies of Single Cases.* New York: Van Nostrand Reinhold.

Dilthey, W. (1883). *Einleitung in die Geisteswissenschaften.* Leipzig.

Downs, A. (1957). *An Economic Theory of Democracy.* New York: Harper and Row.

Easton, D. (1965). *A Systems Analysis of Political Life.* New York: Wiley.

Eckstein, H. (1960). *Pressure Group Politics.* Stanford, Calif.: Stanford University Press.

—————— (1961). *The Theory of Stable Democracy.* Princeton, N.J.: Center of International Studies, Princeton University.

—————— (1964). *Internal War: Problems and Approaches.* New York: Free Press.

—————— (1965). "On the etiology of internal wars." *History and Theory* 4(2):133–163.

—————— (1969). "Authority relations and governmental performance." *Comparative Political Studies* 2:269–325.

Eckstein, H., and D. Apter, eds. (1963). *Comparative Politics: A Reader.* New York: The Free Press of Glencoe.

Finer, H. (1949). *The Theory and Practice of Modern Government.* Revised edition. New York: Holt.

Friedman, M. (1953). *Essays on Positive Economics.* Chicago: University of Chicago Press.

Friedrich, C. J. (1968). *Constitutional Government and Democracy.* Waltham, Mass.: Blaisdell.

Glaser, B. G., and A. L. Strauss (1967). *The Discovery of Grounded Theory, Strategies for Qualitative Research.* Chicago: Aldine.

Greenstein, F., and S. Tarrow (1971). *Political Orientations of Children: Semi-Projective Responses from Three Nations.* Beverly Hills, Calif.: Sage Professional Papers in Comparative Politics.

Gurr, T. R. (1970). *Why Men Rebel.* Princeton, N.J.: Princeton University Press.

Gurr, T. R., and M. McClelland (1971). *Political Performance: A Twelve-Nation Study.* Beverly Hills, Calif.: Sage Professional Papers in Comparative Politics.

Hempel, C. G. (1965). *Aspects of Scientific Explanation and Other Essays in the Philosophy of Science.* New York: Free Press.

Holt, R. R. (1962). "Individuality and generalization in the psychology of personality." *Journal of Personality* 30:377–404.

Holt, R. R., and J. M. Richardson, Jr. (1968). *The State of Theory in Comparative Politics.* Minneapolis, Minn.: Center for Comparative Studies in Technological Development and Social Change, University of Minnesota.

Hurewitz, L. (1971). "An index of democratic political stability." *Comparative Political Studies* 4(1):41–68.

Kaufmann, H. (1958). "The next step in case-studies." *Public Administration Review* 18:52–59.

Kemeny, J. G. (1959). *A Philosopher Looks at Science.* Princeton, N.J.: Van Nostrand.

Lipset, Seymour M., and Stein Rokkan (1967). *Party Systems and Voter Alignments.* New York: Free Press.

Lowi, T. H. (1964). "American business, public policy, case-studies, and political theory." *World Politics* 16(4):677–715.

Macridis, R. C., and B. C. Brown, eds. (1955). *Comparative Politics: Notes and Readings*. Homewood, Ill.: Dorsey Press.

Malinowski, B. (1926). *Crime and Custom in Savage Society*. New York: Harcourt, Brace, and World.

Merton, R. K. (1957). *Social Theory and Social Structure*. Glencoe, Ill.: Free Press.

Michels, R. (1962). *Political Parties: A Study of the Oligarchical Tendencies of Modern Democracy*. New York: Collier Books.

Newman, J. R., ed. (1963). *The Harper Encyclopedia of Science*. New York: Harper and Row.

Osgood, C. E., and Z. Luria (1954). "A blind analysis of a case of multiple personality using the semantic differential." *Journal of Abnormal and Social Psychology* 49:579–591.

Platt, J. R. (1966). *The Step to Man*. New York: Wiley.

Popper, K. R. (1959). *The Logic of Scientific Discovery*. London: Hutchinson.

Przeworski, A., and H. Teune (1970). *The Logic of Comparative Social Inquiry*. New York: Wiley.

Pye, L. (1962). *Politics, Personality, and Nation Building*. New Haven, Conn.: Yale University Press.

Pye, L., and S. Verba, eds. (1965). *Political Culture and Political Development*. Princeton, N.J.: Princeton University Press.

Rickert, H. (1899). *Kulturwissenschaft und Naturwissenschaft*. Freiburg.

Riker, W. H. (1962). *The Theory of Political Coalitions*. New Haven, Conn.: Yale University Press.

Riley, M. W. (1963). *Sociological Research: A Case Approach*. New York: Harcourt, Brace, and World.

Rogowski, R. (1969). *Social Structure and Stable Rule: A General Theory*. Princeton, N.J.: Princeton University, Center of International Studies, TR-3.

Rudolph, L. I., and S. H. Rudolph (1967). *The Modernity of Tradition: Political Development in India*. Chicago: Chicago University Press.

Singer, C. (1959). *A Short History of Scientific Ideas*. London: Oxford University Press.

Verba, S. (1967). "Some dilemmas in comparative research." *World Politics* 20:111–127.

Wallis, W. A., and H. V. Roberts (1962). *The Nature of Statistics*. New York: Free Press.

Weiner, M. (1975). *Party Politics in India*. Princeton, N.J.: Princeton University Press.

Whyte, W. F. (1943). *Street Corner Society: The Social Structure of an Italian Slum*. Chicago: Chicago University Press.

Willey, R. J. (1971). "Democracy in the West German trade unions: a reappraisal of the 'Iron Law.'" Beverly Hills, Calif.: Sage Professional Papers in Comparative Politics.

Windelband, W. (1894). *Geschichte und Naturwissenschaft*. Strassburg.

4

POLIMETRICS: ITS DESCRIPTIVE FOUNDATIONS

HAYWARD R. ALKER, JR.

Without a constant counterfeiting of the world by means of numbers, man could not live.

NIETZSCHE

INTRODUCTION

Political science in the 1970s finds itself with an embarrassment of statistical riches: substantial progress in the collection and quantification of data on political processes, a rapid expansion in the variety of statistical procedures already applied or potentially applicable to the analysis of political data, and a growing body of exemplary statistical studies combining professional standards of logical and empirical rigor with theoretical and practical relevances. The embarrassment comes from growing uncertainties in public and governmental support of the social sciences, continuing graduate student resistance to the advancing requirements of adequate statistical training, and a professional *methodenstreit* among behavioralists, postbehavioralists, and antibehavioralists that produces sharply contested associational elections, rival professional groupings, and a plethora of specialized, competing, or mutually noncomprehending journal-reading populations. The use and abuse of political quantification is frequently at issue in each of these arenas of controversy and debate.

As a contribution to these debates, this chapter raises the issue of the historical, philosophical, and scientific foundations of political statistics, especially its descriptive or measurement procedures. As a whole, at least in the North American and western European context,[1] political statistics (polimet-

---

This chapter derives from a research project on the analysis of complex political processes financed by grant GS-2429 from the National Science Foundation to the Center for International Studies, Massachusetts Institute of Technology. Its completion has been aided by NSF grant GS-41518 to the Department of Political Science, M.I.T. I am grateful for their support and for the continuing contributions to my understanding of statistical practices of many teachers, colleagues, friends, and students. An earlier version of this chapter was given to the VIIIth World Congress of the International Political Science Association, Munich, 1970.

rics) can be shown to have at least two other important branches: one dealing with probabilistic estimation and explanatory inference, the other dealing with the invention and evaluation of policy or system alternatives. In practice, descriptions are interpenetrated by explanations and evaluations. Nonetheless, because current debates and most statistics courses usually begin with the problem of metricization, I shall here give detailed consideration only to descriptive statistics, including heuristic, interpretive, and representational statistical practices.[2]

The present chapter is not a substitute for a statistics course or the related materials provided by Zinnes (1975)—at least one semester of social statistics will be assumed. For many with such a background, the material covered will be relatively novel. But such novelty is not for its own sake: This chapter is designed to help political statisticians to be more critically and creatively aware of the possibilities and limitations of measurement procedures. And I here acknowledge a larger purpose, that of enriching the analytical tools we can use to make qualitative and quantitative political descriptions.

A further presupposition of the present chapter is that the reader has read and mastered Moon's impressive chapter in Volume 1 of this *Handbook* reviewing naturalistic (positivistic) and humanistic (hermeneutic) interests underlying recent debates about quantification and the logic of political inquiry (Moon, 1975). Many of the philosophical terms used here are carefully defined there. Indeed Moon's chapter has played a major role in suggesting a set of questions concerning the proper analysis of often consciously purposive, intentional human actions within hopefully cumulative scientific research programs. The examples of descriptive statistics given below are all chosen to be doubly relevant to both naturalistic and hermeneutic concerns. I shall conclude that doubly relevant but rarely used descriptive procedures do exist, or are being created: intentionally interpretive descriptive procedures that point toward valid explanations and perhaps even appropriate remedial actions.

Their applications raise many issues about adequate explanations and evaluations, however, when autonomous, conscious, consensually described intentional action cannot automatically be assumed. Adequate causal analysis in such cases often challenges intentionalist rationalizations or suggests unconscious interests and intentions. But work reviewed here and elsewhere (Alker, 1974a) suggests that many causal (or "structural") modelling successes need to be reinterpreted as providing less than universally valid nomic explanations. Depending on the adequacy of their specificational and *ceteris paribus* assumptions, structural models may even be useful as partial outlines for interpreting or manipulating, within limits, relatively invariant, but multilevel sociopolitical action systems. How then should we join political action with descriptive, interpretive, evaluative, and explanatory statistics? Answering this question is a task left to the reader.

AN OVERVIEW OF POLIMETRICS

Before intensively reviewing descriptive procedures, I will provide an overview of political statistics as a whole, including an introduction to the foundations of particular techniques: statistical practices, statistical traditions, and research programs (paradigms).

The Origins of Statistics

Even the briefest survey of the origins of modern statistics shows a mixture of motivating interests and situations. Most surprising for those new to the subject is the political focus of the earliest statistical writers. Thus Lazarsfeld (1961) notes that two seventeenth-century roots of modern statistics were William Petty's "political arithmetic" and Hermann Conring's "university statistics." Petty's *Political Anatomy of Ireland* (1971; first published in 1672) accepted Bacon's analogy between the natural body and the "body politic," going on to argue that the "arts of preserving both in health and strength" had their best foundation in the empirical study of corresponding anatomies. As Lazarsfeld (1961) argues further, Petty searched for causal relationships between quantitative variables because of Baconian empiricism, the rational spirit of British capitalism, the need in major states for an abstract predictive basis for public administration, and the mercantilist's belief that size of population was a crucial factor in the power and wealth of the state. Here we see a strong emphasis on positivist, naturalistic, and practical interests as well as suggestive links with a sociopolitical context.

Living amidst 300 small German principalities shortly after the Thirty Years War, Conring and the original university statisticians had practical and interpretive interests: civil reconstruction and survival in a confusing, precarious, and changing international system. Yet important commonalities existed with their English counterparts. As one of Conring's successors was to say in an eighteenth-century work:

> . . . that branch of political knowledge, which has for its object the actual and relative powers of the several modern [European] states, the power arising from their natural advantages, the industry and civilization of their inhabitants and the wisdom of their governments, has been formed . . . — into a separate science . . . distinguished by the new-coined name of *statistics*. (E. A. W. Zimmermann, as quoted in Yule and Kendall, 1958)

Treating the state as his unit of analysis, Conring derived largely qualitative categories of comparative description, interpretation, and prescription from within a teleological Aristotelian framework of causation. As summarized in Alker (1970, p. 246), "Classification of states in terms of their 'formal causes'— their constitutions and laws—were presented along with descriptions of 'material causes', such as economic and demographic resources. More important from the statesmen's view . . . were the 'final causes' or goals of states and their 'efficient causes'—various elite activities, including informal administrative practices." Here a more purposive and humanistic concept of causality (Moon might say "quasi-causality") links statistics with the qualitative Aristotelian ancestors of contemporary hermeneutic thought. Power considerations are again evident.

Thus we find that "statistics," etymologically "the study of states," has its origins not in abstract mathematics or natural science, but in two causally oriented, proto-scientific, data-based traditions of political analysis, one inductive and positivist, the other more hermeneutic and teleological. Both were decision-oriented. Practical problems were Eurocentric, aggregate versions of modern policy analysis, but often defined in medical terms. Rephrasing Lasswell (1975) or Moon (1975), and maintaining the broad focus of early statistical work on alternate forms of political organization, we can describe these problems as the search for (1) insightful data-based descriptions of political actors, including contextual interpretations of their purposes, structures, and processes; (2) appropriate causal inferences allowing both explanations and conjectural anticipations; and (3) appropriate normative appraisals or policy recommendations. At this point, the extent to which advanced statistical practices will continue to be linked to the interests of the most industrially advanced states must remain an open question.

Modern Statistics and Polimetrics

As a professional discipline, statistics has evolved well beyond its original political subject matter. It now has an elaborate and abstract theoretical basis and numerous ancillary fields of application, linking this base to the problems and data of different substantive disciplines in the natural, engineering, and social sciences.

How could we describe the modern branches of the subject? Commenting on a famous reconceptualization of the central field by Mosteller and Tukey (1968), Raiffa (1968) has presented a tripartite characterization of statistics in terms of its purposes: practical decision, scientific inference, and data analysis. Splitting the last set of practices into interpretive and descriptive subbranches (see Fig. 1), I accept these categories but amend their significance better to fit the tripartite historically derived definition of the previous section. Like Raiffa and the classical statisticians, I assume these to be complementary, nonexclusive concerns. Many of the specific illustrations at the bottom of Fig. 1 will be further discussed below.

Statistical procedures leading to the choice of practical social actions or policies in terms of their more general normative appeal and/or their evaluated consequences are most frequently taught in political philosophy, political ethics, or operations research courses, in business schools or public policy programs. When consequences are evaluated, utilities or loss functions are often defined and calculated to assess practical actions, usually in uncertain situations. The leftmost branch of Fig. 1 clusters these concerns, further distinguishing Bayesian and non-Bayesian approaches. Like benefit-cost analysis, Bayesian inference procedures are currently used ways for a decisionmaker to calculate the effects of new evidence on what he already believes about the probabilities of certain future outcomes. Concrete proposals justified in terms of individual needs or collective welfare (Kramer and Hertzberg, Chapter 7 of this volume) may even invoke some normative version of the Aristotelian practical syllogism, as discussed by Von Wright (1971) and Moon (1975). Clearly this normative branch of the field corresponds in important ways to classical statistics.

The second branch of the field, which might be called "inferential statistics," has as its most significant contributor Ronald Fisher. He is most likely to be known to social scientists for his development of inductive, often experimental procedures for generating useful scientific knowledge (e.g., testing hypotheses concerning the yields of different seed–fertilizer combinations using analysis of variance designs and associated statistical significance levels: these of course tell us the probabilities of rejecting a null hypothesis). In a predictive mode the calculation of point estimates and confidence interval elaborates on a very similar logic. Most political scientists trained in the 1950s or early 1960s used textbooks like Blalock's (1960) that treated regression analyses in just this fashion. An additional refinement is due to Neyman and Pearson, who complemented Fisherian statistics by codifying procedures for calculating probabilities of a second type of inferential error: failing to reject a false null hypothesis. Such considerations clearly help the biometrician called on to recommend one seed over another, even though the Neyman–Pearson approach does not assign subjective probabilities and utilities to various possible states of nature. Alker (1965, Appendix) gives a decision-oriented example using type I and type II errors.

Looking further down the middle branch of the figure, we see other important distinctions accepted by inferential statisticians, but only gradually coming into use among polimetricians. A powerful general standard violated by significance tests and confidence intervals is the Likelihood Principle. "This principle asserts that any information about an experiment [or nonexperimental inferential data analysis] and its outcome over and above the likelihood function is irrelevant for inferences or decisions about the population parameter" (Raiffa, 1968, p. 286). Likelihood functions give probabilities for observed sample/ experimental results conditional on the values of underlying population parameters. Occasionally psychometric, econometric, or "covariance structure" estimation of such parameters proceeds by maximizing the likelihood function, rather than the sometimes equivalent procedure of minimizing squared errors. Observed outcomes are assumed to be those most likely to occur given the true likelihood function. Bayesian analysts accept likelihood summaries of experimental outcomes, and use them to modify their prior beliefs, *expressed in subjective probability terms,* about true population parameters.

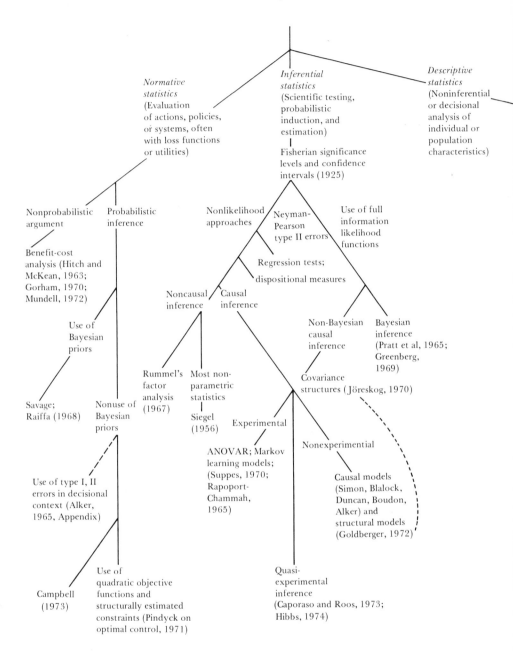

Fig. 1. An evolutionary picture of contemporary statistical practices. This figure is inspired by Raiffa (1968), but is quite different in detail. Neither the branching options, nor the antecedent connections, nor the social sciences applications are intended to be completely exclusive or exhaustive.

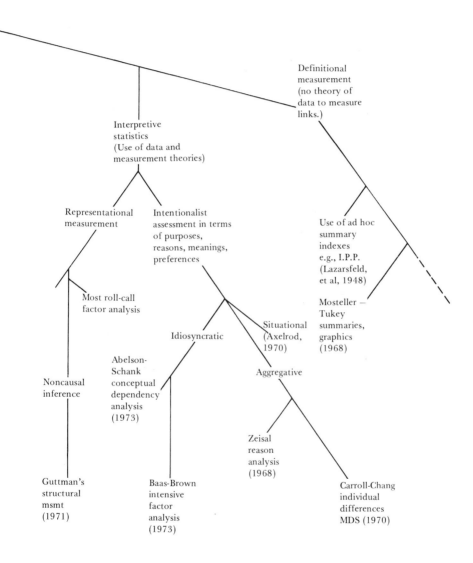

Definitional
measurement
(no theory of
data to measure
links.)

Interpretive
statistics
(Use of data and
measurement theories)

Representational
measurement

Intentionalist
assessment in terms
of purposes,
reasons, meanings,
preferences

Use of ad hoc
summary
indexes
e.g., I.P.P.
(Lazarsfeld,
et al, 1948)

Most roll-call
factor analysis

Idiosyncratic

Situational
(Axelrod,
1970)

Mosteller —
Tukey
summaries,
graphics
(1968)

Noncausal
inference

Abelson-
Schank
conceptual
dependency
analysis
(1973)

Aggregative

Guttman's
structural
msmt
(1971)

Baas-Brown
intensive
factor
analysis
(1973)

Zeisal
reason
analysis
(1968)

Carroll-Chang
individual
differences
MDS (1970)

In the 1960s, North American political science discovered causal inference practices using experimental or quasi-experimental controls, or their non-experimental analog—systems of simultaneously valid regression equations. The key epistemological ideal was the search for equations with manipulative, politically *productive* significance. Miller and Stokes (1963), Blalock (1964), Alker (1966a), Duncan (1966), and Campbell and Stanley (1963) helped spark a flurry of innovative practices, which in retrospect may be seen as largely remedial efforts at catching up with methodological developments in biometrics, psychometrics, and econometrics. Concurrently, some inferential procedures, such as Rummel's use of factor analysis (1967), flourished in noncausal terms. (I shall suggest below that these practices are often misguided in their specificational assumptions.)

As a third branch of statistics, descriptive statistics might also be called "population statistics." Raiffa (1968) too narrowly calls it "data analysis." It focuses on data from a given population—for example, the German principalities—and tries to describe, summarize, insightfully picture, or make interpretetive sense out of them. Mosteller and Tukey's (1968) eyecatching uses of novel graph papers and logit-like transformations are influential instances of what I call "definitional measurement." I will argue below that humanistic, interpretive, intentionalist concerns are also clearly at work in many currently available descriptive statistical procedures. Zeisel's (1968) reason analysis is an example; much of Louis Guttman's school of interpretive data analysis is also directed at elucidating reasons for, as well as causes of, human choices. Game-theoretic approaches to utility measurement (Luce and Suppes, 1965), liberal and Marxian treatments of welfare assessment (Mundel, 1971; Brody, 1970), and Axelrod's situationally oriented conflict of interest analysis (1970) also appear to be intentionalist in orientation. More modern, intentionalist, content analytic coding schemes [for example, Abelson–Schank (1973) conceptual dependency analysis] rely on linguistic near-universals in trying to understand individual differences in political beliefs and behavior.

We shall return again to the ways in which political analysis relates to these major branches of statistical analysis. For now we note that not even a good name exists for the field we want to describe: "Statistics" is no longer an adequate label for it. (Nor does the field of political science have a journal closely corresponding to *Psychometrika, Econometrica, Sociometry* or *Technometrics*.) "Polimetrics" has been used by Alker (1970) and the International Studies Association, using the Greek roots *polis* (the Greek city-state) and *metrikos* (measured) in a construction such as *psyche + ometrics*. Others prefer "politometrics" (derived from *politea,* the Greek citizen, and *ometrics*), or "politimetrics" (Gurr, 1972) as constructions analogous to econometrics (*oikonomos,* Greek for household steward, and *ometrics*). Such phrasing may also connote the principles as well as the practices of measurement. Classical statistics did, however, focus more on the state than on the citizen, and "polimetrics" is a more literal substitute for what we now describe as "political statistics," so we shall use it here. A definition for "polimetrics" that paraphrases *Webster's Third New International Dictionary* on modern econometrics seems suitable in both a classical and a modern sense: polimetrics is the application of mathematical forms and statistical techniques [or procedures] to [the qualitative labelling and quantitative metricizing of possibly observable] political phenomena, the scientific testing of political theories, and the solution of present and future political problems. Note the implicit trichotomy of tasks reminiscent of Lazarsfeld, Lasswell (1975), and Fig. 1. And compare Kramer and Hertzberg (Chapter 7 of this volume) for a compatible conception of formal theorizing in political science.

Statistical Practices, Research Paradigms, and Methodological Controversies

Under the impetus of naturalistic philosophies of scientific practice, the major accomplishment of statistical research and training has been the development, justification, and application of procedurally describable, more or less intersubjectively replicable and objectively valid techniques of statistical analysis. The associated interest in "operational" research has led to the increased use of explicit coding rules for data generation and reproducible, often theory-based procedures for normative, inferential, or descriptive data analysis. Statistical procedures have increasingly been formalized into computer programs (themselves sometime called "procedures") for data definition and analysis. Characterizing such statistical *techniques* as research *procedures* helps highlight action sequences, contingencies, and alternatives associated with the researcher's use of more complex statistical techniques. It also makes more explicit the use of and need for contextual, epistemological, and methodological bases for motivating or justifying the choices thus delimited.

To argue for or against a particular technique (or procedure) *in general* is absurd. Its use may or may not be justified, depending on the purposes of the investigation and on the circumstances. Foundationally, statistical procedures are grounded in statistical practices and statistical traditions. The *internal* test of appropriateness should be made in terms of methodological standards of logico-empirical rigor and problem relevance adhered to by the investigator and/or his copractitioners. These are extremely important parts of larger, evolving traditions of statistical practice surrounding the use of particular techniques. Procedural representations of techniques should also help us see where and how intrinsically preferable alternate practices might be defined and implemented.

But surely methodological or epistemological controversies can go deeper than this. One may proceed further *externally* to criticize statistical practices in terms of (1) different statistical traditions, e.g., Raiffa's Bayesian perspective (1968); (2) the associated research problem-defining substantive research program (see Kuhn, 1970a,b; Lakatos, 1970; and Alker, 1973b); or even (3) the sponsorship/application context (e.g., Horowitz, 1967). This latter type of criticism is often in terms of the social and political interests, advocated by the investigators or inherent in the research situation itself, that are benefitting from, and encouraging, sustaining, opposing, or suppressing the use of a particular technique such as macrosystem computer simulation or benefit-cost analysis. External philosophical attacks on metascientific conceptualizations, including the data-theoretical assumptions and problems definitions inherent in a statistical procedure are also often attempted, but only rarely successful because of the practitioner's deep commitments to internal standards, which should in part be self-correcting of their practices.

Whether the argument is internal or external, criticism can and should be relevant to *statistical practices:* one or more *investigators* with metascientific *conceptual (including epistemological) orientations* trying to solve differently motivated *research problems* in particular *contexts* by applying data generation and analysis *procedures* to (possibly) observable *phenomena*. This is accomplished according to professionally shared *methodological standards* of logico-empirical rigor and problem relevance, with various *results*. Without this perspective on the foundations of statistical techniques, issues are rarely joined, and preferable relevant procedures, if any can exist, are not well conceptualized.

As the distinction between internal and external criticisms makes clear, we need additional process-oriented concepts to describe the intersection and overlap between substantive research activities and statistical practices. Substantively oriented statistics may be multipurpose (appearing in several branches of Fig. 1), or context-assumption-purpose specific (a subbranch of that figure). My preference is to use two broad notions: traditions of statistical practice on the one hand, and substantive research paradigms on the other. By a tradition of statistical practice I mean a naturally occurring, coherent, relatively large and enduring cluster of statistical practices. One cannot understand the current richness of polimetric practices, or begin to elaborate *internal* criticisms of their procedures without being aware of the different purposes and standards of statistical analysis that are suggested by Fig. 1. Benefit-cost analysis, Bayesian analysis, causal modeling, and quasi-experimental analysis are surely statistical "traditions" with overlapping but distinct purposes and standards.

As indicated by the "evolutionary" description of post-Fisherian developments in Fig. 1, there have been considerable changes in the motivating purposes and guiding standards applied to the formulation, reformulation, and application of statistical procedures. Yet some coherent patterns and trends emerge. The growing awareness of subjective beliefs, decisional uncertainties, and implementational costs in making practical and theoretical choices is one such trend identified with the Bayesian tradition. So too is the spread of causal inference, and the increasing popularity in some traditions of compatibility with the maximum-likelihood, full-information estimation ideal, which wants inferences from data based on all the information they provide codified in hypothesis-specific terms. I might even suggest the possibility of an emerging intentionalist tradition in that branch of descriptive statistics I have called interpretive statistics. Major differentiations in the practices of content analysis, factor analysis, and regression analysis make it less clear that traditions can be holistically defined in terms of these methods or techniques. An awareness of such developments, and their more careful description, is important for any assessment of polimetric practices themselves, as well as of their potential impacts on substantive research.

Table 1 compares the notion of a tradition of statistical practice with an analogous, more substantively oriented concept, that of an empirical "research paradigm" (Lakatos prefers the term "research program," meaning the rational reconstruction of a research paradigm or tradition) and its associated disciplinary community or paradigm complex. My multifaceted definition of a research paradigm in Table 1 is based primarily on a partial synthesis in Alker (1973b) of Kuhn's (1970b) much discussed notion of paradigms and Lakatos' influential, anti-Kuhnian description of "The Methodology of Scientific Research Programs" (1970), both reviewed by Moon (1975). My assumption is that growing and decaying research paradigms based on series of more or less exemplary research problem solutions do exist in some areas of political science, and that they embody different metascientific beliefs and values. Both substantive research paradigms and statistical traditions suggest analytically respectable, external epistemological and methodological grounds for criticizing and defending different polimetric practices. When successfully developed, these practices may in turn be used to criticize substantive research paradigms and provide new alternatives to hoary statistical traditions.

As summarized in Table 1, substantive research paradigms differ from statistical practices and more nearly comparable statistical traditions in several major respects. First of all, statistical traditions and ongoing research paradigms are necessarily institutionalized in disciplinary communities, while statistical practices, as we have defined them, are not. The multidisciplinary sources/ applications of statistical traditions and the inherent abstractions of their formal generalizations suggest a clearer, more tolerant pluralism of statistical traditions than we might expect of a tightly integrated, content specific and technically monopolistic research paradigm complex. Moreover, the institutionalization of the statistics profession, given its structure of associated fields, has helped to improve standards of statistical practice, which have in turn had interdisciplinary integrative methodological impacts in the social sciences above, beyond, and through the operations of narrower research paradigm complexes.

A second major difference between research paradigms and traditions of statistical practice is the substantive focus of the former in contrast to the methodological directions of the latter. As we have defined them, research paradigms are empirically oriented, even if value-based and heuristically guided. They include the scientific commitment to describe, explore, interpret, predict, and perhaps change Nature. The statistical practices shown in Fig. 1, on the other hand,

TABLE 1   Correspondences between research paradigm complexes and traditions of statistical practice

Elements of a research paradigm complex	Elements of a statistical tradition (compared to corresponding elements to the left)
1. Metascientific beliefs and values	1. Metascientific beliefs and values
a) metaphysical paradigms, nonfalsifiable "cores" protected by negative heuristics, ontologies	+*a) Such "cores" may exclude model classes and delimit *ceteris paribus* strategies. They differ in fields such as econometrics, biometrics, polimetrics.
b) research-related value commitments, and epistemological standards, including policy interests	+ b) Statistical traditions, like benefit-cost analysis, have normative interests that may be more explicit than those of empirical research paradims.
c) paradigm schemas, problem definitions, question sets	+ c) Problem definitions in statistics have roughly followed the distinctions shown in Fig. 1. Abstraction has decreased specific contents.
2. Originating exemplars and positive heuristics	2. Originating exemplars and positive heuristics
a) applications of analogues or preoperational mechanistic models in a problematic context	a) Note the naturalistic and hermeneutic origins of various statistical practices.
b) technical exemplars including experimental devices, mathematical manipulations, and statistical procedures	+ b) Data generation designs plus associated analytical procedures, e.g., Fisher's analysis of variance or D. T. Campbell's quasi-experimental design and analysis strategies fit here.
c) positive heuristics of model development	c) Such heuristics are often part of a tradition, never of a single practice (e.g., allowable complications with Markov or general linear models).
d) original evidence of exemplar success	d) This evidence is orignally part of a substantive field, but influential in a residual way upon more abstract statistical training.
3. Symbolic generalizations	3. Symbolic generalizations
a) ideal types or constructs	+ a) These include, for example, causal path diagrams, and multivariate normal error distributions. These and the tautologies in 3b and 3c below have effects independent of their content, describable as "model platonism."
b) quasi-tautological symbolic laws	+ b) Since many statistical procedures are completely formalized, these laws, whether general linear model or variance decomposition theorems, are strict tautologies. Interpretive practices are often important as in the assumption of random errors in the general linear model, and the identification of "dependent" variables as caused effects, etc.

c) preliminary or revised theoretical specifications of exemplars

4. A cumulative literature, based on exemplars, mediated through symbolic generalizations
   a) new evidence from new contexts of descriptive and explanatory success of possibly updated exemplars (2a, 2b) and applied positive heuristics
   b) new data discoveries; changing and usually tougher standards; corroborated auxiliary measurement theories
   c) a linearized literature of successful puzzle solutions
   d) a renewed list of phenomena seen as puzzles and anomalies worth trying to explain by those trained in an exemplary way of seeing

5. A scholarly community sharing the research paradigm (1–5 above), normally universal, and tending to be monopolistic

6. The research situation of a scholarly community may be divided into the following:
   a) The immediate or past research contexts, as in 2a:
   b) associated sponsorship/application contexts (Kuhn and Lakatos, but not most radical critics, treat this as extrinsic to the paradigm complex)

+ c) Probabilistic models are frequently used as hypothetical specifications in statistical practice; sometimes, as with Guttman's work, error probability assumptions are not made explicit because of a rejection of associated epistemological arguments.

4. A cumulative literature, based on exemplars, mediated through symbolic generalizations
+ a) Any statistical practice generates a record of at least one or more successes or failures of application associated with it.
+ b) Measurement theories are part of most statistical practices. Standards are basis of most statistical "theory." Auxiliary theories informing intentional coding practices or conflict of interest axiomatizations are good examples.
   c) Statistical textbooks apply traditional standards to increasingly rich, abstract model formulations and data analysis procedures.
+ d) Phenomena come from substantive fields and their problems, but statistical training does generate ways of seeing and subsequent puzzles and anomalies (e.g., where's the causal model?).

+ 5. Trained statisticians are usually more professionally eclectic, given their multitradition training. Technique practitioners thus may or may not constitute a larger, natural community: Bayesians probably do, while factor analysts do not.

6. These are most influential in statistical traditions given statisticians' explicit evaluative roles.
+ a) the current context may be substantively and methodologically significant.
   b) The same debates apply to statistical practices.

---

* + means a definitional characteristic of a novel or a nonoriginal statistical practice.

are methodologically normative in character. With respect to social practices, they argue how scholarly practices should be carried out in a wide variety of evaluative, inferential, and descriptive contexts. This is not to argue that empirical research practices exclude methodological aspects; nor is it to deny that some evaluative statistical procedures have strong empirical bases to them. It is to suggest that statistical practices can constructively or destructively affect one or many more empirically focused research paradigms.

The choice of descriptive polimetric procedures, based upon particular statistical practices and traditions, as the unit of subsequent expositional discussions and critiques means that intrinsic review standards will be emphasized. But I do not intend to ignore the metascientific beliefs and values that clearly inform problem definitions from various substantive traditions of social research and that also help to distinguish among the broader statistical traditions suggested above. Rather, I shall assume from the start that the metascientific and pretheoretical aspects of various substantively oriented political research traditions—or more tightly integrated and focused research paradigms—should be influential in shaping statistical practices within various branches of polimetrics. The process of shaping statistical practices to substantive concerns need not always be traumatic, given historical similarities of concern in political and statistical analysis. Neither should it be a totally insular and one-sided affair, for polimetric practices should be influenced by developments in statistics as well. Certain statistical research traditions (for example, ideological content analysis, the factor analysis of voting data, and cross-national causal modeling) have been quietly and beneficially revolutionized by the impact of external technical exemplars (e.g., computerized nonmetric multivariate analysis, the semantic coding procedures emanating from Chomsky's work on transformational grammars, and the development of simultaneous equation time-series estimation procedures).

When we come externally to criticize (and defend) certain statistical practices, the role of political research paradigms or programs should become clear. Take, for example, the notions of positive and negative heuristics attributed by Lakatos (1970) to any evolving or degenerating research program. As implied in Table I, positive heuristics indicate which paths of research to pursue, including sequences of increasingly complex model specifications that, it is assumed, will give better empirical fits as they are deployed. Negative heuristics suggest which components of a research paradigm should be assumed nonfalsifiable or not directly testable. And they suggest the extent to which certain research paths, including outstanding anomalies and model classes should, at least temporarily, be ignored. Accepting this view means that the kind of statistical practices we adopt must accord with the substantive commitment expressed by the research program.

For example, certain kinds of oversimplified "model platonism" inform both multidimensional scaling approaches and Markovian statistical treatments of sequential Prisoner's Dilemma games. These suggest "natural" complication strategies: the introduction of higher order dimensions or processes rather than fundamentally different cognitively oriented specifications. Behavioristic theorists, with naturalistic notions of scientific philosophy, often defended such heuristics methodologically and substantively. Only recently, with the emergence of richer alternative specifications and the persistence of unexplained phenomena, have these anomalies been attended to in a less behavioristic way. Without some notion comparable to such metascientific heuristics and their associated "model platonisms," it is not possible to make sense of Lakatos' (1970, p. 119) remarkable, yet well-documented claim: "no experiment, experimental report, observation statement or well-corroborated low-level falsifying hypothesis alone can lead to falsification. There is no falsification before the emergence of a better theory."

A Preview Example: Factor Analyses of Cross-National Data

To sketch in more detail the type of critical arguments this chapter will make by using the above concepts, let us consider a well-known but very loose cluster of statistical practices: factor analysis.

Referring allegorically to Tom Swift and his theory-inventing factor analysis machine, Armstrong (1967) has castigated Raymond Cattell and his followers in social science, e.g. Rummel (1970), for a defective descriptive practice, that is, for mindlessly attempting heuristically to discover theories using inappropriate statistical techniques. From a different perspective, Wolin (1969) has attacked quantitative "methodism" in general and factor analysis studies in particular, charging that such statistical practices are dehumanizing, normatively irrelevant, and atheoretical. Later in this discussion I will show how factor analysis can be used for the *intensive* Lasswellian analysis of unconscious interpretive frameworks, clearly a "humanistic" and "theoretical" concern. For now I will only elaborate on these criticisms, showing how they depend on standards that are internal to this particular descriptive practice, and on criteria that are, in some respects, external to it.

More precisely, Armstrong's criticism is partly an internal one couched in terms of an evolving inferential statistical tradition (partly subscribed to by Cattell), which is generally critical of inductive statistical techniques. Restated and expanded, Armstrong's arguments are developed along the following lines. Because the psychological and cross-national phenomena being analyzed by Cattell and his followers have *not* been carefully described (i.e., theoretically conceptualized), the use of Cattell's orthogonal varimax factor analysis procedure is a kind of "phenomena-disregarding" model platonism. It is unlikely to produce valid inferences or even valuable insights. If the investigator's problem is to find meaningful descriptive dimensions and associated measurements of cultural or behavioral variation in his data, he needs additional arguments concerning political phenomena to justify his assumptions about the linear, uncorrelated, dimensional nature of underlying factors and his procedures for extracting only those factors with variances greater than that of a single variable in the original data matrix.

Moreover, if the investigator's problem is one of inferring causally valid measurements, he should be able to justify the assumption, inherent in the use of factor analysis for causal inference purposes, that the phenomena he has observed and measured are not themselves causally related, but linearly, causally dependent on underlying, uncorrelated causal factors.

Given that Cattell subscribes to the standard of empirically replicable and validated measurements, this criticism is internal to Cattell's tradition of dispositional measurement (noted in Fig. 1). Armstrong's criticism is in fact a counterargument to one made by Cattell and Dickman (1962), who were arguing *for* the heuristic utility, if not the inductive validity, of scientific measurements derived through factor analysis. Other users of factor analysis often do not even try to make such arguments and could be internally criticized in terms of this tradition, but Cattell has also developed and occasionally used procedures such as Ahmavaara's (1957) for inferentially *testing* prior factor-specific hypotheses.

Despite Armstrong's catchy title, it should be emphasized that both Armstrong and Cattell are part of a broader Fisherian statistical tradition that takes very seriously the question: How do we make reliable and valid empirical measures? With the emergence of such multi-equation statistical procedures as psychometric factor analysis, biometric path analysis, and simultaneous equation econometrics, the classical inferential tradition of statistics has come to recognize a prior principle or standard in terms of which the inductive, heuristically oriented factor analysis tradition is gradually but revolutionarily being transformed. Valid measurement, like hypothesis testing or explanation, requires that data-theoretic specifications be overidentified (hence, falsifiable) and successfully corroborated, or at least exactly identified and specificationally noncontroversial. When its data-theoretic assumptions (including simply structural rotations and linear orthogonal factors) are not *a priori* unproblematic (according to some Platonistic negative heuristic that fewer and fewer psychometricians are willing to accept), factor models are underidentified.

This criticism can be made very specific in the problem context of trying to understand and explain the phenomena of the United Nations votes (the V_{1i}, V_{2i} indicated for Nation i in Fig. 2). Much previous research (e.g., Alker, 1964) has tried to accomplish this in terms of underlying conflict factors or predispositions (F_{1i} and F_{2i} in Fig. 2), themselves causally dependent on environmental determinants such as aid, alliances, and levels of development (X_{1i}, X_{2i}, X_{3i} in Fig. 2).

For example, votes on operations in the Congo apparently avoided typical Cold War predispositions (F_{3i}, not shown in Fig. 2), but reflected more heavily self-determination and United Nations supranationalism predispositions (F_{1i}, F_{2i}), which are in turn responsive to such environmental determinants as levels

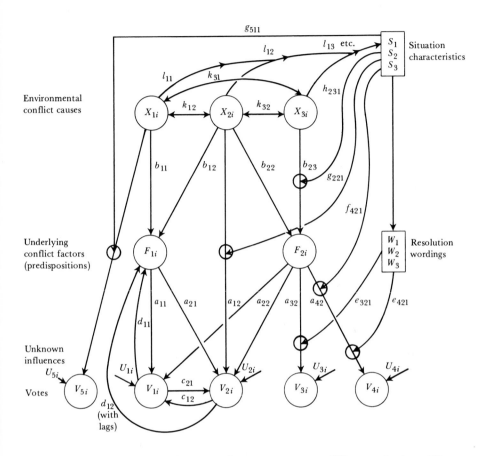

Fig. 2. Some possible causal connections among votes (V), vote factors (F), un-known influences (U), subjectively interpreted situational characteristics (S), resolution wordings (W), and environmental determinants (X) in the United Nations General Assembly for a hypothetical country i. Simple arrows represent direct causal relations. Exogenously correlated variables are represented by double-headed arrows. Time lags in causal chains are not precisely specified. Each type of coefficient is given a different letter. Thus factor loadings are a's with dependent variables first in their subscripts; b's link factors to their environmental determinants; c's refer to vote trading effects; d's indicate modifications in basic predispositions due to vote commitments; e's suggest multiplicative effects of resolution wordings on factors affecting particular votes; f's measure how situations similarly enhance or diminish factors affecting particular votes; etc. (Adapted from H. R. Alker, Jr., 1974b).

of development, economic links to the West, etc. The ordinary factor model, like the regression equation approach originally used to measure environmental effects, assumes both universally valid, additive causal effects (the a and b coefficients of Fig. 2) and independent causal impacts (no k correlations or X_{2i}'s making some of the F's correlated).

The study of the Congo case, as it evolved through time, makes one skeptical about such simplifications (see Alker, 1966b, 1971a, 1974b). Relevant examples could be adduced to suggest a whole world of nonuniversal, often non-additive situational (f, g, h) effects, symbolic maneuvering (the e's), diplomatic vote trading (the c's), and learning or feedback relationships (the d's and l's). Thus, the unknown influences (the U's of Fig. 2) cannot, with adequate causal justification, be assumed to account only for independent, additive factors with variances below unity. That is, there are more distinct parameters to estimate than there are independent constraints to be used in identifying them even with a great amount of data. Thus an infinite set of measurement results can result. The realization of this problem by such social statisticians as Blalock, Cattell, Rummel, and Alker has led them to devise ad hoc procedures for replicating and validating certain factor analytic specificational assumptions, while assuming others.

A major technical breakthrough in this regard has been Jöreskog's development (1969, 1970) of computable maximum likelihood *confirmatory* factor analysis *procedures*. This concept is based on earlier work that placed factor analysis within the inferential, likelihood-based statistical tradition (Lawley and Maxwell, 1963). This procedure, for those skilled enough to understand the structural modeling tradition, allows the *testing* of prior specifications or theoretical hypotheses about patterns of variable-factor correlation (loadings), the number of statistically significant factors, and the degree of interfactor correlation. Linear factor relationships and simple (causal) relations *from* factors *to* variables are still assumed; even higher order "factors underlying factors" are allowed! Despite this Leibnitzian metaphysics, interesting higher order factors have been discovered on occasion using a similar data-theoretic logic, as reported in Rummel (1970, ch. 18). The more liberating awareness generated by such psychometricians as Guttman (1954), Lord and Novick (1968), and Shepherd, Romney, and Nerlove (1972) is that a wide range of differently specified, overidentified data theories and models exist for relating observed phenomena to underlying, unobserved measurement categories or dimensions. None of them is in principle more platonically applicable than any other. Unless model platonisms clearly correspond to substantive heuristics within empirically progressive research programs, their validity must be suspect.

Wolin's (1969) critique of the methodist literature touches the problem of underspecification, but emphasizes larger extrinsic issues, some going back to the split between the two roots of modern statistics and beyond. Without claiming to represent his views exactly, and without repeating his hermeneutic critique of behaviorism, it would appear appropriate that I offer several related arguments. Training graduate students intensively in multivariate quantitative methods such as factor analysis makes less time available for developing a sophisticated awareness of what has classically been thought and said about political life. This latter type of education is quite pertinent to empirical theory specification and to the imaginative construction and critical, prequantitative evaluation of policy and system alternatives. Unfortunately these important problems of political analysis are those least well developed in contemporary polimetric practice. Thus modern training is particularly inappropriate for understanding modern politics in which many questions about systems restructuring are continually raised.

Nonetheless, statistical approaches need not ignore the intentional, occasionally revolutionary character of political phenomena. As I pointed out previously, there is a distinction between the British empiricists' lawlike causal explanations and the German statisticians' more teleological and Aristotelian notions of qualitative causal interpretation. Revivified, this latter statistical root may have much to say about such phenomena.

No doubt, part of the "inhumaneness" of many statistical techniques is their gross oversimplification of human behavior. Moreover, in those contexts in which human intentionality provides rich and varying meaning structures for political actions, this explains the unreliability and invalidity of such techniques. Content analysis research, ably reviewed by Holsti (1968), acknowledges the focal role of such intentionality, but it homogenizes meaning structures in its aggregative, coding, and factor analytic procedures. Further factor analytic and multidimensional scaling improvements (Alker, 1970; Brown, 1974; Carroll and Chang, 1970) dehomogenized meaning structures, allowing for the intensive study of particular nations or individuals. Thus some relevant progress in polimetric practice has slowly been made, but it falls short of Wolin's goals.

In subsequent sections of this chapter I will show that these methodological issues arise in the context of other descriptive statistical procedures—issues rooted in the application of both internal and external standards to particular polimetric practices. And I will be most concerned with showing that polimetrics can profit from the external criticisms directed at its procedures from a "humanist" point of view, by developing techniques that more adequately capture the rich structures of meaning and intentionality so central to political life.

REPRESENTATIONAL MEASUREMENT PROCEDURES

Distinguishing Between Description and Inference

Since I am critically reviewing the foundations of descriptive polimetric procedures, I am departing from the typical practice of statistical textbooks, which generally derive or review techniques (procedures), assuming an inferential rather than a descriptive purpose. The more abstract and formal the treatment, the more attention is given in these textbooks to methodological foundations (e.g., such standards as identifiability, unbiasedness, efficiency, informational sufficiency that are used to justify derivations). Applied treatments spend more time on other foundational elements: results, conditions, and illustrations of applicability. Rarely is critical mention made of the extremely wide range of alternative statistical practices; this usually occurs implicitly, or even unintentionally. Nor is much time usually given to the phenomena under investigation, the theoretical issues that are part of the research problem, the sociopolitical context of the research, or the theoretical and epistemological orientations taken by the investigator.

But I have argued that techniques should be seen as grounded in statistical practices and traditions with associated descriptive, including representational, commitments. In a limited space, I will try to give more equal attention to all these elements of descriptive statistical practices, and to alternate methods of handling these elements.

In previous discussion, I distinguished between descriptive and inferential statistical practices. The manifest dividing line at first appeared to be that descriptive practices concerned themselves with individual cases or entire populations, and not samples from which inferences are to be drawn. A clear interest of the investigator in population description, not policy/system evaluation, was assumed further to differentiate this branch of activities from other branches. But some techniques such as factor analysis (and Guttman scaling) can be used descriptively, heuristically, or in a hypothesis-testing, inferential way. The purposes of the investigator are the crucial discriminating variables. In psychometrics and econometrics there is considerable sophistication in probabilistic estimation and testing with data sets that are *not* random samples from some predefined universe. The associated logic of inference often talks about underlying lawlike (nomic) structures, invariant across all members of a population at least for a certain contextual period. These structures underlie particular observations, obscured either through measurement error or by external random effects. I consider both rationales to be inferential ones.

In attempting to distinguish more specifically between inferential and descriptive practices, therefore, I have considered nomologically oriented hypothesis testing and probabilistic induction or estimation to be conventional inferential practices, and the less ambitious measurement of individual, collective, or situational properties, as well as heuristic data manipulations, to be descriptive practices, typical of many case study efforts (Eckstein, Chapter 3 of this volume). In the descriptive realm, formal relations between observations or data and derived measures may be used in analyzing data. However, checking or testing, if used at all, primarily serves the interpretive and heuristic interests of better representational fits or more accurate intentionalist assessments. I begin a review of representational polimetrics with the problem of interpretively quantifying United Nations peacekeeping involvements, seen through the eyes of Guttman's (1971) structural measurement.

An Example of Structural Measurement

Most roll call-oriented studies of particular (quasi-) legislative institutions (e.g., MacRae, 1958, 1970; Alker, 1964, 1970) use Guttman scaling, cluster, or factor analysis for representational purposes; they do not assume that the American Congress or the United Nations Assembly will be governed from year to year by the same scaling, clustering, or factoring relationships. In a related example, let us assume that we are trying to represent eleven United Nations' peacemaking actions (mediation, committee of experts, calling for ceasefire, etc.) by a cumulative Guttman scale that measures the degree of United Nations involvement resulting from quasi-legislative decisions about more or less serious disputes.

Data theory considerations are part of problem-relevant epistemology; they suggest a number of obvious and not so obvious points. Clearly recorded observations on United Nations actions can be formally represented as dichotomous, nominal scale attributes of a number of units—72 collective security cases, in our example. Assuming that every diplomatic activity used in a particular case gets a +1 score (rather than 0), we are interested in finding a "dominance" relationship among actions (i.e., which actions represent the most intense involvement) on the basis of a "proximity" relationship between actions and cases (a +1 indicates the closeness of the action to the case).

Another set of applied epistemological assumptions belongs in the area of measurement theory (Coombs, Dawes, and Tversky, 1970). Our assumptions as to how our action data reflect an underlying involvement/intensity dimension are at first those of Guttman scaling: Cumulative tracelines such as those shown in Fig. 3(a) imply that above a certain level of direct intensity, a certain kind of action will always occur. The low intensity and involvement cases, on the other hand, would be limited to actions such as referral of the issue to direct negotiations or the use of a committee of inquiry.

A number of statistics have been developed to handle measurement errors or inaccuracies in the present case. But perhaps Guttman's original idea, a coefficient of reproducibility above 0.90, will help ensure sufficient measurement reliability.

Using some type of algorithm (perhaps even a computer program) for generating scales, is the reproducibility criterion all we need to look at? Figure 4 generalizes the practice we have been following, and raises new questions concerning alternatives. It asks: "Do we really want to claim the existence of a phenomenon with demonstrated cumulative properties, or do we just want to get some 'useful' ranks or numbers?" In fact we have been ignoring some of Guttman's most important original criteria for scaleability. Besides a large number of items with a variety of not-too-extreme marginals, Guttman (1950) asked for a random scattering of errors from the by now familiar cumulative scale pattern of Fig. 3(a). [As seen from a probabilistic inferential viewpoint, tracelines

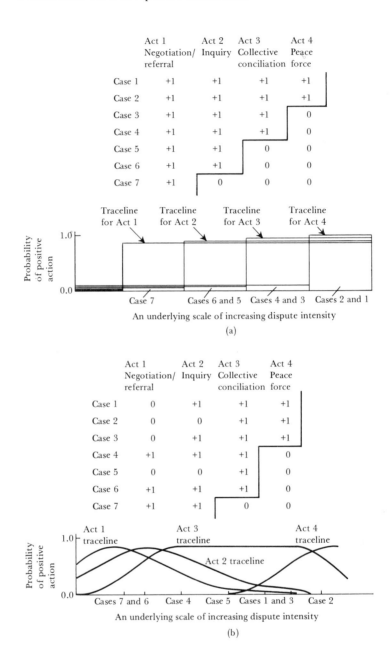

Fig. 3. Two response patterns, measurement theories, and possible scale implications. (a) A perfect cumulative response patterns and measurement theory.
(b) A response pattern with systematic errors suggesting a noncumulative,
single-peaked measurement theory.

involve many estimation problems (Jackson, 1973); Guttman (1950) objects to this kind of "normal" error analysis, however, as epistemologically implausible].

What our hypothetical data set in Fig. 3(b) suggests is that a cumulative or dominance theory is inappropriate as a method of ordering the various diplomatic actions being considered. The use of troops is surely "high involvement" in some sense, but it does not imply that all lesser degrees of involvement necessarily go along with troop use. Another data and measurement theory seems more appropriate—high involvement actions seem to coincide with each other and with high intensity disputes. Perhaps some kind of proximity scaling could be found that takes this correlational insight into account. Single-peaked tracelines of various breadths might be allowed, as suggested by the lower part of Fig. 3(b).

To continue our example for a moment, however, let us suppose that our hypothetical United Nations data analyst has a computer program with no plots, no alternate measurement models, and a clever facility for grouping items in order to increase reproducibilities. The path of measurement by technique shown in Fig. 4 is likely to be followed. Several dichotomous recodings of the data, and perhaps a lowering of the reproducibility requirement to a level at which nearly random items would form a Guttman scale, would cycle the data analyst through the measurement by technique route until some form of "illusory measurement" emerged. He would probably call it something like a "quasi-scale," and be quite vague as to what it measured and why it did so.

Or perhaps, suffering from the lack of statistical theory, high technology, and a large research budget, our investigator would decide to skip the error theory problems of Guttman scaling and construct a quantitative index of UN involvement by adding the number of actions taken, or by prejudging the ranking question and scoring each case solely in terms of its most intense action. This measurement by definition might correlate positively and quite highly with any other measurement that he could use. An influential example of measurement by definitional fiat (noted in Fig. 1 and in Mokken, 1970, p. 5) is the Index of Political Predispositions, designed to predict party voting on the bases of urban economic and religious pressures and cross-pressures (Lazarsfeld, Berelson, and Gaudet, 1948). A more honest but nonparsimonious retreat would be to give up ranking aspirations and use separate nominal scale dummy variables for each type of involvement action. Figure 4 even suggests the possibility of giving up on measurement altogether.

Rather than quit or rush to the next available quantification technique or program (likely at many computer centers in the United States to be "electric factor analysis machines"), should we not ask the phenomenal question: What are we looking for? Political and hermeneutic interests suggest that an important answer might be some way of explaining UN successes and failures. If that is the case, then a success measure would be an important criterion against which to validate prior hypotheses as to the appropriate way of quantifying an

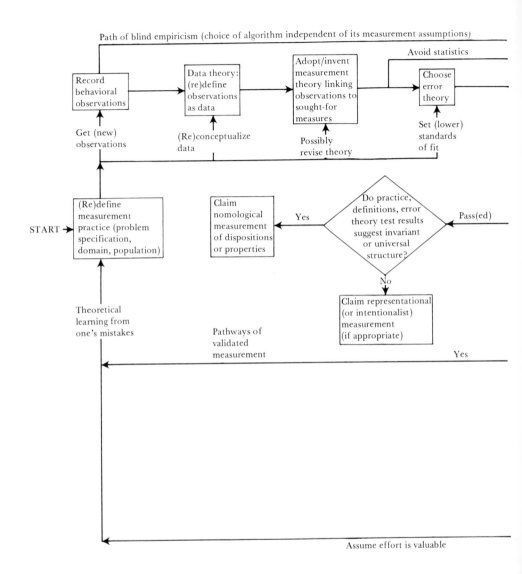

Fig. 4. A Coombsian model of measurement practices.

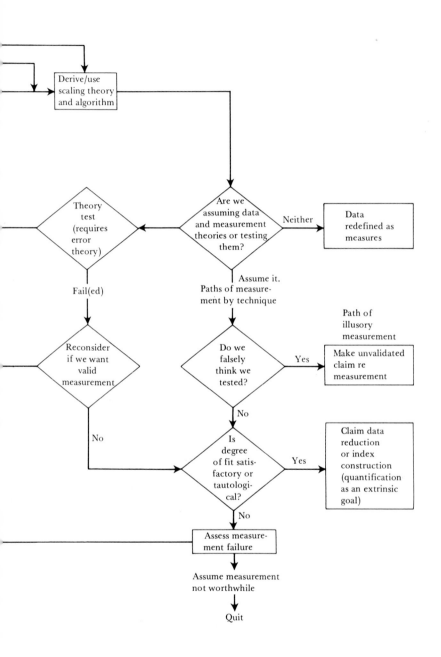

involvement index or indexes. Using several success criteria might also be desirable if it leads to a more stable and generally valid index.

From a substantive, processual point of view, this suggestion might be described as means-outcomes scaling. Actions should be metricized in terms of simple, meaningful relationships with their outcomes. A particularly attractive version of such a relationship would be a linear one restating in part the dominance and proximity ideas mentioned above: More involvement, trying harder, *ceteris paribus*, should bring more success than would less involvement. Whether or not a linear relationship holds is something we would like to be able to investigate.

What if our success variable is itself not metricized? An antiquantitative process theorist might revel in the complex set of qualitative means-outcomes relationships, reasons, and rationalizations that such a possibility suggests. A table generator would look for order in a whole series of bivariate cross-tabulations. Given the great richness of analytic methodology for handling quantitative, multiequation, causal relationships and an interest in causally explaining UN successes, I would like to be able to obtain meaningful interval scales, if possible.

The key to this seemingly hopeless task may be the data-theoretic idea of treating action-success occurrences as "proximities." The methodological principle used by the Guttman–Lingoes series of nonmetric programs (Lingoes, 1973) is that one should assign quantitative weights to each nominal scale category so that when involvements and success outcomes are empirically clustered, Euclidean geometric representations of the related actions and the outcome categories will be close together. A slight bit of statistical manipulation can be used to show that the category weights obtained by Lingoes' eigenvectoring algorithm also maximize the sum of linear squared correlation coefficients among the variables being considered. In the tradition of nonmetric multidimensional scaling, Guttman is not alone in adopting such a quantitative representational criterion and judging measurement accuracy in terms of departures from configurations of various dimensionalities. Guttman (n.d.) states: "The multivariate frequency distribution of a universe of attributes for a population of objects is a perfect scale if it is possible to derive from the distribution a quantitative variable with which to characterize the objects such that each attribute is a simple [traceline] function of that quantitative variable." In his earlier papers (e.g., 1950) a very similar interest in quantification was evident; but his regression-maximizing algorithms for quantifying qualitative information have largely been ignored.

The present example assumes the researcher's intent is heuristic description, but accuracy is here still an issue. Assuming that an error theory is possible in terms of notions not unlike χ^2 tabular analysis (and it is), how shall we avoid the fallacy of measurement as technique rather than as validated quantitative representation? Guttman and Lingoes suggest a prior commitment of varying degrees of firmness to hypothesized orders or partially ordered metrics in the variables being considered. Allowing for the grouping of proximate categories along such an order, we should also hypothesize, roughly, the expected range and signs of our derived correlation coefficients. And we should insist that the dimensions be extracted and statistically distinguished from tabular noise. Parsimony, in the form of finding those metricized category scores that maximize intervariable correlations, now takes over to produce the numbers shown in Table 2.

We leave to the reader the judgment of the validity of these quantifications (see Table 2), all of which are statistically significant. First note that involvement correlations with success indexes are in the $+0.50$ to $+0.60$ range while involvement-HOSTP1 correlations are around $+0.70$ to $+0.80$. These signs and relative magnitudes were anticipated theoretically ahead of time. Moreover, except for the fascinating nonlinear relationship between MNCIV5 and MSCIX1 (which the reader is urged to plot), all the orders correspond closely to United Nations Charter descriptions of the stages and/or levels of coercive and noncoercive involvement. The distinction between coercive and noncoercive involvement is found both in the data and in Charter discussions of the settlement of international disputes, breaches of the peace, or acts of aggression. It should also be noted that the simpler, MSCIXL index is a merging of MSCIX1 in order to achieve a more perfect and less controversial linear relationship. The issue, of course, is whether referring an issue to another organization or the parties concerned, who themselves settle it, should be considered a UN success or a failure of competence.

Critical Discussion

Stepping back from this example, were we right to consider it to be representational measurement, a case of descriptive polimetrics based on a testable measurement theory? Does not the testing of hypothesized relationships between means and outcomes point us toward inferential statistics (the category of dispositional measurement near the middle branch of Fig. 1, or the corresponding nomological measurement box in Fig. 4)? The use of nonmetric information as inputs to the MAC3 program could imply either practice: the avoidance of "normal" or transformed normal error assumptions on epistemological grounds is suggestive, but not decisive given Guttman's commitment to regression-based quantification procedures and Lingoes' significance tests, which were used to test for the nonrandomness of additional quantification dimensions. Both authors suggest ordinal, nonprobabilistic methods of testing the validity of these measurement results. The absence of any claims about invariant structures also points in the descriptive, interpretive, and heuristic directions. Guttman's (1971) presidential address before the Psychometric Society, while controversial in its narrow view of statistics, certainly corroborates the present, descriptive interpretation given here.

TABLE 2   MAC3 metricizations of five UN involvement and success variables*

Variable name (and label)	Categories	Means-outcome metricization	N
MCINVR (metricized recoded coercive involvement index)	No coercive involvement	0.000	52
	Ceasefire ordered, truce established	0.965	9
	Police force, enforcement, boycott, embargo	1.000	11
MNCIVR (metricized noncoercive involvement index)	No coercive actions	0.000	19
	Committee of experts, inquiry, referral of negotiations	0.326	18
	SG presence, mediation, conciliation, adjudication	1.000	35
MNCIV5† (metricized noncoercive involvement index 5)	No noncoercive actions	0.000	19
	Referral of negotiations	−0.370	13
	Committee of experts, inquiry	0.160	5
	SG presence, conciliation, mediation, adjudication	1.000	35
HOSTP1 (stopping hostilities or maintaining truce)	No stopping of hostilities or truce maintenance	0.000	58
	Stopping hostilities and/or maintaining truce	1.000	14
MSCIXL (metricized last recorded success index)	No success bilateral or multilateral settlement with UN referral	0.000	55
	UN helps settle issue	0.990	10
	UN settles issue	1.000	7
MSCIX1† (metricized success index 1)	No success	0.000	48
	Negotiation referral with bilateral/ multilateral settlement	−2.050	7
	UN helps settle	0.870	10
	UN settles	1.000	7

* Substantive normalizations are given in terms of meaningful zero points and maximums, 0.0 and 1.0, respectively. Data are taken from a current study by the author, Cheryl Christensen, and Bill Greenberg.
† MNCIV5 and MSCIX1 are from the same MAC3 run (also involving HOSTP1) ; the rest of the table is from another four-variable run.

A brief review of some of the (1971) arguments might help here. Philosophically, Guttman is interested in logics of discovery more than those of verification. His methodological purpose is heuristic, rather than probabilistically inductive: the development of new insights and the discovery of new forms of lawfulness in data. While statistical theory is seen as the theory of drawing inferences about aspects of a universe from a sample of observations, structural measurement theory "deals with the construction of structural hypotheses rather than with inference from samples," and restricts itself to the structure of linear, rarely lawful regressions among variables measured for appropriate populations.

In some studies, repeated applications of nonmetric measurement techniques may reveal invariant configurations justifying lawlike status, but single applications of Guttman's techniques, even when tested for their relevance, are rarely sufficient for such purposes. Moreover, the investigators generating the measures in Table 2 made no lawlike claims about them. Hence, an interpretive, heuristic, relatively accurate summary representation, rather than a nomologically valid measurement, has been provided.

What critique can we make of this representational measurement example? Certainly a positive, epistemological interest in quantification is dominant. The standard argument is that Guttman scales transform nominal data into *ordinal* measures. But for 30 years Guttman's intent and practice has been to go further, to produce interval scale measures. The dominant logic here is one of empirical parsimony, maximizing representational accuracy with theoretically meaningful and testable structural models. An important incentive was to provide attitudinal and ability measurement theories as alternatives to those of factor analysis, which would have probabilistic, linear, slanted tracelines (unlike either alternative pictured in Fig. 3). Second, Guttman's structural measurement is grounded in psychological and sociological phenomena. His formal treatment comes as a progressive, even revolutionary transformation of early psychometric traditions of attitude measurement practice. Many of their arbitrary assumptions concerning normal distributions have been dropped. When psychometric and polimetric training allows such a pluralistic set of interpretive possibilities, the researcher's freedom of choice and the possibility of greater insight have surely been enhanced. Third, the nonmetric multidimensional revolution, spurred on by the exemplars of Guttman, Coombs, and Shepard (see Shepard *et al.*, 1972), has allowed the recasting and assessment of a whole range of statistical practices with different underlying data theories from nonmetric factor analysis and regression analysis, to Coombsian unfolding of preferential data. Lower levels of quantification are assumed of original data; interval scale measures come from testable, model-based parsimony ideas that have been shown to be remarkably powerful. If such analysis is naturalistic in inspiration, it does show remarkable sensitivity to social context and the variability of human capabilities and social structural possibilities. And it implies the possibility of dispositional alternatives to intentionalist assessments.

INTENTIONALIST ASSESSMENT PRACTICES:
AGGREGATIVE APPROACHES

Let us now concern ourselves wth intentionalist assessments, those seeking to interpret and understand political acts explicitly in terms of actor purposes, preferences, reasons, or meanings. While it is true that the previous example of means-outcomes scaling came close to such a perspective, a serious limitation (in the interest of parsimony) was the absence of explicit information on specific cases of UN conflict containment or resolution goals. A much larger analytical effort would be necessary in order to ascertain whether an organization made up of so many powerful, but conflicting, actors behaved in a teleological fashion consistent with stated UN Charter goals about saving "succeeding generations from the scourge of war." (See Alker, 1971b, for a suggestion as to how to make an emergent functionalist assessment like this using Sommerhoff's concept of directive correlation.)

Reason Analysis

We can get some insights into the involvement decisions of the United Nations by talking more specifically and in more detail about decisions by key states in the Security Council or General Assembly, keeping in mind the possibilities suggested by Fig. 2. Why, for example, did the Soviet Union unexpectedly support (and thus help make possible) a Security Council resolution sending UN troops into the Congo? Our hypothetical review of the reasons for this decision by the Soviet Union and other countries will support the Moon–von Wright analysis of practical inference, modified to take into account changing governmental predispositions and situational characteristics. The link between an actor's reasons or intentions and his actions will not depend on some separate, empirically valid general laws for its validity. Hence the appropriate polimetric branch for Lazarsfeld–Sills–Zeisel "reason analysis," which we are about to review, is the interpretive, rather than the probabilistic, inference one. Recall that the rules of Security Council voting on substantive questions require not only that there be no vetoes, but also that there be substantial majorities in favor of the proposal. It becomes clear that a teleological explanation of how the UN Operation in the Congo (UNOC) action was *possible* because of individual nonvetoes must be complemented by a causal-type, naturalistic explanation of why it was *necessary* for a winning majority to form in support of sending UN peace forces to the Congo. Moreover, aggregative Cold War, supranationalism and self-determination predispositions are relevant. Operational Charter norms help provide an aggregative logic of causal necessity complementing intentionalist possibility arguments (representable as practical syllogisms) governing the behavior of particular actors or actor classes. The net result is a quasi-causal explanation, rather similar to some of Moon's (1975) examples.

Hans Zeisel (1968) gives a clear exposition of the various statistical practices associated with "reason analysis." It is a statistical tradition with origins in the market-research/voter-choice paradigm initiated at Columbia University by Paul Lazarsfeld and his colleagues some 30 years ago. We shall review and criticize this practice in terms of a fictionalized treatment of possible answers to the above question concerning UN intervention in the Congo. Previous studies

(Dallin, 1962; Gross, 1966; and Alker, 1966b, 1968, 1971a, 1974b) make this review somewhat realistic, but the requisite, intensive interviews never took place. The five steps suggested for reason analysis are:

1. Formulating the problem in terms of research purpose.
2. Selecting the action types to be considered.
3. Developing appropriate accounting schemes.
4. Searching for reasons.
5. Assessing and interpreting statistics.

Zeisel's (1968) interest is interpretive and manipulatively causal. He suggests that problem formulation should be responsive to the interests of the research sponsor, emphasizing the controllable influences leading to desirable outcomes. Because the United States does not control Soviet votes in the United Nations, an official researcher could see why a different problem formulation, taking into account American influences on Congo outcomes through private and public extra-UN channels, might be called for. Nonetheless, I will remain with the present problem formulation.

As for types of action, Zeisel (1968) calls for separate treatments of those likely to have different rationale structures. In the context of the Security Council, Charter rules point us toward the veto powers, those countries most likely to have autonomous rationales for decisions. When cleansed of propaganda influences, possibly divergent reasons might profitably be investigated for four groups: the United States and dependent states; the Soviet Union and dependent states; France and Britain (veto powers with colonial interests such as those of the Belgians in Katanga, and with vivid memories of American–Soviet cooperation in stopping their Suez intervention); and unaligned, nondependent states in Europe or the Third World. Off the record, retrospective interviews might show rather similar rationales for the voting positions each group took in the Security Council and General Assembly.

Does this mean that we should require separate accounting schemes in order to "understand" the decisions of each actor (type)? An original interest in at least a quasi-causal explanation of UN action leads us to a form of idiosyncratic, interpretive analysis of each type of actor. The causal significance of aggregative voting rules requires this! Perhaps, however, a reasonably exhaustive tabulation of possible reasons given by different types for supporting or opposing UN involvement will suggest conceptual reformulations of these reasons in a way that makes idiosyncratic positions both more comparable and more understandable in terms of the conventions of plausible state behavior shared by most international observers and participants. Such, at least, is the aggregative goal of reason analysis. The complementary nature of hermeneutic and naturalistic treatments of intentionalist action, as argued by Moon (1975), should become even clearer with this example. The problematical nature of rationale explanations in changing political contexts should also become apparent.

Investigators are told by Zeisel (1968) to develop a provisional feel for the separate dimensions in terms of which interviewees will answer questions about particular actions. Distinct, conceptually related clusters of reasons suggest different dimensions that should be taken into account in designing final interviewing schedules. These are formalized into an accounting scheme.

Let us assume that we begin to develop an accounting scheme with a few trial interviews. A Soviet delegate might suggest in a frank, private interview that the strong support for an anti-imperialist UN intervention by Afro-Asian states was a deciding factor. An American diplomat, resentful of suspicious academics, might emphasize the potential bloody consequences for Belgian citizens of the breakdown of civil order (and the attendant troop mutinies) if a UN presence were not quickly established; he might further argue that these humanitarian concerns, plus the official request of the Congolese government for UN help, at least neutralized their strongly held position against UN interference in decolonization matters.

Would the suggested strategy lead to an adequate account? If one asked diplomats or third-party observers why they thought states other than their own were taking the positions they did, a lot more reasons (or unconscious interests) would emerge. These would probably look a lot more like the conflict predispositions discussed in consideration of Fig. 2. French, Belgian, and other Western economic interests in Katangese mining, Britain's foreign policy views concerning post-Suez confrontations with the United States, popular sentiments in developed Western countries concerning racial warfare, African and Asian leaders' fear of both the great powers and of precedents sanctioning redrawn national boundaries, and United States and USSR Cold War-motivated jockeying for influence in the Third World might then emerge as important complements to off-the-record rationales. Certainly one would hear about the Suez precedent, even if the delegates of the veto powers had not mentioned it. When elaborated on, this reference suggests issues of administrative capabilities, logistical needs, force composition, and obligatory financing. Legal questions are also thorny in gray-area conflicts where the UN's presence is by consent of the host government and veto power support is not solid.

Several comments are in order at this point. First of all, notice that our trial diplomatic interviewees pictured themselves as representing autonomous, intentionalist actors in pursuit of general, attractive interests, but like the factor analytic studies, the interviewees were much more likely to impute less attractive, less autonomous, and more specific goals, interests, and compulsions to others. Second, self-assessments like the above fit the practical inference schema of von Wright as follows.

From now on A (the US, USSR, France) intends to bring about p (peace, the defeat of imperialism, the saving of Belgian lives) at t (as soon as possible).

From now on A considers that, unless he does a (supports a UN peace force) no later than at t' (the next Security Council meetings on the Congo), he cannot bring about p at time t.

Therefore, no later than when A thinks t' has arrived, A sets himself to do a (support UNOC), unless A forgets about the time t' or is prevented. (von Wright, 1971, p. 107, with revisions)

Third, the actors discussed are complex aggregates we call states, even though we particularly have in mind their governments' ambassadorial representatives. Fourth, the candor of each of these interpretations is not incontestable, but rarely totally irrefutable. Ideologically laden general goals are sometimes pure covers for naked power politics, but usually such off-the-record arguments combine a degree of vague validity with some conscious distortion. Zeisel (1968) allows, and even suggests, imputing the more embarrassing goals (reasons) when appropriate.

Fifth, the *combined* set of preliminary interviews suggests a relatively rich (but probably not exhaustive) delineation of a common domain of possible answers to a subsequent, more exhaustive survey. The dimensions of the corresponding accounting scheme might be describable in generalized, nonidiosyncratic terms such as those of Table 3, which cumulatively reflects several of the variables shown in Fig. 2.

Looking at Table 3 we note a tendency to describe positions in favor of alliance solidarity or other interests as voluntaristic, even in those cases where governmental or elite autonomy is historically suspect. This points to a related problem, that is probably paradigm-linked: the inadequacy of volitional tests implied by the reserve clause of the practical syllogism—"unless A ... is prevented." Saying that A was prevented implies theoretical expectations of what would have happened otherwise. Not all hermeneutic authors are willing to accept counterfactional assessments, which perhaps should be based on causal theories (Simon and Rescher, 1966). How deeply must rationale interpretations take into account historical-environmental effects, including the replacement of role incumbents and the structuring of political rewards by economic interests? For example, Congo policies and Soviet voting changed with the assassination of Patrice Lumumba by Katangese interests. To what extent, then, were the post-Lumumba Congolese and Soviet votes autonomously volitional?

Another fairly general methodological observation is the need for an historically based, *augmented means-ends scheme* for fully describing UN practices. *Reasons* related to Charter norms and instrumental UN precedents, as well as general and specific interests or objectives and situational characteristics,

TABLE 3   An accounting scheme for UNOC Security Council votes
(Hypothetical positions of the United States, the USSR, France, and black African
countries are on the left.)

Veto weighted acceptability	Hypothetical positions	I. *Interests of the actors*	
		A. General interests	
−	(+,−,?,−)	1.	Interest in solidarity with Free World bloc leader
−	(−,+,−,?)	2.	Interest in solidarity with anti-imperialist cause
?	(+,?,+,?)	3.	Interest in saving (white) lives, preventing bloodshed
?	(?,+,−,+)	4.	Interest in Third World independence, self-determination
−	(+,?,−,+)	5.	Interest in enhanced UN capabilities
		B. Specific objectives	
−	(+,−,+,+)	1.	Interest in preventing Soviet foothold in the Congo
−	(+,−,+,−)	2.	Interest in supporting colonial governments and settlers in Africa
−	(+,−,+,−)	3.	Interest in transnational economic investments in Katanga
?	(?,?,−,+)	4.	Concern for enlarging UN role in other decolonization/postcolonial disputes
+	(+,+,?,+)	5.	Concern that Soviet-American conflict might devastate the Congo and spread elsewhere
+	(?,+,+,+)	6.	Concern that a precedent for new boundaries not be created by successful Katangese succession
		II. *Nature of the conflict situation*	
		A. Inside the Congo	
−	(−,+,+,+)	1.	The conflict is seen as basically anti-imperial.
?	(+,?,+,−)	2.	The dispute is between Belgium and the Congo.
−	(+,−,+,−)	3.	The primary conflicts are due to a breakdown in public order, as evidenced by mutinies.
+	(?,+,+,+)	4.	The government of the Congo wants UN help vis-à-vis the Belgian troops (and their support of the Katangese).
?	(+,?,+,?)	5.	The Congolese request really involves an admission of civil incapacity to govern.

Veto weighted acceptability	Hypothetical positions	II. *Nature of the conflict situation (cont.)*
		B. Outside of the Congo
		1. The conflict is pivotal in the emergence and maintenance of
?	(?,+,+,?)	a) anti-imperialist coalitions.
?	(?,+,+,?)	b) neutral states friendly to the West.
?	(?,?,+,+)	c) independent Africa.
		2. The conflict is pivotally important for the definition of the UN's role in
?	(?,?,?,+)	a) containing the Cold War.
+	(?,+,+,+)	b) speeding decolonization.
+	(+,+,+,?)	c) peacekeeping questions where veto powers may not all completely agree.
		III. *Expectations about UN actions and alternatives*
		A. Historical-legal justifiability of UN peacekeeping role
?	(+,?,−,+)	1. Willingness to see UN involvement as binding Security Council action
−	(+,+,−,+)	2. Validity of Suez peacekeeping precedent
?	(?,?,+,+)	3. Domestic interventions only valid when host state agrees.
		B. The UN can mobilize sufficient
+	(+,+,?,+)	1. troops
+	(+,?,+,+)	2. logistics
?	(+,?,−,+)	3. administrative personnel
?	(+,?,−,?)	4. financing
		to be quickly effective.
		C. Considerations regarding alternate influence actions
+	(+,+,+,?)	1. Awareness of vulnerabilities of their own large-scale direct intervention attempt
		2. Awareness of some options for continued
+	(+,+,+,?)	a) United States influence
+	(+,+,?,?)	b) Soviet influence
+	(+,+,?,?,)	c) European influence
+	(?,+,+,+)	d) Afro-Asian influence
		within the confines of a UN operation.

are all necessary for a full understanding of UN Congo involvement decisions. Including these variables as part of an augmented analytical scheme makes possible a much richer analysis than the truncated means-outcome treatment in the previous example of Guttman–Lingoes structural measurement.

Let us assume that the above accounting scheme helps us elicit interpretations of national positions from ambassadors and their critics. The judgmental problems in step four of reason analysis, "the search for reasons," should be noted. It may also turn out that a number of actors, such as those simulated in Table 3, have more than one reason per category of the accounting scheme.

We now come to the last stage of reason analysis, that of assessing and interpreting statistical data. In our hypothetical example, "+" indicates that a state subscribes to the interest, perception, or expectation noted in Table 3; "−" means that a state articulates or is observed to take an opposed viewpoint; "?" refers to cases in which no unambiguous information is available. Given our double interest in understanding and explaining the original UNOC involvement decision, the data ascriptions of Table 3 contribute significantly. They suggest formalizable *episode accounts* (see Harré and Secord, 1972, ch. 8 for a related treatment).

Thus by using the information given in Table 3, we may summarize the reasons for initial Soviet support as follows.

The Soviet Union saw the original Congo dispute as a pivotal showdown (II.B.1.a and b in Table 3) in the emergence of anti-imperialist coalitions (I.A.2) able to stunt American influence attempts (I.A.1) directed toward neutralist nations. The situation of an official Congolese request for UN intervention reflects the exacerbating role of capitalist interests in Katanga (I.B.3) and associated colonial (II.A.1, II.B.2) instabilities (II.A.4), not a simple incapacity to govern (II.A.3) as some have claimed. The UN can (III.B.1) and should (II.B.2.b) send forces to speed Belgian withdrawal, even when some imperial powers (France) protest (II.B.2.c, II.A.2). Given their awareness of the difficulties of large-scale support for Lumumba (III.C.1), a prudent strategy (I.B.5) suggests relying on anticolonial majorities (I.A.4, III.C.2.d) to exercise greater influence (III.C.2.b) than in the past (III.A.1, an implicit reference to Korea and other influence seekers, III.C.2.a,c) on this kind of issue.

Rather different episode accounts for the United States, France, and a typical black African state could be constructed from Table 3 as well. This exercise is left to the reader.

How should we aggregate these different perspectives and the variables of Fig. 2 in giving a fuller quasi-causal explanation of UNOC creation? A certain similarity between Fig. 2 and Table 3 should first be noted. As previously suggested, Security Council-weighted majority rules suggest an appropriate method of aggregating perspectives. The comparable categories of Table 3 make it possible to summarize expectations about the nature of the enabling resolution with greater assurance as to their nonspurious character. Allowing vetoes to the United States, the Soviet Union, and France, and estimating these states and Afro-Asian Council members to have about 4, 3, 2, and 2 votes respectively, a nonvetoed positive vote of 7 would occur for only those proposals and preambular decision premises with a "+" in the left-hand column of Table 3. We arrive in this manner at a point where we have partially explained and plausibly reconstructed the main points and some of the wording of the original Congo intervention resolution. A force is established under the Secretary General's leadership, without financially binding Charter citations, in response to Kasavubu's letters of invitation and complaints about Belgian troops. This is accomplished with the tacit understanding that UN troops will not come from the veto powers, and that various groups of states will have some say as to the troops' further actions through a variety of formal, administrative, and informal channels.

Even without going more deeply into the underlying causal processes, one can see that a major, intrinsic statistical problem in reason analysis is the assessment of the relative importance of various reasons. Zeisel (1968) prefers that each major category of the accounting scheme have one and only one positive reason. When there are more actors, one can make cross-tabulations of a collection of comparable actors to suggest which reasons are more often decisive (perhaps these could be weighted as in our example). For a single actor, a notion such as the cost of substituting some other similarly positive reason is suggested as a measure of importance.

These comments suggest some other technical problems intrinsic to reason analysis that may have partially accounted for its declining use in scientific work, despite its rich intentionalist character. First, multiple positive reasons, like multiple, partially sufficient premises in the practical syllogism, lead to assessment problems now frequently handled by multivariate statistical generalizations of cross-tabulation, such as the General Linear Model. And reasons, like causes, can be handled causally in nonadditive ways. The supporting nature of some beliefs in different or even opposed rationale structures (e.g., about Kasavubu's request) suggests more careful, more difficult to aggregate, nonadditive distinctions among reasons, their supports, and genuine motivational or environmental causes. Finally, from an external perspective, market research images of rational choice raise a number of questions about the ideological bias of this approach. These need not overturn, however, the preliminary descriptive utility of such intentionalist analyses.

Carroll–Chang Individual Differences Scaling (INDSCAL)

If the previous example used a minimum of statistical technology in its aggregative mode of intentionalist assessment, Carroll–Chang (see Carroll and Chang, 1970; Carroll, 1972; Wish and Carroll, 1973) Individual Differences Scaling (INDSCAL) represents an individuating technical breakthrough in the use of computer technology. It is comparable to the earlier demonstration that proximity ranks imply tremendous constraints on possible object locations in a small-dimensional Euclidian space, constraints that are usually sufficient to generate rather tight interval scale measurements from nonmetric data and parsimony assumptions. We mention these developments here because of their usefulness for studying individual differences in the way political alternatives are both conceptualized and evaluated. Moreover, like the previous example of aggregative reason analysis, INDSCAL permits a very careful examination of the extent to which individual perceptions can be merged into common spatial representations.

Figure 5, suggested by Anthony Coxon's (1972) helpful expositions (see also Coxon and Jones, 1975 forthcoming), indicates what this statistical practice typically looks like. The problem of political interest is usually the desire to map subjects' cognitions and preferences concerning important social or political objects (eg., occupations or politicians or nations or program alternatives). Individual differences may mean that a common "group space" that summarizes a collectivity's judgments inevitably distorts those judgments of particular individuals. Perhaps their vantage points or legal points differ; perhaps they use differently configured spaces. Aggregatively, INDSCAL allows exploring *the extent that* differences in weightings on the same set of dimensions suggest a satisfactory method of aggregating different perspectives without distorting them. As indicated in the pathway of valid measurement shown in Fig. 4, we should not accept such an aggregation before knowing how much or how little violence it does to individual perceptions.

Figure 5, a hypothetical example basically similar to published results for larger data sets, shows how this kind of checking takes place. The analysis starts with interval or ordinal scale similarity/proximity data for separate subjects (in the ordinal case, a program variant called N(onmetric)-INDSCAL is used). In our example we shall assume these data to be ranked/paired similarity judgments for all distinct pairs of the nations shown in Fig. 5. A common space and comparable separate individual spaces are calculated from these matrices. Of the three individual spaces shown in the figure (those of individuals 2 5, 8) each seems governed by "developed–underdeveloped" discriminations, but only two of these (those from individuals 2 and 4) reflect left–right differences. The national scale positions derived from the similarities are similar, but not identical across individuals. The common space allows oblique (nonperpendicular) axes and has a natural orientation.

Roughly speaking, in the normalized subject space of the figure, for axes that are not too oblique, squared distances from the origin to the subjects' position correspond to the proportion of the subject's individual data accounted for by the common space. And the coordinates in the subject space show to what extent, if at all, particular axes are emphasized in a subject's perceptions. When certain dimensions are totally idiosyncratic, real incomparabilities have been discovered, and subject regroupings should be considered.

(a) *Inputs*

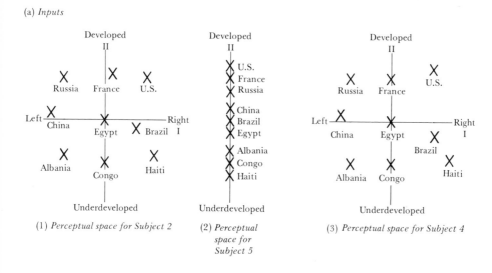

(1) *Perceptual space for Subject 2*

(2) *Perceptual space for Subject 5*

(3) *Perceptual space for Subject 4*

(b) *Outputs*

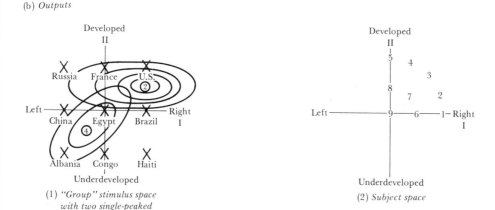

(1) *"Group" stimulus space with two single-peaked preference contour sets*

(2) *Subject space*

Fig. 5. Individual differences scaling, inputs and outputs: three "private" spaces, a subject space, and some preference ellipses. Source: *configurations suggested by Carroll-Chang (1970).*

What makes this example "intentionalist assessment," when the "means-outcome scaling" reviewed earlier seems so similar? Both are multidimensional scaling (MDS) practices. Like Baas and Brown's (1973) extremely interesting use of factor analysis to study one individual's cognitive and affective projection of different politicians into a multidimensional space with the same structure as a space of family members, this example allows considerable attention to individual or unit differences. And, more than the particular example of structural measurement given above, the meaning and relationships of preferences vis-à-vis cognitions are given a central role.

Assuming that spatial relations among objects and preferences peak, one may use a PREFMAP routine (rather like the one described in Alker, 1970, Appendix) that generates preference peaks and associated, descendingly preferred preference ellipses. Such Carroll–Chang results look like those shown in Fig. 5. We can then see, on the bases of previously established cognitive spaces, the extent to which individual (or group) preferences reinforce or cut across their perceptual differentiations. Such an approach would be an improvement on the Baas–Brown procedure reviewed below, which does not allow the disentangling of cognitive and affective dimensions. Because we also have individual cognitive spaces, we are prevented from making the mistake of accusing someone like Individual 4, with preferences untypical of most Americans, of not being able to discriminate left and right from developed and underdeveloped, the problem of Observer 5. Another possible way of getting at preferential cognition effects, a key issue in the discussion of the inputs of political orientations to social scientific analyses, is to start directly with paired preferences data and see what type of dimensional structure can be derived from them.

A critical review of this example can best be continued after a thorough discussion of Baas–Brown intensive factor analysis.

Baas–Brown Intensive Factor Analysis

Although it is oriented toward the study of individual cases, we shall discuss here Baas and Brown's (1973) approach to comparing the personal and public worlds of a single individual, because it is quite similar to INDSCAL. On separate days 15 objects from each of these two worlds were ranked (Q-sorted) in terms of 40 evaluative descriptions (e.g., dominant, loving, shrewd) derived from a Lasswellian typology of values (power, affection, skill, etc.). A single factor analysis of the 40 traits, giving factor scores for the 30 objects, was used indirectly to test Lasswell's developmental formula, the core of their Lasswellian research program:

> Political Man = p (private motives) d (displaced onto the
> public arena) r (and rationalized in terms of the common good).

They found public and private objects in each of their four factor dimensions.

Does this result support the existence of a naturalistic universal law? The same question can be asked of INDSCAL. Type A laws (those such as Newton's laws, with universally constant parameters) and Type B laws (which, like certain chemical relations and most causal modelling, allow parameter differences, but require the same functional relationships to be universally valid) are eschewed by Baas and Brown. One would expect Carroll and Chang to do likewise when exploring culturally variant subjective spaces. Somewhat like Guttman, Baas and Brown do suggest that Lasswell's formula may be a Type C law, one claiming that certain *generating rules* for revealing or demonstrating functional relationships and parameters are invariant. As in Fig. 4, auxiliary measurement theories and formula-based data-generating rules are used (e.g., about the coverage of value universes, the adequacy of Q-sort procedures for revealing subjective feelings, and the substantive technical criteria of factor extraction).

Analogously, the practical syllogism, linked to "reason analysis" and some substantive ideas about voting intentionality, could give a deeper test than less intentionally sophisticated statistical procedures for studying rational voting using MDS (e.g., Cahoon, Hinich, and Ordeshock, 1973). In any case, the resulting notion of lawlikeness, as Guttman (1971) argued, would be a far cry from conventional positivist conceptions, describable as Types A and B laws.

Even in the Baas–Brown example, and certainly in our INDSCAL illustration, a descriptive purpose may predominate. Like the practical syllogism, Lasswell's formula and Carroll–Chang's group spaces may be assumed as a basis for the intentionalist description of individual cases. The logically similar role of the interpretive frames in these cases—one Freudian, one aggregative, one rationalist—should be suggestive of further inferential issues. In particular, the disparity of interpretive frames cries for further explanatory studies of which frame applies here.

Third, it must be observed that INDSCAL developed rather late in a vigorous statistical tradition, multidimensional scaling, that has a bibliography of well over 1000 articles in the last 15 years. The same can be said of intensive factor analysis. Both INDSCAL and related complex versions of factor analysis would allow revealing checks of coder disagreements in other areas of quantitative measurement (e.g., the events data movement given impetus by Moses *et al.*, 1967). Rarely are procedures more attuned to contemporary substantive concerns. But unlike simple, *a priori* index constructions, they are hard to create and master. Hence the external critique that students may spend too much time learning statistics is likely to be valid, but not easily remedied if a theory-relevant polimetrics is desired.

Fourth, despite the considerable improvement taking place in the quality of options available within the MDS and descriptive factor analysis traditions, the particular nature of the symbolic formalisms within the nonfalsifiable core of the traditions needs highlighting. Whether the assumption is Euclidean geometry or its non-Euclidean generalizations, the key epistemological presupposition of MDS is that social reality is spatially representable. Reorderings of the original data are assumed to have distance properties. But spatial acuity is a differentially distributed human capability. Thus both the descriptive and the inferential validity of spatial representations must be at least partially problematical. Modelling alternatives such as cluster analysis and factor analysis represent different epistemological viewpoints: They do not assume each of the same, spatially valid data-theoretic and measurement relations assured by INDSCAL. But their linear additive or nonadditive measurement assumptions may be equally problematic in certain contexts, as was made clear in our preliminary discussion. Thus, either for descriptive or inferential purposes, we are left with the need to validate our interpretational schema.

INTENTIONAL ASSESSMENT: SITUATIONAL AND STRUCTURAL MEASURES

A rather different subject of measurement interest is the opportunity structures facing political actors. Intentionalist issues abound. In terms of realizing their objectives, what should we say about their possibilities for cooperation and conflict, for example? In opportunity cost terms, what are the values of various resources? Another set of related questions, not asked by aggregative approaches reviewed so far, has to do with the capabilities of collectivities to realize their objectives—questions of power, integration, and development fit within this rubric.

As an illustration of this class of intentionalist concerns, I shall review Axelrod's (1970) stimulating work on measuring conflict of interest in game-like situations, extending it to the question of power assessment. In subsequent discussions of explanatory statistical practices, the special case we review (Prisoner's Dilemma games) will be analyzed again. Before beginning with this example, it is also worth noting that the game-theoretic rational choice literature is the source of Moon's exposition of Lakatos' idea of progressive, within paradigm, problem shifts. The reader should also compare this discussion with the well-written exposition by Kramer and Hertzberg (Chapter 7 of this volume) on how to model public goods generation through pollution control. Formally, public goods analysis is a generalized case of the Prisoner's Dilemma (Hardin, 1971). Depending on one's sympathies, however, it needs to be clarified whose definition of the "good" is to be adhered to, that of the District Attorney or that of the Prisoners' seeking to preserve District Attorney ignorance and their own solidarity. To ease comparisons with the Kramer–Hertzberg treatment, and because of its inherent suggestiveness concerning paradigm development, I shall begin from the prisoners' collective perspective.

The story or episode account that goes with such payoff matrices as the following was probably developed *after* its numerical entries and the game-theoretic conventions (reviewed by Kramer and Hertzberg) that are used to

| | | *B* | |
		Confess	Be silent
A	Confess	−1, −1	−5, 0
	Be silent	0, −5	−3, −3

(In each cell, *A*'s payoffs are followed by *B*'s)

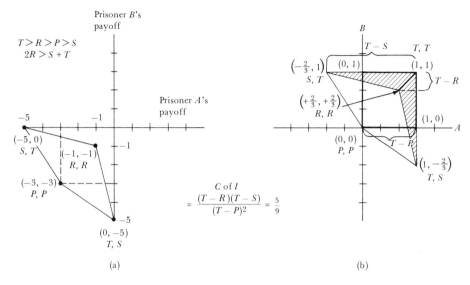

Fig. 6. Axelrod's measure of conflict of interest in a Prisoner's Dilemma. (a) Prisoner payoff space (utilities measured in jail years). (b) Normalized Prisoner's Dilemma, with shaded conflict of interest area.

describe such a two-person, noncooperative, nonzero-sum game in normal form. This may be an important reason for the imperfect selective match of the game with the story. But the perpetuation of the game-theoretic representation of the intentionalist context may also suggest more paradigm-linked limitations.

A typical variant, in brief, of that story is that two prisoners have been caught in circumstances incriminating enough to be likely to lead to short jail sentences, perhaps of one year each (a *Reward* for nondefection of −1 in the above matrix and in Fig. 6a).

The District Attorney, however, suspects the prisoners to be guilty of a more serious crime, holds the prisoners incommunicado, and offers each separately the prospect of a suspended sentence (a *Temptation* payoff of $T = 0$ in the matrix and Fig. 6) if the prisoner "rats" on his co-worker, providing the State with evidence sufficient to convict him for a five-year sentence (a *Sucker* payoff of −5). Exactly the same proposal is made to the other prisoner, and is symmetrically reflected in the payoff matrix, whose first row and column may now be thought of as referring to each prisoner's strategic option of confessing the more serious crime. The prisoners are further told that each has been given the same options, confessing or keeping silent, but that were both to confess independently of each other, the D.A. would not be able, in his opinion, to secure such favorable terms for the prisoner becoming the government's chief witness; hence the *Penalty* payoff entries (−3, −3) in the matrix and Fig. 6, interpretable as three-year jail terms. The game is usually interpreted as presenting a dilemma of collective action, because the penalty (–3, –3) outcome is stable but inefficient. The defection choice is strictly preferred in terms of a major criterion of individualistic rationality theories: It leads to better payoffs *whatever* the choice the other prisoner makes. Those assuming this vantage point also usually use a singular possessive description: prisoner's dilemma. Yet both prisoners would prefer the (–1, –1), "cooperative," joint nondefection reward; hence the prisoners' dilemma has an individualistic component.

An attempt to measure, explain, and control conflicts of interest is one potential way out of this dilemma. But given such a mixture of knowledge interests, note that this account is phenomenally incomplete. It does not make clear whether Prisoners *A* and *B* really are guilty in terms of a just law, for what crime they may be given a five-year sentence, or why they are assumed to be committed to individualistic rationality. [Approximately half of the Michigan students studied by Rapoport and Chammah (1965) *do not* defect in a situation formally equivalent to the above example.] Nor is the option raised of talking with one's attorney before interrogation. Surely this would provide a legal means (according to decisions related to the *Miranda* v. *Arizona* case) of *indirect* interprisoner communication enhancing the chances of cooperative nondefection. Most important, the behavioral options suggested in the above phenomenal analysis and problem definitions exclude the District Attorney's participation as a third party in the Prisoners' Dilemma, and the discussion or analysis of his reasons, objectives, interests, or utilities obtained in doing so. The formal representation abstracts away from crucial legal issues that would help the observer determine whether the system in question is democratic or authoritarian, or just or unjust. It also hides the manipulative, perhaps unduly coercive control relationships of the District Attorney vis à vis (perceptions of) jury decisions and prisoner's legal counsel, relations that are key concerns in the study of political power (Frey, 1974). A similar critique of the representational accuracy of game theory formalism, plus suggested alternative formalisms for descriptive, explanatory, and evaluative purposes, is given in an article entitled "The Prisoners' Dilemma Game as a System of Social Domination" (Burns and Buckley, forthcoming).

Axelrod proposes a procedure for measuring conflict of interest in laboratory or field bargaining games where utility payoffs are quantitatively measured (Luce and Suppes, 1965, review some relevant practices for doing so). After generalizing his measure to include Prisoners' Dilemma games, he then shows how some of Rapoport and Chammah's (1965) experimental data can be reanalyzed more adequately, under the assumption, *ceteris paribus,* that more conflict of interest increases the likelihood of defection. His rationale for his measuring procedure is the most sophisticated data theory we have yet encountered in this chapter. First, five reasonable properties of a measure of conflict of interest are proposed, then a proof is given that one and only one measure satisfied these properties for bargaining games. Then the measure is generalized (but not necessarily uniquely) to the Prisoners' Dilemma game.

Slightly restated, Axelrod's five desired properties for the case of the Prisoners' Dilemma are the following:

1. *Symmetry.*   The measure should not be different if we merely renamed or relabeled the prisoners (but did not change the payoff matrix).

2. *Independence.*   The measure should be independent of any interval level rescaling of prisoners' utilities. This decreases the extent to which the measure requires interpersonal comparisons of utilities, according to the core negative heuristics of liberal choice theory. It also allows the rescaling necessary in the computational algorithm, which uses a normalized rescaling of the payoff space, as indicated in Fig. 6(b). See how the required normalization rescales each player's highest possible payoff (here, T for each player, set to 1.0) and his lowest secure payoff (again in our symmetrical game the same for each player, P, set to 0.0).

3. *Additivity.*   After games have been normalized, this means that if the cost to one player of meeting a demand by another equals the sum of the costs of meeting the same demand in two other games, then the conflict of interest of the first game equals the sum of the conflicts of interest of the latter two games.

4. *Continuity.*   If the payoff regions for two normalized games with the same (P, P) point differ in shape by a very small degree (e.g., one R payoff is slightly larger than the other), then their conflict of interest measures should also be very close.[3]

5. *Permissible range.*   The conflict of interest measure is assumed to go from zero upward. For non-Prisoners' Dilemmas, an upper limit may also be the case, but in Prisoners' Dilemmas, only positive finiteness appears appropriate. (Axelrod, 1970)

Most of the above requirements are designed to make games with different payoff matrices comparable; in fact, the idea of normalization implicitly makes utility *ranges* comparable across actors, since the proposed procedure for calculating conflict of interest is based on area calculations where these two ranges [$(T - P)$ in Fig. 6(b) for each prisoner] are set equal to unity. The core idea of the procedure is then defined in terms of the "amount" of utility payoffs unrealizable because of opposed players' desires. As suggested by the additivity principle, the costs of meeting a demand for a particular payoff pair depend on how far it is from the optimum line for each player. Look at Fig. 6(b), where we have enclosed in and shaded a region that is in one sense desirable—its outer limits are achievable if the other prisoner were self-destructive—but in fact are not attainable assuming players prefer alternatives with higher payoffs. The more covetable, unrealizable outcomes, the more conflict of interest. Axelrod's proposed measure is the area of this tempting but infeasible region, calculated after the payoff space has been normalized for the sake of comparability. In Fig. 6(b) this tempting infeasible region consists of two symmetric triangles with bases $(T - S)$ in length and heights of $(T - R)$. The normalization of this area amounts to dividing it by the area of the rectangle that becomes the unit square after normalization. In the present symmetric case, this rectangle is already square, with area $(T - P)^2$. Hence for symmetric PD games,

$$CI = \text{conflict of interest} = \frac{(T - R)(T - S)}{(T - P)^2} \tag{1}$$

Having attempted briefly to make this result plausible, I shall not try to give a formal proof of the appropriateness of the resulting measure. That Axelrod's index does better in predicting defection behaviors in sequential PDs than several previously proposed by Rapoport, is a suggestive sign of its utility. That it proves effective in the study of Italian cabinet formation is additional evidence for the validity of Axelrod's measure (which in this sense does fit the path of validated measurement in Fig. 4, with error theories specific to the testing relationship).

Because of the unexplicated *ceteris paribus* assumptions in his treatment, however, we cannot really be sure of the timeless or universal validity of Axelrod's measure. Despite its elegant rationale, like the practical syllogism in Moon's analysis, this set of assumptions came before any statistic was ever calculated from them; and it may last in our minds long after other empirical measures have been found to be more convenient or provocative. The measure is intentionally descriptive; it is only potentially explanatory.

As a way of critiquing Axelrod's statistical practices, I shall propose an extension of his work, from the perspective of an external research paradigm partially compatible with his own orientation toward behavioral power analysis. This elaboration starts from my earlier remarks about the inadequacies of game-theoretic approaches in highlighting the essential characteristics of conflicting interests. In particular, I shall try to be responsive to the hypothetical prisoner's question: Doesn't the above description of our conflict of interest obscure our true common interests, which the District Attorney is actively forcing us to deny? A power analyst following the Lasswell–Dahl–Harsanyi research program (see Dahl, 1968; and Alker, 1973a) would translate this question into an analysis of the power exercised by the D.A. over the prisoners—the D.A. is getting the prisoners to do something that they otherwise would not do. The ability to do this is called power. Simultaneously, this conception implies the possibility of the prisoners doing something else plus their coerced prevention from doing so.

Measuring both power and the extent to which it is exercised are polimetric questions par excellence. Relevant distinctions among the bases, opportunity costs, amounts, domains, means, extents, and the costs of noncompliance must also be made. An important way of making nontautological statements about power is to make these statements and associated measures theory-dependent, with the theory being concerned with the causal mechanisms and situational manipulation possibilities for getting people to do what they would not do otherwise. Formally, measurement of this sort requires specification of power *schedules,* functional relations linking resistance costs and/or compliance amounts to the instrumental means/bases of power, perhaps additionally costed in opportunity terms.

In such a spirit, one might ask if power is related to the size of the tempting infeasible region in our prisoners example. Does Axelrod's conflict of interest measure the degree of power exercised by the D.A. over the prisoner? Although at first plausible, I shall suggest how this interpretation is incorrect. To see this, we need a theoretical model of the influence relations of our story, which will include the power schedules mentioned above. In the present exposition, our treatment will of necessity be considerably oversimplified.

What we will attempt to show is a functional relation linking the costs of Prisoner A's noncompliance to the instrumental means of the D.A.'s power. We define this in terms of A's expectations of utility payoffs in the case in which he cooperates minus his utility expectations for the case in which A defects.

$$A\text{'s costs of noncompliance} = \quad EV_A(C_A) \quad - \quad EV(D_A)$$
$$\text{(Expected value} \qquad \text{(Expected value}$$
$$\text{of } C_A) \qquad\qquad \text{of } D_A)$$

Note that at this point the role of the D.A. is completely implicit. Now the conventional way of defining expected utility payoffs from a particular action is in terms of the value of the possible outcomes, each weighted by their expected probability of occurring. Given two prisoners in a conflict situation, we of course should not assume that they both have the same expectations in this regard. Relevant equations are the following:

$$EV_A(C_A) = \quad V_A(C_A, C_B)\hat{p}_A(C_B) \quad + \quad V_A(C_A, D_B) \cdot \hat{p}_A(D_B) \qquad (2a)$$
$$\text{(Probable reward payoff)} \quad \text{(Probable sucker payoff)}$$

$$EV_A(D_A) = \quad V_A(D_A, C_B) \cdot \hat{p}_A, (C_B) \quad + \quad V_A(D_A, D_B) \cdot \hat{p}_A(D_B) \qquad (2b)$$
$$\text{(Probable temptation payoff)} \quad \text{(Probable penalty payoff)}$$

The above equation pair still leaves the role of the D.A. implicit. What in fact does he do? How does it affect payoff valuations (the V's of the equations) and their probability expectations (the $\hat{p}$'s of the equations)? His control of communications is crucial in two respects. First, he uses it (plus the absence of counsel) to decrease the *trust* that Prisoner A has in Prisoner B; we shall label this variable Trust$_{AB}$. Its minimum is $-3/4$. Second, he uses it to paint an uncorrected, rather black picture of the other prisoner, thus motivating him to diminish altruism, α, used in defining A's utility for the various possible outcome payoffs noted in the above equation. Behaviorally, we shall assume that trust has a reciprocal influence on A's probability estimate of B's defection $[\hat{p}_A(D_B)]$. And we shall assume that our prisoners need not follow exactly the golden rule of liberal individualism: think only of thyself. Rather, when $\alpha = 0$, we shall assume a pure rivalrous utility calculation, made in terms of payoff differences for the two prisoners. Pure self-interest corresponds to an α of 1; values of α greater than 1 mean that the other prisoner's payoffs are increasingly, positively taken into account. Plausible equations for these relations, for a conflict of interest CI_{AB} are as follows:

$$V_A(C_A, C_B) = \alpha R_A + (1 - \alpha)(R_A - R_B) \tag{3a}$$
$$V_A(C_A, D_B) = \alpha S_A + (1 - \alpha)(S_A - T_B) \tag{3b}$$
$$V_A(D_A, C_B) = \alpha T_A + (1 - \alpha)(T_A - S_B) \tag{3c}$$
$$V_A(D_A, D_B) = \alpha P_A + (1 - \alpha)(P_A - P_B) \tag{3d}$$

$$\hat{p}_A(D_B) = \min\left(\frac{\log_5 (1 + CI_{AB})}{1 + \text{Trust}_{AB}}, 1\right) \tag{4}$$

The logarithm to the base 5, roughly estimated from Rapoport and Chammah's experimental data, indicates that CI must be fairly high before random pairs of college students almost always defect.

Working in a range $(CI < 4)$ where $\hat{p}_A(D_B)$ is not at its maximum, we can ignore the minimum expression. Solving for the costs of noncompliance, as defined in Equation (2) gives:

$$\begin{array}{l} A\text{'s expected payoff} \\ \text{from noncompliance} \end{array} = 4\alpha - 5 - \frac{9\alpha \log_5 (1 + CI_{AB})}{1 + \text{Trust}_{AB}} \tag{5}$$

This power schedule measures noncompliance costs in terms of variables that the D.A. can influence: α (altruism), Trust_{AB}, and CI_{AB}. For a CI_{AB} of 5/9 (the case in Fig. 5), in the case where Trust is kept to zero and altruism is absent $(\alpha = 1)$, the cost of noncompliance is -1.3. A more general plot of this power schedule is given as Fig. 7. The D.A. has an ability to bring about net costs of noncompliance and probabilities of defection over a large range of α's, Trusts, and CI's. He can get the prisoners to do what is against their true interest (say, their $\alpha > 1$ *before* he talks to them) even without modifying α. Making CI large and preventing Trust will also give negative noncompliance payoffs.

One way of quantitatively measuring power as an ability in this case is to calculate (and perhaps normalize) an area or volume denoting the range of easily induced behavioral change (as in Fig. 7). Using legal means (a certain degree of CI manipulation) but not manipulating α or Trust would be a case of less controversial, smaller, but still considerable D.A. power. If we could assume a degree of certainty about guilt regarding a larger crime, legally deserving a five-year jail term, then we could ask if the discretionary power of the

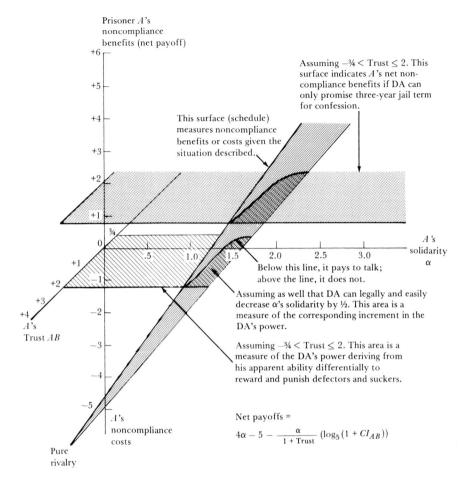

Fig. 7. A simple power schedule: the strength of a D.A.'s power (assuming $CI_{AB} = 5/9$).

District Attorney (and a judge or jury?) exceeeded or fell short of that justifiably needed.

A fuller, intentionalist treatment of this example would move us toward a genuine explanation of why the D.A. does what he does and omits what he omits. Is he running for reelection, desirous of a record of significant convictions? If so, the area measures of power in Fig. 7 suggest ranges of prisoner types for which he can get major convictions. What are the effective constraints, assumed until now without discussion, that keep the D.A. from trying to push distrust below $-3/4$? Why, presumably, has torture not been used? Could it be used safely, from the D.A.'s point of view, to produce Trust$_{AB}$ scores so near to -1 that A's position on the power schedule of Fig. 7, and the schedule itself, would sink below the payoff $= 0$ plane of the figure? The example heuristically suggests that D.A.–prisoner bargaining, a nonuniversal practice, may serve as a substitute for physical coercion. Again we find that our attempt to provide a more accurate interpretation of the intentions and the context of the prisoners in our story points toward a more adequate analysis.

Calculating expected payoffs derived from a matrix of individual jail terms is part of such a reanalysis. R', S', T', and P' could even be redefined in such a fashion. One can then find, as an exercise, the value of α (altruism) necessary in these terms to transform the original game into a non-Prisoners' Dilemma.

This analysis suggests a richer range of questions than those usually studied and statistically analyzed in experimental political science (as ably reviewed in Brody and Brownstein, Chapter 5 of this volume). As summarized by Baumgartner *et al.*, "The social structural context and, in particular, the existing or anticipated social relations among [all three] actors significantly influence their responses to a situation or issue and their interactions in that situation" (1974, p. 15). Game modeling, game playing, and game restructuring are parts of a multilevel process that takes place in both experimental and nonexperimental contexts.

INTENTIONALIST ASSESSMENT: THE INDIVIDUAL CASE

Abelson–Schank Conceptual Dependency Analysis

Positivistically trained, modern political scientists rarely devote themselves exclusively to the understanding of a single case. Comparative analyses allow the observation of effects associated with different, possibly causal conditions. Yet as Eckstein (Chapter 3 of this volume) argues, case studies can be heuristically suggestive in a number of ways that go beyond the conventional argument that they may serve to test a well-formed, prior hypothesis. When the analyst has some degree of belief in general theory but is also willing to modify his theories, he may profitably move back and forth between the particular and the general. Moreover, many representational problems are raised and sometimes solved in the attempt to develop a progressive series of model specifications.

The development of a series of models by Robert Abelson and his associates for explaining how the Barry Goldwater of 1960 and similar True Believers understood their world has been such an effort (Abelson and Rosenberg, 1958; Abelson, 1959; Abelson and Carroll, 1965 Abelson and Reich, 1969; Abelson, 1973). Rather than see these studies as purely idiosyncratic—as one variant of the humanistic concern with the unique—I see them as important, methodologically generalizable exemplars for a kind of polimetrics that seeks better to understand before it explains and evaluates. These studies are enormously suggestive with respect to intentionalist understanding of Barry Goldwater's own, unique public thinking in the 1960s as well. That he no longer is susceptible to quite so simplistic a treatment is a tribute to him, not a refutation of the earlier models. Their authors did not aspire to universal, timeless, nomic validity.

It is not my purpose here to review all the above work. Rather, I would like to suggest that it should serve as an exemplar within a growing tradition of statistical practice that is intentionalist in orientation, that seeks constitutive meanings without taking conscious intentions for granted, and that relates such meanings to their social structural, situational context as suggested above. Neither do I want to limit my interpretation of this exemplar to a hermeneutic interest in the political speeches of important actors, although a fragment of an address by Sheik Yamani of Saudi Arabia before the United Nations will be my major example. Rather, I shall argue that work by Abelson and others (e.g., Shapiro and Bonham, 1973; and Axelrod, 1973) helps us better to explain how political actors understand and therefore shape political realities. This argument is compatible with Moon's emphasis on quasi-causal explanations noted above. But it suggests going further to seek deeper, but inevitably partial explanatory understanding of political interpretive practices.

The text of the speech fragment we shall look at is taken from an address before a Special Session of the United Nations General Assembly called by Algeria, over the objections of the United States, to discuss problems of energy, raw materials, and development. Because Sheik Yamani has become a principal spokesman for the Middle Eastern oil producers and OPEC (the Organization of Petroleum Exporting Countries) as well, it is of more than routine interest. An excerpt is as follows:

> The advanced industrial nations have long been able to dominate and monopolize, directly or indirectly, the four elements of development [raw materials, including energy, capital, technology, markets]. Being the owners of capital and technology, those nations were enabled through their international companies to dominate the sources of raw materials and energy and to place these elements at the disposal of their own industries, which in turn controlled their markets throughout the world, allowing no outsider to approach them.

> On the other hand, the countries of the third world, or the developing countries, devoid of capital and technology, had no real power over the raw materials or sources of energy of which, in many cases, they were the rightful owners. Their role in the international economic game was merely that of exporter of raw materials and energy at unrealistically low prices, the supplier of cheap labour, and as an open market for the manufactured goods that inundated them, making it impossible for them to establish industries in their own territories except within the narrow limits permitted by the advanced industrial countries. (Yamani, 1974)

Some preliminaries. Before giving an illustrative conceptual dependency analysis of parts of this speech, we need to review some methodological preliminaries. These are: (1) the background of conceptual dependency analysis; (2) the possibility rules for formulating conceptual interpretations of English language sentences; and (3) the rules for combining such "atomic" conceptualizations into higher-order constituent meanings, called molecules, themes, plans, and scripts by Abelson (1973). In a sense these rules for an almost operational procedure are like the data and measurement theories of less complex statistical practices.

In developing conceptual dependency analysis, Schank, a computer scientist trained in linguistics, was interested in writing computer programs to help one understand ordinary English. Such efforts have had limited but significant successes (see Schank and Colby, 1973) in what is now known to be an enormously complex and difficult task; hence, the limitation of currently operational systems to limited content areas (excluding UN debates). Schank assumes from the start that unique, prelingual conceptualizations underlie every independent sentence fragment. Driven by the need to write efficient parsing algorithms of incoming texts, Schank uses a "post-Chomskian" representation of syntactic and semantic meaning structures. In particular, once the independently understandable components of an incoming conceptualization are tentatively identified, they are processed in the search for a plausible interpretation. In what must be thought of as a kind of formal hermeneutics, syntactic/semantic meaning structures are described precausally in terms of the conceptual independence, interdependence, and dependence of elementary parts of a particular conceptualization. (A rather similar emphasis on the noncausal nature of interpretive analysis is given by Habermas, 1971.)

Schank's four basic semantic units are concepts similar to those used in high school syntactic parsing exercises: nouns, verbs, adjectives, and adverbs. But, emphasizing their semantic role, Schank uses a slightly different typology. Because they can be thought of without any need for additional relations, *nominal concepts* are referred to as PPs (Picture Producers). For something to be an *action concept* (ACT), it must be something that an animate nominal can be said to be doing (to some nominal object). Picture Aiders (PAs) and Action Aiders (AAs) are *modifier concepts* which have no independent significance, that serve to specify an attribute, respectively, of a nominal or an action.

The seven kinds of permissible dependency/interdependency relations among elementary concepts are described in Table 4, where the examples have mostly been drawn from the Yamani speech fragment quoted above. The first thing to note about the arrows in the qualitative, but data-based formalism, is that they are not causal. In fact, causal relations are not even defined at the atomic level of meaning; they come at a higher molecular level, where purposive behavior and practical inferences can also be defined. Given the need to predict what types of sentence parts should be looked for in completing a not yet fully interpreted sentence, the arrows in conceptual dependence analysis tell us that within a particular conceptualization, the conceptual element at the foot of an arrow predicts to, or is predicated on, a previously defined concept of the type indicated at the head of an arrow. Arrows point to "governor" concepts on which other concepts are "dependent" for their meaning within a given conceptualization.

There are six classes of arrows in Table 4: double-headed, double-lined "actor-act interdependencies"; double-headed, triple-lined "attributive interdependencies" of two sorts; unlabeled, single-arrowed "attributive dependencies"; various types of single-headed, double-lined "prepositional dependencies"; four labeled attributive "case dependencies"; and a complexly drawn "state change dependency" that combines features of case relationships with attributive interdependence. Except for a few complications, including ACT tenses which we shall usually ignore here, these possible relations nearly exhaust the component possibilities within elementary, that is, atomic (and often but not always sentential) conceptualizations.

One comment from the table must be expanded upon, that elaborating on the need for semantic conditions before Actor–Act bonds ($\Longleftrightarrow$) may be realized. Very much like von Wright's discussion of "how possible" teleological explanations, deriving from the Chomskean nondeterministic practice of formulating grammatical possibility rules, the rules of Table 4 are conditional possibility rules. (In general, AA, PA, PP, ACT combinations other than those mentioned in such rules are not allowed.) But possibility rules without concept-specific plausibility conditions should not be conceptually allowed—planes do not swim, nor LDCs change locations without dramatic, attendant changes in state. Hence, the general possibility rules of Table 4 must be supplemented by conceptual and contextual semantic plausibility or state enablement conditions before a concrete conceptualization instance is allowed.

In addition to the comments in the table, the reader should be aware that Schank and Abelson have gone to considerable lengths to reduce the elementary meaning concepts needed to conceptualize actor-act interdependencies to perhaps two dozen primitive acts, such as CONC (meaning "conceptualize"), PTRANS (meaning "physical transfer"), MTRANS (meaning "mental transfer"), ATRANS (meaning "possession transfer"), WANT (a motivational disposition with object specified), sense acts such as SMELL, LOOK-AT, LISTEN-TO, SPEAK, etc.

Special kinds of atomic relations can also be defined. Thus *A*(ction) atoms are made up of a single actor-act bond, necessarily including an instrumental (and thus potentially observable) case and possibly including other case dependencies as well. *S*(tate) atoms are attributive interdependencies, usually thought of as outcomes of or enablers of *A*(ction) atoms. A number of exam-

TABLE 4 Permissible conceptual dependencies at the atomic level (ignoring tense complications). *Source:* Schank, 1973, with revisions.

Conceptual rule in symbolic form, plus name	Comment	Example, plus its English conceptualization
1. PP < = > ACT (Actor-act conceptualization interdependence)	A syntactic, conceptual, action possibility rule – which PPs can do which acts is given by contextual semantics.	LDC < = > supply $\begin{array}{c} \xleftarrow{o} \text{labor} \\ \uparrow \\ \text{cheap} \end{array}$ A_1 "LDCs supply (cheap labor)."
2. PP <≡> PA (attributive conceptualization interdependence)	Used to say PP is in state PA.	DC <≡> poss $\begin{bmatrix} \text{capital and} \\ \text{technology} \end{bmatrix}$ S_1 "DCs possess capital and technology."
3. PP <≡> PP (Attributive conceptualization interdependence)	Used to indicate set membership of lefthand PP in righthand PP.	LDC <≡> $\begin{array}{c} \text{market} \\ \uparrow \\ \text{open} \end{array}$ S_2 "LDCs are open markets."
4. PP $\uparrow$ PA (Attributive dependency)	By definition, the dependent concept (PA) predicts the existence of the governing concept (PP); an (implicit) prior predication of conceptual attribute is assumed.	$\begin{array}{c} \text{market} \\ \uparrow \\ \text{open} \end{array}$ (in the above example.)
5. PP $\uparrow$ PP (type) (Prepositional dependency)	The three most common types are containment (CONT), location (LOC), and possession (POSS-BY)	LDC <≠> poss $\xrightarrow{o}$ industries $\begin{array}{c}\text{many}\uparrow\end{array}$ $\begin{array}{c}\text{LOC}\\ \Uparrow \\ \text{territory} \\ \Uparrow \text{POSS-BY} \\ \text{LDC}\end{array}$ S'_2 "LDCs cannot establish many industries in their own territories."

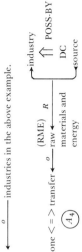

Conceptual rule	Comment	Example, plus its English conceptualization
6. Conceptual case dependencies	Although often implicit, these can be considered as part of, required by, dependent on various ACTS within a full ACT conceptualization; the PP is an object governed by the ACT.	$\overset{o}{\longrightarrow}$ industries in the above example.
(a) ACT $\overset{o}{\longrightarrow}$ PP [Objective dependency (O)]	The PP is an object governed by the ACT.	
(b) ACT $\overset{R}{\longrightarrow}$ (to) PP, (from) PP [Recipient dependency (R)]	Recipient relation (from possession by lower PP to possession by higher PP) is dependent on an ACT, usually through an objective dependency.	one <=> transfer $\overset{o}{\longrightarrow}$ raw materials and energy (RME) $\overset{R}{\longrightarrow}$ industry / source, POSS-BY DC "(Someone) transfers raw materials and energy from their sources to the Developed Countries' own industries."
(c) ACT $\overset{D}{\longrightarrow}$ (to) PP, (from) PP [Directive dependency (D)]	Directive relation is dependent on some ACTS, involving place/directional changes as indicated.	Some <> mover $\overset{D}{\longrightarrow}$ DCs / LDCs "Some move from LDCs to DCs."
(d) ACT $\overset{I}{\longrightarrow}$ PP or ACT $\overset{I}{\longrightarrow}$ ↑ (Instrumental dependency)	Every act requires an instrumental case (means) which is more fully an action or just a PP.	DC <=> dominate $\overset{o}{\longrightarrow}$ sources $\overset{I}{\longrightarrow}$ international companies, CONT raw material and energy, POSS-BY DC "DC dominate sources of RME through their international companies."
7. PP $\ll\equiv$ PA / PA (State change dependency)	A PP can change from one state to another.	LDC $\ll\equiv$ developed / underdeveloped (S'_0) "An underdeveloped country becomes developed."

ples are indicated in Table 4 as circled *A*'s and *S*'s. *P*(urpose) atoms are formed
from the ACT "WANT" plus its objective case specifications, e.g.:

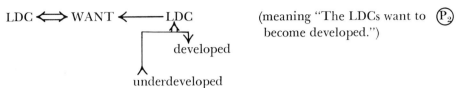

(meaning "The LDCs want to P_2
become developed.")

In Schank's system, purposive wanting of this sort is assumed to imply that if
the objective concept were to be the case, then the wanting actor would be
pleased. Conscious, purposeful wanting can be defined as a *P* atom for which
the CONC(eptualization) of the objective state and its instrumental case has
taken place. For those familiar with von Wright's thought model of a Tractatus
World (1971), or the logical positivist ideal of a logically rigorous formal language with a small number of operationally describable primitive concepts,
Schank's computer language is an impressive, powerful, partly operational realization of this ideal.

We are now ready briefly to review the ways in which elementary, that is,
atomic, conceptualizations are allowed to combine (or "bond") into molecular
forms. The perceptive reader will already have noticed that Table 4's alternate representation of instrumental case relationships in fact combined two independently describable action atoms at the atomic level. We shall indeed continue to treat atomic sentences with other atoms in attributive, prepositional
or case relationships as conceptual atoms. Here, rather than further explore
such alternate representations, we shall depart somewhat from Abelson's definitions, considering a molecule to be any collection of atoms bonded in a
permissible fashion by *molecular* bonds: positive or negative, intentional or unintentional varieties of action, causation, enablement, or equality ties. Molecular ties will be single or double lines without arrows (but read in left-to-right
or top-down order). They should only connect circled atoms. Intended bonds
should be represented as unbroken lines; unintended links are dashed. Negative, blocked, or vitiating relations are indicated by *X*'s, equalities by =, and
conditional gating by ⤳ symbols.

Simple molecular relationships of particular interest are functional and
purposeful actions (formed by (P)– – –(A) and (P)———(A) action bonds), causal
relations (formed by (A)———(S) or reflexive (A)– – –(S) causation bonds), enablement relations (formed by ordinary enablement bonds (S)———(A), allowing
A to happen); or by gating enablement bonds determining whether an action
(A), if taken, leads to a particular outcome (S_1), depending on (S_2), such as

For example, (P)———(A) refers to functional action which unintentionally serves the purpose P, in the sense that some consequences S_i of (A) are consciously or unconsciously part of the object of P, but A does not enable S_i in the sense to be defined below. For (P)———(A) to occur, the "purposive action" bonding rule requires relation A actually to be causing the S included in P and the actor of A to be an agent of the actor of P.

(S)———(A) refers to condition (S) enabling action (A) in one of two senses: i. *(instrumental control)*. Here the actor within the S-atom has or is able to use the instrument(s) of the A-atom, or their equivalents; ii. *(social contract)*. The S-atom is an attributional interdependence (involving previously predicated actors, proposals, agreements, or their equivalents) indicating that the actor in the A-atom has become another's agent with respect to the act in A. An atom (A) is equivalent to another, perhaps more elaborately definite (A_1)———(S)———(A_2) or indefinite (A_1) ... (A_n) molecule,

$$(A) = (A_1)——(S_1)——(A_2) \; ... \; (S_{n-1})——(A_n)$$

if and only if all the constituent elements of the less elaborated molecule are found in semantically corresponding parts of the more elaborated one. Each link in this definition need not be intentional. But wherever such intentional links exist among atoms, we shall assume conscious conceptualization (CONC) also to be present. As another example,

refers to a causal relation of multiple consequences, one of which is the intentional blockage of state S_1. Here, for an (A)———(S) link to be intentional, we assume a conscious purpose to have been already predicated, with the nonrealization of (S_1) as part of its goal object (or an equivalent elaboration thereof). Similarly,

refers to a state S_1 enabling action A as had previously been consciously wanted, except that (S_2), although not intentionally foreseen, plays a necessary-for-action-A gating role.

Clearly, one of the most exciting features of this list is the way it includes, but goes beyond, causal relations. Thus, much of von Wright's (1971) book is dedicated to distinguishing partly tautological relations among parts of an intentional action description from causal statements about actions and their consequences. The P—A molecular link defined above is just such a noncausal bond; similar ties could have been defined involving resulting instrumental actions that are somehow part of an intentional action, not causal consequences of it. Von Wright also argues that we should distinguish enabling conditions from sufficient causes (which we have done in the case of unintentional gating above). And he calls for treating outcomes beyond the instrumental behavior that is part of an action itself as revised system states. His insistence, following Anscombe, that behaviors may be intentional under one description but not another, fits exactly with the semantic criteria of coherence that we have learned to require of conceptual dependency formalisms. Clearly, conceptual dependency analysis provides a quite compatible formalism for intentionalist analyses. Moreover, the introduction of nonadditive, nonintentional action gating, the reflexive causation of actions, and functional (von Wright would say purpose*ful*) actions are but slight revisions of Abelson's presentation. They are designed to accommodate the dispositional and contextual caveats expressed in previous examples in which purely and wholly autonomous intentionalist explanations were suspect. Colby (1973), for example, has used a somewhat similar computer semantics system to model the compulsive behavior of psychiatric patients that may well exhibit the Lasswellian projective tendencies described above.

We are now in a position to present some of the most interesting molecules in the Abelson extension of Schank's system, in particular his formal conceptualizations of purposive implicational molecules and his definition of intentional action and plan molecules. An earlier paper (Abelson and Reich, 1969), discussed the idea of psychological implication in terms of molecules which in use tend to be completed when all but one of their elements are known. These implicational molecules correspond almost exactly in their semantic and pragmatic character to the practical inference schema discussed in various forms by Moon (1975) and von Wright (1971): It is turned around in order to suggest answers to the question: how is it possible that A does X? Abelson calls the resulting molecule "Purpose (Y, A, X)":

$$\text{Purpose } (Y, A, X) = \begin{array}{l} A : A \text{ does } X \\ + \\ S : X \text{ causes } Y \\ + \\ P : ? \text{ (tend to fill in } A \text{ wants } Y) \end{array} \qquad \begin{array}{l} \text{"}A \text{ does } X \text{ because } X \text{ causes} \\ Y \text{ (and } A \text{ wants } Y).\text{"} \end{array}$$

We have labeled and connected atoms in an unconventional way because their formation and bonding rules do not fit the above exposition exactly. But the whole point of such a device in Abelson's simulation is clearly the same as von Wright's claim that we make "how possible" practical inferences in intentionalist contexts all the time.

In his update of this prototype of the practical inference, Abelson (1973, p. 299) defines P—A—S molecules to represent "an action undertaken in order to attain a goal desired by the sponsor of the action." We shall call such constructions "intentional action molecules." Because our description of the WANT ACT did not presume Schank's condition of self-consciousness, the phrase "conscious intentionalist action" will be used unambiguously to imply the existence of the appropriate consciousness, conceptualized as part of the wanting act described in the P atom. Abelson's definitional conditions for an intentional action molecule are:

1. (PS) The S-atom (or its equivalent) is in the objective location of the WANT of the P-atom.
2. (AS) The A atom is causally bonded to the S-atom.
3. (PA) P—A is a purposive action bond, i.e., the actor in the A-atom is an agent (including the special case of self-agency) for the actor in the P-atom and (2) holds.

Plans can be described as "extended, conscious intentionalist actions." They must have been made up of one or more alternating A and S sequences following an initial P-atom. Four conditions for their existence (Abelson, 1973, p. 305) are:

1. The final S in such a sequence must be the same or equivalent to the S in the objective case of the P "want."
2. Each A is causally bonded to the subsequent S.
3. The actor in each A is either the actor in the initial P or the agent of the A or intial P.
4. Each S "enables" the subsequent A.

Since much practical action involves the elaboration of higher-level plans into more specific ones, a natural extension of this definition is to define plans "recursively," that is, in terms of specifiable subplans. Most list processing languages are in fact structured recursively to facilitate such elaborations or transformations, which are taken as evidence of fundamental human cognitive capabilities by linguists influenced by Chomsky's syntactic or semantic research paradigms.

Two of the more complex generative semantic structures in Abelson correspond to what Moon (1975) calls constitutive meanings. Themes are concatinations of plans held by two (or more) different actors. One such theme structure very much in evidence in the Yamani script is "domination." Whether in his speech fragment domination is also an action is not altogether clear, but one could easily build up most of the components necessary for a theme ascription, as will be done in Fig. 9.

Theme descriptions and permissible constructions are in terms of pairs of plan molecules put in boxes. Molecular facilitating and inhibiting relations are used as before, even when indefinite (sketchy) molecular representation rules are used. These are supplemented by specificational conventions describing ways in which the different parties enter as agents, goal objects, or interested parties pleased or displeased with their role in another's plans. According to Abelson (1973), the components of a DC-LDC dominance theme would be schematized as follows.

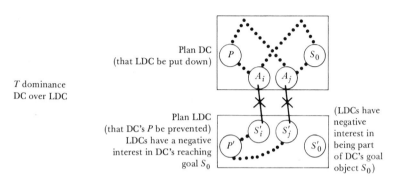

T dominance
DC over LDC

Plan DC
(that LDC be put down)

Plan LDC
(that DC's P be prevented)
LDCs have a negative
interest in DC's reaching
goal S_0

(LDCs have
negative
interest in
being part
of DC's goal
object S_0)

In general, possible semantic conceptualizations at this level are less explicit about their atomic and molecular components, allowing easy manipulations both cognitively and analytically. "Quasi-causal" determinative relations are loosely defined as meaning "naturally following one from another." Scripts are a high-level constitutive meaning structure defined in terms of theme sequences. "Rebellion of E against F" is a script (as well as a theme) which starts with F dominating E and ends with E dominating F; in between are rebellion, conflict, and victory stages, "naturally" following each other. Each of these component themes can be defined in ways analogous to dominance, as defined above.

An Illustrative Example [4]

Returning now to the search for constitutive meaning structures in Yamani's text can we infer a rebellion script involving DSs and LDCs? Or is a structural transformation from dominance to cooperative interdependence appropriate? These options might be schematized as in Figs. 8(a) and 8(b). Note first that the scripts start out the same, but that in the second one a "natural" gating relationship is posited as codetermining a cooperative finale.

Figure 9 suggests something like a functional dominance theme. It cannot be completely described without knowing how much of it and of the remaining parts of Yamani's speech are political propaganda. And we really need insights into his politically relevant memory content as well. Nor are all the parts nicely fitted together in isolated, intentionally pure plans. Nonetheless Yamani probably does see a kind of quasi-planned, dominated past.

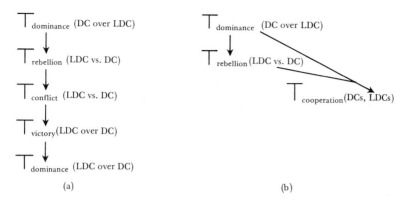

Fig. 8. *Two thematically related interpretations of the revolt by oil-producing LDCs. (a) From dependency to dominance; (b) from dependency to cooperative interdependence.*

Figure 9 points toward some key inferential questions. For example, what are the purposes of the DCs in seeking to maintain their economic advantages? Should they be coded as domination, or only their own development maximization that amounts *functionally* (via dashed links) to the same thing, without all the *conscious* negative interests required of dominance theme. Similarly, we can ask about the situational interests underlying intentionalist assessments. Are all the developing countries (Saudia Arabia, in particular) genuinely interested in economic development (with its attendant socioeconomic transformations) or would they be satisfied with reversing functional dominance, and the associated wealth and power enhancement? Furthermore, is it still correct to identify the industries in the LDCs as possessed by the developed countries, as Yamani does?

We cannot here answer these questions, but the heuristic utility of descriptions that point toward systemic process explanations and emancipatory responses should be emphasized. Figure 9 is a controversial, testable *process theory* of domination relations consistent with alternate specifications at the script level (Fig. 8) of how the international system may be changing. Action, function, causation, enablement, and "between-theme determination" relations are implied. The formalism of Table 4 and Figs. 8 and 9 give us a descriptively rich, suggestive way of renewing the scientific analysis of power relationships.

CONCLUSION

In this chapter, I have called for a new and more careful look at the descriptive foundations of polimetrics, particularly its representational practices. This ex-

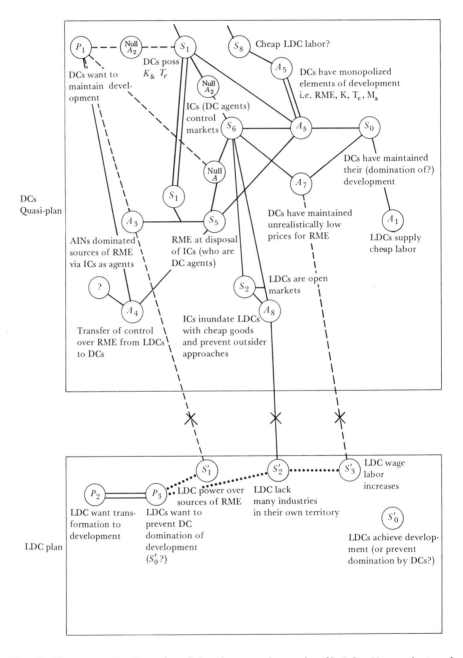

Fig. 9. Elements of a functional-dominance theme implied by Yamani speech fragment. Many atoms are defined in Table 4. When two or more lines go into a single atom they may combine as alternatives or as conjunctive causes. RME

hortation has been made on the assumption that political statistics is developing enough coherence as a subject matter to justify a distinctive name. Polimetrics may be defined, I argued, as the application of mathematical forms and statistical procedures to the quantitative description or qualitative labeling of political phenomena, the inferential testing of explanatory political theories, and the invention or evaluation of political alternatives. This definition extends the conventional definition in terms of nominal, ordinal, and interval measurement.

Polimetrics should be described, criticized, and taught in terms of a variety of foundational statistical traditions and practices, which inform and give rise to particular techniques or procedures. Statistical practices may themselves be thought of as constellations of investigators, with theoretical orientations and methodological standards, trying to solve research problems in various contexts by applying data generation and analysis procedures to hypothetical or observable phenomena with varying results. This "sociological/philosophical" view is necessary if both external and internal criticisms are to be addressed.

The emphasis on descriptive practices derived from several sources. First, these practices often are presented as preceding explanatory and evaluative efforts. Second, the major thrust of recent philosophical critiques of behavioral positivism (or naturalism) in political science, as summarized by von Wright (1971) and Moon (1975), is the concern that formalized data generation and analysis procedures have ignored the consciously or unconsciously intentionalist, interpretive character of political actions and theories. Finally, the author has recently published critical reviews of explanatory statistical practices (Alker, 1970, 1974) which suggested very similar concerns.

Examples of procedures such as reason analysis and conflict of interest analysis that do reflect hermeneutic interests were reviewed. They raised the issue, not taken to be problematic by von Wright, whether polimetrics could *assume* voluntaristic behavior, intentionalist action, and practical inferences in contexts where political capabilities were very equally distributed. Politics always challenges hermeneutics. Even in noncoercive contexts, the Lasswellian formula of political man as a projector and rationalizer of private needs directly challenged this conscious, voluntaristic conception. The Marxian analysis of political interests underlying popular and professional knowledge systems also makes a pure intentionalist perspective problematic (see Habermas, 1971). One

---

= *raw materials, including energy; K* = *capital; T_e* = *technology; M_a* = *markets; DCs* = *AINs* = *developed countries or advanced industrial nations; ICs* = *international companies or corporations; LDCs* = *less developed countries. Note also that causation, enablement, etc., flow from left to right. Dashed lines represent unintentional links; dotted lines are incompletely specified links.*

major implication of the above examples of various forms of intentionalist polimetric practices, including single-peaked preference maps, then, was that they should be augmented in a way that allowed dispositional, situational, counterintentionalist, or covert-intentionalist data theories to contribute to the analysis.

The fact that conceptual dependency analysis allows the representation of practical inferences, plus conscious and unconscious purposive behavior recommends it highly in this regard [Colby (1973) uses a similar computerized qualitative data processing system to analyze the unconscious motives of a psychiatric patient.] Moreover, capabilities of this data-analytic formalism to include intentional and unintentional enabling, gating, vitiation, and blocking relationships in addition to purposive behaviors pointed toward its representational relevance for future political research. "Causal models" in this new formalism, like Fig. 9, are much more phenomenally accurate than currently used polimetric practices.

As part of the theoretical foundations of polimetrics, there must be an underlying conceptualization of politics. The above analysis points toward some of the components of such a conceptualization, which surely should include, but go beyond, the insightful contributions of the previous examples and the Kramer–Hertzberg exposition of formal modelling approaches (see Chapter 7 of this volume). An earlier review of several major theoretical traditions and causal modelling practices resonates with the critical findings of the above analyses (Alker, 1974a). It suggested that polimetrics should be based on the following.

1. The explicit recognition of distinct norms, ends, means, costs, contexts, outcomes, and conditions of individual and collective human actions, as well as often unintended or emergent longer-range institutional consequences of such actions (*an augumented means-ends schema*).

2. The *inclusion of irreducible cognitive mentalistic, linguistic, or conceptual variables* in the definition of action situations, such as normative rules, principles, intentions, symbolic interpretations, constitutional formulas enhancing or limiting power relationships.

3. The existence in at least some cases of norms, ends, or purposes of independent causal significance in choice situations after heredity and environment are taken into account (*a contextually limited freedom of the will perspective*).

4. The existence, development, or decay in social action patterns of *power-relevant emergent properties at multiple system levels,* such as noncoerced consciously purposive behavior, linguistic communication, stable dominance relationships, a normatively regulated political order encouraging market exchange relationships, or collective value solidarities.

5. *An interdisciplinary, precausal conceptualization of the partly routinized nature of social process,* legitimizing the simultaneous use of psychological, social, economic, or political variables, giving meaning and
direction to synthetic process modelling efforts, allowing casual analyses
within a broader class of determinative possibilities. (Alker, 1974a. p. 203ff)

This set of representational foundations frequently undermines the inferential adequacy of nomically justified, simple structural/causal models of
political behavior. Causal models in the formalism of Table 4 and Fig. 9 can
be extended to the power schedule of our Prisoners' Dilemma example. Lasswell's previously cited type *C* law, as analyzed by Baas and Brown, or the
Abelson–Schank generative principles of Fig. 8 may be more appropriate
representations of nomic regularities in the political sphere. An earlier review
showed how simulational respecifications were also necessary for systems of
regression, factor or path equations that have been used to explain UN
voting. A similar critique has been made of Markovian learning models used
causally to model sequential Prisoners' Dilemmas (Alker, 1974a). The conclusion was again representational, hence essentially a descriptive, heuristic
one. Those attempting statistical analyses of political practices must have at
least provisionally adequate descriptive/representational specifications of the
processes they are investigating before real-world explanatory or problem-
solving efforts are likely to be cumulatively fruitful. As a research program,
conceptual dependence analysis and its relatives provide relatively adequate
descriptive formalisms for doing so. The incorporation of quantitative descriptions in such a formal system, and the elaboration of specific representations of
intertheme determination are two areas in which work is currently needed and
progressing.

Given the progress that has been made in modelling and understanding
some natural and artificial (experimental, hypothetical) political systems, polimetrics need not and cannot stop with hermeneutics. Causal, quasi-causal, or
noncausal explanations are relevant and sometimes possible within a richer
repertoire of descriptive and explanatory formalisms. But polimetrics must
frequently pass through hermeneutics before its explanatory and emancipatory
interests can be realized.

NOTES

1. My ignorance of statistical practices outside of North America, Japan, and parts
of western Europe, plus obvious international differences in epistemological orientation and computer access (necessary for much multivariate analysis), make me limit
the presumed relevance of the present remarks to the North American context. A number of arguments and examples will be taken from my earlier papers on political statistics. These and other relevant references appear in the references at the end of the
chapter.

2.   The reader is referred to Goldberger (1972), Alker (1970, 1974a), Gurr (1972), and Kahn (Chapter 8 of this volume) for somewhat parallel reviews of explanatory and predictive statistical practices. Unfortunately, no adequate review of evaluative practices exists, but the reader is urged to consult Raiffa (1968), Pratt, Raiffa, and Schlaifer (1965), Rivlin (1971), Tufte (1974), Campbell (1973), Grumm (1975), and Taylor (1975) for this purpose.

3.   A more rigorous version of this topological idea may be stated in terms of an infinite sequence of game payoff regions, each with the same (P, P) point as a given payoff region, and each closer to the boundaries of the given region than the previous one. The continuity requirement is that the conflict of interest measures for this sequence in the limit become the same as the conflict of interest measure for the given payoff region.

4.   I have been greatly helped in this example by D. Scott Ross's original, unpublished analysis of it.

REFERENCES

Abelson, Robert P. (1959). "Modes of resolution of belief dilemmas." *Journal of Conflict Resolution* 3:343–352.

_____(1973). "The structure of belief systems." In Roger C. Schank and Kenneth M. Colby, eds., *Computer Models of Thought and Language*. San Francisco: W. H. Freeman.

Abelson, Robert P., and J. D. Carroll (1965). "Computer simulation of individual belief systems." *American Behavioral Scientist* 8:24–30.

Abelson, Robert P., and C. M. Reich (1969). "Implicational modules: a method for extracting meaning from input sentences." In D. E. Walker and L. M. Norton, eds., *Proceedings of the International Joint Conference on Artificial Intelligence*. Boston: Mitre Corporation.

Abelson, Robert P., and Milton J. Rosenberg (1958). "Symbolic psychologic: a model of attitudinal cognition." *Behavioral Science* 3:1–13.

Ahmavaara, Y. (1957). "On the unified factor theory of mind." *Annales Academiae Scientiarum Fennicae* 106:1–176.

Alker, Hayward R., Jr. (1964). "Dimensions of conflict in the general assembly." *American Political Science Review* 56:642–657.

_____ (1965). *Mathematics and Politics*. New York: Macmillan.

_____ (1966a). "Causal inference and political analysis." In Joseph Bernd, ed., *Mathematical Applications in Political Science* 2:7–43. Dallas: Southern Methodist University Press.

_____ (1966b). "Supranationalism in the United Nations." *Papers of the Peace Research Society (International), III (1965)*:197–212. Reprinted in James N. Rosenau, ed. (1969). *International Politics and Foreign Policy*. New York: Free Press.

_____ (1968). "The long road to international relations theory: problems of statistical nonadditivity." *World Politics* 23:4 (July 1966), 623–655. Reprinted in Morton

Kaplan, ed. (1968). *New Approaches to International Relations*. New York: St. Martins Press.

_____ (1970). "Statistics and politics: the need for causal data analysis." In Seymour Martin Lipset, ed., *Politics and the Social Sciences*. New York: Oxford University Press.

_____ (1971a). "Assessing the impact of the U.N. collective security system: an operational multicultural approach." *Proceedings of the American Society of International Law* 65:33–39.

_____ (1971b). "Le Comportement Directeur (Directive Behavior)." *Revue Français de Sociologie* (Numero Special):99–122.

_____ (1973a). "On political capabilities in a schedule sense: measuring power, integration and development." In H. R. Alker, Jr., K. W. Deutsch and A. Stoetzel, eds., *Mathematical Approaches to Politics*. New York: Elsevier.

_____ (1973b). "Research paradigms and mathematical politics." Mimeographed. Forthcoming in Rudolph Wildemann, ed., *Proceedings of the Mannheim IPSA Conference*.

_____ (1974a). "Are there structural models of voluntaristic social action?" *Quality and Quantity* 8:199–246.

_____ (1974b). "Computer simulations: inelegant mathematics and worse social science?" *International Journal of Mathematical Education in Science and Technology* 5:139–155.

Armstrong, J. Scott (1967). "Derivation of theory by means of factor analysis or Tom Swift and his electric factor analysis machine." *American Statistician* 21, 5:17–21.

Axelrod, Robert (1970). *Conflict of Interest: A Theory of Divergent Goals with Applications to Politics*. Chicago: Markham.

_____ (1973). "Schema theory: an information processing model of perception and cognition." *American Political Science Review* 67:1248–1266.

Baas, Larry R., and Steven R. Brown (1973). "Generating rules for intensive analysis: the study of transformations." *Psychiatry* 36 (May):172–183.

Baumgartner, T., T. Burns, L. D. Meeker, and B. Wild (1974). "Generalized prisoners' dilemma as a multi-level game: methodological implications of multi-level processes for social research." Paper presented to the VIIIth World Congress of Sociology, Toronto.

Blalock, Hubert M., Jr. (1960). *Social Statistics*. New York: McGraw-Hill.

_____ (1964). *Causal Inferences in Nonexperimental Research*. Chapel Hill: University of North Carolina Press.

Brody, Andras (1970). *Proportions, Prices and Planning*. New York: American Elsevier.

Brown, Steven R. (1974). "Intensive analysis in political research." *Political Methodology* 3:1–25.

Burns, Tom, and Walter Buckley (forthcoming). "The prisoners' dilemma game as a system of social domination." *Journal of Peace Research*.

Cahoon, Lawrence, Melvin J. Hinich, and Peter C. Ordeshook (1973). "A methodology for spatial analysis." Paper delivered at the Montreal Meetings of the International Political Science Association.

Campbell, Donald T. (1973). "Reforms as experiments." In J. A. Caporaso and L. L. Roos, Jr., eds., *Quasi-Experimental Approaches: Testing Theory and Evaluating Policy.* Evanston, Ill.: Northwestern University Press.

Campbell, Donald T., and Julian C. Stanley (1963). "Experimental and quasi-experimental designs for research on teaching." In N. L. Gage, ed., *Handbook of Research on Teaching,* pp. 171–246. Chicago: Rand McNally.

Caporaso, James A., and Leslie L. Roos, Jr., eds. (1973). *Quasi-Experimental Approaches: Testing Theory and Evaluating Policy.* Evanston, Ill.: Northwestern University Press.

Carroll, J. Douglas (1972). "Individual differences and multidimensional scaling." In Roger N. Shepard, A. Kimball Romney, and Sara B. Nerlove, eds., *Multidimensional Scaling: Theory and Application in the Behavioral Sciences.* Two volumes. New York: Seminar Press.

Carroll, J. Douglas, and J. J. Chang (1970). "Analysis of individual differences in multidimensional scaling via an n-way generalization of 'Eckart-Young' decomposition." *Psychometrika* 35:283–319.

Cattell, Raymond B., and Kern Dickman (1962). "A dynamic model of physical influences demonstrating the necessity of oblique simple structure." *Psychological Bulletin* 59:389–400.

Colby, Kenneth M. (1973). "Simulations of belief systems." In Roger C. Schank and Kenneth M. Colby, eds., *Computer Models of Thought and Language.* San Francisco: W. H. Freeman.

Coombs, Clyde, Robyn Dawes, and Amos Tversky (1970). *Mathematical Psychology: An Elementary Introduction.* Englewood Cliffs, N.J.: Prentice-Hall.

Coxon, Anthony P. M. (1972). "Differential cognition and valuation: an introduction to Carroll and Chang's multidimensional scaling models." Research Memorandum. Project on Occupational Cognition, Department of Sociology, University of Edinburgh, Edinburgh, Scotland.

Coxon, Anthony P. M., and Charles L. Jones (1975). "The development and extension of multidimensional scaling models." To be published in revised form in *Quality and Quantity,* forthcoming.

Dahl, Robert A. (1968). "Power." In David Sills, ed., *International Encyclopedia of the Social Sciences,* Volume 12, pp. 405–415. New York: Macmillan.

Dallin, Alexander (1962). *The Soviet Union at the United Nations.* New York: Praeger.

Duncan, Otis Dudley (1966). "Path analysis: sociological examples." *American Journal of Sociology* 72: 1–16.

Fisher, Ronald A. (1925). *Statistical Methods for Research Workers.* Edinburgh: Oliver and Boyd.

Frey, Frederick W. (1974). "Political power." *Encyclopedia Britannica, 14,* Macropaedia 697–702.

Goldberger, Arthur S. (1972). "Structural equation methods in the social sciences." *Econometrica* 40 (6):979–1001.

Goldberger, Arthur S., and Otis Dudley Duncan, eds. (1973). *Structural Equation Models in the Social Sciences.* New York: Seminar Press.

Gorham, William (1970). "Some uses of quantitative analysis to improve the allocation of public funds." In Jean H. P. Paelink, ed., *Programming For Europe's Collective Needs.* New York: American Elsevier.

Greenberg, William J. (1969). "A learning model simulation of United Nations response to crisis." Masters thesis, Department of Political Science, Massachusetts Institute of Technology.

Gross, Leo (1966). "Domestic jurisdiction, enforcement measures and the Congo." In *Australian Yearbook of International Law, 1965*:137–158.

Grumm, John G. (1975). "The analysis of policy impact." In Fred Greenstein and Nelson Polsby, eds. *The Handbook of Political Science,* Volume 6. Reading, Mass.: Addison-Wesley.

Gurr, Ted Robert (1972). *Politimetrics: An Introduction to Quantitative Macropolitics.* Englewood Cliffs, N.J.: Prentice-Hall.

Guttman, Louis (1950). Chapters 3–6, 9 in S. A. Stauffer *et al., Measurement and Prediction.* Princeton, N.J.: Princeton University Press.

——————— (1954). "The radex: a new approach to factor analysis." In P. F. Lazarsfeld, ed., *Mathematical Thinking in the Social Sciences.* Glencoe, Ill.: Free Press.

——————— (1971). "Measurement as structural theory." *Psychometrika* 36(4):329–347.

——————— (n.d.) "On the relationship of scale analysis to 'measurement.' " Jerusalem: The Israel Institute of Applied Social Research. Mimeographed.

Habermas, Jurgen (1971). *Knowledge and Human Interests.* Boston: Beacon Press.

Hardin, Russell (1971). "Collective action as an agreeable *n*-prisoners' dilemma." *Behavioral Science* 16:472–481.

Harré, Rom, and P. F. Secord (1972). *The Explanation of Social Behavior.* Oxford: Basil Blackwell.

Harsanyi, John (1962). "Measurement of social power, opportunity costs, and the theory of two-person bargaining games." *Behavioral Science* 7:67–80.

Hibbs, Douglas (1974a). "On analyzing the effects of policy interventions: Box-Jenkins and Box-Tiao vs. structural equation models." Cambridge, Mass.: Center for International Studies, Massachusetts Institute of Technology.

——————— (1974b). "Problems of statistical estimation and causal inference in time-series regression models." In H. L. Costner, ed., *Sociological Methodology, 1973–1974.* San Francisco: Jossey-Bass.

Hitch, Charles J., and Roland McKean (1963). *The Economics of Defense in the Missile Age.* Second edition. Cambridge, Mass.: Harvard University Press.

Holsti, Ole (1968). "Content analysis." In Gardner Lindzey and Elliott Aronson, eds., *The Handbook of Social Psychology,* Volume 2. Reading, Mass.: Addison-Wesley.

Horowitz, Irving L., ed. (1967). *The Rise and Fall of Project Camelot: Studies in the Relationship Between Social Science and Practical Politics.* Cambridge, Mass.: Massachusetts Institute of Technology Press.

Jackson, John (1973). "Senate voting: problems of scaling and function of form." In Arthur S. Goldberger and Otis Dudley Duncan, eds., *Structural Equation Models in the Social Sciences*. New York: Seminar Press.

Jöreskog, K. G. (1969). "A general approach to confirmatory maximum likelihood factor analysis." *Psychometrika* 34:183–202.

_____ (1970). "A general method for the analysis of covariance structures." *Biometrika* 57:239-251.

Kuhn, Thomas (1970a). "Logic of discovery of psychology of research?" and "Reflections on my critics." In Imre Lakatos and Alan Musgrave, eds., *Criticism and the Growth of Knowledge*. Cambridge: Cambridge University Press.

_____ (1970b). *The Structure of Scientific Revolutions*. Second edition, England. International Encyclopedia of Unified Science, Volume II, Number 2. Chicago: University of Chicago Press.

Lakatos, Imre (1970). "Falsification and the methodology of scientific research programmes." In Imre Lakatos and Alan Musgrave, eds., *Criticism and the Growth of Knowledge*. Cambridge: Cambridge University Press.

Lakatos, Imre, and Alan Musgrave, eds. (1970). *Criticism and the Growth of Knowledge*. Cambridge: Cambridge University Press.

Lasswell, Harold D. (1975). "Research in policy analysis: the intelligence and appraisal functions." In Fred Greenstein and Nelson Polsby, *The Handbook of Political Science*, Volume 6. Reading, Mass.: Addison-Wesley.

Lawley, D. N., and A. E. Maxwell (1963). *Factor Analysis as a Statistical Method*. London and Washington, D.C.: Butterworths.

Lazarsfeld, Paul F. (1961). "Notes on the history of quantification in sociology—trends, sources and problems." In H. Woolf, ed., *Quantification: A History of Its Meaning in the Natural and Social Sciences*. Indianapolis: Bobbs-Merrill.

Lazarsfeld, Paul F., Bernard Berelson, and Hazel Gaudet (1948). *The Peoples Choice*. Second edition. New York: Columbia University Press.

Lingoes, James C. (1973). *The Guttman-Lingoes Nonmetric Program Series*. Ann Arbor: Mathesis Press.

Lord, Frederick M., and Melvin R. Novick (1968). *Statistical Theories of Mental Test Scores*. Reading, Mass.: Addison-Wesley.

Luce, R. Duncan, and Patrick Suppes (1965). "Preference, utility, and subjective probability." In R. Duncan Luce, Robert R. Bush, and Eugene Galanter, eds., *Handbook of Mathematical Psychology*, chapter 19. New York: Wiley and Sons.

MacRae, Duncan, Jr. (1958). *Dimensions of Congressional Voting*. Berkeley: University of California Press.

_____ (1970). *Issues and Parties in Legislative Voting: Methods of Statistical Analysis*. New York: Harper & Row.

Miller, Warren, and Donald Stokes (1963). "Constituency influence in Congress." *American Political Science Review* 57:45–56.

Mokken, Robert J. (1970). *A Theory and Procedure of Scale Analysis: With Applications in Political Research.* 's-Grovenhage: Mouton and Co.

Moon, J. Donald (1975). "The logic of political inquiry: a synthesis of opposed perspectives." In Fred Greenstein and Nelson Polsby, *The Handbook of Political Science,* Volume 1. Reading, Mass.: Addison-Wesley.

Moses, E., Richard A. Brady, Ole R. Holsti, Joseph B. Kodane, and Jeffrey S. Milstein (1967). "Scaling data on inter-nation action." *Science* 156:1054–1059.

Mosteller, Frederick, and John W. Tukey (1968). "Data analysis, including statistics." In Gardner Lindzey and Elliot Aronson, eds., *The Handbook of Social Psychology.* Reading, Mass.: Addison-Wesley.

Mundel, David S. (1971). *Federal Aid to Higher Education and the Poor.* Ph.D. dissertation, Department of Political Science, Massachusetts Institute of Technology.

Natanson, Maurice (1963). *Philsophy of the Social Sciences: A Reader.* New York: Randon House.

Petty, William (1971). *Political Anatomy of Ireland.* (First published in 1672.) Totowa, N.J.: Rowman and Littlefield.

Pindyck, Robert (1973). *Optimal Planning for Economic Stabilization Policy.* Amsterdam: North-Holland.

Pratt, John W., Howard Raiffa, and Robert Schlaifer (1965). *Introduction to Statistical Decision Theory.* New York: McGraw-Hill.

Raiffa, Howard (1968). *Decision Analysis: Introductory Lectures on Choices Under Uncertainty.* Reading, Mass.: Addison-Wesley.

Rapoport, Anatol, and Albert M. Chammah, with the collaboration of Carol J. Orwant (1965). *Prisoner's Dilemma: A Study in Conflict and Cooperation.* Ann Arbor: University of Michigan Press.

Rivlin, Alice M. (1971). *Systematic Thinking for Social Action.* Washington, D.C.: Brookings.

Rummel, Rudolph J. (1967). "Understanding factor analysis." *Journal of Conflict Resolution* 11:444–480.

——————— (1970). *Applied Factor Analysis.* Evanston, Ill.: Northwestern University Press.

Schank, Roger C., and Kenneth M. Colby, eds. (1973). *Computer Models of Thought and Language.* San Francisco: W. H. Freeman.

Shapiro, Michael J., and G. Matthew Bonham (1973). "Cognitive process and foreign policy decision-making." *International Studies Quarterly* 17:147–174.

Shepard, Roger N., A. Kimball Romney, and Sara B. Nerlove, eds. (1972). *Multidimensional Scaling: Theory and Applications in the Behavioral Sciences.* Two volumes. New York: Seminar Press.

Siegel, Sidney (1956). *Nonparametric Statistics for the Behavioral Sciences.* New York: McGraw-Hill.

Simon, Herbert, and Nicholas Rescher (1966). "Cause and counterfactual." *Journal of Philosophy* 33:323–340.

Suppes, Patrick (1970). *A Probabilistic Theory of Causality*. Amsterdam: North-Holland.

Taylor, Michael (1975). "The theory of collective choice." In Fred Greenstein and Nelson Polsby, eds., *The Handbook of Political Science*, Volume 3. Reading, Mass.: Addison-Wesley.

Theil, Henri, ed. (1972). *Statistical Decomposition Analysis*. Amsterdam: North-Holland.

Tufte, Edward (1974). *Data Analysis for Politics and Policy*. Englewood Cliffs, N.J.: Prentice-Hall.

von Wright, George H. (1971). *Explanation and Understanding*. London: Routledge and Kegan Paul.

Wish, Myron, and J. Douglas Carroll (1973). "Applications of 'INDSCAL' to studies of human perception and judgment." In E. C. Carterette and M. P. Friedman, eds., *Handbook of Perception*. Academic Press.

Wolin, Sheldon S. (1969). "Political theory as a vocation." *American Political Science Review* 63:1062–1082.

Yamani, Sheik Ahmed Zaki (1974). Speech before Sixth Special Session of United Nations General Assembly.

Yule, G. U., and M. G. Kendall (1958). *An Introduction to the Theory of Statistics*. 14th ed. New York: Hafner.

Zeisel, Hans (1968). *Say It With Figures*. Fifth edition, revised. New York: Harper & Row.

Zellner, Arnold (1971). *An Introduction to Bayesian Inference in Econometrics*. New York: Wiley and Sons.

Zinnes, Dina (1975). "Scientific international politics." In Fred Greenstein and Nelson Polsby, eds., *The Handbook of Political Science*, Volume 8. Reading, Mass.: Addison-Wesley.

5

EXPERIMENTATION AND SIMULATION

RICHARD A. BRODY
CHARLES N. BROWNSTEIN

It has always been the case that man has sought to bring intellectual order out of the chaos that greets his senses when be observes the physical or social world. Primitive religion, metaphysical speculation, the observing and classifying of existential regularities, and the creation of artificial experiences (experiments) have all played a role in aiding man to uncover the constant structure postulated to lurk beneath the chaos.

The search for "hidden likenessses" is not an activity exclusive to science, but rules of the search have been more self-consciously formulated and applied by practitioners and philosophers of science. This emphasis on procedural rules —scientific "method" or methods—has been a result of the rejection by science of private experience, intuition, and revelation as sources of *confirmed* knowledge.

It is not the case that private insight has been stripped of any role in science (Margenau, 1961, pp. 21–24; Popper, 1961, pp. 31–32); rather, its role has been delimited. The value of private knowledge (personal insight, intuition) to the enterprise of science is symbolized by the familiar distinction between the "logic of discovery" and the "logic of verification" (Cohen and Nagel, 1934, p. 245; Snyder, 1962, p. 99). Insight and intuition are accorded a major role in the formulation of hypotheses, the creation of theory, and similar activities that are at the heart of the logic of discovery. In short, despite their emphasis on "public" knowledge, as the result of scientific method, philosophers of science give to private knowledge processes an important and creative (perhaps, the more creative) role.

In accord with the distinction between "discovery" and "verification," this chapter is predicated on the belief that the purpose of science is to contribute an understanding of physical and social reality by providing criteria for choosing between alternative constructions of that reality. The history of social thought (as well as the history of physical science) is replete with instances of mutually contradictory theories purporting to explain social (or physical) phenomena. Most of these efforts, insofar as they suggest hypotheses, are within the domain of the logic of discovery. The logic of verification and the philosophy of science it represents offer a set of rules to guide the exploration of such alternative hypotheses.

Arnold Brecht succinctly outlines the logic of verification as follows:

In every inquiry—and that means inquiry within the social as well as the natural sciences—Scientific Method concentrates on the following "scientific actions," "scientific operations," or "steps of scientific procedure":

1. *Observation* of what can be observed, and tentative acceptance or nonacceptance of the observation as sufficiently exact.

2. *Description* of what has been observed, and tentative acceptance or nonacceptance of the description as correct and adequate.

3. *Measurement* of what can be measured; this being merely a particular type of observation and description, but one sufficiently distinct and important to merit separate listing.

4. *Acceptance* or nonacceptance (tentative) as *facts* or *reality* of the results of observation, description, and measurement.

5. *Inductive generalization* (tentative) of accepted individual facts (No. 4), offered as a "factual hypothesis."

6. *Explanation* (tentative) of accepted individual facts (No. 4), or of inductively reached factual generalizations (No. 5), in terms of relations, especially causal relations, offered as a "theoretical hypothesis."

7. *Logical deductive reasoning* from inductively reached factual generalizations (No. 5) or hypothetical explanations (No. 6), so as to make explicit what is implied in them regarding other possible observations (No. 1), or regarding previously accepted facts (No. 4), factual generalizations (No. 5), and hypothetical explanations (No. 6).

8. *Testing* by further observations (Nos. 1–4) the tentative acceptance of observations, reports, and measurements as properly made (Nos. 1–3), and their results as facts (No. 4), or tentative expectations as warranted (No. 7).

9. *Correcting* the tentative acceptance of observations, etc., and of their results (Nos. 1–4), of inductive generalizations (No. 5) and hypothetical explanations (No. 6), whenever they are incompatible with other accepted observations, generalizations, or explanations; or correcting the previously accepted contribution.

10. *Predicting* events or conditions to be expected as a consequence of past, present, or future events or conditions, or any possible constellation

of such, in order either (a) to test factual or theoretical hypotheses (Nos. 5 and 6), this being identical with steps 7 and 8; or (b) to supply scientific contribution to the practical process of choosing between several possible alternatives of action.

11. *Nonacceptance* (elimination from acceptable propositions) of all statements not obtained or confirmed in the manner described here, especially of "a-priori" propositions, except when "immanent in Scientific Method" or offered merely as "tentative assumption" or "working hypotheses" . . .*

Much contemporary research in political science attempts to adhere to procedures conformant with these rules of scientific method. The emphasis on both methods and methodology (Kaplan, 1964, p. 23) signals a fundamental concern for the development of coherent sets of testable (i.e., falsifiable) hypotheses purporting to explain political phenomena. Whether such hypotheses derive from venerated political philosophies or contemporary political theories, or are borrowed from the pool of confirmed propositions in other social sciences is immaterial. What is material, for the goal of a cumulative science built on confirmed hypotheses relevant to politics, is the widespread acceptance of standards and techniques of confirmation.

Strictly speaking, propositions are never fully confirmed, that is to say, validated for all times and circumstances. Practically, a proposition is said to be confirmed when all plausible alternative explanations of the cause of the phenomenon in question have been disconfirmed. The task of confirmation thus involves not only giving the hypothesized causal factor an opportunity to produce the effect in question, but also, by one means or another, "controlling" other plausible causes.

The notion of "plausibility" is an aesthetic principle. It is among those a priori propositions Brecht (1959, p. 29) refers to as being "immanent in Scientific Method." Decisions about plausibility are made "in the judgment of the scientist" and not in accord with any well-established set of rules.

This is no less true in the physical sciences than it is in the social sciences. Newton's (1846, p. 385) "Fourth Rule of Philosophizing" can be read in support of restricting investigation to plausible hypotheses. Newton asserts that if we reserve judgment on the truth of a proposition until every conceivable alternative is disproved, it would follow that no theory, irrespective of the quality of direct experimental evidence for it, could be adequately established so long as any imagined alternative remained untested. While it is true that any hypothesis, however little the probability or plausibility, cannot be absolutely excluded, Newton insists that such considerations should not be permitted to

---

* Selections from Arnold Brecht, *Political Theory: The Foundations of Twentieth Century Political Thought* (copyright © 1959 by Princeton University Press), pp. 28–29. Reprinted by permission of Princeton University Press.

affect our judgment if science is to be allowed to reach any conclusions at all (Blake, Ducasse, and Madden, 1960, pp. 126–127).

The problem of discovering which plausible alternative is more likely to be causal comes down to the problem of eliminating competing explanations. The process of removing competing factors is called "control": controls can be designated as "correlational" or "design," the controls that are more or less associated with research done in the field and laboratory, respectively. The correspondence between the type of control and the research site is a rough one because many laboratory studies use "afterthought" correlation controls, and field experiments, as experiments, begin with controls for alternative causal factors.

The two methods of control can be contrasted as to the time, in a study, when the effect of a plausible alternative cause is removed. Correlational controls are typically applied *ex post facto* (Zetterberg, 1963, pp. 56–70; Rosenberg, 1968); design controls are affected prior to the gathering of data.

The use of correlational controls is ubiquitous in political science research. It is quite common, for example, in voting studies seeking to account for the impact of political factors (e.g., party identification), to control, by means of partial correlation, the effect of demographic factors (e.g., age, sex, or socioeconomic status), institutional factors (e.g., ballot form or restrictions on enfranchisement), and situational factors (e.g., whether the election took place in a presidential or an off year) (Campbell, 1962, pp. 31–46). The reader will have little difficulty adding dozens of studies, using this form of control, to this example.

This popularity of correlational controls, as a means of inferring causality by eliminating competing explanations, stems primarily from how and where most political science research is conducted: In breaking with the traditional method of political science research, i.e., "descriptive accounts of what exists and occurs [in legal governments]" (Hyneman, 1959, p. 36), most students of political behavior retain the traditional research site, that is, some aspect or agency of legal government. This is accomplished because, as Hyneman (1959, p. 163) asserts of "traditional" political scientists, "they believe that legal government provides all of the manifestations of influence that need to be examined in the course of constructing a science. They believe that properly designed studies of legal government will disclose many regularities and support many generalizations applicable to influence in all manner of human associations." Given the twin desires of doing research where politics takes place and also seeking to confirm causal theories (a very nontraditional goal), correlational techniques for sorting out causality are, if imperfect, at least an appropriate first step.

Thus, political scientists have by and large not sought an experimental science; they have chosen to observe ongoing processes rather than create or otherwise intervene in these processes. Intervention, when it has taken place, has largely consisted of the introduction of measures (such as questionnaires) used to produce data that is otherwise unobtainable. These interventions are seldom used to elicit consequential behavior. In this sense, they are not experimental interventions but informational probes. Experiments are performed on the data but not on the system itself.

Such procedures are no less scientific but at a certain point in the development of understanding they become very inconvenient. In the development of multifactor theories, the moment arises when the theorist wishes to know the comparative causal importance of the several factors comprising the explanation. Feigl (1953, p. 411) would identify this comparative importance with the functional relationships of the factors to the phenomenon. With correlational techniques (including so-called "causal modeling" techniques), the probable need for the presence of one or another factor in an explanation may be established but estimates of relative contribution cannot be. Beyond correlation, the validity of multivariate estimation procedures for the determination of functional relationships, such as multiple regression, path analysis, and analysis of variance, depends on the degree of the approximate independence of the independent variables. In nonexperimental settings this mutual independence is hard to approximate. Indeed, the scale of much political science research renders inappropriate the available techniques for testing the nonindependence (multicollinearity) of the independent variables (Brody and Verba, 1972, pp. 318–321); thus, it is not only difficult to approximate the requirement of mutual independence, it also is uncertain whether one can get an estimate of how far one has departed from the requirement.

One can expect these difficulties because causes are confounded in the political system. To the extent that confounded variables are central to competing explanations, the political system will not permit the researcher to choose between those explanations. Confounding can be eliminated by design, if the researcher has control over the system. Otherwise, there is the choice of living with the inability to discipline one's causal models or of developing a system over which one has control. Most fields of science faced with this choice have opted for experimentation in created systems; political scientists, by and large, have thus far chosen not to create an experimental science.

Since experimental design is a guarantor of statistical independence, one might expect to find more political science experiments than one does. Why is this the case? One cannot dismiss the explanations suggested by the sociology of science: lack of training, lack of a tradition of experimentation, a consequent lack of familiarity with the technique, and for these reasons a lack of legitimation of its use. But neither can one dismiss the fact that along with the benefits of experimentation one incurs intellectual costs. These have deterred many political scientists from taking the step from the real world into the laboratory.

We are advocates of experimentation. As such it is incumbent on us not only to clarify procedure, as we hope to do in this chapter, but also to detail the burden of assumptions one takes on as a correlate of the benefits of experimenting. But in order to do this we must begin with first principles.

EXPERIENCE AND EXPERIMENT

Leonardo da Vinci offers this capsule of the scientific enterprise: "... nature begins with the cause and ends in experience, we must follow a contrary procedure—that is, begin ... with experience and with that seek for the cause." (Blake, Ducasse, and Madden, 1960, p. 17). At base, science is the process of converting experience into knowledge. The senses of the scientist (including their extension through instrumentation) and the rules of scientific method are the ingredients of the process; its end product is knowledge about reality that conforms to certain agreed-upon desiderata: (1) that the ordering of the facts of experience be better understood; (2) that some critical light be shed on a hypothesis or a system of hypotheses (i.e., a theory); (3) that the knowledge be public (i.e., capable of being communicated to other individuals); and (4) that it be reproducible (i.e., that another researcher following the same procedures will arrive at the same conclusions).

In sum, science employs experience to achieve stable, reliable, valid knowledge. This knowledge, in turn, becomes the subject of further investigations in the continuing quest for simpler, more powerful explanatory generalizations. Science is experience in the service of theory.

It is pointless to enter the debate over whether theory or experience takes precedence in the process of inquiry. If we grant that scientific experience is not aimless, passive exposure to sensations, then we must also grant that theory (in one or another of its manifestations) enters to produce pointed, active inquiry. The term "theory" covers a variety of more or less systematic formulations; and the more systematic may not be required before inquiry can begin. Joseph Priestley (1772, p. 181) put it more forcefully. "Very lame and imperfect theories," he opined, "are sufficient to suggest useful experiments which serve to correct those theories, and give birth to others more perfect."

If we accept the standard tripartite model of scientific inference—the formulation of hypotheses about phenomena, the encountering of the phenomena, and the making of decisions with respect to the hypotheses in light of the encounter—we must acknowledge the literally central role of the encounter (i.e., experience) in the process. But how do we achieve this encounter?

The choice is simple: The investigator can wait for it to happen or he can make it happen. Traditionally we speak of the former means of encounter, with phenomena relevant to making decisions about hypotheses, as "observation"; the latter is usually termed "experiment." But it is important to note that the two means of achieving an encounter with phenomena are used with the same intellectual purpose in mind—namely, the confrontation of hypothesis with fact in order to generate knowledge.

It is also important to understand that one means is not inherently preferable to the other. Gosnell (1927) was not necessarily being any more scientific when he, as an experimenter, *injected* "get-out-the-vote" propaganda into the 1924 Chicago ward elections, than were the astrophysicists who had to *wait* for a total eclipse of the sun in order to *observe* the accuracy of a hypothesis from the theory of relativity.

If the intellectual purpose is the same, why all the fuss about what Leonardo da Vinci called *esperienza*? Why manipulate nature in search of causes instead of waiting for natural causes to produce critical experiences? The attempt to answer these questions takes us first to the need for a clear statement of what we meant by "experiment."

R. A. Fisher points to some important characteristics of experimentation and its relationship to other modes of research when he observes:

> Men have always been capable of some mental process of the kind we call "learning by experience!" Doubtless this experience was often a very imperfect basis, and the reasoning processes used in interpreting it were very insecure but there must have been in these processes a sort of embryology of knowledge, by which new knowledge was gradually produced. Experimental observations are only experience carefully *planned in advance* and *designed to form* a secure basis of *new knowledge;* t*hat is, they systematically related to the body of knowledge already acquired, and the results are deliberately observed, and put on record accurately. (Fisher, 1935, p. 9; italics added)

Thus, for Fisher, an experiment is a planned observation designed to add new knowledge to an existing body of theory.

Most philosophers of science would agree with Fisher that these represent *necessary* elements of experimental inquiry, but are they *sufficient* unto themselves? Here we encounter problems, since there is no definitive answer to this question. Different scientific disciplines and different problem domains within a discipline have requirements that yield equally valid but nonuniform answers to the question of sufficiency. Campbell and Stanley (1966), for example, identify experimentation as ". . . that portion of research in which variables are *manipulated* and their effect upon other variables observed." But this emphasis on manipulation is absent from Fisher's list of characteristics; perhaps he simply took manipulation for granted (all the experiments he describes involve this act). On the other hand, Fisher may have presaged Kaplan (1964, p. 161), who does not hold manipulation to be a necessary condition for experimentation.

The point of view expressed in this chapter stems from a narrower conception of experimentation than that held by Kaplan. This conception holds manipulation to be a necessary characteristic of experimentation but does not contend that experimentation is a necessary process in the production of scientific knowledge. However, in declining to accept Kaplan's very broad definition of experimentation, we are not accepting B. F. Skinner's (1964, p. 337) assertion that nonexperimental (i.e., in his view, nonlaboratory) approaches to knowledge are "divertissements in the growth of a science of human behavior."

Kaplan (1964) also construes manipulation quite broadly; he minimizes the distinction between manipulations of substantial aspects of a social system (for which we reserve the term "experiment") and interventions that are designed to obtain data but not to affect the behavior of the system. The distinction is evident if we contrast, for example, Gosnell's and the Michigan Survey Research Center's research on voting. Gosnell (1926) was interested in the effects on voting turnout of nonpartisan appeals to "get out the vote"; by sending such appeals to experimental groups (and withholding them from control groups) in 12 Chicago voting districts, Gosnell was attempting a manipulation designed to affect behavior. Campbell and his associates (1954, 1960), in pursuit of their interest in why Americans vote the way they do, have introduced questionnaires into a number of elections not in order to affect whether and how their respondents vote but to aid the researcher's understanding of the voting decision.

In Kaplan's (1964, p. 162) use of the term, both of these efforts are experimental; neither study was based on "merely taking what comes . . . ," and both involved "going after what we want and taking steps to make sure we get it. . . ." And yet there are important methodological differences between the approaches used in these studies. To cite only the most important distinction, Gosnell's approach eases the task of inferring causality: The effect of his experimental intervention can be directly assessed; the effects of the Michigan questionnaires cannot.

There are two senses of the term "experiment" that could pertain to sample surveys: The studies made by Campbell and his associates (1954, 1960) could have been considered *methodological* experiments if they had focussed on the reaction of respondents to the questionnaires. Indeed, Glock's (1952) work, which has sought to assess the effects of repeated questioning on a panel of respondents, does provide an example of methodological experimentation. In another sense of "experimentation," the repeated study of elections provides opportunities for so-called "natural experiments" (i.e., studies of some novel variation introduced by the system itself). Studies of the impact of the Korean War on the 1952 election (Belknap and Campbell, 1952) and of John F. Kennedy's Catholicism on the 1960 election (Converse et al., 1961) are examples of the utilization of natural experimental circumstances. However, even in these senses of the term "experimentation," the lack of control over alternative explanations leaves the task of inferring causality not entirely free of hazard.

Thus far, in listing characteristics of experiments, we have asserted that "planned observation" is a necessary but not a sufficient condition for this style of inquiry. We have also taken sides in the debate over the necessity for manipulation to emphasize its advantages. But observation and manipulation together are still insufficient to the task of clearly explicating causality—the key is control.

We can speak about control in a general and a technical sense. Since technical aspects of control will be discussed at a later point, control will be discussed here as a general attribute of experimentation.

In the most general sense, experimentation is distinguished from other methods of inquiry by the mastery of the experimenter over parts of the situation; by his control over inputs (i.e., independent variables), the experimenter has an advantage with respect to understanding how system processes affect outputs (i.e., dependent variables). If, for example, we are curious about which factors attendant to the introduction of a piece of legislation (the inputs) would dispose a committee (the system) to favor or oppose the bill's passage (the output), we are faced with a very complex job of analysis. Even in the realm of legislation, where data abound and are relatively accessible, it is difficult to determine the relative impact on committee reception of sponsorship, content, controversy, and other characteristics of a proposed measure. By contrast, an approach such as the one used by Barber (1966) which utilizes firm control over input, has a fighting chance to clarify such relationships.

Given an experimental study, controls (especially those to which the label "design controls" has been applied) allow the experimenter to answer two central questions: (1) How likely is it that the outcomes observed are due to the experimental variable(s)? and (2) How far beyond the experimental setting can I generalize the relationships I have observed? Donald Campbell (1963, p. 214) refers to these as problems of "internal" and "external" validity and points out that "they are frequently at odds, in that features increasing the solution of one may jeopardize the other." Thus, there may be a paradox involved in the most crucial characteristic of experimental inquiry: *The more effective the controls, the more general the laws; the more general the laws, the harder it is to see them operating in manifestly different empirical situations.* Scientific laws, particularly those derived experimentally, contain an implicit *ceteris paribus* which may not be met in any given empirical situation. But without general laws no comparison between empirical instances could be made. Thus, the operation of a political system in a controlled experiment, like the "perfect gas," provides a standard of comparison.

The final characteristic of experimentation to be considered relates to the site of the inquiry. Is it a necessary condition of experimentation that it be conducted in a laboratory? Is the fact that a study is conducted in a laboratory sufficient to qualify it as experimental? We think the answer to both questions is, no. The discussion of the relative merits of field and laboratory will be postponed, but there is little doubt that planned observation of political phenomena in manipulated, designed-controlled field studies is a valid experimental approach (French, 1953). Gosnell, Eldersveld, and other political scientists performing field experiments have amply demonstrated this.

Field experiments can be distinguished from field studies by virtue of the presence or absence of other experimental characteristics, especially manipulation and design controls. On the other hand, to the extent that such characteristics are absent from research conducted in laboratory settings, this research takes on the problems of field studies with the additional burden of being artificially contrived. That research takes place in a laboratory does not guarantee its experimental nature.

THE VALUE OF EXPERIMENTAL METHOD

Having indicated the characteristics of experimentation, it seems appropriate to indicate the advantages that derive from these characteristics. It is generally conceded, even by those who argue against the technique on other grounds, that experimentation relative to other modes of inquiry offers a superior insight into causal relationships among variables. This relative superiority derives from experimentation's most distinctive characteristics: manipulation of the system by the researcher, and the researcher's ability to control the effect of competing causes.

The logic of causation has troubled philosophers of science since Hume; nevertheless, the working scientist trying to explain phenomena has sought and will continue to seek beyond constant conjunction and concomitant variation to relationships that meet operational criteria of causality.

From Mill's (1882, p. 245) definition of "cause," we can infer the centrality of control among these operational criteria: "The cause of a phenomenon," according to Mill, "is the antecedent, or the concurrence of antecedents, on which it is invariably and *unconditionally* consequent." Mill emphasizes "unconditionality" in order to avoid accepting as a true causal relationship the fallacious invariable sequence (i.e., *post hoc, ergo propter hoc*). The test of conditionality is control. By means of control the researcher can ascertain whether the invariant relationship holds with the effect of some hypothetically conditioning factor removed.

Modern notions of causality, for example, that of Blalock, directly specify the importance of control. Blalock (1964, p. 19) states that in order to speak of a direct causal relationship between variables X and Y, *"we first assume that all other variables* $X_2 \ldots X_n$ *explicitly included in the causal model have been controlled or do not vary . . .* we shall then say that X *is a direct cause of Y if and only if a change in X produces a change in the mean value of Y."*

This notion of cause, no less than Mill's, presents logical difficulties that are immune to eradication but are minimized in the experimental situation. It is important that we mention two of these difficulties.

First of all, while we speak of X (the cause) acting on the system to produce Y (the effect), we are really restricted to observing the concurrence of X and Y. We can never determine empirically whether X *produced* the change in Y (or the mean value of Y). This is to say, processes (the acting of X on Y) are inferred, not observed. However, while logically this difficulty is unremovable, as a matter of practice the closer we come to ideal experimental conditions, the more plausible it seems to infer process. Since under these conditions X_1 is manipulated by the experimenter and competing X's $(X_2 \ldots X_n)$ are controlled, it is plausible to speak of a causal link.

Second, we can never know for sure whether we have omitted a crucial variable from our causal model $(X_1 \ldots X_n)$ and therefore failed to take account of it (Cohen and Nagel, 1934, p. 266). If the crucial variable is substantive, its absence will be noted in the weakness of the relationship between X_1 and Y. If the relationship is not weak, the cruciality of the omitted variable is questionable. But the uncontrolled inclusion of a variable is also a possibility. Consider, for example, the eight threats to internal validity specified by Campbell (1957).

Experiments are designed to minimize the latter possibility; the better the design, the lower the probability of an uncontrolled intervening variable and the clearer the estimate of the strength of the relationship between X_1 and Y. By virtue of this clarified relationship, the absence of crucial variables will be made manifest. There is, however, nothing in the method of experimentation to indicate *which* variable is absent; this task lies outside of the logic of verification and, thereby, beyond the capability of experimental method. But the experimental setting can provide a convenient and disciplined site in which to carry out the search.

THE DESIGN OF THE LABORATORY: THE SIMULATION OF POLITICAL PHENOMENA

On the whole, political scientists have been far more concerned with the damage to inference stemming from the omission of crucial variables and relationships than they have been with the damage stemming from uncontrolled inclusion of confounded explanatory variables. The absence of good explanatory theory has meant that the "crucial" is often identified with the "palpable." In this respect, political science has been ideographic in its conceit, resembling history and anthropology and distinguished from psychology and sociology, whose conceit is nomothetic.

Such an attitude is clearly antipathetic to experimentation. A laboratory that includes all the palpable features of the situation it represents is inconceivable. If we cannot say which features of a situation were essential to what took place and we do not feel comfortable with findings from a setting that include some features and omitted others, we are not going to feel at ease with an experimental science. Paradoxically, this anxiety, focussed on the absence from the experiment of palpable features of the situation being modeled or simulated by the experimental arrangement, is directed at the central intellectual strength of experimental method. Experimentation is unrivaled in its capacity to aid in distinguishing features that are merely present from those that are essential to the phenomena of concern.

And yet it cannot be denied that there is a basis for this anxiety. Not invariably but frequently, experiments do take place in simulated systems and thus the degree of essential similarity between the laboratory and the system it simulates is at the heart of the question of what can be learned from experimentation (Campbell, 1957; Hermann, 1967; Guetzkow, 1968; Brody, 1969b; Van Horn, 1971). The question of validity, under this formulation, becomes the general one of the utility of knowledge gained in one social system as a source of insight into behavior in another social context (Brunswik, 1956). Both the laboratory and the sociopolitical setting it represents are social contexts for behavior. The question is whether features of the laboratory context affect the legitimacy of transfer of knowledge to the nonlaboratory context (Campbell, 1957). This question cannot be answered without study of both contexts.

If in experimentation there is a problem of method artifacts affecting insight, it is not unique to experimentation. It is not even clear that the problem of external validity is more serious with experimentation than with other methods of eliciting data (Webb *et al.,* 1966). We are prepared to argue that this problem should not deter the further development of experimentation as a tool of political research. Bearing in mind the problem of method artifacts, the question becomes one of using the strengths of experimentation to improve the quality of simulations as loci for better experimentation.

Under this conception of the development of a science, a simulation is a device for achieving an understanding about some domain of interest by *representing crucial features* (entities and/or relations) of that domain through deductive and/or analogous systems. A simulation may be wholly deductive or wholly analogous or a mix of the two types of system. Likewise, a simulation may emphasize the entities that populate the domain, or relations among the entities, or the interconnection (interaction) of entities and relations.

Our emphasis on "representing crucial features" of the system being simulated signals the intimate connection between simulation and theory. Our theory about the system is our guide in the selection of features of reality that must be included in the simulation. That we can simulate at all requires the assumption that some of the palpable entities and relations in the observed system are epiphenomenal—that is, that they produce no substantial effect on the behavior of the system being studied—and that some features are crucial, that is, their presence or absence is a matter of consequence to the behavior of the system being studied. The decision that one feature is epiphenomenal and another one consequential is (or should be) dictated by such confirmed theory as exists about the empirical domain.

Theory also enters into the decision concerning the manner in which a feature is represented in the simulation. Other things being equal, the more we know (the better confirmed our theory) about some feature of reality, the more likely we are to represent it by a deductive rather than an analogous system.

A wholly deductive representation (an all-computer simulation or, for that matter, a mathematical model of the domain) is based on the assumption that all the laws concerning entities and relationships among entities are known. What remains to be learned from such a simulation is the variation in output (or outcome) associated with variations in input under various "states of the system" ("initial conditions" in John Stuart Mill's *Logic* (1882). Such studies proceed through the production of logical deductions (new theorems) from the axioms and existing theorems of the model. De Sola Pool, Abelson, and Popkin's (1965) simulation of the 1960 electorate and the explorations within it of electoral outcomes associated with differing emphases among campaign strategies is an obvious example of such an all-deductive simulation. So too are Oliver Benson's "Simple Diplomatic Game" (1961) and the Joint War Games Agency's TEMPER model (JWGA/JCS, 1965).

The assumptions about the status of our knowledge of a particular domain of interest are less stringent for *mixed simulations* than for wholly deductive systems and even less stringent for *wholly analogous* systems. An all-analog simulation (i.e., one comprised entirely of analogous elements) implies that our knowledge of a domain is only sufficient to point to features that must be included in the model. For example, in many games, such as the RAND Corporation's cold war crisis simulations, that focus on top-level decision making, analogic elements (such as those listed in Table 1) are designed to parallel the crucial features of the referent system. These crucial features are physically juxtaposed but they are not related with the specificity that would be required in an all-deductive system. Typically, in such simulations, once the features have been juxtaposed the analog is left free to operate. It is the action (behavior) of the analog that is of interest to the researcher.

All-analogous systems are not restricted to games of the RAND type, nor are they restricted to the laboratory; the survey sample is such an analog. So too is the panel in a panel study. Guided by sampling theory and certain aspects of political theory, the sample is our best analog for obtaining estimates of the distribution of opinions, attitudes, and so forth, in a given population at a given point in time. The panel provides our best estimate of the effects of matters related to the passage of time on distributions in the population. It is not always clear for what behavior in the population the interview response is an analog—sometimes the response is a simulation of an overt act such as a vote; other times the response is analogous to an unarticulated feeling. Nor is it always clear to what the interviewer is analogous. Because of these ambiguities it is not clear what the total interview situation simulates. Is it a political conversation, a step into the voting booth, a search of census records, or all three that are being simulated in this best of all analogs of the population?

TABLE 1 Sample analogic representation of real world structures in a cold war simulation.

Real world structure	Analogic representation
The world	The game
The Soviet decision system	Red team
The United States decision system	Blue team
The rest of the nations	Control team*
The history of international relations between the present and the point at which the game begins	The scenario
The occasion for decision	The scenario
The decisionmakers	The participants
Decision-group process	Group process
Decisional output	The move and position papers
Decisional consequences	Control feedback

* These games are fairly flexible as to the number of nations represented.

The armchair analyst who, for example, tries to anticipate what Sadat's reaction to an Israeli offer in Geneva will be, is also engaged in experimentation in a simulation. Unlike the interview situation, in this simulation the relationship between the input in the referent system and the input in the simulation is known; the two are presumably isomorphic. Again, unlike the interview situation, the relationship between the referent decision system (Sadat) and the analog decision system (the analyst's mental model of Sadat) is unknown.

It is sometimes the case that the referent system serves as its own analog. In these cases, controlled, simulated inputs can be introduced and outputs and/or processes can be studied. J. David Barber's (1966) study of the group aspects of political decision making is a fine example of controlled experimentation with the referent system as its own analog.

There are many examples of simulations that are a mixture of deductive and analogic systems. In principle, any all-deductive simulation with modular subroutines could become a mixed simulation by replacing a given module with an analogic system. By the same logic, the set of deductive components of a mixed simulation can be enlarged as the laws describing the behavior of analogic components are discovered and formalized.

The "Inter-nation Simulation" (Guetzkow *et al.*, 1963) is an example of a mixed simulation that has been widely used in research. In this model the domestic environment for decision making (the nation's economy and aspects of its polity) are represented by deductive programs, but live research subjects (participants) are the analogic decisionmakers who function in this environment. What makes this an "inter-nation simulation" (INS) is the inclusion of a number of "nations" (that differ on the parametric settings on variables included in the deductive model) that are free to interact with each other. In the INS and in mixed simulations in general, the focus of research is on the interaction among the analogic elements and on the interaction between the analogic and deductive systems.

The three types of simulation used singly or in combination go a long way toward providing the conditions that facilitate the development of science in a particular domain of interest. Just as theory is indispensable in the construction of a simulation, the process of simulation building can also contribute to the development of theory and more generally to the cybernetic process of science. This is to say that the steps one goes through in developing a simulation, particularly if deductive systems are included, sharpen existing theory and, even more to the point, indicate pockets of apparent disorders. Beyond this, the ability to repeat the same situation with or without variation, which is a feature of all simulation, is a source of insight into what is regular and what is random.

A program of research can use one or another type of simulation depending on the state of theory and knowledge. Such a research program (i.e., one seeking to develop nomothetic theory for a particular empirical domain) is not a unilinear process. Depending on the state of theory and knowledge about the domain, several alternative paths are available. We can imagine a process such as the one outlined in Fig. 1 which specifies the considerations that indicate one path of development rather than another. (The following discussion of "stages" and "questions" directly refers to Fig. 1.)

*Stage 1. **Defining the domain of interest.*** Few criteria for the selection of "proper" topics are to be found. Surely, in the final analysis, the interests of

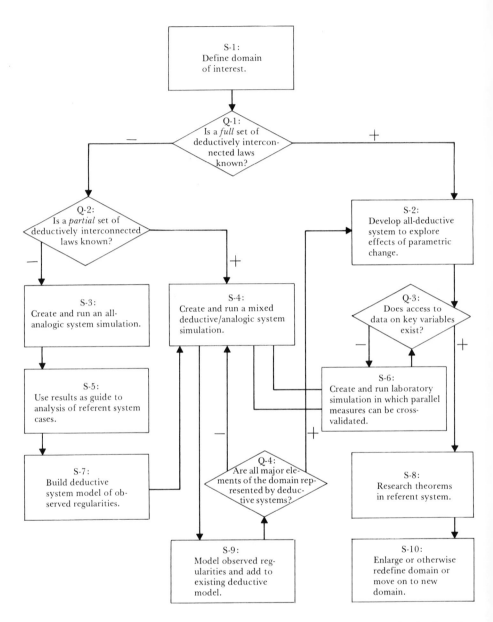

Fig. 1. Idealized flow diagram of research program. (Courtesy of the University Press of Virginia.)

the scholar are dominant but once the selection is made a certain degree of self-consciousness is desirable. For example, it is useful to be told how limited or general in time and/or in space are the sought-after laws.

Question 1. The state of theory. Having defined and otherwise delimited the domain of interest, we encounter the first consideration that serves to indicate the path to follow. This consideration involves questioning the extant theoretical development. Gustav Bergmann (1958) has defined theory as "a deductively interconnected set of laws"; using this definition, if the researcher is satisfied that a theory covering the domain of interest is available, the development of an all-deductive simulation is a live option for him. In general, we might assume that a narrower domain of interest is more apt to have had sufficient theoretical development to lend itself to this style of treatment, whereas a broader domain might not. But the question cannot be answered in general. If theoretical development is insufficient, a subsidiary question needs to be asked, but more of this in a moment.

Stage 2. The development of an all-deductive simulation. By the terms of our definition a theory that is sufficient to offer this option—that is, a theory containing the laws of entities—would simply have to be reexpressed in some appropriate computer language to yield a computer simulation (see Alker, Chapter 4 of this volume). From an experimental perspective, computer simulations: (1) have their prime virtue in their great flexibility for studying the effects of parametric change (i.e., sensitivity analysis); (2) produce results that are predetermined by the model (but the complexity of most models may make this statement of no practical consequence); and (3) yield output having no empirical content, as such; they are theorems that remain to be validated (Van Horn, 1971).

Before one could test theorems derived from the simulation as hypotheses about the referent system, the availability of measures of the variables in the simulation must be taken into consideration.

Question 3. The availability of measurement techniques. Data for the variables in the hypotheses generated by the running of the simulation may or may not be readily accessible in the referent system. If they are, the researcher can move directly to Stage 8 and carry out his research. If they are not accessible (in the situation, for example, in which psychological variables enter into a model but direct measurement access is not available to the researcher), parallel measures that do not require access must be developed (Brody, 1969a). One of the uses to which a simulation, with participants in analogic roles, can be put is the development of parallel research instruments (Stage 6).

Since in such simulation access to the participants is available, both standardized measures and measures that do not require direct access (e.g., content analysis) can be applied. This provides an opportunity for cross-validation (with the standardized instrument as criterion), refinement, and the reduction of measurement error. When the researcher is satisfied that the answer to Question 3 is positive, he can move on to Stage 8 and carry out his research.

Returning to Question 1, let us consider the roles of simulation if the answer is negative. If the researcher is not satisfied with the state of theory about the domain of interest, two general paths of development are open to him; the path he chooses can again be guided by considering the state of theory.

Question 2. The availability of partial theory. If a theory covering all entities and relationships is not available, is there a theory covering part of the domain of interest? If the answer is positive, research can proceed through a mixed-system simulation. If the answer is negative, a wholly analogous system simulation is the most viable option. Stages 3 and 4 reflect these options.

Stage 3. Research with a wholly analogous system simulation. From the point of view of tightening theory, sharpening measurement, and eliminating ideology, there are many reasons for using an all-analog simulation. Research access of the sort unavailable in the referent system is present here; the effect of this is to provide an opportunity for taking into account precise types of measurement. These, in turn, yield richer and more precise concepts with which to view cases in the real world (Stage 5) and also opportunities for formalizing subsystems within the domain of interest (Stage 7). De Rivera's (1968) work is an example of the link between Stages 3 and 5. The analogic simulation is the social-psychological laboratory from which generalizations are drawn; he then uses these generalizations to inform his investgation of a number of actual instances of foreign policy decision making in the United States.

The link between Stages 3 and 7 creates in effect a new answer to Question 2; that is to say, after observed regularities have been formalized, a partially deductive model exists and Stage 4 in the flow diagram has been reached.

Stage 4. Research with a mixed deductive/analogic system simulation. Stages 3 and 4 differ primarily in the extent of theory, about the domain of interest, in possession of the researcher. The researcher, in effect, accepts that theory as given and thus operates with a narrower range of uncertainty than he would in an all-analogic simulation. Research with a mixed system does not correct the deductive portion of the simulation; it seeks to add new deductive elements to it. If the deductive subsystem is not a good model of the referent system—as Chadwick (1967) asserts of the programmed parts of Inter-nation Simulation—since the deductive system is a part of the experimental setting, the external validity of behavior of the analogic elements is threatened. Within the simulation itself the deductive subsystem cannot be corrected; this requires treating this theory as an all-deductive model and taking it through Stage 2,

Question 3, and Stage 8. If the researcher is satisfied with the deductive model, he then moves through Stages 4 and 9 sufficiently often to answer Question 4 positively. Once all the major elements of the domain have been formalized, the researcher has, in effect, reached Stage 2 and he may proceed from there.

In general the more complex the domain, the more interactions of this subsystem (i.e., Stage 4, Stage 9, and Question 4) will be required.

We have taken a fast tour through a multifaceted program of research that could use several forms of simulation in the development of science through both experimentation, modeling, and measurement building. We cannot cite a single research program that has completely followed this developmental pattern, but many mirror the logic of one or more phases. The concern with the quality of the laboratory simulation amounts to a concern with external validity of the results produced in that laboratory. If intelligently conceived, constructed, and operated, a program of laboratory development cannot but produce more reasonable results.

The question of internal validity (Campbell, 1957) is less a matter of the laboratory than of experimental design; it is to that question that the next section is addressed.

THE DESIGN OF SYSTEM OF OBSERVATION: EXPERIMENTAL TECHNIQUES FOR OBSERVING POLITICAL PHENOMENA

From our previous discussion it should be obvious that experimentation is neither new in political research nor does it differ in intent from more commonly practiced and thus more familiar data-gathering techniques. Experimentation is used to generate data in which systematic and regular properties can be observed among variables, and from which tests of hypotheses can be made.

The term "experiment" has been used in many ways. The United States system of government was historically termed the "great experiment." This is the common language usage referring quite simply to trying something previously untried. In this case neither recorded measures of success nor criteria need be established. The spirit of the experiment is in the doing. This type of experimentation, not uncommon to students of politics, is "action" experimentation and requires no design for research into understanding or explaining the "experimental" activity. By way of exteme contrast, the term experiment also has technical usage applied to abstract logical thought processes.

Our focus in this section on experimental design is on experiments as ways of generating data for researching political phenomena. We concentrate specifically on the main elements of experimental research designs, the logic behind them, and the techniques employed in using the logic to answer questions raised by political scientists as they seek to explore, describe, and explain the phenomena that interest them. To be sure, experiments have others uses as well, including the refinement of research techniques, the pretesting of manipulations and measures, and the training of students. Such uses, which Kaplan (1964) terms "methodological," "pilot," and "training" experiments respectively, are no less important than the more theoretical and heuristic purposes for doing experiments in political research. However, we shall concentrate primarily on aspects of experimental design in the context of substantive empirical research.

Experimental design has been approached in various ways. Consider a definition from social psychology, an academic discipline that has traditionally relied on experimentation as its primary data generation procedure:

> a recording of observations, quantitative or qualitative, made by defined and recorded operations and in defined conditions, followed by examination of the data, by appropriate statistical and mathematical rules, for the existence of significant relations. (Cattell, 1966, p. 20)

This definition cautiously avoids restrictive terms such as "manipulation," "control," "abstract," or "laboratory" which the term "experiment" often invokes in contrast to "survey research." In fact, Cattell's reason for scrupulous avoidance of these aspects of experimentation in his definition was part of an attempt to reconcile a conflict in social psychology. That conflict was based on two competing methodological schools: those who relied on limited, bivariate, manipulated laboratory experiments as the principal method of testing hypotheses and building theory, and those who used multivariate and possibly unmanipulative approaches for the same purposes. Rather than assign the label "experiment" invariably to either approach, Cattell proposed a general model of experimental design composed of six basic dimensions. These dimensions include the following: (1) *the number of variables,* ranging from bivariate to multivariate; (2) the aspects of *manipulation,* ranging from those circumstances in which there is great interference or manipulation by the researcher to those in which variations occur freely and naturally; (3) the aspect of the *time of observation,* ranging from those made simultaneous to the experiment to those incorporating dated or historical information; (4) the degree of *situational control,* ranging from conditions held constant to conditions freely varying; (5) the *representativeness of variables* chosen for inclusion, ranging from abstract to actual; and finally (6) *the nature of the population sampling,* ranging from purposely biased to purposely representative (Cattell, 1966, p. 28). Recognition of the variety implied by the dimensions may forestall claims of "correctness" or "truth," that accompany the accepted single methods of conducting experiments or sets of procedures for evaluating those done by other students of political phenomena. Reviewing these dimensions focuses attention on experimental procedures as useful ways to understand political phenomena.

Cattell's notion of separable experimental design dimensions implies active decision making by the researcher. Systematic research requires active and purposeful decision making by the researcher, typically involving the specification of theoretically relevant variables and elaborating the conditions in which variables operate and in which their interaction may be assessed. It is fair to say that experimental designs are formal representations of these decisions.

Virtually all experimental designs include decisions about the following things. First, there must be a clear specification of the behavior to be investigated. That is, one must select a dependent variable (or several) and a way to measure it. Second, there must be an equally unambiguous selection of factors that influence or are causally related to the dependent variable whose effects are to be explored. When the variation in a causal factor, or independent variable, is manipulated or systematically observed for its impact on a dependent variable, it is conventionally called an *experimental variable*. Third, the experimenter must decide on a way to handle independent variables whose effects are not of primary interest. The effects of such variables on the dependent variable are considered bias or error when compared to the effects of the independent variables of primary concern, and these variables are termed *extraneous*. Finally, units for analysis whose behavior is to be studied, or *experimental subjects,* must be selected (Meyers, 1966, p. 1).

Still another way of understanding experimental design is by consideration of the logic that underlies experimentation. According to Campbell and Stanley (1966), experimental designs are particular arrangements in the way in which a phenomenon is observed. Experiments are arrangements that permit the testing of hypotheses about causal relationships occurring among a set of variables uninterrupted by either the system of observation or by other extraneous biasing factors.

Campbell and Stanley (1966) characterize theoretically extraneous sources of variation in a dependent variable measure as plausible rival hypotheses to the substantively interesting hypotheses being examined in any research. That is, the extraneous biases that contribute to variation in a dependent variable are independent causal factors unrelated to theoretically relevant causal factors, but that could plausibly explain the event under study. When this occurs the explanation is confounded. Campbell identifies two types of confounding factors. Those which may confound understanding of whether experimental treatments have a systematic impact in specific experimental instances are termed threats to the internal validity of the experiment. Eight broad classes of alternative hypotheses relate to the possible effects of the following factors:

1. History, or the effect of nonexperimental events which might occur between measurements of the dependent variable.

2. Maturation, or natural developmental changes among experimental subjects or units which might be mistakenly attributed to the experimental variables.

3. Testing, or the effect on subjects of being tested (measured) once upon a subsequent test (measurement).

4. Instrumentation, or variations in the measurement instrument from one measurement to another.

5. Statistical regression, or probabilistic variations in dependent variable scores where subjects have been selected on the basis of extreme scores on an independent variable.

6. Selection, or sample-related dependencies between independent and dependent variables.

7. Experimental mortality, or the loss of subjects from comparison groups.

8. Selection-maturation interaction, or the interaction of any of the above sources of bias which might be confused with the effects of experimental variables. (Campbell and Stanley, 1966, p. 5)

Taking these factors into account, minimizing or eliminating them as explanatory factors is vitally necessary for determining the precise nature of the impact of substantively interesting independent variables.

The other types of threats to validity are those extraneous biases that might make the results of an experiment non-generalizable. That is, although one may have high confidence in one's findings, certain factors could limit the findings to the particular setting or sample of subjects, thereby severely reducing the utility of the research. These limiting factors include the following:

1. The reactive effect of testing, or the changes within subjects due to the measurements taken that render them unrepresentative of the population from which they were selected.

2. Interaction of selection and the experimental variable.

3. The reactive effect of being in an experiment, which might be different from an encounter with the experimental variable in a nonexperimental setting.

4. Multiple treatment interference or the effect of one experimental variable on another in designs where subjects are exposed to several treatments.

Campbell and Stanley (1966) conceive of many types of designs that eliminate the threats to validity outlined above. These will be discussed within a more general discussion of applications of experimentation for studying political phenomena.

Before proceeding, it must be made clear that little attention will be devoted to the statistical and mathematical procedures typically used to describe experimental data or to the philosophical assumptions that underlie their use. There is a symbiotic relationship among designs and methods of statistical analysis, and the normal research practice is to create a design with specific statistical or mathematical analysis procedures in mind. However, there is a sense in which they are independent. Many different statistical and mathematical techniques can be used on a particular set of experimental data. By and large all aim at discovering relationships among variables and comparing relationships with those that might exist on the basis of chance or prior expectation. In combination with nonstatistical, nonmathematical understanding of the sequences in which variables occur, determinations are made as to what thing or combination of things probably caused another. Although we will touch on these topics to illustrate aspects of experimental design, the major focus of this section will be on the six dimensions of design that were outlined above.

The Number of Variables

Our initial consideration is the number of variables chosen for inclusion in an experiment. As was previously stated, the phenomena of politics generally include more variables than a researcher can observe in studying the particular phenomenon selected for research. Political researchers thus constantly face difficult questions concerning which variables they examine at any one time and about the degree to which the variables actually selected are adequate for the purpose of the research. The former question is discussed here as the design dimension, "number of variables." The latter is discussed below as the "representativeness" dimension. In practical and philosophical terms the dimensions are intimately related. We have separated them only to make some specific points about experimentation *in use* in studying politics. While in principle there are only practical limits on the number of variables examined at any time, based on computational ease and statistical necessities, experiments normally include fewer numbers of variables than other political research techniques. As mentioned earlier three kinds of variables are included: dependent variables that measure the effect (behavior or result) of the experimental or independent variables; independent variables that are theoretically relevant to the phenomenon of interest; and extraneous variables that may influence the dependent variables but are not part of the theoretical concern of the researcher and are thus conceived as biasing factors or error. In general, experimental design controls are used to remove the effects of extraneous variables at the time that the data are collected. Thus, there are generally fewer variables analyzed in experimental studies than in other types of political research, which rely on post-data adjustments and analysis to separate the extraneous from the relevant variation in the dependent variable measures.

Of course, post hoc statistical techniques are available to experimenters, and are used when effects due to uncontrolled variables are present to a noticeable degree.

As in other types of research there is a relationship between the number of variables and the complexity in procedures for untangling the relationships among them. Since the world of political activity is generally multivariate, the gains in analytic simplicity and directness from using very small numbers of variables are often offset by losses in being able to generalize from experiment the worldly phenomenon. That is, representativeness may be jeopardized. The problems inherent in choosing how many variables to consider are generally solved by theory, either in the formal sense of a deductive system of interrelated laws about the relationships among a bounded set of variables, or more loosely, in the sense of selecting information to meet some satisfactory criterion of explanation at a particular level. The amount of resources that are available to the researcher also acts as a practical limit on the number of variables. (Ignorance may do the same thing, of course.)

Let us demonstrate, with several experimental studies in voting behavior, some considerations about the number of variables to include. Hartmann (1936) intervened in a local election to test the impact of emotional and rational political leaflets on the vote for a candidate of a minor political party. A minor-party candidate was selected because of the ethical and political difficulty of intervening on behalf of the major parties, one of which was quite likely to win. The limited focus of the research, while not specifically referred to by the author, was also a result of working in the *actual* setting of an on-going electoral campaign. There were relatively few things the researcher could actually do or manipulate. The analysis was based on a comparison of the estimated increase in the party's vote in different areas of the city: where no leaflets were distributed, where "rational" leaflets were distributed, and where "emotional" leaflets were distributed. Other factors known to affect voting behavior were also controlled. Statistical adjustment procedures were used to attempt to remove the impact of naturally varying independent variables that could be considered extraneous with reference to the specific questions for which answers were sought. Thus there was one experimentally manipulated variable, the type of leaflet, with three levels of variation or "conditions": no leaflet, an emotional leaflet, and a rational leaflet. There was one primary dependent variable, party turnout rate.

Similarly, Eldersveld and Dodge (1954) and Eldersveld (1956) undertook examinations of campaign communications in experiments using two multi-level variables. The type of appeal of mailed propaganda, "rational" or "moral," was contrasted with the communication mode of personal contact with voters by student canvassers, by party canvassers, by telephone, or by combined student canvassers and mail. As in the Hartmann (1936) study, theoretically extraneous sources of variation in the dependent variable were removed through a combination of design control procedures and statistical adjustments. Of course, data collection is not necessarily limited to the experimental variables. Occasionally experimental data resemble survey data in the breadth of information generated. In the examples just cited the researchers buttressed their understanding of the situation by using additional information in ways similar to those of survey researchers.

In these field experiments and others (Kamin, 1958; Gertzog, 1970; Blydenburgh, 1971; Reback, 1971; Gosnell, 1927; Darley and Cooper, 1972; Nesbitt, 1972; Mann, Rosenthal, and Abeles, 1971; Bartell and Bouxsein, 1973), the number of variables selected was a function of both the practicality of working in the actual complex environment of the ongoing electoral process, and the limited interests of the researchers.

In comparison to nonexperimental voting research, experimental projects are generally highly focussed, a fact which is occasionally confused with their being "trivial." However, because the researchers actually create the variables and make them operate in the electoral environment, there is strong assurance that the data collected will directly approach the questions raised. Let us make the point another way. No one with much knowledge of politics expects voting behavior to be solely a function of the nature of the propaganda distributed by the candidates. Still, the best information available to students of campaigns about the effects of types of information has come from the studies that have been devoted to asking, "What are the effects and what must be done to assess them?" It would not be unfair therefore to think of experiments as molecular rather than molar in their approach to theory. They aim at answering very specific questions in a very specific manner. This does not mean that the questions are simple or that only two variables can be assessed at a time. Consider the following laboratory experiments in voting behavior. Brownstein (1971) assessed the impact of the style of message (programmatic, ambiguous, or both), the medium of presentation (radio, television, or print), and the context of information use (individual or group discussion) on the voter's perception of competing candidates and also on their vote choice. The design incorporated three multilevel factors, and the analysis produced a clear picture of their effects, both individually and in interaction. Dyson and Scioli (1972, 1974) used a laboratory setting to assess the impact of an actual televised political information program. By manipulating a videotape of the program they assessed the impact on a sample of student voters of party identifications, issue positions, styles of appeal, and amount of information on attitude modification and the process of candidate selection.

These few examples drawn from a single field of inquiry, voting behavior, indicate that the determination of how many variables to include is both a theoretical and practical matter. Most students of politics recognize the political world as a complex, multivariate behavior setting. As an attempt to understand what goes on in that setting, experiments generally limit the theoretical reality to component portions and consider variables a few at a time. When the complexity of a phenomenon is overwhelming, experiments are performed in multiples as part of a program of research. In programmatic research, limited questions are answered with each experiment and used both to generate new questions and to build an inventory of findings about related concepts. Given the experience of other scientific fields, this seems a particularly viable route to theory construction.

The programmatic approach is rare, however, in political experimentation. One outstanding example is the work of Warr and Knapper (1968) in which 40 related experiments are reported. The result is an extensive and fairly complete analysis of how people perceive people and events. (The theoretical focus of the book is not strictly political, but the psychology of perception is explored using political stimulus materials.)

More recently, Axelrod (1973) has constructed an information processing model of perception and cognition that is of direct interest in many areas of political study. Axelrod's theory, which he terms schema theory, is constructed from the findings of a large number of separate experiments.

Control Dimensions in Political Experimentation

Manipulation, temporal relation, and situational control are three subdimensions of experimental design which conventionally differentiate experiments from nonexperimental research. To a great extent these are the dimensions which together imply control, both in the sense of knowing the temporal sequences that underlie the concept of causality in the situation in which a phenomenon occurs, and in the sense of making things occur in ways which are precise, specified, and therefore known. It is through procedures for attaining control that the relevant variables are specified, that their effects are separated from the effects of extraneous variables, and that their effects are elaborated. In most experimental designs, these three control dimensions are used simultaneously through the active intervention of the researcher. At times the situation of study will *itself* lend or imply control and the researcher may use it to gain analytic control just as powerfully as if he had intervened. In this section, we consider some techniques for gaining control and illustrate through examples of political experimentation how and why the techniques are used.

Manipulation of the independent or experimental variable(s) means that the researcher intervenes to physically vary the independent variable(s) and observes the impact of each variation by measuring the value of the dependent variable. Variation in a dependent variable directly attributed to an independent variable is the *effect* of that variable. The actual situation occurring during the presence of each manipulation is called a treatment or condition. The familiar representation of the conditions that make up an experiment is the design layout. A layout is a logically constructed set of conditions that permit an effect to be assessed. For example, if one wished to create a situation for testing the impact of several policy alternatives, one might delineate precisely what constitutes each alternative, and then try each one out on a target group of subjects. Thus one might select one group of subjects and observe their behavior on some specified dependent variable (or set of variables) in the absence of the policy, and compare that to another group in the presence of a policy. Ignoring for the moment other factors that might confuse the analysis, the design might resemble the one shown in Table 2.

TABLE 2   Static group comparison design

	Group 1	Group 2	Group 3
Treatment	The absence of policy	Policy alternative 1	Policy alternative 2
Measure	Observation on variable, O_1	Observation on variable, O_2	Observation on variable, O_3

In this design the control of which group received a particular policy established comparison groups necessary for an accurate evaluation of the policy alternatives. We could, for example, compare each group to see which behaved most in accord with the policy objectives (providing they too were specified in advance) symbolized as the dependent variable measurement O in Table 2. Had only one treated group from this design been observed, the design would be the familiar case study design. We would attribute the behavior (variation in O) to the policy. But suppose that *in fact* the policy had no effect at all on O. Without some means of comparison we could not discover this fact. All experimental design controls create contrasts to meet logical needs such as this. In Fig. 1, a treated group could be contrasted with the untreated or "control" group (Group 1) and the difference between observed measures, $O_1 - O_2$, attributed to the policy (Alternative 1). But suppose further that the policy actually had no effect and there was still a difference between O_1 and O_2. Perhaps the individuals in Group 1 just happened to have different patterns of behavior from those in Group 2. We might then plausibly assert that the way in which the groups were *selected* might have produced the difference, or that Group 2 behaved differently because they *reacted* to the fact that they were in an experiment. Actually, to the extent that any of these rival hypotheses and the others specified by Campbell and Stanley (1966) are plausible, some type of design layout could be constructed to provide the conditions to test them against more substantively interesting hypotheses.

The Solomon Four Group Design is a particularly useful experimental layout for demonstrating how variations in treatment assignments may be used to establish comparisons for checking the validity of hypotheses. This design, as illustrated by Campbell and Stanley (1966), is represented in Table 3.

TABLE 3   Solomon four group design

	Pretest (T_1)	Exposure to experimental variable	Post-test (T_2)
Group 1 (R)*	O_1†	exposed	O_2
Group 2 (R)	O_3	not exposed	O_4
Group 3 (R)		exposed	O_5
Group 4 (R)		not exposed	O_6

Source: Campbell and Stanley, 1966, p. 24.
* Denotes random assignment.
† Denotes a measure or observation.

This design permits a multitude of comparisons for testing the effect of the experimental variable and assessing the effect of most of the rival hypotheses that Campbell and Stanley outline. For example, the assumption that random assignment of subjects to treatments creates truly comparable test groups prior to experimentation may be assessed by comparing pretest scores (in O_1 and O_3) of suspected important variables in Groups 1 and 2. If no systematic differences are found between these groups, confidence will be lent to explanations of differences between the groups due to the exposure of the subjects in Group 1 to the experimental variable generated by comparing post-test (postexperimental) observations O_2 to O_4 and O_5 to O_6. In addition, two plausible hypotheses rivaling that of the effect of the exposure to the experimental variable are rejected if the random assignment of subjects actually created equivalent groups: selection biases and perturbations in dependent variable scores due to statistical regression will have been made unsystematic, having been distributed randomly throughout the design.

The Solomon Four Group Design permits the researcher to assess the impact of testing the subjects prior to the experiment through comparisons of the untested groups' scores, O_5 plus O_6, with the pretested groups' scores, O_2 plus O_4, on any dependent variable. In addition, the effect is controlled in Groups 1 and 2 in the sense that it has an equal impact on post-test measurements. Similarly, the interactive effects of testing and exposure to the experimental variable, and of maturation and history, and the other possible biasing factors such as systematic subject mortality may be determined. Campbell and Stanley (1966) and Wiggins (1968) discuss the logic and analysis procedures for testing rival hypotheses. The interested reader is referred to these excellent discussions for further details.

Despite the obvious advantages of the Solomon Four Group Design, few political scientists have used it in their research. Two examples are available, however, in the works of Steinert (1973) and Robinson (1974). Using issues recently considered by the Supreme Court, Steinert explored the potential for attitude change resulting from exposure to majority opinion only, or both majority and dissenting opinions of the Court. Robinson used a similar design (within a larger study which used survey data) in an attempt to determine the impact of mediated communications on mass opinion and its consequences for the American political system.

The ability to manipulate independent variables provides a way to explore events that may not occur naturally. This aspect of manipulation is most useful to students of politics. Correctly used it might permit the exploration of theoretically interesting or important events that might not otherwise be accessible for study, or that might occur in a way that makes their study difficult or impossible. It is precisely in this fashion that the Institute for Research on Poverty has examined the impact of alternative negative income tax policies prior to the legislative institution of a policy (Elesh *et al.*, 1971). The design was a somewhat more complex version of the simple design discussed previously. Two independent variables were manipulated simultaneously to create a matrix of treatment and control groups. The experiment tested both income guarantee levels and tax rates and used other control techniques to remove a number of potentially confusing factors from the study. But basically the design was similar to that shown in Table 4.

TABLE 4   Partial factorial design

	Tax rates		
Guarantee levels	30%	50%	70%
.50 poverty line	.5 pl/30% tr	.5 pl/50% tr	
.75 poverty line	.75 pl/30% tr	.75 pl/50% tr	.75 pl/70% tr
1.00 poverty line		1.00 pl/50% tr	1.00 pl/70% tr
1.25 poverty line		1.25 pl/50% tr	

Source: Elesh *et al.*, 1971, Table 1.

Each cell in Table 4 corresponds to a treatment representing a possible policy alternative. By filling the cells with subjects and measuring several dependent variables within and across tax rates and guarantee levels, the design permits the comparative assessment of the particular policy mixes aimed at reducing poverty. This particular design is termed a partial factorial design, and may be generalized to include more factors. For example, the Urban Institute has conducted a three-factor experiment which involves the manipulative control over variables relevant to the operation of household allowance policies (Buchanan and Heinberg, 1972). (See also Watts *et al.*, 1971.)

Since large-scale social programs are expensive to undertake and very important to the recipients and society as a whole, the ability to try out the alternatives prior to making the oftentimes irreversible final choices represents one of the more promising potentials of experimentation for students of public policy. Both the advantages and disadvantages of this approach to policy decision making have been extensively discussed (Fairweather, 1967; Suchman, 1967; Campbell, 1971; Cook and Scioli, 1972; Scioli and Cook, 1973; Rossi and Williams, 1972; Weiss, 1972; Weiss and Rein, 1969).

Not all manipulation in political experimentation is oriented toward such a "mundanely" realistic end as that used by students of public policy impacts. In fact, the most frequently cited advantage offered by manipulative control is that it creates treatment combinations unavailable in nature which meet purely theoretical necessities. Consider the Dyson–Scioli (1974) experiment in campaign communications previously mentioned. The researchers were interested in separating the impact of partisan label from the personal attributes of candidates as they appeared to a television viewing audience and also from the content of each candidate's presentation. They could create the treatments from a videotape of the television program in which the candidates appeared, and by careful editing could vary party label and the total length and content of any created treatment, so that each candidate could be presented as either a Republican, Democrat, or whatever. In this way they produced a design of treatment combinations which could hold party label constant and permitted the separation of its effect from the effect of the candidate's personal characteristics. As a result, conditions unavailable in natural campaigns were tested.

Other manipulations are used as well for creating the test conditions needed to assess a host of factors intrinsic to the experiment itself which might confound the analyses of theoretical independent variables. The means of creating test conditions for assessing their impact is derived in part from the ability of the experimenter to manipulate the independent variables as he sees fit. This is not to imply in any way that the intervention of the researcher, in the form of physically creating treatment variations, is absolutely necessary for an experimental study. Where fortuitous natural circumstances themselves create the variety of events to correspond to the appropriate test conditions, there will be little necessity for the interference of the experimenter. This aspect of "as if" manipulation has been used by political scientists to explore the impact of educational curricula and educational institution on the political attitudes of students. (See especially Jaros and Darcy, 1972; Baker, Steed, and Benson, 1973; and Dabelko and Caywood, 1973.) Because of the disruptive effects of manipulation on organizational settings, students of organizational behavior have considered the possibilities for nonmanipulative or partially manipulative experimentation in detail (Barnes, 1971).

We have used the term manipulation in the sense of elaborating conceptual variables into the test conditions for the purpose of meeting the logical needs of a theoretical test. In addition, manipulation may be thought of as something physically done to create a condition or to prepare the experimental units for the experiment. As an example of the former, consider an experiment designed to investigate formal models of strategic behavior in coalition formation. Beal (1973) created a behavior context, a three-person bargaining game, as the test situation. He isolated the subjects (campaign managers attending a preelection training seminar), informed each of the payoff or "reward" he could receive for joining a particular coalition, and instructed them to attempt to maximize their profit. In addition, unknown to the subjects, confederates were used, instructed to play prearranged strategies as the "others" in the triad. By varying the strategies of the confederates, test situations were created to examine the behavior of the subjects in each of five experimental conditions corresponding to differing likelihoods that certain coalitions would form. Similar use of manipulative control has been made by other students of coalition behavior (Riker, 1967, 1968; Riker and Zavoina, 1970; Zavoina, 1971). The general utility of experimentation for this substantive area has been discussed at length by Wissel (1973).

Manipulative control in its broadest sense has been used by political researchers to create complex behavioral environments in which to observe the systematic interaction of individuals conceived of as representations of individuals (or groups) in analog situations. These creations are manual or "manned" simulations. They range in structure from highly constrained role-playing models such as the Inter-Nation Simulation (Guetzkow *et al.,* 1963), to minimally structured and loosely constrained behavioral environments such as the *N*-Person Prisoner's Dilemma Simulation (Powell, 1973). They range in use from instructional settings for training students (Boocock and Schild, 1968) to testing grounds and generation devices for theory (Brody, 1963; Elder and Pendley, 1966; Hermann, 1967). It must be noted that there is considerable variation in the degree to which the users of simulation express confidence in whether the complex environments they create *actually* represent the analog situation or referent their simulation purports to model (Snyder, 1963; Powell, 1969, 1973). The arguments central to this debate are for the most part concerned with the problems of variable specification and the extent to which generalization from the simulation to the referent is possible.

Both in simulation and in more traditional modes of experimentation, manipulative control is frequently used to prepare experimental units (typically human subjects) for the manipulation of the experimental variables. The purpose of this type of manipulation is to make each unit (subject) comparable, by making them similar with respect to some performance variable that might influence behavior in the experiment. For example, simulators may use the early stages of their simulation to train subjects in roles appropriate to the "game" or model, and, when there is certainty that everyone comprehends the rules or other game parameters, to systematically induce an experimental manipulation by varying one or several parameters at a time and observing the subject's responses. Other modes of reducing variation in an extraneous performance variable include limiting information, i.e., using minimal information settings (Scioli, 1971; Dyson and Scioli, 1971; Fleitas, 1971; Brownstein, 1971), constraining behavior by removing behavior options, and the use of nonhuman, mechanical apparatus.

A typical method of reducing variation in the presentation of a treatment involves using written or recorded instructions (to minimize the possible impact of the researcher) or the use of computer-assisted instruction devices to provide experimental stimuli. As an illustration, consider an experiment designed to investigate the utility of psychological learning theory in explaining political attitude formation (Dyson, Sheffield, and Zavoina, 1973). The design included a fixed schedule of reinforcement in the form of common praise words ("good," "very good," "excellent") to attempt to induce attitude change in specified directions (liberal, conservative, or random). The stimuli (in the form of questions) and the reinforcers were displayed on a cathode ray computer terminal in an attempt to remove the impact of a human authority figure who might bias the responses. Of course, the machine itself could introduce a reactive component to the response patterns. In this case the researchers were willing to take that chance because the particular model being tested called for a reinforcement source that did not vary at all.

The examples of manipulative control just cited overlap a second major dimension of control, that is, the control of constancy of conditions. By this control, the impact of certain extraneous variables is made uniform over the entire sample of experimental units. The instructions, time, location, and characteristics of the room or setting are typically controlled in laboratory experiments through the use of this technique. Attention is devoted to making these aspects of the experimental experience identical for all subjects, while the experimental variable is varied as different subjects are exposed to different treatments. In nonlaboratory experimentation it is often difficult to use this control, but as a general rule experimenters attempt to maintain the constancy of any variable or set of variables which might influence a dependent variable measure and confuse the assessment of the impact of the experimental independent variable or variables.

Occasionally, constancy of experimental conditions can be maintained through the design layout. Typically used are balanced or counterbalanced designs to remove the impact of an extraneous variable. One specific technique for balancing is to use matched groups of units (subjects) selected according to some independent variable. In essence this is like replicating the design in blocks, each of which uses one group of the subjects partitioned according to variation in the independent variable being controlled. When the matching is done *prior* to the experiment and the units within blocks are assigned randomly, matching is not the same as the post hoc control typically used in survey research. In experiments with random assignment of subjects, the possibility of selection bias interacting with the experimental variable is simply eliminated as a plausible rival hypothesis for explaining the relationship.

While matching may make the impact of a suspected extraneous variable obvious by permitting unambiguous assessment of experimental effects, it may also severely limit the generality of the experiment if only one or two specific values (out of all possible values) of the criterion variable are tested (Plutchik, 1968, p. 191). Although there are instances in which matching may be the only practical way to remove an extraneous variable, caution must be exercised that other inequalities between matched groups that are created by the matching are not correlated with the dependent variable. Despite the availability of statistical adjustment procedures such as covariance analyses, there is a risk of confounding the determination of experimental effects when this occurs (Campbell, 1970).

It is therefore preferable to remove the systematic impact of extraneous variables through the control technique of randomization. Randomization refers here to the technique of assigning experimental units to the treatment conditions of the design in such a fashion that each unit has the same chance of receiving a given treatment or combination of treatments. Random assignment accomplishes several useful things. First, it distributes all biasing factors related to the units or subjects throughout the design, theoretically eliminating any relationship between treatments and treatment groups that is unrelated to the experiment. That is another way of saying that chance assignment removes the impact of factors related to the selection of the sample as an extraneous independent variable by *equalizing* the treatment groups at the time of randomization. Similarly, bias caused by the probability of regression toward the mean of extreme scores on the dependent variable is removed in that each treatment group (experimental or control) theoretically regresses equally (Campbell and Stanley, 1966, p. 15). As a result, contrasts observed between treatment groups (or between experimental and control groups) are fairly certain to be related only to the experimental treatment. Of course, if the experiment is conducted sequentially (i.e., some groups at one time, some at others), then special care must be taken that extraneous independent variables related to the *time* of treatment do not confuse the interpretation of the data. This might occur if any factor related to the time of experimental manipulation uniquely affects one treatment group (or combination of groups) but not another. In that case history, maturation, or selection–maturation interaction, rather than the independent (experimental) variable, may be the cause of variation in the dependent variable.

The power of random assignment as a control technique should not be underestimated. In addition to removing extraneous bias from known sources, it removes bias from unknown or unelaborated sources as well. Since highly manipulated experiments are generally limited with respect to the number of variables included, randomization represents the most elegant way to maintain confidence that the research will be internally valid.

In addition, random assignment enhances the interpretability of various statistical analysis techniques for determining effects, such as analysis of variance, which offer further advantages to researchers. Brown (1971) has pointed out that even with fairly small samples one may confidently identify nonrandom differences between treatment groups. In fact, the use of empirical rather than theoretical error estimates may lend greater confidence to observed contrasts than is typically the case in nonexperimental, correlational studies, where random assignment is not possible.

However, random assignment techniques may at times be difficult to apply. This is particularly true in field settings where randomization may not be conceived of as fair, convenient, or practical. In such a case a great deal of analytical power must be sacrificed. Students of program evaluation in particular have considered this problem. Although no general solutions have emerged, several suggestions have been made. Campbell (1971), for example, has proposed that samples for policy impact field experiments be drawn by randomized invitations to prospective participants, or that experiments be conducted without subject awareness. On ethical grounds he reasons that the former seems preferable, and in general we agree. Perhaps as Campbell suggests, the only ethical way to secure randomization in field settings is to instill in the subject population (and society as a whole) a willingness to experiment.

Along with ethical restrictions, the problems of using experiments for policy evaluation revolve about the costs in time and other resources of creating large-scale experiments in the field. Light (1973) has called for whole programs of experiments, each dealing with a few locally controllable variables, sequentially linked, and conducted *until* some desired effect was produced. This combination of action and evaluation is one possibility for overcoming the difficulties inherent in field settings.

Actually, other researchers with interests in the field rather than the laboratory have made similar suggestions. Barnes (1971), for example, has suggested the use of "non-classical," special purpose designs in organizational experimentation.

Temporality

The third major control dimension is control of the temporal sequence of events. In some respects it is so obvious that it might seem unnecessary to discuss it. We conventally consider causality a temporal concept. That is, causality is in part determined by noting that a change in a dependent variable *follows* the presence of an independent variable. It is therefore necessary in making a causal inference to know the time sequence of related variables in addition to knowing the degree and probability of the relationship. Such knowledge does not inherently depend on experimentation. Frequently temporal relationships are derived by determining what plausibly occurred first, or observations made at one point in time are related to those made subsequently. However, in complex systems of variables in which there may be multiple causes for a particular reaction, multiple reactions caused by a single independent variable, or multiple reactions caused by multiple independent variables, the determination of causality may become quite difficult. Techniques familiar to political scientists who are approaching such a problem are the use of theory, which directs the search for particular factors, and the use of statistical models of causal systems which employ a variety of partialing techniques to specify the variance explained by each competing factor with others held constant (Blalock, 1964).

In contrast to research designs which deal with causality assessment "post hoc," experimental designs develop time sequences directly. Since the experimenter usually produces the independent variable and observes the reaction in the dependent variable, temporality is clearly established. And since a design must include cases in which a causal factor is present, absent, or combined with other factors, there is great certainty concerning the specification of the causal effects among variables. Manipulation is not essential, however, if naturally occurring situations provide the necessary comparisons. In such instances externally derived knowledge of the sequence of events is sufficient to provide a clear picture of causality.

The other two dimensions of experimental design identified by Cattell (1966) are the "degree of representativeness of the choice of relatives" and the "representativeness of the distribution of population entities." The former is concerned with what variables are to be included in a research project and the latter with the units of analysis (most typically, the subjects). Apart from the methodological and ethical problems raised in our discussion of control, these dimensions of experimental design represent some of the most important operational problems for political experimentation.

Representativeness of Variables

Representativeness of the choice of relatives is portrayed by Cattell (1966) as a dimension that ranges from abstract to representative. Explicit in Cattell's discussion of this dimension is the idea that in conducting systematic research, one necessarily simplifies the complex "reality" which the senses encounter in the existential world, setting bounds on what constitutes the phenomenon of immediate concern, and representing the components by concepts and constructs or operational substitutes. All the while some correspondence must be maintained between the complex of relationships in the data and those in the referent "reality."

As students of science have repeatedly pointed out, data are not the reality itself, but a reasonably constituted substitute from which additional information may be culled. In turn, the use of data in understanding the referent reality is properly thought of as interpretation. Since interpretation is the ultimate objective of data generation, all data-collection activities raise questions of whether the data will provide an adequate basis on which to begin interpretation. Often such questions take the following form. Does the research underway explore a loosely defined array of variables which are suspected to "contain" the phenomenon? Then perhaps a great many variables might be used, even if they overlap. In fact, multiple measures for each variate might be desirable to adequately capture the conceptual variable completely (Campbell and Fiske, 1959). Does the research aim at discovering in a very precise way the relative impact of two variables identified by prior research? Then a bivariate study might prove most useful.

Consider simulations in international relations on one hand, and laboratory investigations of attitude modification in the other. Both purport to be scientific, systematic ways to either test or generate theory. Typically, simulations of international relations have included very large numbers of variables, many of which are unspecified. For example, the Inter-Nation Simulation (Guetzkow *et al.*, 1963) is an operating model of a multination system, with multiple "fixed" decision structures (in the form of deductive programs representing each national economy and polity) and a "free" decision environment for the human subjects, in which the "nations" interact. In the INS, and other mixed man-machine simulations, the focus of research is on the interaction between the human decisionmakers and their deductively derived "national systems" and between the decisionmakers of the various nations. In this case the deductive systems represent political phenomena which the researchers accept either as assumptions or as known quantities, and the decision making of the subjects represents an analog to the referent "unknown" international decision system. The analog is used because it is more immediately observable than the referent system and because it resembles it to a sufficient degree to be interesting. In this way the research conducted using the simulation makes use of known variables (in the nation models), creates the environment for exploring suspected variables such as information levels and communication modes, and enhances the discovery or elaboration of previously unknown variables and relationships. The INS, in addition, has traditionally aimed at understanding the referent. That is, it is meant to be relevant to the actual world of international behavior. It has as a prime concern the external validity or generalizability of its findings.

It is instructive to note that at least one other simulation of international processes, the Prisoner's Dilemma Simulation (Powell, 1973) which in many ways resembles the INS, has also been used as an analog to international behavior. Yet it has been primarily intended to produce findings at a different level of abstraction, that of the relational world of complex interactive behavior between and among groups of subjects. Powell has suggested that a concern with the analog system itself, the simulation treated as the "reality," may logically be a prior research task to dealing with the ultimate referent, the international system (Powell, 1973). This position corresponds to a concern for internal validity as a prerequisite to external validity. In both of these simulations, the researchers are working at a high level of abstraction with some variables specified, some partially specified, and some unspecified. As a result, the procedures for analyzing simulations have proven problematic. The problems occurring in analyzing the analog are like those in analyzing any experimental data, and then some. Processes and outcomes are specified, and relationships to manipulated variables are determined. Treated as experiments in abstract political behavior the analysis would then be complete. However, to make the findings relevant to the actual or "real" world of international behavior, as opposed to merely considering them as heuristics, requires strong confidence that the variables present in the simulation *represent* those present in the referent. The difficulties of extrapolating, from the findings obtained with the simulation, to the object referent (that is, establishing correspondence), have led to a series of validation criteria which have yet to be used with success, but have suggested ways to analyze other sorts of international data. The students of "event" data are in many ways doing the same things with nonsimulation, historical data that simulators have been doing with data generated in the laboratory. Perhaps some convergence in the stable processes each uncovers will become the criterion validity of simulations. To the extent that the lawful aspects of behavior in the theoretical domain of interest (cooperative, conflictive, and interactive behavior) are robust across levels of abstraction, simulation may be placed at both ends of the continuum of representativeness that Cattell has identified.

Experimentation in the field, using as the object of study an ongoing political phenomenon, might at first seem to typify the representative end of the dimension. Certainly the variables observed are worldly rather than abstract. However, the quality of mundaneness is not the defining characteristic of the dimension. Rather, it is the degree to which all factors validly conceived of for a given level of abstraction and validly measured are *included* in the data system undergoing analysis. To the extent that they are included, the design is representative. In practical terms a representative design is one in which the procedure for variable selection is one of random sampling. That is, from the total population of variables that subtend the phenomenon, the researcher would systematically sample to select the variables for experimentation. This is an extension of the logic used in sampling the subjects or units for experimentation. But here we are concerned with using a sampling procedure to select from among the conditions in which the phenomenon might occur, sampling to select the responses (or measures of response) which might be produced, and, if the experimenter is suspected of affecting the results, sampling even the experimenters (Rosenthal, 1966, 1969). It is thus fair to say that *almost* all experimentation in political research is highly biased. Variables are selected on the basis of particular theories and limited in nonrandom ways.

Although the concept of representativeness is fairly old (Brunswick, 1952, 1956), relatively few examples of political research stressing representative design are available. The previously cited studies of person–event perception by Warr and Knapper (1968), the programs of simulation development of Guetzkow and Powell, and the loosely structured series of experiments on attitude modification by Dyson and others could be considered attempts to research a representative collection of variables within given theoretical domains. Rather more systematic attention to representativeness in political studies may be found among a small group of students of political psychology (Brown and Ungs, 1970; Brown, 1971; Nimmo and Savage, 1971a, 1971b; Brown and Taylor, 1970; Brown and Scioli, 1973; Cook, Scioli, and Brown, 1975). These students have used Q techniques and factor analysis to reduce a representative sample of attitude statements to a few attitude dimensions across a theoretically derived, nonrandom, but representative sample of subjects. (For a discussion of Q techniques, see Stephenson, 1953, 1967; Kerlinger, 1964; North *et al.,* 1963.) In these studies, Q methods are used to place emphasis on the self-defined attitude structures of the purposely selected samples of respondents. This contrasts sharply with more familiar survey methods placing emphasis on researcher-defined attitude structures of representative samples of respondents (Converse, 1964).

Concern for representative design overlaps some standard problems of measurement. A primary concern is whether dependent variable measures are valid, whether independent variables are valid, and whether independent variables are valid representations of causal factors in nature.

Whatever the level of abstraction, representativeness, or complexity of the research enterprise, a dependent variable must be selected and ways to measure it devised. The thing to be assessed naturally depends on the theoretical theme and frame of reference of the research. Virtually all experimental dependent variables may be thought of as a response of some type which is stimulated by exposure to an experimentally manipulated independent variable, and by which the differential effects of variation in the experimental independent variable or treatment may be assessed. For example, Eldersveld used as dependent variables *turnout rates* and *candidate preference* scores to test the effects of three different types of campaign communication techniques in a field experiment on campaign propaganda effectiveness (Eldersveld and Dodge, 1953;

Eldersveld, 1956). Laboratory experiments (Brownstein, 1971; Dyson and Brownstein, 1974; Dyson and Scioli, 1974) used subjects' attitude change on campaign-relevant issues and measures of person perception as dependent variables to determine the relative effects of different styles of campaigning and different media of communication. Reported changes in earnings and hours of work time (obtained through questionnaires) were used to test the effects of a public policy, the negative income tax (Elesh *et al.,* 1971). The behavior of signing a petition was the dependent variable in a field experiment seeking to determine the effect of style of attire ("hip" or "straight") on social "helping" behavior at a peace demonstration (Suedfeld, Bochner, and Wnek, 1971), and in assessing the impact of attire on the responses of middle-class residents to paraphrases of the Bill of Rights (Samuel, 1972).

The variables used in these studies differ in the *way* in which they represent the theoretical dependent variable that they stand for. Aronson and Carlsmith (1968) conceive of a continuum of dependent variables ranging from actual behaviors (behavioral), to "almost" behaviors such as expressions of commitment (quasi-behavioral), to indicators based on written reports of behavior, and to paper and pencil tests measuring psychological concepts that cannot actually be observed, such as attitudes and perceptions. Any or all may be equally useful—providing the subject *takes seriously* the activity or response sought by the researcher (Aronson and Carlsmith, 1968, p. 57). The key phrase here is "taking seriously," which refers to the question of validity in general (for all behavioral research) but which is sadly often misinterpreted by critics of experimental research. It is, for example, occasionally implied that the activity or response measured as a dependent variable is trivial in most laboratory situations. That is, it is claimed that experimental situations are so unrealistic that the behavior which occurs is not truly representative of the critical behavior of interest and thus cannot be used to generalize or make useful theoretical statements. Occasionally this is true, but the question of whether it is a general phenomenon is an empirical one. There is overwhelming evidence that experimental realism is quite obtainable. That is, subjects become truly involved in the experimental situation and behave with the same degree of involvement that they would in the nonexperimentally induced analogous situation. It must be noted that experimental realism differs from mundane realism (where the experiment is made to "look like" the real world). Mundane realism may promote experimental realism but is in no way crucial to questions of internal validity (Aronson and Carlsmith, 1968, pp. 25–27). If the *process* of behavior and the explanation of the process are *general,* and presumably correspondent or homomorphic to the same behavior in nonexperimental settings, true validity may be obtained. To illustrate this point, consider a test of the "free rider" theory of rational decision making (Olson, 1968). An experiment was conducted in order to compare an individual's contribution to the public good in the presence and absence of personal private benefit, in groups differentiated by their size, and to observe whether a contribution to the public good was recorded or anonymous (Sweeney, 1971). The mundane referents for Olson's theory and Sweeney's experimental test include such examples as vaccination, national defense, and other public goods. The theoretical referents, however, are cues to contributive behavior and information that permit an individual to make and evaluate social comparisons. In this experiment, the dependent variables selected to stand for an individual's contribution to the collective welfare was a behavioral performance—the rate at which they peddled bicycles under the various experimentally controlled conditions. So mundanely unrealistic a dependent variable is experimentally realistic in its correspondence to the theoretical variable of the experiment.

On the other hand, the threat to validity generated by subjects performing in trivial fashion is not to be lightly dismissed. Facetious or random responses by subjects introduce errors into measures of dependent variables which render experiments *internally* invalid. The experience of social psychologists is particularly useful to deal with such threats to internal or "experimental" validity. Two general strategies are used to manage it. The first is to remove or avoid the threat; the second is to measure it and account for it in the interpretation of data.

Techniques to remove subject noninvolvement and response triviality include making the behavior of interest (dependent variable) one of several which the subject must do during the experiment, and/or concealing it with "blinds" by providing false information regarding the aspect of the experiment that might "trivialize" it. The avoidance of subject "nonseriousness" is also accomplished by the use of unobtrusive measuring devices and through involvement of the subject as though he or she were "aiding" the experimenter. The key feature is always the same: involving the subject to such a degree as to have the subject emit a behavior which is a response to the relevant independent variables and not a response to his perception of irrelevant variables, including the experiment itself. (For a general discussion of these considerations, see Aronson and Carlsmith, 1968. For an application of this logic to nonexperimental survey research, see Atkin and Chaffee, 1972.)

The technique is not limited to laboratory experimentation. Kamin (1958) polled registered voters in two Canadian cities asking them to choose, as part of a public opinion poll, among fictitious candidates and parties, when the candidate names were obviously "ethnic-sounding." The displayed behavior was systematic in the direction of his hypothesis, showing that the ethnic character of candidate names influenced the respondent's perception of the candidate. Although the choices presented to the subjects were for fictitious candidates and even a fictitious office, Kamin reported that only one person polled questioned the existence of the office he had devised! Kamin concluded that the dependent variable measure, candidate selection, was valid and that the processes of making the selection were theoretically valid and generalizable to nonexperimental situations. Quite clearly the validity of a dependent variable measure is closely related to the validity of the independent variable.

In some circumstances, excessive concern with mundane variables is inappropriate and possibly misleading. This occurs when one has in mind testing a "pure" abstract theory which by its nature does not apply directly to actual events, yet is useful to understand them. In such cases, empirically observed deviations from behavior predicted by the theory may be explained by or attributed to other factors. In the absence of an alternative theory that encompasses these additional factors and still explains the event of primary concern, the "incomplete" theory may be satisfactory for explaining the phenomenon, or at the least may be useful as a benchmark for testing competing explanations.

Representativeness of Experimental Units of Analysis

The sixth design dimension suggested by Cattell (1966) is that of the representativeness of the "referee" sample from which measurements of variables are taken. This dimension ranges from highly selective, or biased, to actually representative. Political scientists are in general familiar with the need to study whole populations or to use samples that represent some population to which the findings of research may be generalized. The question of the generalizability of findings, or the external validity of an experiment, rests substantially on whether the units are selected in a way that precludes the possibility of systematic bias and provides the basis for eliminating correlations among dependent variables unrelated to the experimentally manipulated or unmanipulated independent variables.

As with survey methods some type of random sampling procedure provides the best confidence in the representativeness of relationships discovered in the sample. However, the samples generally used in political experiments only rarely look like the samples used by survey researchers. Experimental samples are generally smaller. As previously explained, this is partially a function of the analytic procedures which the random assignment of subjects and other control techniques permit. The careful attention to reducing extraneous variance implied by the use of experimental designs practically always permits relatively smaller samples than are used in nonexperimental research with equivalent levels of statistical confidence in the results.

The small size of experimental samples (relative to nonexperimental samples) occasionally alarms political researchers schooled only in the survey tradition. In general the alarm is misplaced, because sample size alone does not determine the utility of information available in the experimental data. The level of risk the researcher is willing to assume in making an incorrect judgment about a hypothesis being tested or a parameter being estimated must also be considered. Such risks are reflected (statistically) in the variance of dependent variable measures, which, as we previously discussed, is composed both of extraneous variance as "noise" and variance related to relevant independent variables (information). Quantities of useful information can be increased by either reducing extraneous variance or by increasing sample size. (For an excellent discussion of the statistical reasoning, see Mendenhall, 1968, ch. 2.)

There is also great variation in the surface (apparent) representativeness of experimental samples. The typical small-group experiment, for example, uses subjects from readily accessible student populations; field experiments in campaign propaganda rarely use populations more expansive than those in the immediate environs of the researcher, which are mainly small towns with campaigns of "manageable" proportions; the large-scale policy evaluation experiments are conducted among quite large target groups of the policy being tested but within some defined governmental administrative boundary.

Are the latter "valid" as opposed to the former in the sense that the results are more general? The answer is, of course, that in practical use, external validity is never established absolutely, but only in the form of the *degree of confidence* to which the findings are accepted.

Confidence in the generalizability of a finding may be established through replication (easier to do if samples are drawn from accessible populations but incomplete) as well as through sampling from entire populations (which is usually more costly).

The needs of the researcher, in the form of the level of theory or understanding sought, may also influence the appearance of samples. For example, consider the differences in the level of conceptual abstraction between a small-group experiment in communications and conflict, and a policy impact experiment in compensatory education. The small-group experimenter might well be able to generate precisely the circumstances needed to assess, for example, the relative effect of incomplete versus complete information on stipulated criterion of "rationality of decision making" by members of the group using any group of normal subjects. In this case the phenomenon is so general that the population of interest is "human decisionmakers." Students, members of natural groups, or subjects selected from the local townspeople might be representative enough to delve into the research question at this level of abstraction. On the other hand, the population of interest and the level of understanding for exploring a compensatory education policy such as the Head Start program, might be based on more stringent sampling criteria because the questions asked and answers sought are of a far less general, far more specific nature. In addition, the nature of the research effort might influence the stringency of the sampling design. If the research is undertaken in the context of justification, testing well-developed theory derived from a long line of prior empirical findings, greater efforts at securing a truly representative sample might be taken than if the research is exploring virgin theoretical territory. In the latter case, failure to proceed in the absence of a conventionally defined sample may preclude discovering interesting phenomena or theories to pursue. As with other strategies for empirical research, such "cost-benefit" considerations can seldom be precluded as decisions are made in the process of research.

Donald Campbell (1971) has outlined many considerations that might be crucial in determining the sample for an experimental policy research. There is first an ethical aspect to the problem. Are the participants subjects or "victims"? Is there potential *harm* in the treatments? This may interact with whether the subjects are to be aware or unaware of their participation, or if the benefits or losses (in whatever terms) are really substantial to subjects. There are also political questions. Is there some institutional risk to be incurred from findings? Do methodologically ideal "random selection–random assignment" procedures institute some sort of authoritarian control over peoples' lives? Who, even among a target group, should benefit and who should not?

Finally, there are also methodological questions. Is a field experiment absolutely required to overcome possible reactive effects of the lab? Is there a reasonable way to prevent or compensate for experimental mortality? Do appropriate measures exist for evaluation, perhaps in the form of previously collected institutional records?

Any or all of these considerations may influence the researcher's decisions concerning the exact nature of the sample in experimental research. However, in the end, sampling questions join philosophical and statistical reasoning. A sample drawn from a sampling unit rather than the true population of interest may reasonably be used as the basis for statistical hypothesis testing. Contrasts and effects observed within such a sample are in a strict sense limited to the sample. However, they do provide the basis for exploring the hypotheses with other samples in other circumstances. Confidence in the generality of a hypothesis may be increased most rapidly with the number of successful replications obtained across the widest variety of circumstances. Confidence will be misplaced when it is based on the results of a single experiment, no matter what care is taken to make the sample representative of the population.

CONCLUSION

No claim has been made here that experimentation is the only route to understanding or theorizing about political phenomena. Such a presumption would necessarily ignore the degree to which experimenters have used findings generated by other research approaches in structuring their experiments. It would similarly mislead one from a variety of other approaches that often better fit available data and research circumstances. Rather, the claim is made that experimentation has a useful place in political research, and that it represents a powerful tool. Some researchers are comfortably skilled at using the most appropriate tool for a particular job. In cases where the theory or hypothesis one is testing is particularly clear with regard to the causal structure involved, where independent variables may be manipulated directly, where subjects or units may be randomly assigned to experimental conditions or treatment groups, and where a universe or population of experimental units can be appropriately sampled, experimental designs have a clear analytic advantage over other types of research designs. In cases in which all of these conditions save random assignment of experimental units obtained, partial or quasi-experimental designs may be used. Elsewhere, nonexperimental, post hoc designs are available and the data which they produce should not be neglected.

Some students of politics have argued that little of interest is amenable to experimental techniques because political researchers can never achieve the degree of control required. The growing numbers of experiments in political research suggest that this argument stems from either ignorance of the technique or lack of imagination or a failure to observe the literature. Others have suggested that experimental techniques are necessarily reactive, or that "artificial" variation is somehow inferior to naturally occurring variation in independent variables. Specific design techniques have been developed to test these hypotheses, and little systematic empirical evidence has accumulated to verify them. As more examples of experimentation in use become available, it can be expected that these myths about the technique will be dispelled.

Thus far, most of the available examples of experimentation in political research have been in the substantive areas of political psychology and policy analysis. In the case of political psychology, this seems fairly natural, because experimentation has proven itself so useful a tool in psychological research. In policy analyses, the almost complete failure of nonexperimental techniques to provide adequate information about the comparative impact and relative effectiveness of alternative policies and programs has encouraged experimentation.

With its long history as a useful tool in scientific research, and apart from the early examples of political experimentation, the more general application of the logic of experimentation is long overdue in political research.

REFERENCES

Anderson, Barry F. (1966). *The Psychology Experiment*. Belmont, Calif.: Wadsworth.

Aronson, Elliot, and J. Merill Carlsmith (1968). "Experimentation in social psychology." In Gardner Lindzey and Elliot Aronson, eds., *Handbook of Social Psychology*, Second edition. Reading, Mass.: Addison-Wesley.

Atkin, Charles R., and Steven H. Chaffee (1972). "Instrumental response strategies in opinion interviews." *Public Opinion Quarterly* 36:69–79.

Axelrod, Robert (1973). "Schema theory: an information processing model of perception and cognition." *American Political Science Review* 67:1248–1266.

Azar, Edward, Richard A. Brody, and Charles McClelland (1972). *International Events Interaction Analysis*. Beverly Hills, Calif.: Sage Publications.

Baker, Todd A., Robert P. Steed, and Paul R. Bensen, Jr. (1973). "A note on the impact of the college experience on changing the political attitudes of students." *Experimental Study of Politics* 2:76–88.

Barber, J. David (1966). *Power in Committees*. Chicago: Rand McNally.

Barnes, Louis B. (1971). "Classical versus nonclassical designs in field experimentation." In William M. Evan, ed., *Organizational Experiments: Laboratory and Field Research*. New York: Harper & Row.

Bartell, Ted, and Sandra Bouxsein (1973). "The Chelsea project: candidate preference, issue preference, and turnout effects of student canvassing." *Public Opinion Quarterly* 37:269:275.

Beal, Richard Smith (1973). "The coalition strategy of the powerful." *Experimental Study of Politics* 2, no. 3:16–36.

Belknap, George, and Angus Campbell (1952). "Political party identification and attitudes toward foreign policy." *Public Opinion Quarterly* 15:601–623.

Benson, Oliver (1961). "A simple diplomatic game." In James N. Rosenau, ed., *International Politics and Foreign Policy: A Reader in Research and Theory,* pp. 504–511. Glencoe, Ill.: Free Press.

Bergmann, Gustav (1958). *Philosophy of Science,* Madison: The University of Wisconsin Press.

Blake, Ralph M., Curt J. Ducasse, and Edward H. Madden (1960). *Theories of Scientific Method: The Renaissance Through the Nineteenth Century*. Seattle: University of Washington Press.

Blalock, Hubert M. (1964). *Casual Inferences in Nonexperimental Research*. Chapel Hill: University of North Carolina Press.

Blydenburgh, John C. (1971). "A controlled experiment to measure the effects of personal contact campaigning." *Midwest Journal of Political Science* 15:365–381.

Boocock, Sarane S., and E. O. Schild, eds. (1968). *Simulation Games in Learning*. Beverly Hills, Calif.: Sage Publications.

Brecht, Arnold (1959). *Political Theory*. Princeton, N.J.: Princeton University Press.

Brody, Richard A. (1963). "Some systematic effects of the spread of nuclear weapons technology." *Journal of Conflict Resolution* 7:663–753.

——————— (1969a). "The study of international relations qua science: the emphasis on methods and techniques." In Klaus Knorr and James N. Rosenau, eds., *Contending Approaches to International Relations*. Princeton, N.J.: Princeton University Press.

——————— (1969b). "The uses of simulation in international relations research." In Joseph Bernd, ed., *Mathematical Applications in Political Science,* Vol. 4. Charlottesville: The University Press of Virginia.

Brody, Richard A., and Sidney Verba (1972). "Hawk and dove: the search for an explanation of Vietnam policy preferences." *Acta Politics* 7:318–321 and Appendix H.

Brown, Steven R. (1971). "Experimental design and the structure of theory." *Experimental Study of Politics* 1:1–42.

Brown, Steven R., and Frank Scioli (1973). "Apperceptions of urban governance: conviction and ambivalence in response to a political documentary." Mimeographed. Department of Political Science, Kent State University.

Brown, Steven R., and R. W. Taylor (1970). "Objectivity and subjectivity in concept formation: problems of perspective, partition and frames of reference." Paper presented at the American Political Science Association meetings, Los Angeles, September.

Brown, Steven R., and Thomas D. Ungs (1970). "Representativeness and the study of political behavior: an application of Q technique to reactions to the Kent State incident." *Social Science Quarterly* 51:514–526.

Brownstein, Charles N. (1971). "Communications strategies and the electoral decision making process: some results from experimentation." *Experimental Study of Politics* 1:37–50.

Brunswik, Egon (1952). "The conceptual framework of psychology." *International Encyclopedia of Unified Science.* Vol. 1, no. 10. Chicago: University of Chicago Press.

_____ (1956). "Systematic and representative design of psychology experiments." In Egon Brunswik, ed., *Perception and the Representative Design of Psychological Experiments.* Berkeley: The University of California Press.

Buchanan, Garth, and John Heinberg (1972). "Housing allowance household experiment design: part 1, summary and overview." Washington, D.C.: The Urban Institute.

Campbell, Angus (1962). "Recent studies in survey studies of political behavior." In Austin Ranney, ed., *Essays on the Behavioral Study of Politics.* Urbana: University of Illinois Press.

Campbell, Angus, Philip Converse, Warren Miller, and Donald Stokes (1960). *The American Voter.* New York: Wiley.

Campbell, Angus, Gerald Gurin, and Warren Miller (1954). *The Voter Decides.* Evanston, Ill.: Row, Peterson.

Campbell, Donald T. (1957). "Factors relevant to the validity of experiments in social settings." *Psychological Bulletin* 54:297–312.

_____ (1963). "From description to explanation: interpreting trends as quasi-experiments." In Chester W. Harris, ed., *Problems in Measuring Change.* Madison: University of Wisconsin Press.

_____ (1970). "Considering the case against experimental evaluations of social innovations." *Administrative Science Quarterly* 15:110–113.

_____ (1971). "Methods for the experimenting society." Paper presented at the American Psychological Convention, Washington, D.C.

Campbell, Donald T., and Albert Erlebacher (1970). "How regression artifacts in quasi-experimental evaluations can mistakenly make compensatory education look harmful." In J. Hellmuth, ed., *Compensatory Education: A National Debate,* volume 3 of *The Disadvantaged Child.* New York: Brunner/Mazel.

Campbell, Donald T., and Donald W. Fiske (1959). "Convergent and discriminant validation by the multitrait-multimethod matrix." *Psychological Bulletin* 56:81–104.

Campbell, Donald T., and Julian C. Stanley (1966). *Experimental and Quasi-Experimental Designs for Research.* Chicago: Rand McNally.

Cattell, Raymond B. (1966). "The principles of experimental design and analysis in relation to theory building." In Raymond B. Cattell, ed., *Handbook of Multivariate Experimental Psychology*. Chicago: Rand McNally.

Chadwick, Richard W. (1967). "An empirical test of five assumptions in an inter-nation simulation about national political systems." *General Systems* 12:177–192.

Cohen, Morris R., and Ernest Nagel (1934). *An Introduction to Logic and Scientific Method*. New York: Harcourt, Brace.

Collins, Barry E., and B. H. Raven (1969). "Group structure: attractions, coalitions, communication, and power." In Gardner Lindzey and Elliott Aronson, eds., *Handbook of Social Psychology*. Second edition. Reading, Mass.: Addison-Wesley.

Converse, Philip E. (1964). "The nature of belief systems in mass publics." In David E. Apter, ed., *Ideology and Discontent*. New York: Free Press.

Converse, Philip E., Angus Campbell, Warren Miller, and Donald Stokes (1961). "Stability and change in 1960—a reinstating election." *American Political Science Review* 55:269–280.

Cook, Thomas J. (1969). "The application of operant learning theory principles to the study of political socialization." Unpublished Ph.D. dissertation, Florida State University.

Cook, Thomas J., and Frank P. Scioli, Jr. (1971). "An experimental design for the analysis of policy impact." Paper delivered at the Annual Meeting of the American Political Science Association, Chicago, Illinois, 7–11 September 1971.

——————— (1972). "A research strategy for analyzing the impact of public policy." *Administrative Science Quarterly* 17:329–339.

Cook, Thomas J., Frank P. Scioli, Jr., and Steven R. Brown (1975). "Experimental design and Q methodology: optimizing the analysis of attitude change." *Political Methodology,* forthcoming.

Cooper, Joseph, and David Pollock (1959). "The identification of prejudicial attitudes by the galvanic skin response." *Journal of Social Psychology* 50:241–245.

Dabelko, David D., and Craig P. Caywood (1973). "Higher education as a political socializing agent: some effects of various curricula." *Experimental Study of Politics* 2:1–24.

Darley, John M., and Joel Cooper (1972). "The 'clean for gene' phenomenon: the effects of students' appearance on political campaigning." *Journal of Applied Social Psychology* 2:24–33.

de Rivera, Joseph H. (1968). *The Psychological Dimension of Foreign Policy*. Columbus, Ohio: Charles E. Merrill.

de Sola Pool, Ithiel, Robert Abelson, and Samuel Popkin (1965). *Candidates, Issues and Strategies*. Cambridge, Mass.: MIT Press.

Dyson, James W., and Charles N. Brownstein (1974). "Campaign information, attitudinal voting and the electoral context: an experimental investigation." Paper delivered at the Annual Meeting of the Southwestern Political Science Association, Dallas.

Dyson, James W., Daniel W. Fleitas, and Frank P. Scioli, Jr. (1972). "The interaction of leadership, personality, and decisional environments." *Journal of Social Psychology* 86:29–33.

Dyson, James W., Paul H. B. Godwin, and Leo A. Hazlewood (1972). "Political discussion and decision-making in experimental small groups." Paper delivered at the Annual Meeting of the American Political Science Association, Washington, D.C., 5–9 September 1972. Mimeographed.

Dyson, James W., and Frank P. Scioli, Jr. (1970). "Linkage of alternative attitude theories: an experimental test of a model interrelating consistency theory and behavior theory." Paper presented at the Southern Political Science Association Convention, Atlanta, Georgia, November. Mimeographed.

_____ (1971). "An experimental test of consistency theory." *Experimental Study of Politics* 1:118–138.

_____ (1972a). "The campaign as a communication variable." Paper delivered at the Annual Meeting of the Southern Political Association, Atlanta, Georgia, 2 November 1972. Mimeographed.

_____ (1974). "Communication and candidate selection." *Social Science Quarterly* 55:77–90.

Dyson, James W., James Sheffield, and William Zavoina (1972). "Reinforcement contingencies in political attitude formation." Paper presented at the International Political Science Association, Montreal Meeting, August.

Elder, Charles D., and R. E. Pendley (1966). "An analysis of composition standards and validation satisfactions in the Inter-Nation simulation in terms of contemporary economic theory and data." Mimeographed. Evanston, Ill.: Northwestern University.

Eldersveld, Samuel J. (1956). "Experimental propaganda techniques and voting behavior." *American Political Science Review* 50:154–165.

Eldersveld, Samuel J., and Richard W. Dodge (1954). "Personal contact or mail propaganda? An experiment in voting turnout and attitude change." In Daniel Katz, Dorwin Cartright, Samuel Eldersveld, and Alfred McClung Lee, eds., *Public Opinion and Propaganda*. New York: Dryden Press.

Elesh, David, Jack Ladinsky, M. J. Lefcowitz, and Arnold Shore (1971). "After 15 months: preliminary results from the urban negative income tax experiment." *Discussion Papers*. Madison, Wisc.: Institute for Research on Poverty.

Evan, Williams M., ed. (1971). *Organizational Experiments: Laboratory and Field Research*. New York: Harper & Row.

Fairweather, G. A. (1967). *Methods for Experimental Social Innovation*. New York: Wiley.

Feigl, Herbert (1953). "Notes on causality." In Herbert Feigl and Mary Brodbeck, eds., *Readings in the Philosophy of Science*. New York: Appleton-Century-Crofts.

Festinger, Leon (1953). "The laboratory experiment." In Leon Festinger and Daniel Katz, eds., *Research Methods in the Behavioral Sciences*, pp. 136–172. New York: Holt, Rinehart and Winston.

Fisher, R. A. (1935). *The Design of Experiments*. Edinburgh: Oliver and Boyd.

Fleitas, Daniel W. (1971). "Bandwagon and underdog effects in minimal information elections." *American Political Science Review* 65:434–438.

French, J. P. R. (1953). "Experiments in field settings." In Leon Festinger and Daniel Katz, eds., *Research Methods in Behavioral Science*. New York: Holt, Rinehart and Winston.

Friedell, Morris F. (1968). "A laboratory experiment in retaliation." *Journal of Conflict Resolution* 12:357–373.

Geller, Jesse D., and Gary Howard (1972a). "Some sociopsychological characteristics of student political activists." *Journal of Applied Social Psychology* 2:112–137.

_____ (1972b). "A test of Gamson's theory of political trust orientation." *Journal of Applied Social Psychology* 2:137–157.

Gertzog, Irwin N. (1970). "The electoral consequences of a local party organization's registration campaign: The San Diego experiment." *Polity* 3:247–264.

Glock, Charles Y. (1952). "Participation bias and reinterview effect in panel studies." Unpublished Ph.D. dissertation, Columbia University.

Golembiewski, Robert (1962). *The Small Group,* Chicago: University of Chicago Press.

Gosnell, Harold F. (1926). "An experiment in the stimulation of voting." *American Political Science Review* 20:869–874.

_____ (1927). *Getting Out the Vote*. Chicago: University of Chicago Press.

Guetzkow, Harold (1968). "Some correspondences between simulations and 'realities' in international relations." In Morton Kaplan, ed., *New Approaches to International Relations*. New York: St. Martin's Press.

Guetzkow, Harold, Chadwick Alger, Richard Brody, Robert Noel, and Richard Snyder (1963). *Simulation in International Relations: Developments for Research and Teaching*. Englewood Cliffs, N.J.: Prentice-Hall.

Hartmann, George W. (1936). "A field experiment on the comparative effectiveness of 'emotional' and 'rational' political leaflets in determining election results." *Journal of Abnormal and Social Psychology* 19:99–114.

Hermann, Charles (1967). "Validation problems in games and simulations with special reference to models of international politics." *Behavioral Science* 12:216–231.

Hovland, Carl I. (1959). "Reconciling conflicting results derived from experimental and survey studies of attitude change." *American Psychologist* 14:8–17.

Hyneman, Charles S. (1959). *The Study of Politics*. Urbana: University of Illinois Press.

Jaros, Dean, and R. Darcy (1972). "The elusive impact of political science: more negative findings." *Experimental Study of Politics* 2:14–52.

Jaros, Dean, and Gene L. Mason (1969). "Party choice and support for demagogues: an experimental investigation." *American Political Science Review* 63:100–110.

JWGA/JCS [Joint War Games Agency/Joint Chiefs of Staff] (1965). *TEMPER*, Volumes I–VII. Washington, D.C.: Department of Defense.

Kamin, Leon J. (1958). "Ethnic and party affiliations of candidates as determinants of voting." *Canadian Journal of Psychology* 12:205–212.

Kaplan, Abraham (1964). *The Conduct of Inquiry.* San Francisco: Chandler.

Kelley, Harold H., and John W. Thibaut (1969). "Group problem solving." In Gardner Lindzey and Elliott Aronson, eds., *The Handbook of Social Psychology.* Second edition. Reading, Mass.: Addison-Wesley.

Kerlinger, Fred N. (1964). *Foundations of Behavioral Research.* New York: Holt, Rinehart and Winston.

Kuhn, Thomas S. (1970). *The Structure of Scientific Revolutions.* Second edition. Chicago: University of Chicago Press.

Lamare, J. (1971). "University education in American government: an experimental approach to a growing problem." *Experimental Study of Politics* (February): 122–148.

Lave, Lester B. (1965). "Factors influencing cooperation in the prisoners' dilemma." *Behavioral Science* 10:26–38.

Light, Richard J. (1973). "Experimental design issues in the evaluation of large scale social programs." *Experimental Study of Politics* 2:53–75.

MacDougall, John A., and William M. Evan (1967). "Interorganizational conflict: a labor management bargaining experiment." *Journal of Conflict Resolution* 11:398–413.

Madron, Thomas W. (1969). *Small Group Methods.* Evanston, Ill.: Northwestern University Press.

Mann, Leona, Robert Rosenthal, and Ronald P. Abeles (1971). "Early election returns and the voting behavior of adolescent voters." *Journal of Applied Social Psychology* 1:66–75.

Margenau, Henry (1961). *Open Vistas: The Philosophical Perspectives of Modern Science.* New Haven, Conn.: Yale University Press.

McGrath, Joseph E., and Irwin Altman (1966). *Small Group Research: A Synthesis and Critique of the Field.* New York: Holt, Rinehart and Winston.

Mendelsohn, Harold (1966). "Western voting and broadcasts of results on Presidential election day." *Public Opinion Quarterly* 30:212–225.

Mendenhall, William (1968). *Introduction to Linear Models and the Design and Analysis of Experiments.* Belmont, Calif.: Wadsworth.

Meyers, Jerome L. (1966). *Fundamentals of Experimental Design.* Boston: Allyn and Bacon.

Mills, John S. (1882). *A System of Logic.* 8th Edition. New York: Harper.

Morse, Stanley J., and Kenneth J. Gergen (1971). "Material aid and social attraction." *Journal of Applied Social Psychology* 1(2):150–162.

Nesbitt, Paul D. (1972). "The effectiveness of student canvassers." *Journal of Applied Social Psychology* 2(4):343–349.

Newton, Issac (1846). *The Mathematical Principles of Natural Philosophy*, First American edition. Translated by Andrew Motte. New York: D. Adde.

Niemi, R., and H. Weisberg (1972). "The effects of group size on collective decision making." In R. Niemi and H. Weisberg, eds., *Probability Models of Collective Decision Making.* Columbus, Ohio.: Charles E. Merrill.

Nimmo, Dan, and Robert L. Savage (1971a). "Image typoloties in a senatorial campaign: a comparison of forad vs. free distribution data." Paper delivered at the Annual Meeting of the American Political Science Association, Chicago, Illinois, 7-11 September 1971. Mimeographed.

——————— (1971b). "Political images and political perceptions." *Experimental Study of Politics* 1:1–36.

North, Robert C., Ole R. Holsti, M. George Zaninovitch, and Dina A. Zinnes (1963). *Content Analysis.* Evanston, Ill.: Northwestern University Press.

Olson, Mancur (1968). *The Logic of Collective Action: Public Goods and the Theory of Groups.* New York: Schocken Books.

Phillips, James L., and Lawrence Nitz (1968). "Social contacts in a three-person 'political convention' situation." *Journal of Conflict Resolution* 12:206–214.

Platt, J. R. (1964). "Strong inference." *Science* 146:347–352.

Plutchik, Robert (1968). *Foundations of Experimental Research.* New York: Harper & Row.

Popper, Karl R. (1961). *The Logic of Scientific Discovery.* New York: Scientific Editions.

Powell, Charles A. (1969). "Simulation: the anatomy of a fad." *Acta Politica* 3:299–330.

——————— (1973). "Validity in complex experimentation." *Experimental Study of Politics* 2:61–98.

Priestley, Joseph (1772). *The History and Present State of Discoveries Relating to Vision, Light, and Colour.* London: Printed for J. Johnson.

Rapaport, Anatol (1968). "Prospects for experimental games." *Journal of Conflict Resolution* 12(4):461–470.

Reback, Gary L. (1971). "The effects of precinct-level voter contact activities on voting behavior." *Experimental Study of Politics* 1:65–98.

Riker, William H. (1967). "Bargaining in a three person game." *American Political Science Review* 61:642–656.

——————— (1968). "Experimental verification of two theories about three person games." In Joseph Bernd, ed., *Mathematical Applications in Political Science III.* Charlottesville: University of Virginia Press.

Riker, William H., and William James Zavoina (1970). "Rational behavior in politics." *American Political Science Review* 64:48–60.

Robinson, Michael J. (1974). "Understanding television's effects—experimentation and survey research: an offer one shouldn't refuse." Paper presented at the American Political Science Association Meeting, Chicago. Mimeographed.

Rosen, Benson, and Hillel J. Einhorn (1972). "Attractiveness of the middle of the road political candidate." *Journal of Applied Social Psychology* 2:157–166.

Rosenberg, Morris (1968). *The Logic of Survey Analysis.* New York: Basic Books.

Rosenthal, R. (1966). *Experimenter Effects in Behavior Research.* New York: Appleton-Century-Crofts.

——————— (1969). "Interpersonal expectations: effects of the experimenters hypothesis." In R. Rosenthal and R. L. Rosnow, eds., *Artifact in Behavioral Research*. New York: Academic Press.

Ross, John, and Perry Smith (1968). "Orthodox experimental designs." In H. M. Blalock and A. B. Blalock, eds., *Methodology in Social Research*. New York: McGraw-Hill.

Ross, M., J. Thibaut, and S. Evanbeck (1971). "Some determinants of the intensity of social protest." *Journal of Experimental Social Psychology* 7:401–418.

Rossi, Peter H., and Walter Williams (1972). *Evaluating Social Programs*. New York: Seminar Press.

Samuel, William (1972). "Response to Bill of Rights paraphrases as influenced by the hip or straight attire of the opinion solicitor." *Journal of Applied Social Psychology* 2, 1:47–62.

Scioli, Frank P. Jr. (1970). "Political attitude, verbal behavior, and candidate selection in experimental small groups." Unpublished Ph.D. dissertation, Florida State University.

——————— (1971). "Conformity in small groups: the relationship between political attitude and overt behavior." *Comparative Group Studies* 2:53–64.

Scioli, Frank P. Jr., and Thomas J. Cook (1973). "Experimental design in policy impact analysis." *Social Science Quarterly* (September): 271–281.

Skinner, B. F. (1964). "The flight from the laboratory." In M. H. Marx, ed., *Theories in Contemporary Psychology*. New York: Macmillan.

Snyder, Richard (1962). "Experimental techniques and political analysis." In James C. Charlesworth, ed., *The Limits of Behavioralism in Political Science*. Philadelphia: American Academy of Political and Social Science.

——————— (1963). "Some perspectives on the use of experimental techniques in the study of international relations." In Harold S. Guetzkow, Chadwick Alger, Richard Brody, Robert Hoel, and Richard Snyder, eds., *Simulation in International Relations: Developments for Research and Teaching*. Englewood Cliffs, N.J.: Prentice-Hall.

Stephenson, William (1953). *The Study of Behavior*. Chicago: University of Chicago Press.

——————— (1967). *The Play Theory of Mass Communication*. Chicago: University of Chicago Press.

Stroadbeck, Fred, Rita M. James, and Charles Hawkins (1957). "Social status in jury deliberation." *American Sociological Review* 22:713–719.

Suchman, Edward A. (1967). *Evaluative Research*. New York: Russell Sage Foundation.

Suedfeld, Peter, Steven Bochner, and Carol Matas (1971). "Petitioner's attire and petition signing by peace demonstrators: a field experiment." *Journal of Applied Social Psychology* 3:278–283.

Suedfeld, Peter, Steven Bochner, and Denna Wnek (1971). "Helper-sufferer similarity and a specific request for help: bystander intervention during a peace demonstration." *Journal of Applied Social Psychology* 1:17–23.

Sweeney, John W. (1971). "An experimental investigation of the free-rider problem."

Paper presented at the American Political Science Association Meeting, Chicago. Mimeographed.

Tursky, Bernard, and Milton Lodge (1971). "Compliance, resistance and rebellion: the strength of political conviction under stress." Paper delivered at the Annual Meeting of the American Political Science Association, Chicago, 7–11 September 1971. Mimeographed.

Van Horn, Richard L. (1971). "Validation of simulation results." *Management Science* 17:247–258.

Verba, Sidney (1961). *Small Groups and Political Behavior*. Princeton, N.J.: Princeton University Press.

Wahlke, John, and Milton Lodge (1971). "Psychophysiological measures of change in political attitudes." Paper delivered at the Annual Meeting of the Midwest Political Science Association, Chicago, 28 April–1 May 1971. Mimeographed.

Warr, Peter B., and Christopher Knapper (1968). *The Perception of People and Events*. New York: Wiley.

Watts, Harold W., Mordecai Kurz, Robert G. Spiegelman, Terence F. Kelly, Leslie Singer, and James N. Morgan (1971). "Current status of income maintenance experiments." *American Economic Review* 61:15–42.

Webb, Eugene J., Donald T. Campbell, Richard D. Schwartz, and Lee Sechrest (1966). *Unobtrusive Measures*. Chicago: Rand McNally.

Weick, Karl E. (1965). "Laboratory experimentation with organizations." In James G. March, ed., *Handbook of Organizations*. Chicago: Rand McNally.

_____ (1967). "Organizations in the laboratory." In Victor H. Vroom, ed., *Methods of Organizational Research*. Pittsburgh: University of Pittsburgh Press.

Weiss, Carol H. (1972). *Evaluation Research*. Englewood Cliffs, N.J.: Prentice-Hall.

Weiss, Robert S., and Martin Rein (1969). "The evaluation of broad-arm programs: a cautionary case and a moral." *Annals of the American Academy of Political and Social Sciences* 385:133–142.

_____ (1970). "The evaluation of broad-arm programs: experimental design, its difficulties, and an alternative." *Administrative Science Quarterly* 15:97–109.

Wiggins, James A. (1968). "Hypothesis validity and experimental laboratory methods." In H. M. Blalock and A. B. Blalock, eds., Methodology in Social Research. New York: McGraw-Hill.

Wissel, Peter A. (1973). "Experiments and formal models: a complementary exchange." *Experimental Study of Politics* 2:1–14.

Zavoina, William James (1971). "The rational calculus of coalition formation: evidence from a three person game." *Experimental Study of Politics* 1:87–121.

Zetterberg, Hans (1963). *On Theory and Verification in Sociology*. Totawa, N.J.: Bedminster Press.

6
SURVEY RESEARCH

RICHARD W. BOYD
with
HERBERT H. HYMAN

INTRODUCTION

There is no doubt that survey research has made a major contribution to the postwar growth of political science. In our more expansive and confident moments, we would agree with McClosky's assessment that "within two decades the survey method has become the most important procedure in the 'behavioral' study of politics..." (1967, p. 65). Now and again, however, we are uncomfortably reminded that no method is infallible. With great chagrin the July 1973 issue of the *Current Population Reports'* series, *Consumer Buying Indicators,* announced the end of the Survey of Consumer Buying Expectations. A special study of the survey had revealed the disconcerting fact that from 1967 through the first half of 1972 the correlation between the index of expected car purchases and actual new car purchases was negative. Moreover, the index had such a large standard error that there was no statistically significant change in the predictive index from July 1967 to April 1971, "a time of considerable variability in actual purchases," the report dutifully noted (*Current Population Reports,* Series P–65, 46:1). So we will not argue that the survey method has not had its pratfalls. We simply will not dwell long on them, proceeding instead on the more comfortable assumption that one learns more from examples of successes than failures.

In spite of or, more properly perhaps, because of the variety of surveys, we need to circumscribe our task. Should we begin with the classic nineteenth-century surveys of poverty in England by Booth and Rowntree, even though

---

We would like to thank Russell D. Murphy, Leon V. Sigal, and Clement E. Vose of Wesleyan University for their helpful suggestions of examples included in the chapter and Angus Campbell of the University of Michigan for reading the section on the fusion of research and policy interests in the development of survey techniques.

their work could not take advantage of sampling techniques yet to be invented? Should we include Lasswell's *Psychopathology and Politics* (1930), even though another researcher could not replicate his unstructured interviews? We prefer a more limited definition of a survey in order to eliminate the extraordinary number of studies that form a penumbra around the core group of studies possessing all the components of survey methods. We will restrict the definition of a survey to one formulated for a prior analysis of this literature: "A survey is an inquiry of a large number of people, selected by rigorous sampling, conducted in normal life settings by explicit, standardized procedures yielding quantitative measurements" (Hyman, 1973, p. 324).

As a technique of data gathering, survey research falls into the larger category of field methods. In their rigid requirements of sampling from strictly delimited populations and in their standardized procedures for acquiring information, surveys clearly depart from the more traditional methods of empirical political science. The memory of de Tocqueville, Martineau, and Bryce as exemplars of work based on wise and detached observation and reflection makes one wonder if the accoutrements of modern techniques are really necessary. On the other hand, we might also infer from these notables that a researcher who is not a genius had better bring along his bag of tools.

In addition to the observations of world travelers, surveys contrast also with other traditional methods of data collection. In all, the richest sources of political data have undoubtedly been documents and aggregate data produced by governments and private groups. V. O. Key, Jr., surely a most important political scientist, made most of his major contributions via shrewd analyses of aggregate data. But in his two final books, *Public Opinion and American Democracy* (1964) and *The Responsible Electorate* (1966), he demonstrated how important it is to have data about people as individuals in order to make statements about people as a corporate entity.

Key did not, as E. E. Schattschneider once said of public opinion analysts, confuse the actors with the audience. Key knew that the initiatives for policy change and the selection among alternative programs usually rests even in a democracy with governmental leaders. But his argument in *The Responsible Electorate* (1966) focused political scientists' attention on voters' evaluations of government programs, particularly during what he called "critical" (realigning) elections. His timely argument encouraged researchers to look for key issues as the bases of voter decisions in the United States elections of the 1960s and 1970s. (See, for example, the articles and citations in the June 1972 *American Political Science Review* symposium on issue voting.) It is difficult to imagine how Key could have ever made a credible argument that the electorate is indeed rational without having at his disposal the data on individual voters' opinions that survey research provided.

Similarly, Robert Dahl's first works relied in the main on the traditional sources of data in political science: elite interviewing, government documents, and the writings of major philosophers. To be sure, *Congress and Foreign Policy* (1950), in its analysis of the dilemma of citizen competence and democratic control of foreign policy, did utilize secondary analyses of opinion polls of the 1930s and 1940s. However, Dahl's principal concerns focused on party cohesion and responsibility in Congress on foreign policy issues, for which he relied mainly on roll call votes and interviews with critical members of Congress and its staff. In *Politics, Economics, and Welfare* (with Charles E. Lindblom in 1953) and in *A Preface to Democratic Theory* (1956), Dahl made landmark contributions to the problem he had earlier posed concerning the relationship between citizens and leaders in a democracy. This he termed the "First Problem of Politics": How to prevent leaders from becoming tyrants (1953, p. 273). Dahl noted the importance of training leaders in democratic norms; however, his greater stress was on the pluralistic organization of social and political power, without which "no constitutional arrangements can produce a non-tyrannical republic" (1956, p. 83).

Though Dahl became with these books the leading interpreter of the pluralist school, his work still lacked direct evidence on the character of power relationships between citizens and political leaders. That lack is presumably one reason why he titled his treatise on democratic theory, *A Preface* . . . In the late 1950s, he filled this lacuna with coordinated surveys of the people in New Haven, Connecticut: personal interviews with important local decision makers; a questionnaire sent to all members of a well-defined population of subleaders in political parties, a redevelopment agency, and Board of Education and PTA officials; and finally personal interviews with two samples of registered voters. From this design came empirical answers to the issues he had raised. In *Who Governs? Democracy and Power in an American City* (1961), he detailed a system of power in which there existed a different set of leaders and attentive publics for distinct domains of policy. It was the evidence for pluralism that he needed to support the arguments of *The Federalist Papers* he had analyzed in *A Preface to Democratic Theory* (1956).

What then do we infer from the patterns of research of Key and Dahl? It is certainly not that survey research has supplanted documentary and aggregate evidence as the most important data source in political science. Rather, we have drawn attention to the work of two scholars who made profitable use of multiple data sources and who both came to view information on the policy opinions and democratic values of individuals as critical to lines of inquiry linking, in both cases, several books. This chapter, then, is no brief that empirical research questions can only be answered with surveys; it does suggest, however, that only surveys can answer *some* questions. (Another pointed example is Wilson and Banfield's (1971) use of a survey in an attempt to resolve a controversy over the "political ethos" of immigrant and Anglo-Saxon subcultures.) Beyond this point we emphasize the quite extraordinary range of valid research techniques and the points at which surveys can help settle crucial elements in a broad gauged theoretical investigation.

To summarize, surveys provide data on a large number of people in their varied and normal life settings. They provide quantifiable measures on a notable range of behaviors and beliefs, thus opening to the researcher the analytic powers of an increasingly sophisticated statistics. And they do so using scientific bases for sample selection that justify confidence about the broader universe to which findings can be generalized.

Looking ahead, it is not our purpose to present a minitext on survey design and analysis. Our bibliography lists numerous examples of both general and specialized works on survey research methods. Instead, we will ask the questions that someone examining the potential of survey methods for the first time might ask: What kinds of belief and behavior can be studied? For what purposes? With what effect on substantive theory? Our goal is to suggest the ways in which surveys can answer particular questions by pointing to examples in the substantive literature of political science, though in our search for apt illustrations we will occasionally stray outside the domains of politics and policy analysis.

WHAT KINDS OF BELIEF AND BEHAVIOR CAN BE STUDIED?

Demographic Attributes and the Social Survey Movement

A primary use of surveys is in demography. Indeed, the origin of modern survey research lies in the social and health survey movement of the nineteenth century. Parten (1950, p. 6) credits Charles Booth with conducting the first comprehensive social survey in London in 1886, published as *Life and Labour of the People of London* in 17 volumes (1892–1897). This survey of economic and social conditions was designed to show, as Parten quotes Booth, "the numerical relation which poverty, misery, and depravity bear to the regular earnings and comparative comfort and to describe the general conditions under which each class lives" (Parten, 1950, p. 6). B. Seebohm Rowntree followed Booth with an investigation of the conditions of the working class in York, England: *Poverty, A Study of Town Life,* first published in 1901.

The Discovery of Poverty in the United States, as Bremner so neatly subtitles his book *From the Depths* (1956), provides a good history of the development of America's counterpart to the European social survey movement. Complementing portraits on slum life in the nineteenth century by popular writers such as Jacob Riis were Carrol D. Wrights' survey of unemployment in Massachusetts during the depression of 1873–1879 and the Association for Improving the Condition of the Poor's Survey of New York City in 1873 (Stephan, 1948,

p. 18). Similarly, the Citizens Association of New York sponsored the *Report of the Council of Hygiene and Public Health* (1865), an extensive investigation of sanitation facilities and disease in New York.

The question of whether or not we would label these early demographic investigations as surveys is ambiguous. Several meet our criterion of standard-ized procedures of measurement. For example, the latter report on New York City includes a detailed list of instructions to investigators on the delimitation of the area surveyed, methods of inspecting houses, and queries of household residents on sickness and mortality (pp. xxiv–xxxv). These nineteenth-century social surveys fail to meet our criteria for surveys only for their lack of scientific sampling. As Stephan notes (1948, p. 21), "although the theory of probability was well established in the eighteenth century, its applications to the practical drawing of samples were delayed until the twentieth." Not until 1912, when Arthur Bowley surveyed the economic conditions of the working class of Read-ing, England, were the principles of scientific sampling first used. Moreover, even after Bowley's sampling innovations had been published, United States surveys still followed Booth's procedures of attempting to catalogue complete populations of cities on a broad range of subjects (Parten, 1950, p. 9).

The social survey movement illustrates one rather common feature of sur-veys of social and demographic data: the interpretation of the data is typically grounded in politics and policy preferences.

First of all, the motive of the social surveyors was to dramatize the prob-lems of the poor in order to affect policy in areas of health, sanitation, living conditions, and working conditions. The perspectives of the investigators, of course, varied. Some saw the problems from the point of view of the poor and hoped to stimulate substantial changes in their lives. The fruits of their efforts were realized in such social legislation as the New York Tenement Inspection Act of 1901, the first effective inspection law and one that became a model for other cities (Beard, 1912, ch. 11; Davies, 1966, p. 4).

Others in the social survey movement seemed more concerned with the threat to social order posed by the living conditions of the poor than by a re-gard for the welfare of the poor as such. For example, the introduction to the survey report of the previously mentioned Council on Hygiene and Public Health commented:

But beyond the physical, the mental, and the economical losses resulting from prevailing ill-health, there are certain political and social aspects of the same agencies that ought to be studied by every intelligent citizen. The mobs that held fearful sway in our city during the memorable outbreak of violence in the month of July, 1863 [the Civil War draft riots], were gath-ered in the overcrowded and neglected quarters of the city. As was stated by a leading journalist at that time: "The high brick blocks and closely-packed houses where the mobs originated seemed to be literally *hives of sickness and vice.* It was wonderful to see, and difficult to believe, that so much misery, disease, and wretchedness can be huddled together and hidden by high walls, unvisited and unthought of, so near our own abodes ... Alas! human faces look so hideous with hope and self-respect all gone! And female forms and features are made so frightful by sin, squalor, and debasement! To walk the streets as we walked them, in those hours of conflagration and riot, was like witnessing the day of judgment, with every wicked thing revealed, every sin and sorrow blazingly glared upon, every hidden abomination laid before hell's expectant fire. The elements of popular discord are gathered in those wretchedly-constructed tenant-houses, where poverty, disease, and crime find an abode." (Citizens Association of New York, 1865, pp. xv–xvi)

In a similar vein, Diamond (1963) details the obvious political motives that underlay many nineteenth-century questionnaires, including one example of a questionnaire taken among plantation owners designed to show that religious instruction did not lead slaves to subversive thoughts.

A second way in which the gathering of social and demographic data is connected to politics is that the type of data collected is a guide to what people view as the major social and political problems of a particular period of history. In the second half of the nineteenth century the problems of the poor were interpreted as the problems of cities, particularly problems linked to the passage of immigrants into city slums, to the political corruption that middle-class reformers saw immigrants as creating, and to the challenge of the then novel experiment with universal manhood suffrage. One can see these concerns in the dates that federal data first became available on a *city-by-city* basis: nativity (1850); occupation and education (1870); blind, deaf-mutes, and insane and feeble-minded (1880); citizenship and inability to speak English (1890); and housing (1900) (U.S. National Resources Commission, 1939).

Third, just as policy concerns cause data to be collected, existing data, however inaccurate, will usually be used to justify policy arguments. For example, Regan (1973) has recently discussed the deficiencies of the first six United States censuses of 1790 through 1840. Interest in reforming existing census procedures was peaked by the use that proslavery forces made of the 1840 figures on the proportion of "insane and idiots" among free and slave Negroes. The figures suggested that the proportion of Negroes enumerated in the North as "insane and idiots" was substantially higher than the proportion indicated for the South. Regan quotes Calhoun's use of the data, "Here is proof of the necessity of slavery ... The African is incapable of self-care and sinks into lunacy under the burden of freedom. It is a mercy to him to give him this guardianship and protection from mental death" (Regan, 1973, p. 541).

The figure for "insane and idiots" among Negroes was just one error of many produced by poor administration and non-standard interview schedules.

A young physician named Edward Jarvis campaigned for reform of census ad-ministration, and succeeded in persuading the American Statistical Association to take up the cause. As a result Congress adopted substantial changes in the law in preparation for the 1850 census. Because of the advances made in the administration of the 1850 census, "it marked the beginning," as the Director of the Census said in 1907, "of scientific census inquiry in the United States" (Regan, 1973, pp. 544–545).

Once the 1850 census had begun the process of standardizing interview schedules and adopting uniform procedures for organizing and displaying the data for all the states, the utility of the census for demographic measurements was assured. It only remained for the 1940 census to institute sampling in the United States census, in this case a 5 percent sample of households who were asked a list of supplemental questions in addition to those posed to the remainder of households, including the critical unemployment and income questions that have only been asked of census samples. As Parten notes (1950, p. 14), the adoption of sampling by the United States census blurs a distinction commonly made between a census and other surveys—that a census is a total enumeration, whereas most surveys are samples.

The policy impact of the census is, of course, enormous. United States federal grants-in-aid payments to states and cities are directly tied to census estimates of population, and the systematic underrepresentation of mobile, young members of minority groups often costs cities substantial federal funds to which an accurate census would entitle them. In terms of sample size, mea-surement error, and careful administration, however, the United States census has no peers among academic surveys. Its limitations are those imposed by the political sensibilities of a government that does not want to risk tainting the generally high reputation of the census with charges that it requests politically sensitive information. For example, the census asks neither questions of politi-cal attitudes nor of voting choices, though it does risk asking its sample respondents whether they are registered to vote and if they went to the polls. From these samples the Bureau has published an exceedingly useful series of publications on registration and voting patterns among social groups, the P-20 series of *Current Population Reports.*

Contemporary uses of surveys to measure demographic and social attributes are as intriguing as those of the social survey movement. One such example is the study of social and occupational mobility and its effects on political attitudes. Inter- and intra-generational mobility are two of the fundamental concepts in political sociology, since observing the impact of upward or down-ward movement in status highlights the influence of status relationships on political attitudes. One recurring question is whether or not mobility causes people to abandon the values they formerly held in favor of the values of the class or group into which they have moved.

The effects of mobility on values are nearly always more complex, even intractable, than they first appear. Citing an example of this, Lipset and Bendix suggest that mobility may lead to conservatism in one situation and radicalism in another. Applying this observation to South Africa, they observe:

> ... if a Negro in South Africa obtains a nonmanual position, he is a ready candidate for leadership in a movement of radical protest. But if a White American from a working-class family makes the same move, he usually becomes politically and socially conservative. (Lipset and Bendix, 1964, p. 64)

Lipset and Bendix attribute the difference in the attitude changes of the hypothetical South African and American to a concept that has enjoyed a considerable vogue in recent years. Called variously status inconsistency, status discrepancy, and low status crystallization, this concept derives from the fact that we are all embedded simultaneously in a multidimensional status structure in which a person's position in the eyes of others may be determined by many of his statuses: his ethnic background, income, education, and occupation. Because a person may move up and down his individual status ladders at different rates, he may at once occupy a high position on one status and a low position on another.

Rush (1967) notes that the concept of status inconsistency has been proffered as an explanation of a range of social and political attitudes: a sense of social isolation, desire for fundamental radical change, motivations to action, conservatism, and political liberalism. He, along with others (Bell, 1963), uses the concept to explain right-wing conservatism.

Despite the disparity of the dependent variables to which it has been related, status inconsistency retains its conceptual focus. Most investigators assert that variation in their chosen dependent variable results from the psychological stress that inconsistent statuses produce. This stress is itself the product of frustration and uncertainty that grow in those who occupy inconsistent status positions. Inconsistency creates ambiguous expectations for the particular person as well as for those with whom he interacts. How is the black professional to be treated? How indeed does he see himself? As this example suggests, status inconsistency is usually thought to be particularly stressful for people who have earned a high position on an achieved status, yet occupy a lower position on an ascribed status such as race (Jackson, 1962; Jackson and Burke, 1965). Thus, psychological stress intervenes between status inconsistency and the political attitudes that the stress is presumed to influence.

The theoretical appeal of the concept of status inconsistency is manifest in a number of studies that have made it a central explanatory concept (Lenski, 1954; Goffman, 1957; Kelly and Chambliss, 1966; Treiman, 1966). For our purposes the point is that the concept could never be investigated empirically without survey research. It is not enough to have aggregate statistics on a nation's racial, occupational, or income distributions. The concept requires a look at each individual's status *set*. What are his race *and* his occupation? Only when the individual is the unit of analysis can we investigate such a concept.

The American Occupational Structure, that classic of survey research by Blau and Duncan (1967), provides a second example of the political uses of demographic information in surveys. In a cooperative venture with the United States Census Bureau in 1962, they added a series of questions on inter- and intra-generational mobility to the Bureau's continuing *Current Population Survey.* The sample consisted of about 20,700 males between the ages of 20 and 64. Because the Census Bureau shuns questions on political attitudes for the understandable reason that it does not want to be charged with maintaining a government data bank on the political values of individual citizens, no political attitude items were included on the interview schedule. Nonetheless, Blau and Duncan devote much of their concluding chapter to speculation on the relationship of opportunities for social mobility in a society to its politics—its equality of political influence, its political stability, its capacity for change.

Much of their argument is a critique of Lipset and Bendix's view on the relationship of mobility to egalitarian values and stable democracy. Lipset and Bendix had challenged de Tocqueville's thesis that the opportunity for social mobility in the United States is the source of its political stability. This explanation fails, they say, because rates of movement between blue-collar and white-collar classes are no higher in the United States than in other industrial countries. They suggest instead a variant of Hartz's thesis in *The Liberal Tradition in America* (1955): that the United States possesses an egalitarian value system because it had no feudal past and no conservative aristocracy, and this is responsible for its political stability.

Blau and Duncan find this explanation unpersuasive and question what perpetuates this egalitarian value system if, in fact, rates of mobility in the United States are not higher than those of other countries. Instead, they point to the implications of a finding that Lipset and Bendix, with their more limited data base, could not have known: ". . . the opportunities of men originating in lower social strata to move into *top* positions in the occupational hierarchy are greater in the United States than in other countries," and this sustains its egalitarian values (Blau and Duncan, 1967, p. 437, italics added). Blau and Duncan also note that the "crass materialism of American values" elevates "possessions into the most important distinguishing feature of differential status," which, they argue, "makes it easier to translate economic improvements into advancements in accepted social status" (1967, p. 437).

Bottomore (1968) in turn criticizes this explanation by Blau and Duncan, noting periods in American history when both American intellectual and popular movements challenged as myth the assumption of an egalitarian society. He finds the explanation of political stability in the failure of protest movements to establish themselves as an effective opposition party, a result, he argues, of the ethnic diversity of the population, the "peculiar" situation of Negroes, and ultimately the steadily rising standard of living.

However this argument is resolved, it underscores the importance of theories of social mobility and political values. And to risk the lesson in repetitive argument, one cannot measure mobility, not to mention political attitudes, without the measures of individual characteristics that survey research provide.

Perhaps the most convincing evidence of the usefulness of survey research in demography is the number of projects around the world that are replicating the Blau and Duncan study. These surveys comprise what Featherman and Sewell (1974) have termed a second generation of mobility studies, and the list of nations includes, in addition to their own study of the United States, Australia, Japan, France, Germany, Hungary, Poland, Canada, Denmark, Finland, the United Kingdom, Yugoslavia, Switzerland, and Italy. The Centre for Intergroup Studies of the University of Cape Town has begun a similar study of social mobility among the Coloured population group in the western Cape region of South Africa and plans to extend the study to include Africans and whites as well. In short, studies of social mobility and political values presently constitute an extraordinarily fertile field of research, all directly traceable to the special attributes of the survey technique: the possibility of measuring the characteristics of the individual efficiently and economically.

Attitudes, Beliefs, and Behavior

Attitudes, beliefs, and behavior constitute a second major category of social and political data that can be efficiently studied with surveys. However, simply to use these two words, attitude and belief, is to raise a controversy concerning the definitions of the terms. One group of attitude theorists regards the concept of attitude as a unidimensional concept. For example, Fishbein defines an attitude as pure affect for or against some object, and provides separate operational definitions for beliefs and behavioral intention. In this approach he follows in the steps of others such as Thurstone and Osgood. Other theorists, including Rosenberg and McGuire, regard attitude as a multidimensional concept, with affective, cognitive, and conative components.

The dispute over the more useful definitions of attitude is discussed in articles by Zajonc (1968), Scott (1968), and McGuire (1969) in the companion series to this handbook, *The Handbook of Social Psychology*. Since our task here is to underscore the variety of significant applications of surveys, there is no reason for us to take a position on the proper conception of attitude. Rather, we will be content to note, as Greenstein (1973) said about personality theory, that attitude theory is a pluralistic universe. We will group responses to surveys in various content domains (affect, attitudes and beliefs, judgments, behavior, ideologies and belief systems, and cultural values) and emphasize in the discussion that few surveys are limited to a single domain. Quite the contrary, most surveys explore a constellation of responses across a rich and variable array of subjects, a fact that will be evident in the range of topics we discuss.

Political affect. To search the literature on political affect is to confront a paradox. Surveys of political attitudes and actions are the substance of endless surveys, with beliefs on issues, candidates, and parties repetitively measured with items that catch the subtlety and complexity of people's evaluations of politics. In contrast, surveys of affect, those "emotions and sentiments that accompany political thought and behavior" (Hyman, 1973, p. 345), are quite rare. The paradox is all the more pointed when we reflect that so much of our literature on political behavior argues that many people's expressed opinions are marked by lack of affect, by an absence of feeling and intensity. But how can we know this, when we have invested so few resources in measuring the emotions that people bring to politics?

To be sure there are a few examples of studies of affect, but their presence is marked by the isolation in which they stand. Almond and Verba (1963, pp. 145–146) asked the respondents of their five-nation survey to report whether they found "election campaigns pleasant and enjoyable," whether they "sometimes get angry during campaigns," whether they "sometimes find campaigns silly or ridiculous." The answers suggested substantially different emotional responses to campaigns between countries. For example, the majority of United States citizens admitted that they found them at times pleasant, at others ridiculous. At least one gathers that they found them emotional experiences on some level. In contrast, a majority of Italians reported that they "never enjoy, never get angry, and never feel contempt" during campaigns. These pointed differences in national responses suggest the value of studying political emotions and sentiments, and it is unfortunate that we have not pursued such suggestive research.

There does exist a pair of studies that have focused on measuring affect. In the first study Fishbein and Coombs (1971) sampled an unspecified midwestern American city using a panel design with waves of interviews before and after the 1964 election. In Fishbein's attitude theory, attitudes are defined precisely as "the amount of affect for or against a psychological object" (Fishbein and Coombs, 1971, p. 5). In his terms one can measure an attitude (e.g., toward government medical insurance) with evaluative scales using "good" and "bad" as their anchor points. A "belief" in turn is a cognitive judgment defined as "the probability or improbability that a particular relationship exists between the object of belief and some other object" (1971, p. 6). An example of the two measures will clarify the distinction between attitude (or affect) and belief.

1. An evaluation scale of *attitude (affect)* toward Medicare.
Medicare
Good—— : —— : —— : —— : —— : —— : ——Bad

2. A cognitive scale of *belief* about a candidate's position on Medicare.
Lyndon Johnson is in favor of Medicare.
Probable—— : —— : —— : —— : —— : —— : ——Improbable

In Fishbein's theory the behavioral intention to vote for Lyndon Johnson would be expected to be a function of a person's attitudes (affect) toward some issues such as Medicare and his beliefs about the candidate's views on the issues. As Fishbein and Coombs predicted, there was a high correlation in this sample between the reported vote in the postelection interview and vote predictions made on the basis of attitudes and beliefs toward a series of issue objects measured in the preelection interviews.

The second study by McClure and Patterson in Syracuse, New York is similar to that of Fishbein and Coombs in design, though not in theoretical focus (McClure and Patterson, 1973; Patterson and McClure, 1973; and Patterson, McClure, and Meier, 1974). Patterson and McClure (1973) were concerned with the effects of media, especially paid television advertising, in altering people's attitudes and beliefs about issues and candidates. As in the Fishbein–Coombs study, attitudes were defined as affect measured with evaluative scales, with "good" and "bad" as the polar anchor points. Their findings make important contributions to the conventional wisdom of mass communications theory. Media advertising did not change the viewer's attitude (or affect) toward issues such as defense spending or pulling troops out of Vietnam. But media did change people's *beliefs* about where the candidates stood on those issues, in the main contributing to voters' acquisition of accurate information about candidate positions on those issues.

As interesting as the Fishbein and Coombs, and McClure and Patterson, studies are, they do not alter our judgment that the study of political affect is sadly neglected. In the first place, by defining attitudes toward public policy issues in terms of "good–bad" evaluative scales, a rather strong cognitive component infuses the measures of affect. After all, we likely think that Medicare is good or bad because of other cognitive beliefs about the state of public and private health care facilities and people's ability to pay for them. Thus, affect in this usage is more cognitively based than the kinds of emotions and sentiments that we usually denote as affect.

In the second place, in these two studies affect was measured in only one of its manifestations, the evaluation of good and bad. Surely this is justifiable in terms of the length of time required to administer semantic differential scales. It does mean, however, that *qualitatively* different affective responses are obscured. Ponder the variety of emotions and sentiments that sustain people in politics or repel them from it: anger, disgust, revulsion, fear, alienation, apathy, or the opposing sentiments of satisfaction, gratification, fulfillment. We rarely measure these emotions directly, even though most of us presume they are motive forces in our political behavior. Rather, we tend to infer the emotions from the cognitive content of people's opinions.

Consider, for example, the literature on those venerable political scales of the United States voting studies—the indexes of political efficacy and political cynicism. Taken singly, both bear consistent relationships to the act of voting. Feelings of low political efficacy typify those who rarely vote. Political cynicism, a mistrust of officials in office, is related to a disposition to vote against the candidates of the party in office in national elections (and to vote against bond and policy referenda in local elections) (Campbell *et al.*, 1960; Boyd, 1967; Gamson, 1968).

Taken together, low political efficacy and political cynicism are often considered as the cognitive and the affective components of political alienation. (See Table 1.) That is, an alienated person not only believes that he is powerless, he also resents the fact that he is, an inference from his cynicism and mistrust of public officials (Gamson, 1968). In fact, the alienated voter is but one of a number we can define using the extremes of the efficacy and mistrust indexes (Boyd, 1967).

TABLE 1   Combinations of political efficacy and political trust

		Trust of public officials		
		Low	Medium	High
Sense of political efficacy	Low	Alienated voter		Acquiescent voter
	Medium			
	High	Protest voter		Allegiant voter

Clearly, these four voter types are distinguished as much by their feelings or emotions about politics as by cognitive beliefs about their own ability to influence the course of politics through the voting process. The estrangement of the alienated voter has just been described: it is resentment grounded in felt impotence. This is a different attitude from that of the protest voter, who acts on his mistrust of political leaders because of his own convictions of political potency. The belief, as Gamson put it (1968, p. 48) that influence is both "possible and necessary," has been one of the distinctive features of postwar American politics, establishing what Converse has called a "prime setting for the effective mobilization of discontent" (1972, p. 336).

We may think of cynicism as a direct measure of affect, but it is surely grounded in cognitive beliefs about the behavior of candidates in office. More accurately, we *infer* that emotional intensity must infuse people's political behavior, when particular combinations of feelings of political power and political mistrust interact. Thus, we have been content to measure the cognitive components of the attitudes directly and assume the affect that underlies them.

We have not, of course, exhausted treatments of affect in survey research. Sears, for example, in his review of the literature on political behavior for the *Handbook of Social Psychology* (1969), interprets the political socialization of children as the acquisition of partisan loyalties and allegiances toward public figures through the role of the family and schools in nurturing positive affect toward politics. Surely it is right that in the child's world, feelings about politics precede cognitive beliefs about the political system. Hyman (1959), Greenstein (1965), Hess and Torney (1967), Easton and Dennis (1969), and Jennings and Niemi (1974), as well as many others, have contributed to these theories of the development of affective loyalties toward the political system, exploring feelings of political legitimacy toward what they term the political community, the regime, and its authorities. In a series of articles, Arthur Miller has examined the breakdown of those affective allegiances in the United States and the growth of feelings of estrangement from politics (1973, 1974a, 1974b). Yet, when we reflect on the variety of qualitatively different emotional responses to politics, responses ranging from revulsion to adoration, we wonder why researchers have devoted so little of their energies to measuring those feelings that so strongly influence the character of our political behavior.

Political attitudes and beliefs. Measures of attitudes and beliefs comprise the bulk of most surveys. The usefulness of attitude surveys is so evident that we will not pause to make the argument. What may not be quite so obvious is the multidimensionality of this content domain, which we sense only when we ask ourselves what it is that we would like to know about a belief. Then the question focuses our attention on the complexity of what first might have appeared as a simple entity.

For example, we would ask the kinds of questions that Smith, Bruner, and White (1956), Lane and Sears (1964), and Best (1973) have asked: What is the *direction* of an opinion? Are the respondents in the survey in favor of more or less control of wages and prices? How much more? How much less?

How *intensely* does the person hold this view? With what level of conviction does he imbue this belief? Lane (1962) and Riesman (1950), for example, have argued that Americans rarely hold intense opinions, rarely look with outrage on those whose opinions are contrary or who convert their political opinions into moral crusades. Freidson (1955) has emphasized the developmental processes that inhibit the formation of such extreme views. In a similar vein Almond, in his influential book *The American People and Foreign Policy* (1950), argued that the public is largely indifferent to most issues in foreign affairs:

> The characteristic response to questions of foreign policy is one of indifference. A foreign policy crisis, short of the immediate threat of war may transform indifference to vague apprehension, to fatalism, to anger; but the reaction is still a mood. (Almond, 1950, p. 53)

This "mood theory" of foreign policy opinion is consistent with the arguments of many who assert that the public lacks the conviction and interest to support a sustained, costly role in foreign affairs. Still others argue on the same premise that the public will not likely support a long-term, conventional war, preferring instead either isolationism or extreme escalation of conflict (Key, 1964; Brzezinski and Huntington, 1964). Caspary (1970), among others (Boyd, 1972, p. 443), has raised questions concerning the mood theory. The controversy is an important one, and it underlines why we must know whether an opinion is crystallized, intensely held, and stable or whether it is weakly held, fluid, and easily changeable or manipulatable.

We would also ask about the attitudinal *structure* in which an opinion is embedded. Is the opinion part of a constellation of other beliefs? Is it organized into and supported by a more abstract political ideology? We will consider this issue in a later section on surveys designed to explore ideologies and belief systems, but we mention it here to note that the most important aspect of what we may want to know about one belief is its relationship to another.

We would want to ask as well about the *level of information* that supports a belief. Even at a minimal level many people lack information on major policy choices of their government. For example, in 1969 the United States Senate Foreign Relations Committee held televised hearings on President Nixon's proposal to build an antiballistic missile system, and these hearings were prominently featured on national network news. At the height of the controversy, the Gallup Poll asked whether its respondents had heard or read about the ABM program (Gallup, 1972, p. 2190). Thirty-one percent were willing to admit that they had not heard of the program. In all probability many of those who said they had heard of the proposal were simply too embarrassed to admit they had not, for an additional 29 percent of those polled stated that they had no opinion on the issue. Questions on the information level of the ordinary voter raise some of the most intractable issues in democratic theory, particularly on the question of whether a government or its leaders are ultimately accountable for the success or failure of policy.

Sears (1969) provides a good discussion of the evidence concerning the political knowledge of the average citizen. Suffice it to say that most of our measures of information tap such issues as whether or not a person knows his elected leaders or knows basic facts about the constitutional structure of the government. Measures of knowledge about political controversies or practical politics are quite rare. For example, numerous surveys chart the growth of disapproval of Richard Nixon as the Watergate crisis unfolded. However, no published survey through 1974 has actually measured what knowledge people gained of the materials on the Watergate tapes or the nature of the charges of the House Judiciary Committee's impeachment report. Without such knowledge it is not at all clear what kind of impact, if any, the events had upon people's perspectives on government. This is simply one illustration of a general point, that in the main we have only the most tentative information about people's information.

Finally, we would want to know about the *context* of a belief. Taken together, how do the opinions of individuals aggregate to form a *public* opinion? How far is a particular opinion from the modal view? What is the character of aggregated opinions as a distribution? And as Key (1964) and Dahl (1972) asked, What distribution denotes a consensus? polarization? a constitutional crisis?

To inquire of the context of a belief is also to ask about the relationship between a person's beliefs and those of political leaders. Does a person see significant differences in policies between a Democratic candidate and a Republican? That, of course, depends on the attitudinal distance of the two candidates from the observer's own position. Or, as someone once put it, the difference between a Methodist and a Baptist may not seem like much to a Buddhist, but it's like night and day to the Baptist.

Another aspect of context includes beliefs about *other* people's beliefs. Allport (1924) and Katz and Schanck (1938) have underlined the importance of *pluralistic ignorance,* the false ideas we have of the attitudes of others. Allport warned against the "illusion of universality" which sustains people in action through the belief that they are supported by an army of like-minded supporters. Allport spoke of pluralistic ignorance as an important source of prejudice. It reminds us that in an "other-directed" culture, the perception of beliefs of others may have as great an influence on our behavior as our own beliefs. Madison, in *Federalist* No. 49, knew that people are hesitant to act on opinions unless they perceive that others support them. In the context of a warning against Jefferson's proposition in *Notes on the State of Virginia* that constitutions should be amended by conventions of the people, Madison remarked:

> If it be true that all governments rest on opinion, it is no less true that the strength of opinion in each individual, and its practical influence on his conduct, depend much on the number which he supposes to have entertained the same opinion. The reason of man, like man himself is timid and

cautious, when left alone; and acquires firmness and confidence, in proportion to the number with which it is associated. (Cooke, 1961, p. 340)

Another component of the context of a belief has to do with the expectations in which the beliefs are grounded. We have expectations, for example, based on our perceptions of the fate of others in situations similar to our own. Theorists of *relative deprivation* tell us that satisfaction with one's material life is less determined by one's objective situation than it is by our perception of the situation of others. As an illustration, Stouffer *et al.* (1949, vol. 1, pp. 250–253) found that soldiers in units with few promotions were more satisfied with promotion opportunities than soldiers in units with a high record of promotions.

Our beliefs are also embedded in the context of what Lewin (1943) has termed a "time perspective." We see ourselves and the world in which we live against the backdrop of the past and the unfolding of the future. Thus, a person's policy beliefs are not simply a function of his preferences but also of the difference between what he prefers and what he foresees realistically as the probable course of his life. To take a hypothetical example, two white citizens of South Africa may share the same attitudes toward apartheid laws, but if one believes in the inevitability of African enfranchisement while the other does not, the two are likely to have very different stances on the liberalization of race legislation.

Political judgments. Quite often a survey solicits not so much a respondent's attitude as it does a judgment, for example, not what candidate does a person *want* to win in an election but who does he *expect* to win. Respondents will surely blur the distinction between an attitude and an appraisal, no matter how much the item wording may entreat him to suppress his own opinions. Nonetheless, judgments or appraisals are a distinct analytical category, and we should so treat them.

A clear example of a judgment measure is the "self-anchoring striving scale," developed by Hadley Cantril and Lloyd A. Free (Cantril, 1965 and Free and Cantril, 1968) for a series of studies in 18 countries between 1958 and 1964. Each person was asked to evaluate the nation's achievements in relation to his own hopes and fears for it. Thus, the scale is distinctive not only as a measure of judgment, but also because the anchor points of the index are provided by the respondent himself. Each person is first asked to describe "the best possible situation for our country," then "the worst." He is then shown a ten-point ladder with the explanation that the tenth or top rung represents the best he could hope for the nation and the bottom rung the worst. Having set the anchor points in terms of his own best hopes and worst fears, he then indicates where the nation stands on the ladder at present, where he believes it stood five years ago, and where he expects it to stand five years in the future. (It is worth noting that this is a time perspective of five years imposed on the respondents. A different time frame might have produced quite divergent findings.)

Most people in most countries render favorable judgments on their country's progress. In the 18 countries surveyed by Cantril and Free, only once (in the Philippines in 1959) did a nation judge its present to be worse than its past. Notably, a recent survey by Albert Cantril and Charles Roll (1971) established the United States in 1971 as a second example of a country whose population has judged its present as inferior to its past. Such has been the growth of disaffection in the United States since the mid 1960s (Boyd, 1974, p. 181).

An example of a judgment measure that is part appraisal, part attitude and affect is the "presidential popularity" question, which Gallup has asked regularly since 1945: "Do you approve of the way (the incumbent) is handling his job as president?" Mueller (1973) has given us an interesting analysis of why presidents have always declined in the nation's estimate during office. He finds that the positive judgments suffer in times of increased unemployment (though good times do not necessarily benefit a performance rating). Flash crises produce a rallying to the president, but this kind of approval quickly fades. And presidents can always expect to suffer a loss of approval the longer they have served in office, because people seem to remember the failures of policy more acutely than the successes. Counterintuitively, Mueller found that when the several causes of unpopularity are considered, "the Korean War had a large, significant independent negative impact on President Truman's popularity of some 18 percentage points, but the Vietnam War had no independent impact on President Johnson's popularity at all" (Mueller, 1973, p. 277). This is but one of a number of arresting findings about an item that has been asked perhaps as many times as any other political question in any survey series, but which had never been subjected to rigorous analysis prior to that of Mueller.

Behavior. Many of us, if asked to state the primary uses of survey research, would respond quickly, "Why to measure opinions, of course." So prevalent is this assumption that we often use public opinion surveys and survey research as synonymous terms. So we pause here to emphasize that measures of behavior are invariably important components of surveys and to dispute in the process the common charge that surveys of behavior are necessarily unreliable.

Voting choice is a type of behavior we often survey. Butler and Stokes, in their analysis of *Political Change in Britian* (1969), offer us a sophisticated interpretation of the shifts in party support during the period from 1959 to 1966 that reveals the complexity of seemingly simple changes in voting behavior. In 1959 the Conservative Party strengthened the margin it had enjoyed over the Labour Party since 1951, emerging with a 107-seat advantage. In 1964 Labour won a narrow victory of 13 seats over the Conservatives. With a margin so slim and prospects for a bigger victory so bright, Labour called another election in 1966 and triumphed with a 109-seat victory over the Conservatives.

Butler and Stokes were prescient enough to have captured this period of change with a sophisticated, three-wave panel survey of the United Kingdom (excluding Northern Ireland): a first in the summer of 1963, a second after the autumn election of 1964, and a third after the spring election of 1966. Having asked the 1963 sample about its 1959 voting choice, Butler and Stokes had a single sample of voters who had been interviewed at three different points of a formative political period. By cross-classifying voting choices in one election with those of another, they could precisely estimate the several sources of change (Butler and Stokes, 1969, pp. 275ff):

1. *Replacement of the electorate.* The coming of age of a new voter cohort and the death of a political cohort since the preceding election.
2. *Differential turnout.* The changes caused by people who vote in one election but not the other.
3. *Circulation of the Liberals.* Those "floating voters" who supported the Liberal Party in one election and the Conservative or the Labour Party in another. (The Liberal Party almost doubled its popular vote from 1959 to 1964.)
4. *Circulation of minor-party supporters.* The vote for Irish, Welsh, and Scottish Nationalist, or Communist candidates.
5. *Straight conversion.* Those who voted for the Conservatives in one election and the Labour Party in another.

The analysis dispelled the notion that most electoral change results from the final category—the change in vote from one major party to another. From 1959 to 1964 the greatest change was based in the replacement of the electorate —the substitution by those who were voting their first time of those who had voted their last. In second place as a cause of change was the circulation of Liberal voters. Straight conversion ranked only fourth of five in its impact. In short, political change was as much actuarial as electoral, an engaging finding that would have been lost were it not for the ability of surveys to capture the character of behavior.

Incidentally, this analysis of the sources of the Labour Party's surge required that the sample estimates be as accurate as possible. In this particular case, the marginals of the change tables could be adjusted to reflect the actual percentage of votes received by each party according to official returns. Mosteller (1968) had previously suggested a method of adjusting the cell frequencies in a table in a way that preserves the existing statistical relationship within the table, but alters the cell and marginal frequencies to reflect a distribution known to be more accurate than the sample results. Axelrod (1972, 1974) used the same adjustment procedures in his calculations of the coalitions that comprised the Republican and Democratic parties from 1952 to 1972.

A second example of using surveys to measure behavior attests to the versatility of the technique. In the summer of 1966 the National Opinion Research Center surveyed for The President's Commission on Law Enforcement and Administration of Justice a full probability sample of 10,000 households in all parts of the United States. Criminal victimization in the United States was the subject of the survey, specifically a comparison of the incidence of crime as reported in the FBI's Uniform Crime Reports with crimes mentioned by the sample respondents. Ennis (1967), the study director, found that the official figures approximated the survey results quite closely for such crimes as homicide and vehicle theft. For other types of crime, the survey estimates greatly exceeded the official figures, robbery being twice as frequent as recorded and rape being four times as frequent. The figures are, we might say, arresting. The survey also included a thorough analysis of why victims did not report crimes against them. And the careful analysis of victims' common dissatisfaction with police treatment in cases that *were* reported suggests some of the reasons for the decisions of many others to keep the crimes secret. In 1973 the Law Enforcement Assistance Administration of the United States Department of Justice initiated what is projected to become a continuing National Crime Panel. Conducted by the Bureau of the Census, the survey includes a sample of 60,000 households and 15,000 businesses throughout the 50 states and the District of Columbia (United States Department of Justice, 1974). Together, these criminal victimization studies cast doubt on the usual premise that survey results provide "softer," less reliable data than other methods of data collection.

Finally, we could not close our discussion of surveys of behavior without reference to perhaps the most extraordinary survey ever undertaken: the Multinational Comparative Time-Budget Research Project. This study, directed by Alexander Szalai in collaboration with Philip E. Converse, Pierre Feldheim, Erwin K. Scheuch, and Philip J. Stone, is based on detailed time-budgets recorded by nearly 30,000 respondents drawn from urban and suburban samples in 1965 and 1966 in 12 countries in Eastern and West Europe, South America, and the United States. From detailed reports of the activities of a 24-hour day, the investigators compare the use that citizens of different countries make of time. The results are illuminating. There could be no more precise support for Dahl's argument (1961) that man is not a political animal than to note that the average American spends fewer than 12 seconds a day on political activities (Szalai, 1972, p. 557).

However, if man is not Dahl's *Homo politicus,* neither does he appear to be *Homo copulatus* or *Homo evacuatus.* Though activities requiring an average of fewer than three seconds were not recorded in the tables, the tables suggest that no one devoted a single moment to sexual intercourse or elimination—not even during the weekend! But perhaps this statistic can only suggest that surveys of behavior are not completely free from measurement error. As the authors so discreetly suggested in a footnote, "For obvious reasons, minor unidentified gaps in the flow of daily activities were by fiat assigned to the 'personal care' category" (Szalai, 1972, p. 129).

Ideologies and belief systems. In the last decade surveys of ideologies and belief systems have been undertaken in some form in most of the industrialized countries of the world. Many of these studies have focused on the problem raised by Converse in his classic article "The Nature of Belief Systems in Mass Publics" (1964). Converse defines a belief system in terms of what he calls a "constraint or functional interdependence" among a person's attitudes. Converse distinguishes two different types of constraint, static and dynamic. By static constraint he means "the success we would have in predicting, given initial knowledge that an individual holds a specified attitude, that he holds certain further ideas and attitudes" (Converse, 1964, p. 207). In contrast, dynamic constraint "refers to the probability that a change in the perceived status (truth, desirability, and so forth) of one idea-element would *psychologically* require, from the point of view of the actor, some compensating change(s) in the status of idea-elements elsewhere in the configuration" (1964, p. 208). Summarizing Converse's long and sophisticated essay invites oversimplification, but in general he argues that a continental shelf exists between elites and ordinary voters in terms of having either constrained belief systems or even stable positions on discrete issues over time.

Converse's work has stimulated numerous critiques, which he evaluates in Volume 4 of this *Handbook of Political Science* (1975). Since our interest is only in arguing that belief systems can be usefully studied with survey research, we will not review the controversy in depth, except to note that Cobb (1973) provides a helpful review of this literature.

Cobb suggests that research has focused on six features of belief systems: (1) the degree of differentiation of beliefs, whether they are cognitively simplistic and undifferentiated or sophisticated and complex; (2) the intensity and commitment of ordinary people to politics; (3) the stability of beliefs, or the extent to which peoples' attitudes remain fixed over time; (4) the internal consistency of attitudes within a belief system, that is, the degree to which one can predict that people who are liberal on one attitude will be liberal on another; (5) the instrumentality of attitudes, or the degree to which beliefs predict behavior; and (6) the insulation of belief systems, or the degree to which ideas in an ideology are vulnerable to change from external pressures.

Arguments on all sides of these issues can be buttressed from evidence gathered through sophisticated survey designs, which suggests two conclusions regarding the usefulness of surveys in studying ideologies. First, the degree to which people possess constrained belief systems in both a static and a dynamic sense can vary substantially in the same political system over a short period of time. For example, Converse's evidence suggesting that voters are ideologically unsophisticated is based on election surveys of 1956, 1958, and 1960. However, as so many have remarked so often, this was indeed a quiescent period in American politics, when politics seemed relatively unimportant to most people. The 1960s, however, brought forth a set of issues that engaged voters' attention, most notably the civil rights movement and the antiwar movement, and candidates such as Barry Goldwater, Lyndon Johnson, George Wallace, and George McGovern took distinct and widely divergent stands on these issues. Voters paid attention to these stands, evidently took cues from them, and responded by holding views on political issues that were both ideologically sophisticated and internally consistent (e.g., Field and Anderson, 1969; Boyd, 1972; Luttbeg, 1968; Nie, 1974; Pierce, 1970; Pomper, 1972; and RePass, 1971, among many others). Taken together these studies clearly document a remarkable change over a short period of time in the degree to which voters think about politics in ideological terms, a change in large part determined by the salience and character of political issues at the time and the clarity of the positions that leaders are taking on those issues. It is not the case that voters do not respond to political issues because they lack the basic cognitive skills to do so. Thus, what surveys disclose about the ideological character of voters' attitudes may say as much about the character of political controversies or the conduct of leaders as it does about immutable features of people's cognitive capacities.

None of this argument is intended to deny the undeniable—that highly educated people, people of high cognitive ability, are more likely to have structured opinions than are people of low cognitive development. For example, Williams and Wright, using a factor analysis conducted separately for each educational stratum, found that "the organization of opinions appear[s] more strongly delineated in the college educated segment" (1955, p. 563). Similarly, Campbell et al. (1960) showed that ideological "levels of conceptualization" were much more common in the college stratum than among lower education groups. This suggests that the secular change toward increased education over the last 20 years might be expected to have a significant effect on the degree to which ordinary citizens possess structured opinions about politics. We commonly think of education as an experience that induces us to think in more sophisticated and complex ways about politics. Yet, we must note that Nie (1974) found that the growth of more structured opinions from 1956 to 1972 was as great in the stratum that had not attended college as in the stratum that had. Thus, it seems clear that it is both the changeable political climate that people confront, as well as their more enduring cognitive abilities, that determine the degree to which they possess structured opinions about the political world.

Second, surveys may be a poor device for exploring what we ordinarily mean when we use the term ideology. By ideology we usually have in mind those abstract social and political values that people can use to justify a set of attitudes or policy preferences. The standard interview schedule, even with its complement of open-ended questions, is not well suited to the in-depth probing exploited by Lane (1962) and Smith, Bruner, and White (1956) to elicit the terms in which a person justifies his beliefs. With the exception of the literature on the "levels of conceptualization scale" introduced in Campbell's *The American Voter* (1960), most studies of belief systems have focused on responses to closed questions and have analyzed the degree of internal consistency in a person's attitudes, asking, for example, whether one can predict that a person who is liberal on one issue will be liberal on another. Where consistency exists we have tended to assume that it is because people's attitudes are integrated into a more encompassing belief system. Where it does not, we have inferred that no such ideology exists. But we have not directly measured the ideological justification; the basis for our interpretation is little more than a statistic, the degree of intercorrelation of beliefs across a sample of respondents. By judging attitudinal consistency in this manner, we require not only that a person have an ideological justification for his beliefs but that the respondents in the sample share the *same* justification.

Axelrod (1967) neatly demonstrated an alternative approach. In his analysis of a 1956 American survey, he found a group of citizens (mainly the politically active and well-educated) whose policy views were consistently liberal or consistently conservative. But he also found another group, commonly less-educated nonvoters, who took consistent positions in support of social welfare policies, of firing suspected communists from public service, and of an isolationist foreign policy. This latter set of beliefs he labeled "populism" because its advocacy of a strong governmental role in domestic affairs, combined with isolationist and anticivil libertarian beliefs, corresponded to Hofstadter's (1955) interpretation of the attitudes of the American Populist movement of the 1890s.

The moral is plain. Axelrod found evidence of consistent beliefs where others did not because he was willing to drop the assumption that all respondents in the sample must evaluate policies in terms of the same dimensions. Instead, he looked for consistency among subgroups of citizens whose social and political character was more homogeneous and who might be expected to share similar perspectives on politics.

As Axelrod's example suggests, the character of belief systems is grounded in the pattern of a nation's social cleavages. In some countries, notably the Netherlands, Belgium, India, and South Africa, the dominant cleavages of class, region, and religion all coincide with ethnic lines. Thus in such countries, there tend to develop separate trade unions, voluntary associations, businesses, newspapers, and religious organizations within each ethnic group. The Dutch word *verzuiling* has become a standard term for describing these systems in which the major social cleavages parallel or reinforce one another, rather than crosscut each other (Lipset and Rokkan, 1967, p. 15; and Lijphart, 1968). When people are embedded in social groups in which everyone tends to have the same religious, ethnic, organizational, and perhaps even class loyalties, it would not be surprising to find substantial attitudinal consistency across a series of political issues, for each of his reference groups reinforces similar political beliefs. In a country of crosscutting cleavages, however, people are constantly placed in positions of cross-pressures because their social groups tend to be more socially and politically heterogeneous. For this reason several of the recent surveys of political beliefs in various countries have focused on the linkages between patterns of social cleavages and the consistency of political attitudes (Barnes, 1971; Barnes and Pierce, 1971; Converse and Pierce, 1970; and the various studies in Lipset and Rokkan, 1967).

Studies of national character. To this point we have been discussing relatively limited domains—affect, attitudes, action. In contrast, surveys are often interested in the most comprehensive analyses of a nation's modal character structure. When such studies are limited to one society, they run the risk of drawing inferences about the distinctiveness of national character on the basis of "pseudo-cross national designs" (Hyman, 1964). That is, the analyst compares the empirical results of a survey in one country to the results of an imagined survey in a second. To avoid this problem there was a widespread, one could almost say worldwide, interest in the 1950s and 1960s in truly cross-cultural surveys of personality in which uniformities and differences in character types could be empirically demonstrated.

One approaches the topic of national character studies as one does a wasp nest, knowing that no matter how careful a person is, he will inevitably be stung. Fortunately, there exists a protective netting—in the form of numerous works aimed precisely at clarifying the difficult problems that cross-cultural research creates, and we will take refuge by citing those works that are most helpful in coping with them. At the beginning of the list is the annotated bibliography compiled by Frey and his associates Stephenson and Smith (1969), who have abstracted over 1600 articles on comparative surveys published up to 1967, classified by topic and area of the world.

Several works delineate the alternative research designs for cross-cultural surveys, including Frey's "Cross-Cultural Survey Research in Political Science" (1970), Przeworski and Teune's *The Logic of Comparative Social Inquiry* (1970), and Hyman's "Strategies in Comparative Survey Research" (1975). Needless to say, our definition of surveys in terms of "explicit, standardized procedures yielding quantitative measurements" confronts nearly intractable problems when interview schedules must be translated into other languages and when research procedures must be equivalent across cultural boundaries. It would be fatuous to seek solutions to linguistic and cultural differences with literal translations of instruments and nominal identity of research procedures. Rather, the cross-cultural researcher strives for functional or conceptual *equivalence* of procedures. Some of the more helpful sources, in addition to those named above, are Hymes, "Linguistic Aspects of Comparative Political Research" (1970); Przeworski and Teune, "Equivalence in Cross-National Research"

(1966–1967); and Strauss, "Phenomenal Identity and Conceptual Equivalence of Measurement in Cross-National Comparative Research" (1969). Specialized problems of equivalence are discussed by Haller and Lewis (1966), Gough and Di Palma (1965), Tiryakian (1958), and Schuman (1966).

Studies of *national character* are a special type of cross-cultural investigation, distinctive in their search for modal personality types arising in particular sociocultural systems. In *The Handbook of Social Psychology*, Inkeles and Levinson carefully state the issues that studies of national character pose:

> The concept of national character is an important but problematic one in the social sciences. It has been strongly rejected in the hereditarian or racist forms in which it was couched by earlier writers. Seen in more modern perspective, however, it poses fundamental problems for social-scientific theory and research: To what extent do the patterned conditions of life in a particular society give rise to certain distinctive patterns in the personalities of its members? To what extent, that is, does the sociocultural system produce its distinctive forms of "social character," "basic personality structure," or "modal personality"? Further, what are the consequences, if any, of this patterning in personality for stability or change in the societal order? (Inkeles and Levinson, 1969, vol. 4, p. 418)

Together with DeVos and Hippler (1969), the essay by Inkeles and Levinson is a valuable guide to this literature.

Controversies in Attitude Research

In our discussion of attitudes and behavior, we deferred examination of issues that continue to be the subject of controversy. Prominent among these are (1) the reliability of attitude measures in light of the sensitivity of responses to slight changes in item wording, (2) the degree to which people's behavior conforms to attitudes expressed in interviews, and (3) the degree to which responses to many items can actually be said to measure political attitudes, when respondents tend to answer such questions in almost random patterns over time (the so-called "non-attitude" argument). Each of these issues poses difficult problems for the survey analyst, both in the design of measures and the interpretation of results.

Response sensitivity to item wording. Perhaps the first warning the survey initiate receives is that subtle changes in the wording of attitude items often alter the frequency of a response by as much as 20 percentage points. Experienced analysts wince at reading a statement that, for example, 80 percent of a sample supports gun control legislation or that 55 percent endorse legalized abortion. They know that a differently worded item could easily turn these majorities into minorities. Indeed, experiments on the effects of item wording were a core concern of those who were the pioneers of modern survey techniques in the 1930s and 1940s (Gallup, 1944; Cantril, 1947; Stouffer et al., 1949; and Payne, 1951).

Philip Converse and Howard Schuman (1970) offer us a recent example of this old problem. In June 1969 the Gallup Poll asked a national sample the following question on Vietnam: "President Nixon has ordered the withdrawal of 25,000 United States troops from Vietnam in the next three months. How do you feel about this—do you think troops should be withdrawn at a faster rate or slower rate?" (The response "same as now" was not presented, but it was accepted if volunteered.) In September–October 1969, the Harris Poll asked a similarly worded item: "In general, do you feel the pace at which the President is withdrawing troops is too fast, too slow, or about right?" The responses to the two items were the following:

The Gallup Poll		*The Harris Poll*	
Faster	42%	Too slow	28%
Same as now	29	About right	49
Slower	16	Too fast	6
No opinion	13	No opinion	18
	100%		101%

The differences in the poll results are striking. One could interpret the Gallup Poll as a plurality in favor of faster withdrawal. Yet the Harris Poll, with a very similar item, shows a plurality in support of administration policy. Why is there a 20 percentage point difference in the two items? Obviously the answer is that the Gallup Poll did not suggest to its sample the response alternative, "same as now." Yet one would hardly expect this change to affect people's stated opinions on an issue so salient as the war, measured at a peak point of its intensity.

Confronted with item wording effects such as these, the prudent analyst is usually given the following advice (Stouffer et al., 1949, vol. 1, p. 45; and James Davis, 1971): Avoid imputing any absolute validity to the total distribution of responses because wording changes can shift the modal response on an attitude dimension. However, one can usually assume, one is told, that the *relative ordering* of people in each response category is still reliable, e.g., that most of the 28 percent in the Harris Poll who supported a faster withdrawal of troops would have also answered the Gallup item by advocating a faster withdrawal. Thus, the two items still measure the same content domain. They simply slice that opinion distribution into groups of somewhat different sizes.

If it were true that the two items measure the same underlying attitude, then it should be the case that the items will have a similar statistical relationship to a third variable such as education. Thus, for either sample one could formulate a generalization such as "the more educated a respondent in each sample is, the more likely it is that he favors a faster withdrawal of troops." Such a generalization would require that respondents of the same educational level interpret the meaning of the differently worded items in a similar way. However, not even this assumption is always valid, as Schuman and Duncan (1974) reveal in a subsequent reanalysis of these same two Vietnam items. Table 2 displays the quite different statistical relationships that responses bear to education.

TABLE 2   Percentage distribution on withdrawal from Vietnam questions by education: Gallup and Harris Polls*

	Advo-cates faster with-drawal	Advo-cates slower with-drawal	Advo-cates present rate†	No opinion	Total %	N
Gallup						
College (13 and over)	42	16	31	11	100	300
High school (9–12)	42	16	30	12	100	765
Grade school (0–8)	41	19	24	16	100	435
						1500
Harris						
College (13 and over)	36	4	42	18	100	320
High School (9–12)	27	7	51	15	100	816
Grade school (0–8)	18	5	61	16	100	468
						1604

Source: Schuman and Duncan, 1974, p. 239.

* See text for wording of Gallup and Harris questions. Responses to the two questions have been equated and relabeled here in terms of intended meaning; for example, "faster" for Gallup question and "too slow" for Harris question are both considered "advocates faster withdrawal."

† This alternative is explicitly presented to respondents in this Harris question but not in the Gallup question.

In the Gallup Poll, those with a college education are more likely than those with a grade school education to favor the existing rate of troop withdrawal. In the Harris Poll this positive relationship becomes negative, as those with a grade school education give more support to the administration policy than the college-educated do. As Schuman and Duncan conclude, "the claim is often made that orderings and associations are invariant in the face of changes in question wording. There are in fact few demonstrations that this assumption is generally true" (1974, p. 236).

Indeed, how can the assumption ever be justified? The 1968 Survey Research Center election study offers us one example that lends it credibility: the effect of item wording on the venerable political efficacy index. The index, which we introduced previously in our discussion of affect, was formulated in the Survey Research Center election survey of 1952, and the questions were phrased in a format common to that period. That is, the items were declaratory statements, with the respondent asked to state his agreement or disagreement with the assertion. Table 3 lists these items in their original versions.

Items stated in this "agree-disagree" format are often invalid measures because of the well-known tendency of many people, especially less-educated respondents, to agree to any statement regardless of its content. This particular form of bias is known as *acquiescence response set.* These items are twice biased because every item is worded such that an agree response denotes a feeling of political powerlessness. Thus, respondents who score high on this powerlessness index are made up of some unknown quantity of people who actually feel powerless, plus another unknown number who are obligingly agreeing with the statements.

To avoid such bias the Michigan Survey Research Center began to drop the agree-disagree format in favor of item wordings in which the respondent is asked to choose among alternatives stated in the question, rather than simply agree or disagree with a statement. The revised version as worded in Table 3 was therefore included on the 1968 preelection survey. Yet, because of the interest of many scholars in keeping the original items for time series analysis, the original versions were included in their usual place in the postelection survey. Thus, the two versions of the index were asked of the same respondents but in interviews separated in time by one to five months. Given the fact that the sample is the same, any substantial variation in responses is likely due to the effects of item wording. The two versions present, then, an attractive experiment in item-wording effects.

As Table 3 clearly indicates, the impact of item wording is considerable. Indeed, the majority position becomes the minority position on three of the four items. Were it not for the presence of the original set we might have inferred extraordinary changes in the public feelings of political efficacy, when in fact the source of much of the change would have been in the typewriters of the items' authors. Item 4 provides the most extreme variation; the proportion expressing feelings of powerlessness is almost 35 percentage points higher than in the original version.

Interestingly, this case supports the maxim that differently worded items may still measure the same content domain even though the items may elicit very different frequency responses. Despite wide variations in the pattern of responses to each pair of items, the responses themselves are highly intercorrelated. That is, those who expressed feelings of powerlessness in one version of the test had a high probability of expressing such feelings in the other. The sta-

TABLE 3 Frequency of responses to two versions of the SRC political efficacy items, 1968.

Original version			Revised version	
1. "I don't think public officials care much what people like me think." (N = 1312)		.61*	1. "Would you say that most public officials care quite a lot about what people like you think, or that they don't care much at all?" (N = 1475)	
	Agree	44%	Don't care	40%
	Disagree	56%	Care	60%
2. "Voting is the only way that people like me can have any say about how the government runs things." (N = 1323)		.69*	2. "Would you say that voting is the only way that people like you can have any say about the way government runs things, or that there are lots of ways that you can have a say?" (N = 1493)	
	Agree	43%	Voting is the only way	58%
	Disagree	57%	Lots of ways	42%
3. "Sometimes politics and government seem so complicated that a person like me can't really understand what's going on." (N = 1336)		.68*	3. "Would you say that politics and government are so complicated that people like you can't really understand what's going on, or that you can understand what's going on pretty well?" (N = 1521)	
	Agree	71%	Can't understand	44%
	Disagree	29%	Can understand	56%
4. "People like me don't have any say about what the government does." (N = 1331)		.67*	4. "Would you say that people like you have quite a lot of say about what the government does, or that you don't have much say at all?" (N = 1507)	
	Agree	41%	Don't have much to say	75%
	Disagree	59%	Have a lot to say	25%

* Gamma coefficient measuring association between two versions of items.

tistical relationships between the two versions of the test are invariant over changes in the item wordings, for the correlations are high and steady within a fairly narrow range from .61 to .69.

Moreover, as Table 4 indicates, responses to the two versions of the index are quite similarly related to the respondent's level of education. In both versions feelings of political powerlessness are concentrated among people with less education. We can also see the effects of acquiescence response set on the original version. Because the less educated also tend toward acquiescence, the disposition of the less educated to feel powerless is reinforced by the response set. Thus, in each of the four items the association of the original items with education is higher than it is with the revised version.

These two examples, attitudes on the Vietnam War and feelings of political powerlessness, offer us illustrations of the range of item-wording effects we

TABLE 4   Relationship of two versions of political efficacy items to Education, 1968: proportion giving inefficacious responses.

	Education of Respondent					
Item	Grade school or less	Less than high school graduate	High school graduate	Some college	College graduate	Gamma
1. Public officials don't care						
Original version	76%*	59	35	28	20	.51
Revised version	62%	44	38	35	27	.25
2. Voting is the only way						
Original version	87%	73	53	44	23	.54
Revised version	83%	68	58	45	27	.46
3. Politics is too complicated						
Original version	88%	86	69	57	46	.50
Revised version	70%	55	41	31	20	.43
4. People don't have say						
Original version	71%	52	36	28	21	.43
Revised version	86%	81	74	69	61	.29

* Each cell entry is the proportion of respondents expressing a feeling of political powerlessness. Because the response categories are dichotomous, the proportion expressing feelings of political efficacy is the difference between the figure and 100 percent. The items are those of Table 3.

should anticipate. In the case of war attitudes, the form of the question affected the frequency of responses to the items and modified the statistical relationships between the war attitudes of the respondents and their education. In the case of political efficacy, item wording had substantial effects on the frequency of of responses but minimal impact on their statistical relationships to another variable, education. Converse and Schuman (1970) also provide other examples in which different wordings of items produced no significant effects of either type. Thus, there are no uniform rules that the researcher can confidently apply to the problem. Perhaps the best advice is given by Stouffer *et al.* (1955) long ago, and elaborated by Donald Campbell and Fiske (1959) and Schuman and Duncan (1974): whenever possible measure a concept with as many different items as practicable and analyze separately the relationships of these multiple indicators to other variables. Similarly, Noelle-Neumann (1970) argues for the routine use of split ballots to control for question wording effects. Though multiple indicators consume scarce questionnaire space and split ballots complicate data analysis, each technique provides a basis for confidence that the relationships one observes are not simply a result of an arbitrary wording of an attitude item.

Even when we find that pleasing situation in which changes in item wordings do not disturb statistical relationships with other variables, the effect of item-wording changes on response frequencies remains troublesome. This is particularly true when we wish to examine changes in attitudes over time. Duncan (1969, p. 28) concisely states the dilemma: "When a study has become old enough to be interesting as a base-line for change measurement, it is likely also to be old enough to have used techniques considered outmoded in some respects. Hence there is a great temptation to substitute improved measurements instead of achieving serious replication [of original measures]." Duncan suggests that researchers should generally use improved measures even for time comparisons, but that whenever possible they should include the old measures on questionnaires along with the new. By this method, the new measures can be calibrated or spliced together with the old one, preserving our investment in time series data.

The United States Bureau of Labor Statistics' measure of unemployment illustrates nicely Duncan's advice. (To be sure, measurement of the labor force is not strictly a "political" variable, but, of course, it has profound political impact.) For many years it was known that the measure of unemployment was defective. However, to have changed it might render impossible the kinds of longitudinal analyses for which the time series on unemployment is so important. However, applying new and old measures to the same years allowed the two indexes to be calibrated in such a way that the unemployment rate for years past could be estimated as though it had always been measured using the newly revised series (Ducoff and Hagood, 1947, pp. 5–7, 28–29, 89).

Unfortunately, the calibration of measures does not always avoid the conflict between the need to correct deficient measures and the desire to protect a time series for longitudinal analysis. This dilemma is apparent in the changes that the Survey Research Center has made in many of its attitude items.

From 1952 through 1960 many Survey Research Center items other than political efficacy were phrased as statements to which the respondents were asked to agree strongly, agree, disagree, or disagree strongly. As we discussed in the example of the political efficacy items, this format is subject to various biases, including acquiescence response set. Presumably, because the 1956, 1958, and 1960 studies were a panel design with a primary emphasis on longitudinal analysis, these measures were retained through 1960 in spite of their probable biases. With the return to a standard cross-section sample in 1964, many of the old items were changed to the format illustrated by the revised political efficacy items of Table 2, in which respondents must choose between response alternatives embedded in the items. In most cases the old item formats were not included for the purposes of calibration, at least not in the final interview schedule. Thus, researchers who wish to use the now substantial series of Survey Research Center election studies for longitudinal analyses should assure themselves that the changes they observe are not artifacts of altered item wordings.

Nie's (1974) study of belief systems provides an illustration of the pains a careful researcher should take to eliminate the possibility that item-wording effects contaminate measures of attitude change. By comparing responses to the Survey Research Center items with differently worded items from a National Opinion Research Center (NORC) sample, Nie found that the revision of the Likert format for measuring opinions on public policy issues did not prevent their use in time series analysis. In other cases (the political efficacy items in Table 2 are a good example) item-wording effects are of such a magnitude that time series analyses combining the original and the revised versions would be difficult. Even though the relationships of the efficacy items to variables such as education were not disturbed, the wording effects were so large that the new version could not be spliced with the original. Evidently, the Survey Research Center decided that scholarly interest in maintaining the time series on the efficacy measures outweighed the advantages of substituting refined measures; in the 1972 survey the original items were included and the revised items discarded.

The nexus of attitudes and behavior. A second controversy concerns what Cobb (1973) calls the instrumentality of attitudes, that is, the degree to which people's behavior conforms to their beliefs. Although Deutscher (1966) argues that the issue remains important, his formulation of the controversy now seems somewhat quaint. Few would dispute that attitudes are sometimes poor predictors of actions. As Liska (1974) points out, the question has been recast in a more complex multivariate form: what conditions affect the correspondence between beliefs and behavior? Reformulated, it simply becomes a theoretically interesting question to ponder why our attitudes and actions so often diverge.

1. A necessary first step in clarifying this controversy is to distinguish surveys of past and future behavior. If we seek to measure past behavior, then conceptually there is no uncertainty about whether the overt behavior on which the respondent is queried actually took place. Presuming the item is itself unambiguous, all that is at issue is the accuracy (memory error) and honesty (bias) of the response.

As Sudman and Bradburn (1974, p. 67) note, psychologists have rather accurately defined the distribution of memory errors. Sudman and Bradburn distinguish two types of memory errors in surveys. The first is *omission error*, in which a respondent simply forgets certain of his past actions. The second is *telescoping error*, when time is compressed and an event is remembered as occurring more recently than it actually did (for example, a respondent reporting a case of criminal victimization in the preceding month when in fact the crime occurred two months in the past).

Sudman and Bradburn specify the amount of response error contributed by omission and telescoping with some precision. Because the validity of survey reports can be measured in many cases, it is merely tendentious to argue that inaccuracy of responses generally invalidates surveys of past behavior. Rather what we wish to know is the magnitude of the errors and their distribution, random or systematic, across groups of respondents. We also wish to know how such errors can be reduced by interview procedures such as aided recall and open-ended questions. Sudman and Bradburn provide exactly these helpful types of guides.

Errors due to bias are often more intractable than random memory errors, since biased responses include systematic distortions into data analysis. Survey researchers have long been aware of the understandable disposition of people to report *socially desirable* responses, that is, what they wish the interviewer to believe about themselves. For example, during World War II the Division of Surveys of the Office of War Information surveyed respondents who were known to have redeemed war bonds in the preceding week. Seventeen percent of the sample denied having redeemed the bonds, an act considered at the time to be harmful to the war effort (Hyman, 1944–1945).

There has come to be a substantial literature devoted to estimating the magnitude of bias in surveys, for example, Dinerman (1948), Parry and Crossley (1950), Zitter and Starsinic (1966), Cahalan (1968–1969), and Clausen (1968–1969) on the systematic inflation of survey reports of voter turnout rates. Substantial efforts are being made to reduce such biases. One of the more exotic examples is the randomized response model, in which a respondent is presented with paired questions (Abernathy *et al.*, 1970; Folsom *et al.*, 1973). One is an innocuous item for which the population parameter is well known; for example, "I was born in the month of April." The second item in the pair is a threatening one, likely to evoke biased responses; for example, "I was pregnant at some time during the past 12 months and had an abortion which ended the pregnancy." A random process dictates to the respondent which of the two questions she should answer. The interviewer, however, does not know whether a "yes" response is an answer to the first or the second question, thus assuring the respondent some degree of privacy of her views. No response can ever be attributed to particular individuals in the sample, but because the proportion of people born in particular months is known, researchers can accurately specify the incidence of actions that respondents would otherwise be hesitant to admit in a standard survey. In general, the more anonymous survey respondents perceive themselves to be, for example, through the use of telephone or self-administered questionnaires rather than face-to-face interviews, the lower will be the response bias for items containing a socially desirable answer (Sudman and Bradburn, 1974, p. 66).

Surveys probing future behavior present an entirely different conceptual problem from surveys of the past. It is possible to measure the direction and magnitude of response error for past behavior because one can construct validating tests for which the actual behavior of the respondent is known. In contrast, there is an irreducible element of uncertainty about reports of intention to take some action in the future, for there are always contingencies that may intervene between an intention to act and the action itself. Epistemologically, a respondent cannot lie to an interviewer about an act that has yet to take place. How indeed can we ever know how we will behave until actually confronted with a situation? All a survey can do is to try to make a necessarily hypothetical event realistic for the respondent. For example, in the midst of a September campaign Gallup does not ask his respondents how they will vote in the coming November election. Rather, he asks them how they would vote if the election were held on the date of the interview. Strictly speaking, then, most polls do not predict elections; they merely measure people's voting intentions at the time of the interview. In the 1948 United States election and the 1970 United Kingdom election, pollsters came to grief for their failure to measure late campaign surges and to predict accurately the turnout rate. But the polls were not necessarily inaccurate on the vote intentions measured during the period of the interviews (Mosteller *et al.,* 1949; and Abrams, 1970). In short, the use of surveys as a tool to forecast future events is often a misuse of survey methodology. The failure of such forecasts is less a criticism of surveys than it is a failure of judgment on the part of the interpreter of the survey. Dollard's (1948) codification of the conditions under which opinions predict behavior remains an important theoretical statement on the reasons why our intentions so often fail to predict our future actions.

We have reason for confidence in surveys of behavior in an intriguing finding of Sudman and Bradburn: the more salient the item to the respondent, the more likely he is to report his behavior accurately in a survey (1974, p. 39). This suggests that people's attitudes on controversial issues may often be fairly reliable guides to their subsequent actions. A convincing test of this hypothesis was executed as a component of the 1969 Detroit Area Study, directed by Irwin Katz and Howard Schuman and reported by Brannon *et al.* (1973). The first phase of this ingenious experiment consisted of a survey of people's attitudes on open-housing legislation. On the basis of the survey, the respondents were placed in two categories, one supporting a nondiscrimination open-housing proposal and a second group supporting an owner's right to sell his house to whomever he chooses.

The action phase of the experiment followed three months later, when a group of graduate students posing as members of an organization of concerned citizens returned to each of the original respondents seeking endorsement of a petition supporting *either* open-housing or owner's rights, corresponding to his previously expressed attitudes. Eighty-five percent of the owner's-rights advocates signed the owner's-rights petition. Seventy percent of the open-housing advocates signed the open-housing petition. In contrast, among a control group of owner's-rights advocates who were presented with an open-housing petition, 78 percent *refused* to sign. On a controversial issue such as race policy, people not only expressed their attitudes to a sympathetic interviewer, they were also willing to commit themselves by name to a position on a document that, so far as they knew, could have been broadly available to the public.

2. Another element affecting the correspondence of attitudes and actions is the degree to which the attitudinal measures capture the genuine complexity of social life. This means, as Rokeach (1968) and Liska (1974) argue, that we must measure specific and often contradictory beliefs about concrete situations as well as those more abstract principles surrounding some controversy. Schuman (1972) provides an example from the 1969 Detroit Area Study that illuminates this point. As Table 5 shows, 85 percent support the principle of nondiscrimination in hiring (item C). Yet, 39 percent agree to discrimination if it is said to be necessary for the harmony of the firm (item A), and 50 percent agree to it if it is the preference of a majority of whites (item B).

Schuman argues that the different responses to the three items reflect the very real situations of our lives. Many of us will support principles stated in the abstract. Real situations, however, usually pose conflicts of principles, just as items A and B pose conflicts between belief in fairness on the one hand and belief in interpersonal harmony and the dominance of majority preferences on the other. When items are written to simulate these clashes of principle, surveys can tap the genuine ambivalence that most people feel when principles they endorse are in conflict and can elicit responses that are likely to bear a close

TABLE 5   Racial attitudes on an abstract principle versus attitudes on a concrete situation

Suppose a good Negro engineer applied for a job as an engineering executive. The Personnel Director explained to him: "Personally I'd never given your race a thought, but the two men you would have to work with most closely—the plant manager and the chief engineer—both have strong feelings about Negroes. I *can* offer you a job as a regular engineer, but *not* at the executive level, because any serious friction at the top could ruin the organization."

A. Was it all right for the personnel director in this case to refuse to hire the Negro engineer as an executive in order to avoid friction with the other employees?

1. Yes	39%
2. No	56
9. Other, D.K., N.A.	5

100(640)

B. Should the personnel manager have asked the other men how they would feel about working with a Negro engineer and then made his decision on the basis of their wishes?

1. Yes	50%
2. No	45
9. Other, D.K., N.A.	5

100(640)

C. In general, do you think employers should hire men for top management without paying any attention to whether they are white or Negro?

1. Yes	85%
2. No	12
9. Other, D.K., N.A.	3

100(640)

Source: Schuman, 1972, p. 348.
The sample was an area probability cross section of white adult heads and wives of heads of household in the metropolitan Detroit area. The response rate was 78 percent, with a final N of 640 individuals.

correspondence to what our behavior would have been in a real situation. As Hyman once observed, "If our aim is to predict a given kind of behavior in a given social setting, we should design our tests so that they incorporate the fundamental aspects of the setting into the test" (1949, p. 40).

Schuman's example of clashes of principles in hiring practices clarifies a dispute over the interpretation of two influential political studies by Prothro and Grigg (1960) and by McClosky (1964). Both had discovered an apparent inconsistency in Americans' support of democratic principles. Although Americans tended to endorse democratic principles stated in abstract terms, they qualified that support substantially when presented with a specific instance of the application of those principles.

For example, respondents in both surveys endorsed the principle of free speech, but large numbers would not give that right to communists, atheists, and other unpopular groups. In the context of the cold war atmosphere of the late 1950s, when both surveys were conducted, it is perhaps not remarkable that people might feel that free speech for communists posed a conflict of principles between support for free speech and a belief that some political groups might pose a threat to that same democratic principle. Similarly, people may have felt a conflict of principles on the question of permitting antireligious advocacy in community forums and schools. Americans, as many others, have never really believed that questions of fundamental values (such as religion) are best settled in the marketplace of ideas. Rather, schools and churches in communities have often been charged with a responsibility for inculcating an appreciation of (most often) Christian doctrine, just as instruction in civics has long been fused into secondary school curricula. Thus, it should not surprise us that we find genuine disagreement on the rights of religious dissenters. We will return to the interpretation of these studies in a later discussion on the influence of survey research on political theory. It is sufficient here to note that the Prothro and Grigg and the McClosky studies provide evidence that survey questions can incorporate realistic conflicts between competing principles.

3. Finally, Liska (1974) emphasizes the impact of social support on the correspondence of attitudes to actions. When social support is congruent with attitudes, the correspondence is of course accentuated. When group pressures run counter to attitudes, social pressure may outweigh beliefs in affecting behavior. Liska's discussion of this point centers principally on the somewhat esoteric matter of whether social support and attitudes combine additively or interactively to affect actions. However, we can extend his point by noting the extensive literature stressing the importance of our location in social groups for our beliefs and behavior.

Primary groups—"those small, face-to-face, solidary, informal and enduring coteries that we commonly experience as family, friendship and occupational peer groups"—possess an "extraordinary capacity for rewarding conformity and punishing deviation" (McClosky and Dahlgren, 1959, pp. 757, 759). In their survey of the literature as of 1959, McClosky and Dahlgren list some of the important ways in which primary groups influence behavior and beliefs:

> Almost every major voting study furnishes additional proof that primary groups are essential links in the complex process by which political norms are indoctrinated and party preferences implanted. They find, for example, that members of the same primary groups characteristically vote alike, think alike on issues, and affiliate with the same party; that voters in doubt about whom to vote for usually resolve their indecision by embracing the

political preferences of their friends; that approximately three out of four young people vote as their parents do; and that the more uniform a group's political outlook the firmer the voting intentions of its members. Homogeneity of opinion among primary group members also affects voting turnout and the level of political curiosity. People who disagree with their families or friends about politics are less apt to vote and less likely to develop or to retain an interest in politics. But primary groups may help to reinforce habits of participation and interest as well as to inhibit them. Patterns of participation, as one study concluded, are "contagious"—likely to be active when voters belong to politically aware groups and apathetic when they belong to politically indifferent ones. (McClosky and Dahlgren, 1959, p. 758)

Many of these findings derive from the sociological focus of Columbia's Bureau of Applied Social Research, which generated *The People's Choice* (Lazarsfeld, Berelson, and Gaudet, 1944), *Voting* (Berelson, Lazarsfeld, and McPhee, 1954), and *Public Opinion and Congressional Elections* (McPhee and Glaser, 1962), and which stimulated replications in the United Kingdom, *Straight Fight* (Milne and Mackenzie, 1954), *How People Vote* (Benney, Gray, and Pear, 1956), and *Marginal Seat* (Milne and Mackenzie, 1958). Since 1959 the emergence of the field of political socialization has added to our knowledge of the impact of family and peer groups on behavior (e.g., Hyman, 1959; Greenstein, 1965; Easton and Dennis, 1969; Hess and Torney, 1967; Jennings and Niemi, 1974; and Sears in Vol. 2 of this *Handbook*).

The role of primary groups is so well known that additional examples are superfluous. Less often noted are the effects of *secondary groups* and the *community* on our behavior, or what Ennis (1962) has termed "the contextual dimension in voting." One of the most intriguing concepts from this tradition of research is the concept of the *breakage effect,* a term Berelson borrowed from horse racing circles. Berelson, Lazarsfeld, and McPhee observed (1954, p. 100) that people who are cross-pressured tend to resolve their conflict by voting with the community majority. For example, in Elmira, New York, if people whose friends and coworkers were 2:1 Republican, the vote divided three-fourths Republican. But if they were divided 2:1 Democratic, only half voted Democratic. The "breakage" for the Republicans reflected the party's dominance in Elmira at that time: "... the Republicans get more than their random share of the adjustment to a conflicting environment, because of the pervasive Republican atmosphere of Elmira that thus tends to perpetuate itself. The surrounding majority gets the benefit of the operation of cross-pressures" (Berelson, Lazarsfeld, and McPhee, 1954, p. 100).

Butler and Stokes used the breakage effect to explain why, in English elections, the greater the proportion of a social class in a constituency, the more politically homogeneous is that class (1969, p. 146). Tingsten had first observed this phenomenon and labeled it "the law of the social centre of gravity" (1937, pp. 177–180, 230). Valen and Katz (1964, p. 149) and Katz and Eldersveld (1961, p. 13) confirmed what they termed this "clustering" effect. Apparently, when it is numerically dominant, a group has more success in reinforcing the political behavior of its members (cf. Putnam, 1966). In addition, Butler and Stokes also found that a clustering or breakage effect explained the anomaly of uniform national election swings in the United Kingdom (1969, pp. 303ff). One might presume, for example, that a national swing of one out of every five normally Conservative voters to Labour would result in very large percentage losses in heavy Conservative constituencies and small losses in dominant Labour constituencies where there would be few normally Conservative votes to gain. In fact, however, there tended to be uniform party swings across constituencies regardless of the previous balance of party supporters. Butler and Stokes explain the uniform losses by noting that the breakage effect tends to offset the extraordinary losses that a party might expect to incur in those constituencies where its dominance would otherwise provide a large pool of potential defectors.

In sum, the primary and secondary groups to which we belong have a major effect on our behavior. It should not surprise us, then, that our actions will oftentimes be more influenced by our perceptions of the attitudes of others than by our own. Indeed, this is what survey research has confirmed, and it cannot be taken as a criticism of surveys that our behavior so often contradicts our beliefs. Given that all of the above findings have been generated from survey evidence, it suggests, quite the contrary, that surveys can be relatively refined techniques for clarifying the complex interrelationships of attitudes and actions.

Do surveys at times measure "non-attitudes"? A final controversy in attitude research is raised by Converse's provocative study, "The Nature of Belief Systems in Mass Publics" (1964). In the course of an essay of considerable scope, Converse examined the question of the degree to which people tend to have stable opinions over time. On what he termed items of "pure affect" (such as party identification is for many people), he expected and found fairly high stability of opinions from 1956 to 1960. On questions that invoked attitude towards groups *qua* groups (e.g., race-related issues such as school desegregation), he found a moderate degree of stability. However, on some policy issues, especially those that were designed to measure political ideologies about the role of the government in social and economic affairs, there tended to be little consistency of responses over time. "Faced with the typical item of this kind, only about 13 out of twenty manage to locate themselves even on the same *side* of the controversy in successive interrogations, when ten out of twenty could have done so by chance alone" (Converse, 1964, p. 239).

Moreover, Converse found a special property in the pattern of attitude stability on this last class of policy issues. The correlation for responses from

1956 to 1958 and from 1958 to 1960 was about .3 in both instances. Thus, one might have expected that the correlation from 1956 to 1960 would not have exceeded .09. In fact, the correlation for 1956–1960 was also .3. One model that would explain such a pattern would be, Converse suggested, a "black–white" distinction in which there might exist "first, a 'hard core' of opinion on a given issue, which is well crystallized and perfectly stable over time. For the remainder of the population [in this hypothetical model], response sequences over time are statistically random" (Converse, 1964, p. 242).

Converse explored a number of attitudes for goodness of fit with this model and found only one—the role of private enterprise and government in housing and electrical power—that fit the model of random change at all well. However, Butler and Stokes (1969, p. 181) found the same pattern of response correlations on the question of British attitudes toward an independent nuclear force. One implication of such findings—that the responses of *some* people to *some* policy items are so random as to properly be called "non-attitudes"—is sufficiently controversial that reinvestigations were inevitable. Converse has explored the issue further in "Attitudes and Non-Attitudes: Continuation of a Dialogue" (1970) and in Volume 4 of this *Handbook*. Pierce and Rose (1974) have examined whether an alternate probability model might not also explain why there appeared to be random responses to some policy items over time.

We will not pass final judgments in the dispute between Converse and Pierce and Rose. The reader is encouraged to make his own. The controversy has served to highlight some cautionary maxims that no one, regardless of his position on the non-attitude controversy, would likely dispute.

First, to pose survey questions of people who have no interest in them is to encourage meaningless, random responses. Thus, Converse notes (1974, p. 651) that the 1956 survey "invited respondents who had no opinions on a particular issue to report that fact directly, instead of laboring to concoct some kind of meaningless data point for us." He suggests that this use of filter questions to weed out random responses ran counter to the trend of that period in which interviewers were trained to probe for responses in order to minimize missing data. The use of such filter questions to ensure that people who do not have opinions on some issue are not asked for an opinion is old and honored advice (Gallup, 1947). Unfortunately, it is too often ignored.

Second, the debate highlights the political situations in which people's opinions are likely to display the most extreme instability across time. Converse took pains to note that instability of responses can occur for two very different reasons: (1) measurement invalidity due to random responses, and (2) real attitude change. In the first case people's responses are unstable because their answers are elicited on topics for which they have no genuine attitudes. In the second case real attitudes are in flux because the level of politics has become sufficiently heated that people reexamine their beliefs.

There is no easy way to distinguish between instability due to random factors and that due to genuine attitude change. Therefore, in order to test his "black–white" model, Converse had to choose from a limited set of items in a special period in history for which he could assume that observed response instability was not due to attitude change. The 1956–1960 period of American politics was one of those quiescent times in which there were few political events that excited people to reflect on their political beliefs. In addition, Converse had to select a *type* of issue on which people's attitudes, if they had them, were relatively settled. By choosing the ideological issue of the role of the state in housing and electrical power, Converse could assume that there was little real attitude change on such a question. In short, Converse never assumed that his "black–white" model with its somewhat elitist implications would apply to more than a restricted type of issue—and then only in particular historical periods. Therefore, Converse's example probably represents a limiting case for the existence of "non-attitudes."

By making explicit the exceptional conditions in which the "black–white" model applies, our attention is focused on the conditions that produce the maximal response instability due to genuine attitude change as opposed to random "non-attitudes." The period would be one in which politics reaches a peak of political intensity for ordinary citizens, and the items would tap issues that had only recently emerged as salient. The late 1960s and early 1970s are obviously such a period in American politics, particularly on the questions of civil disorder and the Vietnam war. We might well assume that anyone who maintained perfectly stable attitudes on these issues during this period was either the most rigid of true believers or oblivious to the world around him.

Bibliography on Measurement and Scaling

The literature on attitude measurement and scaling is both voluminous and arcane; an analysis of it would require another chapter of this length and would be redundant, given that so many specialists have devoted themselves to the task (for example, Scott, 1968). We will merely suggest a small number of works that will prove helpful to the political scientist who wishes an introduction to the field.

To construct an opinion item is to assume, implicitly or explicitly, a theory of attitude measurement. Three recent collections of readings present selections from the classics of attitude theory and measurement: *Readings in Attitude Theory and Measurement* (Fishbein, 1967); *Attitude Measurement* (Summers, 1970); and *Scaling: A Sourcebook for Behavioral Scientists* (Maranell, 1974). The following works also clarify the links between methods of measurement and scaling and the attitude theories the methods assume: *Techniques of Attitude Scale Construction* (Edwards, 1957); *Theory and Methods of Scaling*

(Torgerson, 1958); *A Theory of Data* (Coombs, 1964); and *Political Research* (Leege and Francis, 1974).

Equally important are several compendia of scales describing measures for almost every concept from anomie to xenophobia. By the use of existing measures, one can take advantage of others' work on the validity and reliability of measures and contribute to the comparability of findings. Bonjean, Hill, and McLemore's *Sociological Measurement* (1967), Shaw and Wright's *Scales for the Measurement of Attitudes* (1967), and Miller's *Handbook of Research Design and Social Measurement* (1970) are useful collections, as are three other works produced under the auspices of the Institute for Social Research of the University of Michigan: *Measures of Political Attitudes* (Robinson, Rusk, and Head, 1968), *Measures of Social Psychological Attitudes* (Robinson and Shaver, 1969), and *Measures of Occupational Attitudes and Occupational Characteristics* (Robinson, Athanasiou, and Head, 1969).

Finally, we should note the work of a Social Science Research Council committee, whose mandate it is to encourage the standardization of background items in surveys. The SSRC Center for Coordination of Research on Social Indicators has convened a working committee for the purpose, chaired by Philip Converse, which has reached agreement on a model set of background items and coding procedures for a number of items including (in its preliminary version) age, sex, marital status, color-race, ethnicity, religion, education, employment status, occupation, income, political party preference, and residential characteristics (SSRC, *Social Indicators Newsletter,* May 1974, p. 2). The widespread use of such standardized items promises great improvements in the precision of estimates of the reliability of background measures.

SURVEY RESEARCH: FOR WHAT PURPOSES?

We have concluded our examination of the types of belief and behavior that surveys typically explore; we turn now to the varied purposes that surveys serve. Without ambiguity we can easily distinguish four very different uses of surveys: basic research, public policy analysis, political electioneering, and commercial profit. In our discussion we will give examples of surveys that were inspired by each goal. Our principal argument, however, is that there has been a fortunate compatibility among the research, policy, and commercial uses of surveys. Perhaps among all the techniques commonly used in social science, none approaches survey research in the degree to which the development of the method is simultaneously tied to each of these different needs.

The Fusion of Research and Policy Interests

The history of survey methodology illustrates the close connection between the research and the policy interests of those who pioneered the development of surveys. The distinctive policy concerns of the innovators are evidenced in each of four major periods of the method's growth.

Period 1: The social survey movement. In an earlier discussion we observed that the origins of modern survey research are the social surveys of the nineteenth century. It was in these surveys that respondents, the urban poor, were first selected on a sampling basis (Parten, 1950, p. 9). The immediate goal of the surveys was an accurate description of the conditions of the poor in major industrial cities. As we noted, however, this knowledge was to serve different purposes. Some investigators were clearly concerned with stimulating social legislation that would ameliorate conditions for the urban poor. Others seemed primarily concerned with the threat to social order posed by a discontented lower class. Our only point is to restate that these initial social surveys were motivated by the policy concerns of the researchers.

Period 2: The Depression years. Just as the plight of the urban poor led to the nineteenth century social surveys, the depression of the 1930s created an immediate need for accurate data on the social and economic problems caused by massive unemployment. The survey technique was an obvious means of collecting the data, and numerous studies, supported both privately and publicly, were commissioned to study the depression's consequences for American life. As we shall see, the opportunity to investigate these problems attracted the attention of people who were to make, in the course of their data collections, important contributions to survey methodology.

1. United States federal agencies were one such stimulus to substantive and methodological research in the 1930s. Stephan (1948) presents a comprehensive list of the statistical surveys sponsored by federal agencies during the New Deal. Many provided detailed information where none previously existed. Limiting ourselves simply to the *national* surveys, the list includes: The Financial Survey of Urban Housing (1934), The Study of Consumer Purchases (1935–1936), The National Health Survey of 1935–1936, The Continuous Work History Sample, and The 1937 Enumerative Census of Unemployment.

As Stephan observes (1948, p. 27), these surveys clearly reflect their origins in the depression. Beyond the need for data on depression life, the surveys were conducted by personnel who were hired as part of the federal program to create public jobs for unemployed white-collar workers. As a consequence of this last fact, these surveys tended to be crude. The costs of supervising relief personnel discouraged intensive analysis and limited survey designs to those that could be executed by people with relatively little training. Thus, these surveys, as significant as they were, did not usually take advantage of the more efficient sampling procedures that were being developed at that time in several federal agencies.

Even though many of these depression-period surveys did make use of unreliable or inefficient sampling designs, researchers in several federal agencies were at work formulating the complex, multistage sample designs that have since become the recommended procedures for minimizing sampling error and cost. Beginning in 1936 the Research Division of the Bureau of the Census began a study of sampling procedures that led Frederick Stephan, William Deming, and Morris Hansen to develop the five-percent sample in time for use in the 1940 census. In addition to Hansen, Lester Frankel and William Hurwitz were among the important sampling theoreticians actively involved in the Bureau of the Census in the late 1930s and early 1940s.

The Works Progress Administration (WPA) was itself an active research site on sampling problems in the depression years. Lester Frankel was Chief of the Sampling Section of the WPA from 1936 to 1942. The Research Division of the WPA investigated methods of conducting surveys of unemployment, initiating a monthly nationwide survey in 1939. Enlarged and transferred to the Bureau of the Census in 1942, it developed into the Monthly Survey of the Labor Force (Stephan, 1948).

2. Private foundations were a second stimulus to methodological research, working in concert with federal agencies to refine survey techniques and to generate survey data so essential to the policy needs of depression agencies. Indeed, during this period the cooperation of public and private organizations was so extensive that the distinction between public and private sponsorship of research almost loses its meaning. Foremost among the private agencies fostering research on public problems was the Social Science Research Council, incorporated in 1924 and composed of constituent organizations representing American professional associations of social scientists and statisticians.

Throughout the 1930s the SSRC supported committees that focused on depression policy problems. One, The Committee on Government Statistics and Information Services (cosponsored by the American Statistical Association), conducted a thorough analysis of the adequacy of federal statistics and recommended procedures for the coordination of data collection through the auspices of the Central Statistical Board, which had been established by Executive Order on 27 July 1933, "to effect coordination of the statistical services . . . incident to the purposes of the National Industrial Recovery Act" (Social Science Research Council, 1937, p. 8). Stuart A. Rice, perhaps the "father" of quantitative techniques in political science, was acting chairman of the SSRC committee in 1933.

Still another SSRC committee, The Committee on Studies in Social Aspects of the Depression, produced under the direction of Samuel A. Stouffer a remarkable series of 13 monographs, including a study of depression family life by Stouffer and Lazarsfeld (1937) and an analysis of relief policies by White and White (1937). Of these, Stouffer and Lazarsfeld's study of family life is distinctive for its summary of existing social survey data from several countries.

Another example of the symbiosis of the public policy needs and private research efforts is a series of four works on Negro youth in the depression, sponsored by the American Youth Commission of the American Council on Education. St. Clair Drake sets these studies in context:

> Hundreds of thousands of American youth were unemployed, and the number of Negroes among them was greatly out of the expected proportion. The New Deal had established a National Youth Administration (NYA) and a Civilian Conservation Corps (CCC) to provide emergency employment, but both educators and government officials were concerned over the long-term welfare of the nation's young people. (About 200,000 Negro youth served in the CCC between 1933 and 1939.) The American Council on Education organized an American Youth Commission to conduct research and to recommend action . . . The key question selected for study was, "What are the effects upon the personality development of Negro youth of their membership in a minority racial group?" *

Four volumes compose this series: Allison Davis and John Dollard's *Children of Bondage: The Personality Development of Negro Youth in the Urban South* (1964; orig. pub., 1940), E. Franklin Frazier's *Negro Youth at the Crossways: Their Personality Development in the Middle States* (1940), Charles S. Johnson's *Growing Up in the Black Belt: Negro Youth in the Rural South* (1967; orig. pub. 1941), and W. Lloyd Warner, Buford H. Junker, and Walter A. Adams's *Color and Human Nature: Negro Personality Development in a Northern City* (1941). In addition to these volumes, all of which are based on original research, Ira DeA. Reid prepared a summary volume on previously available knowledge of Negro youth, *In a Minor Key: Negro Youth in Story and Fact* (1940). Donald Sutherland summarized the major findings of the series and recommended a program of educational and social planning in *Color, Class, and Personality* (1942).

Two aspects of this series attract the interests of the historian of surveys. First, it provides some of the earliest survey evidence on the life and attitudes of American blacks and thus stands as an important baseline for measures of change. Of particular interest is Johnson's study of black youth in the South. As Drake notes in his introduction to *Growing Up in the Black Belt*, Fisk University (where Johnson taught) "had the precise data at hand needed for scientific sampling within the Black Belt, something no other institution except the University of North Carolina had" (Johnson, 1967, p. xiii). Johnson selected eight counties as sampling sites, including two with traditional plantation agriculture, two in declining plantation areas, one near the city of Memphis,

---

* Reprinted by permission of Schocken Books Inc. from the Introduction by St. Claire Drake to *Growing Up in the Black Belt* by Charles S. Johnson. Copyright © 1967 by Schocken Books Inc.

and another in which Negroes competed with white farmers in a nonplantation setting. In school classrooms, more than 2000 youths completed several highly structured questionnaires measuring personal attitudes, attitudes toward race, and I.Q. [As Johnson states (1967, p. 334), "I.Q. is used in this study as an indicator of the effects of cultural and educational differences between children assumed to be essentially the same (as groups) in inherent capacity."] These tests were followed by intensive interviews with about 20 percent of the sample and with interviews of parents in 916 families. In short, Johnson's survey was an early example of a complex and sophisticated design.

The other books in this series are also important works, but they are not, strictly speaking, surveys. Davis and Dollard's *Children of Bondage* (1964) is based on intensive case interviews of 30 adolescents interviewed several times a week over a period of four to seven months, supplemented with additional interviews with other black adolescents for insights into methods of child-rearing and attitudes toward whites. Similarly, Frazier's study (1940) is, in large part, a case study approach based on neither structured schedules nor rigorous sampling procedures. Nonetheless, though they lacked the trappings of surveys, these latter works provided informative, early insights into the attitudes of Negro youth in the United States. In fact, the potential of these early studies as measures of change did not escape notice. Almost 20 years after Davis and Dollard had intensively interviewed their sample of black adolescents, a research team returned to study these same individuals, who were by then in their middle age. As Rohrer and Edmonson describe the goal of their work, *The Eighth Generation*:

> We wished not only to discover what had happened to the "Children of Bondage," but also to find out whether they were perpetuating in their relations with their own children the methods by which they themselves had been trained. (Rohrer and Edmonson, 1960, p. 5)

Second, the books in this series are notable for the opportunities they afforded black scholars. Johnson, Frazier, Adams, and Davis are black scholars who produced numerous books before and after those in this series; their staffs were largely black as well. Johnson built Fisk University into an important center for the study of Negro life and later served as its president.

In sum, the depression years in the United States offer a wealth of examples for our argument that the methodology of survey research developed in a context in which policy needs and basic research were knit together. This is perhaps most clearly illustrated in the important advances that were made in sampling theory by scholars working within New Deal action agencies and the Bureau of the Census. The connection of policy and research goals is evident, as well, in the number of government surveys that provided basic data on the impact of the depression on American life. Finally, we note close cooperation between government and private organizations such as the Social Science Research Council and the American Youth Commission that contributed so much to illuminating aspects of American society about which we had previously been so ignorant. Yet, as distinctive as we might regard the depression years in these respects, the onset of World War II simply presented a new category of policy problems for public officials. As we shall see, survey methodology flourished in the next decade, again largely due to the efforts of social scientists working within federal agencies.

Period 3: World war and cold war. As Sheatsley observes (1963), the official use of United States public opinion data began in 1939 with the establishment of the Division of Program Surveys in the Department of Agriculture. Under the direction of Rensis Likert, the division became a center for the development of survey research techniques. For example, under the tutelage of J. Steven Stock, the division developed the Master Sample of Agriculture in 1943, which divided the rural United States into a grid of small sampling units making possible the efficient, repeated selection of many samples from this single sampling frame (Kish, 1965b, p. 478). Likert himself became a central figure in a controversy over his advocacy of the more frequent use of fixed question-free answer items and of the use of batteries of items to form scales and indexes to avoid reliance on single questions. In an article with the self-explanatory title, "The Controversy over Detailed Interviews—An Offer for Negotiation," Lazarsfeld (1944) made the now conventional argument that both closed and open questions have their appropriate place in interview schedules.

After the bombing of Pearl Harbor, other federal agencies began to call on the expertise of the Division of Program Surveys. Dorwin Cartwright, then a staff member, conducted research for the Treasury Department on people's motives for buying and redeeming war bonds, information that was critical to guiding policy on war and postwar inflation control (Cartwright, 1950, p. 55). On the basis of its survey, Cartwright predicted that the rate of bond redemption in 1946 would fall between $4.5 and $6.3 billion and was rewarded with an actual result almost in the center of the interval, $5.4 billion.

Cartwright's study of bond redemption was merely one of many studies of civilian attitudes and behavior conducted by the Division of Program Surveys. But the Division was not first into the field. D. Caradog Jones (n.d.) reminds us that military purposes prompted the first great English survey—in this case, by William the Conqueror in 1086. The survey is known as Domesday "because it was accepted as a faithful record of facts as they were when it was compiled, and no appeal was allowed against its witness in a court of law" (Jones, p. 15). Jones makes the important point that governments making war must know the resources of their citizens.

> But the main purpose of nearly all, if not all, nationwide surveys, undertaken by official direction in different parts of the world in early times, has been to ascertain man-power for waging war and to make an assessment of other resources, in cash or kind, available to fill the coffers of the ruling Sovereign and his Government or those dependent upon them.

This was true of the Domesday Survey. Weak kings had collected tribute (Danegeld) from their people to bribe the Danes from attacking their realms. Others had used the money they collected to arm their soldiers to defend themselves against attack. The more systematic William the Conquerer determined to make a thorough examination of his resources, and to discover incidentally what taxes he could exact from his estates for his own ends. (Jones, n.d., p. 15)

Though far less avaricious than William, the wartime staff of the Division of Program Surveys was no less energetic and quite a bit more expert at surveys. The staff reads as a *Who's Who* of innovators in survey research methods. Besides Cartwright, Likert, and Stock, there were Angus Campbell, Charles Cannell, W. G. Cochran, Richard Crutchfield, Dwight Chapman, Roe Goodman, Herbert Hyman, George Katona, Daniel Katz, Leslie Kish, David Krech, John Lansing, John Riley, David Truman, and Julian Woodward. With war's end support for the division waned. Confronted by a cut in budget support, Likert, Campbell, Cannell, Katona, and Kish left the division to establish the Survey Research Center at the University of Michigan and were later joined by Cartwright and Lansing (Institute for Social Research, *Newsletter*, Winter 1971). One wonders if academic research ever profited more by a slash in a government budget.

The Division of Program Studies was only the first of several agencies conducting survey research on wartime policy problems. In 1942 the Office of War Information established a Surveys Division under the direction of Elmo C. Wilson, which conducted over 100 studies of civilian attitudes on wartime problems (Sheatsley, 1963). Hyman, Katz, Riley, and Woodward, in an agency personnel shuffle that was to become typical, joined other survey research experts such as Hazel Erskine Gaudet and Helen Dinerman at the Office of War Information.

Just as the Survey Research Center was linked in origin with the Division of Program Surveys, so too was there a close connection between the Office of War Information and the fledgling National Opinion Research Center. NORC had been established at the University of Denver in 1941 as the first nonprofit, university-affiliated research center with national survey facilities (Sheatsley, 1968). During those first lean years, NORC sustained its academic research program by conducting surveys for the federal government. All of the field work for the *national* surveys of the Office of War Information was in fact conducted under the direction of Paul Sheatsley of NORC. Hyman joined Sheatsley at NORC in 1947, when the center moved to its present home at the University of Chicago.

In 1944 Likert became director of a new agency, the Morale Division of The United States Strategic Bombing Survey. The USSBS had as its mandate a determination of the "direct and indirect effects of bombing upon the attitudes, behavior and health of the [bombed] civilian population, with particular reference to its effect upon the willingness and capacity of the bombed population to give effective and continued support to the German [and Japanese] war effort" (United States Strategic Bombing Survey, 1947a, vol. 1, p. iv). The following analysis of the survey's findings on the effects of the bombing is adapted largely from Hyman's "Misguided Bombs" (1972a).

The Strategic Bombing Survey consisted of many divisions (for example, an Overall Economic Effects Division was directed by J. K. Galbraith), but we shall limit our discussion to the work of the Morale Division. Towns to be sampled were selected from the cumulative records of the British and American air forces. Using an experimental design, the cities and towns were classified in terms of the nature and severity of the bombing raids to which they had been exposed. In Germany 34 places were chosen to represent communities that had been exposed to no bombing at all, or to "light," "medium," or "heavy" bombing. About 4000 German civilians were interviewed in June and July 1945. In Japan some 60 sample points were similarly chosen, and about 3200 civilians were interviewed in Japanese by military personnel of Japanese ancestry in November and December 1945. The core of the questions dealt with wartime morale—the sense of weariness, defeatism, willingness to surrender, confidence in leadership, patterns of behavior at work and at home—as well as direct questions on experiences and feelings about the bombing.

Given the difficulties of conducting surveys in wartorn foreign countries, the surveys were remarkably well done (as one might expect of a staff that included Likert, Crutchfield, Cartwright, Cochran, Hyman, Katz, Krech, Truman, Gabriel Almond, Howard Longstaff, and Helen Peak). For example, in Germany the survey results were validated by official German documents, samples of civilian mail captured during the war, questionnaires filled out by displaced foreign workers who had experienced bombing in Germany, and interrogation of French escapees and key informants, especially community leaders. Helen Peak's study (1945) of the number and characteristics of Nazi party members stands as simply one example of the care with which bombing survey findings were checked for validity by comparison with such other sources as official German ministerial records.

That bombing was a horrible experience and reduced morale cannot be doubted. Many Germans described the bombing as a great hardship, the source of their weariness with the war, and the basis for their belief that the war was lost. Many reported severe emotional upset and intense fear, some saying that they could not talk about it to the interviewers despite a long passage of time.

As clear as the evidence is that the bombing of civilians terribly depressed their morale, the evidence is also stark that the *prolongation and expansion* of bombing did not serve the Allies' goals. To quote the official report, "The greatest rate of decline in morale tends to occur between unbombed towns and those subjected to total average bombing of about 500 tons. There is some further decline when bombing is stepped up to 6000 tons. There is very little change or, in some cases, slight improvement in morale as a result of increasing bombing up to 30,000 tons" (United States Strategic Bombing Survey, 1947a, vol. 1, p. 22).

Feelings of despair were intense even among people living in *unbombed* towns. The degree of difference in willingness to surrender between those living in bombed cities and those living in unbombed cities was only six percent. Why? "All of the unbombed communities had repeated alerts and many expected that sooner or later they would be the target. Moreover these people had heard much about the devastating consequences of raids from the evacuees in their midst" (United States Strategic Bombing Survey, 1947a, vol. 1, p. 16). If one is intent on bombing civilians, it is not necessary to bomb everyone nor to bomb them with furious intensity.

In Japan, where the total tonnage of bombs was less than in Germany but the toll in destruction and lives far greater, the results were very similar to the German findings. Those with no personal experience with the bombing had only slightly higher morale; repeated personal exposure almost never produced any further decline in morale. Here we do not allude to the effects of the atomic bombs on Hiroshima and Nagasaki, which were so manifestly horrible and were the subject of a separate study (United States Strategic Bombing Survey, 1946).

When evaluated together the bombing surveys of Germany and Japan provide an extraordinarily complete and sophisticated analysis of a range of social and psychological effects induced by civilian bombing. Indeed the research is so persuasive that it underlines a terrible irony regarding the use of massive bombing of North Vietnam by the United States. By 1972 the tonnage of bombs dropped on Vietnam more than doubled the amount dropped on Germany and Japan together, even though Japan alone encompasses a larger area than all of Vietnam and includes twice as many people. Why the authorities made the decision to bomb North Vietnam so intensely despite the prior evidence that heavy bombing serves no purpose in terms of civilian morale is a question that begs for an answer. It is unlikely that those who were responsible for formulating the North Vietnam bombing policy had no one to remind them of the evidence that the government had previously gathered with such care. Among the officers of the Strategic Bombing Survey were Paul H. Nitze and George W. Ball, both of whom were officials in Lyndon Johnson's administration who became disenchanted with the United States policy in Vietnam.

Halberstam (1973) attributes the bombing policy in part to the influence of such key figures as Walter Rostow in the Kennedy and Johnson administrations.

Perhaps all men tend to be frozen in certain attitudes which have been shaped by important experiences in their formative years; for young Rostow, one of the crucial experiences had been picking bombing targets in Europe. It had been a stirring time, a time when he was of great service to his country. He had believed in strategic bombing, in the vital, all-important role it played in bringing victory during World War II, that it had broken the back of the German war machine. His enthusiasm for bombing and for his own role had allowed him to withstand all the subsequent intelligence of the *U.S. Strategic Bombing Survey* . . . (Halberstam, 1973, pp. 199–200)

In sum, the bombing surveys are remarkably candid reports by a government agency of a government excess. (The candor is attributable in part, no doubt, to the fact that the Strategic Bombing Survey was a semi-autonomous agency reporting directly to the president.) The decision to undertake the studies reflects the government's confidence that surveys could contribute importantly to the formulation of public policy. The Vietnam bombing policy stands as a mocking counterexample of the failure of a government to utilize the information it had displayed such foresight in obtaining.

The Strategic Bombing Survey was not the last series of United States government-sponsored surveys in western Europe. When the wartime surveys were completed in the fall of 1945, some of their personnel became available to the Information Control Division of the Office of Military Government, U.S. (OMGUS). As an alien occupation force in Germany, OMGUS confronted numerous policy problems, including general issues such as the attitudes of Germans toward the Allied occupation and denazification programs, and specific problems associated with food rationing, refugees and expellees, currency reform, acceptance of a divided Germany, and the blockade of Berlin. Merritt and Merritt (1970) provide a good summary and analysis of these important OMGUS surveys.

Even with the promulgation of the Federal Republic in September 1949, the United States government remained interested in German political attitudes. The Opinion Survey Section within OMGUS became the Reactions Analysis Staff of the U.S. High Commissioner for Germany (HICOG), which from 1949 until 1955 conducted many more surveys. (Unfortunately, to our knowledge these latter surveys have never been published.)

With the realization of the value of such surveys for guiding public policy in West Germany, the United States Information Agency became a major survey sponsor, commissioning more than 20 surveys in Great Britian, France, Italy, and West Germany. Selected items from these surveys, as well as discussions of the substantive and methodological issues they pose, are presented by Merritt and Puchala (1968). The western European surveys are, of course, only a subset of those produced by a worldwide United States Information Agency survey program. Many of these surveys are available for secondary analysis from the Roper Public Opinion Research Center.

The responsibilities of the several survey organizations operating within the federal government during World War II were rather clearly demarcated. The role of the survey divisions of the Department of Agriculture and the Office of War Information was the assessment of domestic opinion within the United States. The United States Strategic Bombing Survey measured opinion among the civilian citizens of Germany and Japan. Finally, we come to the fourth important survey center within the federal government, the Research Branch in the Information and Education Division of the War Department. The focus of this unit was the study of the social psychology of American soldiers themselves. In collected form these studies became the landmark four volume work *The American Soldier: Studies in Social Psychology in World War II* by Samuel Stouffer and a long list of illustrious associates (1949–1950). Stouffer was the director of the professional staff of the Research Branch, which consisted of two principal analytical sections: a Survey Section headed in 1943–1944 by Leonard S. Cottrell, Jr., and an Experimental Section headed by Carl I. Hovland.

Stouffer's initial chapter provides an interesting history of the decision of the War Department to utilize survey research in the formation of policy toward the treatment of military personnel. Stouffer points to three direct results of their research that had particularly important policy consequences. One was the order with which military units would be demobilized after the defeat of Germany. Though the war with Japan was still to end, the conclusion of the war in Europe made it possible to release several million men. But who? And in what order that would not depress the morale of those who had to continue the war in the Asian theater? President Roosevelt accepted a plan by which soldiers would be released in order of their accumulation of a certain number of points computed from such factors as length of service, time overseas, combat experience, and parenthood. Roosevelt justified this demobilization plan on the ground that the order of release was determined by the preferences of the soldiers themselves. The idea for this point system had been conceived in the Research Branch, Stouffer notes, on the basis of its sample surveys of personnel stationed throughout the world (Stouffer *et al.*, 1949, vol. 1, p. 7; and vol. 2, ch. 11).

A second important policy decision influenced by the surveys of the Research Branch was the level of funding for the proposed GI bill. The Research Branch undertook a series of studies to estimate how many soldiers would go back to college if the bill were drafted to include such aid. Stouffer notes that the survey predictions provided policymakers with a figure that proved to be correct within two or three percentage points (Stouffer *et al.*, 1949, vol. 1, p. 7; vol. 2, ch. 13; and vol. 4, chs. 15–16).

Third, in collaboration with the Neuropsychiatric Division of the Surgeon General's Office, the Research Branch developed a short form of a psychoneurotic inventory that was routinely administered in United States induction stations. Though the inventory was inevitably a crude test, it did predict to a degree the propensity of soldiers for psychiatric and other nonbattle casualties (Stouffer *et al.,* 1949, vol. 1, p. 8; and vol. 2, ch. 1). In a similar fashion the Branch, working with the Adjutant General's Office, constructed tests of aptitudes and abilities for use in the assignment of soldiers to military units (Stouffer *et al.,* 1949, vol. 1, p. 8, and ch. 7).

Finally, we might speculate, though Stouffer did not, on a fourth consequence of the work of the Research Branch. The troops of World War II fought essentially in a Jim Crow army. Although the Selective Service Act of 1940 provided that "there shall be no discrimination against any person on account of race or color," Roosevelt concurred with a War Department policy against integrating regiments on the grounds that integration "would produce situations destructive to morale and detrimental to the preparation for national defense" (John P. Davis, 1966, p. 627). Not only were units segregated but also a much higher proportion of black troops were assigned to service units than to combat duty, in contrast to white troops.

Black spokesmen were incensed at the policy of troop segregation and made numerous calls for the army to integrate. By the end of 1944, casualties of the Battle of the Bulge had created a shortage of infantry riflemen in the European Theater of Operations. The army decided to take this opportunity to experiment with assigning black volunteers to all black combat platoons that would fight within integrated companies. (The response of the black troops was so enthusiastic that three thousand black volunteers had to be turned away [Dalfiume, 1969, p. 99].)

In 1946 "a board of officers charged with reviewing the facts [concerning Negroes in combat] concluded that all-Negro divisions gave the poorest performance of Negro troops, but spoke favorably of the performance of Negro Infantry platoons fighting in white companies" (Stouffer *et al.,* 1949, vol. 1, p. 586). The Gillem report, named for the board's chief officer, became, of course, an exceedingly controversial document. As it happened the Research Branch in Europe had made a separate study of the reactions of white soldiers to this experiment to integrate combat companies, which Shirley Star details in *The American Soldier* (Stouffer 1949, vol. 1, pp. 586ff). The research showed that whites fighting in companies with Negro platoons were much more favorable to integrated companies than soldiers who fought in segregated companies. As Star concludes:

When we note that the proportion of men having no experience with mixed companies who say "they would dislike the arrangement very much" is almost exactly the same (62 percent) as the two thirds proportion of white enlisted men in mixed companies who were previously noted as reporting retroactively that they were initially opposed to the idea [but came to favor it], we can get some conception of the revolution in attitudes that took place among these men as a result of enforced contacts. (Stouffer *et al.,* 1949, vol. 1, pp. 595–596)

Whether the Research Branch study had a significant effect on subsequent policy decisions is uncertain. Major General F. H. Osburn, Chief of the Information and Education Division (which included the Research Branch) and General Benjamin O. Davis (the American armed forces' first black general) wanted the Research Branch survey made public (Nichols, 1954, p. 70; and Dalfiume, 1969, p. 100). However, opponents within the army feared that publication might lose support for the peacetime draft proposal among southern senators and would encourage demands by black organizations for further experiments in integration. Dalfiume concludes:

Those who preferred the *status quo* won. As soon as the war in Europe came to an end, the Negro platoons were unceremoniously detached from their white units and either returned to all-Negro service units or discharged. Although the Negro platoons appeared to be forgotten by the War Department, the few who believed that integration was the solution to efficient utilization of manpower continued to remember this experience as proof that they were right. (Dalfiume, 1969, p. 100)

On 26 July 1948, President Truman issued his well-known executive order 9981 requiring "equal treatment and opportunity for all persons in the armed services" (not necessarily integration) and creating the Fahy Committee, which in its reports to the president hammered at the gaps between the Presidential proclamation and armed forces practice (John P. Davis, 1966, pp. 52ff).

In addition to the substantive contributions of the Research Branch to public policy and social psychological theory, Stouffer's *The American Soldier* (1949–1950) also testifies to the important methodological work the Branch supported. The most important contribution was undoubtedly to scaling theory. Expanding on an idea that he had previously published in 1940, Louis Guttman developed at the Research Branch the method of attitude scaling that bears his name (Stouffer, 1949, vol. 4, p. 5). Similarly, Paul Lazarsfeld, a consultant to the Research Branch, began his own development of the technique for scaling attitudes known as latent structure analysis.

The importance of the studies that comprise *The American Soldier* reflects the abilities of the experts that guided its work. *The American Soldier* includes a long list of the personnel and consultants of the Branch. A partial and more or less arbitrary list of those who were then or have since become important figures within survey research includes, in addition to Cottrell, Hovland, and Stouffer, such staff members as M. Brewster Smith, Arnold Rose, Shirley Star,

Edward Suchman, and Robin Williams, Jr., and such consultants as Hadley Cantril, John Dollard, Louis Guttman, Philip Hauser, Irving Janis, Paul Lazarsfeld, Rensis Likert, Quinn McNemar, Robert Merton, Frederick Mosteller, and Frank Stanton.

In summary, our purpose in our review of the initial three stages in the development of survey research is to emphasize that its growth took place in an environment that inextricably mixed policy and scholarly interests. Scholars and the policy programs of the federal government nurtured one another. For survey research the payoff was counted in several coins: public support of substantive research, encouragement of advances in measurement, statistics, and sampling theory so necessary to survey work, and support given to the growth of a large pool of experts who subsequently left government service to people the research centers of universities. Public policy decisions benefited, in turn, from the availability of basic information on the attitudes and socioeconomic conditions of citizens in the United States and other countries.

The concluding list of prominent scholars who worked in the Research Branch reflects the shared policy goals of scholars and public officials during World War II and stands as a pointed contrast to the relative lack of academic survey experts in the Korean and Vietnam wars. Indeed, outside of the Bureau of the Census, the Bureau of Labor Statistics, and the National Center for Health Statistics, there exist at present no major centers for survey research within agencies of the United States government in any policy field.

It would be wrong, however, to observe the dearth of governmental survey research centers and conclude that the banquet years of surveys for policy applications are on their final course. The site of the feast has simply moved from the agencies of government to the survey research centers of the universities. The postwar period, then, represents a new phase in the fusion of basic research and policy analysis.

Period 4: The postwar years. As Alice Rivlin (1971, p. 9) has noted, "The distribution of social problems has been illuminated by two important technical developments. The first is the improvement and wider use of sample survey techniques. The second is the astonishing increase in the data processing capacity of computers." In her *Systematic Thinking for Social Action* (1971), Rivlin devotes few words to computer analysis, but her review of the policy implications of surveys is perhaps the best discussion of the issue. Because the total number of policy surveys is so large, it is a hopeless task to discuss them all. Therefore, we will take refuge in the limits that Rivlin drew for herself, the subjects of welfare, education, and health; we will rather arbitrarily exclude other fields in the delivery of governmental services.

1. *The Survey of Economic Opportunity.* A special census survey conducted for the Office of Economic Opportunity, the Survey of Economic Opportunity (SEO) stands as an important exception to our argument that most policy

surveys of the postwar years have been conducted by university survey centers. When the war on poverty was being considered in 1963, the government had little data on how many people were poor, who they were, or where they were located. Lacking this important information, the Council of Economic Advisors somewhat arbitrarily selected $3000 as a poverty line for family income (Rivlin, 1971, pp. 10, 29–34).

The SEO, conducted in 1966 and 1967, provided the missing information. The sample consisted of two separate frames: One was a national sample of about 18,000 drawn according to procedures of the continuing Current Population Survey. The second consisted of a supplementary sample of about 12,000 households in areas with a large concentration of nonwhite poor. The same households were surveyed again in 1967, creating a panel design for direct measures of short-term changes in income.

Combined with computer simulations of family earning models, the SEO data allowed policymakers to experiment with different programs in order to judge the costs and benefits of various legislative proposals. *Poverty Amid Plenty,* The Report of the President's Commission on Income Maintenance Programs (The Heineman Commission), used this SEO data to justify the need for new programs on public welfare. Nixon's Family Assistance Plan, submitted in 1969, was the response. Its benefits were directly tied to projections from the SEO (Moynihan, 1973, p. 497).

2. *Negative Income Tax Experiments.* Not all questions can be answered from the projections of simulation models, however. If some form of income maintenance plan such as President Nixon's were adopted, what would be the response of the beneficiaries? Would the social and economic behavior of the recipients change? Would a significant number of people guaranteed $3000 a year quit working? Would fathers that might otherwise desert families remain at home? How many more marriages might take place under this new system of different economic incentives? (Rivlin, 1971, p. 34). Questions such as these require that the circumstances of people's lives actually be changed to see whether their behavior changes. For just this kind of purpose the income maintenance experiments were designed.

Rivlin distinguishes two types of experiments, natural and systematic. By natural experiments she means those that take advantage of a comparison of two situations that *happen* to be similar in all important respects save some critical policy program whose effectiveness is at test. Her examples include comparing school systems with Head Start programs to similar districts that do not have the program. A natural experiment, then, is one similar to the bombing surveys in Germany and Japan, in which the sample of citizens was stratified according to the intensity of the bombing to which their towns had been subjected. But, there were no existing situations where one could exploit a natural experiment on income maintenance effects. Therefore, the Office of Economic Opportunity funded the Institute for Research on Poverty of the

University of Wisconsin to implement a set of income maintenance proposals in a controlled experimental design—first, in Trenton, New Jersey, and successively in a number of other sites.

At this writing the results of the experiments are still being evaluated and debated. (See, for example, Marmor, 1971; and Orr, Hollister, and Lefcowitz, 1971.) Scott and Shore (1974) offer an engaging and self-critical apologia of their role as sociologists in selecting items for inclusion in the survey instruments, in the absence of theory specifying the most pertinent variables for explaining poverty. Nonetheless, we should be charitable toward all such disclaimers. The income maintenance experiments represent one of the first attempts at a strategy revolutionary in its prudence—the testing of proposals in experimental settings prior to their uniform implementation throughout the whole of a system.

3. *Equality of Educational Opportunity Survey* and *Project TALENT*. From Section 402 of the Civil Rights Law of 1964 came the mandate to undertake the *Report on Equality of Educational Opportunity*, popularly known as the Coleman Report (1966). Mosteller and Moynihan (1972, p. 5) describe the survey on which the report was based (the EEOS) as "the second largest social science research project in history." In all the projects surveyed and tested 570,000 pupils and 60,000 teachers, and collected detailed information on 4000 schools. This massive study is exceeded in size only by an earlier survey, Project TALENT, which was conducted by the University of Pittsburgh for the Office of Education (Flanagan *et al.,* 1962).

If the Coleman Report is only second in size, it is first in controversy generated by its policy implications. As Robert Dentler notes:

> More crucially, many of the findings run contrary to the favorite assumptions of three of the most concerned audiences: militant school integrationists, militant school segregationists . . . and the many professional educators who focus their effort too exclusively upon school facilities, curriculum reform, and teacher training. (Quoted in Mosteller and Moynihan, 1972, p. 29)

The outcries from these audiences could have been predicted. Militant integrationists were offended, for example, by the finding that black and white children had nearly comparable school resources within regions. Militant segregationists were incensed at the findings that the quality of black and white schools alike is much poorer in the south than in the north, and that blacks integrated into mostly white schools learn and perform better than blacks attending mostly black schools. Professional educators were angered by the major conclusions of the report—that family background of students has an important effect on student performance and that school facilities and per pupil expenditures have relatively little impact.

Complaints against the Coleman Report are not without grounds. In the first place, the analysis had to proceed quickly; operating under the legal mandate, the survey was completed at the unacademic pace of two years. Thus some conclusions of the Report are weakened by simple mechanical errors in statistical calculations (Smith, 1972). In the second place, for this pathbreaking project, the investigators had to make decisions that the reflections of hindsight would have questioned. Hindsight in this case has materialized in the form of numerous reexaminations of the methods and inferences of the Report (see, for example, Vose, 1967; Rivlin, 1971; Mosteller and Moynihan, 1972; and the series of reviews and articles on the Report in the June 1967 and April 1970 issues of the *American Sociological Review*).

A dominant theme of these criticisms is the call for surveys incorporating systematic experimentation. However, if that conclusion is to be more than cant, we will have to face up to the sensitive political problems that real experiments generate. Parents may be unimpressed by an explanation for a lack of improvement of their child's school facilities, if the explanation is that some school, after all, must be a control group. Many more parents may be equally upset to find their children in an "experimental group." To be sure Donald Campbell (1969) reminds us that randomization is not merely a proper technical procedure but also a democratic rule for allocating the benefits of experiments. However, this is a sophistication likely to be lost on an angry parent. Rivlin's cautionary discussion of the political issues implicit in experimental designs is provocative.

One such call for experimentation raises intriguing questions concerning social research and invasions of privacy. The following statement from Sewell illustrates the dilemma:

> Perhaps the most tragic faults of the survey were due to the administrative decisions apparently made by the Office of Education—decisions which probably seemed expedient at the time but which greatly reduce the current and future usefulness of the research data. Thus, neither school systems nor students were identified so that neither schools, classrooms, principals, teachers, nor students can be selected for further intensive analysis . . . [T]he decision not to tag children means that no true longitudinal study building upon these data will ever be possible. This is unfortunate because it is precisely this kind of information which is so badly needed for determining the future effects of current educational inequalities. (Sewell, 1967, p. 478)

Rivlin as well regrets the cross-sectional nature of the survey, for the problem of explaining what contributes to the development of children is compounded when one is limited to observations at a single point in time. Yet in a study so vast as the EEOS, who is prepared to assume responsibility for abuses of privacy if publicly supported data banks on children and teachers were maintained over time? "Politics," Mr. Dooley reminds us, "ain't bean bag." The sensitivity of the Office of Education to possible charges of invasion of privacy seems entirely understandable.

Finally, we close this note on the Coleman Report with a comment on the consequences of unanticipated, unwanted research findings. Critics of the Coleman Report often wonder why so much effort was made to measure the quality of school facilities relative to aspects of teacher performance. Several answers come to mind. First, it is easier to obtain accurate measures of books in libraries, laboratories, ages of buildings, and per pupil expenditures than it is to assess the qualities that make for good teaching, qualities Rivlin (1971, p. 75) suggests includes a teacher's "sympathy, her sense of humor, or her confidence in her students." Second, school facilities and expenditures are manipulatable, that is, they can be changed by policy decisions. How, in comparison, does one increase a teacher's sympathy for students, confidence in them, humor toward them?

Beyond these points, we are simply reading between the lines of the report. However, it seems plausible that Coleman and his coworkers took particular care to investigate facilities and expenditures because they may have believed that the unequal funding of schools—black and white, north and south—creates unequal educational opportunities and is inherently wrong. But when their survey could not determine important consequences of expenditures on student achievement, they could only accept those findings with honesty and, it seems likely, with regret. The possibility of affecting changes in policy may seem a heady opportunity for an academic. A price is that one must be prepared to accept the unwanted implications of that research.

4. *The National Health Survey.* The health survey program is perhaps sufficiently removed from politics that we can give it briefer notice than the previous three surveys. Prior to 1956 the only illness data collected by the federal government pertained to communicable diseases (Moriyama, 1968). The National Health Survey, begun in 1957, now fills that gap. The survey itself is divided into three separate programs. The *Health Interview Survey* is a continuing nationwide survey of households, soliciting information on the incidence of illnesses and accidents known to the respondents. The *Health Examination Survey* actually conducts diagnostic examinations of sample respondents in several different age cohorts. This survey found, for example, that about two-thirds of American diabetics have never had their illness diagnosed. Finally, the *Health Records Survey* is a series of samples of establishments providing medical, dental, and other services. Taken together, the separate surveys that compose the National Health Survey provide some of the data necessary for national planning for the provision of health services.

In summary, the development of survey research techniques is substantially, if by no means exclusively, an American product. [For discussions of nineteenth-century surveys in Germany and France, see Oberschall (1965); Clark (1973); and Rigaudias-Weiss (1975).] The development of survey research in the United States falls into four crucial periods: the social survey movement, the depression years, World War II, and the postwar years. These periods exemplify a common theme. Though we may think of surveys as fundamentally a tool of academic scholarship, the fact is that the present body of experts and expertise has developed in substantial part from governmental support. This fusion of purposes of policy and scholarship has undoubtedly served the development of survey research. How well it has served to inform policy-makers is a more difficult judgment. Whatever that answer, the costs of surveys are now so great that some form of public or commercial support is necessary to sustain most modern surveys, and the likelihood of public support without a claim of policy payoffs is increasingly uncertain. [The most complete list of figures on trends in survey costs is Lansing and Morgan (1971).]

One solution to the rising costs of surveys is the omnibus survey in which a number of researchers pay fixed prices to piggyback their own items onto an interview schedule. All those who buy into the omnibus survey obtain the responses to the face sheet data describing the respondent as well as the information from their own items. Academic institutions such as the Survey Research Center and the National Opinion Research Center have such ominibus surveys as, of course, do many commercial polling firms.

A second response to the survey costs is the resurgent interest in existing surveys. Secondary analysis of survey data, "the extraction of knowledge on topics other than those which were the focus of the original survey," has become an important mode of research (Hyman, 1972b, p. 1). Secondary analysis, its attractions and limitations, is a separate subject in its own right, recently examined in Hyman's *Secondary Analysis of Sample Surveys* (1972b). The only observation we make here is that a notable number of surveys now available to political analysts were originally collected for commercial rather than academic purposes. That these surveys have proved so valuable to social scientists attest to the scientific interests of many of those who have guided commercial surveys. A brief elaboration of this point will conclude our discussion of the uses of surveys.

The Compatibility of Commercial and Academic Uses of Surveys

The importance of commercial pollsters in survey research may come as a disappointment to those who prefer their research free of the taint of profit. As Jesse Unruh said of politics, money is the mother's milk of survey research.

The 1936 presidential election marked the beginning of modern surveys. Often overlooked in the comical disaster of the *Literary Digest*'s prediction of a Landon victory was that three new polls correctly predicted the result. These were the American Institute of Public Opinion, founded in 1935 by George H. Gallup; The *Fortune* Survey, conducted by Paul T. Cherington and

Elmo Roper; and the Crossley Poll, directed by Archibald M. Crossley (Sheatsley, 1963). These pollsters used small samples of respondents selected by specific quotas and avoided the bloated, but biased samples of the *Literary Digest*. As Sheatsley observes (1968, p. 463), "It was Gallup, Roper, and Crossley who first applied, on a nationwide scale, the techniques of sampling, standardized questionnaire, and personal interview to the measurement of public opinion. The vindication of these methods had enormous consequences for our profession."

In the depression years, of course, there was small support for purely academic research. It is to the gratitude of a succeeding generation of public opinion analysts that commercial pollsters such as Gallup, Roper, and Crossley held the goals of scientific research in such high esteem. Their contributions go well beyond the legitimacy they gave to the techniques of small samples. They produced, as well, much of the early research on opinion measurement. Gallup's *A Guide to Public Opinion Polls* (1944) contains much of this research. More obviously, it is present in Cantril's *Gauging Public Opinion* (1947), for Cantril credits Gallup with making all the data of the American and British Institutes of Public Opinion available to the Office of Public Opinion Research, which Cantril had established at Princeton University in 1940.

The foresight of Gallup and Roper in recognizing the value of their data for scholarly analysis may ultimately have been their most important contribution. The formation of the Roper Public Opinion Research Center at Williamstown, Massachusetts in 1946 as an archive for Roper's surveys was a critical first step. In 1957 it was reorganized as a general archive and has now become the largest repository of social surveys in the world. Such archives offer us our only direct means of exploring opinions in the past. Cantril and Strunk's *Public Opinion 1935–1946* (1951), a huge compendium of the results of surveys from 23 organizations in 19 countries, is only a sample of the data available for secondary analysis for that period. From the Roper Center archive has come such important works as Key's *The Responsible Electorate* (1966), Reed's *The Enduring South* (1972), and Mueller's *Wars, Presidents and Public Opinion* (1973). It is a fortunate fact that contemporary pollsters such as Harris and Yankelovich have followed in the tradition of Gallup, Roper, and Crossley by ensuring that their surveys are available for scholarly research. Many survey archives that now offer such attractive opportunities for the secondary analyst are listed by Hyman (1972b, pp. 330ff.) and by Clubb in Chapter 2 of this volume.

Having discussed the growth of survey research as a mesh of academic research, public policy analysis, and commercial opinion polling, we conclude this topic with a discussion of an article that illustrates several of our arguments. "A Scientific Attempt to Provide Evidence for a Decision on Change of Venue" (Woodward) was published in 1952 in the *American Sociological Review*. It described the case of four blacks who were accused of raping a white woman in Florida in 1949. One black was shot "while resisting arrest." The other three were convicted. One was sentenced to life imprisonment; the other two, to the electric chair. The convictions of the latter two were appealed to the United States Supreme Court, which held that the jury selection procedure involving racial quotas was illegal. Two justices also expressed an opinion that conditions in the trial county had precluded the possibility of a fair trial. The state court ultimately ordered a retrial of the two, but before the new trial took place, both were shot while "attempting to escape." In 1952 the remaining defendant came up for retrial in a county adjacent to the site of his original conviction.

The National Association for the Advancement of Colored People, which undertook the defense, commissioned the polling firm of Elmo Roper to conduct a survey to determine whether prejudgment of guilt in the community precluded a fair trial. The Roper firm drew a sample in four counties: the site of the original trial, the site of the forthcoming trial, and two additional counties far from the first two to serve as control group samples.

Interviews in the two trial counties were not completed. After five Roper interviewers (southern women from nearby states) were interfered with by town constables in one county and the whole staff warned to leave in the other, the survey director withdrew the interviewers with 76 respondents remaining to be contacted. However, comparisons with census data revealed that little or no bias resulted from the missing interviews.

The survey results clearly suggested a substantial prejudgment of guilt. In the county of the original trial, 63 percent responded that they "felt sure" the defendant was guilty. In the new trial site, 43 percent of the whites (as opposed to one percent of the Negroes) said they were sure he was guilty. In contrast, 17 percent and 25 percent of the two control county samples said they were sure the man was guilty. Moreover, in the county of the retrial, 84 percent of the Negroes said they felt something might happen to a juryman who voted not guilty; of the whites in the sample, only 16 percent concurred.

At the new trial the court refused to admit the survey results as evidence that prejudgment of guilt in the community precluded a fair trial. The court sustained the objection of the prosecutor that because the respondents were anonymous, none could be cross-examined to validate their expressed opinions. Thus, the survey results were ruled out as hearsay evidence. The motion of change of venue was denied, and the defendant was again convicted.

Though the judgment against the admissibility of surveys as hearsay evidence was indeed in accord with conventional doctrine, the article noted that several courts had recently declared surveys admissible and that the doctrine on surveys as hearsay evidence was in the process of change. The article concluded, "It will, therefore, be interesting to see what happens to this particular survey at the hands of justices in higher courts." The author proved too optimistic in this case. Barksdale (1957, p. 87) reports that the Florida Supreme Court upheld the view of the trial judge, and the United States Supreme Court in 1954 declined to review this ruling (346 U.S. 927). In general however, if not in this particular case, the author's prediction that survey evidence would increasingly be ruled admissible evidence in United States courts has proved correct (Barksdale, 1957).

The author of the article was also the director of the Roper survey. His name was Julian L. Woodward, and he had died prematurely in the year the article was published. Woodward was a sociologist at Columbia, Dartmouth, and Cornell Universities. At the onset of World War II he took a leave of absence from Cornell University and joined the staff of the Division of Program Surveys of the Department of Agriculture. From 1942 to 1944 he served as Deputy Chief of the Surveys Division of the Office of Facts and Figures. He concluded his service as assistant to the Director of the Office of War Information. In 1946 he resigned from Cornell University to join the market and public opinion research firm of Elmo Roper. In 1950 Woodward was elected president of the American Association for Public Opinion Research.

Woodward's career was illustrative of so many of his generation of survey experts. He was a professor, a bureaucrat, and a commercial executive. His work included academic research, public policy evaluation, public opinion surveys, and market research. In his biography is a microcosm of the history of the development of survey techniques.

CONCLUSIONS: WHAT ARE THE EFFECTS OF SURVEYS ON THEORY?

In this chapter we have explored the usefulness of surveys by asking two broad questions: First, what types of belief and behavior can surveys measure? Second, what academic, policy, and commercial purposes do surveys serve? To the first question we clearly took an eclectic, even permissive position. We pointed to examples in which surveys had been used to measure phenomena so varied as demographic and social characteristics, affect, attitudes, judgments, information, behavior, ideologies, cultural values, and national character. Promiscuous might be a better word than permissive for our inclusive attitudes regarding the uses of surveys. The quality of a survey lies not in its subject but in the care with which the survey is conceived and executed.

To the second question our position is similarly catholic. Surveys are used for basic research, policy analysis, commercial profit, or political electioneering. However, we preferred to treat the boundaries of these fields as permeable. The flow of experts from universities to government to market and opinion research firms was constant during the critical years of the development of survey methodology. In a discussion of the discovery of survey techniques, distinctions between research, policy, and profit are mostly irrelevant.

Moving beyond these two questions of the uses of surveys, we conclude with a final set of observations about the effects of survey research on substantive theories of politics. Here we take our cue from the two classic essays by Robert Merton (1957) concerning the links between theory and methodology. In the first essay Merton pondered the bearing of sociological theory on empirical research. Much of his effort lay in clarifying the multiple meanings of theory, in explaining the paucity of scientific laws in sociology, and, indeed, in cautioning against the premature search for formal theory in the research of an immature science.

In his second essay Merton turns the first problem on its head and inquires of the impact of research methods on substantive theory:

> It is my central thesis that empirical research goes far beyond the passive role of verifying and testing theory: it does more than confirm or refute hypotheses. Research plays an active role: it performs at least four major functions which help shape the development of a theory. It *initiates,* it *reformulates,* it *deflects* and it *clarifies* theory. (Merton, 1957, p. 100)

Merton's observations on the bearing of research on theory apply equally as well to political science as sociology. We will use his thesis to recapitulate our previous arguments on the importance of survey research for the study of politics.

The serendipity pattern: the unanticipated, anomalous and strategic datum exerts pressure for initiating theory. In his essay Merton (1957, p. 103) provides only one example of the role of serendipity ("the discovery, by chance or sagacity, of valid results which were not sought for") in originating new hypotheses—in this case a study of the psychology of social norms.

Writing his essay in 1946, Merton did not yet have a full elaboration of serendipitous discoveries then being made by the Research Branch for Stouffer's *American Soldier* (1949). One such discovery was the concept of *relative deprivation,* which we discussed as an example of the interpersonal expectations in which beliefs are grounded. Once the *American Soldier* was published, Merton and Alice Rossi (Merton, 1957, ch. 9) considered the concept of relative deprivation from the perspective of the theory of *reference group behavior.* Hyman had formulated the concept of reference groups in "The Psychology of Status" (1942). However, it was not until Merton drew attention to the links between relative deprivation and theories of reference groups that reference group became a prominent concept in research (Hyman and Singer, 1968, p. 6).

Another important instance of serendipity resulting from surveys is the "two-step flow of communications" hypothesis. This chain of discovery began with Lazarsfeld, Berelson, and Gaudet's (1944) survey of Sandusky, Ohio during the 1940 presidential campaign. This survey was designed as a study of formal channels of communication media, based on the prevailing assumption that opinions were formed by community leaders. Opinions of these leaders, who control the local media, were presumed to percolate "down from one social stratum to the next until all followed the lead of the conspicuous persons at the apex of the community structure" (Katz and Lazarsfeld, 1955, p. 3). To Lazarsfeld's surprise, the influence of community leaders and the media on voting decisions was quite small compared to interpersonal influence operating within primary groups.

This finding subsequently generated two important lines of research. First, it implied that mass communications (then radio and newspapers) do not directly influence most people's political actions. Rather, the media message first diffuses to group opinion leaders, who then interpret the content of the media to others with whom they have influence. In this way a survey of formal communication led to what Katz and Lazarsfeld (1955) term the periodic "rediscovery" of the importance of the primary group. Merton (1957, ch. 10) further elaborated the theory by exploring his distinction between "local" and "cosmopolitan" influentials. Second, these intermediate opinion leaders were not limited to persons of high social status; rather each stratum had its own opinion leaders. The discovery of intermediate opinion leaders in turn suggested that steeply hierarchical models of community power were probably inaccurate, a finding quite consistent with the spate of research on pluralistic models of community power, so aptly illustrated by Dahl's survey in *Who Governs?* (1961).

The chain of studies from Lazarsfeld, Berelson, and Gaudet's *The People's Choice* (1944) to Katz and Lazarsfeld's *Personal Influence* (1955) illustrates a common pattern for fortuitous findings from survey research. Surveys, as we defined them, require interview schedules containing "explicit, standardized procedures, yielding quantitative measurements." These questionnaires are usually administered by field interviewers who are not themselves attentive to interesting anomalies that appear early in the stages of data collection. Even if the researcher becomes aware of an intriguing line of inquiry in the midst of the fieldwork, a standardized schedule usually cannot be changed to explore this new insight. Thus, nearly all generalizations from serendipitous survey findings are *ex post-facto* and speculative. They are rarely testable with the existing data because the researcher has not directly measured the variables he has conceived to explain the anomalous results. For this reason, *The People's Choice* contains little direct evidence for the "two-step flow of communications" or for primary group "opinion leaders." Tests of these hypotheses had to await the new research designs of Merton, and Lazarsfeld and Katz. Serendipity is merely part of the process of discovery. Verification follows discovery in a chain of inquiries. Nonetheless, the unanticipated findings of surveys have had a major effect on theories of political behavior.

The recasting of theory: new data exert pressure for the elaboration of a conceptual scheme. Survey research has had a profound impact on theories of political behavior—particularly so in areas relating to the interest, knowledge, and values that ordinary citizens bring to political acts. The new data not only brought pressure for the recasting of empirical theories of behavior; normative theories were also seen as vulnerable to the new surveys of the 1950s that seemed to suggest that voters were much less interested and informed than some classical theories of democracy may have assumed. The resulting controversies are wide-ranging. Is the ignorance and apathy of many voters more a consequence of their own cognitive limitations or more a result of the failure of parties and candidates to make clear and distinctive arguments of the issues? Were classical normative theories properly interpreted as assuming an active and informed electorate as an empirical fact rather than a normative ideal? Is there, in any·case, a *single* classical democratic theory? And, most fundamentally, under what conditions can empirical data weaken a normative argument regarding how voters *ought* to behave? [These questions are addressed in the articles in McCoy and Playford (1967) and Kariel (1970), and by Pateman's *Participation and Democratic Theory* (1970) and Moon's (1972) review essay of recent books on these issues.] A careful discussion of these issues would require yet another chapter. We will be content, therefore, with a single example that is posed by the following question: To what degree does a democracy require a consensus among ordinary citizens for the tenets of civil liberties?

This controversy was joined with the publication of Samuel Stouffer's *Communism, Conformity, and Civil Liberties* in 1955. Stouffer's research design was elegant in its inclusion of both a cross-section sample of ordinary citizens and a special sample of community leaders in cities with populations of 10,000 to 150,000. The interviews took place in May through July 1954, the year in which Senator Joseph McCarthy made his attempt to sway United States congressional races with attacks on candidates he considered procommunist.

The results of the survey proved startling in many respects. First, sizable minorities, in some cases even majorities, appeared to favor the denial of such basic rights as freedom of speech for atheists, socialists, and accused and admitted communists. In contrast, the leadership sample expressed much more support for freedom of the press and speech for religious and political radicals. Counterintuitively, however, anticommunism was apparently not much on people's minds, in spite of McCarthy's attempt to generate an anticommunist mass movement. In response to the question, "What kinds of things do you worry about most?," "the number of people who said that they were worried either about the threat of Communists in the United States or about civil liberties was, even by the most generous interpretation of occasionally ambiguous responses, less than 1%!" (Stouffer, 1955, p. 58). It is not clear which of the findings was more unsettling to the study's readers—the lack of expressed support for civil liberties or the lack of expressed interest in political issues of the day.

The Stouffer study became the seed of important successors. Two of the more significant were "Fundamental Principles of Democracy" by Prothro and Grigg (1960) and "Consensus and Ideology in American Politics" by McClosky (1964). McClosky's was an exceedingly ambitious design, including both a cross-section sample of citizens and a leadership sample drawn from party delegates to the 1956 presidential nominating conventions. The Prothro and Grigg cross-section samples were drawn from two university towns: Tallahassee, Florida, and Ann Arbor, Michigan. Both studies shared the same substantive interest—assessing the degree to which Americans would endorse both general principles of democratic government as well as specific applications of those principles. The two studies yielded a common result: substantial majorities would endorse tenets of democracy when stated as general principles, such as "people in the minority should be free to try to win majority support for their opinions." Support tended to erode on specific applications of those principles, such as "A Negro should not be allowed to run for mayor of this city." In addition, McClosky found, as Stouffer had before him, that the sample of leaders was much more prone to "democratic" responses than were ordinary citizens.

It was perhaps inevitable that such findings would lead to the recasting of theories on the forces that sustain democratic systems. Consider Key's conclusion to *Public Opinion and American Democracy*:

> The longer one frets with the puzzle of how democratic regimes manage to function, the more plausible it appears that a substantial part of the explanation is to be found in the motives that actuate the leadership echelon, the values that it holds, in the rules of the political game to which it adheres, in the expectations which it entertains about its own status in society, and perhaps in some of the objective circumstances, both material and institutional, in which it functions. Focus of attention on this sector of the opinion system contrasts with the more usual quest for the qualities of the people that may be thought to make democratic practices feasible. That focus does not deny the importance of mass attitudes. It rather emphasizes that the pieces of the puzzle are different in form and function, and that for the existence of a democratic opinion-oriented system each piece must possess the characteristics necessary for it to fit together with the others in a working whole. The superimposition over a people habituated to tyranny of a leadership imbued with democratic ideals probably would not create a viable democratic order. (Key, 1964, p. 537)

Continuing this line of argument, Key distinguished activists and ordinary citizens in terms of the degree to which it is essential that each stratum possess a consensus on the rules of the game:

> These observations resemble the proposition that a consensus needs to prevail for democracy to exist; yet they should not be taken as the equivalent of that proposition. Perhaps among the upper-activist stratum a consensus does need to prevail on the technical rules of the game by which the system operates. What kind of consensus, if any, extends throughout the population beyond a general acceptance of the regime remains problematic. In the

main, the notion of consensus has sprung from the inventive minds of theorists untainted by acquaintance with mass attitudes. (Key, 1964, p. 550)

Such arguments have met with considerable criticism, on both normative and empirical grounds. [See, for example, the exchange between Jack L. Walker (1966) and Robert A. Dahl (1966).] The debate includes many facets, and we shall not join it, except to comment briefly on the relevance of survey methods to the evidence that is at issue. First, the behavior of ordinary citizens may not pose the threat to civil liberties that their expressed opinions would seem to imply. Prothro and Grigg (1960), for example, are careful to note that in spite of the fact that a large minority (42 percent) agreed that "a Negro should not be allowed to run for mayor of this city," a Negro had in fact only a few months earlier conducted an active campaign for the office in Tallahassee without efforts being made by whites to obstruct the campaign. In a previous discussion we presented several reasons why people often do not act on their attitudes. People live their lives in primary and secondary groups that may have more influence on their behavior than their own beliefs. In the second place, we also noted in the same discussion that a specific application of a general principle may create a conflict between two valued beliefs. Legalization of political activity for communists is surely one deduction that can be made from a general principle that minorities should be free to win majority support for their opinions, but as Prothro and Grigg noted (1960, p. 293), "respondents who repudiate free speech for communists are responding in terms of anti-Communist rather than anti-free speech sentiments." To express disapproval of communism in this case does not mean that the respondent would either endorse the restrictions on Communist party political activities such as were embodied in the Smith Act of 1940 or try actively to prevent a radical from speaking in their own community. And the reasons may not be simply that there are some positive benefits of citizen apathy for democratic order as Berelson, Lazarsfeld, and McPhee (1954) and, more cautiously, Prothro and Grigg (1960) suggested.

In the third place, it may be that survey research is fundamentally hostile to almost any consensus theory of politics. Surveys are instruments to describe and explain individual differences. In that rare instance in which an item does not discriminate among people, the survey researcher almost reflexively discards it. Surveys reflect people in their remarkable variability. To have used a survey to test the existence of consensus is, with only slight exaggeration, to have determined the result. What was not determined, of course, was that leadership samples would have more strongly endorsed the applications of democratic norms than cross-section samples of citizens. This remains a problem which the critics of democratic revisionism must address. Our principal point is to note that surveys, as any research technique, can create genuine pressure to recast theory, and that in this particular case the recasting may not have been entirely warranted by a careful reading of the evidence.

The refocusing of theoretic interest. New methods of empirical research exert pressure for new foci of theoretic interest. To assess the impact of surveys on political science would be, in point of fact, to restate much of our chapter. Moreover, the availability of evidence of citizen attitudes influenced almost every field in the discipline. But we should not overstate the impact of surveys on the development of political science. If we substitute "survey data" for the word "statistics," Merton's comment would accurately reflect our view:

> What we have said does not mean that the piling up of statistics in itself advances theory; it does mean that theoretic interest tends to shift to those areas in which there is an abundance of *pertinent* statistical data. (Merton, 1957, p. 114)

The shift toward fields that are appropriately studied with survey data has been a notable feature of postwar political science. Without citing the works themselves, we will briefly note some of the subfields of political science that have attracted scholarly interest, in part due to the availability of survey evidence.

Empirical Theories of Behavior. The field of public opinion and voting behavior is, of course, almost entirely a product of survey evidence. So, too, is the study of preadult political socialization, a topic that bloomed so quickly in the 1960s that it has been aptly described as a "growth industry." The cross-cultural study of political values is a third field that owes its origins to surveys, as data became available on the people's attachments to and disaffection from political communities, regimes, and authorities. Studies of race and ethnic relations, the political sociology of social cleavages and ideologies, the political psychology of character and values, the values that contribute to political modernization and change—the list of fields of political behavior that attracted new interest after the emergence of survey techniques simply runs on and on.

Policy Process. The study of political institutions is, next to political philosophy, the oldest field in political science. Surveys did not create our interest in institutions, but they did open a window on one of the critical problems of political order, namely, the links between institutional leaders and ordinary citizens. By what means and to what degree can leaders influence the attitudes and behavior of people in a system? To what degree do people take cues from parties and candidates? Under what conditions do people accept the decisions of leaders as authoritative, for example, under what conditions will people comply with court decisions? To what degree does the existence of a new technology such as television provide a leader with leverage for obtaining popular support for his policies? What do conflicts of values between leaders suggest about the organization of political power in a community or nation?

We can also turn the relationship on its head and ask about the influence that people can exert over leaders and policy. To what degree do votes for a particular party reflect common preferences for future policy? Under what conditions (if ever) does opinion become so crystallized that the options of leaders on policy choices become significantly circumscribed? Does domestic opinion significantly influence foreign policy decisions? What influences the fluctuations of public mood between apathy and activism? These are just some of the questions concerning the links between leaders and followers, and the introduction of surveys on mass attitudes resulted in a significant shift in research interest toward providing some answers (cf. Cohen, 1973).

Policy Evaluation. In our history of the development of survey techniques, we emphasized the importance of the United States government's interest in policy issues. The potential of surveys for the assessment of citizen preferences led to substantial public support for the development of survey techniques. Since then the delivery of public services has become a growing field of study in political science. The use of surveys in tandem with the natural and systematic experiments that Rivlin (1971) described is a reflection of the importance of surveys in the assessment of policy options. The burgeoning interest in constructing time series of political and social indicators is simply the successor to the social survey movement of the nineteenth century. All of these are concerns that would not have been practical without the data that surveys provide.

The clarification of concepts. Empirical research exerts pressure for clear concepts. Merton's (1957) final point is sufficiently obvious to require little elaboration. He notes that the necessity of specifying the measurement of a concept disposes one to think with more exactitude of the definitions of concepts within a theory. One can always speak loosely about alienation, power, legitimacy, charisma, or rationality. However, the fundamental ambiguity of such concepts is often revealed by the process of having to construct their operational measures. Constructing survey schedules is an intellectually demanding (and often humbling) task. One does not have to believe, as Bridgman (1927) did, that the meaning of a term is fully and exclusively determined by its means of measurement to be convinced that the task of measurement induces one to think more clearly about just what exactly it is that one seeks to measure.

Conclusion

The discipline that measurement imposes on the researcher is reflected in our definition of a survey as "an inquiry of a large number of people, selected by rigorous sampling, conducted in normal life settings by explicit, standardized procedures yielding quantitative measurements." If we ponder why surveys have been so productive of important discoveries, the discipline this definition implies provides two clues.

First, the requirement of quantification induces one toward clearer concepts and more accurate measures. A less obvious point is that accurately quantified measurements are often essential to the serendipitous discoveries so important to theoretical advances. This is the case because the discoveries themselves often depend on effects of small magnitude. For example, the concept of relative deprivation was revealed by small differences in the frequency of particular attitudes in groups of soldiers (Hyman, 1963, p. 446). Without accurate measures of large numbers of respondents, the effect would not have been distinguishable to the researchers from the ordinary variations of sampling and measurement error.

Similarly, such interesting concepts as status inconsistency and selective perception of media depend on accurately quantified measures. Selective perception, those systematic differences between the world outside and the images of that world in our minds, is an apt example. Berelson, Lazarsfeld, and McPhee's *Voting* (1954, ch. 10) is quite well known for its demonstration that preferences for candidates lead voters to perceive selectively candidate stands on critical issues. In the 1948 United States presidential campaign, Republicans who were in favor of the Taft–Hartley law were much more likely to see Dewey as favoring the law than Republicans who were opposed to the law, even though Dewey's opposition to the law was unambiguous. Democrats who were in favor of the law were more likely to see Truman as favoring the law than were Democrats who opposed the policy, in spite of the indisputable fact that Truman had earlier vetoed the law. What is often overlooked in this example is the fact that most people had an accurate perception of the stands of the two candidates, and this was true in spite of the fact that the perception questions were only asked of the august panel—before people were likely to be attentive to the campaign. The point is that the existence of selective bias in perceptions was not of great magnitude; it was only systematic and in theoretically interesting directions. Without the precision of accurate measures and large samples, the effects might never have been discovered.

A final example is status inconsistency, which we discussed in our section on demography. Status inconsistency is theoretically hypothesized to be small in magnitude compared to the additive effects of status on such dependent variables as psychological stress or political attitudes. In one of the more careful tests of status inconsistency, the phenomena explained only about two percent of the variance in feelings of stress (Jackson and Burke, 1965). Likewise, the effects of techniques of political electioneering, from media advertising to political canvassing, are likely to be of small magnitude in the context of a presidential campaign. Indeed, their influence may be expected to be smaller than some irreducible level of random measurement and sampling error. Small but systematic effects will only be discernable with accurate measures of a large number of respondents in repeated samples. In sum, without the quantification that surveys permit, many of our more theoretically interesting hypotheses would be untestable.

A second reason why surveys have been so productive of important discoveries is that a presurvey social science had no means by which to study a large and representative sample of people in their normal life settings. Lasswell's (1930) intensive investigation of the political personality could not help but slight the impact of community context upon the personality. Conversely, prior to surveys, students of parties and elections had only impressionistic data on the psychology of political behavior. Surveys, which combine the efficiencies of sampling with the rigor of standardized measures, presented a means of studying individual psychology in a social context.

The ability to study the individual in a social setting is clearly evidenced in the example of *relative deprivation,* for this concept is grounded in differences between individual feelings of satisfaction or deprivation within a group of people whose objective situations are quite similar. These contradictions would not have surfaced without a simultaneous and intensive examination of individual feelings in a group context.

In sum, rigorous measures of individual behavior in a social context have made surveys remarkably productive of political discoveries. The substantive chapters of this *Handbook* are themselves witness of the degree to which the rapid development of survey techniques after 1930 has changed the character of the study of politics. In chapter after chapter we see evidence of a sustained and cumulative development of knowledge about politics, much of it derived from survey evidence. If one stripped from each chapter the generalizations that rest on surveys, the gaps would be silent testimony to the contribution of surveys to political science.

REFERENCES

Abernathy, James R., Bernard G. Greenberg, and Daniel G. Horvitz (1970). "Estimates of induced abortion in urban North Carolina." *Demography* 7:19–29.

Abrams, Mark (1970). "The opinion polls and the British election of 1970." *Public Opinion Quarterly* 34:317–324.

Allport, Floyd Henry (1924). *Social Psychology.* Boston: Houghton Mifflin.

Almond, Gabriel A. (1950). *The American People and Foreign Policy.* New York: Praeger.

Almond, Gabriel A., and Sidney Verba (1963). *The Civic Culture: Political Attitudes and Democracy in Five Nations.* Princeton: Princeton University Press.

Asher, Herbert E. (1974). "Some consequences of measurement error in survey data." *American Journal of Political Science* 18:469–485.

Axelrod, Robert (1967). "The structure of public opinion on policy issues." *Public Opinion Quarterly* 31:51–60.

——————— (1972). "Where the votes come from: an analysis of electoral coalitions, 1952–1968." *American Political Science Review* 66:11–20.

——————— (1974). "Communication." *American Political Science Review* 68:717–720.

Babbie, Earl R. (1973). *Survey Research Methods.* Belmont, Calif.: Wadsworth.

Backstrom, Charles H., and Gerald D. Hursh (1963). *Survey Research.* Evanston, Ill.: Northwestern Press.

Barber, James Alden, Jr. (1970). *Social Mobility and Voting Behavior.* Chicago: Rand McNally.

Barksdale, Hiram C. (1957). *The Use of Survey Research Findings as Legal Evidence.* Pleasantville, N.Y.: Printers' Ink Books.

Barnes, Samuel H. (1971). "Left, right, and the Italian voter." *Comparative Political Studies* 4:157–175.

Barnes, Samuel H., and Roy Pierce (1971). "Public opinion and political preferences in France and Italy." *Midwest Journal of Political Science* 15:643–660.

Beard, Charles A. (1912). *American City Government: A Survey of Newer Tendencies.* New York: Century.

Bell, Daniel, ed. (1963). *The Radical Right.* (Originally published in 1955 as *The New American Right.*) New York: Anchor Books.

Benney, Mark, A. P. Gray, and R. H. Pear (1956). *How People Vote: A Study of Electoral Behaviour in Greenwich.* London: Routledge and Kegan Paul.

Berelson, Bernard R., Paul F. Lazarsfeld, and William N. McPhee (1954). *Voting: A Study of Opinion Formation in a Presidential Campaign.* Chicago: University of Chicago Press.

Best, James J. (1973). *Public Opinion: Micro and Macro.* Homewood, Ill.: Dorsey.

Blau, Peter M., and Otis Dudley Duncan (1967). *The American Occupational Structure.* New York: Wiley.

Bonjean, Charles M., Richard J. Hill, and S. Dale McLemore (1967). *Sociological Measurement: An Inventory of Scales and Indices.* San Francisco: Chandler.

Booth, Charles (1892–1897). *Life and Labour of the People in London.* Second edition, nine volumes. London: Macmillan.

Bottomore, T. B. (1968). Review of *The American Occupational Structure* by Peter M. Blau and Otis Dudley Duncan. *American Sociological Review* 33:294–296.

Bowley, Arthur L. (1913). "Working class households in Reading." *Journal of the Royal Statistical Society* 76:672–701.

Boyd, Richard W. (1967). "A theory of voting defection: attitudinal cross-pressures and political alienation." Ph.D. dissertation. Bloomington, Ind.: Indiana University.

——————— (1972). "Popular control of public policy: a normal vote analysis of the 1972 election." *American Political Science Review* 66:439–449.

——————— (1974). "Electoral trends in postwar politics." In James David Barber, ed., *Choosing the President.* Englewood Cliffs, N.J.: Prentice-Hall.

Brannon, Robert, Gary Cyphers, Sharlene Hesse, Susan Hesselbart, Roberta Keane, Howard Schuman, Thomas Viccaro, and Diana Wright (1973). "Attitude and action: a field experiment joined to a general population survey." *American Sociological Review* 38:625–636.

Bremner, Robert H. (1956). *From the Depths: The Discovery of Poverty in the United States.* New York: New York University Press.

Bridgman, P. W. (1927). *The Logic of Modern Physics.* New York: Macmillan.

Brown, Steven R. (1970). "Consistency and the persistence of ideology: some experimental results." *Public Opinion Quarterly* 34:60–68.

Brzezinski, Zbigniew, and Samuel P. Huntington (1964). *Political Power: USA/USSR.* New York: Viking Press.

Butler, David, and Donald Stokes (1969). *Political Change in Britain: Forces Shaping Electoral Choice.* New York: St. Martin's.

Cahalan, Don (1968–1969). "Correlates of respondent accuracy in the Denver validity survey." *Public Opinion Quarterly* 32:607–621.

Campbell, Angus, Philip E. Converse, Warren E. Miller, and Donald E. Stokes (1960). *The American Voter.* New York: Wiley.

Campbell, Donald T. (1969). "Reforms as experiments." *The American Psychologist* 24:409–429.

Campbell, Donald T., and Donald W. Fiske (1959). "Convergent and discriminant validation by the multitrait-multimethod matrix." *Psychological Bulletin* 59:81–105.

Cantril, Albert H., and Charles W. Roll, Jr. (1971). *Hopes and Fears of the American People.* New York: Universe Books.

Cantril, Hadley (1947). *Gauging Public Opinion.* Princeton: Princeton University Press.

_____ (1965). *The Pattern of Human Concerns.* New Brunswick: Rutgers University Press.

Cantril, Hadley, and Mildred Strunk, eds. (1951). *Public Opinion 1935–1946.* Princeton: Princeton University Press.

Carter, Launor F. (1963). "Survey results and public policy decisions." *Public Opinion Quarterly* 27:549–557.

Cartwright, Dorwin (1950). "Survey research: psychological economics." In James Grier Miller, ed., *Experiments in Social Process: A Symposium on Social Psychology.* New York: McGraw-Hill.

Caspary, William R. (1970). "The 'mood theory': a study of public opinion and foreign policy." *American Political Science Review* 64:536–547.

Citizens Association of New York (1865). *Report of the Council of Hygiene and Public Health.* New York: D. Appleton.

Clark, Terry Nichols (1973). *Prophets and Patrons: The French University and the Emergence of the Social Sciences.* Cambridge, Mass.: Harvard University Press.

Clausen, Aage R. (1968–1969). "Response validity: vote report." *Public Opinion Quarterly* 32:588–606.

Cobb, Roger W. (1973). "The belief-systems perspective: an assessment of a framework." *Journal of Politics* 35:121–153.

Cohen, Bernard C. (1973). *The Public's Impact on Foreign Policy.* Boston: Little, Brown.

Coleman, James S., Ernest Q. Campbell, Carol J. Hobson, James McPartland, Alexander M. Mood, Frederic D. Weinfeld, and Robert L. York (1966). *Equality of Educational Opportunity*. Washington, D.C.: U.S. Department of Health, Education and Welfare.

Converse, Jean M., and Howard Schuman (1974). *Conversations at Random: Survey Research as Interviewers See It*. New York: Wiley.

Converse, Philip E. (1964). "The nature of belief systems in mass publics." In David Apter, ed., *Ideology and Discontent*. New York: The Free Press.

_____ (1970). "Attitudes and non-attitudes: continuation of a dialogue." In Edward R. Tufte, ed., *The Quantitative Analysis of Social Problems*. Reading, Mass.: Addison-Wesley.

_____ (1972). "Change in the American electorate." In Angus Campbell and Philip E. Converse, eds., *The Human Meaning of Social Change*. New York: Sage.

_____ (1974). "Comment." *American Political Science Review* 68:650–660.

Converse, Philip E., and Roy Pierce (1970): "Basic cleavages in French politics and the disorders of May and June, 1968." Paper presented at the 7th World Congress of Sociology, Varna, Bulgaria.

Converse, Philip E., and Howard Schuman (1970). " 'Silent majorities' and the Vietnam War." *Scientific American* 222:17–25. (Reprinted by permission.)

Cooke, Jacob E., ed. (1961). *The Federalist*. Middletown, Conn.: Wesleyan University Press.

Coombs, Clyde H. (1964). *A Theory of Data*. New York: Wiley.

Dahl, Robert A. (1950). *Congress and Foreign Policy*. New York: Harcourt, Brace.

_____ (1956). *A Preface to Democratic Theory*. Chicago: University of Chicago Press.

_____ (1961). *Who Governs? Democracy and Power in an American City*. New Haven, Conn.: Yale University Press.

_____ (1966). "Further reflections on 'the elitist theory of democracy'." *American Political Science Review* 60:296–305.

_____ (1972). *Democracy in the United States: Promise and Performance,* Second edition. Chicago: Rand McNally.

Dahl, Robert A., and Charles E. Lindblom (1953). *Politics, Economics, and Welfare: Planning and Politico-Economic Systems Resolved into Basic Social Processes*. New York: Harper & Row.

Dalfiume, Richard M. (1969). *Desegregation of the U.S. Armed Forces: Fighting on Two Fronts 1939–1953*. Columbia: University of Missouri Press. (Reprinted by permission.)

Davies, Richard O. (1966). *Housing Reform During the Truman Administration*. Columbia: University of Missouri Press.

Davis, Allison, and John Dollard (1964). *Children of Bondage: The Personality Development of Negro Youth in the Urban South*. (Originally published in 1940.) New York: Harper & Row.

Davis, James A. (1971). *Elementary Survey Analysis*. Englewood Cliffs, N.J.: Prentice-Hall.

Davis, John P. (1966). "The Negro in the armed forces of America." In John P. Davis, ed., *The American Negro Reference Book*. Englewood Cliffs, N.J.: Prentice-Hall.

Deming, William Edwards (1950). *Some Theory of Sampling*. New York: Wiley.

Deutscher, Irwin (1966). "Words and deeds: social science and social policy." *Social Forces* 13:235–254.

Devine, Richard P., and Laurence L. Falk (1972). *Social Surveys: A Research Strategy for Social Scientists and Students*. Morristown, N.J.: General Learning Press.

DeVos, George A., and Arthur E. Hippler (1969). "Cultural psychology: comparative studies of human behavior." In Gardner Lindzey and Elliot Aronson, eds., *Handbook of Social Psychology*, Volume 4 (Second edition). Reading, Mass.: Addison-Wesley.

Diamond, Sigmund (1963). "Some early uses of the questionnaire: views on education and immigration." *Public Opinion Quarterly* 27:528–542.

Dinerman, Helen (1948). "1948 votes in the making: a preview." *Public Opinion Quarterly* 12:581–598.

Dollard, John (1948–1949). "Under what conditions do opinions predict behavior?" *Public Opinion Quarterly* 12:623–632.

Ducoff, Louis J., and Margaret Jarman Hagood (1947). *Labor Force Definition and Measurement: Recent Experience in the United States*. Bulletin 56. New York: Social Science Research Council.

Duncan, Otis Dudley (1969). *Toward Social Reporting: Next Steps*. New York: Sage.

Easton, David, and Jack Dennis (1969). *Children in the Political System: Origins of Political Legitimacy*. New York: McGraw-Hill.

Edwards, Allen L. (1957). *Techniques of Attitude Scale Construction*. New York: Appleton-Century-Crofts.

Ennis, Philip E. (1962). "The contextual dimension in voting." In William N. McPhee and William A. Glaser, eds., *Public Opinion and Congressional Elections*. Glencoe, Ill.: The Free Press.

——————— (1967). *Criminal Victimization in the United States: A Report of a National Survey*. Chicago: National Opinion Research Center.

Featherman, David L., and William H. Sewell (1974). "Toward comparable data on inequality and stratification: perspectives on the second generation of national mobility studies." *The American Sociologist* 9:18–25.

Field, John Osgood, and Ronald E. Anderson (1969). "Ideology in the public's conceptualization of the 1964 election." *Public Opinion Quarterly* 33:380–398.

Fishbein, Martin, ed. (1967). *Readings in Attitude Theory and Measurement*. New York: Wiley.

Fishbein, Martin, and Fred S. Coombs (1971). "Basis for decision: an attitudinal approach toward an understanding of voting behavior." Paper prepared for delivery at the annual meeting of the American Political Science Association, Chicago.

Flanagan, John C., John T. Dailey, Marion F. Shaycroft, William A. Gorham, David

B. Orr, and Isadore Goldberg (1962). *Design for a Study of American Youth*. Boston: Little, Brown.

Folsom, Ralph E., Bernard G. Greenberg, Daniel G. Horvitz, and James R. Abernathy (1973). "The two alternate questions randomized response model for human surveys." *Journal of the American Statistical Association* 68:525–530.

Frazier, E. Franklin (1940). *Negro Youth at the Crossways: Their Personality Development in the Middle States*. Washington, D.C.: American Council on Education.

Free, Lloyd A., and Hadley Cantril (1968). *The Political Beliefs of Americans: A Study of Public Opinion*. New York: Simon and Schuster.

Freidson, Eliot (1955). "A prerequisite for participation in the public opinion process." *Public Opinion Quarterly* 19:105–111.

Frey, Frederick W. (1970). "Cross-cultural survey research in political science." In Robert T. Holt and John E. Turner, eds., *The Methodology of Comparative Research*. New York: The Free Press.

Frey, Frederick W., with Peter Stephenson and Katherine Archer Smith (1969). *Survey Research on Comparative Social Change: A Bibliography*. Cambridge, Mass.: MIT Press.

Gallup, George (1944). *A Guide to Public Opinion Polls*. Princeton, N.J.: Princeton University Press.

——————— (1947). "The quintamensional plan of question design." *Public Opinion Quarterly* 11:385–393.

——————— (1972). *The Gallup Poll: Public Opinion 1935–1971*. Three volumes. New York: Random House.

Galtung, Johan (1967). *Theory and Methods of Research*. New York: Columbia University Press.

Gamson, William A. (1968). *Power and Discontent*. Homewood, Ill.: Dorsey.

Glock, Charles Y., ed. (1967). *Survey Research in the Social Sciences*. New York: Sage.

Goffman, Irwin W. (1957). "Status consistency and preference for change in power distribution." *American Sociological Review* 22:275–281.

Gough, Harrison, and Giuseppe Di Palma (1965). "Attitudes toward colonialism, political dependence, and independence." *Journal of Psychology* 60:155–163.

Greenstein, Fred I. (1965). *Children and Politics*. New Haven, Conn.: Yale University Press.

——————— (1973). "Political psychology: a pluralistic universe." In Jeanne N. Knutson, ed., *Handbook of Political Psychology*. San Francisco: Jossey-Bass.

Halberstam, David (1973). *The Best and the Brightest*. Originally published in 1969. New York: Fawcett Crest Books. (Reprinted by permission.)

Haller, Archibald O., and David M. Lewis (1966). "The hypothesis of intersocietal similarity in occupational prestige hierarchies." *American Journal of Sociology* 72:210–216.

Hartz, Louis (1955). *The Liberal Tradition in America*. New York: Harcourt, Brace and World.

Hess, Robert D., and Judith V. Torney (1967). *The Development of Political Attitudes in Children*. Chicago: Aldine.

Hofstadter, Richard (1955). *The Age of Reform*. New York: Knopf.

Holt, Robert T., and John E. Turner, eds. (1970). *The Methodology of Comparative Research*. New York: Free Press.

Hyman, Herbert H. (1942). *The Psychology of Status*. New York: Archives of Psychology, No. 269.

––––––––––– (1944–1945). "Do they tell the truth?" *Public Opinion Quarterly* 8:557–559.

––––––––––– (1949). "Inconsistencies as a problem in attitude measurement." *Journal of Social Issues* 5:38–42.

––––––––––– (1955). *Survey Design and Analysis: Principles, Cases and Procedures*. Glencoe, Ill.: The Free Press.

––––––––––– (1959). *Political Socialization: A Study in the Psychology of Political Behavior*. Glencoe, Ill.: The Free Press.

––––––––––– (1963). "Reflections on the relation between theory and research." *The Centennial Review* 7:431–453.

––––––––––– (1964). "Research design." In Robert Ward, ed., *Studying Politics Abroad*. Boston: Little, Brown.

––––––––––– (1969). "Social psychology and race relations." In Irwin Katz and Patricia Gurin, eds., *Race and the Social Sciences*. New York: Basic Books.

––––––––––– (1972a). "Misguided bombs." Unpublished manuscript.

––––––––––– (1972b). *Secondary Analysis of Sample Surveys: Principles, Procedures, and Potentialities*. New York: Wiley.

––––––––––– (1973). "Surveys in the study of political psychology." In Jeanne N. Knutson, ed., *Handbook of Political Psychology*. San Francisco: Jossey-Bass.

––––––––––– (1975). "Strategies in comparative survey research: cross national designs." In Robert Smith, ed., *Social Science Methods: A New Introduction*. New York: The Free Press.

Hyman, Herbert H., with William J. Cobb, Jacob J. Feldman, Clyde W. Hart, and Charles Herbert Stember (1954). *Interviewing in Social Research*. Chicago: University of Chicago Press.

Hyman, Herbert H., Gene N. Levine, and Charles R. Wright (1967). "Studying expert informants by survey methods: a cross-national inquiry." *Public Opinion Quarterly* 31:9–26.

Hyman, Herbert H., and Paul B. Sheatsley (1964). "Attitudes toward desegregation." *Scientific American* 211:2–9.

Hyman, Herbert H., and Eleanor Singer, eds. (1968). *Readings in Reference Group Theory and Research*. New York: The Free Press.

Hymes, Dell (1970). "Linguistic aspects of comparative political research." In Robert T. Holt and John E. Turner, eds., *The Methodology of Comparative Research*. New York: The Free Press.

Inkeles, Alex, and Daniel J. Levinson (1969). "National character: the study of modal personality and socio-cultural systems." In Gardner Lindzey and Elliott Aronson, eds., *Handbook of Social Psychology,* Volume 4 (Second edition). Reading, Mass.: Addison-Wesley.

Institute for Social Research. *Newsletter.* Ann Arbor, Michigan.

Jackson, Elton F. (1962). "Status consistency and symptoms of stress." *American Sociological Review* 27:469–480.

Jackson, Elton F., and Peter J. Burke (1965). "Status and symptoms of stress: additive and interactive effects." *American Sociological Review* 30:556–564.

Jennings, M. Kent, and Richard G. Niemi (1974). *The Political Character of Adolescence: The Influence of Families and Schools.* Princeton, N.J.: Princeton University Press.

Johnson, Charles S. (1967). *Growing Up in the Black Belt: Negro Youth in the Rural South.* (Originally published in 1941.) New York: Schocken Books.

Jones, D. Caradog (n.d.). *Social Surveys.* London: Hutchinson's University Library. (Reprinted by permission.)

Kahn, Robert L., and Charles F. Cannell (1966). *The Dynamics of Interviewing.* New York: Wiley.

Kariel, Henry S., ed. (1970). *Frontiers of Democratic Theory.* New York: Random House.

Katz, Daniel, and Samuel J. Eldersveld (1961). "The impact of local party activity upon the electorate." *Public Opinion Quarterly* 25:1–24.

Katz, Daniel, and Richard Schanck (1938). *Social Psychology.* New York: Wiley.

Katz, Elihu, and Paul F. Lazarsfeld (1955). *Personal Influence: The Part Played by People in the Flow of Mass Communications.* Glencoe, Ill.: The Free Press.

Kelly, K. Dennis, and William J. Chambliss (1966). "Status consistency and political attitudes." *American Sociological Review* 31:375–382.

Key, V. O., Jr. (1964). *Public Opinion and American Democracy.* New York: Knopf. (Reprinted by permission.)

——————— (1966). *The Responsible Electorate: Rationality in Presidential Voting 1936–1960.* Cambridge: Harvard University Press.

Kish, Leslie (1965a). "Sampling organizations and groups of unequal size." *American Sociological Review.* 30:564–572.

——————— (1965b). *Survey Sampling.* New York: Wiley.

Kraut, Robert E., and John B. McConahay (1973). "How being interviewed affects voting: an experiment." *Public Opinion Quarterly* 37:398–406.

Lane, Robert E. (1962). *Political Ideology: Why the American Common Man Believes What He Does.* New York: The Free Press.

Lane, Robert E., and David O. Sears (1964). *Public Opinion.* Englewood Cliffs, N.J.: Prentice-Hall.

Lansing, John B., and James N. Morgan (1971). *Economic Survey Methods.* Ann Arbor, Mich.: Institute for Social Research.

Lansing, John B., Stephen B. Withey, and Arthur C. Wolfe (1971). *Working Papers on Survey Research in Poverty Areas.* Ann Arbor, Mich.: Institute for Social Research.

LaPiere, R. T. (1934). "Attitudes vs. actions." *Social Forces* 13:230–237.

Lasswell, Harold (1930). *Psychopathology and Politics.* Chicago: University of Chicago Press.

Lazarsfeld, Paul F. (1944). "The controversy over detailed interviews—an offer for negotiation." *Public Opinion Quarterly* 8:38–60.

Lazarsfeld, Paul F., Bernard Berelson, and Hazel Gaudet (1944). *The People's Choice: How the Voter Makes Up His Mind in a Presidential Campaign.* New York: Columbia University Press.

Leege, David C., and Wayne L. Francis (1974). *Political Research: Design, Measurement and Analysis.* New York: Basic Books.

Lenski, Gerhard E. (1954). "Status crystallization: a non-vertical dimension of social status." *American Sociological Review* 19:405–413.

Lewin, Kurt (1943). "Defining the 'field at a given time'." *Psychological Review* 50:292–310.

Lijphart, Arend (1968). *The Politics of Accommodation: Pluralism and Democracy in the Netherlands.* Berkeley: University of California Press.

Likert, Rensis (1948). "Opinion studies and government policy." *Proceedings of the American Philosophical Society* 92:341–350.

Lipset, Seymour Martin, and Reinhard Bendix (1964). *Social Mobility in Industrial Society.* Berkeley: University of California Press.

Lipset, Seymour Martin and Stein Rokkan, eds. (1967). *Party Systems and Voter Alignments: Cross-National Perspectives.* New York: The Free Press.

Liska, Allen E. (1974). "Emergent issues in the attitude-behavior consistency controversy." *American Sociological Review* 39:261–272.

Luttbeg, Norman R. (1968). "The structure of beliefs among leaders and the public." *Public Opinion Quarterly* 32:398–409.

Maranell, Gary M. (1974). *Scaling: A Sourcebook for Behavioral Scientists.* Chicago: Aldine.

Marcus, George E., David Tabb, and John L. Sullivan (1974). "The application of individual differences scaling to the measurement of political ideologies." *American Journal of Political Science* 18:405–420.

Marmor, Theodore R., ed. (1971). *Poverty Policy: A Compendium of Cash Transfer Proposals.* Chicago: Aldine-Atherton.

McClosky, Herbert (1964). "Consensus and ideology in American politics." *American Political Science Review* 58:361–382.

——————— (1967). "Survey research in political science." In Charles Y. Glock, ed., *Survey Research in the Social Sciences.* New York: Sage.

McClosky, Herbert, and Harold E. Dahlgren (1959). "Primary group influence on party loyalty." *American Political Science Review* 53:757–776. (Reprinted by permission.)

McClure, Robert D., and Thomas E. Patterson (1973). "Television news and voter behavior in the 1972 presidential election." Paper delivered at the annual meeting of the American Political Science Association, New Orleans.

McCoy, Charles A., and John Playford, eds. (1967). *Apolitical Politics: A Critique of Behavioralism*. New York: Crowell.

McGuire, William J. (1969). "The nature of attitudes and attitude change." In Gardner Lindzey and Elliot Aronson, eds., *The Handbook of Social Psychology*, Volume 3 (Second edition). Reading, Mass.: Addison-Wesley.

McPhee, William N., and William A. Glaser, eds. (1962). *Public Opinion and Congressional Elections*, Glencoe, Ill.: The Free Press.

Merritt, Anna J., and Richard L. Merritt, eds. (1970). *Public Opinion in Occupied Germany: The OMGUS Surveys, 1945–1949*. Urbana: University of Illinois Press.

Merritt, Richard L. (1970). *Systematic Approaches to Comparative Politics*. Chicago: Rand McNally.

Merritt, Richard L., and Donald J. Puchala, eds. (1968). *Western European Perspectives on International Affairs: Public Opinion Studies and Evaluations*. New York: Praeger.

Merton, Robert K. (1957). *Social Theory and Social Structure*. Revised edition. Glencoe, Ill.: The Free Press.

Miller, Arthur H. (1974a). "Change in political trust: discontent with authorities and economic policies, 1972–1973." Paper delivered at the annual meeting of the American Political Science Association, Chicago.

——————— (1974b). "Political issues and trust in government: 1964–1970." *American Political Science Review* 68:951–972.

Miller, Arthur H., Thad A. Brown, and Alden S. Raine (1973). "Social conflict and political estrangement, 1958–1972." Paper delivered at the annual meeting of the Midwest Political Science Association, Chicago.

Miller, Delbert (1970). *Handbook of Research Design and Social Measurement*. New York: McKay.

Milne, R. S., and H. C. Mackenzie (1954). *Straight Fight: A Study of Voting Behavior in the Constituency of Bristol North-East at the General Election of 1951*. London: The Hansard Society.

——————— (1958). *Marginal Seat, 1955: A Study of Voting Behavior in the Constituency of Bistol North East of the General Election of 1955*. London: The Hansard Society.

Moon, J. Donald (1972). "Participation and democracy: a review essay." *Midwest Journal of Political Science* 16:473–485.

Moriyama, Iwao M. (1968). "Problems in the measurement of health status." In Eleanor Bernert Sheldon and Wilbert E. Moore, eds., *Indicators of Social Change: Concepts and Measurements*. New York: Sage.

Moser, C. A. (1958). *Survey Methods in Social Investigation*. London: Heinemann.

Mosteller, Frederick (1968). "Association and estimation in contingency tables." *Journal of the American Statistical Association* 63:1–28.

Mosteller, Frederick, Herbert Hyman, Philip J. McCarthy, Eli S. Marks, and David B. Truman (1949). *The Pre-election Polls of 1948: Report to the Committee on Analysis of Pre-election Polls and Forecasts.* New York: Social Science Research Council.

Mosteller, Frederick, and Daniel P. Moynihan (1972). "A pathbreaking report." In Frederick Mosteller and Daniel P. Moynihan, eds., *On Equality of Educational Opportunity: Papers Deriving from the Harvard University Seminar on the Coleman Report.* New York: Vintage Books.

Moynihan, Daniel P. (1973). *The Politics of a Guaranteed Income: The Nixon Administration and the Family Assistance Plan.* New York: Vintage Books.

Mueller, John E. (1973). *War, Presidents and Public Opinion.* New York: Wiley.

Nichols, Lee (1954). *Breakthrough on the Color Front.* New York: Random House.

Nie, Norman H., with Kristi Andersen (1974). "Mass belief systems revisited: political change and attitude structure." *Journal of Politics* 36:540–591.

Noelle-Neumann, Elisabeth (1970). "Wanted: rules for wording structured questionnaires." *Public Opinion Quarterly* 34:191–201.

Oberschall, Anthony (1965). *Empirical Social Research in Germany, 1848–1914.* New York: Basic Books.

Oppenheim, A. N. (1966). *Questionnaire Design and Attitude Measurement.* New York: Basic Books.

Orr, Larry L., Robinson G. Hollister, and Myron J. Lefcowitz, eds. (1971). *Income Maintenance: Interdisciplinary Approaches to Research.* Chicago: Markam.

Parry, Hugh J., and Helen M. Crossley (1950). "Validity of responses to survey questions." *Public Opinion Quarterly* 14:61–80.

Parten, Mildred (1950). *Surveys, Polls, and Samples: Practical Procedures.* New York: Harper.

Pateman, Carole (1970). *Participation and Democratic Theory.* Cambridge: Cambridge University Press.

Patterson, Thomas E., and Robert D. McClure (1973). "Political advertising: voter reaction to televised political commercials." Study No. 23. Princeton, N.J.: Citizens' Research Foundation.

Patterson, Thomas E., Robert D. McClure, and Kenneth J. Meier (1974). "Issue voting and voter rationality: a panel analysis." Paper delivered at the annual meeting of the American Political Science Association, Chicago.

Payne, Stanley (1951). *The Art of Asking Questions.* Princeton, N.J.: Princeton University Press.

Peak, Helen (1945). "Observations on the characteristics and distribution of German Nazis." *Psychological Monographs* 59:1–44.

Pierce, John C. (1970). "Party identification and the changing role of ideology in American politics." *Midwest Journal of Political Science* 14:25–42.

Pierce, John C., and Douglas D. Rose (1974). "Nonattitudes and American public opinion: the examination of a thesis." *American Political Science Review* 68:626–649.

Pomper, Gerald M. (1972). "From confusion to clarity: issues and American voters, 1956–1968."*American Political Science Review* 66:415–428.

Prothro, James W., and Charles M. Grigg (1960). "Fundamental principles of democracy: bases of agreement and disagreement." *Journal of Politics* 22:276–294.

Przeworski, Adam, and Henry Teune (1966–1967). "Equivalence in cross-national research." *Public Opinion Quarterly* 30:551–568.

——————— (1970). *The Logic of Comparative Social Inquiry*. New York: Wiley.

Putnam, Robert D. (1966). "Political attitudes and the local community." *American Political Science Review* 60:640–654.

Reed, John Shelton (1972). *The Enduring South: Subcultural Persistence in Mass Society*. Lexington, Mass.: D. C. Heath.

Regan, Opal G. (1973). "Statistical reforms accelerated by sixth census errors." *Journal of the American Statistical Association* 68:540–546.

Reid, Ira DeA. (1940). *In a Minor Key: Negro Youth in Story and Fact*. Washington, D.C.: American Council on Education.

RePass, David E. (1971). "Issue salience and party choice." *American Political Science Review* 65:389–400.

Richardson, Stephen A., Barbara Snell Dohrenwend, and David Klein (1965). *Interviewing: Its Forms and Functions*. New York: Basic Books.

Riesman, David (1950). *The Lonely Crowd: A Study of the Changing American Character*. New Haven, Conn.: Yale University Press.

Rigaudias-Weiss, Hilde (1975). *Les Enquêtes Ouvrières en France Entre 1830 et 1848*. Originally published in 1936. New York. Arno Press.

Rivlin, Alice (1971). *Systematic Thinking for Social Action*. Washington, D.C.: Brookings.

Robinson, John P., Robert Athanasiou, and Kendra B. Head (1969). *Measures of Occupational Attitudes and Occupational Characteristics*. Ann Arbor, Mich.: Institute for Social Research.

Robinson, John P., Jerrold G. Rusk, and Kendra B. Head (1968). *Measures of Political Attitudes*. Ann Arbor, Mich.: Institute for Social Research.

Robinson, John P., and Phillip R. Shaver (1969). *Measures of Social Psychological Attitudes*. Ann Arbor, Mich.: Institute for Social Research.

Rohrer, John H., and Monro S. Edmondson, eds. (1960). *The Eighth Generation: Cultures and Personalities of New Orleans Negroes*. New York: Harper.

Rokeach, Milton (1968). *Beliefs, Attitudes, and Values*. San Francisco: Jossey-Bass.

Rosenberg, Morris (1968). *The Logic of Survey Analysis*. New York: Basic Books.

Rossiter, Clinton, ed. (1961). *The Federalist Papers*. New York: New American Library.

Rowntree, B. Seebohn (1901). *Poverty: A Study of Town Life*. London: Macmillan.

Rush, Gary B. (1967). "Status consistency and rightwing extremism." *American Sociological Review* 32:86–92.

Schuman, Howard (1966). "The random probe: a technique for evaluating the validity of closed questions." *American Sociological Review* 31:218–222.

_____ (1972). "Attitudes vs. action *versus* attitudes vs. attitudes." *Public Opinion Quarterly* 36:347–354. (Reprinted by permission.)

Schuman, Howard, and Otis Dudley Duncan (1974). "Questions about attitude survey questions." In Herbert L. Costner, ed., *Sociological Methodology 1973–1974*. San Francisco: Jossey-Bass. (Reprinted by permission.)

Scott, Robert A., and Arnold Shore (1974). "Sociology and policy analysis." *The American Sociologist* 9:51–59.

Scott, William A. (1968). "Attitude measurement." In Gardner Lindzey and Elliot Aronson, eds., *The Handbook of Social Psychology*, Volume 2 (Second edition). Reading, Mass.: Addison-Wesley.

Sears, David O. (1969). "Political behavior." In Gardner Lindzey and Elliot Aronson, eds., *Handbook of Social Psychology*, Volume 5 (Second edition). Reading, Mass.: Addison-Wesley.

Sewell, William H. (1967). Review of James S. Coleman *et al., Equality of Educational Opportunity*. *American Sociological Review* 32:475–479. (Reprinted by permission.)

Shaw, Marvin E., and Jack M. Wright (1967). *Scales for the Measurement of Attitudes*. New York: McGraw-Hill.

Sheatsley, Paul B. (1963). "Public opinion." *Encyclopedia Americana* 22:772–776.

_____ (1968). "Presidential address: AAPOR times 21." *Public Opinion Quarterly* 32:462–475.

Simon, Rita James (1974). *Public Opinion in America: 1936–1970*. Chicago: Rand McNally.

Smith, M. Brewster, Jerome S. Bruner, and Robert W. White (1956). *Opinions and Personality*. New York: Wiley.

Smith, Marshall S. (1972). "Equality of educational opportunity: the basic findings reconsidered." In Frederick Mosteller and Daniel P. Moynihan, eds., *On Equality of Educational Opportunity: Papers Deriving from the Harvard University Seminar on the Coleman Report*. New York: Vintage Books.

Social Science Research Council. *Social Indicators Newsletter*. Washington, D.C.: Center for Social Indicators.

Social Science Research Council (1937). *Government Statistics: A Report of the Committee on Government Statistics and Information Services*. Bulletin 26. New York.

Stephan, Frederick F. (1948). "History of the uses of modern sampling procedures." *Journal of the American Statistical Association* 43:12–39.

Stephan, Frederick F., and Philip J. McCarthy (1958). *Sampling Opinions: An Analysis of Survey Procedure*. New York: Wiley.

Stouffer, Samuel A. (1955). *Communism, Conformity, and Civil Liberties: A Cross-section of the Nation Speaks Its Mind*. New York: Doubleday.

Stouffer, Samuel A., and Paul F. Lazarsfeld (1937). *Research Memorandum on the Family in the Depression*. Bulletin 29. New York: Social Science Research Council.

Stouffer, Samuel A., Edward A. Suchman, Leland C. DeVinney, Shirley A. Star, and Robin M. Williams, Jr. (1949–1950). *The American Soldier: Studies in Social Psychology in World War II*. Four volumes. Princeton, N.J.: Princeton University Press.

Strauss, Murray A. (1969). "Phenomenal identity and conceptual equivalence of measurement in cross-national comparative research." *Journal of Marriage and the Family* 31:233–341.

Sudman, Seymour (1967). *Reducing the Costs of Surveys*. Chicago: Aldine.

Sudman, Seymour, and Norman M. Bradburn (1974). *Response Effects in Surveys: A Review and Synthesis*. Chicago: Aldine.

Summers, Gene F., ed. (1970). *Attitude Measurement*. Chicago: Rand McNally.

Sutherland, Robert L. (1942). *Color, Class, and Personality*. Washington, D.C.: American Council on Education.

Szalai, Alexander, ed. (1972). *The Use of Time: Daily Activities of Urban and Suburban Populations in Twelve Countries*. The Hague: Mouton.

tenBroek, Jacobus, Edward N. Barnhart, and Floyd W. Matson (1954). *Prejudice, War and the Constitution*. Berkeley: University of California Press.

Tingsten, Herbert (1937). *Political Behavior: Studies in Election Statistics*. London: P. S. King and Son.

Tiryakian, Edward A. (1958). "The prestige evaluation of occupations in an underdeveloped country: the Philippines." *American Journal of Sociology* 63:390–399.

Torgerson, Warren S. (1958). *Theory and Methods of Scaling*. New York: Wiley.

Treiman, Donald J. (1966). "Status discrepancy and prejudice." *American Journal of Sociology* 71:651–664.

United States Department of Justice (1974). *Criminal Victimization in the United States: A National Crime Panel Survey Report*. Volume 1. Report No. SD-NCP-N-1. Washington, D.C.

United States National Resources Commission (1939). "Trends in the reporting of urban information." In *Urban Government*. Washington, D.C.

United States Strategic Bombing Survey (1946). "The effects of atomic bombs on Hiroshima and Nagasaki." No. 3. Morale Division, Washington, D.C.

——————— (1947a). "The effects of strategic bombing on German morale." No. 64b. Two volumes. Morale Division, Washington, D.C.

——————— (1947b). "The effects of strategic bombing on Japanese morale." No. 14. Morale Division, Washington, D.C.

Valen, Henry, and Daniel Katz (1964). *Political Parties in Norway: A Community Study*. Oslo, Norway; Universitetsforlaget.

Verba, Sidney, and Norman H. Nie (1972). *Participation in America: Political Democracy and Social Equality*. New York: Harper & Row.

Vose, Clement E. (1967). "School desegregation: a political scientist's view." *Law and Society Review* 2:141–150.

Walker, Jack L. (1966). "A critique of the elitist theory of democracy." *American Political Science Review* 60:285–295.

Warner, W. Lloyd, Buford H. Junker, and Walter A. Adams (1941). *Color and Human Nature: Negro Personality Development in a Northern City.* Washington, D.C.: American Council on Education.

Weinberg, Eve (1971). *Community Surveys with Local Talent: A Handbook.* Chicago: National Opinion Research Center.

Weinstein, Alan G. (1972). "Predicting behavior from attitudes." *Public Opinion Quarterly* 36:355–360.

White, R. Clyde, and Mary K. White (1937). *Research Memorandum on Social Aspects of Relief Policies in the Depression.* Bulletin 38. New York: Social Science Research Council.

Williams, Robert J., and Charles R. Wright (1955). "Opinion organization in a heterogeneous adult population." *Journal of Abnormal and Social Psychology* 51:559–564.

Wilson, James Q., and Edward C. Banfield (1971). "Political ethos revisited." *American Political Science Review* 65:1048–1062.

Woodward, Julian L. (1952). "A scientific attempt to provide evidence for a decision on change of venue." *American Sociological Review* 17:447–452.

Yarmolinsky, Adam (1963). "Confessions of a non-user." *Public Opinion Quarterly* 27:543–548.

Zajonc, Robert B. (1968). "Cognitive theories in social psychology." In Gardner Lindzey and Elliot Aronson, eds., *The Handbook of Social Psychology,* Volume I (second edition). Reading, Mass.: Addison-Wesley.

Zitter, Meyer, and Donald E. Starsinic (1966). "Estimates of 'eligible' voters in small areas: some first approximations." *American Statistical Association: Proceedings of the Social Section* 368–378.

7
FORMAL THEORY

GERALD H. KRAMER
JOSEPH HERTZBERG

INTRODUCTION

This chapter deals with theoretical research on political phenomena, which makes use of formal analytical methods. It should be noted at the outset that this work has been concentrated in certain areas, and there are many other areas and topics in political science on which little or no such research has yet been done. Indeed, political science, to the extent that it is a science, is largely an empirical one at present, rather than a theoretical one. Such theory as does exist —whether normative political philosophy or descriptive functional or systems analyses of political behavior—is for the most part eclectic, informal, and incompletely codified, rather than rigorous scientific theory in the usual sense.

This state of affairs is to some degree simply a reflection of the nature and complexity of the subject. The array of forces and personalities at play in many contemporary or historical political episodes is often too complex, multifaceted, and uncertain to lend itself to any simple all-encompassing theoretical explanation. Similarly, the far-reaching ramifications and layers of complexity surrounding many fundamental issues of social and political philosophy seem beyond the reach of rigorous analysis at present. But while it seems clear that important areas of political science are unlikely ever to be fully susceptible to rigorous scientific analysis, it also seems clear that many such areas contain important components that are amenable to more careful theoretical treatment. Many fundamental questions of political philosophy, for example, involve the relationship between the individual and collective wills, a central concern of the modern theory of collective choice. Much of political life revolves around the interplay of conflicting individual and group interests within some institutional setting, and hence falls within the scope of the theory of games and strategic behavior. An understanding of the functioning of particular structured

351

political institutions, whether agenda or voting procedures for a committee, or large-scale electoral systems, is of central concern to the study of political science, on which a theoretical literature is gradually accumulating. Current theoretical knowledge in all these areas is still incomplete and partial, and clearly much remains to be done. Nevertheless there has emerged a body of concepts, results, and analytical tools that have provided considerable theoretical insight and clarification in certain areas, and that may well be the basis on which important theoretical advances in the future are built. The central purpose of this chapter is to describe this theoretical core, and to selectively review some of the derivative applications in various areas of political science.

Though the title of the chapter refers to "formal" theory, there is no sharp or universal boundary between formal and informal methods. In political science, an article that used the differential calculus, for example, or that involved lengthy algebraic or even graphical derivations, would qualify as relatively formal. However, in more quantitative scientific disciplines, such as economics or the various natural sciences, such methods are the everyday tools of most theoretical research contributions, and an article would not be considered particularly formal or mathematical unless it used more advanced types of mathematics, or met high standards of mathematical rigor. Thus the "formal" theory of political science is essentially the ordinary, garden variety of scientific theory in the usage of most scientific disciplines.

By a theory we mean something like a set of premises and assumptions concerning a certain class of phenomena, from which useful or revealing implications can be derived. Of course even in everyday affairs, our actions and reflections about our surroundings are based on certain implicit assumptions about the nature of things, whose implications guide our conduct and our interpretations of events. Such deductive structures also underlie political commentary or scholarly analyses of current or historical political events. In this sense, it can be said that most intellectual activity involves theory of some sort. However, this everyday type of theoretical reasoning differs in essential respects from scientific theory. Concepts in ordinary language usage carry a variety of different connotations and meanings, and are used in various of these different meanings during the course of ordinary discourse. Only rarely in everyday discussion do we bother to consistently use a word in only one of its senses, or to make precise and explicit the meanings of key terms and underlying premises of the argument. Indeed, permitting terms to carry a degree of ambiguity is usually an efficient way of proceeding, since the listener can generally determine the sense from the context. By the same token it is rarely worthwhile to begin a discussion by listing all the causal and normative premises in terms of which one intends to interpret the subject of interest. Some such premises may be introduced as they are needed, while many of them are normally not made explicit at all, but left implicit, since they are part of a common knowledge that the listener can be assumed to share. These ambiguities, logical lacunae, and potential inconsistencies are generally innocuous in informal discourse. But they also differentiate the "proto-theory" of informal discussion from scientific theory, which by its very nature must be based on a well-defined, delimited, and consistent set of premises and concepts, logically sufficient to imply the conclusions of interest.

In principle, precision, consistency, and logical validity are properties of the argument itself, not of the language in which the argument is expressed. Carefully reasoned argument is possible in any language, formal or informal. As a practical matter, however, the task is easier in some languages than others, particularly for complex arguments with lengthy chains of reasoning. There is a widespread view, for example, that English is inherently a more precise and literal language, and hence more suited to scientific discourse, than is French, for example, or many non-European languages. (Perhaps for this reason English is the common language of many scientific meetings, even among groups that share and use some other tongue for ordinary social discourse.) Formal languages (including mathematics, programming languages, or special purpose formalisms for expressing chemical reactions or syntactic structure in linguistics) are intrinsically even more suited for these purposes. By their very nature, such formal languages demand a degree of precision and explicitness, and provide a codified and structured method of presenting lengthy derivations or chains of implications. These characteristics facilitate precise communication, and provide an efficient method for verifying logical validity, or exploring the consequences of variations in certain premises or relationships. For these reasons, most scientific disciplines in which there exists a substantial body of theoretical knowledge have found it efficient to use formal language, in at least a supplementary role.

Mathematical methods play an even more fundamental role in more theoretically advanced fields. In areas of theoretical physics, for example, the state of theoretical knowledge is such that it simply cannot be accurately grasped, or applied, in nonmathematical terms. A purely verbal treatment of general relativity or quantum mechanics may succeed in conveying the general flavor and broad outlines of the theory, but the essential content is intrinsically mathematical. The situation is a bit different in theoretical economics, where many of the key results are more qualitative in character, and can be accurately described nonmathematically. However, advanced mathematical methods have been crucial in establishing fundamental existence and other results that underlie and tie together the more intuitive partial equilibrium results of applied microeconomic theory. Other types of mathematics have been important in making the theory applicable to realistic problems, permitting qualitative results for two-variable problems to be extended to multiple-variable problems, and providing practical computational methods for obtaining useful quantitative results in large and complex applications. As a consequence, there has been a considerable evolution in the use and acceptance of mathematical methods in economics. Articles that a few decades ago would have been considered suitable only for specialized technical journals, because of their mathematical content, today constitute the preponderance of contributions in the *American Economic Review* and other general economics journals.

Whether any comparable evolution will occur in the field of political science will depend primarily on whether a useful body of analytic scientific theory is developed. No sizable body of such theory exists at present. However, there are several areas in which substantial developments have occurred, which may provide the basis for future cumulative developments. In the remainder of this chapter we will review some of the key concepts and results in several of these areas. Our emphasis will be in areas in which mathematical methods function as an active research tool, rather than merely as a means of communication and codification; and our discussion will be selective with respect to both individual articles and research areas.[1]

The first part of this chapter introduces a simple example of a community faced with a pollution problem. This example is developed in several directions, and serves to introduce the major topics of what might be called modern political economy: the theory of preference and individual choice behavior underlying much of formal theory; the notion of a multiperson behavioral equilibrium, and some of the mathematical tools needed to investigate it; some aspects of social choice theory, and related normative questions; and finally, some of the work on the theoretical analyses of political institutions.

The second section concerns the theory of games and strategy. Key theoretical concepts and results and their applications to political science are reviewed for each of the major branches of game theory (two-player zero-sum, general noncooperative, and cooperative games).

For a more leisurely and detailed review of many of the areas covered in this chapter, the reader is referred especially to Riker and Ordeshook's recent *An Introduction to Positive Political Theory* (1973), which is the most comprehensive survey of formal political theory presently available.

POLITICAL ECONOMY

To illustrate the nature of formal mathematical analysis, and to introduce the major subject areas of the field, we will develop an example from the area of political economy. For expositional convenience we will be very concrete and specific in our example. Consider a community situated on the shore of a lake. The lake is the sole source of drinking water for the community; it may serve as a common source of food, and recreational and esthetic benefits as well. Perhaps inadvertently, it is also used for another purpose: waste of all kinds, unless disposed of at its origin, eventually finds its way into the lake. Thus the lake serves as a common means of waste disposal. This last function, however, is potentially in conflict with the lake's other uses, for as more garbage accumulates, the lake becomes less suitable for other purposes.

The alternative to polluting the lake is to dispose of waste in another manner, but this could be a time-consuming and tedious process. An individual who did this would have to sacrifice other values or goods. Each individual must, therefore, strike a balance between conflicting goals. To investigate his behavior in this situation, we must know something about his preferences.

Individual Preferences and Collective Goods

The set of alternatives from which the individual must choose consists of the possible combinations of water quality and private consumption. To be precise, we shall measure water quality by the rate of aggregate waste discharge into the lake (in tons per year, for example). Water quality, which we will denote by the symbol q, thus ranges from 0 (for perfectly unpolluted water) downward. For example, $q = -100$ signifies the water quality level resulting from the continued discharge at the rate of 100 tons per year. We can similarly suppose that the level of private consumption enjoyed by an individual may be characterized by a single number, which we will call "income." All individuals must use the same lake, so its quality is a *collective* good, shared by all. However, different individuals may have different levels of income, a *private* good. Thus we denote by y_i the income of individual i. The set of combinations of water quality and private consumption with which the individual might conceivably be confronted is thus the set of possible (q, y_i) pairs. Each such combination, or ordered pair, can be represented as a point in a two-dimensional space (see, for example, Fig. 1) whose vertical and horizontal coordinates represent water quality and income, respectively.

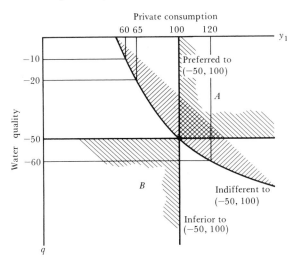

Figure 1

The theory of individual choice which underlies this example (and much of modern economic theory, collective choice theory, and the theory of games) is based on several general assumptions concerning individual choice behavior. An individual's choices are assumed to be as if guided by an underlying *preference ordering* of the possible objects of choice. Given a free choice of any of a set of objects, the individual will choose that alternative which is ranked highest by that ordering. The underlying ordering of each individual is assumed to have the following properties:

1. The ordering is *complete*. Given any pair of alternatives A and B, the individual either prefers A to B, or prefers B to A, or else is indifferent between A and B. There are no "incomparable alternatives."

2. The ordering is *transitive*. If A is preferred or indifferent to B, and B is to C, then A must be preferred or indifferent to C. The various possible paired preferences must be consistent.

These two assumptions apply quite generally to individual preferences, whether the objects of choice are (q, y_i) pairs, competing candidates for office, alternative legislative proposals, or whatever. For the type of alternatives we are considering here (varying amounts of two or more valued quantities, or "goods") several additional assumptions are made. These assumptions—that the preference ordering is continuous, convex, and monotonic—are somewhat more technical, but their thrust is that both "goods" are always positively valued (more of either is always preferred to less) but at a diminishing rate (as the quantity available of either good is increased, an additional unit of it becomes less valuable relative to an additional unit of the other good).

These premises have some fairly definite implications for individual preference structures. Consider an individual and a particular combination of water quality and income, say $q = -50$ and $y_i = \$100$. Our first premise on individual preferences says that the individual can decide whether or not he prefers this particular alternative to any other possible combination. Thus he can divide up the set of possible alternatives into three mutually exclusive subsets: those he prefers to $(-50, 100)$; those that he finds inferior to $(-50, 100)$; and those that are indifferent to $(-50, 100)$. Our assumptions allow us to say a bit more about these subsets. Since water quality and income are both desirable, clearly he prefers any alternative that gives him more of both, or more of one and no less of the other. These alternatives lie in the shaded region A of Fig. 1. By the same token, an alternative that gives him less of one good, with no compensating increase in the other, must be inferior to $(-50, 100)$; the set of such points lies in the region B in Fig. 1.

But not all points preferred to $(-50, 100)$ lie in region A, and not all points to which $(-50, 100)$ is preferred lie in region B. Our individual might, for example, prefer a combination providing him with a smaller income if there were a sufficient improvement in water quality. To complete our identification of these subsets, we must find the subsets of points that the individual finds indifferent to (−50, 100). These points lie on the curve that passes through (−50, 100) in Fig. 1. The combinations (−10, 60), (−20, 65), and (−60, 120) are all on this curve, and all are indifferent to (−50, 100) and to one another. The shape of this curve displays the "diminishing returns" property demanded by our assumptions. At the point (−50, 100), the individual would require an extra $20 in income to compensate him for a 10-unit decline in water quality [since he is indifferent between the points (−50, 100) and (−60, 120)]. At higher levels of water quality, a smaller increase in income is required to offset the same decline. For example, the individual requires only a $5 increase in income to compensate him for a 10-unit quality decline at the point (−10, 60).

If we consider several distinct points, we can draw an indifference curve through each. If any pair of indifference curves were to intersect, we could find three points for which the transitivity assumption (2) (see p. 356) would not be satisfied. Hence, if our assumptions are satisfied and the individual's preferences are consistent, we can represent his preference structure with a "family" of nonintersecting, nested indifference curves. Several representative curves are shown in Fig. 2. Points lying on a higher indifference curve, such as b, are preferred to those on a lower curve, such as a. Given the choice among points a, b, and c, the individual would choose c, which lies on the highest curve.

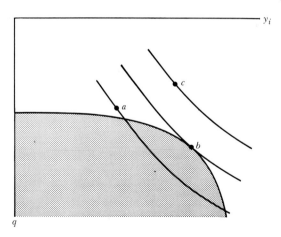

Figure 2

The set of combinations of water quality and income actually available for choice by the individual may be represented in this same space. The shaded region in Fig. 2 might be such a set. The boundary of the region moves in a northwest-southeast direction reflecting a "trade-off" between water quality and income: in general, to achieve purer water some private income must be sacrificed, and vice versa. Confronted with a choice from the points in this region, the individual will select the one that lies on the highest indifference curve: point b in Fig. 2. Of all the combinations available, he prefers this one.

The discussion so far has been in terms of a single individual, acting in an isolated environment in which his actions alone determine the ultimate consequences of his choices. Let us now examine some of the complications that arise when individual choices must be made in a social setting, in which the results of any individual's action are affected by actions and choices of others, who are pursuing their own interests.

Unregulated Individualism

In a state of unregulated anarchy, with no effective intervention from the community, each individual is free to try to choose whichever (q, y_i) pair he prefers most, without regard to the welfare of anyone but himself. Even so, his best choice, or optimal behavior, will depend in part on the behavior of others in the community.

This dependence is explored in Fig. 3. Suppose that everyone except Individual 1 produces a relatively large amount $(-q^*)$ of pollution. If Individual 1 decides not to clean up any of his waste, he will keep all of his private income y_1, but water quality will deteriorate somewhat, and the resulting quality–income state will be B^*, as shown on the figure. Conversely, if Individual 1 chooses to treat all his own waste, water quality will be maintained at q^*, but his income will fall, and the resulting state will be A^*. Other decisions, to clean up varying proportions of his waste, will yield (q, y_i) combinations lying on the line from A^* to B^*; thus the set of states available to Individual 1, from which he must choose, is the set of points in the line A^*B^*. If Individual 1's preferences are described by the indifference curves in Fig. 3, clearly his best choice is to treat all his waste, resulting in the state A^*.

If the other individuals produced a smaller amount $(-q')$ of total pollution, the set of (q, y_i) combinations available to Individual 1 would be shifted upward, to the line $A'B'$; and in this case, his optimal response is not to undertake any waste treatment at all. In intermediate cases, such as $A\ B$, he will choose to treat some, but not all, of his waste.

It is clear from this that no individual can choose his best course of action independently of the actions of others. But this leads to the possibility of an infinite regress, since each individual's action depends on other individuals' choices, which in turn depend in part on the first individual's choice, and so on. Thus the question arises whether there exists any stable set of choices—i.e., a set of choices that are in *equilibrium,* in the sense that if they were realized, no one would then want to modify his decision and hence choose a different state. If no such set exists we may be unable to make any useful predictions or inferences about the consequences of uncontrolled pursuit of private self-interest.

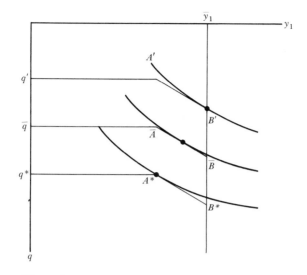

Figure 3

Suppose the community consists of only two individuals. Then if Individual 2 produces a given amount p_2 of pollution, there is a well-defined opportunity set (like $\bar{A}\,\bar{B}$) confronting Individual 1, from which he will choose the best point. Let $\hat{p}_1(p_2)$ be the amount of pollution (which may be zero) which Individual 1 will decide to emit (or leave untreated), when Individual 2 produces p_2 units; since Individual 1's choice is well defined for any feasible p_2, the *response function* $\hat{p}_1(p_2)$ summarizes his responses to all of Individual 2's possible actions. Conversely, by interchanging the rules of Individuals 1 and 2, we can obtain a second function $\hat{p}_2(p_1)$ which summarizes Individual 2's responses to Individual 1's possible actions. The functions $\hat{p}_1(.)$ and $\hat{p}_2(.)$ are not necessarily identical (they depend on the incomes and preferences of the two individuals, which may differ), but they will be of the same general shape. In particular, it is clear from Fig. 3 that each individual will treat more of his own waste as water quality decreases, i.e., as the amount produced by the others pollutes more. A typical response function for Individual 2 is shown in Fig. 4. When Individual 1's pollution is at the level $\bar{p}_1$, Individual 2's response is to emit an amount $\hat{p}_2(\bar{p}_1)$ of untreated waste. If Individual 1's initial level is $\bar{\bar{p}}_1$ (or less), Individual 2 leaves all his waste untreated, while if Individual 1 produces $\bar{\bar{p}}_1$ or more, Individual 2 undertakes 100 percent treatment.

Of course, the behavioral responses summarized in the functions $\hat{p}_1(p_2)$, $\hat{p}_2(p_1)$ still contain the possibility of an infinite regress, since each person's behavior depends on the behavior of the other. To examine this possibility more carefully, consider Fig. 5. The horizontal and vertical axes represent the amounts of pollution produced by Individuals 1 and 2, respectively. The curve

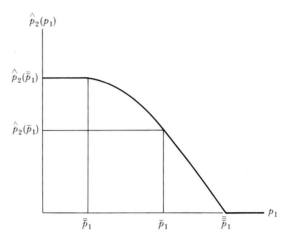

Figure 4

labelled $\hat{p}_2(p_1)$ is the function describing the response of Individual 2, contingent on Individual 1's behavior, while the line $\hat{p}_1(p_2)$ is a graph of the analogous function for Individual 1. Thus if Individual 2's pollution is fixed at a level p_2^0, Individual 1's response is $\hat{p}_1(p_2^0) = p_1^1$, measured on the horizontal axis.

Suppose that at some initial state individuals are discharging untreated

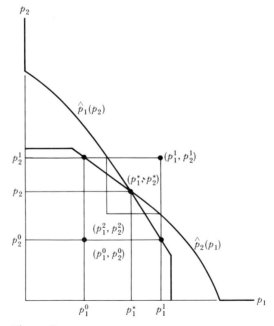

Figure 5

pollution at rates of p_1^0 and p_2^0 units, respectively. As each becomes aware of the other's behavior, he will find it advantageous to readjust his own decision. Thus Individual 1 will seek to increase his own rate to $\hat{p}_1(p_2^0) = p_1^1$, while Individual 2 will similarly tend to move toward the level $p_2^1 = \hat{p}_2(p_1^0)$. If each person can readily readjust his pollution level, and can do so before becoming aware that the other party is also readjusting, the net result will be a movement from the initial point (p_1^0, p_2^0) to a new point (p_1^1, p_2^1). However, this situation will not persist—Individual 1 will tend to move to p_1^2, while Individual 2 moves to p_2^2. This new situation is still in disequilibrium, since a further readjustment will still take place.

However, there is one state in which such readjustments do not arise, namely, the point at which the two response curves cross, (p_1^*, p_2^*). In this situation, Individual 1's optimal response to Individual 2's behavior is $\hat{p}_1(p_2^*) = p_1^*$, so his action is unchanged. The same is true for the other individual, since $\hat{p}_2(p_1^*) = p_2^*$. Thus these two courses of action are mutually consistent, and self-perpetuating.

The state (p_1^*, p_2^*) constitutes an *equilibrium:* a set of actions, one for each individual, which has the property that no individual finds it advantageous to change to some other action if no one else does. It is optimal for Individual 1 to continue at the level p_1^* so long as Individual 2 maintains his pollution rate p_2^*. Similarly, Individual 2 is willing to maintain p_2^* if Individual 1 remains at p_1^*. In our example, such an equilibrium will exist if, and only if, the two schedules $\hat{p}_1(p_2)$, $\hat{p}_2(p_1)$ intersect somewhere on Fig. 5. Under our assumptions there must be such an intersection.

Two points should be made concerning this argument. First, the actions p_1^*, p_2^* are stable in the sense that if both individuals happened to choose them, they would persist over time, but our analysis does not guarantee that these actions actually will be chosen. In this example, if each individual responds naively to the current action of the other, their actions will converge on the point (p_1^*, p_2^*). However under different assumptions about the shapes of the response functions, their successive responses might take them further away from, rather than closer to, the equilibrium. Moreover, even if the functions are as drawn in Fig. 5, convergence need not occur if the individuals are sophisticated and try to anticipate the other's future behavior while formulating their own responses. Our model is basically a static one. It enables us to show the existence of an equilibrium set of actions that would tend to persist, but it tells us little about the dynamic adjustment process that might occur in disequilibrium.

Second, although the point $(p_1^*\ p_2^*)$ is stable, it is by no means necessarily desirable. It is possible that both individuals prefer one of the disequilibrium states, such as (p_1^*, p_2^*), to the equilibrium situation. The "invisible hand" need not work to the benefit of all, or even of any. We will consider this issue—the desirability and social efficiency of unregulated individualism—in the next section.

From a mathematical point of view, the argument developed in this section is a simplified case of an important class of arguments. In our example, the existence of equilibrium turned out to depend on whether the $p_1(p_2)$, $p_2(p_1)$ schedules intersected. In the simple case of two people and one decision variable, it is possible to investigate this question graphically. A graphical analysis of the three-person case might also be feasible, but clearly such methods are inadequate when there are many individuals, or two or more decision variables. The existence of equilibrium in these more general situations can often be shown by a mathematical argument using a *fixed-point* theorem. The question of whether there exists an equilibrium state, which reconciles the actions of several agents pursuing their own mutually conflicting interests, is one that occurs in many areas of the social sciences, and fixed-point theorems are powerful mathematical tools widely used for investigating this type of question.[2]

Individual versus Collective Rationality

We have shown that even in the absence of any social cooperation, there may exist an equilibrium combination of individual decisions about pollution levels, which no individual has any incentive to change. We now turn to the question of whether this equilibrium state is in any sense a desirable one.

Let us suppose that each individual in our two-person society produces the same amount, m, of pollution in the absence of any treatment. Let t_i be the amount that any Individual i treats, so that $p_i + t_i = m$, for each individual. Furthermore, let us suppose it costs r dollars per unit to treat waste, so that the income sacrificed by Individual i to treat t_i units is rt_i. Now consider Fig. 6. If both individuals were to pollute the maximum amount, the water quality would fall to $-2m$. However, at the equilibrium point identified above and labelled C^* on the diagram, each does treat some of his waste.[3] Neither has any incentive to treat more (or less) of his pollution.

Now suppose that both individuals entered into an agreement to treat twice as much of their waste. The situation would change from the equilibrium point C^* to a new point D.[4] This moves Individual 1 from the indifference curve I_1^* to the higher curve I_1' so he prefers the new situation to the equilibrium. The same might well be true of Individual 2 also. However, even if D is preferred to C^* by both individuals, it is not an equilibrium. Because Individual 2 now treats $2t_2^*$ of his waste, the opportunity set confronting Individual 1 is the line $A'B'$, where A' and B' are the states resulting from Individual 1's minimum and maximum levels of pollution (0 and m, respectively). If Individual 1 is free to choose any point on this line, he will move to the point C', which touches his highest indifference curve. At this point, he treats even less of his waste than he did in the equilibrium state C^*. Individual 2 might well be led into a

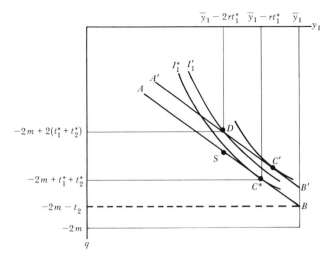

Figure 6

similar decision. Thus, although both parties would benefit from having the agreement in force, each has an incentive to violate it.

It is this tension between individualistic and collective rationality that is at the heart of Olson's (1965) logic of collective action. Each individual finds it personally profitable to violate the agreement, and thus become a *free rider*, reaping the benefits of the collective action without making any contribution of his own. But other individuals have similar incentives to become free riders also. If a substantial number attempt to get free rides, the agreement will become ineffective—even though, as shown above, all are better off with the agreement in force than when it is not. In some small or particularly cohesive societies, individual conscience and sense of civic duty, perhaps reinforced by social pressures and informal sanctions (when violations are relatively visible), may suffice to ensure general compliance. Often, however, the only effective means will involve a measure of compulsion, and the establishment of formal enforcement mechanisms. This divergence between individualistic and collective rationality is thus a powerful stimulus for social organization.

Efficiency, Equity, and Conflicts of Interest

A collective organization, or government, whose purpose is to facilitate and enforce mutually beneficial arrangements faces a complex task, however, for often there will be several possible arrangements. Though everyone will agree that any of these arrangements is superior to the unregulated individualistic equilibrium, some will nevertheless prefer certain of these possible cooperative agreements to others.

To investigate this possibility further, it is useful to look at preferences in a slightly different way. Since overall water quality depends on the treatment expenditures of everyone, each individual's preferences can be reexpressed in relation to the set of possible combinations of treatment expenditures by all other individuals. To derive these indirect preferences in our two-person example, consider Fig. 7, which is a simplified version of Fig. 6. The individualistic equilibrium point is C^*, at which Individual 1 spends rt_1^* on treatment, and Individual 2 spends rt_2^*. The indifference curve I_1^* traces out the set of quality–income combinations that Individual 1 finds indifferent to the equilibrium combination C^*; thus he is indifferent to the three points B, E, and C^*. In Fig. 8, the horizontal and vertical axes represent the treatment expenditures by Individuals 1 and 2, respectively. At the equilibrium point, Individuals 1 and 2 spend rt_1^* and rt_2^*, respectively, for treatment, so the point C^* of Fig. 7 corresponds to the combination (rt_1^*, rt_2^*) in Fig. 8. The other points in Fig. 7, such as B and E, similarly have corresponding points in Fig. 8, and the set of quality–income combinations lying on I_1^* in Fig. 6 corresponds to the similarly labelled set in Fig. 7. For every other indifference curve for Individual 1 in the quality–income space, there will be corresponding indifference curves, such as I_1' and I_1'', in the expenditure space of Fig. 8.

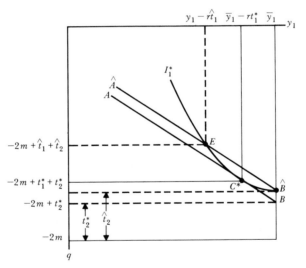

Figure 7

In the same fashion we can translate Citizen 2's preferences for different (q, y_2) combinations into an indifference map in the same space of expenditure combinations. Figure 9 shows some representative indifference curves of both individuals, plotted in the same expenditure space. With the aid of this diagram, let us now reconsider the question of possible social benefits from organization. The individualistic equilibrium point results in the expenditure combination (rt_1^*, rt_2^*), labelled C^* on the diagram. Any point lying above In-

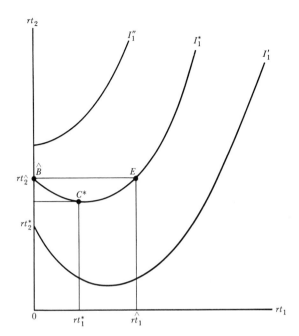

Figure 8

dividual 1's indifference curve I_1^* through C^* will be preferred (to C^*) by Individual 1, while any point to the right of I_2^* is preferred by Individual 2. The point D which results from doubling both the equilibrium expenditure levels satisfies both these conditions simultaneously, and so makes both individuals better off. Point D is not unique in this respect, however, for any point lying in the region bounded by the curves I_1^* and I_2^*, such as point D', is also preferred to C^* by both parties. Moreover, the two individuals clearly have differing views on the desirability of these various alternatives. From the viewpoint of Individual 1, points C^* and B, which lie on his indifference curve I_1^*, are among the least desirable alternatives, since other points in the region, such as D and D', lie on higher indifference curves. The point A lies on the highest of Individual 1's indifference curves which touch the region: of all possible mutually beneficial combinations, point A is best for Individual 1. For Individual 2, the situation is reversed, since A lies on his lowest indifference curve in the region, while B lies on his highest. The distance from A to B is thus a rough measure of the potential conflict of interest inherent in the situation. A fundamental task confronting the collectivity is to reconcile this conflict of interest, and somehow choose among the different alternatives.

One possible way of doing this is to appeal to some ethical principle of equity or fairness. However, difficulties emerge when we attempt to formulate a precise criterion of "equity." One natural criterion might be that both ought

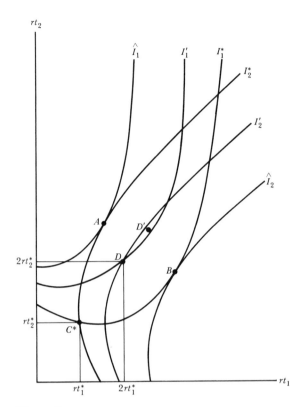

Figure 9

to pay equal amounts for treatment. The set of points for which $rt_1 = rt_2$ lies along a 45° line through the origin, labelled Oe' in Fig. 10. One difficulty is immediately apparent: though many points are not equitable in this sense, all of the points on line Oe' are; and of these, all points that lie on the line segment ee' are better than C^* for both individuals. Hence some way must still be found to resolve the problem of choice that remains.

A second difficulty arises from the fact that there may be differing views as to what constitutes "fairness." If one individual's income is much larger than the other's, for example, the "equal amounts" criterion would result in the poorer person spending a large portion of his income for treatment, while the wealthier individual foregoes only a small portion of his. A plausible alternative criterion, therefore, might be to require each person to spend an equal *proportion* of income on treatment. If Individual 2 is wealthier than Individual 1, the set of points satisfying such a criterion would lie on a line such as Of' in Fig. 10. This criterion, like the earlier one, identifies a set of mutually beneficial, equitable possible solutions (lying on the segment ff'), rather than a single solu-

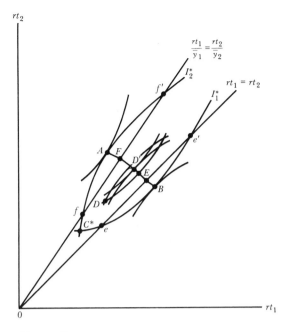

Figure 10

tion. Moreover, the fact that these two criteria lead to such different results poses a more fundamental problem. Individual 1 will generally be better off under the proportional criterion, since the points in *ff'* lie on higher indifference curves than most of the points in *ee'*. The opposite is true for Individual 2, however, and he will tend to prefer the first criterion. In these circumstances, it might be just as difficult to reach agreement on what constitutes equity as it would be to agree directly on an expenditure point.

The point *D* in Figs. 9 and 10 violates another normative criterion. It is clear that both individuals could be better off by moving from *D* to a point such as *D'* in Fig. 9, since *D'* lies above and to the right of the two indifference curves (I'_1 and I'_2, in Fig. 9) through *D*. Thus the point *D* is in a sense a socially wasteful, or inefficient, choice. If for a point *X* there can be found another point *Y* which everyone prefers to *X*, then *X* is *inefficient;* conversely, if *no* such point *Y* can be found, then *X* is efficient, or *pareto optimal*. Though point *D* is inefficient in this sense, the point *A* is efficient, since any movement from *A* to a higher indifference curve for one individual necessarily moves the other person to a lower curve. By this same reasoning, any point such as *D'* or *B* in Fig. 10, at which the indifference curves of the two individuals are just tangent to each other, is efficient. The set of efficient points thus lies on the curve *AB* in Fig. 10. Evidently an efficient point need not be fair, or equitable: the set *AB* of efficient points is quite different from the sets *Of'* and *Oe'* satisfying the two criteria of equality: only F and E are both efficient and fair, in either sense. Even though there may exist no consensus on what constitutes equity in this situation, social efficiency, as we have defined it, is a standard that should command universal assent. However, it is clear that the two individuals' preferences concerning the different alternatives in the efficient set AB are diametrically opposed; hence, the conflict of interest remains, and must still be resolved.

Let us recapitulate the principal points of this analysis. Cooperative action offers potential benefits to all individuals. To realize these benefits, the individuals must become sufficiently well organized to agree on a common course of action, and on mechanisms to ensure that some individuals do not become "free riders." Within the set of possible mutually beneficial collective choices, serious conflicts of interest arise. Ethical principles are unlikely in themselves to resolve these conflicts because they are too broad, and because such principles are themselves likely to conflict. Thus we are led to consider the possibility of establishing political institutions for resolving social conflicts.

Majority Rule

Let us, therefore, consider some possible political decision-making mechanisms that might be adopted by our community. Specifically, we will be concerned with voting mechanisms based on simple majority rule. Because majority rule is uninteresting with only two voters, let us add a third individual to our analysis.

To begin with, suppose our community first agrees to adopt the "equal shares" rule discussed above. Each individual will be required to spend the same amount $K = rt_i$ on pollution control, implying that each will treat the same amount $\hat{t} = K/r$ of waste. If the level of K (and hence of $\hat{t}$) is to be determined by the community through a majority vote, at what level will the standard be set? Individual 1's preferences among alternative values may be derived from Fig. 11. If the other individuals treated none of their waste, the choice set of Voter 1 would be AB. Because the other two individuals must spend the same amount as Individual 1 does for treatment, however, three units of total waste will be treated for every unit treated by Individual 1, and possible quality–income combinations from which Individual 1 must choose are those in the set $A'B$. His most-preferred point in this set is C, so his most-preferred value of K is therefore $r\hat{t}''$. If we consider a lower value of K, i.e., points such as D for which $\bar{y}_1 - \bar{r}t > \bar{y}_i - rt''$, it is clear that the smaller the value of rt', the lower the indifference curve on which the point D lies. The same is true for values of K greater than $r\hat{t}''$, such as rt'''. Individual 1's preference ranking of the alternative treatment amounts $r\hat{t}'$, $r\hat{t}''$, and $r\hat{t}'''$, which are associated with the points D, C, and E, respectively, may hence be read from Fig. 11. This ranking is shown explicitly in Fig. 12. The preference orderings of Individuals 2 and 3 for these same alternatives can be obtained similarly, and under our assumptions, they will be similarly shaped. Each ordering will have a peak at

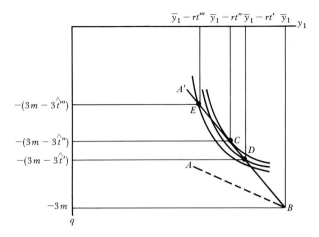

Figure 11

the voter's most-preferred value of K, and will decline as the treatment level increases or decreases from this most-preferred value. A preference ordering of this shape is said to be *single-peaked* (Black, 1958). A possible set of such single-peaked rankings for all three individuals is shown in Fig. 13.

Given a choice between any two alternatives, each individual will vote for whichever one he ranks higher. Thus in a choice between K_1 and K_2 in Fig. 12, Individual 1 will vote for K_1, while Individuals 2 and 3 would vote for K_2; hence, K_2 defeats K_1 by majority rule. Similarly, K_2 will defeat K_3 in a paired vote, while K_1 in turn will defeat K_3. Thus in this case the majority preference relation is *transitive* (it satisfies the consistency property (2) of individual preferences); and there exists an alternative, K_2, which is a *majority winner* in the sense that it wins every paired vote between it and any other alternative.

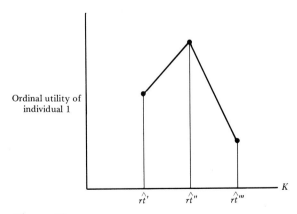

Figure 12

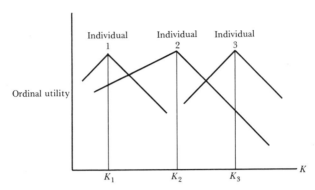

Figure 13

A principal contribution of Black's original and important work *The The-ory of Committees and Elections* (1958) (as subsequently generalized) is a theorem to the effect that such a majority winner necessarily exists, for any number of alternatives and voters, if all individual preference rankings are single-peaked. Thus whenever the single-peakedness condition is satisfied, majority rule is "well behaved," and a political process based on majority voting will lead to a determinate outcome and thus succeed in resolving the underlying conflict of interest.

If the community had begun by defining equity in terms of equal proportions, rather than equal shares, a different set of alternatives would have to be considered. The task facing the community would then be to decide on a common fraction α of everyone's income to be used for pollution treatment. In this case the set of quality–income combinations for an individual resulting from different values of α would also be a straight line, similar to $A'B$ in Fig. 12, but its slope would depend on the individual's income, in relation to the income of the rest of the community. In particular, the line would be steeper (closer to vertical) for the poorer citizens, and more horizontal for the wealthier ones. However each individual's preferences for different points on the line confronting him (and hence for different values of α) would still be single-peaked. Hence, majority rule would still lead to a determinate outcome, though the water quality resulting from this outcome might well be different from that which would result under the "equal shares" criterion.

If the community were unable to agree initially on either principle of equity, majority rule might well be indeterminate. To show this, let us suppose that the community began by agreeing on what level of water quality should be achieved, and then used majority rule to decide how the costs of achieving this quality level should be distributed among the citizenry. For simplicity, suppose the quality level they have agreed on requires total treatment expenditures of $100. This total cost must be somehow apportioned among the three citizens. If we let C_1, C_2, and C_3 be the amounts paid by Individuals 1, 2, and 3, respectively, then clearly the set of possible alternatives, over which the community must vote, is the set of expenditure combinations (C_1, C_2, C_3) such that $C_1 + C_2 + C_3 = 100$. As these assessments are varied, the opportunity set confronting Individual 1 will be the horizontal line segment AB in Fig. 14. Water quality will be the same whatever the value of C_1, so the choice set runs from the point A, at which $C_1 = 100$, to point B, where $C_1 = 0$. Clearly Individual 1 prefers C_1 to be as small as possible, and his most-preferred point is B. Obviously Individuals 2 and 3 will also want their assessments, C_2 and C_3, to be as small as possible.

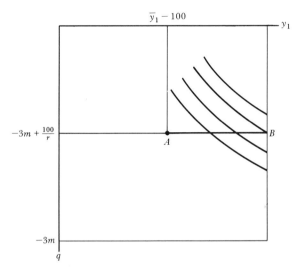

Figure 14

The set of possible assessment combinations (C_1, C_2, C_3) for which $C_1 + C_2 + C_3 = 100$ is shown graphically in Fig. 15. Since each individual cares only about his own assessment, he is indifferent to any combinations in which his own contribution is the same. Individual 3, for example, is indifferent to (100, 0, 0) and (0, 100, 0), and to any intermediate combination such as (50, 50, 0), since his contribution is zero in all such cases. Hence his indifference "curve" I'_3 through these combinations is a straight line, as are his other indifference curves I''_3, I'''_3, I''''_3. Clearly his least-preferred combination is (0, 0, 100) (the point Q), at which he pays all the treatment costs himself, so his "higher" or more-preferred indifference curves are those that are lower on the triangle. The indifference maps of the other two individuals 2 and 3 are similar, though oriented differently; representative curves I^E_1 and I^E_2 for Individuals 1 and 2 are shown.

What is the effect of majority voting over this set of alternatives? If there

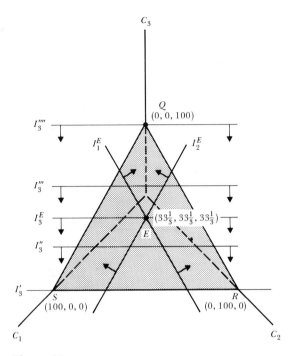

Figure 15

is to be a majority winner, the equal-shares point E, at which each person pays $33\frac{1}{3}$, is a likely candidate. I^E_1, I^E_2, I^E_3 are the indifference curves of the three voters through point E. It is easily seen that E is not a majority winner, for it is defeated by various other points. For example, Individuals 2 and 3 will each prefer the combination (100, 0, 0) (the point S) to E; while Individuals 1 and 2 would prefer the point R to E, and so on. In fact, there are infinitely many points, shown in the shaded areas of the triangle in Fig. 16, which could defeat E in paired majority votes. It is clear from the geometry of the situation and the parallelism of the indifference curves that this is not unique to the point E, for we would find the same situation if the indifference curves were drawn through any other point in the interior of the triangle. The majority preference relation is not transitive: for example, if we consider the three points F, G, and H in Fig. 16, we find that F defeats G (since Voters 1 and 2 prefer F), G defeats H, yet H in turn defeats F. Majority rule is not well behaved [5] in this case, since the majority preference relation forms a cycle:

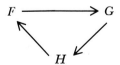

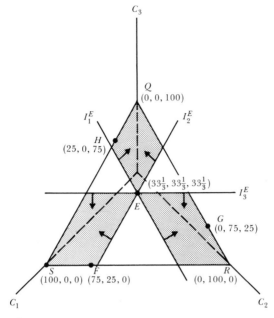

Figure 16

None of the three alternatives is a majority winner, and there is no clear majority will.

This is an instance of the problem of *cyclical majorities,* or the *paradox of voting* (the paradox being that transitive individual preferences can give rise to intransitive collective preferences). This phenomenon was apparently first noted by Condorcet in 1785, and has been of continuing interest in the study of voting methods ever since. (For an interesting and readable historical survey of the earlier literature, see Black, 1958.) The upshot of this work is that, in the presence of cyclical majorities, no method of election, voting procedure, or other political mechanism based on majority rule seems very satisfactory. The outcome finally selected will be more an artifact of the procedure, or order of voting, than a genuine reflection of the electorate's will. It will be unstable, or inconsistent, in the sense that a slight variation in the order of voting, or the reintroduction of a previously rejected alternative into consideration, could produce a very different result. Cyclical majorities thus pose both normative and practical difficulties for the functioning of democratic political institutions based on majority voting.

The Possibility of Other Methods of Social Choice

There is the possibility that these difficulties are in some sense an artifact of simple majority rule, the principle embedded in all the procedures and institutions discussed above. If this were so, it might be possible to find some other principle, such as rule by majorities of two-thirds or greater, or "representative" majority rule, that does not lead to inconsistencies. Political institutions based on such a principle would then be free of the difficulties noted above.

Arrow's *Social Choice and Individual Values* (1963) is, in effect, a very general analysis of the possibility of finding such a principle. In asking whether there exists a method of social choice that is consistent and democratic, we might proceed by examining various possible methods in detail. As we have seen, the basic difficulty with majority rule is its lack of consistency. Other methods of social choice, though consistent, are unacceptable on different grounds. Dictatorship or colonial rule, for example, is undemocratic, though consistent. The principle of unanimity, on the other hand, leads to decisions that are consistent and democratic, but the principle is still unsatisfactory because it is incomplete: it provides no means for resolving questions on which there is less than a unanimous consensus. Clearly there are many other possible methods to be considered: qualified (e.g., two-thirds) and representative majority rule; multistage hierarchical voting procedures of various kinds; methods permitting vote trading or barter across different issues; compensation schemes whereby winners are permitted, or required, to make side payments to compensate losers; and many others. Each of these, if examined in detail, would turn out to be unsatisfactory in one respect or another. However, there are still many other possible methods, and since the total number of conceivable methods is truly enormous, we cannot hope to ever examine them all in detail. An alternative approach is to proceed more abstractly, or *axiomatically,* by attempting to formulate more precisely our standards of what constitutes an "acceptable" method of social choice. By working with these general criteria, or axioms, themselves, we may be able to discover a method or class of methods that meets all our requirements. The particular requirements, or conditions, that Arrow (1963) used to define "acceptability" can be roughly described as follows.

First, the method should yield consistent social choices: the social preference relation should be *transitive* and *complete.*

Second, the method should be general. It should not be a highly specialized mechanism that works only on simple choices (e.g., those with only one or two alternatives) or only in societies in which there already exists substantial consensus on the choice. Thus the scope or *domain* of the method should include choices with any number of alternatives, and societies of any size, in which the citizens rank the alternatives in any possible way.

Third, the social choice concerning a particular set of alternatives should depend only on citizens' preferences for *those* alternatives. There would be something strange, and a bit impractical, about a method that made the choice between two candidates *A* and *B* for president depend on citizens' preferences for popular tunes, their views on chastity, and their opinions about the relative merits of other conceivable candidates, such as Gladstone and de Gaulle, along with their judgments of the suitability of the two actual candidates. It is difficult to envisage any practical election procedure that could efficiently collect all the information required for a decision under a method of this sort. A practical social choice procedure should be such that the decision concerning a set of alternatives is *independent of irrelevant alternatives* not belonging to the set.

In addition to satisfying these essentially technical or procedural conditions, a reasonable method of social choice ought to be "democratic" in some sense. Clearly democracy is a complex concept, and formal explication of the notion is bound to involve a degree of simplification and incompleteness. However, virtually any reasonable formulation of what we mean by a democratic method ought to satisfy at least the following minimal requirements.

First, a democratic method ought to be responsive to a unanimous consensus of the citizenry, at the very least: that is, if every citizen prefers A to B, then the method should be such that A is collectively preferred to B. Clearly this *unanimity principle* is a weak requirement, much less restrictive than the majority principle, for example.

Second, under a democratic method the power to influence social decisions ought to be dispersed broadly among the members of society; or at the very least, it ought not to be concentrated in the hands of any single individual. Thus an acceptable method should be *nondictatorial:* it should not make any single individual a dictator, in the sense that the social preference relation invariably coincides with his preferences, irrespective of the preferences of the rest of the citizenry.

These are minimal conditions, and undoubtedly fall far short of fully characterizing what most people would regard as democracy. One might well argue, for example, that a method that satisfied all these conditions, but that denied power to all but a few (an oligarchy), or that violated the majority principle, is not really democratic in any reasonable sense; hence, the conditions ought to be strengthened, or new ones should be added to the list.

It turns out, however, that the five minimal conditions listed above are already too strong, for no conceivable method of social choice can satisfy them all. This fact is the gist of Arrow's (Im)possibility Theorem.[6] [For a precise statement of the axioms and proof of the result, the reader is referred to Arrow's original work (1963, pp. 96ff.) or, for a lucid and less technical exposition of the argument, to Luce and Raiffa (1957, ch. 9).]

One interpretation of this result is that the cycling problem is not just an artifact of majority rules but is intrinsic to the very nature of the problem of social choice. There has been a great deal of subsequent research (surveyed in Taylor's chapter in Volume 3 of *The Handbook of Political Science*) on the possibility of other acceptable social choice mechanisms, following Arrow's original result. This work has modified the precise statement of the impossibility result somewhat. (For example, methods can be found that satisfy all of Arrow's conditions for infinitely large societies, and that satisfy various modifications of the original axioms for finite societies.) However, the essential point remains valid: no very interesting or general method of social choice has been found that is not affected by the cycling problem, or by other equally serious problems (such as being indecisive when confronted with complex choices).

Analysis of Political Institutions

Even in the presence of cyclical majorities, decisions are made by voting bodies. In such cases, the outcome depends on the voting procedures under which the body operates, or the order in which alternatives are considered. Any of the proposals F, G, and H in Fig. 16 might be chosen by the group under some possible voting order. If F and G are compared first and the winner is then paired with H, the outcome is H. If the first division is between F and H, then the outcome is G. If the first division is between G and H, the outcome will be F. Riker (1958) has examined some consequences of the rules of the United States House of Representatives for voting on several alternative wordings of a particular paragraph of a bill being considered by the House, in the presence of cyclical majorities. He finds that the original wording is in a sense a privileged alternative under these rules.

Even when a majority winner does exist, the voting procedure may affect the outcome. Consider again the preferences displayed in Fig. 13, and recall that K_2 is the majority winner in this case. Suppose the voting procedure involved an initial vote on whether to adopt K_2 forthwith, or to eliminate it from further consideration; if the vote goes against K_2, a second vote is taken between K_1 and K_3, the survivor of this vote being adopted. Under this procedure, Voter 1 would vote against K_2 on the first round, since he prefers K_1; and so would Voter 3, since he prefers K_3. Hence K_2 would be defeated (the final result would be K_1, since it would win on the second round). As we pointed out earlier, however, K_2 is a majority winner in this example; hence, certain perfectly plausible voting procedures may result in violation of the majority principle, i.e., in nonenactment of a majority winner. The role of voting procedures on committee decisions has been incisively analyzed by Farquharson (1969), for the case when committee members vote "sincerely" (as implicitly assumed in the example above), and also when they vote "strategically," by taking account of the actions of other voters. Since Farquharson's approach is game-theoretic, we defer detailed description of his work to a later section.

Much of the theoretical structure we have described is relevant to the analysis of large-scale political systems in which the basic political mechanism is electoral competition by rival political parties. In this type of model (see Downs, 1957), the parties compete for votes by advocating particular policies, or alternatives; each voter votes for whichever party advocates the policy he would most prefer. A central question is whether there exists an electoral *equilibrium,* that is, a set of policies or platforms, one for each party, with the property that no party could increase its vote share by changing its platform, if the other parties do not change theirs.

Returning to our lakeside community, suppose our citizens—rather than directly voting in a referendum on proposals to treat pollution—instead elect a government to deal with the problem. In the situation outlined in Fig. 13, the strategies available to the competing parties are the different possible values of the expenditure level K. If there are only two parties, and if voters' preferences are single-peaked as in the figure, then there is an electoral equilibrium. In particular, if each party adopts the same (majority winner) policy K_2 as its platform, neither can gain votes by changing to a different platform. This is the thrust of Downs's (1957) famous analysis of two-party competition. The result provides an explanation of the often-noted tendency of political parties in two-party systems to avoid extreme policy positions, and converge toward the middle ground of moderate policy.

This basic framework has been extended in several directions to take account of some of the complexities of real electoral competition ignored in Downs's original simplified, though insightful, model of two-party competition over a single dimension or issue. Stokes (1963) has pointed out some of the limitations of the simple Downsian formulation. Elections are often contested over several issues or policy questions, rather than just one; hence, the underlying choice space of possible platforms is multidimensional. (This would occur in our example if the set of platforms were the points in Fig. 15, rather than those of Fig. 13.) Under these conditions an electoral equilibrium is unlikely to exist. Davis, Hinich, and Ordeshook, in a series of papers (e.g., 1966, 1970; Hinich, Ledyard, and Ordeshook, 1973) investigated two-party competition in several dimensions, and have obtained a variety of conditions for the existence of an electoral equilibrium. Their initial conditions were quite special though they have been progressively relaxed in subsequent analyses. Even so, the underlying preference assumptions on which this tradition of spatial modelling rests still seem restrictive. This, and the fact that there has been no really successful analysis of multiparty competition (including Downs's own), suggest that real progress may depend on more fundamental modifications of the basic Downsian framework. The assumption that parties are motivated solely by a desire to maximize votes, for example, is both restrictive and unrealistic: incumbents are often more concerned with preserving their own seats than with expanding their party's overall vote, while many parties and politicians have serious policy views and preferences that influence their actions independently of any considerations of electoral gain. Though there have been a few unpublished attempts to construct electoral models based on more realistic motivational assumptions, a really serious analysis along these lines remains to be made.

To remove this discussion of political institutions from the realm of the hypothetical, let us conclude with an outline of an analysis of a set of political mechanisms actually used in pollution management drawn from Klevorick and Kramer (1973). In the Ruhr industrial region of West Germany, pollution treatment is financed through effluent taxation—polluters are taxed in proportion to the amount of their waste discharge. The rate of this taxation is set by the *Genossenschaften,* a collection of regional political bodies responsible for water quality within their jurisdictions. Both industrial firms and communities are represented in the General Assembly of each *Genossenschaft,* which must vote to establish quality standards and effluent charges. Each member's voting strength is roughly proportional to its financial contribution to the association, and since these contributions consist of the taxes each member pays for its pollution discharges, the largest polluters have the most votes in determining the water quality standard—and the effluent tax rate—to be enforced in the area. This structure seems somewhat anomalous, and indeed potentially unstable, since some firms' levels of pollution, and hence their voting strengths, will increase or decrease in response to changes in the effluent tax rate. In fact, as the rate is lowered, industrial pollution increases, thus increasing firms' voting strengths and hence their ability to vote in still further decreases in the rate. Thus, we might expect the rate to be driven to zero, at which no pollution treatment at all is undertaken.

In fact, the *Genossenschaften* have functioned rather well, both in the sense of not having been incapacitated by instability (with some exceptions, noted below), and of having undertaken quite extensive treatment, resulting in water quality that is remarkably high, considering the level of industrialization in the area.

Klevorick and Kramer (1973) develop a simple theoretical model to investigate the existence and nature of equilibrium in these rather unusual political institutions. The general idea of the analysis is as follows. A given tax rate t implies a particular set of "contributions," and hence, a particular distribution of voting strengths in the General Assembly. Under fairly general conditions, there will be a rate (or set of rates) $\tau(t)$ which is a voting equilibrium, or majority winner with respect to the prevailing vote distribution. If $\tau(t)$ is different from t, enactment of the new rate will result in changes in voting strengths, and hence lead to a different equilibrium $\tau[\tau(t)]$; so evidently the condition for overall stability is that $t = \tau(t)$ for some t. The analysis shows that such a stable rate exists under quite general conditions. It also yields conditions for this stable rate to be greater than zero. These conditions seem quite plausible substantively, and shed light on difficulties certain of the *Genossenschaften* have encountered, and have solved by modifying the representation laws in specific ways that in effect guarantee satisfaction of one of these sufficient conditions previously mentioned.

THEORY OF GAMES

The theory of games is a general framework for the analysis of interactions among several agents who are mutually interdependent (in the sense that the effect of any agent's action depends in part on the actions taken by the others), and whose interests are to some degree conflicting. These features of strategic interdependence and conflicting interests are characteristic of much of social and political interaction among individuals, groups, and nations (as well as of parlor "games").

Consider a simple example. Two people play. One hides a penny in either his right hand or his left. The other guesses which hand the penny is in. Each therefore has two alternative ways of playing, or strategies. If the second player guesses correctly, he wins the penny; otherwise he pays the first player a penny. Such a game may be represented by a payoff matrix.[7] (See Fig. 17.) The payoff to Player 1 is shown above the diagonal in the cell representing each combination of strategies, or actions, while Player 2's payoff appears below the diagonal. Player 1's strategies are represented by the row of the matrix, Player 2's by the columns.

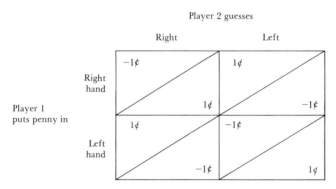

Figure 17

Most games are considerably more complicated than this. Parlor games such as chess and bridge involve literally millions of possible strategies, while many real-world "games" are more complex still. Nevertheless, the essential elements of complex strategic situations can often be captured in simple abstract games. The game introduced above, for example, might describe with some accuracy the essential problems of decision confronting two military commanders, one choosing between two routes for sending supplies, the other deciding how to intercept them (Luce and Raiffa, 1957; Rapoport, 1960). Game theory is not a comprehensive overall theory, but rather a general analytical framework that encompasses a body of related but distinct concepts and special theories. Our coverage here will be highly selective, emphasizing areas that have been or promise to be most useful for the analysis of political problems.[8]

Two-Player Constant-Sum Games

An important type of game for which the theory is highly developed is the class of two-player games in which whatever one player wins, the other loses. For example, in a two-party electoral contest in a parliamentary system, the seats that one party captures are lost by the other, since the total number of seats is fixed. In such games, the interests of the players are diametrically and inalterably opposed.

Implicit in the definition of a two-person constant-sum game is the assumption that the payoffs can be measured on an interval scale (and that the sum of payoffs to the two players is constant[9]). This is a natural assumption in parlor games or electoral contests, where the relevant payoffs are dollars or votes. It is less plausible in more general situations, where the payoffs might be income–water quality combinations, or a particular candidate elected, or set of bills passed. In such cases the player may have a consistent preference ordering of the alternatives, but often it will not be possible to express these preferences in terms of an interval scale of value. Zero-sum theory is applicable only to those situations in which it is possible to measure preferences in terms of such an interval scale of value (which is usually referred to as a *cardinal utility function*).

The essence of a two-person constant-sum game is (1) a set of alternative strategies for each player, and (2) a pair of payoffs associated with each pair of strategy choices, one for each player. These always add to the same total, so that one player loses what the other wins. The game shown in Fig. 18 is an example.

Let us examine the choice problems confronting the two players. From Player 2's point of view, the choice is obvious, for no matter which strategy his opponent plays, B_1 will yield a lower payoff than B_2. Hence B_1 is an inferior,

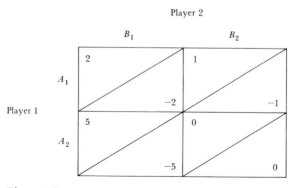

Figure 18

or *dominated,* strategy, and Player 2 will never have any incentive to choose it. The choice is not so simple from Player 1's perspective, since if Player 2 plays B_1, A_2 is Player 1's best choice, while against B_2, A_1 is his best choice. If Player 1 knew the strategies and payoffs confronting his opponent, and were sure that Player 2 was clever enough to avoid playing his dominated strategy, then he could predict Player 1's choice (B_2) and choose his own best strategy, A_1, accordingly. The resulting strategy pair (A_1, B_2) would yield payoffs of 1 and -1, respectively, to the two players.

In many constant-sum games, however, even after eliminating obviously inferior choices such as B_1, both players will have several strategies left. This is true, for example, of the game shown in Fig. 19, described in more detail below. In such situations a player cannot confidently predict his opponent's choice, so none of his own strategies is an obvious best choice. How should a reasonable player act in such a case?

In view of the unpredictability of his opponent, a somewhat conservative player might well proceed on the pessimistic assumption that his opponent will choose the worst possible strategy. A particular strategy for Player 1 (such as A_1 of Fig. 18) which might yield him any of several payoffs (2 or 1), is thus conservatively assumed to yield the minimum (one unit) of these. A prudent choice for Player 1 would then be to adopt that strategy with the largest minimum payoff. This choice maximizes the player's "security level," since it ensures that the minimum payoff he may get is as large as possible. The strategy with this property is the player's *maximin* strategy (or equivalently, since it also minimizes his maximum *loss,* his *minimax* strategy).

In the example shown in Fig. 18, A_1 is minimax, since it guarantees a payoff of at least one unit, while A_2 guarantees only 0. Similarly B_2 is minimax for Player 2. The resulting strategy pair (A_1, B_2) is the same as that arrived at by the dominance argument above. Moreover, in this example, if the minimax strategies are played, the pessimistic assumptions of each player turn out to be true, since the resulting payoffs to Players 1 and 2 are indeed the smallest of those associated with A_1 and B_2, respectively. The payoff to Player 1, one unit, is a minimum in the B_2 column of payoffs to him: so long as his opponent plays B_2, Player 1 can do no better than stick to his minimax strategy, A_1. Similarly the payoff (actually a loss) to Player 2, -1, is a maximum in the A_1 row of payoffs to Player 2, so he also has no incentive to abandon his minimax strategy. Such a pair of payoffs is often referred to as a *saddle point.*[10] A pair of strategies whose payoff pair is a saddle point is an equilibrium, in the sense that neither player has any incentive to play differently so long as his opponent sticks to his same strategy.

Not all two-person constant-sum games have saddle points, however. For example, in the penny-matching game described in Fig. 17, it is readily verified that there is no payoff to Player 1 that is both a row minimum and a column maximum. No pair of strategies is an equilibrium, since in any combination of choices, one of the players always has an incentive to change to his other strategy. If this matching game were played repeatedly by intelligent players, each player would soon realize that if he acts in a consistent or predictable fashion, his opponent can gain a decisive advantage. Hence the best course is to make his strategy choices irregular, or random; indeed, the best course (for each player) would be to do something like flip a coin on each trial, to decide between right and left.

The possibility of adopting a random or statistical device for selecting a strategy is itself a type of strategy: It is referred to as a *mixed* strategy, to distinguish it from the deterministic or *pure* strategies we have been considering so far. A mixed strategy is characterized by its probabilities of selecting each of the pure strategies. Thus in the penny-matching game, the set of mixed strategies includes those with probabilities of choosing left or right of $1/2$ and $1/2$, $2/3$ and $1/3$, 1 and 0, 0 and 1, and so on. Clearly the set of such strategies is infinite. With mixed strategies permitted, the relation between strategy choices and payoffs is no longer deterministic, since an element of randomness or statistical variability is present: The same pair of mixed strategies may lead to any of several different pairs of pure strategies being subsequently played, and hence to different payoffs. However, a pair of mixed strategies can be characterized by the average or *expected* payoffs they would yield, if played repeatedly, and the notions of minimax strategies, saddle points, and equilibrium pairs of strategies can be defined in terms of these expected payoffs.

The fundamental theorem of two-person zero-sum theory asserts that in such a game, if the number of pure strategies is finite and mixed strategies are admissible,[11] a saddle point (possibly involving mixed strategies) necessarily exists. The pair of strategies yielding the saddle point constitutes an equilibrium, and each member of the pair is a minimax strategy (von Neumann and Morgenstern, 1947; Luce and Raiffa, 1957). Saddle points also exist in certain classes of games with infinite sets of pure strategies (Burger, 1963).

Let us briefly examine an example of real political behavior to illustrate the mixed-strategy concept. In the 1964 New York Senate race the incumbent Kenneth Keating was challenged by Robert Kennedy. During the course of the campaign, Keating made a live television broadcast, sitting next to an empty chair. The scene was intended to dramatize Kennedy's supposed unwillingness to confront the incumbent in an open debate; but unfortunately for Keating, his opponent showed up at the studio during the broadcast, making it clear he had never been invited. The ploy backfired, and may well have cost Keating some votes. His staff, in planning the broadcast, evidently failed to take account of the possibility that the Kennedy organization might become aware of the plan and find a way to counteract it.

Once this possibility is recognized, the problem of deciding whether to use the "chair" tactic takes on the character of a two-player game. If the relevant payoffs are the incremental gains or losses to each candidate's expected plural-

Kennedy

Comes   Does not come

| Keating appears | with chair | −3000 | 2000 |
| | without chair | 1000 | 0 |

Figure 19

ity resulting from the broadcast, the game is zero-sum. The available strategies (assuming other possible counteracting strategies are either infeasible or dominated) and payoffs might have been as shown in Fig. 19. The payoffs are in incremental votes for Keating: he loses votes if he uses the chair tactic and Kennedy shows up, but in every other contingency at least breaks even.

What strategies should the candidates have chosen? It is readily verified that this game has no saddle point in pure strategies. From the minimax theorem, however, we know that a mixed-strategy saddle point will exist. Mixed strategies do seem operationally meaningful in this situation. For the Keating organization, for example, a mixed strategy would mean deciding statistically whether or not to use the chair, and keeping the decision secret until the last moment. The minimax mixed strategy for Keating turns out to be to use the chair tactic with probability 1/6 (and not to with probability 5/6), while Kennedy's minimax strategy is to appear with probability 1/3.[12]

The strategy actually chosen by the Keating organization, apparently, was to use the chair with probability 1. This is clearly far from optimal, and it is difficult to imagine any plausible set of assumptions that would make it optimal. For example, even if the Keating organization believed they would not lose votes if Kennedy counteracted the chair tactic (i.e., if the −3000 payoff were changed to 0), the minimax mixed strategy still gives the chair tactic a probability of only 1/3.

Two-person zero-sum theory has been applied to several political problems, especially in the analysis of two-party electoral competition. Sawyer and Mac-Rae (1962) used a game-theoretic framework in their study of nomination strategies used by the two parties competing for seats in three-membered legislative districts in Illinois. The Sankoff–Mellos (1972) model focused on resource-allocation strategies by two parties competing for seats across a set of single-membered districts, assuming that each district is won by whichever party spends the most money in it. They argue that this simple model (in which no pure strategy saddle point exists, in general) can account for empirically observed values of the aggregate seat-vote, or "swing," ratio. A number of related models of this same general type were used by Brams and Davis (1974) in their analysis of resource allocation in presidential campaigns. They find that the effect of the electoral college is to exaggerate the influence of large states, in the sense that the minimax resource allocation strategies result in disproportionate spending in those states by both parties.

The Downsian (1957) model of electoral competition, in which parties compete by advocating policies rather than spending resources, can also be formulated as a two-player zero-sum game. Under Downs's original assumptions—that the set of possible policies is one-dimensional, and voters have single-peaked preferences—there exists a pure strategy saddle point: The minimax strategy for each party is to adopt the median policy as its platform. There have been several analyses of electoral competition in multidimensional policy spaces (Davis and Hinich, 1966; Davis, Hinich, and Ordeshook, 1970). These studies indicate that except in special cases, there is in general no pure strategy equilibrium point for the parties, once the classic Downsian assumptions are weakened. If the number of policies or possible platforms is finite, the minimax theorem ensures the existence of an equilibrium in mixed strategies, and Shubik (1970) has investigated some of the properties and implications of these strategies. As Ordeshook (1971) has pointed out, however, there are some potential difficulties in interpreting mixed strategies in this context. In particular, they cannot be interpreted as ambiguous or uncertain policy commitments by the parties, for in that case the set of possible (ambiguous) platforms is infinite, and the minimax theorem no longer applies. Moreover, voters in this case are in the position of choosing between ambiguous platforms, or lotteries over policies, so their behavior must be analyzed in terms of the theory of decision making under risk. This has been done by Shepsle (1972a, 1972b). He finds that under certain conditions ambiguity may benefit either party. In general these results depend on asymmetry between the incumbent and challenging parties: if both parties are free to adopt ambiguous platforms without restriction, no saddle point need exist, even if the classic Downsian assumptions are otherwise satisfied.

Noncooperative Games

In a two-person constant-sum game, the interests of the two players are diametrically opposed: Whatever one wins is at the expense of the other. There are many situations, however, in which both the players' motives are not entirely antagonistic, since certain outcomes may benefit both simultaneously: their interests are partially convergent, and partially conflicting. Our two-person pollution example is an instance of this, since both individuals could benefit from certain cooperative actions, yet they also had conflicting views about which such action should be adopted. In such situations, the motives of the players are mixed. Axelrod (1970) has suggested a measure of the *degree* of conflict of interest among the players in such a game, and has applied it to a variety of political situations.

Issues of communication and collaboration become important in the study of mixed-motive games. This is in contrast to two-person constant-sum games, in which there is no incentive for cooperation, and communication between the players is essentially pointless. Mixed-motive games are commonly divided into two classes, *cooperative* and *noncooperative,* depending on the opportunities for communication and collaboration present. In noncooperative games, the players cannot collude to coordinate their strategies, cannot make binding agreements, and cannot bargain. Cooperative games, on the other hand, are characterized by the possibility of negotiations among players to make binding agreements to coordinate strategies in mutually beneficial ways. This possibility in some ways simplifies and in some ways complicates the analysis of the game, but in either event, the analysis of the cooperative game differs from that of the noncooperative. Here we will review some elements of the noncooperative theory; cooperative theory will be discussed in the following section.

The game usually called "the battle of the sexes" is a straightforward noncooperative mixed-motive game. In a political context, this game might reflect the situation arising when two liberal politicians—Charles Goodell and Richard Ottinger, say—are involved in a three-way race for Senator in a state with a generally liberal electorate. The third candidate, James Buckley, is a conservative, whose election would be regarded by both Goodell and Ottinger as the worst possible outcome. Only a plurality is required to win, and though either liberal candidate could defeat the conservative in a two-way race, the conservative candidate is likely to receive a plurality of votes in a three-way race. Each of the liberal candidates would of course most prefer to win himself, which is possible only if the other liberal drops out of the race. Each liberal would also prefer that his liberal rival win, rather than the conservative. This strategic situation is shown with hypothetical payoffs in Fig. 20.

If communication between the candidates is impossible, their decision problems are different from those in a constant-sum game. If mixed strategies are feasible, minimax mixtures can be found for each player. In particular, as the reader may verify, the minimax strategy for each candidate is to stay in the race with probability $2/5$. If this were a constant-sum game, the pair of minimax strategies would necessarily be an equilibrium, in the sense that neither player could benefit from some other choice, so long as his opponent plays his minimax strategy. However, in the game described above, if Ottinger plays his minimax strategy, Goodell will find it advantageous to play his pure "stay-in" strategy.

However, equilibrium pairs (which are not necessarily minimax) still exist quite generally in mixed-motive games. A *Nash equilibrium point* is a pair of

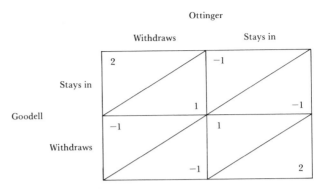

Figure 20

strategies (s_1, s_2) [or more generally, in a multiperson game with n players, an *n-tuple* of strategies $(s_1, s_2, \ldots, s_n)$], one for each player, with the property that no player can benefit by switching to some different strategy, so long as the others stick to their *s*-strategies. An important theorem of Nash (1951) showed that a mixed-motive game in which the set of pure strategies is finite necessarily has an equilibrium, if mixed strategies are permitted. Equilibrium points have also been shown to exist in other classes of games, including some games with infinite strategy sets (Burger, 1963). Indeed, our pollution example is, in game-theoretic terms, a noncooperative game with infinite strategy sets (the strategies being various emission levels), and the equilibrium identified in Fig. 5 is a (pure strategy) Nash equilibrium point. Many games have more than one Nash equilibrium point. In the above example concerning the election, if Goodell stays in the race and Ottinger withdraws, the pair is an equilibrium; but an equilibrium also results if Goodell drops out and Ottinger stays in. In contrast to constant-sum games, when several equilibria exist in a mixed-motive game they are not necessarily of equal value to the players.

Another feature of mixed-motive games introduced by this example is the usefulness of threats. Suppose Goodell makes it clear to Ottinger that he will not under any circumstances withdraw from the race. If Ottinger is convinced that this is true, his only sensible strategy is to drop out himself. Each candidate, in such a case, may be expected to proclaim that he is in the race for keeps and to make efforts to make his threat credible. In a constant-sum game, threats are of course pointless.

A different, rather famous, example of a noncooperative game is the Prisoner's Dilemma, an abstraction of a type of situation arising in many real-world political situations. Suppose the nations of Uplandia and Downlandia have signed an arms limitation treaty restricting the construction and deployment of new weapons. Both wish to honor the treaty, but neither fully trusts the other. Uplandian leaders fear that Downlandia will secretly rearm. They are compelled themselves to consider secret rearmament. Downlandian leaders, of

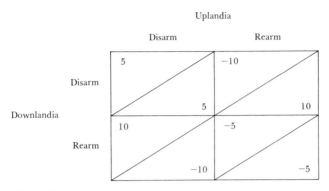

Figure 21

course, have complementary fears. The game's payoff matrix is shown in Fig. 21.

It is easily verified that the one and only equilibrium point in this game is for both sides to play their "rearm" strategies. Each country fails to benefit, and indeed loses, by playing its disarm strategy (or any mixed strategy that gives positive probability to disarming) so long as the other country plays its rearm strategy (or in fact, any other strategy—all strategies except rearming are *dominated* strategies). In this game, in contrast to the previous one, the equilibrium point is unique, and moreover each of the strategies involved is minimax. The paradox of the Prisoner's Dilemma is the conflict between individual (noncooperative) and collective (cooperative) rationality. If both sides could effectively cooperate without fear of betrayal by the other, the sensible thing would be for both to disarm. Yet in the absence of mutual trust, or of effective mechanisms for enforcing cooperative agreements, it is individually irrational for either country to do other than rearm, even though the resulting payoff pair (−5, −5) is considerably inferior to that which could be achieved by cooperation.

It should be clear that the "free rider" phenomenon encountered in the discussion of the pollution example is also a Prisoner's Dilemma type of situation. Though all citizens would benefit by a mutual reduction of pollution levels, each finds it individually profitable not to abide by the agreement, if there are no effective penalties for such violations. Hardin (1971) has discussed the problem of collective action in terms of an n-person Prisoner's Dilemma.

Elements of noncooperative game theory have been used in several areas of political science, most extensively in the study of international relations (e.g., Ellsberg, 1961; Ikle, 1962, 1964; Schelling, 1960; and the "gaming" articles in almost any issue of the *Journal of Conflict Resolution*).

Probably the most significant application of noncooperative theory outside of the areas of international affairs and deterrence is Robin Farquharson's

Theory of Voting (1969). His analysis does not apply to situations characterized by such essentially collusive phenomena as vote-trading and block voting; a cooperative analysis would be appropriate for such situations. There are many real-world situations, however, in which collusion and coalition formation are severely restricted. Legal provisions, or institutional devices such as the secret ballot, may make collusive agreements impractical or unenforceable; while in many voting bodies (nonpartisan committees, courts, faculty meetings) there are strong informal but effective norms against explicit collusion or vote-trading. Farquharson (1969) provides an insightful and compelling noncooperative analysis of voting in such bodies.

His analysis is primarily concerned with situations in which the body proceeds to a decision by a sequence of paired votes (on amendments or individual sections of a bill, for example). Such *binary* voting procedures are an important class of procedures, widely used in actual practice. (The Rules of Order of parliamentary procedure, for example, in effect prescribe certain binary procedures for various kinds of issues.) However Farquharson's basic approach, and the concepts of sincere, straightforward, and sophisticated voting, are quite general and potentially applicable to other types of voting situations as well.

In voting games, the usual noncooperative solutions (the Nash equilibrium points) turn out not to be very helpful, since there are too many of them. For example, every strategy n-tuple that gives unanimity on every vote is a Nash equilibrium,[13] so every possible outcome is produced by at least one equilibrium point. The notion of equilibrium points gives no useful prediction of the outcome, or of what strategies a voter might be led to use in such situations.

One strategy a voter might consider is his *sincere* strategy, the one in which he votes for his most-preferred alternative on each ballot. A sincere voter is thus one who always votes "honestly" (or naively). Sincere voting strategies may well not yield a noncooperative equilibrium, however, since some individuals may be able to get a better outcome by voting differently. For example, under the plurality rule, sincere voting may require an individual to "waste" his vote on a candidate who has no chance of winning, whereas by voting for his second-best candidate (hence, "insincerely"), he would be able to influence the outcome.

A *straightforward* strategy is one whose use is never unprofitable: that is, one from which the voter in question never has any incentive to change, no matter how everyone else votes. Though obviously a rational voter will use such a strategy if he has one, Farquharson shows that under most binary procedures, they do not exist for most (or all) voters. In such cases, however, a rational voter might well use his *sophisticated* strategy. The idea of this somewhat subtle concept is as follows: A rational voter will not use a strategy that is dominated. Neither will the other voters (if they are as clever as the voter in question). Hence our voter can eliminate his rivals' dominated strategies from consideration, and reconsider his decision problem in this reduced game.

A strategy that is dominated in this smaller game can now be deleted. Moreover, assuming the other voters are clever enough to go through the same reasoning, he may also be able to eliminate some of their strategies, thus obtaining a still smaller game. The same argument can then be applied again to this reduced game. Farquharson shows that if this reasoning is applied repeatedly, each voter will eventually be left with a single voting strategy: his *sophisticated* strategy. Though sophisticated voting strategies are defined in somewhat abstract game-theoretic terms, they seem quite plausible as choices for a clever voter in an actual sequential voting situation. For example, in deciding whether to vote to amend a particular proposal, a sophisticated voter would use his knowledge of the preferences of the other voters to predict the result of the two possible final votes for adoption (of the amended and unamended proposals, respectively). He would then vote on the amendment according to which of these *predicted* outcomes he prefers (irrespective of whether he actually prefers the amendment).

Cooperative Games

If players are able to communicate and make binding agreements to collude, the strategic aspects of a game are considerably changed, and the analysis of such cooperative games proceeds along rather different lines. The original von Neumann–Morgenstern (1947) analysis of cooperative games was based on restrictive assumptions—notably, the assumption that utilities were cardinal and transferable among players—which made their theory of limited applicability. However, in the past decade there have been a number of developments and extensions that have eliminated many of these restrictive assumptions, and the current theory, as recast in a strictly ordinal framework, is potentially much more applicable to real-world political situations. Because of their recentness, these developments are not discussed in the surveys recommended at the beginning of the section on game theory. Aumann (1967) provides an excellent, though somewhat technical, survey; Shubik's (1972) nontechnical review paper is more comprehensive, though less detailed.

A key concept in the cooperative approach is that of a *coalition,* a subset of players, acting in concert. Instead of considering the strategies and security levels of individual players, the focus in cooperative theory is on the various possible coalitions of players, and the payoffs they can guarantee their members by collusive action. Cooperative games are usually represented in *characteristic function* form. Until now, we have presented games in *normal* form, showing the strategies available to each player and the payoffs resulting from each combination of strategy choices. The characteristic function describes a game, instead, in terms of what payoffs can be achieved by each player or coalition of players, abstracting away from the question of which combinations of strategy choices give rise to these payoffs. If $N = \{1, 2, \ldots, n\}$ is the set of players, a coalition C is a subset of N. The characteristic function specifies, for every coalition C, the set of payoffs that the coalition can ensure its members.

As an example, consider a three-person body, which decides by majority vote whether to pass a particular bill B, an amended version A of the bill, or to preserve the status quo S by not passing any bill. Suppose the three players' utilities for these outcomes are as shown in Fig. 22. Under majority rule, any coalition of two players is powerful enough to produce any of the three outcomes. Thus the coalition consisting of Players 1 and 2, for example, can, by passing B, obtain a payoff of 4 for Player 1 and 8 for Player 2, so it can ensure the set of payoff pairs (u_1, u_2) such that $u_1 \leqslant 4$ and $u_2 \leqslant 8$. Similarly, by passing A it can ensure any $(u_1, u_2) \leqslant (10, 0)$, and by preserving the status quo S, any $(u_1, u_2) \leqslant (0, 6)$. Thus the characteristic function associates with the coalition $\{1, 2\}$ the region of payoffs shown in Fig. 23. The payoff combinations associated with the two other two-player coalitions $\{1, 3\}$, $\{2, 3\}$ are determined similarly. The one-player coalitions are powerless in a majority game, so they can ensure only their minimum payoffs; for example, $\{1\}$ can ensure only $u_1 \leqslant 0$. The coalition of all three players can, like the two-player coalitions, produce any of the outcomes, so the characteristic function associates with it the set of combinations (u_1, u_2, u_3) which are less than or equal to $(10, 0, 5)$, or $(4, 8, 0)$, or $(0, 6, 9)$.

		Outcome		
		A	B	S
Player	1	10	4	0
	2	0	8	6
	3	5	0	9

Figure 22

It should be noted that this representation makes no assumption about the possibility of "side payments" or utility transfers among players. If the payoffs were dollars rather than utilities, and if the members of a coalition were free to pool their winnings and reallocate them in any fashion, the set of payoffs a coalition can ensure would be rather different. For example, the $\{1, 2\}$ coalition described in Fig. 23 could win a total of 6, 10, or 12 dollars, depending on which outcome it voted for, and by reallocating these winnings, it could ensure any pair of payoffs (u_1, u_2) for which $u_1 + u_2 \leqslant 12$. Thus its characteristic function would be the region lying below the dotted line in Fig. 23. Early cooperative theory was based on the premise that all characteristic functions were of this form; but while this is plausible for situations in which the outcomes are varying quantities of some divisible, tradeable commodity (such as dollars or perhaps patronage jobs), there are clearly many situations in which this assumption is quite unrealistic. Much of the game-theoretic literature in

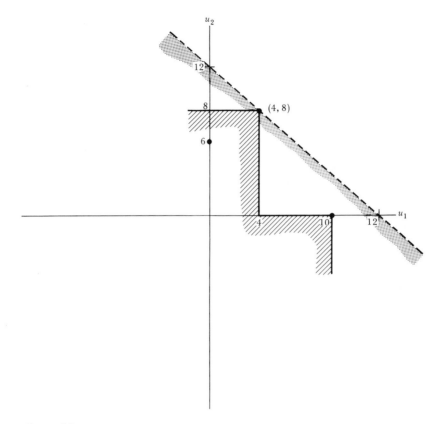

Figure 23

political science, both theoretical and experimental, has been primarily concerned with games with transferable utility. Hopefully this emphasis will change, for the transferability assumption has turned out to be unnecessary for much of cooperative theory, and it is obviously of rather limited applicability to real-world political situations.

The notion of what a coalition can "ensure" itself is obvious in the above example. In other games, such as those described in our discussion of noncooperative theory, the notion is not so obvious. Alternative definitions of the characteristic function for such games have been proposed. We shall consider only one, the so-called "beta" definition (cf., Aumann, 1967). According to this definition, a coalition such as $\{1, 2\}$ can ensure itself a pair of payoffs (u_1, u_2) if for each combination of strategy choices of the nonmembers of the coalition (Voter 3 in the example) there is some combination of strategies available to the members of the coalition such that the resulting set of strategy choices yields a payoff of at least u_1 to Player 1, and u_2 to Player 2.

Let us apply this to the Prisoners' Dilemma, described in Fig. 21. Clearly the coalition of both players can ensure any of the four outcomes so it can attain the set of payoffs shown in Fig. 24. What about the single-player coalitions? If Player 2 chooses his "disarm" strategy, Player 1 can obtain a payoff of 10 for himself by defecting; but if Player 2 chooses his "rearm" strategy, Player 1 can do no better than -5. Hence, under our definition, Player 1 can ensure himself only -5, and the coalition $\{1\}$ ensures the set of all payoffs $u_1 \leqslant -5$. Reasoning similarly about Player 2, $\{2\}$ ensures all $u_2 \leqslant -5$.

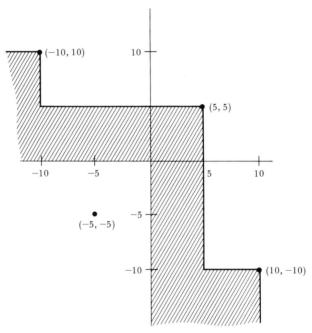

Figure 24

Having described the characteristic function representation of an n-person game, let us now consider how an equilibrium in such a game should be characterized. It will be recalled that a noncooperative (Nash) equilibrium is, roughly speaking, a state such that no single player can improve his position unilaterally. A natural extension of this idea is to think of a cooperative equilibrium as a state such that no *coalition* of players can collude to improve their *joint* position relative to that state. The *core* of an n-person game is an equilibrium concept of this type.[14] It is defined as follows: First, we shall say a combination or vector of payoffs is *blocked* by a coalition C if the coalition is able to ensure each of its members a better payoff. The vector of payoffs $(u_1, u_2, u_3, \ldots, u_n)$ is blocked by $C = \{1, 2\}$, for example, if C can ensure itself (i.e., if its characteristic function contains) a pair of payoffs (u_1', u_2') such that $u_1' > u_1$ and $u_2' > u_2$. If such a payoff vector can be blocked by some coalition C, it is not in equilibrium, since the members of C will benefit by colluding to overturn it in favor of some other outcome. Conversely, a feasible payoff combination that cannot be blocked is in equilibrium, since there is no coalition that has both the incentive and the power to overturn it. The *core* of an n-person game thus consists of the set of payoff combinations $(u_1, u_2, \ldots, u_n)$ which (1) can be attained by some combination of strategy choices; and (2) cannot be blocked by any coalition.

Let us now determine whether the Prisoners' Dilemma, whose characteristic function we have already described, has a core. To do this, we must see whether there is any attainable pair of payoffs (u_1, u_2) that would not be blocked. The pair $(-10, 10)$ which results from Player 1 disarming while Player 2 rearms would be blocked by the coalition $\{1\}$, since by rearming Player 1 can ensure himself a higher payoff of -5. Similarly, $(10, -10)$ would be blocked by the coalition consisting of Player 2 alone. If both players play their rearm strategies, the resulting payoff combination $(-5, -5)$ cannot be blocked by either single-person coalition, since neither can independently improve upon -5. However, this pair is blocked by the $\{1, 2\}$ coalition, since it can ensure $(5, 5)$, which is obviously superior for both coalition members. The only remaining possible outcome is the $(5, 5)$ vector which results from both players using their disarm strategies. Obviously neither one-player coalition can block this outcome—the best they can obtain is -5. Nor can the coalition $\{1, 2\}$ improve on this pair of payoffs. Hence, this outcome is not blocked by any coalition, so the game has a core. As one would expect from a cooperative theory, the solution results from both players agreeing to play their cooperative ("disarm") strategies.

Implicit in the formulation of this equilibrium concept is the assumption that the members of the potential coalitions are free to communicate and to make binding collusive commitments among themselves. Of course there are many real-world situations where these conditions are not satisfied. Overt communication is sometimes impossible or very costly, and legal or other means of enforcing agreements on those who enter into them are often absent. These features are characteristic of many situations that have been analyzed as Prisoners' Dilemmas (such as international arms races), and in such cases, a noncooperative treatment may be more appropriate.

Even when overt communication is impossible, however, it is sometimes possible for players to communicate implicitly. Schelling (1960) has introduced the intriguing notion of "tacit communication." Some joint strategy choices may seem so prominent or obvious to the players that they can be achieved without real collaboration. If, for example, two people are each asked to claim a share of a dollar without communication and told that each will receive the amount he claims if the total of the two does not exceed one dollar, the obvious strategy is for each to claim 50 cents. Schelling argues that such tacit communication is important even in relations among nations. He attributes the fact that poison gas was not used in World War II to the fact that "no gas" is an unambiguous rule that could be tacitly adopted more easily than "gas only in certain situations."

Another sort of implicit communication is possible in games played repeatedly by the same players. In such situations the players, through trial and error or through "signalling" one another with their strategy choices in subsequent play of the game, may reach an effective cooperative solution even in the absence of overt communication or enforcement mechanisms. A theorem by Aumann (1967) has provided a rigorous theoretical formulation of this process. Consider a two-person Prisoners' Dilemma game that is to be played repeatedly by the same players. These players, instead of considering anew in each play of the game which strategy to choose, might instead view the entire sequence of plays as one big "supergame." Each player may try to choose a strategy for the whole supergame. Such a strategy might be for Player 1 to play his "cooperate" strategy on the first trial and to continue to do so on subsequent trials so long as Player 2 also plays "cooperatively"; but if Player 2 plays "defect" on the first trial, Player 1 will "punish" him by playing "defect" on the second trial, then returning to "cooperate" on the third to see whether Player 2 has gotten the message. If he has, Player 1 will continue to "cooperate," if not . . . , and so on. This complex and infinitely large set of contingent decisions constitutes a *single* supergame strategy, and the number of such supergame strategies is itself infinite. Despite the complexity of the supergame, we can still ask whether it has an equilibrium. We might look for the Nash equilibrium points or, alternatively, for the core of the supergame. The relevant solution concept turns out to be neither of these, but rather the somewhat intermediate, "semicooperative" concept of the *strong equilibrium point*.[15] Roughly speaking, Aumann's result is that the strong equilibrium points of the supergame correspond to the payoff combinations in the core of the individual game (cf., Aumann, 1967, pp. 22–23). Thus there is a very strong sense (which we have not attempted to make precise) in which cooperative play in each trial of a repeated game is equivalent to long-run stability or equilibrium in the supergame.

There are multiperson games in which every feasible combination of payoffs is blocked by some coalition, so the core is empty. Unfortunately, many situations of interest to political scientists, when modelled as cooperative games, are of this type. Consider, for example, the voting game detailed in Fig. 20. The payoff combination associated with each of the three possible outcomes is blocked by some coalition. The combination (10, 0, 5) resulting from the passage of amended bill *A* is blocked by coalition {2, 3}, which can ensure its members payoffs of 6 and 9 units, respectively (by voting for the status quo). The status quo results in the payoff combination (0, 6, 9), which can be blocked by {1, 2} (by passing the bill *B*). Similarly, *B* is associated with a combination of payoffs (4, 8, 0) which can be blocked by {1, 3}. Thus no available combination of payoffs is in the core: the core is empty. There is a close connection between the voting paradox, discussed earlier, and the existence or nonexistence of a core in voting situations modelled as cooperative games.

Even when it is not empty, the core does not always identify a unique outcome to a cooperative game. In such cases, where all the players must agree on a single outcome and joint strategy choice to achieve it, the result might well depend on negotiation or bargaining among the players. What is a "fair" outcome of bargaining in such a situation? And what outcome might we reasonably expect, or predict, in such a bargaining process? An answer to the former question is provided by the *Nash bargaining solution* (not to be confused with the noncooperative *Nash equilibrium point*) (Nash, 1950; Luce and Raiffa, 1957, ch. 6). Nash proposed four reasonable criteria or axioms that a "fair" solution ought to satisfy, and then demonstrated that there is only one solution that satisfies these four conditions. The Nash framework does assume utility to be cardinal (though not necessarily transferable); in such situations, if we accept the axioms as reasonable, the Nash bargaining solution is the unique fair outcome. Harsanyi (1956), building on an earlier model of Zeuthen (1930), has argued that the Nash solution is also an accurate *prediction* of the outcome of a bargaining process. His model assumes that each party proceeds by first proposing a particular outcome, and then revising the proposal by making concessions that are proportional to the "cost" to him of not reaching agreement. This process of successive concessions continues until an agreement is concluded, and Harsanyi showed that this final agreement will be the Nash bargaining solution. Coddington (1968) also reviews the formal literature on bargaining in some detail.

The "threat point," or payoff vector that would result if no agreement is reached, plays an important role in bargaining games of this type (Nash, 1953); and indeed, threats by individuals or coalitions play an important role in many multiperson game situations. The role of threat strategies has been informally though perceptively discussed by Schelling (1960). The formal cooperative solution concept with which we have been mainly concerned here, the core, does implicitly take account of certain kinds of threats, but only in a rather restrictive way (e.g., the cost to a coalition itself of actually enforcing a threat is in effect ignored). There are other cooperative solution concepts, such as the Aumann–Maschler (1964) *bargaining set* (discussed by Shubik, 1972), that do attempt to deal with threats in a more explicit and comprehensive fashion.

The bargaining set, and other cooperative equilibrium concepts, have been applied to some political problems. In a series of experiments, Riker (1967a, 1967b) and Riker and Zavoina (1970) found the bargaining set to be an accurate predictor of payoff distributions in a three-person cooperative game. Leiserson (1966) tested several of the concepts experimentally in a study of payoffs in coalition governments. A variant of the bargaining set was also used by Wilson (1971) in a theoretical analysis of equilibrium in majority-voting games.

A rather different cooperative concept is the *Shapley value* of an *n*-person game (Shapley, 1953; Luce and Raiffa, 1957; and most straightforwardly, Riker and Ordeshook, 1973). The *value* of a game (with cardinal utilities) to a player is, roughly speaking, the payoff he can expect to receive by playing it. The precise measure of value is defined axiomatically, but in a cooperative game it turns out to be the incremental payoff a player adds to a coalition if he joins it, averaged over all the possible coalitions. In voting games, the Shapley value is the likelihood or probability that a member's vote will be decisive, i.e., that by joining a coalition he will change it from one that cannot win to one that can. The value of a voting game can also be interpreted as a measure of an individual's *a priori* voting power. Shapley and Shubik (1954) applied this to the United States federal government, and measured the distribution of voting power among the members of the two houses of congress, and the president The Shapley value has also been used to analyze the distribution of power among the states in the electoral college, and to investigate the effects of reapportionment, weighted voting, and other possible methods for reforming malapportioned legislative districts (Mann and Shapley, 1964; Riker and Shapley, 1968; Banzhaf, 1968).

The theory of political coalitions makes extensive use of cooperative game-theoretic concepts. Its central proposition is Riker's size principle: "In social situations similar to *n*-person, zero-sum games with side-payments, participants create coalitions just as large as they believe will ensure winning and no larger" (Riker, 1962, pp. 32–33). Many efforts have been made to test and apply the size principle empirically, with data from elections, tribal politics, the Constitutional Convention, and particularly, the process of cabinet formation in multiparty parliamentary systems (Leiserson, 1966; Groennings, Kelley, and Leiserson, 1970; De Swaan, 1973). Other principles have also been proposed to account for cabinet formation. Leiserson (1968) argues that the internal bargaining costs for a coalition are critical, and that these are minimized when the number of *parties* in the coalition is minimized, irrespective of the size of its parliamentary majority. Axelrod (1970) argues that coalitions with the least internal conflict of interest among their members will tend to prevail, and that these will be *minimal connected winning coalitions,* that is, minimal coalitions whose members are adjacent along the ideological spectrum.

Rohde (1972a, 1972b) has investigated the formation of coalitions, or voting blocs, in the United States Supreme Court. He argues that opinion coalitions will be connected, in Axelrod's sense, though for some issues not necessarily minimal, and tests these propositions with a set of cases involving First Amendment issues. Krislov (1963), and subsequently Schubert (1964) have investigated the distribution of power, as measured by the Shapley–Shubik power index, among supreme court opinion blocs of varying configurations. The formation of such blocs is examined less formally by Ulmer (1965).

A rather different issue studied by coalition theorists is whether an individual ought to join a coalition, and if so, when. The basic idea is that the reward a member can expect from joining is proportional to his incremental value to the coalition (value being measured by a variant of the Shapley value, or increase in the "probability" that the coalition will become a winning coalition); thus he should join when that reward is largest (Brams and Riker, 1972; Coleman, 1968, 1970). The basic premise of these models—that the incremental change in voting power of a coalition is an important factor in inducing members to join it—was tested empirically (though inconclusively) in Riker's (1959) interesting analysis of defection and recruitment among legislative voting blocs in the French Fourth Republic.

Another sort of collusive political behavior that has attracted attention by theorists is the strategy of logrolling or vote-trading. This is a form of strategic voting in which one player agrees to cast a vote not in strict accord with his preferences on the issue, in exchange for another player's promise to recipro-cate on some other issue. Models of this phenomenon have been constructed and their implications analyzed by Coleman (1966), Wilson (1969), Tullock (1970), Riker and Brams (1973), and others. The tenor of much of this work is that vote-trading somehow leads to determinate outcomes and removes the instability inherent in a voting paradox solution. Because of the varying frame-works and assumptions, however, it is not clear that this has really been firmly established except in special cases.

NOTES

1. One omission is the work on power, aimed at arriving at a precise formal explica-tion or definition of the concept. Much of this literature is covered in Nagel's (1975) recent survey. Another omission is the work on mathematical models of the dynamics of arms races; for an overview of that literature the reader is referred to Busch's (1970) survey. There have also been individual contributions in a number of isolated areas, such as mathematical prediction of court decisions, which we have not attempted to cover.

2. Such arguments have been used to show the existence of a saddle point in two-person zero-sum game theory (Luce and Raiffa, 1957, Appendix 2) and its generalization, the Nash equilibrium point of an n-person noncooperative game (Luce and Raiffa, 1957, Section 7.8; Burger, 1963). In the theory of general economic equilibrium the Kakutani fixed-point theorem is a basic tool used in modern proofs of the existence of a competitive equilibrium. Such arguments are developed in Quirk and Saposnik (1968) and Debreu (1959). Our example is essentially a demonstration of the existence of a competitive equilibrium in the presence of externalities, and is thus an illustration of a more general result (e.g., Arrow and Hahn, 1971, Theorem 2, p. 135). Fixed-point theorems have also been employed in studying the existence of equilibria in political

process based on voting mechanisms of various kinds (Kramer, 1972; Klevorick and Kramer, 1973).

3.   Specifically, Individual 1 treats t^*_1 of his waste and Individual 2 treats t^*_2 of his. The resulting water quality is $-2m + t^*_1 + t^*_2$ and Individual 1's income is $y_1 - rt^*_1$, as shown in Fig. 6.

4.   Individual 1 now treats $2t^*_1$ of his waste at a cost of $2rt^*_1$, and Individual 2 treats $2t^*_2$. Water quality improves to $-2m + 2(t^*_1 + t^*_2)$, while Individual 1's income drops to $\bar{y}_1 - 2rt^*_1$. Hence the point D in Fig. 6.

5.   As it turns out, each of the corner points Q, R, and S (see Fig. 16) is a majority winner in this example, suggesting that the effect of majority rule is for some majority to form and exploit the minority, forcing it (him) to bear the entire burden. This is something of an artifact of our example, for in general there is no majority winner in "division-of-the-pie" situations of this sort. If the rules of the game permitted bribes or side payments, a point such as S would no longer be a majority winner, since Voter 1 could offer a bribe of $5 to Voter 2 to shift the burden to Voter 3 [i.e., the combination (5, −5, 100) would defeat the original point (100, 0, 0)].

6.   Arrow himself refers to the basic results as the General Possibility Theorem, since it is a theorem about the possibility of an acceptable social choice method. Since it shows that such methods are impossible, however, it is often referred to as the Impossibility Theorem.

7.   This is the *normal* form representation of the game, in terms of the strategies available to each player and the payoffs resulting from each combination of strategy choices. Other representations are the *extensive* form, in terms of the sequential moves available to each player, and the *characteristic function* form, described later.

8.   Excellent introductions to the theory of games are available to readers at all levels of mathematical sophistication. The best for social scientists with some mathematical facility is Luce and Raiffa's (1957) *Games and Decisions*. This is a thorough and lucid survey of game theory up to that date. Rapoport (1960) and Williams (1954) provide readable nontechnical introductions to the field. Somewhat more technical are Rapoport's works on two-person (1966) and n-person (1970) game theory and Davis's (1970) introduction. Burger (1963) demands more technical sophistication.

9.   Since the choice of unit and zero-point for each player's utility scale is arbitrary, a constant-sum game can easily be changed (by adjusting the zero-points) to one that is zero-sum, and the two types of game are strategically equivalent.

10.   Since the point is a minimum in the column of payoffs to Player 2, it is (in a constant-sum game) necessarily a maximum of the column of payoffs to Player 1. A point that is both a row minimum and column maximum is like the point on a saddle that is simultaneously the lowest point looking sideways, and the highest point in a cross-section: hence, the term saddle point.

11.   There are social situations that can be accurately modelled as zero-sum games, but in which no course of action corresponding to a mixed strategy is possible. For a possible example, see the discussion of Shubik (1970) and Ordeshook (1971).

12.   According to the minimax theorem, the pair of minimax strategies must yield a saddle point, or equilibrium. It is easily verified that they do. To see this, note that if

Kennedy chose to come to the studio, Keating's expected gain with his minimax strategy is

$$\tfrac{1}{6}(-3000) + \tfrac{5}{6}(1000) = 333 \text{ votes},$$

while if Kennedy does not come, the expected payoff is still

$$\tfrac{1}{6}(2000) + \tfrac{5}{6}(0) = 333.$$

If Kennedy used a mixed strategy of coming with probability p, evidently the expected payoff would be

$$p(333) + (1 - p)333 = 333 \text{ votes},$$

again; hence, the payoff is a row minimum, since none of Kennedy's choices can give a smaller payoff. It is also a column maximum, in the sense that if Kennedy plays his own minimax strategy ("appear" with probability $\tfrac{1}{3}$), no mixed or pure strategy of Keating can yield a higher payoff. In particular, if Keating chose an arbitrary mixed strategy of appearing with the chair with probability p, his expected payoff would be

$$p[\tfrac{1}{3}(-3000) + \tfrac{2}{3}(2000)] + (1 - p)[\tfrac{1}{3}(1000) + 0] = 333 \text{ votes},$$

so no value of p can give Keating a higher payoff against Kennedy's minimax strategy than his $(\tfrac{1}{3}, \tfrac{2}{3})$ minimax strategy.

13. Since no single vote can affect the outcome when the vote is unanimous (under simple majority rule), no voter can profit by changing to a different voting strategy.

14. There are other cooperative equilibrium concepts as well (including the original von Neumann–Morgenstern solution, the Aumann–Maschler bargaining set, and others), which we will not attempt to review in detail here. Descriptions and references can be found in Shubik (1972).

15. A Nash equilibrium point of a game is a combination of strategy choices with the property that no *single player* can profit from switching to a different strategy if the other players continue to play their equilibrium strategies. A strong equilibrium point is a combination of strategy choices such that no *coalition* of players can all profit by jointly switching to other strategies if nonmembers continue to play their equilibrium strategies. This is a natural extension of the Nash equilibrium concept. The strong equilibrium notion was the solution concept used in one of the first rigorous game-theoretic analyses of voting, the important work of Dummett and Farquharson (1961).

REFERENCES

Arrow, Kenneth (1963). *Social Choice and Individual Values*. Second edition. New York: Wiley.

Arrow, Kenneth, and F. H. Hahn (1971). *General Competitive Analysis*. San Francisco: Holden-Day.

Aumann, Robert (1967). "A survey of cooperative games without side payments." In Martin Shubik, ed., *Essays in Mathematical Economics in Honor of Oskar Morgenstern*. Princeton, N.J.: Princeton University Press.

Aumann, Robert, and Michael Maschler (1964). "The bargaining set for cooperative games." In M. Dresher, L. S. Shapley, and A. W. Tucker, eds., *Advances in Game Theory*. Princeton, N.J.: Princeton University Press.

Axelrod, Robert (1970). *Conflict of Interest.* Chicago: Markham.

Banzhaf, John (1968). "One man, 3.312 votes: a mathematical analysis of the electoral college." *Villanova Law Review* 13:304–332.

Barth, Fredrik (1959). "Segmentary opposition and the theory of games: a study of Pathan organization." *Journal of the Royal Anthropological Society* 89:5–21.

Black, Duncan (1958). *The Theory of Committees and Elections.* Cambridge: Cambridge University Press.

Brams, Steven, and Morton Davis (1974). "The 3/2's rule in presidential campaigning." *American Political Science Review* 68:113–134.

Brams, Steven, and William Riker (1972). "Models of coalition formation in voting bodies." In James Herndon, ed., *Mathematical Applications in Political Science, VI.* Charlottesville: University of Virginia Press.

Burger, Ewald (1963). *Introduction to the Theory of Games.* Translated by John Freund. Englewood Cliffs, N.J.: Prentice-Hall.

Busch, Peter (1970). "Mathematical models of arms races." Appendix to Bruce Russett, *What Price Vigilance?* New Haven, Conn.: Yale University Press.

Coddington, Alan (1968). *Theories of the Bargaining Process.* London: George Allen and Unwin.

Coleman, James (1966). "The possibility of a social welfare function." *American Economic Review* 56:1105–1122.

——————— (1968). "The marginal utility of a vote commitment." *Public Choice* 5:39–53.

——————— (1970). "The benefits of coalition." *Public Choice* 8:45-61.

Davis, Morton (1970). *Game Theory.* New York: Basic Books.

Davis, Otto, and Melvin Hinich (1966). "A mathematical model of policy formation in a democratic society." In Joseph Bernd, ed., *Mathematical Applications in Political Science, II.* Dallas: Southern Methodist University Press.

Davis, Otto, Melvin Hinich, and Peter Ordeshook (1970). "An expository development of a mathematical model of the electoral process." *American Political Science Review* 64:426–448.

Debreu, Gerard (1959). *Theory of Value: An Axiomatic Analysis of Economic Equilibrium.* New York: Wiley.

De Swaan, Abram (1973). *Coalition Theories and Cabinet Formations.* San Francisco: Jossey-Bass.

Downs, Anthony (1957). *An Economic Theory of Democracy.* New York: Harper and Brothers.

Dummett, Michael, and Robin Farquharson (1961). "Stability in voting." *Econometrica* 29:33–43.

Ellsberg, Daniel (1961). "The crude analysis of strategic choices." *American Economic Review* 51 (Proceedings): 472–478.

Farquharson, Robin (1969). *Theory of Voting.* New Haven, Conn.: Yale University Press.

Groennings, Sven, E. W. Kelley, and Michael Leiserson, eds. (1970). *The Study of Coalition Behavior.* New York: Holt, Rinehart, and Winston.

Hardin, Russell (1971). "Collective action as an agreeable *n*-prisoners dilemma." *Behavioral Science* 16:472–481.

Harsanyi, John (1956). "Approaches to the bargaining problem before and after the theory of games: a critical discussion of Zeuthen's, Hicks's, and Nash's theories." *Econometrica* 24:144–157.

Hinich, Melvin, John Ledyard, and Peter Ordeshook (1973). "A theory of electoral equilibrium: a spatial analysis based on the theory of games." *Journal of Politics* 35:154–193.

Ikle, Fred (1964). *How Nations Negotiate.* New York: Harper and Row.

Ikle, Fred, in collaboration with Nathan Leites (1962). "Political negotiation as a process of modifying utilities." *Journal of Conflict Resolution* 6:19–28.

Klevorick, Alvin, and Gerald Kramer (1973). "Social choice on pollution management: the *Genossenschaften.*" *Journal of Public Economics* 2:101–146.

Kramer, Gerald (1972). "Sophisticated voting over multidimensional choice spaces." *Journal of Mathematical Sociology* 2:165–180.

Krislov, Samuel (1963). "Power and coalition in a nine-man body." *American Behavioral Scientist* 6:24–26.

Leiserson, Michael (1966). *Coalitions in Politics.* Unpublished Ph.D. dissertation, Yale University.

_____ (1968). "Factions and coalitions in one-party Japan: an interpretation based on the theory of games." *American Political Science Review* 62:770–787.

Luce, R. Duncan, and Howard Raiffa (1957). *Games and Decisions.* New York: Wiley.

Lumsden, Malvern (1973). "The Cyprus conflict as a prisoner's dilemma game." *Journal of Conflict Resolution* 17:7–32.

Mann, Irwin, and Lloyd Shapley (1964). "The *a priori* voting strength of the electoral college." In Martin Shubik, ed., *Game Theory and Related Approaches to Social Behavior.* New York: Wiley.

Nagel, Jack (1975). *The Descriptive Analysis of Power.* New Haven, Conn.: Yale University Press.

Nash, John (1950). "The bargaining problem." *Econometrica* 18:155–162.

_____ (1951). "Non-cooperative games." *Annals of Mathematics* 54:286–295.

_____ (1953). "Two-person cooperative games." *Econometrica* 21:128–140.

Olson, Mancur (1965). *The Logic of Collective Action.* Cambridge, Mass.: Harvard University Press.

Ordeshook, Peter (1971). "Pareto optimality in electoral competition." *American Political Science Review* 65:1141–1145.

Quirk, James, and Rubin Saposnik (1968). *Introduction to General Equilibrium Theory and Welfare Economics.* New York: McGraw-Hill.

Rapoport, Anatol (1960). *Fights, Games, and Debates.* Ann Arbor: University of Michigan Press.

Rapoport, Anatol (1966). *Two-Person Game Theory*. Ann Arbor: University of Michigan Press.

——————— (1970). *N-Person Game Theory*. Ann Arbor: University of Michigan Press.

Riker, William (1958). "The paradox of voting and congressional rules for voting on amendments." *American Political Science Review* 52:349–366.

——————— (1959). "A test of the adequacy of the power index." *Behavioral Science* 4: 120–131.

——————— (1962). *The Theory of Political Coalitions*. New Haven, Conn.: Yale University Press.

——————— (1967a). "Bargaining in a three-person game." *American Political Science Review* 61:642–656.

——————— (1967b). "Experimental verification of two theories about *n*-person games." In Joseph Bernd, ed., *Mathematical Applications in Political Science, III*. Charlottesville: University of Virginia Press.

Riker, William, and Steven Brams (1973). "The paradox of vote trading." *American Political Science Review* 67:1235–1247.

Riker, William, and Peter Ordeshook (1973). *An Introduction to Positive Political Theory*. Englewood Cliffs, N.J.: Prentice-Hall.

Riker, William, and Lloyd Shapley (1968). "Weighted voting: a mathematical analysis for instrumental judgments." In Roland Pennock, ed., *Nomos X: Representation*. New York: Atherton.

Riker, William, and William Zavoina (1970). "Rational behavior in politics: evidence from a three-person game." *American Political Science Review* 64:48–60.

Rohde, David (1972a). "Policy goals and opinion coalitions in the supreme court." *Midwest Journal of Political Science* 16:208–224.

——————— (1972b). "Policy goals, strategic choice and majority opinion assignments in the U.S. supreme court." *Midwest Journal of Political Science* 16:652–682.

Sankoff, David, and Koula Mellos (1972). "The swing ratio and game theory." *American Political Science Review* 66:551–554.

Sawyer, Jack, and Duncan MacRae (1962). "Game theory and cumulative voting in Illinois: 1902–1954." *American Political Science Review* 56:936–946.

Schelling, Thomas (1960). *The Strategy of Conflict*. Cambridge, Mass.: Harvard University Press.

Schubert, Glendon (1964). "The power of organized minorities in a small group." *Administrative Science Quarterly* 9:133–153.

Shapley, Lloyd (1953). "A value for *n*-person games." In H. W. Kuhn and A. W. Tucker, eds., *Contribution to the Theory of Games, II*. Princeton, N.J.: Princeton University Press.

Shapley, Lloyd, and Martin Shubik (1954). "A method for evaluating the distribution of power in a committee system." *American Political Science Review* 48:787–792.

Shepsle, Kenneth (1972a). "The paradox of voting and uncertainty." In Richard Niemi and Herbert Weisberg, eds., *Probability Models of Collective Decision Making*. Columbus, Ohio: Merrill.

——————— (1972b). "The strategy of ambiguity: uncertainty and electoral competition." *American Political Science Review* 66:555–568.

Shubik, Martin (1970). "Voting, or a price system in a competitive market structure." *American Political Science Review* 64:179–181.

——————— (1972). Game Theory and Political Science. Cowles Foundation Discussion Paper No. 351. Cowles Foundation for Research in Economics at Yale University, New Haven, Conn.

Stokes, Donald (1963). "Spatial models of party competition." *American Political Science Review* 57:368–377.

Tullock, Gordon (1970). "A simple algebraic logrolling model." *American Economic Review* 60:419–426.

Ulmer, S. Sidney (1965). "Toward a theory of sub-group formation in the United States Supreme Court." *Journal of Politics* 27:133–152.

von Neumann, John, and Oskar Morgenstern (1947). *Theory of Games and Economic Behavior*. Second edition. Princeton, N.J.: Princeton University Press.

Williams, J. D. (1954). *The Compleat Strategist*. New York: McGraw-Hill.

Wilson, Robert (1969). "An axiomatic model of logrolling." *American Economic Review* 59:331–341.

——————— (1971). "Stable coalition proposals in majority rule voting." *Journal of Economic Theory* 3:254–271.

Zeuthen, Frederik (1930). *Problems of Monopoly and Economic Warfare*. London: G. Routledge & Sons.

8

ON STUDYING THE FUTURE

HERMAN KAHN

While man has often been interested in the future, its systematic and serious study as a rational discipline is a relatively new phenomenon. In fact, it is still a precarious activity and any claim to full professional or scholarly status is shaky. Nonetheless, interest in the subject is high, and much study and thought concerning the future now play a relatively important part in governmental, intellectual, and even popular discussions, particularly in the United States. Indeed, hundreds of United States high schools and colleges have more or less serious courses in futurology as part of their ordinary curricula. While much of the most interesting work on the future still comes from subject-oriented specialists or talented amateurs, the more or less professional futurologists or policy-oriented analysts are playing a much greater role in such studies and investigations.

The term "futurology" is of European origin and many Americans, particularly policy research analysts, dislike it. They concede, of course, that they are spending considerable professional time in dealing with the future; but usually they do not feel that even a "systematic and rational preoccupation with the future" is, by itself, a profession. In addition, they argue that the term implies an unjustified pretension to being scientific. Others, particularly professional futurologists, dislike the term even more because it seems more likely to suggest distasteful connotations than honorific ones; in other words, the term is more apt to suggest a connection to astrology than to a scientific discipline.

Actually, many activities that are subsumed under futurology do have a strong basis in reasonably careful, scholarly, and even scientific research. It is true, however, that futurology studies also include pursuits that may be described as fashionable, literary, artistic, political, ideological, scientistic (or sciency[1]), and occasionally creative.

Some of the best futurology studies have all these elements. As in any field, but particularly in a new and popular one, there are the fashionable, banal, polemical, and sometimes even charlatanical elements. And even much of the "legitimate" work does not attain very high levels of originality, creativity, or scholarly rigor. The publicist and expositional literature is even more mixed. Nevertheless, it is often possible to project many specific, long-term trends, particularly technological and economic trends, with surprising accuracy and insight. Of course one need not be a professional to do this. Indeed some novelists such as H. G. Wells and Jules Verne have projected remarkably well—the former with historical trends, the latter with technological devices.

As a notable example of an area in which successful projection can be made, many of the forces of the industrial revolution and some of its technological and economic consequences have a staying power and intensity that have not been disturbed greatly even by surprising events or setbacks. As Peter Drucker (1968) points out, if an analyst in the early 1900s had engaged in projecting the economic and technological forces for half a century later (i.e., 1950–1960), in the style that is common today, these projections might have been surprisingly accurate for the United States and many European countries, and for many specific industries within those countries. This would have been true despite two world wars, the Great Depression, a number of bloody revolutions, and many economic and technical innovations. Despite the sharp changes in world history, basic trends in technology and economic growth continued predictably, at least on the average, by "catching up" in "good years," although deviating from the basic trends in "bad years." (This implies, of course, that the trends disclosed during the period 1890–1910 were basic and that much of the rest of the first half of the 20th century was "aberrant"—a position I would largely accept.) These projections might not have been so accurate for the last decade because some recent, and relatively spectacular, innovations were not predictable at the turn of the century, at least not by any techniques normally used today.

Even longer-range projections have sometimes proved to be remarkably valid. An excellent example was a projection by Alexis de Tocqueville in 1830:

> There are at the present time, two great nations in the world, which started from different points, but seem to tend towards the same end. I allude to the Russians and the Americans. Both of them have grown up unnoticed; and while the attention of mankind was directed elsewhere, they have suddenly placed themselves in the front rank among the nations, and the world learned their existence and their greatness at almost the same time.
>
> All other nations seem to have nearly reached their natural limits, and they have only to maintain their power; but these are still in the act of growth. All the others have stopped or continue to advance with extreme difficulty;

these alone are proceeding with ease and celerity along a path to which no limit can be perceived. The American struggles against the obstacles that nature opposed to him; the adversaries of the Russian are men. The former combats the wilderness and savage life; the latter, civilization with all its arms. The conquests of the Americans are therefore gained by the plow-share; those of the Russians by the sword. The Anglo-American relies upon personal interest to accomplish his ends and gives free scope to the un-guided strength and common sense of the people; the Russian centers all the authority of society in a single arm. The principal instrument of the former is freedom; of the latter, servitude. Their starting point is different and their courses are not the same; yet each of them seems marked out by the will of heaven to sway the destinies of half the globe. (de Tocqueville, 1966, p. 452)

But it is important to note that this projection would probably not have been correct if a new trend, the rise of Prussia after 1870, had continued and been allowed to interfere with the basic projection. Thus, if the Kaiser had won the war of 1914 or Hitler the war of 1939, de Tocqueville would not read so well today. Like all predictions, his could only be made with an "other things being equal" caveat. The projection was based on very simple notions regarding the then current trends in population and economic growth, and the persistence of national character; both the strength and weakness of the projection derive from these simple ideas.

WHY STUDY THE FUTURE?

Speculation about the future is almost always interesting and is often useful—indeed, often unexpectedly useful. In particular, it may generate many new insights about important *current* trends and possibilities as well as the future.

One reason for this usefulness in the past is less likely to be as apparent today and for some time to come: in the Kingdom of the Blind, the one-eyed man is king. If hardly anyone is studying future possibilities, then those who do so are almost certain to obtain noteworthy findings; in many cases these are findings of the "obvious": one only needed to look. They are often not only the easiest to find but also the most useful and persuasive of all findings. Thus, many an organization has found its first serious look at the future to be sur-prisingly productive; later looks did not return as much product per unit of effort.

It can also be helpful to adopt a perspective from the future looking back-ward, in order to permit the observer to generate new insights about the present. Moreover, long-term speculation and study often provide useful con-texts for practical policy studies that deal with the next two to ten years. They can be useful even if the context turns out to be inadequate, since it is usually better to have some such context than none at all. Thus, an interesting viewpoint on both future and current events can often be derived from long-term projections done superficially and naively, though this is no reason for making such projections in that way.

Another motivation for futurology is to make it more practical, eventually, to conduct serious policy studies to cover the next 10 to 30 years. This possibility is extremely important, since many projects, such as those dealing with large public works, most arms control issues, many aspects of the education of the individual, new weapons systems, antipollution programs, and so on, typically require 5 to 15 years to be implemented, and then are expected to have a useful operational life for an additional 5 to 20 years or longer. Unlike the situation in the more slowly changing past, it now often seems to be too difficult to design programs and systems so as to take account seriously and explicitly of the likely relevant changes over the entire life cycle of these programs and systems.

Nevertheless, decisions and policies are still necessary. They are usually based on current and past factors, with a large and mostly unexamined mixture of intuitive, pragmatic, or ideological concepts concerning the long-term future. One common practical compromise is to base decisions on "near-term studies," which are close enough to the present to allow the uncertainties to be relatively manageable. The results are then extrapolated into the future, usually implicitly or unconsciously, but sometimes explicitly and with real sophistication.

Yet a great need exists for improved 10-, 20-, or 30-year guidelines and perspectives. Even though most current methodologies and applications of futurology may be imperfect, biased, or illusioned, futurology is still likely to be one of the main tools used to improve our ability to conduct longer-term studies and to develop longer-term policies.

Fred Polak (1973) has argued that there is an interaction between images of the future and the future itself. This is most important for both society as a whole and for elite groups and decision-makers. As a result of this interaction, society is often pulled forward by its own "magnetic images of an idealized future." Thus Polak points out that the Marxist image was powered by eschatological and Utopian images of the future, and this unshakeable and optimistic belief in the future continues to influence Russian politics and policy. One can also argue persuasively that the "revolution of rising expectations" has played a similar role in spurring economic development, while the current "neo-Malthusian" movement may also act, mostly unintentionally, as a self-fulfilling prophecy.

Despite their intrinsic uncertainties, the long-term projections (or even simply images of the future) are usable (and abusable) in many important ways. If they are credible, they can be the basis for the following.

1. They can provide a context and guideline for practical plans and decision making at all levels. This can include official or unofficial ideologies for national and international organizations, agencies, or cadres. Basing a discussion, at least in part, on relatively specific or exciting images of the future may improve enormously the quality and usefulness of debate, consideration, and communication at all levels and among all groups.

2. If used in the form of alternative futures they can often provide a surprisingly useful, and usable, context for a relatively apolitical and objective institutional discussion of ends and means, particularly if the debate can be largely shifted from ends to means.

3. If these scenarios are sufficiently clear, exciting, and persuasive, they may play a similar role for various less formally organized groups, such as academics, journalists, publicists, or intellectuals in general. In any case, they provide an almost ideal context and mechanism for explication, feedback, revision, and elaboration.

4. Public relations and morale, both internal and external, can often be enhanced by these projections.

5. Indeed, these images of the future can provide an ideology, or quasi-ideology, for the masses that is useful in improving public understanding of, and gaining support and cooperation for, government programs and policies.

6. Future contexts are also useful in educating individuals, both young and old, at almost any educational and social level, to deal with a rapidly changing cultural and physical environment.

7. They can be similarly applied to education for citizenship and public service, i.e, to elicit and guide the active cooperation of the general public in attaining some public objective.

8. A future context may provide a clear and dramatic example of what should be done or what can be done—or the converse. This can be used as a very specific and realistic possibility, or as a literary or political metaphor.

9. An ideology of the future may enable one group or institution to deal better with some other group or institution. In particular, it may serve as an ideology of the intellectuals, by the intellectuals, or for the intellectuals, and yet be used by governments to achieve specific purposes, such as rapid economic growth or the exercise of political leadership.

10. In short, futurology studies can strongly influence the agenda of discussion and the perspectives and emphases of those who take part in the discussion.

While these are all valuable uses of future projections, we are particularly interested in the first three—as the context and guideline for practical plans and decision making, for discussion and feedback, and eventually for explication, revision, testing, and documentation. In other situations the fact that these images of the future can act as a kind of ideology or context for achieving unity, direction, meaning, and purpose may be even more important. In particular, they may have an important and active political and ideological role in creating a self-fulfilling or self-destroying prophecy. In order to serve these ends, images of the future must usually (1) be projected far enough into the future to allow time for the achievement of significant results; (2) be near enough to be meaningful—or at least promise to show significant results soon enough so as to motivate specific actions; and (3) contain images or target dates that are charismatic enough to create excitement and commitment.

Anniversaries such as the United States bicentennial in 1976 and charismatic dates such as the year 2000 can easily be used to create an occasion and focus for such studies.

There are many other reasons for studying the future. It is generally a pleasurable and interesting activity that can be accomplished for the reasons stated above. Or there may be ideological, political, religious, or ritualistic reasons for these studies; in fact, arguments based on future images often serve these last purposes very effectively.

Thus, almost by definition, an ideology must include some image of the future. This is particularly true of ideologies that contain a built-in bias (perhaps even an explicit vision) of either progress or decay, of either redemption or destruction. Many religious groups conceive of God working His will through the manipulation of history. Alternatively, they may emphasize that the entire historical drama has been preordained according to God's will. Such ideological or religious emphasis is often the main reason why a study is well received in some groups but creates a skeptical or hostile reception in others.

While the ideological and political attitudes of those who support futuristic studies often encourage rather low-quality work to be accepted (e.g., futurology as a kind of religious art), ideological and political studies can also often be quite valuable and even of good quality. Futurology studies can also be almost purely inspirational in character and still promote didactic objectives. Harsh ideological or extreme polemical emphases are more likely to be motivated by a requirement for internal consumption and external propaganda (usually to increase the morale, unity, or commitment of individual members of an organization), rather than by any objective need to improve the understanding of internal or external reality.

Policy studies may contain elements of these biases, and yet still be valuable. In general, however, policy-oriented studies should maintain a disciplined use of emotional and normative elements. While few policy studies can, or should, be "value-free," it is preferable to study the future as objectively and carefully as possible, recognizing the existence of difficult, contradictory, and unpleasant elements as well as the beneficial, desirable, and enjoyable ones, and minimizing the inescapable biases (if only in terms of selection and focus) that inevitably exist.

From a general humanistic viewpoint, possibly the most important reason for studying the future is that it now seems as though the end of the 20th century will constitute a major historical turning point. As has been discussed elsewhere, it seems likely that both "superindustrial" [2] and "postindustrial" [3] economies will emerge in much of the world during this period, to be followed later by superindustrial and postindustrial societies and, eventually, cultures. There are many practical, academic, and human reasons for studying these last two trends in as much detail as possible, as well as with imagination and judgment. Others believe that almost the opposite will occur: the neo-Malthusian forces will take over. The two views are compared in Table 1. One can learn much about our subject by considering the consequences of the two hypotheses set forth in the two columns and by determining how one would go about choosing between them or coping with them.

THE CHOICE OF PERSPECTIVE

While in principle the facts should speak for themselves, initially at least, it is typical in studying or speculating about the future to choose a relatively narrow perspective or theory and to fit everything within the given framework as much as possible. This also usually happens in the conclusionary stage. The big change in perspective usually occurs, if at all, at some intermediate stage of investigation. We have suggested the need to choose between the neo-Malthusian and postindustrial perspectives (or some in-between or mixed position) and will argue later that data and analysis can help in making this choice. A number of other themes can be emphasized; thus, a very common concept in the past was that the future is static, and that a number of traditional ideas and themes are repeated many times. Almost as common in the past was a pessimistic view: that culture and society have shown a process of decay, with an emphasis on a lost golden age, a tragic view of history (often involving nostalgic and conservative concepts), or a feeling that a particular society is no longer competitive or otherwise viable. Just as common was a Malthusian (or neo-Malthusian) belief in an approaching catastrophe because of an assumed or demonstrated inability of nature or society to supply important physical needs; because economic, technological, or other growth turns out to be counterproductive; or perhaps because of some kind of decadence, i.e., members of the society can no longer cope with the problem.

In the last 200 years, first Western culture and then most of the world have held a basic perspective that is progressive and optimistic. There has been a concept of a worldwide revolution of rising expectations: a view of the future as an enormous improvement over the present or the past, at least so far as material aspects and standard of living are concerned. A further implication has been that most people will share in that improvement and be entitled to do so. Traditional liberal thinking has sustained this concept of progress, as

TABLE 1   Two characteristic current views on technological and economic growth

A. Neo-Malthusian beliefs and conclusions	
1. **Fixed pie.** We have a fairly good idea of what this world can provide. Therefore, "the finite pie" or "fixed bowl" are good metaphors, particularly in thinking about non-renewable or limited resources. We must share more fairly the limited supplies and room of "spaceship earth." Otherwise, even if the rich grow richer, the poor will grow poorer. Nor should we irresponsibly deny our grandchildren by using up or destroying the common patrimony of man.	**Basic Model**
2. **Diminishing returns.** New technology and additional capital investment, necessary to extract marginal resources, will vastly increase pollution, probably to lethal levels, and markedly accelerate the approaching exhaustion of resources. In any case, we shall have to cope increasingly with diminishing marginal returns and utilities—increasingly facing situations in which the effort required for the returns gained increases dramatically.	**More Technology and More Capital**
3. **Likely failure.** The rapidity of change, the growing complexity of problems, and increasing by conflicting interests will all make the effective management of resources, control of pollution, and resolution of other conflicts surprisingly difficult. Some sort of slow-down of change, simplification of issues, and centralized region-wide (or worldwide) decision making is imperative—even if this requires revolutionary or other drastic action.	**Management and Decision Making**
4. **Rapid depletion.** Man is rapidly depleting the earth's food, energy, and mineral resources, and even running out of space for getting rid of pollution products. Many key resources will soon be seriously depleted. While most of these problems will not arise in catastrophic form until early in the next century, current pollution problems, food and energy shortages, and increasing shortages of materials and resources generally, are not only becoming critical now but are clearly precursors of more disastrous events in the medium- and long-term future.	**Resources**
5. **Uncontrolled exponential and/or cancerous.** Even if the current level of population and production could be sustained indefinitely, current exponential growth in both (for example, gross world product doubles every 14 years, world population every 33) will accelerate dramatically the approaching exhaustion of resources and of our ability to cope with pollution—indeed unless stopped soon by drastic programs, it will make an early and catastrophic collision with resource limitations or pollution constraints inevitable.	**Current Growth**

B. Postindustrial (and superindustrial) perspective

1. **Growing pie.** No one knows accurately what the earth holds or can produce—or what new uses may be made of new or old materials. But "growing pie," "expanding bowl," "exercised muscle" (or skill) are all good metaphors—i.e., within limits, the more one produces, the more one can produce. Furthermore, increases in productivity, wealth, and affluence anywhere often create conditions that allow or encourage similar increases almost everywhere.

2. **Absolutely necessary.** New technology and capital investment are necessary not only to increase production to desirable levels, but to help protect and improve the environment, to keep resource costs down, and to provide an economic surplus for problems and crises. In any case, if we are reasonably prudent and flexible we will not have to contend with any really serious shortages in the medium run and the long run looks even better. *(But we must be on alert for far-fetched and unlikely but potentially catastrophic events due to misunderstood innovations or inappropriate growth.)*

3. **Probable success.** The systematic internalization of relevant external costs and the normal use of the price and other market mechanisms can deal with most issues. Some low but practical degree of public regulation and international cooperation can deal with most or all of the rest. *With some possible exceptions, the level of management required is not remarkably high,* particularly if the system normally learns from experience—even if slowly and painfully. (But good management can increase the speed and accuracy of reaction and reduce the pain.)

4. **Adequacy.** *Leaving aside for the moment some very specialized and/or far-fetched issues,* it would be possible to support, more or less satisfactorily *(at least by likely middle class standards)* world populations of 20 or 30 billion at levels of 20 or 30 thousand (1974) dollars per capita for centuries; indeed, we could do this largely using only current and near current technology. Given likely technological progress we should do much better. Further, it is exactly technological progress and large economic surpluses which make it likely that we can deal with these specialized and/or far-fetched issues if they arise.

5. **Eventually a transition to stability.** While such long run projections are inherently uncertain, one can make a plausible case for world population stabilizing in the 21st century at about 15 billion, GWP/cap at about $20,000, and GWP at about $300 trillion. Give or take factors of, say, two, three, and four respectively. (In other words, population should be between 7 and 30 billion, GWP/cap between $5,000 and $60,000 and GWP between $50 and $1000 trillion.)

have both the Marxist and postindustrial scenarios of the future, given earlier. These perspectives have often included considerable Utopian or chiliastic thinking.

A common perspective, certainly for many macrohistorians, emphasizes relatively cyclical phenomena. Great emphasis is placed on the rise and fall of a culture, or on concepts of growth, maturity, and decay. This basic viewpoint has been common to Chinese thinkers for the last 2000 years, and was developed in our own culture by the ancient Greeks to describe both their city-states and their culture as a whole. Thus, for example, Aristotle studied the constitutions of 158 Greek cities and concluded that any form of government tended to decay or change into another form in a cyclical or circular fashion. Rather than searching for the best form of government, he preferred an interpretation of history that argued that good forms would degenerate into bad ones but that these bad ones would in turn generate new good forms. Many modern writers, including Sorokin, Quigley, Toynbee, Spengler, Berdyaev, and Vico, have also observed in history some rise and fall or cyclic pattern of events.

These philosophers often think of civilization in terms of three phases of experience: an early phase in which the crucial issues involve man's relationship to God, to other supernatural concepts, or to ethics; a second heroic and dynamic phase that mixes these early ideational religious concepts with increasing pragmatism, materialism, and secularism; and finally, a third phase producing almost a complete, indeed excessive, secularization of culture that ends up either in an anarchic collapse or a polarization, pitting egoistic-hedonistic attitudes in competition with the revival of old religious and ethical attitudes —or sometimes both the collapse and the polarization.

It is common to all these perspectives and theories that the future is held to be more or less unitary and coherent—or at least to have a thesis-antithesis-synthesis structure. However, there is also a basic view which emphasizes discontinuity, inconsistency, arbitrariness, disorder, and chance; that is, unpredictability or the specificity and uniqueness of actual events and conditions. In this case, an emphasis may be placed on probabilistic events, with a calculation of odds for and against these occurrences. A more agnostic attitude may be adopted: that the future is more like an unexplored continent, a *terra incognita* that is intrinsically unknowable. Such arguments can be sophisticated or naive. They can emphasize the uncertainty of the future, but include the concept that much of this uncertainty is basic and not governable by either objective or subjective probabilities, or indeed any serious analysis; or they can emphasize that the future is uncertain but governed by probabilistic or statistical laws.

The two types of uncertainty are very different—the uncertainties of the *terra incognita* concept are very different from those involved in a throw of fair dice or the running of a horse race, in which one can calculate or intuit reasonable and credible odds. In an extreme case of *terra incognita* the observer may not only be ignorant about the fairness of the dice or the track record of the horses but may also not know how many dice are being thrown or which horses are competing, or even how win and lose are defined. These limitations would make calculations about future possibilities basically irrelevant. In such situations even subjective probabilities can be largely meaningless, except for describing the beliefs and behavior of individuals who hold these subjective probabilities; in other situations or perspectives one may have some respect for the intuitive judgment of certain individuals. Sometimes, in this last case, about all that can be usefully done by the analyst is to poll the subjective probabilities of these observers who are believed to be expert, insightful, or of good judgment. The Delphi technique discussed later can be used in this fashion.

EIGHT APPROACHES TO FUTURIBLES [4]

Three basic choices must be made in the construction of basic contexts, alternative futures, and scenarios. The first is to choose between the extrapolative approach and the goal-seeking (or goal-avoiding), normative approach. In the extrapolative technique one examines an existing situation, selects certain tendencies that seem important or relevant, and then extrapolates these tendencies in a more or less sophisticated fashion. Various policy measures that might affect these projections and change the trends or results can then be examined. By contrast, the normative (or goal-oriented) approach involves first setting up some future context or scenario that is either desirable to achieve or to avoid, and then asking what sequence of events might lead to the realization of this objective. In many cases, a relatively implausible goal is examined, such as the achievement of a world government or total arms control, and then this goal is compared with the current situation and its most likely extrapolation. In order to connect the present and the postulated goal, it may be necessary to modify the image of the current world and that of the future world, and perhaps to use relatively implausible scenarios. These distortions are justified because of the aim of focusing attention or discussion on some unlikely but absolutely important event or educational dimension.

In principle, either the normative or the extrapolative approach may lead eventually to the same results if carried through rigorously and in detail. Usually, though, the analyst has no intention of being detailed and rigorous, nor has he the ability to be so if he wishes to, and then it is usually more convenient to apply one approach than the other. The results will, of course, depend on what approach is used.

A second basic choice must be made between a synthetic approach and a morphological approach. In the synthetic technique, separate themes or issues are chosen to be examined and then put together into a whole. In the morphological technique, a general description of the whole is first chosen and then detailed issues and themes are specified to fit within the chosen whole. In other words, the synthetic approach begins with actors and situations and then creates a suitable environment for them; the morphological approach begins with the environment itself and then seeks the most appropriate actors and situations.

Third, it is necessary to choose whether to work with intuitive and empirical concepts and images taken from the existing real world, or to apply fairly abstract and theoretical archetypes, concepts, and other generalizations. The intuitive, empirical approach is most natural to either the amateur or the area expert, usually in combination with one of the extrapolative techniques. In this method, the concrete aspects of the familiar everyday world are first identified and explicated, and then used to construct a picture of the future. In the alternative approach, the emphasis is usually on theories, or abstract formulations and general hypotheses. An abstract model of the real situation is first constructed, and then the variables of the model are examined. The model may be quite primitive and intuitive so long as the variables can be defined and specified.

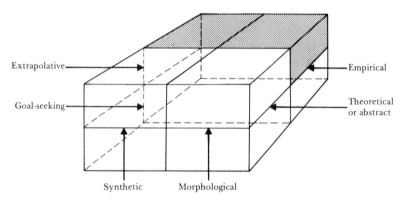

Fig. 1. Eight approaches to futuribles which emerge from three dichotomies.

Figure 1 illustrates that, according to how these three basic choices are approached, it is possible to employ eight different techniques for constructing future scenarios. All eight combinations have their own various uses. Actually, these dichotomies are not rigid "go–no go" or yes–no choices, but are really *continuous* questions of mixture and degree and allow for a continuity and variety of choices. Therefore, much more freedom exists than is indicated in the figure. In the end, all these approaches may lead to much the same result, but since analyses are rarely carried to the limit, each of these approaches is often quite different in practice. Theoretically, the use of any one technique does not seem *a priori* to have overwhelming or general advantages. In any particular case, the opposite is often true; it all depends on the individual researcher and the issues on which he chooses to focus.

In extrapolating some system of events, whether it is the world as a whole or as a very small segment, it is possible to apply the eight basic types of extrapolation shown in Fig. 1, which are characterized as being synthetic or morphological, extrapolative or goal-seeking, empirical or theoretical and abstract. The analyst could first consider the degree to which it is desirable to describe a situation by showing its gross characteristics and working out the components that would be reasonably consistent with these overall characteristics. Alternatively, the analyst may describe the components and then synthesize the whole from the components, working out the inconsistencies and the tensions between them. For example, if future technologies are extrapolated by simply providing future cost and performance, but not initially describing how these costs and performances are to be attained, then we would describe that method as being morphological—or more directly as "working in performance/cost space." On the other hand, the details of how a system operates might be provided, including all of the components which, when specified, make it possible, at least in principle, to calculate later the cost and performance. This would be the synthetic method of specifying a future system or systems, sometimes described as "operating in engineering, tactical, or operational space." (But it should be noted that the same example could be used as illustrative of the difference between theoretical and abstract on the one hand and intuitive and empirical on the other.)

Except for the possibility, when appropriate, of working in performance/cost space, my own usual preference is for the synthetic, extrapolative, and empirical approaches, but many other professional futurologists favor being morphological, abstract, and/or goal-seeking.

THE PREDICTABILITY OF VARIABLES

My attitude, and that of many analysts, toward the future is largely determined by a desire to do policy-oriented studies with practical applications. Such analysts therefore tend to be pragmatic, eclectic, and synthetic in their thinking. In particular, they make distinctions between various classes of future variables and various purposes for making statements about their future. Even if they have an overall perspective of the sort suggested earlier, they are willing to recognize that not all questions and issues will manifest the same phenomenon nor can they be treated in the same manner.

Some kinds of futuribles depend on variables that are almost completely unpredictable, at least in terms of our current technical abilities. These include such events as the timing and location of hurricanes and earthquakes, at least within the geographic areas in which they occur. In other geographic areas, the prediction is simple; they will usually not occur. Thus it is possible to isolate regions where phenomena tend to occur, and other areas where they are relatively uncommon; in that sense we may still make limited predictions for their nonoccurrence. There are important, but less rigorous analogies here with many societal issues. Sometimes the unpredictability arises from the possibility of events that are currently incalculable, but that may become more predictable in the future. This is likely to be true of both hurricanes and earthquakes; it has become true for certain astronomical events such as the appearance of catalogued comets or the path of comets that are discovered early. Progress is increasingly being made in predicting many economic and technological variables and, to a lesser extent, social, political, and cultural variables.

The essence of good futurology is often to identify those variables that are relatively predictable, and then to explore the future of these variables on an "other things being equal" basis. More accurately we should say "other things, *so far as they count,* being more or less equal." Insofar as other events and forces do not count, they may change dramatically in the future, yet the variables being examined may still evolve in the predicted manner. Moreover, other events need not be exactly equal; it is necessary only that their effects on the variable being considered be limited or such that these effects allow or create catching up, correction, or other counteraction. As Justice Cardozo once said, "Danger invites rescue."

Experience has shown that relatively predictable variables associated with the rate of economic growth or of technological development often have (at least under today's conditions) an extremely strong internal dynamic, that can be changed, but not easily, over a long period of time. Nevertheless, many political and intellectual movements are terribly sensitive to seemingly minor phenomena—and once changed, they may stay changed, or at least not have any behavior equivalent to the "catching up" phenomena of economics and technology. Thus, in questioning how much and how far we can predict, we must first isolate various kinds of variables, and then ask, "If other things are more or less equal, how predictable is this variable?" Then we may ask, "How sensitive is this prediction to various events?"; "What will be the immediate effect of various perturbations?"; "How long will these effects last?" We can often respond by characterizing a variable as belonging to one of the following categories.

1. Genuinely unpredictable because it is:
   a. Patternless and incoherent.
   b. Currently incalculable.
   c. Accidental and nonprobabilistic.
   d. *Terra incognita.*

2. Relatively unpredictable as are:
   a. Many fashions and transitory trends.
   b. Events that are unstable in relation to small perturbations.
   c. Unusual men, movements, or events.

3. Relatively predictable (at least in the absence of great perturbations) by the use of:

    a. Systematic variations.
    b. Extrapolation.
       (1) Relatively stable or only slowly changing.
       (2) Exponential, logistic, or other theoretical growth curves.
       (3) Envelope curves.
       (4) Other smooth extrapolations from past trajectories.
    c. Identification of simple and perhaps overwhelming forces or trends.
    d. Analysis.
       (1) Rigorous and quantitative.
       (2) Phenomenological and quantitative.
       (3) Relatively nonquantitative but logical.
       (4) Reasonable and plausible argumentation.
       (5) Intuitive and literary.

PREDICTING THE RATE OF INNOVATION

In dealing with relatively predictable variables, how far can we project them into the future?

Almost any trend will eventually move toward leveling out or topping out, or will create countervailing forces and trends. Depending on the area and the individual involved, there seem almost always to be very strong biases of either estimating too early peaking or topping out, too early creation of countervailing forces and trends, or an almost total ignorance of these possibilities and an assumption that current tendencies will continue almost indefinitely. The first group is fond of the analogy of the growing boy, and argues that the second group would extrapolate a growth rate of a teenage youth more or less indefinitely, not realizing that processes are under way that will rapidly limit his growth. The latter group often accuses the former of insufficient imagination and creativity: the former group allegedly doesn't understand that, even though countervailing forces and trends would arise, the forces behind the growth are strong enough or the people behind the forces ingenious and creative enough to surmount these countervailing forces and trends, at least for a while. Thus, for a long time, many professional analysts overestimated the staying power of the West German and Soviet economic growth rates. But even more common has been the underestimation in the last 20 years of the staying power of Japanese growth rates, an underestimation that I believe is still present. Or to take another example, in *Things to Come* (Kahn and Bruce-Briggs, 1972), I point out that a relatively unknown individual regularly made better predictions for a period of almost ten years concerning the future capabilities of United States weapons systems, particularly nuclear weapons, than did the most prestigious scientists in the country. He did so mainly by assuming that the recent rate of innovations would continue, while the most knowledgeable people all too often could not believe that the current momentum could be maintained; that the genius they and their colleagues had exhibited in the past would be matched, or even exceeded, in the future. This is an important point. Experts speculating about the long-term future will typically extrapolate from the currently most dynamic technology or currently most dynamic economic activity, and then note that this current driving force or technique clearly has only limited possibilities of growth in the medium- or long-term future. But in most dynamic situations, the crucial issue is usually the estimation of the rate and character of innovation as it may be generated, for example, by new technologies, new policies, or other new forces and innovations. In many situations the best, easiest, and perhaps only way to estimate this is to extrapolate the past rate of innovation.

For many reasons an expert who has specialized in the subject of study may have great difficulty in accepting this idea. He may be unwilling to consider seriously likely corrective and blocking actions, or more likely, he may not consider innovations that would negate these blocking or corrective actions. A less specialized outsider who may have a better feel for the techniques of extrapolation and for what has happened in other areas can often develop better predictions. The expert may not understand his own incapacity to accept the likelihood of such innovations occurring and may feel that the outsider has given insufficient attention to obvious bottlenecks, countervailing forces, or other problems. The expert may also consider "mindless" extrapolations of the rate of innovation to be foolish, irresponsible, or incomprehensible.

METHOD OF FORECASTING RELATIVELY PREDICTABLE VARIABLES

To a remarkable degree, the two most important and basic methods for conjecturing, forecasting, or studying the future are (1) relatively straightforward *simple extrapolations* from current trends (but with the rate of innovation included in the "current trend"), and (2) the more or less obvious use of historical examples. Many futurologists seem to have contempt for both methods because of their apparent naivete. They object to "simplistic" extrapolation. It is a matter of record, however, that in many cases journalists and social commentators have used simple extrapolations to predict the future better than have very skilled scientists and engineers; furthermore, those knowledgeable in history have done better than those confined to a shallow present in their thinking. Of course, any method may be abused, and the very simplicity of extrapolation and historical analogy lends these areas to abuse; nevertheless, they are the most basic, important, useful, and flexible tool that we have.

The simplest extrapolation model is a straight-line projection in which past data fit a more or less linear function, and in which it is assumed that future data will also fit this same linear function. Normally this is true for uncomplicated phenomena, or because a particular coordinate system producing a straight-line curve is chosen. For example, an exponential curve in which the rate of growth is a percentage of the current value of the variable will be graphed as a straight line on semilog paper. Similarly, the so-called "S-shaped" or logistic curve appears as a straight line on logistic paper.

It is important not to confuse these two basic models. Many phenomena of interest to futurologists show a rate of change basically similar to the logistic curve. These appear to increase more or less exponentially for a period of time, perhaps at a varying rate of growth, but they reach a maximum growth rate and then pass through a point of inflection. From that point on, the rate of growth decreases until the curve more or less flattens out. This is the expected curve for world population or gross world product. In fact, it seems likely that the point of inflection for world population will be 1975 or within a few years of this year.

It is of the utmost importance to try to understand when and why these curves will turn over or flatten out. It is exactly this distinction that is at the heart of the two perspectives shown in Table 1. For example, in a Hudson study of the Prospects for Mankind, it is argued that the expected S-curve for world population and gross world product will turn over mainly as a result of urbanization, affluence, literacy, new birth control technology, the adoption of current middle-class values and style of life, and other changes in values and priorities; that is, from the effects of relatively free choice by billions of people who will decide to have fewer children and who will decide eventually not to work so hard to increase their income. We do not expect that, worldwide, the S-shaped curve for population and gross product growth will be strongly influenced by famine, pollution, or limitations of nonrenewable resources.

Projections may be developed from functional forms other than straight lines, exponentials, or logistic curves; but in general the future can typically be predicted best by the use of relatively simple but appropriate extrapolations of past experience. One very special type of extrapolation is the so-called "envelope" curve—the curve that is, in effect, the tangent to a family of curves. The envelope curve is applicable usually in a dynamic technical or economic projection in which the most important variable is the rate of innovation, rather than the rate of change of some specific current phenomena. This type of projection means anticipating the driving forces behind the rate of dynamism and innovation. It means anticipating how these forces will vary as one force becomes exhausted and another force becomes important. Two typical examples of the use of envelope curves are shown in Fig. 2, describing the rate of increase of operating energy in particle accelerators, and illustrating the growth of computer capacity.

Each labeled point on the computer trends chart indicates a new technology. The curve was originally drawn at the Hudson Institute in 1963, and turned out to be quite successful in predicting innovations in the next decade. Rather interestingly, the two practical failures in innovation, the Philco 2000 and the IBM Stretch, are also the two cases in which the engineer tried to go

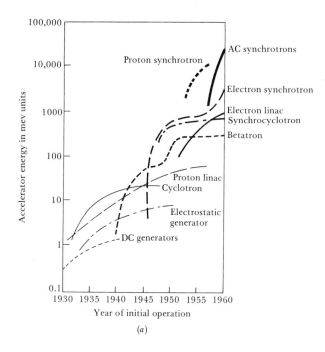

(a)

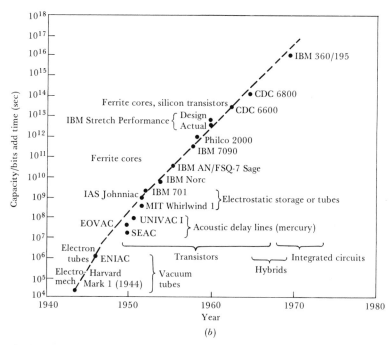

(b)

Fig. 2. (a) The rate of increase of operating energy in particle accelerators. (b) Computer trends.

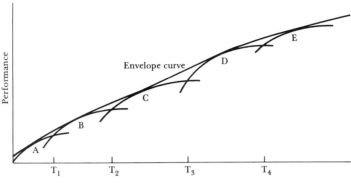

Figure 3

faster than the trend curve (i.e., the "mindless" trend curve was better than the best engineering experts in judging how fast to go in attempting to improve current technology).

A general illustration of an envelope curve is shown in Fig. 3. The illustration might represent five different technologies whose functions are shown by the curves A, B, C, D, and E—i.e., these five technologies are five different ways (over time) in which to accomplish the same functions, each one being introduced, improved for a time, and then replaced by a superior technology. At time T_1 technology A would be obsolete and technology B would be coming into full flower. Technology C would not have been invented yet and would not yet be studied. At this point, the expert would be very knowledgeable about technology B and might predict the future performance in this field according to the rate of change of technology B, which will soon be slowing down in its rate of increase of performance. The expert might not realize that technology C is feasible in the future—after all, it has not yet been invented. The amateur, however, might simply assume that technology C would be introduced in the future in order to maintain the overall rate of change that is represented by the envelope curve. New technology is almost always being introduced, often to the surprise of specialists who, proud of their technical ability, are firmly convinced that they are pushing the state of the art to its limits—and that further dramatic innovation surpassing their current ability and understanding is unlikely.

At time T_2, new technology has come into existence that may not perform as well as technology B has. The expert may at this point still not predict the full development of technology C, particularly if it is a technology that is not in his narrow field of expertise. In any case he will almost certainly be unaware of the possibility of technology D (which will not show up as a serious idea until T_4). In these dynamic situations, an envelope curve of all the technologies, present and likely in the future, tangent to all their growth rate curves, is often the best means of prediction, even in those situations where some technologies have not yet been invented.

It is often difficult to explain why new technology should be introduced at a rate of innovation which is similar to the rate in the past. Nevertheless, this has been true, particularly in the last two or three decades, in literally hundreds of technologies. It suggests certain characteristics about organizations, the rate at which they innovate or accept change, and the need to make significant changes combined with the difficulties of making changes that are considered to be too great at a certain time. The usefulness of envelope curves relies not so much on these arguments, however, but rather on the empirical observation that envelope curves have maintained rather steady rates of change in such disparate fields of technology as computer power, memory size, costs of storing, bits, maximum speed of airplanes, engine input temperature, power of lasers, creep strength of new alloys, yield per pound in nuclear weapons, and so on. The dynamism of change in performance because of technical innovation in these and other areas seems to be reasonably constant—at least until fundamental limitations come into play, or there is a basic institutional change.

An overall envelope curve can also be used to project future economic growth rates in much the same way that it may be applicable to future new technologies. An excellent example is provided by Japanese postwar economic growth, as shown in Fig. 4. One can get some intuition about this process by examining certain fundamentals of the Japanese national character, their political and socioeconomic systems, and their opportunities. (For a discussion of the Japanese national character and the reasons for the continuation of Japan's growth rate, see Kahn, 1971.)

In dynamic situations, particularly in technology and economic growth rates, the crucial issue, particularly of this year, is the estimation of the rate and character of innovation. The experts often have the greatest difficulty in dealing with this. After all, if they knew how something was going to be done in the future, they would do it now. Indeed, often the expert does not really understand his own incapacity to accept the fact that such innovations will occur. He may feel, therefore, that a less expert individual who does accept this must be giving insufficient attention to countervailing forces or other problems.

Clearly the dynamism of demographic, technological, or economic change will depend very much on the surrounding social, political, and cultural milieu, as well as on the innate characteristics of the population, technology, or economy. These sociopolitical factors are especially important in the case of population growth. For the world as a whole in the last 30 years, population growth has been relatively steady; but for many individual countries, the fluctuations have been relatively erratic. Few projections for individual

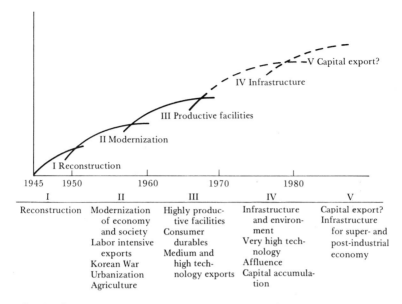

I	II	III	IV	V
Reconstruction	Modernization of economy and society Labor intensive exports Korean War Urbanization Agriculture	Highly produc- tive facilities Consumer durables Medium and high tech- nology exports	Infrastructure and environ- ment Very high tech- nology Affluence Capital accumula- tion	Capital export? Infrastructure for super- and post-industrial economy

Fig. 4. Five states of Japanese postwar economic growth.

countries have been successful in making 20-year or 30-year projections of population growth. Thus, when the analyst typically projected low, medium, and high rates of change, the actual results have often turned out to be lower than the low estimate or higher than the high estimate.

Where political and socioeconomic factors dominate a rate of change, it is very often difficult to project ahead of time how rapidly these factors will be dealt with by the governing institutions. In countries within northwest Europe and North America, we can be reasonably confident that problems of environ- mental pollution and ecological damage will bring about major corrective actions rapidly, and in fact, progress in these areas in the last decade has often been remarkable. This points out that it is necessary not only to rely on past data, but also to analyze and make judgments about the character of the driving forces behind the rate of change. It is essential to decide whether past data should be relied on as a reasonable projection of the future, and how much it should be modified. Often, past data is used as a basic trend, and analysis is applied to suggest the extent to which the basic trend should be modified.

An equally difficult choice concerns the appropriate baseline on which to base an extrapolation. Consider the example of a country that has main- tained a two percent growth rate for a long period, but has shown a six percent growth rate for the past ten years. Either the previous decade or the long-term trend could be chosen as the base that would be most relevant, or some average between the two could be selected. The choice would depend very much on the analyst's judgment about the underlying forces responsible for the growth rates and for the change in growth rates. The more recent data could be considered a special situation related to highly specific and no longer continuing causes, some other kind of aberration, a "catching up," or as a fundamental change in the country's dynamism. It is usually possible to rationalize the choice of a baseline and the choice of the determining socioeconomic forces used in making a projection—and very often the rationalization is justified.

These remarks illustrate that it is often essential to examine the mechanisms behind the data or functions that are being extrapolated. In relatively complex situations, some set of interacting phenomena is being projected, and not all the interactions will play the same role in the future as they have in the past.

In examining these complex situations, two very different attitudes and types of analysts might be described, using an analogy from the stock market, as "the chartists" and "the basics." The chartists concentrate on examining the prices on the stock exchange, and argue that the flow of stock prices, by integrating the judgments of buyers and sellers, is the best predictor of future prices. The basics, on the other hand, examine the data and institutions behind these prices, and analyze companies, the economy, and other economic, technical, political, or social factors that may affect the flow of prices. They will use current price information, but will not be dominated by the pattern of these transactions. The extra information and analysis are often rejected by the chartists, who feel that they will be inundated with too much information, and thereby will lose the value of their intuitive and perhaps subconscious judgment. They may substitute instead the use of regression formulas, methods of extrapolation derived from statistical theory, or special theories in order to impose a pattern on the flow of economic data. A similar difference in attitude and technique separates bettors on horse races—some focus attention on the track record and others on the heredity and other basic characteristics of the horse. All these attitudes and techniques are applied in futurology studies as well as in the stock market and at the race track, and they each have their own strengths and weaknesses.

THE USE OF DELPHI

The Delphi technique is basically a variation of an instinctive method of consulting a group of experts or requiring them to interact informally through a committee, organized working group, or by interviews and questioning by a skilled analyst. This technique is a much more systematic and perhaps objective method of polling experts, though it is not always more efficient or creative.

It is usually organized among a set of experts by distributing to each one a form with a series of questions regarding the probability, feasibility, or timing of some future development. The various estimates are then combined into one synthetic estimate, or into a distribution of estimates. The experts are then provided with a considerable amount of information derived from the initial responses and judgments of the group; the whole exercise is then repeated. This can be done a number of times with different feedback and different rules of organization. Normally anonymity, objective feedback, and rapid convergence are emphasized. Eventually the process will produce a relatively stable estimate (or distribution of estimates) of future probabilities, and this is the desired output of the exercise.

One great virtue of the Delphi technique is that it gives a very respectable result, and a very quotable one. This does not mean that the result is highly valid. But it does provide a consensus of opinion, derived by a method that seems to produce convergence among any fixed group of people in fixed circumstances.

One basic disadvantage of the Delphi technique is that the results are typically very fashionable. This is especially likely because it is usually not possible to elicit more than superficial thinking, and often the experts are not really very expert. They may be quite distinguished, but examination of their experience will often show that, while they are very knowledgeable in their own field, they may not be very expert in the specific issues that are being examined.

In recent years a large number of Delphi exercises have been run. This has created a new problem: the novelty of the Delphi technique has worn off and it is becoming more difficult to obtain the serious participation of first-rate specialists.

Despite these weaknesses, it seems likely that variations of the Delphi method will continue to be used as a very basic technique for generating futuribles and related estimates; and in many contexts and circumstances, the virtues of the technique do outweigh its defects.

"BUSINESS-AS-USUAL" AND "SURPRISE-FREE" SCENARIOS

The word scenario is carefully chosen to emphasize that it is an artificial sequence of events or an artificial description of a possible future. Some scenarios involve considerable documentation and analysis, while others are simply based on speculation or sheer imagination. The two most important types of scenarios are obtained by taking some trends or aspects of society and projecting them in what we call the "business-as-usual" or "surprise-free" modes. Both types of scenarios may be based on current trends, and they may furnish the same future projection. But more often they provide different projections.

The business-as-usual forecast is often used more as an illustrative or base scenario than as a predictive device. It is often thought by critics to be another name for the so-called "naïve projection" of economics or the straight-line projection. While it is similar in spirit to these it can, in fact, include many nonlinear functions. It does imply, however, the absence of basic changes in current policies and practices, except for those that are already in the mill or already clearly going to be in the mill even without any special actions or recommendations by the group doing the study.

The business-as-usual scenario does not include all plausible and likely reactions to new conditions. It leaves out those reactions of and solutions by governments and peoples to perceived problems that, however needed in a clear and immediate fashion, may not be effected unless there is active intervention or pressure. Such reactions usually include those that are expensive, threatening, unprecedented, or otherwise uncomfortable or difficult—but still in the postulated circumstances quite plausible—the kind of reaction suggested by the previously quoted Cardozo remark, "Danger invites rescue."

Thus the business-as-usual projection is often unrealistic, even in its own terms. Many "expensive, threatening, unprecedented, or otherwise uncomfortable or difficult" reactions will be undertaken more or less as a matter of course, though skeptics and critics will not believe this. The business-as-usual projection is especially useful as a kind of control case that can be applied by policymakers in comparing current policies with possible changes they are considering. It is a most obvious way to generate future scenarios for "the base case" and other polemic or pedagogic uses.

By contrast, the surprise-free scenario implies that in a reasonably dynamic society or institution with a reasonably competent leadership, it is to be expected that there will be reaction to problems in order to prevent the situation from getting out of control. The business-as-usual description indicates what would happen if no counteractions were taken and if events continued as they had in the past. But it is usual to change behavior so as to counteract harmful new events or to exploit favorable ones. The surprise-free description applies where an expected or normal exploitative or counteraction occurs. It is probably the most useful projection we have because it covers such a multitude of ideas and techniques. Nevertheless, it must be remembered that usually the business-as-usual and the surprise-free projection would be very surprising if they actually occurred exactly as the analyst projected. These are likely to be both surprising and unsurprising modifications. Very often the business-as-usual projection results in a satisfactory or acceptable condition. In this case it may also be surprise-free—no new policies being very much needed or perhaps very plausible either.

Normally though, the surprise-free projection incorporates many changed conditions and policy choices. These are not necessarily rigorously derivable from past or present circumstances, and are not necessarily simple continuations of current trends. The phrase means that the projection would not be unlikely if it occurs, at least not unlikely to the analysts or group making the prediction. It is possible to have a number of different surprise-free projections from one analyst or from one group, since they may be uncertain and wish to allow for the possibility of a number of different, even contradictory, series of future events. This variety, even if well chosen, will not necessarily be representative of the real possibilities because it will leave out, by definition, many unexpected discontinuities or genuine surprises. It would usually be quite difficult to include these more radical possibilities in a systematic and representative way, because there will always be so many of them. Some surprising projections may be included in the hope that the ones left out will not be such serious possibilities as to negate the analysis, or they may be included merely because the enhanced richness of analysis is felt to justify the increased complexity and effort.

Where surprising events are included, we generally focus on those that may be comparatively unlikely, but very significant if they occurred. Alternatively, surprising events may be included if they involve interesting methodological or practical issues, in order to show the nature and consequence of the interaction of important trends; if they are useful in the creation and testing of deferred decision and other hedging strategies; or sometimes just to remind the reader that surprises are to be expected.

Many of these projections may be considered to be "what-if" scenarios. A set of circumstances and events is imagined, then analyzed and developed to produce various consequences. This stems from a triggering scenario or a "what-if" situation; it leads to a number of consequential scenarios in which possible consequences and ripple effects are identified. It often begins with a surprise-free projection that is close to the business-as-usual situation without being surprising. A number of elaborating scenarios are then developed that are usually of a less surprise-free nature, if only because they are more specific than the general context.

In constructing surprise-free projections, an individual analyst or a group applies some trend of events or other theory, one that he may not necessarily believe to be the most likely, but feels would not be surprising if it occurred. Therefore a surprise-free scenario may not be the most probable projection, but it is at least a projection that is judged not so improbable as to be surprising. It has some credibility at least to the individual or group making the projection and, as has already been mentioned, it is possible to have a number of contradictory surprise-free projections for different assumptions, since the analyst would not be surprised if any one of these different possibilities occurred.

Actually, surprise-free projections have always been, and still are, the normal tool of discussion and planning ahead. During all of human history, people everywhere have applied projections of the future that they believed would occur, or at least that they thought would not be surprising. They have always understood that while a surprise-free projection is not necessarily the most probable one, it is at least probable enough so that its occurrence would not be considered to be extreme good or bad luck, or extremely improbable.

One major criticism of the scenarios normally generated by professional policy analysts is that of overreliance on surprise-free projections. It is certainly not difficult to generate projections that would be very surprising. But which of many surprises should be taken seriously as future projections? By definition, these surprises will not be plausible to those analysts who are surprised. There are so many ways in which surprises may occur; furthermore, the timing and sequence of these surprises may often make a considerable difference to the result. This does not mean, however, that no surprises should be studied. Some surprises could be so important if they occurred that they must be seriously considered; other surprises are interesting from a pedagogical point of view. But there should be some method of selecting which surprises should be studied. Unfortunately, no method has gained a consensus. It is exactly our difficulty in dealing with surprising events that is one of the greatest weaknesses of policy research and other applications of futurology. But this reflects the real world's complexity and unpredictability as much as the weakness of current theories and empirical knowledge.

RELATIVE PROBABILITY

It is important to consider the systematic use of what is sometimes called a *double negative*. If an event is said to be probable, it means an assertion that the occurrence of the event is more likely than not. The analyst is assigning a probability of between 0.5 and 1.0 to the likely occurrence of this event—say, a probability of about 0.7 or 0.8. When an event is said to be improbable, it clearly means that its probability is less than 0.5, or more often that it is less than 0.1 or some relatively small number. Therefore, if it is said that an event is "not improbable," the two negatives do not cancel each other but suggest that the event might still have a probability of 0.2 or 0.3 or so. Such an event is not "probable" (i.e., its probability is not greater than 0.5) but it is not surprising either (i.e., of probability less than 0.1).

The use of such a double negative may be important in polemics. A debater may not be willing to assert that some event is probable because the burden of proof would then be on him. But he may be willing to assert that it is "not improbable" and therefore worth considering seriously, which would put the burden of proof on his opponent to deny the statement and show that the event is so improbable as not to be worth serious consideration. Many discussions leave out this possibility—that events that are "not improbable" may often be important enough so that they should be seriously considered, even though they are not "probable." Similar use of the double negative may be extended to phrases such as "not important," "not unlikely," or "not insignificant."

It may also be valuable to consider slightly surprising scenarios or even extremely improbable ones in which the examination may be very enlightening in an expository sense. The scenario would then provide a better understanding of the design and performance of a particular system or series of events. It is also possible to use unrealistic examples in constructing *a fortiori* arguments.

OTHER EXTRAPOLATIONS AND EXCURSIONS

Another type of excursion into a scenario is to ask whether a situation might develop which would be analogous with a situation in past history. Thus, it could be described as a kind of Munich, or a Cannae, or a Cuban missile crisis, or an Agadir crisis. These analogies can often enrich discussion and suggest what might be some important issues, even if the analogy is not perfect. One of the weaknesses of current discussions is that so many participants often have a weak knowledge and sense of history or their images and expectations are dominated by *one* significant or dramatic recent event. One way or another, certain historic events may have made such a deep impression on certain groups that they always see an analogy with that event, even when they should not. Thus, having experienced Munich once, we may be too fearful of flexibility, bargaining, and compromise (at least over the short run). But even if the likelihood of a Munich may be exaggerated, the reference could still be a useful countereffect to the typical tendency not to worry enough that events and situations can go very badly—particularly in a case of wishful thinking and a very natural dislike to face up to facts and hard decisions. One substitute for the use of historic analogies is to create a relatively *systematic taxonomy*. This is an attempt to formulate, in a more or less systematic way, all the relevant possibilities, and to provide names, labels, numbers, or some method of categorizing many of the relevant possibilities so that they may be easily identified and discussed. It is often particularly important to do so in a "context scenario." In this type of scenario, the data, assumptions, and details are given in a bare outline. The context can be filled in or used in different ways by the participants in the study. A set of context scenarios may be especially helpful in considering a range of possibilities or frameworks.

PREDICTION

When conjectures, speculations, or imaginary scenarios are described, they may be simply elucidations of events that are asserted to be in the future tense, without any strong sense that they are really probable or realistic. All these descriptions of the future can be constructed without concern about how much one believes that they will happen or not, or worrying what degree of reality and emphasis to ascribe to either the whole or the part. This raises the issue of prediction. Futurologists often describe their work as simply an attempt to educate people, at most to provide "if-then" observations, to offer more alternatives, to stimulate more constructive thinking about the future, to provide more sensitivity to future issues, to provoke discussion or imagination, or to increase consciousness of what may happen—all without actually claiming to be able to predict the future. All these are legitimate and relatively achievable objectives. Indeed they are rather modest objectives. Rather surprisingly, such a position can also be self-serving. It disarms criticism and reduces the burden of proof on the futurologist. Yet at times, futurologists are trying to predict the future, even if at other times they are playing a much more modest role. In surprise-free projections, the futurologist is asserting that it would not be surprising if the predicted events occurred. Or the situation may be dominated by such an overwhelming trend or force, or be so stable, that relatively firm (or even highly certain) assertions about some aspect of the future can be made.

In the normal situation, if it is feasible, the most useful prediction is the forecast. This consists of a listing of a number of possible outcomes and a description of their relative probability. Clearly this would be the ideal type of prediction. It admits that the future is uncertain but describes exactly the quality and degree of uncertainty and asserts that all the theorems of probability theory and statistics apply. But in most situations there is genuine uncertainty about the future. One cannot make such clearcut or precise statements, but it may still be possible to offer useful observations about the relative probability of these uncertainties. This may be the most information that can be given; the rest is not up to chance but in genuine *terra incognita*. Often it is feasible only to list the more important or useful possibilities, and to provide a very qualitative and vague description of the relative probabilities, i.e., going as far as possible in the direction of a forecast without indulging in illusioned thinking about what can be realistically achieved in the way of quantitative analysis. Sometimes it is possible to use numerical and precise information in a situation that is intrinsically qualitative and vague in order to describe primarily the state of the author's subjective beliefs about the external reality, rather than the external reality itself. This can be quite useful but is very prone to the generation of misconceptions—the very attempt to improve the preciseness of the communication obviates the true state of information. Despite the frequency of genuine *terra incognita,* of intrinsically uncertain situations, it is often necessary to make choices or policies on actions. In effect, the policy process is an attempt to make desirable events more probable, easier to achieve, and of greater benefit if they occur; or else to influence the probability of less desirable events so that they become even less likely and easier to avoid, or at least to hedge against them should they occur, so that their undesirable characteristics will be alleviated. This is often less a selection process than one of design, of balancing and hedging against a range of assumptions and criteria.

Often it is not possible to judge whether calculations or intuition are based on reasonable considerations. Nevertheless, many people have shown consistent good judgment over long periods of time, using their intuitive mechanisms, subliminal stimuli, and unconscious reasoning to make a selection and evaluation of possible future events. Many important decisions and public policies are developed on the basis of intuitive, qualitative, and subjective reasoning. Therefore, it should be included, as much as possible, as part of the process of policy planning, even if there is simultaneously an attempt to make things as explicit and quantitative as can usefully be done.

One type of prediction in a class by itself is prophecy, a prediction formed and informed with moral fervor. It is often mythic in character and thus need not depend on whether it is realistic. It is a moral and dramatic image of the future designed to convert or transform, whether or not it is practical to do so. Mythic scenarios and projections can play an important role in history. Nevertheless, prophecy and mythic projections are not part of the usual futurology studies, at least not consciously and explicitly.

TECHNOLOGY ASSESSMENT

We turn now to an area related to futurology—or to perhaps a very important subarea. The basic concept behind technology assessment is so simple and clear that one wonders why it has not always been at the center of attention. It is only when one looks at the details that one understands that it is a very controversial activity. Basically, the idea is that one should not introduce a new technology without reasonably fully understanding all its consequences, including by-products and unintended effects. Only after one has done this, can one add up all the pros and cons and then and only then can one assess whether the innovation is, on balance, desirable or not. Or one can decide what modification and controls are needed before the innovation is judged, on balance, to be acceptable.

There are several difficulties with this simple concept, even though it is a valuable one whose time has clearly come. First and foremost, it is almost impossible to make a reasonably satisfactory study in which one can claim the kind of competence and confidence one would like to have in making such an assessment, particularly if one really is to use the assessment as the basis for a final decision. I have seen many such studies and I have failed yet to find any that seemed to me' to be as adequate as even a moderately prudent person would wish.

Of course one can say that what is worth doing well is probably worth doing badly. I accept this. Not all the potential value of a theoretically adequate study is lost if the study is done less well. After all, accepting practical and theoretical constraints, one should still assess the technology as well as one can, even though admittedly the process will of necessity be basically inadequate. However, if one takes technology assessment too seriously, the studies become so elaborate and complex—and expensive and time-consuming—and the assertions and caveats must be made so clearly, that the activity might be an extraordinarily strong roadblock on the way to further technological progress at a time when such technological progress is very much needed to deal with various present and future problems. Prudence and caution are essential, but too great an emphasis on these could be disastrously contraproductive. This is an obvious remark but a fact that is much overlooked. This danger seems to be particularly true if one accepts the basic concept of our likely future that I do: that the world as a whole is basically in the middle of a 500-year process of transition from preindustrial to postindustrial society that will be much facilitated if we are relatively affluent as soon as possible and have rapid and convenient access to many new technologies. While current Hudson studies indicate that this transition could be accomplished relying pretty much on current and near-current technology, it will not only be greatly facilitated by improvements in technology, but the amount of tragedy, disorder, time, and suffering that accompanies this transition could be reduced enormously, if one uses new technologies in a reasonably intelligent fashion (even though some avoidable tragedies and mistakes will also result from such use). And being rich has the great virtue of providing a cushion of excess resources, economic flexibility, and available capital.

Another problem involves the adding up of the pluses and minuses that are disclosed by the study. Even this limited activity is a much more difficult process than one might think. Let us start by considering one of the most dramatic and clearer examples: thalidomide. I have been told that thalidomide was about the only available reasonably effective sleeping pill for which it was almost impossible to take a fatal overdose, and that more lives were saved because of this valuable property than were damaged because of the genetic mutation problem. Nevertheless, the particular kind of damage thalidomide caused was so dramatic and so prone to create great tragedy that I suspect almost everybody would agree it was a mistake to introduce the drug despite almost any pluses it may have had.

The withdrawal of the artificial sweetener cyclamate, because of fear of carcinogenic effects, is much more controversial. I have asserted many times, in public and before experts, that I have yet to find a serious professional who believes that cyclamates are dangerous enough to justify the ban. At the time the Americans banned it, the Swedes, Dutch, Germans, and Swiss continued to use it. These are not the most ignorant or reckless people in the world. But cyclamates did cause cancer (under rather extreme circumstances) in experimental animals and therefore were judged to be too dangerous for human consumption.

Or take the example of the automobile. Who could have imagined in the middle of the late 19th century that the United States would be willing to be largely dependent on a transportation system that kills more than 50,000 people a year and injures more than a million? And despite all the current upper middle-class and intellectual opposition to the automobile, I believe that most Americans feel, and correctly, that this is a very reasonable transportation system even under current conditions. Furthermore, many of its defects (particularly the pollution-causing aspects and traffic conditions) will be gradually alleviated or cured over the next decade, at least in most of the developed world. But it is primarily because people value the automobile's flexibility, comfort, economy, and speed that we will probably have to wait somewhat longer for a very large increase in safety. It is hard to believe that technology assessment would have predicted the problem accurately, and, if it did, would have concluded that the system was still acceptable despite these casualties—annual fatalities that equal the battle deaths in the entire Korean or Vietnamese wars.

Or consider such a widely used medicine as aspirin. Many doctors regard it as one of the most useful, if not the most useful, item in pharmacology. Nevertheless, if it were introduced as a new medicine under current conditions, it would almost certainly not be approved, because of its many side effects. For example, even small amounts often cause some intestinal bleeding. Sometimes these side effects are such that in fact another medicine is preferred to aspirin, but even then aspirin would normally be acceptable if the other medicine were not available.

The point of the above discussion is not that we should not be using technology assessment with a great deal of intensity and in as many areas as possible, but that we should be aware of the fact that it is simply not true that we will necessarily gain much by such activity. It is extremely important to apply common sense and good judgment to technology assessment; we must not only be willing to face hard facts but also be able to recognize that, unless we are willing to take some risks, unless we are willing indeed to gamble to some extent, we will find ourselves in very serious trouble. There is simply no totally safe and prudent strategy that mankind can follow in the immediate years to come. Attempts to increase safety—particularly if motivated by excessive, illusioned, or biased expectations and assumptions—are just as likely as not to increase risks.

It is probably not necessary to point out that whether or not technology assessment is a subarea of futurology (as many practitioners in both fields claim), the problems and difficulties are often much the same; almost everything discussed in the last section applies, often in exaggerated form, to many futurology studies.

I will close this chapter with a number of anecdotes illustrating some practical and much overlooked principles that are terribly useful to policy research analysts in particular and very often to the futurologist in general, particularly insofar as the latter's interests and aspirations overlap those of the policy research analyst. I will also illustrate the application of these anecdotes to some of the current concerns about limits to growth.

The first anecdote concerns what we call the "hot snowload" and is mostly true (if incomplete). It seems that there was once an individual in Los Angeles who had designed some aluminum housing and submitted his design to the Department of Building and Safety for approval. They noted that aluminum is weakest when the temperature is hot and since it sometimes gets to be about 100° in Los Angeles, they assumed, for safety, a temperature of 130°. They noted that the strain on the proposed structure was greatest when there was snow on the roof. Every 5 or 10 years one gets about a half inch of snow in Los Angeles. Therefore assume, again for safety's sake, two inches of snow. They then informed the applicant that his housing would not withstand a two-inch snowload at 130°. He replied that that was a very interesting but academic fact. They replied that since his housing would not accept the hot snowload, they would not accept the design as safe. He objected that one cannot get two inches of snow at 130°." They replied, "We are not meteorologists. If you wish you can have a court hearing and bring in expert opinion."

From some perspectives, the Department of Building and Safety was right. If one can have housing that passes a hot snowload, it is really a safe kind of housing indeed. Sometimes, however, there is no system that will pass this kind of requirement; it may then be terribly important to make one's tests in systematic consistent contexts or scenarios in which hot snowloads simply do not occur. Many times the "limits to growth" advocates hold concerns that would be characteristic of both a very wealthy world, in terms of the sheer volume of gross world product, and at the same time of a very poor world, in terms of concerns about elementary levels of nutrition. Although there are scenarios that could give a combination of an excessive pollution due to excessive product in combination with insufficient gross world product per capita, in most cases, this combination really cannot occur—except as a local and limited phenomenon. As a matter of fact, one of the best arguments for increased economic growth and technology is that they provide a surplus enabling one to deal with other problems as they come up.

A cartoon once appeared in a Pentagon publication showing a number of ants running up and down a log that was floating down a river; the caption indicated that each of the ants thought he was steering the log. It is terribly important to realize that fundamental movements (such as the current of the river) can often be much more important than any particular government policies, or that even when such policies have important effects, they still tend to be at the margin (i.e., in addition to the basic current). This is particularly true again for the growth rates for world population and gross world product which, as we have already indicated, seem likely, as a result of natural forces, to peak in the next decade or so and then drop rapidly. As a result the whole model of exponential growth in the medium and even more in the long-term future is terribly simplistic and misleading. Nor is it necessarily true that one can always err on the side of safety by being concerned about these problems, by assuming the worst case. Again, taking an example we have already used, consider the growth rate of a young adolescent. It is true that if this is naively extrapolated for the next 20 or 30 years, the individual can grow into a monster, but that doesn't mean one errs on the side of safety by denying the "potential monster" essential nutrients during the period when he needs them most. We believe the analogy here is very good: that any attempt to starve the world during this crucial growth period can well result in very counterproductive policies and in self-defeating or self-fulfilling prophecies of the worst kind.

A similar comment can be made about the alleged need for explicit models in the explication of assumptions of public policies. It is important to realize that civilization has been around for about 10,000 years. During most of this time, many governments, countries, and areas have been run rather well by a kind of intuitive technique that, in good hands, is really terribly effective. The current mania for rationalizing policies by explicit model making and systematic rational calculation would be a little bit like selecting a baseball pitcher or a bird as if one were hiring a theoretical aerodynamics engineer. Indeed, most likely the more the pitcher (or the bird) has the usual qualities of the theoretician, the more likely he will be a bad pitcher (or bird). But pitchers do throw balls with great skill and the bird (and the bee[5]) does fly quite well, thank you; and they do it, relatively speaking, without being self-consciously aware of many explicit quantitative relationships. A good deal of governing is performed in much the same way. Indeed it is most difficult to beat the performance of skilled individuals by trying to duplicate the capabilities by explicit professionalism and expert objective analyses and calculations.

One desirable system for the use of explicit theory would be through a kind of a management by exception. One uses the new techniques and methodologies and the new ideas where they have a clear competitive advantage, but one is terribly careful, as much as possible, to preserve the virtues of the pre-scientific era. We simply are not in a scientific era today—not at least so far as policymaking is concerned. But the critics often argue "after all you do have assumptions; you might as well make them explicit." The answer is very often that the assumptions on which actions are based are kind of a phenomenological model (or close to what we have called morphological approach or the price/performance approach) in which one knows very little about the specific details underlying these mechanisms but knows a good deal (mostly as a result of experience) about overall performance. To the extent that one does know a good deal about specific mechanisms, the knowledge tends to be gained because one is dealing with other human beings and one can introspect and/or empathize and get some real understanding of what is going on; but again, only if one has a practical and useful contact with reality and understands the individuals with whom one is dealing.

I have discussed elsewhere my belief that the biggest single current and future problem in what I call the Atlantic Protestant Culture Area (Scandinavia, Atlantic Germany, Holland, England, the United States, Canada, Australia, and New Zealand) and in Japan is likely to have in the next decade or two is that of "educated incapacity." The phrase is basically a modification of Veblen's phrase "trained incapacity." It refers to the tendency of academic and expert people in particular—and upper middle-class elites in general—to be unable to deal with relatively simple issues, with which they often would have been able to deal if they had had a more practical background or emphasis, or other effective emphasis or reality testing, rather than academic training.

I close with a list of reasons for educated incapacity, all of which seem to be important in the field we have just been discussing.

1. Classic tendency to exercise favorite or accustomed muscles (skills or formulations).

2. Normal parochial professionalism and emphasis.

3. Misleading or constraining bureaucratic or organizational ground rules or commitments.

4. Misplaced glamour or incentives.

5. Ideological (political or apolitical) biases.

6. Insufficient imagination, courage, expertise, etc., for useful innovation or creativity.

7. An increasing use of irrelevant experience and intuition: a growth of simplistic, theoretic, illusioned, and/or wishful thinking and Utopian objectives; and a general lack of reality testing and hard-headed or tough-minded analysis (perhaps most important of all).

8. Being immersed in a political and cultural milieu in which one communicates only with likeminded individuals.

NOTES

1. "Sciency" is to science as "arty" is to art.

2. The most obvious aspect of the superindustrial economy will be its sheer size in terms of gross world production, typical organization, business firms, projects, equipment, and potential impact on the environment. Another foremost quality of the superindustrial economy is its scope; for the first time the entire world will participate in the industrial revolution and in modern technology and science. Another important property is the difficulty of fitting the superindustrial economy into the world. The

"externalities" become more important; that is, the costs of external or unintended problems and benefits created as a by-product of large or pervasive technical or industrial activities will become central.

3. In the postindustrial economy the two major types of service activities will predominate: tertiary, which helps primary (extractive) and secondary (industrial) activities; and quaternary, which are services done for their own sake as consumption goods. The predominance of high-level and professional quaternary services may be the main characteristic of the truly postindustrial economy.

4. "Futuribles" is a term coined by Bertrand de Jouvenal to denote "future possibilities" or what are often called "scenarios of the future," "scenarios in the future tense," or "alternative futures."

5. A reference to the well-known calculations about the aerodynamics of the bee which show that the bee cannot fly, though in fact it can, and quite well at that.

REFERENCES

I conclude this chapter with some remarks on important literature in the field, taking as a principle of organization a form no more profound than that of the alphabet, since the field is not so closely joined that individual contributions readily and easily cluster. The principle of selection is, necessarily, even more arbitrary, since I have included only a very small sampling of what might be included.

Bell, Daniel, ed. (1968). *Toward the Year 2000: Work in Progress.* Boston: Houghton Mifflin. A number of papers written by well-known authors, and edited by Daniel Bell under the aegis of the Academy of Arts and Sciences. An extremely seminal, readable, and still worthwhile collection of articles.

_____ (1973). *The Coming of Post-Industrial Society; A Venture in Social Forecasting.* New York: Basic Books. The magnum opus of one of the early pioneers and one of the most original, creative, and scholarly thinkers in the field of futurology. It is a rather eclectic book; some readers may find it difficult at times, but nevertheless, to date, it is the most serious and systematic discussion of the topics he addresses. It is, however, more interesting for the insights it collects than for the unpersuasive theoretical structure to which the author seems to attach more importance.

Bright, James R., ed. (1968). *Technological Forecasting for Industry and Government; Methods and Applications.* Englewood Cliffs, N.J.: Prentice-Hall. Perhaps the best collection of articles on this subject.

Dalky, Norman C. (1969). *The Delphi Method: An Experimental Study of Group Opinion.* Santa Monica: Rand. The basic discussion of perhaps the most popular formal technique of prediction by a group.

Drucker, Peter (1968). *The Age of Discontinuity.* New York: Harper & Row. From the viewpoint of the futurologist or the policy research analyst, this book offers one of the best discussions of current issues. The author is creative, imaginative, almost always sound, and always interesting. The reader might also be interested in consulting almost any of Mr. Drucker's earlier books: *The New Society, Landmarks of Tomorrow, The End of Economic Man,* or *The Future of Industrial Man.* Many of today's most topical issues were approached by Drucker some ten or twenty years ago and his discussions are basic enough so as to seem still fresh and relevant. Perhaps because of his lack of interest in the usual academic formulations, Mr. Drucker has been largely underestimated by the academic community and much of his earlier formulations stand in danger of being neglected or reinvented.

Forrester, Jay W. (1971). *World Dynamics.* Cambridge, Mass.: Wright Allen Press. This is the first of the popular studies of highly advocated computer models with basically five variables. Such input-output models usually underestimate possibilities of innovation and creativity and often have dubious assumptions (for example, that it is difficult to reduce pollution by 90–95 percent when in fact almost every current program against pollution will do exactly that in the next ten years, to say nothing of the next 100 or 200 years), overestimate the harshness and rigidity of adjustment mechanisms (arguing as if we were trying to keep a house at a reasonable temperature by freezing it as soon as it hit the boiling point of water and heating it with large furnaces as soon as we hit the freezing point, when in fact the actual heating elements and the friction processes are much more gentle and flexible). Such studies can be terribly interesting from a methodological point of view (as is often emphasized by the authors) but much less so substantially. Unfortunately the authors of this and similar studies often argue that they are primarily methodological when discussing the recommendations that come out of them. The foregoing remarks apply in general to *The Limits to Growth* by Donella Meadows, Dennis Meadows, Jurgen Randers, and William Behrens III. New York: University Books, 1972. This highly publicized book was sponsored by the Club of Rome's project on "The Current Predicament of Mankind"—phraseology suggesting an inclination toward pessimistic findings.

Gabor, D. (1964). *Inventing the Future.* New York: Alfred A. Knopf.

Jantsch, Erich (1967). *Technological Forecasting in Perspective.* Paris: OECD. This is certainly one of the most serious and systematic surveys of the "state of the art" of technological forecasting. It is important to note, however, that Dr. Jantsch has deliberately focused on the technique and trends of technological forecasting most commonly used and discussed, without providing much critical analysis of his findings.

Jouvenel, Bertrand de (1967). *The Art of Conjecture.* New York: Basic Books. In some ways, this has become the classic book on the subject of futurology and "futuribles." The author is one of the moving spirits in the attempt to create a professional discipline of futurology.

Kahn, Herman (1971). *The Emerging Japanese Superstate: Challenge and Response.* London: Andre Deutsch Ltd. This book attempts to give a comprehensive overview of Japan and its prospects, judging the effects of traditional and changing Japanese national character and the changing economic, political and social milieu. It indicates some of the main driving forces behind the growth of the Japanese economy and argues that these are not likely to slacken much until the late 1980s or early 1990s.

——————— ed. (1974). *The Future of the Corporation.* New York: Mason & Lipscomb. This is a collection of papers given at a conference held at Malmo, Sweden and sponsored by PLM (Aktiebolaget Platmanufactur). It addresses many of the issues that are likely to affect the corporate environment in the 1970s and 1980s. It includes brilliant discussion by Peter Drucker, Daniel Bell, and others.

Kahn, Herman, and Barry Bruce-Briggs (1972). *Things to Come: Thinking About the Seventies and Eighties*. New York: Macmillan. As the subtitle indicates, this work sets a context for thinking about the seventies and eighties. It is somewhat more popular and "practical" and thus less concerned with methodological and philosophical issues than *The Year 2000*.

Kahn, Herman, and Anthony Wiener (1967). *The Year 2000: A Framework for Speculation on the Next Thirty-Three Years*. New York: Macmillan. The first three chapters offer an extensive discussion of various applications, both quantitative and qualitative, of different kinds of trend analyses. The rest of the book applies these concepts to the creation of basic contexts and a wide range of scenarios to create "a framework for speculation."

Lapp, R. E. (1973). *The Logarithmic Century*. Englewood Cliffs, N.J.: Prentice-Hall. An interesting and sometimes useful collection of relatively specific curves describing the past and some future trends. Gives a good sense of how things have occurred and how they may go. It shows that the argument for relatively smooth projections can be made terribly persuasive. However, it fails to take account of the likely S-shaped curve of the future GWP and population.

Morgenstern, O., K. Knorr, and K. P. Heiss (1973). *Long-Term Projections of Power*. Cambridge, Mass.: Ballinger. This is a rather eclectic book that discusses various methodologies for making projections of the future. It presents a rather good summary and critique of these, with particular emphasis on future technology and international power. It is well worth reading but, as one would expect and as the authors themselves recognize, it is not very conclusive with regard to the central issues indicated by the title.

Polak, F. L. (1973). *The Image of the Future*. Amsterdam: Elsevier Scientific Publishing Co. A very exciting and illuminating discussion about what may eventually be the most important application of futurology.

Quigley, C. (1961). *The Evolution of Civilizations*. New York: Macmillan. A very clear summary and reformulation of some of the most useful concepts and other findings of the macrohistorian.

Sorokin, P. (1941). *The Crisis of Our Age*. New York: E. P. Dutton. This readily available and readable paperback gives a reasonably adequate summary, for the general reader, of Sorokin's four-volume opus *Social and Cultural Dynamics*. Whether or not the reader accepts the perspective of the macrohistorians, this book remains terribly useful from the viewpoint of description and stimulation.

Tocqueville, Alexis de (1966). *Democracy in America*. Edited by J. P. Mayer and Max Lerner; translated by George Lawrence. New York: Harper & Row. This is a truly seminal and creative book and, to an extraordinary degree, still largely current with regard to the issues of United States national character. It not only applies to the American people but also provides insights on how to study the role of national character in general. A very wise and sound book.

Toffler, Alvin (1970). *Future Shock*. New York: Random House. The all-time bestseller in this area and the one book that has become a household word. It is an extremely competent, if journalistic account of most of the current issues. However, its major thesis, "future shock," is greatly overstated; it is reasonable to say that most of the immigrants that came to this country in the 19th and 20th centuries and most of the peasants that moved to urban centers doubtlessly experienced a bigger change than the one we will be experiencing. Under normal conditions, they did not suffer from future shock.

Toynbee, Arnold (1939). *A Study of History*. Vol. 4, Breakdown of Civilizations; Vol. 5, Part 1 and Vol. 6, Part 2, Disintegration of Civilizations. New York: Oxford University Press. Despite much current criticism and neglect, this is still a masterpiece and the author, at least for his time, a giant.

INDEX

Abeles, Ronald P., 235
Abelson, Robert, 146, 188, 189, 191, 194, 196, 197, 198, 203, 223
Abernathy, James R., 297
Abrams, Mark, 298
Adams, Walter A., 309
Affect
  definition of, 275
  political, 275-278
Ahmavaara, Y., 154
Aiken, Michael, 64
Alger, Chadwick, 225, 241, 246
Alker, Hayward R., 64, 140, 141, 143, 146, 147, 149, 154, 156, 157, 159, 168, 169, 184, 201, 202, 203, 204, 227
Allen, Howard W., 47
Allport, Floyd Henry, 280
Allport, Gordon, 96
Almanacs, 16
Almond, Gabriel A., 99, 105, 110, 121, 275, 279
American Association for Public Opinion Research, 327
American Institute of Public Opinion, 324
American Youth Commission, 309
Analysis of variance, 215, 244
Anderson, Frank Maloy, 4
Anderson, Ronald E., 286
Apartheid, 281
Apter, D. E., 82, 99

Archive on Political Elites in Eastern Europe, 50
Archives, 27-34, 45-67
Armstrong, J. Scott, 153, 154
Aronson, Elliot, 249, 250
Arrow, Kenneth, 374, 375, 376, 397
Arrow's (Im)possibility Theorem, 375
Ashby, C. M., 33
Athanasiou, Robert, 306
Atkin, Charles R., 250
Attitude formation, 242
Attitude measurement
  acquiescence response set, 292, 294
  bias, 297
  controversies in, 289-305
  filter questions, 304
  index of political cynicism, 277
  index of political efficacy, 277, 292, 296
  latent structure analysis, 318
  levels of conceptualization, 286, 287
  memory error, 297
  multiple indicators, 295
  omission error, 297
  randomized response, 297-298
  scaling theory, 318
  self-anchoring striving scale, 281
  semantic differential scales, 276
  social desirability response set, 297
  split ballots, 295
  telescoping error, 297